American Foreign Policy and National Security
A Documentary Record

Edited by

Paul R. Viotti
University of Denver

PEARSON
Prentice
Hall

Upper Saddle River, New Jersey 07458

Library of Congress Cataloging-in-Publication Data

American foreign policy and national security: a documentary record / [compiled and
edited by] Paul R. Viotti.
    p. cm.
    Includes bibliographical references.
    ISBN 0-13-040027-0
    1. United States—Foreign relations—Sources.   2. National security—United
States—History—Sources.   I. Viotti, Paul R.

E183.7.A557 2005
327.73'009—dc22   2004046601

Editorial Director: Charlyce Jones-Owen
Acquisitions Editor: Glenn Johnston
Assistant Editor: John Ragozzine
Editorial Assistant: Suzanne Remore
Production Liaison: Joanne Hakim
Marketing Manager: Kara Kindstrom
Marketing Assistant: Jennifer Lang
Manufacturing Buyer: Sherry Lewis
Cover Art Director: Jayne Conte
Cover Design: Bruce Kenselaar
Cover Images: Getty Images, Inc.
Composition/Full-Service Project Management: Michael Bohrer-Clancy/ICC
Printer/Binder: Phoenix Book Tech Park

*Dedication—To Ambassador George Lane and
Alan Francis, the late William Heath, and the
late Edward Schweikardt, early mentors, who
underscored the importance of the documentary
record to understanding American foreign policy
and national security.*

Credits and acknowledgments borrowed from other sources and reproduced, with
permission, in this textbook appear on appropriate page within text.

Pearson Education LTD., London
Pearson Education Singapore, Pte. Ltd
Pearson Education, Canada, Ltd
Pearson Education—Japan
Pearson Education Australia PTY, Limited

Pearson Education North Asia Ltd
Pearson Educación de Mexico, S.A. de C.V.
Pearson Education Malaysia, Pte. Ltd
Pearson Education, Upper Saddle River, New Jersey

10 9 8 7 6 5 4 3 2 1
ISBN 0-13-040027-0

Contents

PART TWO: *Constitutional Interpretations on the Conduct of American Foreign Policy   67*

Chapter 5:   *The Federal Role in Foreign Policy   68*

Chapter 6:   *Separation of Powers and Treaties   78*

Chapter 7:   *Executive-Legislative War Powers   88*

Chapter 8:   *Civil Liberties in Wartime   99*

PART THREE: *Statements on Foreign and National Security Policy*   *141*

Chapter 9: *Pre–World War II: Foreign Policy and National Security Statements*   *142*

Chapter 10: *World War II and Its Settlement: Foreign and National Security Policy Statements*   *174*

Chapter 11:   *The Onset of the Cold War: Foreign and National Security Policy Statements*   **190**

Chapter 12:   *The Cold War: Foreign and National Security Policy Statements*   **216**

Chapter 15: *Arms Control Through Geographic or Spatial Measures   294*

Chapter 16: *Arms Control Through Functional Measures   308*

Preface

We bring together in this volume a select few of the many documents that inform the making and implementation of American foreign and national security policy. The choice of which documents to include in a single volume and which to set aside is by no means easy. How much to include of those documents that make the short list is another difficult editorial challenge. Although historical documents from previous centuries are included, this collection is not intended to be a comprehensive diplomatic history. Because of the single-volume constraint, our purpose is to provide only a selective documentary record on which to base an understanding of the factors that influence American foreign and national security policy processes, decisions, and actions.

To assist the reader, we have taken the liberty to italicize those parts of the documents that we have identified either as keys to understanding American foreign policy and national security in general or as the main points of the document. Although space limitations preclude reprinting most of the documents in their entirety (except those of particular significance such as the U.S. Constitution and the United Nations Charter), readers may find reading the original, full-text versions of many of these and other documents worthwhile. Indeed, many of these documents also address important matters beyond the scope of this volume's focus on matters of foreign policy and national security interest.

Brief introductions before each document as well as an index facilitate use of this volume. Organized by topic, we have grouped the documents categorically into five parts and eighteen chapters. We begin in Part 1 with foreign policy and national security aspects of seventeenth- and eighteenth-century documents related to constituting the American republic. Constitutional interpretations on the actual conduct of American foreign and national security policy are the focus of Part 2—the federal role in relation to states on such matters, separation of powers and treaties, executive-legislative understandings on war powers, and civil liberties in wartime. In Part 3 we turn to actual foreign and national security policy "statements" of lasting or present-day importance, grouped chronologically in five separate chapters (viz., pre–World War II, World War II and its settlement, the onset of cold war, the cold war itself, and the post–cold war period to date). Part 4 takes up a substantial number of arms control agreements in three chapters organized categorically—controlling armaments themselves by institutionalizing qualitative and quantitative measures, establishing geographic (or spatial) prohibitions or limitations, and routinizing various functional measures. Finally, in Part 5 we look at American foreign policy and national security institutions and processes in two last chapters cast separately at domestic and international levels of analysis—one on the National Security Council and the Departments of

State, Defense, and Homeland Security and the other on a select few of the international organizations to which the United States has joined or was instrumental in forming—the League of Nations, United Nations, Organization of American States, North Atlantic Treaty Organization, Organization for Security and Cooperation in Europe, and North American Free Trade Agreement.

The editor deeply appreciates the assistance others have given him in this project. This began with Michelle Viotti's early help with identifying those parts of the Federalist Papers that deal with foreign policy and national security. Organization assistance and discussions with Radia d'Aoussi and other students in the Graduate School of International Studies, University of Denver, helped in the difficult process of identifying and then narrowing the list of documents that should be included in this single volume. The editor also acknowledges beneficial discussions with Paul Viotti, Jr., and the encouragement offered by his friends and colleagues—Mark Kauppi and David Goldfischer, as well as the efforts of those who agreed to review parts of the manuscript in which they have particular expertise—Claude d'Estrée, Jeffrey Larsen, James Smith, Bernard Udis, and David Viotti.

Many thanks to the following reviewers of this text: Fred Hertrich, Middlesex County College; Carlos Yordan, Visiting Assistant Professor, Hamilton College; Robert Blanton, University of Memphis; and William Kelly, Auburn University. The author found their suggestions helpful. Thanks are also due to Beth Gillette Mejia at Prentice Hall, who originally saw value in this project, and her colleagues, most recently Glenn Johnston. Thanks are also due to Michael Bohrer-Clancy for the production of the volume. Finally, this volume owes much to the love and support over many decades of Linda Viotti.

Paul R. Viotti
University of Denver

Foreword

One of the most vivid moments in modern drama occurs in the memorable play, "The Lion in Winter." When the king challenges the queen to "face the facts," she responds, plaintively, "Which ones? We have so many."

The perplexity captured in that exchange radiates through many realms of human existence, nowhere more acutely than in the field of foreign policy and national security. Policymakers and scholars alike confront myriad realities that impede their understanding of the factors, the actors and the options they must consider. Seldom, if ever, can the student or the practitioner of American foreign policy claim a grasp of the issues in play sufficient to reach firm conclusions or make flawless choices.

When confronted with perpetual issues of statecraft—shaping a sound balance of constitutional power among the several branches of government, decisions regarding war and peace, setting prudent tradeoffs between defense and diplomacy, pursuing America's national interests in a multi-nation system that requires attention to the competing interests of other states—insights are almost always limited and policies almost never adequately informed. In the twenty-first century America's global engagement imposes ever-increasing demands to ground policy in analyses that are both informed historically and responsive to contemporary realities. It is to that task that this book is addressed.

Context is crucial to analysis and the burden of providing valid descriptions of the policy context falls heavily, though not exclusively, on scholars. That is true for two reasons. First, the tempo of decision-making in the modern era is so hectic and the pressures on those responsible for policy so great that those in authority have precious little time to study fast-breaking issues and to give them the necessary reflection. Second, while modern bureaucracies are massive, turnover in key positions is so great that institutional memory suffers and discontinuities are common; it often falls to analysts outside of government to compensate for those shortcomings by providing the longer view and the independent perspective. There is a premium on scholarship that blends empathy for the policymaker with detachment from the immediate responsibilities that may distort the policymaker's judgment. An essential element in such scholarship is knowledge of the roots from which current policy questions have grown.

This volume is a remarkable contribution to that scholarly mission. Any construction of the documentary record of U.S. foreign and national security policy must overcome a daunting task of selection from archives too vast for even the most assiduous scholars to master. For such a record to be most useful the editor must play the role of scout, exploring more widely than others are able to do, marking the heights and valleys, and—most important—providing sophisticated assessments of the key features arising in this terrain. Professor Viotti proves himself a veritable Meriwether Lewis of foreign policy scouts.

The documents assembled here present a rich chronological panorama, ranging from the early contours of American foreign and security policy to today's efforts to adapt the country's historic concepts to a complex world in which the lines between foreign and domestic policy, between international and homeland security, grow less distinct. Especially noteworthy are the volume's attention to the evolving constitutional framework for policymaking and its integration into that framework of major innovations that have been undertaken during the opening years of the new century. By relating the dramatic recent developments in U.S. foreign and security policy to the precedents on which they have built or from which they have departed, the editor equips the reader to cast a fresh eye on America's unfolding role in the wider world.

What is most valuable in this book is its juxtaposition of scrupulous, concise commentary with the original documents that enable readers to form their own opinions. Commentary without documentation risks veering toward polemic, while documents without context may breed incomprehension. French President Jacques Chirac once said that "elections are like policemen—people behave better when they are around." So, too, with documents that have defined policy over the years: it behooves policymakers and scholars to ground their views in the originals, rather than in the myths or inaccuracies that often accrue to them. As teachers, students and practitioners will discover, that purpose is well served by this admirable volume.

Alton Frye
Counselor and Presidential Senior Fellow
Council on Foreign Relations
March 1, 2004

PART ONE

Constituting the American Republic

Foreign policy and national security decision making in the United States exhibits many of the same characteristics as U.S. decision making on other issues of political importance. This is not surprising, given the American constitutional framework that guides the way in which all such political choices are made. By design, the framers of the U.S. Constitution drew up a document (1787–89) that avoided the extreme decentralization of authority to the states under the Articles of Confederation (1781–89) while keeping the central government from becoming too strong. *Separating* powers among the branches of central government (executive, legislative, and judicial) and *dividing* them between the central and state governments became the framers' prescription for keeping government in check. It also assured representation of diverse points of view.

In their focus on domestic matters, many scholars tend to overlook the foreign policy and national security aspects of the historical documents contained in this book. The editor's rather liberal use of italics in these documents is intended not only to focus our attention on these aspects, but also to reveal just how much of these documents is, in fact, devoted to foreign policy or national security issues.

Chapter 1

The Earliest Documents

These documents are included here because they underscore how even the earliest settlers were deeply concerned not just with day-to-day running of a colony, but also with the colony's external (or foreign) relations essential to both commerce and domestic security. Many of the spellings in these documents have been modernized; italicized portions of the text refer to security, commerce, or other external matters.

1. The Virginia Charters
(1606 and 1608)

Before their landing in Virginia, the settlers received written instructions from the English government not to be "hasty in landing your victuals and munitions" until finding "the strongest, most wholesome and fertile place." For security of the colony, the settlers were urged to find an upriver location, perhaps "a hundred miles from the river's mouth, and the further up the better." Particular focus was put on threats to the colony from the French or Spanish. Rather than confront an enemy on the coast, an upriver site would provide a defensive advantage allowing the settlers "from both sides of the river where it is narrowest, so [to] beat them with your muskets as they shall never be able to prevail against you." The settlers were also warned lest "the native people of the country . . . grow discontented with your habitation, and be ready to guide and assist any nation that shall come to invade you; and if you neglect this, you neglect your safety." More formally, the Virginia Charters of 1606 and 1608 put the same emphasis on security in relation to external threats to colonial Virginia, which began with the Jamestown settlement of 1607. The welfare of Virginia settlers depended fundamentally on security against external threats and on success in both domestic and international commerce, concerns amply reflected in these charters and also in subsequent documents.

(1606)

James, by the grace of God, King of England, Scotland, France, and Ireland, Defender of the Faith, &c. Whereas our loving and well disposed subjects . . . have been humble suitors unto us that we would vouchsafe unto them our licence to make habitation, plantation and to deduce a colony of sundry of our people into that part of America commonly called Virginia. . . .

We, greatly commending and graciously accepting of their desires to the furtherance of so noble a work which may, by the providence of Almighty God, hereafter tend to the glory of His Divine Majesty in propagating of Christian religion to such people as yet live in darkness and miserable ignorance of the true knowledge and worship of God and may in time bring the infidels and savages living in those parts *to humane civility and to a settled and quiet government*, do by these our letters patents graciously accept of and agree to their humble and well intended desires . . . and [they, i.e., the residents of colonies] shall and may inhabit and remain there; and shall and may also *build and fortify within any the same for their better safeguard and defence*, according to their best discretions and the direction of the Council of that Colony. . . .

And we do also ordain, establish . . . that each of the said Colonies shall have a Council which shall govern and order all matters and causes which shall arise, grow, or happen to or within the same several Colonies, according to such laws, ordinances and instructions as shall be in that behalf, given and signed with our hand . . . and pass under the Privy Seal of our realm of England. . . .

And moreover we do grant and agree . . . that the said several Councils of and for the said several Colonies shall and lawfully may . . . *dig, mine and search for . . . gold, silver and copper . . . to the use . . . of the same Colonies* and the plantations thereof. . . . And that *they shall or lawfully may establish* and cause to be made a *coin . . . for the . . . traffic and bargaining between and*

amongst them and the natives there. . . . And we do likewise . . . give full power and authority to . . . the said several Companies, plantations and Colonies . . . *with sufficient shipping and furniture of armour, weapon, ordnance, powder, victuals, and all other things necessary for the said plantations and for their use and defence.* . . .

Moreover, we do . . . give and grant license . . . *for their several defences . . .* [to] *repel and resist . . . by sea as by land, by all ways and means whatsoever*, all and every such person and persons as without special license of the said several Colonies and plantations shall attempt to inhabit . . . any of them, or that shall enterprise or attempt at any time hereafter the hurt, detriment or annoyance of the said several Colonies or plantations. . . . And we do further . . . give and grant . . . that *they . . . may transport the goods, chattels, armor, munition and furniture, needful to be used by them for their said apparrel* [sic], *defence or otherwise* in respect of the said plantations, out of our realms of England and Ireland and all other our dominions from time to time, for and during the time of seven years . . . without any custom, subsidy or other duty. . . .

Also we do . . . declare . . . that all . . . shall have and enjoy all liberties, franchises and immunities within any of our other dominions to all intents and purposes as if they had been abiding and born within this our realm of England or any other of our said dominions. . . .

We do hereby declare *to all Christian kings, princes and estates*, that if any person or persons . . . shall . . . *rob or spoil by sea or by land* or do any act of unjust and unlawful hostility to any the subjects of us . . . or any of the *subjects of any . . . state being then in league or amity with us* . . . and that upon such injury . . . we . . . shall make open proclamation within any the ports of our realm of England . . . that the said person or persons having committed any such robbery or spoil shall . . . make full restitution or satisfaction of all such injuries done . . . and that if the said person or persons . . . shall not . . . , then it shall be lawful . . . to put the said person or persons . . . out of our allegiance and protection; and that it shall be lawful and free for all princes and others to pursue with hostility the said offenders. . . .

(1608)

. . . And for their further encouragement, of our special grace and favor, we do . . . Grant . . . that they and every of them *shall be free . . . of all subsidies and customs in Virginia for the space of one and twenty years, and from all taxes and impositions forever, upon any goods or merchandise* at anytime or times hereafter, *either upon importation* thither *or exportation* from thence into our realm of England or into any other of our . . . Dominions. . . . *except only the five pound per centum due for custom . . . according to the ancient trade of merchants,* which five pounds per centum only being paid, it shall be thenceforth lawful and free for the said Adventurers the same goods . . . *to export and carry out of our said dominions into foreign ports without any custom, tax or other duty to be paid* . . . provided, that the said goods and merchandise be shipped out within thirteen months after their first landing within any part of those dominions.

And we do also confirm and grant . . . *power and authority of government and command* in or over the said Colony or plantation . . . *for their several defence and safety, encounter, expulse, repel and resist by force and arms, as well by sea as by land,* and all ways and means whatsoever, all and every such person and persons whatsoever as without the special license . . . shall attempt to inhabit within the said . . .

Colony and plantation; and also, *all . . . as shall enterprise, or attempt at any time hereafter, destruction, invasion, hurt, detriment or annoyance. . . .*

Also we do . . . declare by these presents, that all and every the persons being our subjects which shall go and inhabit within the said Colony and plantation, and every of their children and posterity which shall happen to be born within . . . the limits thereof, shall have . . . all liberties, franchises and immunities of free . . . and natural subjects within any of our other dominions to all intents and purposes as if they had been abiding and born within this our kingdom of England or in any other of our dominions.

And forasmuch as it shall be necessary for all such our loving subjects as shall inhabit within the said precincts of Virginia aforesaid to determine *to live together in* the fear and true worship of Almighty God, Christian *peace and civil quietness,* each with other, whereby every one may *with more safety,* pleasure and profit enjoy that where unto they shall attain with great pain and peril, we . . . do give and grant unto the said Treasurer and Company and . . . to such governors, officers and ministers as shall be, by our said Council, constituted and appointed . . . that they shall and may from time to time for ever hereafter, within the said precincts of Virginia . . . have full and absolute power and authority to correct, punish, pardon, govern and rule all such the subjects of us . . . as shall from time to time adventure themselves in any voyage thither or that shall at any time hereafter inhabit in the precincts and territory of the said Colony . . . so always as the said statutes, ordinances and proceedings . . . be agreeable to the laws, statutes, government and policies of this our realm of England.

2. *The Mayflower Compact*
(1620)

The idea of a formal social contract among the first English settlers in Massachusetts (referred to here as Virginia, the lines among colonies not yet having been drawn) is embodied in this early covenant designed to achieve security—"better Ordering and Preservation" and "for the General Good of the Colony." The short Mayflower Compact is reprinted here in its entirety; spellings for the most part have been modernized.

In the name of God, Amen. We, whose names are underwritten, the Loyal Subjects of our dread Sovereign Lord, King James, by the Grace of God, of Great Britain, France, and Ireland, King, Defender of the Faith, &c. Having undertaken for the Glory of God, and Advancement of the Christian Faith, and the Honour of our King and Country, a Voyage to plant the first colony in the Northern Parts of Virginia; do, by these Presents, solemnly and mutually in the Presence of God and one of another, covenant and combine ourselves together into a civil Body Politik, *for our better Ordering and Preservation,* and Furtherance of the Ends aforesaid; And by Virtue hereof do enact, constitute, and frame, such just and equal Laws, Ordinances, Acts, Constitutions, and Offices, from time to time, as shall be thought most meet and convenient for *the General Good of the Colony;* unto which we promise all due Submission and Obedience. In Witness whereof we have hereunto subscribed our names at Cape Cod the eleventh of November, in the Reign of our Sovereign Lord, King James of England, France, and Ireland, the eighteenth, and of Scotland, the fifty-fourth, Anno Domini, 1620.

Chapter 2

Constructing a Constitutional Republic

Given our foreign policy and national security focus, we do not include the many colonial documents relating to the formation and development of the thirteen English colonies. We turn to the period in which certain colonial leaders in these colonies unite in 1776 under a Declaration of Independence to seek and eventually establish their independence in a war with Britain.

We italicize those portions of the Declaration of Independence and the Articles of Confederation that relate to foreign policy and national security. Although these documents are not always represented or recognized or understood for their foreign policy and national security content, the italicized portions reveal how much of these two important documents (as with the Constitution that in 1789 would succeed the Articles) pertains to these matters.

3. *The Declaration of Independence*
(July 4, 1776)

Often overlooked are the foreign policy and national security aspects that are core to understanding the Declaration of Independence, which was drafted by Thomas Jefferson with some changes made in final draft by other colonial leaders. The Declaration explicitly challenges British sovereignty in the person of the king. Although there is reference to the British people (viz., their parliamentary representatives)—"brethren" who have been unresponsive to the plight of fellow subjects in the colonies—the British parliament is spared the blame for these circumstances because in the colonial (and Jefferson's) view it is the king as sovereign who retains responsibility for the colonies. The king allegedly not only has failed to carry out his responsibility to provide for the security and welfare of the thirteen American colonies and their inhabitants, but also has violated their rights as British subjects. By this Declaration, the signers construct a vision of colonies becoming states in their own right, newly defining Britain as an external power no different in kind from France, Spain, or other states. As states, the thirteen are seen as having new authority or "full power to levy war, conclude peace, contract alliances, establish commerce, and to do all other acts and things which independent states may of right do." Focus is thus as much on their external sovereign claim to a right to be independent or autonomous in foreign relations with other states as it is on their domestic sovereign claim to a right to exercise complete political and legal jurisdiction on their own territories.

When, in the course of human events, it becomes necessary for *one People to dissolve the political bonds which have connected them with another,* and to assume among the powers of the earth, the *separate and equal station* to which the laws of Nature and of Nature's God entitle them, a decent respect to the opinions of mankind requires that they should declare the causes which impel them to the separation.

We hold these truths to be self-evident, that all men are created equal, that they are endowed by their Creator with certain unalienable rights that among these are life, liberty and the pursuit of happiness—That to secure these rights, Governments are instituted among men, deriving their just powers from the consent of the governed, that whenever any form of Government becomes destructive of these ends, it is the right of the People to alter or to abolish it, and to institute new Government, laying its foundation on such principles, and organizing its powers in such form, as to them shall seem most likely *to effect their safety* and happiness. Prudence, indeed, will dictate that Governments long established should not be changed for light and transient causes; and accordingly all experience hath shown, that mankind are more disposed to suffer, while evils are sufferable, than to right themselves by abolishing the forms to which they are accustomed. But, when a long train of abuses and usurpations, pursuing invariably the same object, evinces a design to reduce them under absolute despotism, it is their right, it is their duty, to throw off such Government, and to *provide new guards for their future security.* Such has been the patient sufferance of these Colonies, and such is now the necessity which constrains them to alter their former systems of Government. The history of *the present King of Great-Britain* is a history of repeated injuries and usurpations, all having in direct object *the establishment of an absolute tyranny over these States.* To prove this, let facts be submitted to a candid world.

He has refused his assent to laws, the most wholesome and necessary for the public good.

He has forbidden his Governors to pass laws of immediate and pressing importance, unless suspended in their operation till his assent should be obtained; and when so suspended, he has utterly neglected to attend to them.

He has refused to pass other laws for the accommodation of large districts of people, unless those people would relinquish the right of representation in the Legislature, a right inestimable to them, and formidable to tyrants only.

He has called together legislative bodies at places unusual, uncomfortable, and distant from the depository of their public records, for the sole purpose of fatiguing them into compliance with his measures.

He has dissolved Representative Houses repeatedly, for opposing with manly firmness his invasions on the rights of the People.

He has refused for a long time, after such dissolutions, to cause others to be elected; whereby the legislative powers, incapable of annihilation, have returned to the people at large for their exercise; *the State remaining in the meantime exposed to all the dangers of invasion from without, and convulsions within.*

He has endeavoured to prevent the population of these States; for that purpose *obstructing the laws for naturalization of foreigners; refusing to pass others to encourage their migration hither,* and raising the conditions of new appropriations of lands.

He has obstructed the administration of justice, by refusing his assent to laws for establishing judiciary powers.

He has made judges dependent on his will alone, for the tenure of their offices, and the amount and payment of their salaries.

He has erected a multitude of new offices, and sent hither swarms of officers to harass our people, and eat out their substance.

He has *kept among us, in times of peace, standing armies, without the consent of our Legislature.*

He has *affected to render the military independent of, and superior to, the civil power.*

He has combined with others, to subject us to a jurisdiction foreign to our constitution, and unacknowledged by our laws; giving his assent to their acts of pretended legislation:

For *quartering large bodies of armed troops among us:*

For *protecting them, by a mock trial, from punishment for any murders which they*

should commit on the inhabitants of these States:

For *cutting off our trade* with all parts of the world:

For imposing taxes on us without our consent:

For depriving us, in many cases, of the benefits of trial by jury:

For *transporting us beyond seas to be tried for pretended offenses:*

For abolishing the free system of English laws in a neighboring province, establishing therein an arbitrary Government, and enlarging its boundaries, so as to render it at once an example and fit instrument for introducing the same absolute rule in these Colonies:

For taking away our charters, abolishing our most valuable laws, and altering fundamentally the forms of our Governments:

For suspending our own Legislatures, and declaring themselves invested with power to legislate for us in all cases whatsoever.

He has abdicated Government here, by *declaring us out of his protection and waging war against us.*

He has *plundered our seas, ravaged our coasts, burnt our towns, and destroyed the lives of our people.*

He is, at this time, *transporting large armies of foreign mercenaries to complete the works of death, desolation and tyranny,* already begun with circumstances of cruelty and perfidy scarcely paralleled in the most barbarous ages, and totally unworthy the Head of a civilized nation.

He has constrained our fellow *citizens taken captive on the high seas to bear arms against their country* to become the executioners of their friends and brethren, or to fall themselves by their hands.

He has *excited domestic insurrections amongst us,* and has *endeavoured to bring on the* inhabitants of our frontiers, the merciless Indian savages, whose known rule of warfare, is undistinguished destruction of all ages, sexes and conditions.

In every stage of these oppressions we have petitioned for redress in the most humble terms: Our repeated petitions have been answered only by repeated injury. A Prince, whose character is thus marked by every act which may define a tyrant, is unfit to be the ruler of a free people.

Nor have we been wanting in attention to *our British brethren*. We have warned them from time to time of attempts by their legislature to extend an unwarrantable jurisdiction over us. *We have reminded them of the circumstances of our emigration and settlement here.* We have appealed to their native justice and magnanimity, and we have conjured them by the ties of our common kindred to disavow these usurpations, which, would inevitably interrupt our connections and correspondence. *They too have been deaf to the voice of justice* and consanguinity. We

must, therefore, acquiesce in the necessity which denounces our separation, and *hold them, as we hold the rest of mankind, enemies in war, in peace, friends.*

We, therefore, the Representatives of the United States of America, in general Congress assembled, appealing to the Supreme Judge of the World for the rectitude of our intentions, do, in the name, and by the authority of the good People of these Colonies, solemnly publish and declare, *That these United Colonies are, and of right ought to be, free and independent states; that they are absolved from all allegiance to the British Crown, and that all political connection between them and the State of Great Britain, is and ought to be totally dissolved;* and that *as free and independent states, they have full power to levy war, conclude peace, contract alliances, establish commerce, and to do all other acts and things which independent states may of right do.* And for the support of this Declaration, with a firm reliance on the protection of divine Providence, we mutually pledge to each other our lives, our fortunes, and our sacred honor.

---

4. *The Treaty of Alliance with France*
(1778)

In this important, first treaty the united States secure an external recognition of the legitimacy of its cause in forming a "defensive" alliance with France that would prove to be decisive in the ultimate defeat of British forces at Yorktown in 1781. Significantly, this was a pact by thirteen states acting in union and represented in France by Benjamin Franklin, lead negotiator. (As befits these original circumstances, in the French language one refers to the United States in the plural; i.e., les États-Unis sont—the United States are rather than the United States is, as would be said in American usage.) We include this important document in its entirety here not only because it marks the initiation of an American foreign policy outside the British realm, but also because as an act of diplomacy it proved to be an essential step in the process of separating from Britain and, in time, constituting a republic. For the most part, spellings in this document have been modernized.

The most Christian King and the United States of North America, to wit, New Hampshire, Massachusetts Bay, Rhodes island, Connecticut, New York, New Jersey, Pennsylvania, Delaware, Maryland, Virginia, North Carolina, South Carolina, and Georgia, having this Day concluded a Treaty of amity and Commerce, for the reciprocal advantage of their Subjects and Citizens have thought it necessary to take into consideration the means of strengthening those engagements and of rendering them useful to the safety and tranquility of the two parties, particularly in case Great Britain in Resentment of that connection and of the good correspondence which is the object of the said Treaty, should break the Peace with France, either by direct hostilities, or by hindering her commerce and navigation, in a manner contrary to the Rights of Nations, and the Peace subsisting between the two Crowns; and his Majesty and the said united States having resolved in that Case to join their Councils and efforts against the Enterprises of their common Enemy, the respective Plenipotentiaries, empowered to concert the Clauses & conditions proper to fulfil the said Intentions, have, after the most mature Deliberation, concluded and determined on the following Articles.

Article 1. If War should break out between France and Great Britain, during the continuance of the present War between the United States and England, his Majesty and the said united States, shall make it a common cause, and aid each other mutually with their good Offices, their Counsels, and their forces, according to the exigence of Conjunctures as becomes good & faithful Allies.

Article 2. The essential and direct End of the present defensive alliance is to maintain effectually the liberty, Sovereignty, and independence absolute and unlimited of the said united States, as well in Matters of Government as of commerce.

Article 3. The two contracting Parties shall each on its own Part, and in the manner it may judge most proper, make all the efforts in its Power, against their common Enemy, in order to attain the end proposed.

Article 4. The contracting Parties agree that in case either of them should form any particular Enterprise in which the concurrence of the other may be desired, the Party whose concurrence is desired shall readily, and with good faith, join to act in concert for that Purpose, as far as circumstances and its own particular Situation will permit; and in that case, they shall regulate by a particular Convention the quantity and kind of Succor to be furnished, and the Time and manner of its being brought into action, as well as the advantages which are to be its Compensation.

Article 5. If the united States should think fit to attempt the Reduction of the British Power remaining in the Northern Parts of America, or the Islands of Bermudas, those Countries or Islands in case of Success, shall be confederated with or dependent upon the said united States.

Article 6. The Most Christian King renounces for ever the possession of the Islands of Bermudas as well as of any part of the continent of North america which before the treaty of Paris in 1763, or in virtue of that Treaty, were acknowledged to belong to the Crown of Great Britain, or to the united States heretofore called British Colonies, or which are at this Time or have lately been under the Power of The King and Crown of Great Britain.

Article 7. If his Most Christian Majesty shall think proper to attack any of the Islands situated in the Gulf of Mexico, or near that Gulf, which are at present under the Power of Great Britain, all the said

Isles, in case of success, shall appertain to the Crown of France.

Article 8. Neither of the two Parties shall conclude either Truce or Peace with Great Britain, without the formal consent of the other first obtained; and they mutually engage not to lay down their arms, until the Independence of the united states shall have been formally or tacitly assured by the Treaty or Treaties that shall terminate the War.

Article 9. The contracting Parties declare, that being resolved to fulfil [sic] each on its own Part the clauses and conditions of the present Treaty of alliance, according to its own power and circumstances, there shall be no after claim of compensation on one side or the other whatever may be the event of the War.

Article 10. The Most Christian King and the United states, agree to invite or admit other Powers who may have received injuries from England to make common cause with them, and to accede to the present alliance, under such conditions as shall be freely agreed to and settled between all the Parties.

Article 11. The two Parties guarantee mutually from the present time and forever, against all other powers, to wit, the united states to his most Christian Majesty the present Possessions of the Crown of France in America as well as those which it may acquire by the future Treaty of peace: and his most Christian Majesty guarantees on his part to the united states, their liberty, Sovereignty, and Independence absolute, and unlimited, as well in Matters of Government as commerce and also their Possessions, and the additions or conquests that their Confederation may obtain during the war, from any of the Dominions now or heretofore possessed by Great Britain in

North America, conformable to the 5th & 6th articles above written, the whole as their Possessions shall be fixed and assured to the said States at the moment of the cessation of their present War with England.

Article 12. In order to fix more precisely the sense and application of the preceding article, the Contracting Parties declare, that in case of rupture between France and England, the reciprocal Guarantee declared in the said article shall have its full force and effect the moment such War shall break out and if such rupture shall not take place, the mutual obligations of the said guarantee shall not commence, until the moment of the cessation of the present War between the united states and England shall have ascertained the Possessions.

Article 13. The present Treaty shall be ratified on both sides and the Ratifications shall be exchanged in the space of six months, sooner if possible.

In faith where of the respective Plenipotentiaries, to wit on the part of the most Christian King Conrad Alexander Gerard royal syndic of the City of Strasbourgh & Secretary of his majesty's Council of State and on the part of the United States Benjamin Franklin Deputy to the General Congress from the State of Pennsylvania and President of the Convention of the same state, Silas Deane heretofore Deputy from the State of Connecticut & Arthur Lee Councellor at Law have signed the above Articles both in the French and English Languages declaring Nevertheless that the present Treaty was originally composed and concluded in the French Language, and they have hereunto affixed their Seals

Done at Paris, this sixth Day of February, one thousand seven hundred and seventy eight.

5. *The Articles of Confederation and Perpetual Union*

(proposed in 1777, ratified in 1781, and effective 1781–89)

Foreign policy and national security were difficult to administer under the Articles of Confederation, which at the outset made clear that each of the thirteen states remained sovereign except for what was "expressly delegated to the United States" as a whole. This confederation was merely "a firm league of friendship" formed in large part "for their common defence." A nine-vote majority of the thirteen states was necessary to empower the central government to exercise many of its powers. Because each state retained substantial authority, many of the passages in the Articles of Confederation dealt with external relations among the thirteen states themselves. Foreign policy and national security prerogatives were centralized to some degree on matters of war and peace, diplomatic representation, and the making of treaties; however, the responsibility for raising armies for national use was reserved to the states. Subject to some restrictions, the states could also earn revenues by taxing international trade. Beyond borrowing on the credit of the United States, finance for "all charges of war . . . incurred for the common defence or general welfare" was to come "out of a common treasury" that was to "be supplied by the several states." The apparent inadequacy of so heavy a reliance on states for both revenue and the manning of units in the armed forces was a principal motivation for "amending" these Articles, a process that resulted in a new U.S. constitution that went into effect in 1789.

To all to whom these Presents shall come, we the undersigned Delegates of the States affixed to our Names send greeting. . . .

Article I. The Stile [sic] of this confederacy shall be "The United States of America."

Article II. *Each state retains its sovereignty, freedom and independence, and every Power, jurisdiction and right, which is not by this Confederation expressly delegated to the United States*, in Congress assembled.

Article III. The said states hereby severally enter into *a firm league of friendship with each other, for their common defence, the security of their Liberties, and their mutual and general welfare, binding themselves to assist each other, against all force offered to, or attacks made upon them, or any of them, on account of religion, sovereignty, trade, or any other pretence whatever.*

Article IV. *The better to secure and perpetuate mutual friendship and intercourse among the people of the different states in this union, the free inhabitants of each of these states, paupers, vagabonds and fugitives from Justice excepted, shall be entitled to all privileges and immunities of free citizens in the several states; and the people of each state shall have free ingress and regress to and from any other state, and shall enjoy therein all the privileges of trade and commerce, subject to the same duties, impositions and restrictions as the inhabitants thereof respectively, provided that such restriction shall not extend so far as to prevent the removal of property imported into any state, to any other state of which the Owner is an inhabitant* provided also that *no imposition, duties or restriction shall be laid by any state, on the property of the united states, or either of them.*

If any Person guilty of, or charged with *treason*, felony, or other high misdemeanor in any state, shall flee from Justice, and be found in any of the united states, he shall, upon demand of the Governor or executive power of the state from which he fled, be delivered up and removed to the state having jurisdiction of his offence. *Full faith and credit shall be given in each of these states to the records, acts and judicial proceedings of the courts and magistrates of every other state.*

Article V. For the most convenient management of the general interests of the united states, delegates shall be annually appointed in such manner as the legislatures of each state shall direct, to meet in Congress. . . .

In determining questions in the united states, in Congress assembled, each state shall have one vote.

Freedom of speech and debate in Congress shall not be impeached or questioned in any Court, or place out of Congress, and the members of congress shall be protected in their persons from arrests and imprisonments, during the time of their going to and from, and attendence on congress, except for *treason,* felony, or breach of the peace.

Article VI. *No state without the Consent of the united states in congress assembled, shall send any embassy to, or receive any embassy from, or enter into any conference, agreement, or alliance or treaty with any King, prince or state; nor shall any person holding any office of profit or trust under the united states, or any of them, accept any present, emolument, office or title of any kind whatever from any king, prince or foreign state; nor shall the united states in congress assembled, or any of them, grant any title of nobility.*

No two or more states shall enter into any treaty, confederation or alliance whatever between them, without the consent of the united states in congress assembled, specifying accurately the purposes for which the same is to be entered into, and how long it shall continue.

No state shall lay any imposts or duties, which may interfere with any stipulations in treaties, entered into by the united states in congress assembled, with any king, prince or state, in pursuance of any treaties already proposed by congress, to the courts of France and Spain.

No vessels of war shall be kept up in time of peace by any state, except such number only, as shall be deemed necessary by the united states in congress assembled, for the defence of such state, or its trade; nor shall any body of forces be kept up by any state, in time of peace, except such number only, as in the judgment of the united states, in congress assembled, shall be deemed requisite to garrison the forts necessary for the defence of such state; but every state shall always keep up a well regulated and disciplined militia, sufficiently armed and accoutered, and shall provide and constantly have ready for use, in public stores, a due number of field pieces and tents, and a proper quantity of arms, ammunition and camp equipage.

No state shall engage in any war without the consent of the united states in congress assembled, unless such state be actually invaded by enemies, or shall have received certain advice of a resolution being formed by some nation of Indians to invade such state, and the danger is so imminent as not to admit of a delay till the united states in congress assembled can be consulted; nor shall any state grant commissions to any ships or vessels of war, nor letters of marque or reprisal [This refers to the practice at the time of allowing private vessels to engage enemy vessels and seize commercial cargoes.—Ed.], *except it be after a declaration of war by the united states in congress assembled, and then only against the kingdom or state and the subjects thereof, against which war has been so declared, and under such regulations as shall be established by the united states in congress assembled, unless such state be infested by pirates, in which case vessels of war may be fitted out for that occasion, and kept so long as the danger shall continue, or until the united states in congress assembled shall determine otherwise.*

Article VII. *When land forces are raised by any state for the common defence, all officers of or under the rank of colonel, shall be appointed by the legislature of each state respectively, by whom such forces shall be raised, or in such manner as such state shall direct, and all vacancies shall be filled up by the state which first made the appointment.*

Article VIII. *All charges of war, and all other expenses that shall be incurred for the common defence or general welfare, and allowed by the united states in congress assembled, shall be defrayed out of a common treasury, which shall be supplied by the several states, in proportion to the value of all land within each state, granted to or surveyed for any Person, as such land and the buildings and improvements thereon shall be estimated according to such mode as the united states in congress assembled, shall from time to time direct and appoint.* The taxes for paying that proportion shall be laid and levied by the authority and direction of the legislatures of the several states within the time agreed upon by the united states in congress assembled.

Article IX. *The united states in congress assembled, shall have the sole and exclusive right and power of determining on peace and war, except in the cases mentioned in the sixth article—of sending and receiving ambassadors—entering into treaties and alliances, provided that no treaty of commerce shall be made whereby the legislative power of the respective states shall be restrained from imposing such imposts and duties on foreigners, as their own people are subjected to, or from prohibiting the exportation or importation of any species of goods or commodities whatsoever—of establishing rules for deciding in all cases, what captures on land or water shall be legal, and in what manner prizes taken by land or naval forces in the service of the united states shall be divided or appropriated—of granting letters of marque and reprisal in times of peace* [This is

another reference to the practice of allowing private vessels to engage enemy vessels and seize commercial cargoes.—Ed.]— *appointing courts for the trial of piracies and felonies commited on the high seas and establishing courts for receiving and determining finally appeals in all cases of captures,* provided that no member of Congress shall be appointed a judge of any of the said courts.

The united states in congress assembled shall also be the last resort on appeal in all disputes and differences now subsisting or that hereafter may arise between two or more states concerning boundary, jurisdiction or any other cause whatever. . . .

All controversies concerning the private right of soil claimed under different grants of two or more states, whose jurisdictions as they may respect such lands, and the states which passed such grants are adjusted, the said grants or either of them being at the same time claimed to have originated antecedent to such settlement of jurisdiction, *shall on the petition of either party to the congress of the united states, be finally determined.* . . .

The united states in congress assembled shall also have the sole and exclusive right and power of regulating the alloy and value of coin struck by their own authority, or by that of the respective states—fixing the standards of weights and measures throughout the united states—*regulating the trade and managing all affairs with the Indians, not members of any of the states,* provided that the legislative right of any state within its own limits be not infringed or violated— *establishing or regulating post offices from one state to another,* throughout all the united states, and exacting such postage on the papers passing through the same as may be requisite to defray the expenses of the said office—*appointing all officers of the land forces, in the service of the united states, excepting regimental officers—appointing all the* officers of the naval forces, and commissioning all officers whatever in the service of the united states—making rules for the government and regulation of the said land and naval forces, and directing their operations.

The united states in congress assembled shall have authority to appoint a committee, to sit in the recess of congress, to be denominated "A Committee of the States," and to consist of one delegate from each state; and to appoint such other committees and civil officers as may be necessary for managing the general affairs of the united states under their direction—to appoint one of their members to preside, provided that no person be allowed to serve in the office of president more than one year in any term of three years; to ascertain the necessary sums of Money to be raised for the service of the united states, and to appropriate and apply the same for defraying the public expenses—to borrow money, or emit bills on the credit of the united states, transmitting every half year to the respective states an account of the—sums of money so borrowed or emitted—to build and equip a navy—to agree upon the number of land forces, and to make requisitions from each state for its quota, in proportion to the number of white inhabitants in such state; which requisition shall be binding, and thereupon the legislature of each state shall appoint the regimental officers, raise the men and clothe, arm and equip them in a soldier like manner, at the expense of the united states; and the officers and men so clothed, armed and equipped shall march to the place appointed, and within the time agreed on by the united states in congress assembled. But if the united states in congress assembled shall, on consideration of circumstances judge proper that any state should not raise men, or should raise a smaller number than its quota, such extra number shall be raised, officered, clothed, armed and equipped in the

same manner as the quota of such state, unless the legislature of such state shall judge that such extra number cannot be safely spared out of the same, in which case they shall raise, officer, clothe, arm and equip as many of such extra number as they judge can be safely spared. And the officers and men so cloathed [sic], armed and equipped, shall march to the place appointed, and within the time agreed on by the united states in congress assembled.

The united states in congress assembled shall never engage in a war, nor grant letters of marque or reprisal in time of peace, nor enter into any treaties or alliances, nor coin money, nor regulate the value thereof, nor ascertain the sums and expenses necessary for the defence and welfare of the united states, or any of them, nor emit bills, nor borrow money on the credit of the united states, nor appropriate money, nor agree upon the number of vessels of war, to be built or purchased, or the number of land or sea forces to be raised, nor appoint a commander in chief of the army or navy, unless nine states assent to the same: nor shall a question on any other point, except for adjourning from day to day be determined, unless by the votes of the majority of the united states in congress assembled.

The congress of the united states shall have power to adjourn to any time within the year, and to any place within the united states, so that no period of adjournment be for a longer duration than the space of six Months, and shall publish the Journal of their proceedings monthly, except such parts thereof relating to treaties, alliances or military operations, as in their judgment require secrecy; and the yeas and nays of the delegates of each state on any question shall be entered on the Journal, when it is desired by any delegate; and the delegates of a state, or any of them, at his or their request shall be furnished with a transcript of the said Journal, except such parts as are above excepted, to lay before the legislatures of the several states.

Article X. The committee of the states, or any nine of them, shall be authorized to execute, in the recess of congress, such of the powers of congress as the united states in congress assembled, by the consent of nine states, shall from time to time think expedient to vest them with; provided that no power be delegated to the said committee, for the exercise of which, by the articles of confederation, the voice of nine states in the congress of the united states assembled is requisite.

Article XI. *Canada acceding to this confederation, and joining in the measures of the united states, shall be admitted into, and entitled to all the advantages of this union;* but no other colony shall be admitted into the same, unless such admission be agreed to by nine states.

Article XII. All bills of credit emitted, monies borrowed and debts contracted by, or under the authority of congress, before the assembling of the united states, in pursuance of the present confederation, shall be deemed and considered as a charge against the united states, for payment and satisfaction whereof the said united states, and the public faith are hereby solemnly pledged.

Article XIII. Every state shall abide by the determination of the united states in congress assembled, on all questions which by this confederation are submitted to them. And the Articles of this confederation shall be inviolably observed by every state, *and the union shall be perpetual;* nor shall any alteration at any time hereafter be made in any of them; unless such alteration be agreed to in a congress of the united states, and be afterwards confirmed by the legislatures of every state.

And whereas it hath pleased the Great Governor of the World [This is a Masonic reference to the creator; Freemasonry was an important influence on many of those constructing the confederation and the constitutional federation that would succeed these Articles.—Ed.] to incline the hearts of the legislatures we respectively represent in congress, to approve of, and to authorize us to ratify the said articles of confederation and perpetual union. Know Ye that we the undersigned delegates, by virtue of the power and authority to us given for that purpose, do by these Presents, in the name and in behalf of our respective constituents, fully and entirely ratify and confirm each and every of the said articles of confederation and perpetual union, and all and singular the matters and things therein contained: And we do further solemnly plight and engage the faith of our respective constituents, that they shall abide by the determinations of the united states in congress assembled, on all questions, which by the said confederation are submitted to them. And that the articles thereof shall be inviolably observed by the states we respectively represent, *and that the union shall be perpetual.* In Witness whereof we have hereunto set our hands in Congress. Done at Philadelphia in the State of Pennsylvania the ninth day of July in the Year of our Lord one Thousand seven Hundred and Seventy-eight, and in the third year of the independence of America.

6. *The Treaty of Paris*
(1783)

This important document restores peace, thus ending the Revolutionary War fought between 1776 and 1781. Britain terminates its claims to the now former colonies and refers to them collectively as the United States of America. In Article 1 Britain understands them "to be free sovereign and independent states." Thus achieved were the aspirations in the Declaration of Independence: "That these United Colonies are, and of right ought to be, free and independent states; that they are absolved from all allegiance to the British Crown. . . ."

In the name of the most holy and undivided Trinity. It having pleased the Divine Providence to dispose the hearts of the most serene and most potent Prince *George the Third, by the grace of God, king* of Great Britain, France, and Ireland, defender of the faith, duke of Brunswick and Lunebourg, arch-treasurer and prince elector of the Holy Roman Empire etc., and of *the United States of America, to forget all past misunderstandings and differences* that have unhappily interrupted the good correspondence and friendship which they mutually wish to restore, and *to establish such a beneficial and satisfactory intercourse,* between the two countries upon the ground of reciprocal advantages and mutual convenience as may promote and *secure to both perpetual peace and harmony* . . . his Britannic Majesty and the United States of America . . . have constituted and appointed, that is to say his Britannic Majesty on his part, David Hartley, . . . and the said United States on their part, John Adams, . . . Benjamin Franklin . . . , [and] John Jay . . . to be plenipotentiaries for the concluding and signing the present definitive treaty; who after having reciprocally communicated their respective full powers have agreed upon and confirmed the following articles.

Article 1. *His Britannic Majesty acknowledges the said United States,* viz., New Hampshire, Massachusetts Bay, Rhode Island and Providence Plantations, Connecticut, New York, New Jersey, Pennsylvania, Maryland, Virginia, North Carolina, South Carolina and Georgia, *to be free sovereign and independent states,* that he treats with them as such, and for himself, his heirs, and successors, *relinquishes all claims to the government, propriety, and territorial rights of the same and every part thereof.*

Article 2. And that all disputes which might arise in future on the subject of the boundaries of the said United States may be prevented, it is hereby agreed and declared, that the following are and shall be their boundaries. . . . [Detailed description of territorial boundaries is not reprinted here.]

Article 3. It is agreed that the people of the United States shall continue to enjoy unmolested the right to take fish of every kind on the Grand Bank and on all the other banks of Newfoundland, also in the Gulf of Saint Lawrence and at all other places in the sea, where the inhabitants of both countries used at any time heretofore to fish. . . .

Article 4. It is agreed that creditors on either side shall meet with no lawful impediment to the recovery of the full value in sterling money of all bona fide debts heretofore contracted.

Article 5. It is agreed that Congress shall earnestly recommend it to the legislatures of the respective states to provide for the restitution of all estates, rights, and properties, which have been confiscated belonging to real British subjects; and also of the estates, rights, and properties of persons resident in districts in the possession on his Majesty's arms and who have not borne arms against the said United States. . . . And it is agreed that all persons who have any interest in confiscated lands, either by debts, marriage settlements, or otherwise, shall meet with no lawful impediment in the prosecution of their just rights.

Article 6. That there shall be no future confiscations made nor any prosecutions commenced against any person or persons for, or by reason of, the part which he or they may have taken in the present war, and that no person shall on that account suffer any future loss or damage, either in his person, liberty, or property; and that those who may be in confinement on such charges at the time of the ratification of the treaty in America shall be immediately set at liberty, and the prosecutions so commenced be discontinued.

Article 7. There shall be a firm and perpetual peace between his Britannic Majesty and the said states, and between the subjects of the one and the citizens of the other, wherefore all hostilities both by sea and land shall from henceforth cease. All prisoners on both sides shall be set at liberty, and his Britannic Majesty shall withdraw all his armies. . . .

Article 8. The navigation of the river Mississippi, from its source to the ocean, shall forever remain free and open to the subjects of Great Britain and the citizens of the United States.

Article 9. In case it should so happen that any place or territory belonging to Great Britain or to the United States should have been conquered by the arms of either from the other before the arrival of the said Provisional Articles in America, it is agreed that the same shall be restored without difficulty and without requiring any compensation.

Article 10. The solemn ratifications of the present treaty expedited in good and due form shall be exchanged between the contracting parties in the space of six months or sooner. . . .

Done at Paris, this third day of September in the year of our Lord, one thousand seven hundred and eighty-three.

Chapter 3

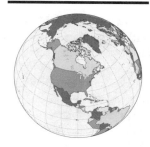

A Constitutional Republic Constructed

Cognizant of weaknesses in the Articles of Confederation, the delegates who assembled in Philadelphia in 1787 decided to propose amendment to them. Article XIII of the Articles required that any "alteration" of these provisions "be agreed to in a congress of the united states, and be afterwards confirmed by the legislatures of every state." There was by no means unanimity on need for amending the Articles; however, convening a committee finally became possible when George Washington agreed in 1787 to lend his legitimacy to the proceedings by attending and chairing these meetings in Philadelphia. More than just a few amendments here and there, the delegates drafted a new document. A comparison of the Articles of Confederation with the new Constitution reveals that some of the clauses in the original document survived; however, the new document markedly strengthened the new central or federal government, particularly in relation to foreign policy and national security matters as well as revenue-raising authority that would secure the government's financial base.

In Chapter 4, we include selections from the *Federalist Papers* because they so clearly delineate much of the thinking that gave rise to the formal provisions in the U.S. Constitution. Beyond *Federalist* Nos. 10 and 51 described here (and the brief excerpt from *Federalist* No. 37 that depicts a rather dark ontological perspective on human nature that informed the constitutional construction), we look at views expressed by John Jay and Alexander Hamilton on security through national unity (to include important commentary on civil-military relations) as well as on the treaty-making power and the role of the judiciary on foreign policy and related matters.

In their focus on domestic politics and processes, many scholars of American politics have tended to overlook or discount as relatively less important the foreign policy and national security arguments that Hamilton and Jay present in the *Federalist Papers*. Close reading, however, reveals how important *union* was to their view of both *domestic security* in relation to other states (avoiding breakdown into competing states or alliances among different coalitions among the thirteen states) and to Native American or Indian tribes and *external security* (strength in numbers against any would-be foe). Quite apart from the ineffectiveness of central government and its troubling finances under the Articles of Confederation, without these compelling security arguments it would have been most difficult to bring these diverse states to form the federation they eventually constructed under the U.S. Constitution.

The power and the balance of power that Hamilton and Jay saw as dominating international politics reflected what today we would call a *realist* view of the external environment within which the new republic was immersed. (This mode of thinking also was, of course, part of the same Madisonian formula domestically—setting competing interests or factions at odds with each other within a checks-and-balances system at both federal and state-and-local levels.) At the same time, however, the *Federalist* writers also sought to avoid unnecessary international conflicts that would be contrary to U.S. commercial and other interests abroad. This required sensitivity to the interests of great powers beyond the American shore, particularly the British, French, and Spanish.

7. *The Constitution of the United States*
(drafted in 1787 and ratified in 1789)

Reprinted here in its entirety, the U.S. Constitution replaced the Articles of Confederation and established a much stronger central government. At the same time, it established within a federal state a bicameral legislature and the further separation of powers among three branches of the central government. Key parts of foreign policy and national security interest are in Article I, particularly Section 8, and Article II, particularly Sections 2 and 3.

The Constitution vests Congress with revenue and appropriations authority—the "purse strings" essential to financing government operations in foreign policy, national security, and a wide range of domestic programs. As with all other federal government spending, appropriations bills originate in the House of Representatives, whose members are elected to represent the people in their respective districts. (After all, a key issue in the American Revolution was British taxation of the colonies without their being represented in the British parliament.)

The Constitution grants Congress an extensive charter to provide for the common defense and general welfare, regulate international commerce and the value of U.S. currency in relation to foreign currencies, make rules for naturalization of immigrants as citizens, define and provide for punishment of piracy and other violations of international law, raise and provide for the armed forces, and declare war. Article II empowers the president with the advice and consent of the Senate to make treaties and appoint diplomats and all other government officers, names the president as commander in chief of the armed forces, requires him to report to Congress on the state of the union, and designates him in his capacity as chief executive responsible for receiving foreign diplomats. The "advice and consent" clause on treaty ratification specifies a substantial role for the Senate in which each state has equal representation, thus giving states through their senators a preeminent role in foreign policy matters that would have been separate state prerogatives were they not part of the union.

That said, Article I (see Sections 9 and 10) explicitly centralizes foreign policy authority, denying states power to make treaties or, without consent of Congress, to enter into alliances, engage independently in warfare (except when invaded), or tax foreign trade. Beyond designating the president as commander in chief in Article II, key passages relating to civil-military relations are found in Article I, Section 8, and in the Second, Third, Fifth, and Fourteenth Amendments. Clauses related to American foreign policy and national security have been italicized.

We the People of the United States, in Order to form a more perfect Union, establish Justice, *insure domestic Tranquility, provide for the common defence,* promote the general Welfare, and secure the Blessings of Liberty to ourselves and our Posterity, do ordain and establish this Constitution for the United States of America.

Article I

Section 1. All legislative Powers herein granted shall be vested in a Congress of the United States, which shall consist of a Senate and House of Representatives.

Section 2. The House of Representatives shall be composed of Members chosen every second Year by the People of the several States, and the Electors in each State shall have the Qualifications requisite for Electors of the most numerous Branch of the State Legislature.

No Person shall be a Representative who shall not have attained to the Age of twenty five Years, and been seven Years a Citizen of the United States, and who shall not, when elected, be an Inhabitant of that State in which he shall be chosen.

Representatives and direct Taxes shall be apportioned among the several States which may be included within this Union, according to their respective Numbers, which shall be determined by adding to the whole Number of free Persons, including those bound to Service for a Term of Years, and excluding Indians not taxed, three fifths of all other Persons [See the Four-teenth Amendment, which changes this provision.—Ed.]. The actual Enumeration shall be made within three Years after the first Meeting of the Congress of the United States, and within every subsequent Term of ten Years, in such Manner as they shall by Law direct. The Number of Representatives shall not exceed one for every thirty Thousand, but each State shall have at Least one Representative; and until such enumeration shall be made, the State of New Hampshire shall be entitled to choose three, Massachusetts eight, Rhode-Island and Providence Plantations one, Connecticut five, New-York six, New Jersey four, Pennsylvania eight, Delaware one, Maryland six, Virginia ten, North Carolina five, South Carolina five, and Georgia three.

When vacancies happen in the Representation from any State, the Executive Authority thereof shall issue Writs of Election to fill such Vacancies.

The House of Representatives shall choose their Speaker and other Officers; and shall have the sole Power of Impeachment.

Section 3. The Senate of the United States shall be composed of two Senators from each State, chosen by the Legislature thereof [See the Seventeenth Amendment, which changes this provision.—Ed.], for six Years; and each Senator shall have one Vote.

Immediately after they shall be assembled in Consequence of the first Election, they shall be divided as equally as may be into three Classes. The Seats of the Senators of the first Class shall be vacated at the Expiration of the second Year, of the second Class at the Expiration of the fourth Year, and of the third Class at the Expiration of the sixth Year, so that one third may be chosen every second Year; and if Vacancies happen by Resignation, or otherwise, during the Recess of the Legislature of any State, the Executive thereof may make temporary Appointments until the next Meeting of the Legislature, which shall then fill such Vacancies [See the Seventeenth Amendment, which changes this provision.—Ed.].

No Person shall be a Senator who shall not have attained to the Age of thirty Years, and been nine Years a Citizen of the United States, and who shall not, when elected, be an Inhabitant of that State for which he shall be chosen.

The Vice President of the United States shall be President of the Senate, but shall have no Vote, unless they be equally divided.

The Senate shall choose their other Officers, and also a President pro tempore, in the Absence of the Vice President, or when he shall exercise the Office of President of the United States.

The Senate shall have the sole Power to try all Impeachments. When sitting for that Purpose, they shall be on Oath or Affirmation. When the President of the United States is tried, the Chief Justice shall preside: And no Person shall be convicted without the Concurrence of two thirds of the Members present.

Judgment in Cases of Impeachment shall not extend further than to removal from Office, and disqualification to hold and enjoy any Office of honor, Trust or Profit under the United States: but the Party convicted shall nevertheless be liable and subject to Indictment, Trial, Judgment and Punishment, according to Law.

Section 4. The Times, Places and Manner of holding Elections for Senators and Representatives, shall be prescribed in each State by the Legislature thereof; but the Congress may at any time by Law make or alter such Regulations, except as to the Places of choosing Senators.

The Congress shall assemble at least once in every Year, and such Meeting shall be on the first Monday in December [See the Twentieth Amendment, which changes this provision.—Ed.], unless they shall by Law appoint a different Day.

Section 5. Each House shall be the Judge of the Elections, Returns and Qualifications of its own Members, and a Majority of each shall constitute a Quorum to do Business; but a smaller Number may adjourn from day to day, and may be authorized to compel the Attendance of absent Members, in such Manner, and under such Penalties as each House may provide.

Each House may determine the Rules of its Proceedings, punish its Members for disorderly Behaviour, and, with the Concurrence of two thirds, expel a Member.

Each House shall keep a Journal of its Proceedings, and from time to time publish the same, excepting such Parts as may in their Judgment require Secrecy; and the Yeas and Nays of the Members of either House on any question shall, at the Desire of one fifth of those Present, be entered on the Journal.

Neither House, during the Session of Congress, shall, without the Consent of the other, adjourn for more than three days, nor to any other Place than that in which the two Houses shall be sitting.

Section 6. The Senators and Representatives shall receive a Compensation for their Services, to be ascertained by Law, and paid out of the Treasury of the United States. They shall in all Cases, except

Treason, Felony and Breach of the Peace, be privileged from Arrest during their Attendance at the Session of their respective Houses, and in going to and returning from the same; and for any Speech or Debate in either House, they shall not be questioned in any other Place.

No Senator or Representative shall, during the Time for which he was elected, be appointed to any civil Office under the Authority of the United States, which shall have been created, or the Emoluments whereof shall have been increased during such time; and no Person holding any Office under the United States, shall be a Member of either House during his Continuance in Office.

Section 7. *All Bills for raising Revenue shall originate in the House of Representatives; but the Senate may propose or concur with Amendments as on other Bills.*

Every Bill which shall have passed the House of Representatives and the Senate, shall, before it become a Law, be presented to the President of the United States: If he approve he shall sign it, but if not he shall return it, with his Objections to that House in which it shall have originated, who shall enter the Objections at large on their Journal, and proceed to reconsider it. If after such Reconsideration two thirds of that House shall agree to pass the Bill, it shall be sent, together with the Objections, to the other House, by which it shall likewise be reconsidered, and if approved by two thirds of that House, it shall become a Law. But in all such Cases the Votes of both Houses shall be determined by yeas and Nays, and the Names of the Persons voting for and against the Bill shall be entered on the Journal of each House respectively. If any Bill shall not be returned by the President within ten Days (Sundays excepted) after it shall have been presented to him, the Same shall be a Law, in like Manner as

if he had signed it, unless the Congress by their Adjournment prevent its Return, in which Case it shall not be a Law.

Every Order, Resolution, or Vote to which the Concurrence of the Senate and House of Representatives may be necessary (except on a question of Adjournment) shall be presented to the President of the United States; and before the Same shall take Effect, shall be approved by him, or being disapproved by him, shall be repassed by two thirds of the Senate and House of Representatives, according to the Rules and Limitations prescribed in the Case of a Bill.

Section 8. *The Congress shall have Power To lay and collect Taxes, Duties, Imposts and Excises, to pay the Debts and provide for the common Defence and general Welfare of the United States; but all Duties, Imposts and Excises shall be uniform throughout the United States;*

To borrow Money on the credit of the United States;

To regulate Commerce with foreign Nations, and among the several States, and with the Indian Tribes;

To establish an uniform Rule of Naturalization, and uniform Laws on the subject of Bankruptcies throughout the United States;

To coin Money, regulate the Value thereof, and of foreign Coin, and fix the Standard of Weights and Measures;

To provide for the Punishment of counterfeiting the Securities and current Coin of the United States;

To establish Post Offices and post Roads;

To promote the Progress of Science and useful Arts, by securing for limited Times to Authors and Inventors the exclusive Right to their respective Writings and Discoveries;

To constitute Tribunals inferior to the supreme Court;

To define and punish Piracies and Felonies committed on the high Seas, and Offences against the Law of Nations;

To declare War, grant Letters of Marque and Reprisal [This refers to the practice at the time of allowing private vessels to engage enemy vessels and seize commercial cargoes.—Ed.], *and make Rules concerning Captures on Land and Water;*

To raise and support Armies, but no Appropriation of Money to that Use shall be for a longer Term than two Years;

To provide and maintain a Navy;

To make Rules for the Government and Regulation of the land and naval Forces;

To provide for calling forth the Militia to execute the Laws of the Union, suppress Insurrections and repel Invasions;

To provide for organizing, arming, and disciplining, the Militia, and for governing such Part of them as may be employed in the Service of the United States, reserving to the States respectively, the Appointment of the Officers, and the Authority of training the Militia according to the discipline prescribed by Congress;

To exercise exclusive Legislation in all Cases whatsoever, over such District (not exceeding ten Miles square) as may, by Cession of particular States, and the Acceptance of Congress, become the Seat of the Government of the United States, and *to exercise like Authority over all Places purchased by the Consent of the Legislature of the State in which the Same shall be, for the Erection of Forts, Magazines, Arsenals, dock-Yards, and other needful Buildings;*—And

To make all Laws which shall be *necessary and proper* for carrying into Execution the foregoing Powers, and all other Powers vested by this Constitution in the Government of the United States, or in any Department or Officer thereof.

Section 9. *The Migration or Importation of such Persons as any of the States now existing shall think proper to admit, shall not be prohibited by the Congress prior to the Year one thousand eight hundred and eight, but a Tax or duty may be imposed on such Importation, not exceeding ten dollars for each Person* [This provided for at least a twenty-year continuance of the slave trade.—Ed.].

The Privilege of the Writ of Habeas Corpus shall not be suspended, unless when in Cases of Rebellion or Invasion the public Safety may require it.

No Bill of Attainder or ex post facto Law shall be passed.

No Capitation, or other direct, Tax shall be laid, unless in Proportion to the Census or Enumeration herein before directed to be taken.

No Tax or Duty shall be laid on Articles exported from any State.

No Preference shall be given by any Regulation of Commerce or Revenue to the Ports of one State over those of another; nor shall Vessels bound to, or from, one State, be obliged to enter, clear, or pay Duties in another.

No Money shall be drawn from the Treasury, but in Consequence of Appropriations made by Law; and a regular Statement and Account of the Receipts and Expenditures of all public Money shall be published from time to time.

No Title of Nobility shall be granted by the United States: And *no Person holding any Office of Profit or Trust* under them, shall, *without the Consent of the Congress, accept of any present, Emolument, Office, or Title, of any kind whatever, from any King, Prince, or foreign State.*

Section 10. *No State shall enter into any Treaty, Alliance, or Confederation; grant Letters of Marque and Reprisal* [This is another reference to the practice of allowing private vessels to engage enemy vessels and seize commercial cargoes.—Ed.]; coin Money; emit Bills of Credit; make any Thing but gold and silver Coin a Tender in Payment of Debts; pass any Bill of Attainder, ex post facto Law, or Law impairing the Obligation of Contracts, or grant any Title of Nobility.

No State shall, without the Consent of the Congress, lay any Imposts or Duties on Imports or Exports, except what may be absolutely necessary for executing it's [sic] inspection Laws; and the net Produce of all Duties and Imposts, laid by any State on Imports or Exports, shall be for the Use of the Treasury of the United States; and all such Laws shall be subject to the Revision and Control of the Congress.

No State shall, without the Consent of Congress, lay any Duty of Tonnage, keep Troops, or Ships of War in time of Peace, enter into any Agreement or Compact with another State, or with a foreign Power, or engage in War, unless actually invaded, or in such imminent Danger as will not admit of delay.

Article II

Section 1. *The executive Power shall be vested in a President of the United States of America.* He shall hold his Office during the Term of four Years, and, together with the Vice President, chosen for the same Term, be elected, as follows:

Each State shall appoint, in such Manner as the Legislature thereof may direct, a Number of Electors, equal to the whole Number of Senators and Representatives to which the State may be entitled in the Congress: but no Senator or Representative, or Person holding an Office of Trust or Profit under the United States, shall be appointed an Elector.

The Electors shall meet in their respective States, and vote by Ballot for two Persons, of whom one at least shall not be an Inhabitant of the same State with themselves. And they shall make a List of all the Persons voted for, and of the Number of Votes for each; which List they shall sign and certify, and transmit sealed to the Seat of the Government of the United States, directed to the President of the Senate. The President of the Senate shall, in the Presence of the Senate and House of Representatives, open all the Certificates, and the Votes shall then be counted. The Person having the greatest Number of Votes shall be the President, if such Number be a Majority of the whole Number of Electors appointed; and if there be more than one who have such Majority, and have an equal Number of Votes, then the House of Representatives shall immediately choose by Ballot one of them for President; and if no Person have a Majority, then from the five highest on the List the said House shall in like Manner choose the President. But in choosing the President, the Votes shall be taken by States, the Representation from each State having one Vote; a quorum for this Purpose shall consist of a Member or Members from two thirds of the States, and a Majority of all the States shall be necessary to a Choice. In every Case, after the Choice of the President, the Person having the greatest Number of Votes of the Electors shall be the Vice President. But if there should remain two or more who have equal Votes, the Senate shall choose from them by Ballot the Vice President [See the Twelfth Amendment, which changes this provision.—Ed.].

The Congress may determine the Time of choosing the Electors, and the Day on which they shall give their Votes; which Day shall be the same throughout the United States.

No Person except a natural born Citizen, or a Citizen of the United States, at the time of the Adoption of this Constitution, shall be eligible to the Office of President; neither shall any Person be eligible to that Office who shall not have attained to the Age of thirty five Years, and *been fourteen Years a Resident within the United States.*

In Case of the Removal of the President from Office, or of his Death, Resignation, or Inability to discharge the Powers and Duties of the said Office, the Same shall devolve on the Vice President, and the Congress may by Law provide for the Case of Removal, Death, Resignation or Inability, both of the President and Vice President, declaring what Officer shall then act as President, and such Officer shall act accordingly, until the Disability be removed, or a President shall be elected [See the Twenty-fifth Amendment, which changes this provision.—Ed.].

The President shall, at stated Times, receive for his Services, a Compensation, which shall neither be increased nor diminished during the Period for which he shall have been elected, and he shall not receive within that Period any other Emolument from the United States, or any of them.

Before he enter on the Execution of his Office, he shall take the following Oath or Affirmation:—"I do solemnly swear (or affirm) that I will *faithfully execute the Office of President of the United States, and will* to the best of my Ability, *preserve, protect and defend the Constitution of the United States.*"

Section 2. *The President shall be Commander in Chief of the Army and Navy of the United States, and of the Militia of the several States, when called into the actual Service of the United States;* he may require the Opinion, in writing, of the principal Officer in each of the executive Departments, upon any Subject relating to the Duties of their respective Offices, and he shall have Power to grant Reprieves and Pardons for Offences against the United States, except in Cases of Impeachment.

He shall have Power, by and with the Advice and Consent of the Senate, to make Treaties, provided two thirds of the Senators present concur; and *he shall nominate, and by and with the Advice and Consent of the Senate, shall appoint Ambassadors, other public Ministers and Consuls,* Judges of the supreme Court, *and all other Officers of the United States,* whose Appointments are not herein otherwise provided for, and which shall be established by Law: *but the Congress may by Law vest the Appointment of such inferior Officers, as they think proper, in the President alone,* in the Courts of Law, *or in the Heads of Departments.*

The President shall have Power to fill up all Vacancies that may happen during the Recess of the Senate, by granting Commissions which shall expire at the End of their next Session.

Section 3. *He shall from time to time give to the Congress Information of the State of the Union, and recommend to their Consideration such Measures as he shall judge necessary and expedient;* he may, on extraordinary Occasions, convene both Houses, or either of them, and in Case of Disagreement between them, with Respect to the Time of Adjournment, he may adjourn them to such Time as he shall think proper; *he shall receive Ambassadors and other public Ministers; he shall take Care that the Laws be faithfully executed, and shall Commission all the Officers of the United States.*

Section 4. The President, Vice President and all civil Officers of the United States, shall be removed from Office on Impeachment for, and Conviction of, *Treason,*

Bribery, or other high Crimes and Misdemeanors.

Article III

Section 1. The judicial Power of the United States shall be vested in one supreme Court, and in such inferior Courts as the Congress may from time to time ordain and establish. The Judges, both of the supreme and inferior Courts, shall hold their Offices during good Behaviour, and shall, at stated Times, receive for their Services a Compensation, which shall not be diminished during their Continuance in Office.

Section 2. *The judicial Power shall extend to all Cases, in Law and Equity, arising under this Constitution, the Laws of the United States, and Treaties made, or which shall be made, under their Authority;—to all Cases affecting Ambassadors, other public Ministers and Consuls;—to all Cases of admiralty and maritime Jurisdiction;—to Controversies to which the United States shall be a Party;—to* Controversies between two or more States;—between a State and Citizens of another State [This was modified by the Eleventh Amendment.—Ed.];—between Citizens of different States;—between Citizens of the same State claiming Lands under Grants of different States, and *between a State, or the Citizens thereof, and foreign States, Citizens or Subjects.*

In all Cases affecting Ambassadors, other public Ministers and Consuls, and those in which a State shall be Party, the supreme Court shall have original Jurisdiction. In all the other Cases before mentioned, the supreme Court shall have appellate Jurisdiction, both as to Law and Fact, with such Exceptions, and under such Regulations as the Congress shall make.

The Trial of all Crimes, except in Cases of Impeachment, shall be by Jury; and such Trial shall be held in the State where the said Crimes shall have been committed; but when not committed within any State, the Trial shall be at such Place or Places as the Congress may by Law have directed.

Section 3. *Treason against the United States shall consist only in levying War against them, or in adhering to their Enemies, giving them Aid and Comfort. No Person shall be convicted of Treason unless on the Testimony of two Witnesses to the same overt Act, or on Confession in open Court.*

The Congress shall have Power to declare the Punishment of Treason, but no Attainder of Treason shall work Corruption of Blood, or Forfeiture except during the Life of the Person attainted.

Article IV

Section 1. Full Faith and Credit shall be given in each State to the public Acts, Records, and judicial Proceedings of every other State. And the Congress may by general Laws prescribe the Manner in which such Acts, Records and Proceedings shall be proved, and the Effect thereof.

Section 2. The Citizens of each State shall be entitled to all Privileges and Immunities of Citizens in the several States.

A Person charged in any State with *Treason,* Felony, or other Crime, who shall flee from Justice, and be found in another State, shall on Demand of the executive Authority of the State from which he fled, be delivered up, to be removed to the State having Jurisdiction of the Crime.

No Person held to Service or Labour in one State, under the Laws thereof, escaping into another, shall, in Consequence of any Law or Regulation therein, be discharged from such Service or Labour, but shall be delivered up on Claim of the Party to whom such Service or Labour may be due [The Thirteenth Amendment changes this slavery provision.—Ed.].

Section 3. New States may be admitted by the Congress into this Union; but no new State shall be formed or erected within the Jurisdiction of any other State; nor any State be formed by the Junction of two or more States, or Parts of States, without the Consent of the Legislatures of the States concerned as well as of the Congress.

The Congress shall have Power to dispose of and make all needful Rules and Regulations respecting the Territory or other Property belonging to the United States; and nothing in this Constitution shall be so construed as to Prejudice any Claims of the United States, or of any particular State.

Section 4. *The United States shall guarantee to every State* in this Union a Republican Form of Government, and shall *protect each of them against Invasion;* and on Application of the Legislature, or of the Executive (when the Legislature cannot be convened), *against domestic Violence.*

Article V

The Congress, whenever two thirds of both Houses shall deem it necessary, shall propose Amendments to this Constitution, or, on the Application of the Legislatures of two thirds of the several States, shall call a Convention for proposing Amendments, which, in either Case, shall be valid to all Intents and Purposes, as Part of this Constitution, when ratified by the Legislatures of three fourths of the several States, or by Conventions in three fourths thereof, as the one or the other Mode of Ratification may be proposed by the Congress; Provided that *no Amendment which may be made prior*

to the Year One thousand eight hundred and eight shall in any Manner affect the first and fourth Clauses in the Ninth Section of the first Article [This passage precludes from amendment the 1788–1808, twenty-year, slave-trade compromise embodied in the first clause of Article I, Section 9 supra.—Ed.]; and that no State, without its Consent, shall be deprived of its equal Suffrage in the Senate [See also the Seventeenth Amendment.—Ed.].

Article VI

All Debts contracted and Engagements entered into, before the Adoption of this Constitution, shall be as valid against the United States under this Constitution, as under the Confederation.

This Constitution, and the Laws of the United States which shall be made in Pursuance thereof; *and all Treaties made, or which shall be made, under the Authority of the United States, shall be the supreme Law of the Land;* and the Judges in every State shall be bound thereby, any Thing in the Constitution or Laws of any State to the Contrary notwithstanding.

The Senators and Representatives before mentioned, and the Members of the several State Legislatures, and all executive and judicial Officers, both of the United States and of the several States, shall be bound by Oath or Affirmation, to support this Constitution; but no religious Test shall ever be required as a Qualification to any Office or public Trust under the United States.

Article VII

The Ratification of the Conventions of nine States, shall be sufficient for the Establishment of this Constitution between the States so ratifying the Same.

Done in Convention by the Unanimous Consent of the States present the

Seventeenth Day of September in the Year of our Lord one thousand seven hundred and Eighty seven and of the Independence of the United States of America the Twelfth In witness whereof We have hereunto subscribed our Names.

Constitutional Amendments

Bill of Rights
(proposed in 1789 and ratified in 1791)

I

Congress shall make no law respecting an establishment of religion, or prohibiting the free exercise thereof; or abridging the freedom of speech, or of the press; or the right of the people *peaceably to assemble,* and to petition the Government for a redress of grievances.

II

A well regulated Militia, being necessary to the security of a free State, the right of the people to keep and bear Arms, shall not be infringed.

III

No Soldier shall, in time of peace be quartered in any house, without the consent of the Owner, nor in time of war, but in a manner to be prescribed by law.

IV

The right of the people to be secure in their persons, houses, papers, and effects, against unreasonable searches and seizures, shall not be violated, and no Warrants shall issue, but upon probable cause, supported by Oath or affirmation, and particularly describing the place to be searched, and the persons or things to be seized.

V

No person shall be held to answer for a capital, or otherwise infamous crime, unless on a presentment or indictment of a Grand Jury, *except in cases arising in the land or naval forces, or in the Militia, when in actual service in time of War or public danger;* nor shall any person be subject for the same offence to be twice put in jeopardy of life or limb; nor shall be compelled in any criminal case to be a witness against himself, *nor be deprived of life, liberty, or property,* without due process of law; nor shall private property be taken for public use, without just compensation.

VI

In all criminal prosecutions, the accused shall enjoy the right to a speedy and public trial, by an impartial jury of the State and district wherein the crime shall have been committed, which district shall have been previously ascertained by law, and to be informed of the nature and cause of the accusation; to be confronted with the witnesses against him; to have compulsory process for obtaining witnesses in his favor, and to have the Assistance of Counsel for his defence.

VII

In Suits at common law, where the value in controversy shall exceed twenty dollars, the right of trial by jury shall be preserved, and no fact tried by a jury, shall be otherwise re-examined in any Court of the United States, than according to the rules of the common law.

VIII

Excessive bail shall not be required, nor excessive fines imposed, nor cruel and unusual punishments inflicted.

IX

The enumeration in the Constitution, of certain rights, shall not be construed to deny or disparage others retained by the people.

X

The powers not delegated to the United States by the Constitution, nor prohibited by it to the States, are reserved to the States respectively, or to the people.

Other Amendments

XI

[proposed in 1794 and ratified in 1798]

The Judicial power of the United States shall not be construed to extend to any suit in law or equity, commenced or prosecuted against one of the United States by Citizens of another State, or by Citizens or Subjects of any Foreign State.

XII

[proposed in 1803 and ratified in 1804]

The Electors shall meet in their respective states, and vote by ballot for President and Vice-President, one of whom, at least, shall not be an inhabitant of the same state with themselves; they shall name in their ballots the person voted for as President, and in distinct ballots the person voted for as Vice-President, and they shall make distinct lists of all persons voted for as President, and of all persons voted for as Vice-President, and of the number of votes for each, which lists they shall sign and certify, and transmit sealed to the seat of the government of the United States, directed to the President of the Senate;—The President of the Senate shall, in the presence of the Senate and House of Representatives, open all the certificates and the votes shall then be counted;—The person having the greatest number of votes for President, shall be the President, if such number be a majority of the whole number of Electors appointed; and if no person have such majority, then from the persons having the highest numbers not exceeding three on the list of those voted for as President, the House of Representatives shall choose immediately, by ballot, the President. But in choosing the President, the votes shall be taken by states, the representation from each state having one vote; a quorum for this purpose shall consist of a member or members from two-thirds of the states, and a majority of all the states shall be necessary to a choice. And if the House of Representatives shall not choose a President whenever the right of choice shall devolve upon them, before the fourth day of March next following, then the Vice-President shall act as President, as in the case of the death or other constitutional disability of the President.—The person having the greatest number of votes as Vice-President, shall be the Vice-President, if such number be a majority of the whole number of Electors appointed, and if no person have a majority, then from the two highest numbers on the list, the Senate shall choose the Vice-President; a quorum for the purpose shall consist of two-thirds of the whole number of Senators, and a majority of the whole number shall be necessary to a choice. But no person constitutionally ineligible to the office of President shall be eligible to that of Vice-President of the United States.

XIII

[proposed and ratified in 1865]

Section 1. Neither slavery nor involuntary servitude, except as a punishment for crime whereof the party shall have been duly convicted, shall exist within the

United States, or any place subject to their jurisdiction.

Section 2. Congress shall have power to enforce this article by appropriate legislation.

XIV
[proposed in 1866 and ratified in 1868]

Section 1. *All persons born or naturalized* in the United States, and subject to the jurisdiction thereof, *are citizens* of the United States and of the State wherein they reside. No State shall make or enforce any law which shall abridge the privileges or immunities of citizens of the United States; nor shall any State deprive any person of life, liberty, or property, without *due process of law*; nor deny to any person within its jurisdiction the *equal protection of the laws.*

Section 2. Representatives shall be apportioned among the several States according to their respective numbers, counting the whole number of persons in each State, excluding Indians not taxed. But when the right to vote at any election for the choice of electors for President and Vice President of the United States, Representatives in Congress, the Executive and Judicial officers of a State, or the members of the Legislature thereof, is denied to any of the male inhabitants of such State, being twenty-one years of age, and citizens of the United States, or in any way abridged, *except for participation in rebellion,* or other crime, the basis of representation therein shall be reduced in the proportion which the number of such male citizens shall bear to the whole number of male citizens twenty-one years of age in such State.

Section 3. *No person shall* be a Senator or Representative in Congress, or elector of President and Vice President, or *hold any office, civil or military,* under the United States, or under any State, *who, having*

previously taken an oath, as a member of Congress, or as an officer of the United States, or as a member of any State legislature, or as an executive or judicial officer of any State, *to support the Constitution of the United States, shall have engaged in insurrection or rebellion against the same, or given aid or comfort to the enemies thereof.* But Congress may by a vote of two-thirds of each House, remove such disability.

Section 4. *The validity of the public debt* of the United States, authorized by law, including debts incurred *for payment of pensions and bounties for services in suppressing insurrection or rebellion, shall not be questioned.* But *neither the United States nor any State shall assume or pay any debt or obligation incurred in aid of insurrection or rebellion against the United States,* or any claim for the loss or emancipation of any slave; but all such debts, obligations and claims shall be held illegal and void.

Section 5. The Congress shall have power to enforce, by appropriate legislation, the provisions of this article.

XV
[proposed in 1869 and ratified in 1870]

Section 1. The right of citizens of the United States to vote shall not be denied or abridged by the United States or by any State on account of race, color, or previous condition of servitude.

Section 2. The Congress shall have power to enforce this article by appropriate legislation.

XVI
[proposed in 1909 and ratified in 1913]
The Congress shall have power to lay and collect taxes on incomes, from whatever source derived, without apportionment among the several States, and without regard to any census or enumeration.

XVII

[proposed in 1912 and ratified in 1913]

The Senate of the United States shall be composed of two Senators from each State, elected by the people thereof, for six years; and each Senator shall have one vote. The electors in each State shall have the qualifications requisite for electors of the most numerous branch of the State legislatures.

When vacancies happen in the representation of any State in the Senate, the executive authority of such State shall issue writs of election to fill such vacancies: Provided, That the legislature of any State may empower the executive thereof to make temporary appointments until the people fill the vacancies by election as the legislature may direct.

This amendment shall not be so construed as to affect the election or term of any Senator chosen before it becomes valid as part of the Constitution.

XVIII

[proposed in 1917 and ratified in 1919 but repealed in 1933 by the Twenty-first Amendment]

Section 1. After one year from the ratification of this article the manufacture, sale, or transportation of *intoxicating liquors* within, *the importation thereof into, or the exportation thereof from the United States and all territory subject to the jurisdiction thereof for beverage purposes is hereby prohibited.*

Section 2. The Congress and the several States shall have concurrent power to enforce this article by appropriate legislation.

Section 3. This article shall be inoperative unless it shall have been ratified as an amendment to the Constitution by the legislatures of the several States, as provided in the Constitution, within seven years from the date of the submission hereof to the States by the Congress.

XIX

[proposed in 1919 and ratified in 1920]

The right of citizens of the United States to vote shall not be denied or abridged by the United States or by any State on account of sex. Congress shall have power to enforce this article by appropriate legislation.

XX

[proposed in 1932 and ratified in 1933]

Section 1. The terms of the President and Vice President shall end at noon on the 20th day of January, and the terms of Senators and Representatives at noon on the 3d day of January, of the years in which such terms would have ended if this article had not been ratified; and the terms of their successors shall then begin.

Section 2. The Congress shall assemble at least once in every year, and such meeting shall begin at noon on the 3d day of January, unless they shall by law appoint a different day.

Section 3. If, at the time fixed for the beginning of the term of the President, the President elect shall have died, the Vice President elect shall become President. If a President shall not have been chosen before the time fixed for the beginning of his term, or if the President elect shall have failed to qualify, then the Vice President elect shall act as President until a President shall have qualified; and the Congress may by law provide for the case wherein neither a President elect nor a Vice President elect shall have qualified, declaring who shall then act as President, or the manner in which one who is to act shall be selected, and such person shall act accordingly until a President or Vice President shall have qualified.

Section 4. The Congress may by law provide for the case of the death of any of the persons from whom the House of Representatives may choose a President whenever the right of choice shall have devolved upon them, and for the case of the death of any of the persons from whom the Senate may choose a Vice President whenever the right of choice shall have devolved upon them.

Section 5. Sections 1 and 2 shall take effect on the 15th day of October following the ratification of this article.

Section 6. This article shall be inoperative unless it shall have been ratified as an amendment to the Constitution by the legislatures of three-fourths of the several States within seven years from the date of its submission.

XXI
[proposed and ratified in 1933]

Section 1. The eighteenth article of amendment to the Constitution of the United States is hereby repealed.

Section 2. *The transportation or importation into any State, Territory, or possession of the United States for delivery or use therein of intoxicating liquors, in violation of the laws thereof, is hereby prohibited.*

Section 3. This article shall be inoperative unless it shall have been ratified as an amendment to the Constitution by conventions in the several States, as provided in the Constitution, within seven years from the date of the submission hereof to the States by the Congress.

XXII
[proposed in 1947 and ratified in 1951]

Section 1. No person shall be elected to the office of the President more than twice, and no person who has held the office of President, or acted as President, for more than two years of a term to which some other person was elected President shall be elected to the office of the President more than once. But this Article shall not

apply to any person holding the office of President when this Article was proposed by the Congress, and shall not prevent any person who may be holding the office of President, or acting as President, during the term within which this Article becomes operative from holding the office of President or acting as President during the remainder of such term.

Section 2. This article shall be inoperative unless it shall have been ratified as an amendment to the Constitution by the legislatures of three-fourths of the several States within seven years from the date of its submission to the States by the Congress.

XXIII
[proposed in 1960 and ratified in 1961]

Section 1. The District constituting the seat of Government of the United States shall appoint in such manner as the Congress may direct: A number of electors of President and Vice President equal to the whole number of Senators and Representatives in Congress to which the District would be entitled if it were a State, but in no event more than the least populous State; they shall be in addition to those appointed by the States, but they shall be considered, for the purposes of the election of President and Vice President, to be electors appointed by a State; and they shall meet in the District and perform such duties as provided by the twelfth article of amendment.

Section 2. The Congress shall have power to enforce this article by appropriate legislation.

XXIV
[proposed in 1962 and ratified in 1964]

Section 1. The right of citizens of the United States to vote in any primary or other election for President or Vice

President, for electors for President or Vice President, or for Senator or Representative in Congress, shall not be denied or abridged by the United States or any State by reason of failure to pay any poll tax or other tax.

Section 2. The Congress shall have power to enforce this article by appropriate legislation.

XXV
[proposed in 1965 and ratified in 1967]

Section 1. In case of the removal of the President from office or of his death or resignation, the Vice President shall become President.

Section 2. Whenever there is a vacancy in the office of the Vice President, the President shall nominate a Vice President who shall take office upon confirmation by a majority vote of both Houses of Congress.

Section 3. Whenever the President transmits to the President pro tempore of the Senate and the Speaker of the House of Representatives his written declaration that he is unable to discharge the powers and duties of his office, and until he transmits to them a written declaration to the contrary, such powers and duties shall be discharged by the Vice President as Acting President.

Section 4. Whenever the Vice President and a majority of either the principal officers of the executive departments or of such other body as Congress may by law provide, transmit to the President pro tempore of the Senate and the Speaker of the House of Representatives their written declaration that the President is unable to discharge the powers and duties of his office, the Vice President shall immediately assume the powers and duties of the office as Acting President. Thereafter, when the President transmits to the President pro tempore of the Senate and the Speaker of the House of Representatives his written declaration that no inability exists, he shall resume the powers and duties of his office unless the Vice President and a majority of either the principal officers of the executive department or of such other body as Congress may by law provide, transmit within four days to the President pro tempore of the Senate and the Speaker of the House of Representatives their written declaration that the President is unable to discharge the powers and duties of his office. Thereupon Congress shall decide the issue, assembling within forty-eight hours for that purpose if not in session. If the Congress, within twenty-one days after receipt of the latter written declaration, or, if Congress is not in session, within twenty-one days after Congress is required to assemble, determines by two-thirds vote of both Houses that the President is unable to discharge the powers and duties of his office, the Vice President shall continue to discharge the same as Acting President; otherwise, the President shall resume the powers and duties of his office.

XXVI
[proposed in 1971 and ratified in 1971]

Section 1. The right of citizens of the United States, who are eighteen years of age or older, to vote shall not be denied or abridged by the United States or by any State on account of age.

Section 2. The Congress shall have power to enforce this article by appropriate legislation.

XXVII
[proposed in 1789 as part of original Bill of Rights, but not ratified until 1992]

No law, varying the compensation for the services of the Senators and Representatives, shall take effect, until an election of Representatives shall have intervened.

Chapter 4

Justifying the Construction of a Constitutional Republic

Written by Alexander Hamilton (New York), James Madison (Virginia), and John Jay (New York) under the pen name Publius, the *Federalist Papers* were newspaper columns advocating ratification of the newly drafted U.S. Constitution. Although *Federalist* No. 10 and No. 51, which give justification for *federalism* and *separation of powers*, are widely cited, we include in this chapter those papers that underscore the often over-looked foreign policy and national security motivations for forming a federal republic that were core to the *Federalist* writers. Indeed, constituting this federal republic that united thirteen states was seen as essential not only to maintaining security against external threats as from Britain and Spain, but also to maintaining peace among the thirteen states themselves lest they break into competing coalitions or alliances as in the customary European fashion.

The other *Federalist Papers* in this chapter treat the quest for security through a stronger union (*Federalist* Nos. 1 and 6–9 by Alexander Hamilton) and the problem of civil-military relations; a similar justification of security through national unity (*Federalist* Nos. 2–5 by John Jay); treaty-making powers and executive-legislative concurrence (*Federalist* No. 64 by John Jay); and the judiciary, foreign policy, and national security (*Federalist* Nos. 78–81 and 83 by Alexander Hamilton).

8. Federalist Papers Nos. 10, 37, and 51

(1787–88)

The political theory underlying American government and the formula for separation of powers in a federal state are provided most succinctly in these two papers. Federalist No. 37 *and* No. 51 *were the work of Madison as was* Federalist No. 10, *which reflects the thought of both Madison and Hamilton. They were not so much interested in providing efficiency of government as they were in keeping central governance from becoming too powerful. Read together, Federalist No. 10 and No. 51 provide insight into the rationale for dividing and separating power—a fragmentation of governmental structure into many, often competing parts that to the present day profoundly affects all aspects of American government and political processes to include* the making of American foreign and national security policy. *Subheads have been added in brackets for ease of reading.*

No. 10

(1787)

This paper provides a justification for federalism—division of powers between the central (or federal) government and the governments of separate states. Even separate county (or local) governments within a state are part of this federal design to divide powers seemingly as much as possible. It is a design intended to contain factions if they become radical majorities. The participation of states in foreign policy and national security is assured in a federal system that gives voice not only to governors and state legislatures, but also to the U.S. Senate, a body that represents each state equally. Indeed, following the U.S. Constitution, the Senate performs an "advice and consent" role on treaties and assumes a prominent role on other foreign policy and national security matters. Key passages related to Madison's theory of faction and his federal, republican remedy have been italicized (as is one reference to international commerce he uses as an example of class conflict of interest).

Among the numerous advantages promised by a well constructed Union, none deserves to be more accurately developed than its tendency to break and control the violence of faction. . . . Complaints are everywhere heard . . . that our governments are too unstable, that the public good is disregarded in the conflicts of rival parties, and that measures are too often decided, not according to the rules of justice and the rights of the minor party, but by the superior force of an interested and overbearing majority. . . . It will be found . . . that other causes will not alone account . . . for that prevailing and increasing distrust of public engagements, and alarm for private rights, which are echoed from one end of the continent to the other. These must be chiefly, if not wholly, effects of the unsteadiness and injustice with which a factious spirit has tainted our public administrations.

[Factions Defined and Remedies Considered]

By a faction, I understand a number of citizens, whether amounting to a majority or a minority of the whole, who are united and actuated by some common impulse of passion, or of interest, adverse to the rights of other citizens, or to the permanent and aggregate interests of the community.

There are two methods of curing the mischiefs of faction: the one, by removing its causes; the other, by controlling its effects.

There are again two methods of removing the causes of faction: the one, by destroying the liberty which is essential to its existence; the other, by giving to every citizen the same opinions, the same passions, and the same interests.

It could never be more truly said than of the first remedy, that it was worse than the disease. Liberty is to faction what air is to fire, an aliment without which it instantly expires. But *it could not be less folly to abolish liberty,* which is essential to political life, because it nourishes faction, than it would be to wish the annihilation of air, which is essential to animal life, because it imparts to fire its destructive agency.

The second expedient is as impracticable as the first would be unwise. As long as the reason of man continues fallible, and he is at liberty to exercise it, different opinions will be formed. . . . The diversity in the faculties of men, from which the rights of property originate, is not less an insuperable obstacle to a uniformity of interests. The protection of these faculties is the first object of government. From the protection of different and unequal faculties of acquiring property, the possession of different degrees and kinds of property immediately results; and from the influence of these on the sentiments and views of the respective proprietors, ensues a division of the society into different interests and parties.

[Causes of Faction: An Interest-Based Class Analysis]

The latent causes of faction are thus sown in the nature of man; and we see them everywhere brought into different degrees of activity, according to the different circumstances of civil society. A zeal for different opinions concerning religion, concerning government, and many other points, as well of speculation as of practice; an attachment to different leaders ambitiously contending for pre-eminence and power; or to persons of other descriptions whose fortunes have been interesting to the human passions, have, in turn, divided mankind into parties, inflamed them with mutual animosity,

and rendered them much more disposed to vex and oppress each other than to cooperate for their common good. So strong is this propensity of mankind to fall into mutual animosities, that where no substantial occasion presents itself, the most frivolous and fanciful distinctions have been sufficient to kindle their unfriendly passions and excite their most violent conflicts. But the most common and durable source of factions has been the various and unequal distribution of property. *Those who hold and those who are without property have ever formed distinct interests in society.* Those who are creditors, and those who are debtors, fall under a like discrimination. A landed interest, a manufacturing interest, a mercantile interest, a moneyed interest, with many lesser interests, grow up of necessity in civilized nations, and *divide them into different classes, actuated by different sentiments and views. The regulation of these various and interfering interests forms the principal task of modern legislation,* and involves the spirit of party and faction in the necessary and ordinary operations of the government.

No man is allowed to be a judge in his own cause, because his interest would certainly bias his judgment, and, not improbably, corrupt his integrity. With equal, nay with greater reason, a body of men are unfit to be both judges and parties at the same time; yet what are many of the most important acts of legislation, but so many judicial determinations, not indeed concerning the rights of single persons, but concerning the rights of large bodies of citizens? And what are the different classes of legislators but advocates and parties to the causes which they determine? Is a law proposed concerning private debts? It is a question to which *the creditors are parties on one side and the debtors on the other. Justice ought to hold the balance between them. Yet* the parties are, and must be, themselves the judges; and *the most numerous party, or, in other words, the most powerful faction must be expected to prevail. Shall domestic manufactures be encouraged, and in what degree, by restrictions on foreign manufactures?* are questions which would be differently decided by the landed and the manufacturing classes, and probably by neither with a sole regard to justice and the public good. . . .

It is in vain to say that enlightened statesmen will be able to adjust these clashing interests, and render them all subservient to the public good. Enlightened statesmen will not always be at the helm. Nor, in many cases, can such an adjustment be made at all without taking into view indirect and remote considerations, which will rarely prevail over the immediate interest which one party may find in disregarding the rights of another or the good of the whole.

[Remedy Lies in Controlling Effects of Factions]

The inference to which we are brought is, that the CAUSES of faction cannot be removed, and that relief is only to be sought in the means of controlling its EFFECTS.

If a faction consists of less than a majority, relief is supplied by the republican principle, which enables the majority to defeat its sinister views by regular vote. It may clog the administration, it may convulse the society; but it will be unable to execute and mask its violence under the forms of the Constitution. *When a majority is included in a faction, the form of popular government, on the other hand, enables it to sacrifice to its ruling passion or interest both the public good and the rights of other citizens. To secure the public good and private rights against the danger of such a faction, and at the same time to preserve the spirit and the form of popular government, is then the great object to*

which our inquiries are directed. Let me add that it is the great desideratum by which this form of government can be rescued from the opprobrium under which it has so long labored, and be recommended to the esteem and adoption of mankind.

By what means is this object attainable? Evidently by one of two only. Either the existence of the same passion or interest in a majority at the same time must be prevented, or the majority, having such coexistent passion or interest, must be rendered, by their number and local situation, unable to concert and carry into effect schemes of oppression. If the impulse and the opportunity be suffered to coincide, we well know that *neither moral nor religious motives can be relied on as an adequate control.* They are not found to be such on the injustice and violence of individuals, and lose their efficacy in proportion to the number combined together, that is, in proportion as their efficacy becomes needful.

[Republics: Representative Rather Than Direct Democracy]

From this view of the subject it may be concluded that *a pure democracy,* by which I mean a society consisting of a small number of citizens, who assemble and administer the government in person, *can admit of no cure for the mischiefs of faction.* A common passion or interest will, in almost every case, be felt by a majority of the whole; a communication and concert result from the form of government itself; and there is nothing to check the inducements to sacrifice the weaker party or an obnoxious individual. Hence it is that *such democracies* have ever been spectacles of turbulence and contention; *have ever been found incompatible with personal security or the rights of property;* and have in general been as short in their lives as they have been violent in their deaths. Theoretic politicians, who have patronized this species of government, have erroneously supposed that by reducing mankind to a perfect equality in their political rights, they would, at the same time, be perfectly equalized and assimilated in their possessions, their opinions, and their passions.

A republic, by which I mean a government in which the scheme of representation takes place, opens a different prospect, and promises the cure for which we are seeking. Let us examine the points in which it varies from pure democracy, and we shall comprehend both the nature of the cure and the efficacy which it must derive from the Union.

The *two great points of difference between a democracy and a republic* are: first, *the delegation of the government, in the latter, to a small number of citizens elected by the rest;* secondly, the greater number of citizens, *and greater sphere of country, over which the latter may be extended.*

The effect of the first difference is, on the one hand, to refine and enlarge the public views, by passing them through the medium of a chosen body of citizens, whose wisdom may best discern the true interest of their country, and whose patriotism and love of justice will be least likely to sacrifice it to temporary or partial considerations. Under such a regulation, it may well happen that the public voice, pronounced by the representatives of the people, will be more consonant to the public good than if pronounced by the people themselves, convened for the purpose. On the other hand, the effect may be inverted. Men of factious tempers, of local prejudices, or of sinister designs, may, by intrigue, by corruption, or by other means, first obtain the suffrages, and then betray the interests, of the people. The question resulting is, whether small or extensive republics are more favorable to the election of proper guardians of the public weal; and it is clearly decided in favor of the latter. . . . As each representative will be chosen by a greater number of citizens in the large than in the small republic, it will be more difficult for unworthy candidates to practice with success the vicious arts by which elections are too often carried; and the suffrages of the people being more free, will be more likely to centre in men who possess the most attractive merit and the most diffusive and established characters.

It must be confessed that in this, as in most other cases, there is a mean, on both sides of which inconveniences will be found to lie. By enlarging too much the number of electors, you render the representatives too little acquainted with all their local circumstances and lesser interests; as by reducing it too much, you render him unduly attached to these, and too little fit to comprehend and pursue great and national objects. *The federal Constitution forms a happy combination* in this respect; *the great and aggregate interests being referred to the national, the local and particular to the State legislatures.* The other point of difference is, the greater number of citizens and extent of territory which may be brought within the compass of republican than of democratic government; and it is this circumstance principally which renders factious combinations less to be dreaded in the former than in the latter. The smaller the society, the fewer probably will be the distinct parties and interests composing it; the fewer the distinct parties and interests, the more frequently will a majority be found of the same party; and the smaller the number of individuals composing a majority, and the smaller the compass within which they are placed, the more easily will they concert and execute their plans of oppression. *Extend the sphere, and you take in a greater variety of parties and interests; you make it less probable that a majority of the whole will have a common motive to invade the rights of other citizens; or if such a common motive exists, it will be more difficult for all who feel it to discover their own strength, and to act in unison with each other.* Besides other impediments, it may be remarked that, where there is a consciousness of unjust or dishonorable purposes, communication is always checked by distrust in proportion to the number whose concurrence is necessary.

[Federal Republics Contain the Effects of Radical Factions]

Hence, it clearly appears, that *the same advantage which a republic has over a democracy, in controlling the effects of faction, is* enjoyed by a large over a small republic,— *is enjoyed by the Union over the States composing it.* Does the advantage consist in the substitution of representatives whose enlightened views and virtuous sentiments render them superior to local prejudices and schemes of injustice? It will not be denied that the representation of the Union will be most likely to possess these requisite endowments. Does it consist in the greater security afforded by a greater variety of parties, against the event of any one party being able to outnumber and oppress the rest? In an equal degree does the increased variety of parties comprised within the Union, increase this security. Does it, in fine, consist in the greater obstacles opposed to the concert and accomplishment of the secret wishes of an unjust and interested majority? Here, again, the extent of the Union gives it the most palpable advantage.

The influence of factious leaders may kindle a flame within their particular States, but will be unable to spread a general conflagration through the other States. A religious sect may degenerate into a political faction in a part of the Confederacy; but the variety of sects dispersed over the entire face of it must secure the national councils against any danger from that source. A rage for paper money, for an abolition of debts, for an equal division of property, or for any other improper or wicked project, will be less apt to pervade the whole body of the Union than a particular member of it; in the same proportion as such a malady is more likely to taint a particular county or district, than an entire State.

In the extent and proper structure of the Union, therefore, we behold a republican remedy for the diseases most incident to republican government. And according to the degree of pleasure and pride we feel in being republicans, ought to be our zeal in cherishing the spirit and supporting the character of federalists.

No. 37

(1788)

Madison's (and Hamilton's) negative view of human nature is apparent in Federalist No. 10 *and No. 51, but it is perhaps most clearly and eloquently stated in the following passage by Madison. Madison's reference here to "depravities of the human character," (echoed in Hamilton's observation in* Federalist Paper No. 78 *about "the ordinary depravity of human nature") underscores the negative view of humankind on which both were in agreement. The governmental structure of federalism and the separation of powers are a practical remedy designed to channel human behavior or contain its adverse consequences.*

... The history of almost all the great councils and consultations held among mankind for reconciling their discordant opinions, assuaging their mutual jealousies, and adjusting their respective interests, is a history of factions, contentions, and disappointments, and may be classed among *the most dark and degraded pictures which display the infirmities and depravities of the human character.* If, in a few scattered instances, a brighter aspect is presented, they serve only as exceptions to admonish us of the general truth; and by their lustre to darken the gloom of the adverse prospect to which they are contrasted. . . .

No. 51

(1788)

This paper provides a justification for separation of powers among separate branches (referred to in the text as "departments" of government in the central [or federal] government, which would then be replicated in the states). Not only are legislative, executive, and judicial branches separated, but the legislature itself is composed of distinctly separate houses—a bicameral formula adopted subsequently by forty-nine of the fifty states, only Nebraska being unicameral. It is a "checks-and-balances" design intended to keep any one branch (and government as a whole) from becoming too strong. As reflected in the U.S. Constitution, authority for foreign and national security policy is separated primarily between the executive and legislative branches with relatively more authority on foreign policy (viz., treaties) in the Senate, the chamber affording equal representation to the states. Key passages have been italicized that relate to a theory of a compound republic, which both separates powers *within government and, as discussed in* Federalist *No. 10, divides powers* among federal and state-and-local governments.

To what expedient, then, shall we finally resort, for maintaining in practice the necessary partition of power among the several departments, as laid down in the Constitution? The only answer that can be given is, that as all these exterior provisions are found to be inadequate, the defect must be supplied, by so *contriving the interior structure of the government as that its several constituent parts may, by their mutual relations, be the means of keeping each other in their proper places.* . . .

In order *to lay a due foundation for that separate and distinct exercise of the different powers of government,* which to a certain extent is admitted on all hands to be essential to the preservation of liberty, it is evident that *each department should have a will of its own; and consequently should be so con-stituted that the members of each should have as little agency as possible in the appointment of the members of the others.* . . .

It is equally evident, that *the members of each department should be as little dependent as possible on those of the others,* for the emoluments annexed to their offices. Were the executive magistrate, or the judges, not independent of the legislature in this particular, their independence in every other would be merely nominal.

But *the great security against a gradual concentration of the several powers in the same department, consists in giving to those who administer each department the necessary constitutional means and personal motives to resist encroachments of the others.* The provision for defense must in this, as in all other cases, be made commensurate to the danger of attack. *Ambition must be made to counteract ambition.* The interest of the man must be connected with the constitutional rights of the place. It may be a reflection on human nature, that such devices should be necessary to control the abuses of government. But *what is government itself, but the greatest of all reflections on human nature? If men were angels, no government would be necessary. If angels were to govern men, neither external nor internal controls on government would be necessary. In framing a government which is to be administered by men over men, the great difficulty lies in this: you must first enable the government to control the governed; and in the next place oblige it to control itself. A dependence on the people is, no doubt, the primary control on the government; but experience has taught mankind the necessity of auxiliary precautions.*

This policy of supplying, by opposite and rival interests, the defect of better motives, might be traced through the whole system of human affairs, private as well as public. We see it particularly displayed in all the subordinate distributions of power, where the constant aim is to divide and arrange the several offices in such a manner as that each may be a check on the other that the private interest of every individual may be a sentinel over the public rights. These inventions of prudence cannot be less requisite in the distribution of the supreme powers of the State.

But it is not possible to give to each department an equal power of self-defense. *In republican government, the legislative authority necessarily predominates. The remedy for this inconveniency is to divide the legislature into different branches; and to render them, by different modes of election and different principles of action, as little connected with each other as the nature of their common functions and their common dependence on the society will admit.* It may even be necessary to guard

against dangerous encroachments by still further precautions. As the weight of the legislative authority requires that it should be thus divided, *the weakness of the executive may require, on the other hand, that it should be fortified.* An absolute negative [i.e., veto power] on the legislature appears, at first view, to be the natural defense with which the executive magistrate should be armed. But perhaps it would be neither altogether safe nor alone sufficient. On ordinary occasions it might not be exerted with the requisite firmness, and on extraordinary occasions it might be perfidiously abused. . . .

There are, moreover, two considerations particularly applicable to the federal system of America, which place that system in a very interesting point of view. First. In a single republic, all the power surrendered by the people is submitted to the administration of a single government; and the usurpations are guarded against by a division of the government into distinct and separate departments. *In the compound republic of America, the power surrendered by the people is first divided between two distinct governments, and then the portion allotted to each subdivided among distinct and separate departments. Hence a double security arises to the rights of the people. The different governments will control each other, at the same time that each will be controlled by itself.*

Second. It is of great importance in a republic not only to guard the society against the oppression of its rulers, but to guard one part of the society against the injustice of the other part. Different interests necessarily exist in different classes of citizens. *If a majority be united by a common interest, the rights of the minority will be insecure.* There are but two methods of providing against this evil: the one by creating a will in the community independent of the majority that is, of the society itself; the other, by comprehending in the society so many separate descriptions of citizens as will render an unjust combination of a majority of the whole very improbable, if not impracticable. The first method prevails in all governments possessing an hereditary or self-appointed authority. This, at best, is but a precarious security; because a power independent of the society may as well espouse the unjust views of the major, as the rightful interests of the minor party, and may possibly be turned against both parties. The second method will be exemplified *in the federal republic of the United States. Whilst all authority in it will be derived from and dependent on the society, the society itself will be broken into so many parts, interests, and classes of citizens, that the rights of individuals, or of the minority, will be in little danger from interested combinations of the majority.* In a free government the security for civil rights must be the same as that for religious rights. It consists in the one case in the multiplicity of interests, and in the other in the multiplicity of sects. . . . *Justice is the end of government. It is the end of civil society.* It ever has been and ever will be pursued until it be obtained, or until liberty be lost in the pursuit.

In a society under the forms of which the stronger faction can readily unite and oppress the weaker, anarchy may as truly be said to reign as in a state of nature, where the weaker individual is not secured against the violence of the stronger; and as, in the latter state, even the stronger individuals are prompted, by the uncertainty of their condition, to submit to a government which may protect the weak as well as themselves; so, in the former state, will the more powerful factions or parties be gradually induced, by a like motive, to wish for a government which will protect all parties, the weaker as well as the more powerful. . . . *In the extended republic of the United States, and among the great variety of interests, parties, and sects which it embraces, a coalition of a majority of the whole society could seldom take place on any other principles than those of justice and the general good;* whilst there being thus less danger to a minor from the will of a major party, there must be less pretext, also, to provide for the security of the former, by introducing into the government a will not dependent on the latter, or, in other words, a will independent of the society itself. It is no less certain than . . . that the larger the society, provided it lie within a practical sphere, the more duly capable it will be of self-government. And happily for the REPUBLICAN CAUSE, the practicable sphere may be carried to a very great extent, by a judicious modification and mixture of the FEDERAL PRINCIPLE.

---

9. *[The Quest for Security through a Stronger Union]:* Federalist Papers *Nos. 1, 6, 7, 8, and 9*

Alexander Hamilton
(1787)

Here we find Hamilton's compelling arguments for a strengthened union as essential to the security of the component states from both foreign invasions and wars among themselves into which they might otherwise be drawn. Later manifestations of these concerns were the British invasion in the War of 1812 and the union's division into two parts or competing coalitions in the

Civil War (1860–65), referred to in the South as the War Between the States—the United States of America (USA) and the Confederate States of America (CSA). Particularly informative are Hamilton's perspectives on civil-military relations, concerns shared by many of the framers about the challenge standing armies can pose to civil liberties and civil society as a whole. Seventeenth-century English history (the Cromwell period) and the American colonial experience under a British standing army were informative in this regard.

No. 1 After an unequivocal experience of the inefficiency of the subsisting federal government, you are called upon to deliberate on a new Constitution for the United States of America. The subject speaks its own importance; comprehending in its consequences nothing less than the existence of *the UNION, the safety and welfare of the parts of which it is composed.* . . . The vigor of government is essential to *the security of liberty.* . . . I propose, in a series of papers, to discuss . . . THE UTILITY OF THE UNION TO YOUR POLITICAL PROSPERITY, THE INSUFFICIENCY OF THE PRESENT CONFEDERATION TO PRESERVE THAT UNION, THE NECESSITY OF A GOVERNMENT AT LEAST EQUALLY ENERGETIC WITH THE ONE PROPOSED, TO THE ATTAINMENT OF THIS OBJECT THE CONFORMITY OF THE PROPOSED CONSTITUTION TO THE TRUE PRINCIPLES OF REPUBLICAN GOVERNMENT ITS ANALOGY TO YOUR OWN STATE CONSTITUTION and lastly, *THE ADDITIONAL SECURITY WHICH ITS ADOPTION WILL AFFORD* TO THE PRESERVATION OF THAT SPECIES OF GOVERNMENT, TO LIBERTY, AND TO PROPERTY. . . . It will therefore be of use to begin by examining the advantages of that Union, the certain evils, and the probable dangers, to which every State will be exposed from its dissolution. . . .

No. 6 The three last numbers [i.e., *Federalist Papers* 3, 4, and 5 by John Jay] of this paper have been dedicated to an enumera-

tion of *the dangers to which we should be exposed, in a state of disunion, from the arms and arts of foreign nations.* I shall now proceed to delineate *dangers* of a different and, perhaps, still more alarming kind—those *which will in all probability flow from dissensions between the States themselves, and from domestic factions and convulsions.* . . .

A man must be far gone in Utopian speculations who can seriously doubt that, if these States should either be wholly disunited, or only united in partial confederacies, the subdivisions into which they might be thrown would have frequent and violent contests with each other. To presume a want of motives for such contests as an argument against their existence, would be to forget that *men are ambitious, vindictive, and rapacious.* To look for a continuation of harmony between a number of independent, unconnected sovereignties in the same neighborhood, would be to disregard the uniform course of human events, and to set at defiance the accumulated experience of ages.

The *causes of hostility among nations* are innumerable. There are some which have a general and almost constant operation upon the collective bodies of society. Of this description are *the love of power* or the *desire of pre-eminence and dominion*—the jealousy of power, or the desire of equality and safety. There are others which have a more circumscribed though an equally operative influence within their spheres. Such are the *rivalships and competitions of commerce between commercial nations.* And there are others, not less numerous than either of the former, which take their origin entirely in *private passions;* in the attachments, enmities, interests, hopes, and fears of leading individuals in the communities of which they are members. Men of this class, whether the favorites of a king or of a people, have in too many instances abused the confidence they possessed; and assuming the pretext of some public motive, have not scrupled *to sacrifice the national tranquillity to personal advantage* or personal gratification.

The celebrated Pericles, in compliance with the resentment of a prostitute [This is Plutarch's account.—Ed.], at the expense of much of the blood and treasure of his countrymen, attacked, vanquished, and destroyed the city of the SAMNIANS. The same man, stimulated by private pique against the MEGARENSIANS, another nation of Greece, or to avoid a prosecution with which he was threatened as an accomplice of a supposed theft of the statuary Phidias, or to get rid of the accusations prepared to be brought against him for dissipating the funds of the state in the purchase of popularity [Phidias was accused (along with Pericles) of having taken Athenian gold improperly for use in a statue of the goddess Minerva.—Ed.], or from a combination of all these causes, was the primitive author of that famous and fatal war, distinguished in the Grecian annals by the name of the PELOPONNESIAN war; which, after various vicissitudes, intermissions, and renewals, terminated in the ruin of the Athenian commonwealth.

The ambitious cardinal, who was prime minister to Henry VIII, permitting his vanity to aspire to the triple crown [worn by the popes] entertained hopes of succeeding in the acquisition of that splendid prize by the influence of the Emperor Charles V. To secure the favor and interest of this enterprising and powerful monarch, he precipitated England into a war with France, contrary to the plainest dictates of policy, and at the hazard of the safety and independence, as well of the kingdom over which he presided by his counsels, as of Europe in general. For if there ever was a sovereign who bid fair to realize the project of universal monarchy, it was the Emperor Charles V, of whose intrigues Wolsey was at once the instrument and the dupe. The influence which the bigotry of one female [Madame de Maintenon], the petulance of another [Duchess of Marlborough], and the cabals of a third [Madame de Pompadour], had in the contemporary policy, ferments, and pacifications, of a considerable part of Europe, are topics that have been too often descanted upon not to be generally known.

To multiply examples of *the agency of personal considerations in the production of great national events, either foreign or domestic,* according to their direction, would be an unnecessary waste of time. Those who have but a superficial acquaintance with the sources from which they are to be drawn, will themselves recollect a variety of instances; and *those who have a tolerable knowledge of human nature will not stand in need of such lights to form their opinion either of the reality or extent of that agency.* Perhaps, however, a reference, tending to illustrate the general principle, may with propriety be made to a case which has lately happened among ourselves. If Shays had not been a DESPERATE DEBTOR, it is much to be doubted whether Massachusetts would have been plunged into a civil war.

But notwithstanding the concurring testimony of experience, in this particular, there are still to be found *visionary or designing men, who stand ready to advocate the paradox of perpetual peace between the States, though dismembered and alienated from each other.* The genius of republics (say they) is pacific; the spirit of commerce has a tendency to soften the manners of men, and to extinguish those inflammable humors which have so often kindled into wars. Commercial republics, like ours, will never be disposed to waste themselves in ruinous contentions with each other. They will be governed by mutual interest, and will cultivate a spirit of mutual amity and concord.

Is it not (we may ask these projectors in politics) the true interest of all nations to cultivate the same benevolent and philosophic spirit? If this be their true interest, have they in fact pursued it? *Has it not, on the contrary, invariably been found that momentary passions, and immediate interest, have a more active and imperious control over human conduct than general or remote considerations of policy, utility or justice? . . .* Is it not well known that their determinations are often governed by a few individuals in whom they place confidence, and are, of course, liable to be tinctured by the passions and views of those individuals? Has commerce hitherto done anything more than change the objects of war? Is not the love of wealth as domineering and enterprising a passion as that of power or glory? Have there not been as many wars founded upon commercial motives since that has become the prevailing system of nations, as were before occasioned by the cupidity of territory or dominion? Has not the spirit of commerce, in many instances, administered new incentives to the appetite, both for the one and for the other? Let experience, the least fallible guide of human opinions, be appealed to for an answer to these inquiries.

Sparta, Athens, Rome, and Carthage were all republics; two of them, Athens and Carthage, of the commercial kind. Yet were they as often engaged in wars, offen-

sive and defensive, as the neighboring monarchies of the same times. . . . Venice, in later times, figured more than once in wars of ambition. . . . The provinces of Holland, till they were overwhelmed in debts and taxes, took a leading and conspicuous part in the wars of Europe. They had furious contests with England for the dominion of the sea, and were among the most persevering and most implacable of the opponents of Louis XIV.

In the government of Britain the representatives of the people compose one branch of the national legislature. Commerce has been for ages the predominant pursuit of that country. Few nations, nevertheless, have been more frequently engaged in war; and the wars in which that kingdom has been engaged have, in numerous instances, proceeded from the people. There have been . . . almost as many popular as royal wars. The cries of the nation and the importunities of their representatives have, upon various occasions, dragged their monarchs into war, or continued them in it, contrary to their inclinations, and sometimes contrary to the real interests of the State. In that memorable struggle for superiority between the rival houses of AUSTRIA and BOURBON, which so long kept Europe in a flame, it is well known that the antipathies of the English against the French, seconding the ambition, or rather the avarice, of a favorite leader [This is understood to be a reference to the Duke of Marlborough.—Ed.], protracted the war beyond the limits marked out by sound policy, and for a considerable time in opposition to the views of the court.

The wars of these two last-mentioned nations have in a great measure grown out of commercial considerations,—the desire of supplanting and the fear of being supplanted, either in particular branches of traffic or in the general advantages of trade and navigation. . . . From this summary of what has taken place in other countries, whose situations have borne the nearest resemblance to our own, what reason can we have to confide in those reveries which would seduce us into an expectation of peace and cordiality between the members of the present confederacy, in a state of separation?

Have we not already seen enough of the fallacy and extravagance of those idle theories which have amused us with promises of an exemption from *the imperfections, weaknesses and evils incident to society* in every shape? Is it not time to awake from the deceitful dream of a golden age, and to adopt as a practical maxim for the direction of our political conduct that we, as well as the other inhabitants of the globe, are yet remote from the happy empire of perfect wisdom and perfect virtue? . . .

So far is the general sense of mankind from corresponding with the tenets of those who endeavor to lull asleep our apprehensions of discord and hostility between the States, in the event of disunion, that it has from long observation of the progress of society become a sort of axiom in politics, that vicinity or nearness of situation, constitutes nations natural enemies. An intelligent writer [This is a reference to the Abbé de Mably, *Principes de Negociations.*—Ed.] expresses himself on this subject to this effect: "NEIGHBORING NATIONS (says he) are naturally enemies of each other unless their common weakness forces them to league in a CONFEDERATE REPUBLIC, and their constitution prevents the differences that neighborhood occasions, extinguishing that secret jealousy which disposes all states to aggrandize themselves at the expense of their neighbors." This passage, at the same time, points out the EVIL and suggests the REMEDY.

No. 7 It is sometimes asked, with an air of seeming triumph, what inducements could the States have, if disunited, to make war upon each other? It would be a full answer to this question to say—precisely the same inducements which have, at different times, deluged in blood all the nations in the world. But, unfortunately for us, the question admits of a more particular answer. There are causes of differences within our immediate contemplation, of the tendency of which, even under the restraints of a federal constitution, we have had sufficient experience to enable us to form a judgment of what might be expected if those restraints were removed.

Territorial disputes have at all times been found one of the most fertile sources of hostility among nations. Perhaps the greatest proportion of wars that have desolated the earth have sprung from this origin. This cause would exist among us in full force. *We have a vast tract of unsettled territory within the boundaries of the United States. There still are discordant and undecided claims between several of them.* . . . In the wide field of Western territory . . . we perceive an ample theatre for hostile pretensions, without any umpire or common judge to interpose between the contending parties. To reason from the past to the future, we shall have good ground to apprehend, that the sword would sometimes be appealed to as the arbiter of their differences. . . .

We may trace some of the causes which would be likely to embroil the States with each other, if it should be their unpropitious destiny to become disunited. *The competitions of commerce would be another fruitful source of contention.* The States less favorably circumstanced would be desirous of escaping from the disadvantages of local situation, and of sharing in the advantages of their more fortunate neighbors. Each State, or separate confederacy, would pursue a system of commercial policy peculiar to itself. This would occasion distinctions, preferences, and exclusions, which would beget discontent.... The spirit of enterprise ... characterizes the commercial part of America.... It is not at all probable that this unbridled spirit would pay much respect to those regulations of trade by which particular States might endeavor to secure exclusive benefits to their own citizens. The infractions of these regulations, on one side, the efforts to prevent and repel them, on the other, would naturally lead to outrages, and these to reprisals and wars. . . .

The public debt of the Union would be a further cause of collision between the separate States or confederacies. The apportionment, in the first instance, and the progressive extinguishment afterward, would be alike productive of ill-humor and animosity. How would it be possible to agree upon a rule of apportionment satisfactory to all? ... *Foreign powers would urge for the satisfaction of their just demands, and the peace of the States would be hazarded to the double contingency of external invasion and internal contention.* . . . There is, perhaps, nothing more likely to disturb the tranquillity of nations than their being bound to mutual contributions for any common object that does not yield an equal and coincident benefit. For it is an observation, as true as it is trite, that there is nothing men differ so readily about as the payment of money.

Laws in violation of private contracts, as they amount to aggressions on the rights of those States whose citizens are injured by them, *may be considered as another probable source of hostility.* We are not authorized to expect that a more liberal or more equi-table spirit would preside over the legislations of the individual States hereafter, if unrestrained by any additional checks ... and we reasonably infer that ... *a war, not of PARCHMENT, but of the sword, would chastise ... atrocious breaches of moral obligation and social justice.* The probability of incompatible alliances between the different States or confederacies and different foreign nations, and the effects of this situation upon the peace of the whole, have been sufficiently unfolded in some preceding papers. From the view they have exhibited of this part of the subject, this conclusion is to be drawn, that *America, if not connected at all, or only by the feeble tie of a simple league, offensive and defensive, would, by the operation of such jarring alliances, be gradually entangled in all the pernicious labyrinths of European politics and wars;* and by the destructive contentions of the parts into which she was divided, would be likely to become a prey to the artifices and machinations of powers equally the enemies of them all. *Divide et impera* [divide and command] must be the motto of every nation that either hates or fears us.

No. 8 Assuming it therefore as an established truth that the several States, in case of disunion, or such combinations of them as might happen to be formed out of the wreck of the general Confederacy, would be subject to *those vicissitudes of peace and war, of friendship and enmity,* with each other, *which have fallen to the lot of all neighboring nations not united under one government,* let us enter into a concise detail of some of the consequences that would attend such a situation.

War between the States, in the first period of their separate existence, would be accompanied with much greater distresses than it commonly is in those countries where regular military establishments have long obtained. The disciplined armies always kept on foot on the continent of Europe, though they bear a malignant aspect to liberty and economy, have, notwithstanding, been productive of the signal advantage of rendering sudden conquests impracticable, and of preventing that rapid desolation which used to mark the progress of war prior to their introduction. The art of fortification has contributed to the same ends. The nations of Europe are encircled with chains of fortified places, which mutually obstruct invasion. Campaigns are wasted in reducing two or three frontier garrisons, to gain admittance into an enemy's country. Similar impediments occur at every step, to exhaust the strength and delay the progress of an invader. Formerly, an invading army would penetrate into the heart of a neighboring country almost as soon as intelligence of its approach could be received; but now a comparatively small force of disciplined troops, acting on the defensive, with the aid of posts, is able to impede, and finally to frustrate, the enterprises of one much more considerable. The history of war, in that quarter of the globe, is no longer a history of nations subdued and empires overturned, but of towns taken and retaken; of battles that decide nothing; of retreats more beneficial than victories; of much effort and little acquisition.

In this country the scene would be altogether reversed. The jealousy of military establishments would postpone them as long as possible. The want of fortifications, leaving the frontiers of one state open to another, would facilitate inroads. The populous States would, with little difficulty, overrun their less populous neighbors. Conquests would be as easy to be made as difficult to be retained. War, therefore, would be desultory and preda-

tory. PLUNDER and devastation ever march in the train of irregulars. The calamities of individuals would make the principal figure in the events which would characterize our military exploits. This picture is not too highly wrought; though, I confess, it would not long remain a just one. *Safety from external danger is the most powerful director of national conduct.* Even the ardent love of liberty will, after a time, give way to its dictates. *The violent destruction of life and property incident to war, the continual effort and alarm attendant on a state of continual danger, will compel nations the most attached to liberty to resort for repose and security to institutions which have a tendency to destroy their civil and political rights. To be more safe, they at length become willing to run the risk of being less free.*

The institutions chiefly alluded to are STANDING ARMIES and the correspondent appendages of military establishments. Standing armies, it is said, are not provided against in the new Constitution; and it is therefore inferred that they may exist under it. [This objection will be fully examined in its proper place, and it will be shown that the only natural precaution which could have been taken on this subject has been taken; and a much better one than is to be found in any constitution that has been heretofore framed in America, most of which contain no guard at all on this subject.] Their existence, however, from the very terms of the proposition, is, at most, problematical and uncertain. But *standing armies*, it may be replied, *must inevitably result from a dissolution of the Confederacy. Frequent war and constant apprehension, which require a state of as constant preparation, will infallibly produce them.* The weaker States or confederacies would first have recourse to them, to put themselves upon an equality with their more potent neighbors. They would endeavor to supply the inferiority of population and resources by a more regular and effective system of defense, by disciplined troops, and by fortifications. They would, at the same time, be necessitated to strengthen the executive arm of government, in doing which their constitutions would acquire a progressive direction toward monarchy. *It is of the nature of war to increase the executive at the expense of the legislative authority.*

The expedients which have been mentioned would soon give the States or confederacies that made use of them a superiority over their neighbors. Small states, or states of less natural strength, under vigorous governments, and with the assistance of disciplined armies, have often triumphed over large states, or states of greater natural strength, which have been destitute of these advantages. Neither the pride nor the safety of the more important States or confederacies would permit them long to submit to this mortifying and adventitious superiority. They would quickly resort to means similar to those by which it had been effected, to reinstate themselves in their lost pre-eminence. Thus, we should, in a little time, see established in every part of this country the same engines of despotism which have been the scourge of the Old World. This, at least, would be the natural course of things; and our reasonings will be the more likely to be just, in proportion as they are accommodated to this standard.

These are not vague inferences drawn from supposed or speculative defects in a Constitution, the whole power of which is lodged in the hands of a people, or their representatives and delegates, but they are solid conclusions, drawn from the natural and necessary progress of human affairs.

It may, perhaps, be asked, by way of objection to this, why did not standing armies spring up out of the contentions which so often distracted the ancient republics of Greece? Different answers, equally satisfactory, may be given to this question. The industrious habits of the people of the present day, absorbed in the pursuits of gain, and devoted to the improvements of agriculture and commerce, are incompatible with the condition of a nation of soldiers, which was the true condition of the people of those republics. *The means of revenue, which have been so greatly multiplied by the increase of gold and silver and of the arts of industry, and the science of finance, which is the offspring of modern times, concurring with the habits of nations, have produced an entire revolution in the system of war, and have rendered disciplined armies, distinct from the body of the citizens, the inseparable companions of frequent hostility.*

There is a wide difference, also, between military establishments in a country seldom exposed by its situation to internal invasions, and in one which is often subject to them, and always apprehensive of them. The rulers of the former can have a good pretext, if they are even so inclined, to keep on foot armies so numerous as must of necessity be maintained in the latter. These armies being, in the first case, rarely, if at all, called into activity for interior defense, the people are in no danger of being broken to military subordination. The laws are not accustomed to relaxations, in favor of military exigencies; the civil state remains in full vigor, neither corrupted, nor confounded with the principles or propensities of the other state. *The smallness of the army renders the natural strength of the community an over-match for it;* and the citizens, not habituated to look up to the military power for protection, or to submit to its oppressions, neither love nor fear the soldiery; they view them with a spirit of jealous acquiescence in a necessary evil, and stand ready to resist a power which they suppose may be exerted to the prejudice of their rights. The army under such circumstances may usefully aid the magistrate to suppress a small faction, or an occasional mob, or insurrection; but it will be unable to enforce encroachments against the united efforts of the great body of the people.

In a country in the predicament last described, the contrary of all this happens. *The perpetual menacings of danger oblige the government to be always prepared to repel it; its armies must be numerous enough for instant defense. The continual necessity for their services enhances the importance of the soldier, and proportionably degrades the condition of the citizen. The military state becomes elevated above the civil.* The inhabitants of territories, often the theatre of war, are unavoidably subjected to frequent infringements on their rights, which serve to weaken their sense of those rights; and by degrees the people are brought to consider the soldiery not only as their protectors, but as their superiors. The transition from this disposition to that of considering them masters, is neither remote nor difficult; but it is very difficult to prevail upon a people under such impressions, to make a bold or effectual resistance to usurpations supported by the military power.

The kingdom of Great Britain falls within the first description. An insular situation, and a powerful marine, guarding it in a great measure against the possibility of foreign invasion, supersede the necessity of a numerous army within the kingdom. A sufficient force to make head against a sudden descent, till the militia could have time to rally and embody, is all that has been deemed requisite. No motive of national policy has demanded, nor would public opinion have tolerated, a larger number of troops upon its domestic establishment. There has been, for a long time past, little room for the operation of the other causes, which have been enumerated as the consequences of internal war. This peculiar felicity of situation has, in a great degree, contributed to preserve the liberty which that country to this day enjoys, in spite of the prevalent venality and corruption. If, on the contrary, Britain had been situated on the continent, and had been compelled, as she would have been, by that situation, to make her military establishments at home coextensive with those of the other great powers of Europe, she, like them, would in all probability be, at this day, a victim to the absolute power of a single man. 'T is possible, though not easy, that the people of that island may be enslaved from other causes; but it cannot be by the prowess of an army so inconsiderable as that which has been usually kept up within the kingdom.

If we are wise enough to preserve the Union we may for ages enjoy an advantage similar to that of an insulated situation. Europe is at a great distance from us. Her colonies in our vicinity will be likely to continue too much disproportioned in strength to be able to give us any dangerous annoyance. Extensive military establishments cannot, in this position, be necessary to our security. But if we should be disunited, and the integral parts should either remain separated, or, which is most probable, should be thrown together into two or three confederacies, we should be, in a short course of time, in the predicament of the continental powers of Europe— our liberties would be a prey to the means of defending ourselves against the ambition and jealousy of each other. . . .

No. 9 A firm Union will be of the utmost moment to the peace and liberty of the States, as a barrier against domestic faction and insurrection. It is impossible to read the history of the petty republics of Greece and Italy without feeling sensations of horror and disgust at the distractions with which they were continually agitated, and at the rapid succession of revolutions by which they were kept in a state of perpetual vibration between the extremes of tyranny and anarchy. If they exhibit occasional calms, these only serve as short-lived contrast to the furious storms that are to succeed. . . . From the disorders that disfigure the annals of those republics the advocates of despotism have drawn arguments, not only against the forms of republican government, but against the very principles of civil liberty. . . .

The utility of a Confederacy, as well to suppress faction and to guard the internal tranquillity of States, as to increase their external force and security, is in reality not a new idea. It has been practiced upon in different countries and ages, and has received the sanction of the most approved writers on the subject of politics. The opponents of the plan proposed have, with great assiduity, cited and circulated the observations of Montesquieu on the necessity of a contracted territory for a republican government. . . . Montesquieu . . . explicitly treats . . . a CONFEDERATE REPUBLIC as the expedient for extending the sphere of popular government, and reconciling the advantages of monarchy with those of republicanism. "It is very probable," says he, that mankind would have been obliged at length to live constantly under the government of a single person, had they not contrived a kind of constitution that has all the internal advantages of a republican, together with the external force

of a monarchical government. I mean a CONFEDERATE REPUBLIC.

"This form of government is a convention by which several smaller STATES agree to become members of a larger ONE, which they intend to form . . . to provide for the security of the united body. . . . A republic of this kind [is] able to withstand an external force. . . . Should a popular insurrection happen in one of the confederate states the others are able to quell it. Should abuses creep into one part, they are reformed by those that remain sound. The state may be destroyed on one side, and not on the other; the confederacy may be dissolved, and the confederates preserve their sovereignty. . . . As this government is composed of small republics, it enjoys the internal happiness of each; and with respect to its external situation, it is possessed, by means of the association, of all the advantages of large monarchies." [See Montesquieu's *Spirit of the Laws*, Book IX, ch. 1, para. 3, 4, 8, 10, and 11.—Ed.]

I have thought it proper to quote . . . these interesting passages because . . . they . . . have . . . an intimate connection with *the more immediate design of this paper; which is, to illustrate the tendency of the Union to repress domestic faction and insurrection.* The proposed Constitution, so far from implying an abolition of the State governments, makes them constituent parts of the national sovereignty, by allowing them a direct representation in the Senate, and leaves in their possession certain exclusive and very important portions of sovereign power. This fully corresponds, in every rational import of the terms, with the idea of a federal government. . . .

10. [Security Through National Unity]: Federalist Papers Nos. 2, 3, 4, and 5

John Jay
(1787)

As do the other framers, John Jay advances national security as the driving imperative for form-ing a stronger union. He is concerned not just with the danger of foreign invasion, but also lest the states divide into competing confederacies with multiple standing armies or outbreaks of war among them the result. His sensitivity here to the importance of maintaining good relations with foreign countries as a way to avoid wars was reflected in his role as part of the peace delegation that negotiated the Treaty of Paris (1783) that ended the Revolutionary War and later when he served as chief negotiator in what came to be called the Jay Treaty (1794) with Britain.

No. 2 . . . Nothing is more certain than the indispensable necessity of government, and it is equally undeniable, that whenever and however it is instituted, the people must cede to it some of their natural rights in order to vest it with requisite powers. . . . It has until lately been a received and un-contradicted opinion that the prosperity of the people of America depended on their continuing firmly united. . . . But politi-cians now appear, who insist that this opin-ion is erroneous, and that instead of looking for *safety and happiness in union,* we ought to seek it in a division of the States into distinct confederacies or sovereignties. . . . It cer-tainly would not be wise in the people at large to adopt these new political tenets. . . . Providence has been pleased to give this one connected country to one united people—a people descended from the same ancestors, speaking the same language, professing the same religion, attached to the same principles of government, very similar in their manners and customs, and who, *by their joint counsels, arms, and efforts, fighting side by side throughout a long and bloody war,* have nobly established general liberty and independence. . . . To all general purposes we have uniformly been *one peo-ple each individual citizen everywhere enjoying the same* national rights, privileges, and

protection. As a nation *we have made peace and war;* as a nation *we have vanquished our com-mon enemies;* as a nation *we have formed alliances, and made treaties, and entered into various compacts and conventions with foreign states.* A strong sense of *the value and bless-ings of union* induced the people, at a very early period, *to institute a federal government to preserve and perpetuate it. . . .* being pur-suaded that ample security . . . could only be found in a national government more wisely framed. . . .

No. 3 . . . It is not a new observation that the people of any country (if, like the Americans, intelligent and well informed) seldom adopt and steadily persevere for many years in an erroneous opinion re-specting their *interests. . . .* Among the many objects to which a wise and free peo-ple find it necessary to direct their atten-tion, that of providing for their SAFETY seems to be the first. The SAFETY of the people doubtless has relation to a great va-riety of circumstances and considerations, and consequently affords great latitude to those who wish to define it precisely and comprehensively. At present I mean only to consider it as it respects *security for the preservation of peace and tranquillity,* as well as against *dangers from FOREIGN ARMS*

AND INFLUENCE as from *dangers of the LIKE KIND arising from domestic causes. . . .* Let us therefore proceed to examine whether the people are not right in their opinion that *a cordial Union, under an efficient national government, affords them the best security* that can be devised against HOSTILITIES from abroad.

The *number of wars* which have happened or will happen in the world will always be found to be in proportion to the number and weight of the causes, whether REAL or PRETENDED, which PROVOKE or INVITE them. If this remark be just, it becomes useful to inquire whether so many JUST causes of war are likely to be given by UNITED AMERICA as by DISUNITED America; for if it should turn out that *United America will probably give the fewest*, then it will follow that in this respect *the Union tends most to preserve the people in a state of peace with other nations.*

The *JUST* causes of war, for the most part, *arise* either *from violation of treaties or from direct violence. America has already formed treaties with no less than six foreign nations,* and all of them, except Prussia, are maritime, and therefore able to annoy and injure us. *She has also extensive commerce* with Portugal, Spain, and Britain, and, with respect to the two latter, has, in addition, the circumstance of neighborhood to attend to.

It is of high importance to the peace of America that she observe the laws of nations towards all these powers, and to me it appears evident that this will be more perfectly and punctually done by one national government than it could be either by thirteen separate States or by three or four distinct confederacies. . . . The administration, the political counsels, and the judicial decisions of the national government will be more wise, systematical, and judicious than those of individual States, and consequently more satisfactory with respect to other nations, as well as more SAFE with respect to us.

Because, under the national government, treaties and articles of treaties, as well as the laws of nations, will always be expounded in one sense and executed in the same manner,—whereas, adjudications on the same points and questions, in thirteen States, or in three or four confederacies, will not always accord or be consistent . . . the wisdom of the convention, in committing such questions to the jurisdiction and judgment of courts appointed by and responsible only to one national government, cannot be too much commended. . . . So far, therefore, as either designed or accidental violations of treaties and the laws of nations afford JUST causes of war, they are less to be apprehended under *one general government* than under several lesser ones, and in that respect the former *most favors the SAFETY of the people.*

As to those just causes of war which proceed from direct and unlawful violence, it appears equally clear to me that *one good national government affords vastly more security* against dangers of that sort than can be derived from any other quarter. . . . Not a single Indian war has yet been occasioned by aggressions of the present federal government, feeble as it is; but there are several instances of Indian hostilities having been provoked by the improper conduct of individual States, who, either unable or unwilling to restrain or punish offenses, have given occasion to the slaughter of many innocent inhabitants.

The neighborhood of Spanish and British territories, bordering on some States and not on others, naturally confines the causes of quarrel more immediately to the . . . bordering States. . . . who, under the impulse of sudden irritation, and a quick sense of apparent interest or injury, will be most likely, by direct violence, to excite war with these nations; and nothing can so effectually obviate that danger as a national government, whose wisdom and prudence will not be diminished by the passions which actuate the parties immediately interested.

But not only fewer *just causes of war* will be given by the national government, but it will also be more in their power *to accommodate and settle them amicably.* They will be more temperate and cool, and in that respect, as well as in others, will be more in capacity to act advisedly than the offending State. . . . The national government, in such cases, will not be affected by this pride, but will proceed with moderation and candor to consider and decide on the means most proper to extricate them from the difficulties which threaten them.

Besides, it is well known that acknowledgments, explanations, and compensations are often accepted as satisfactory from a strong united nation, which would be rejected as unsatisfactory if offered by *a State or confederacy of little consideration or power.* In the year 1685, the state of Genoa having offended Louis XIV, endeavored *to appease* him. He demanded that they should send their . . . chief magistrate, accompanied by four of their senators, to FRANCE, to ask his pardon and receive his terms. They were obliged to submit to it for the sake of peace. Would he on any occasion either have demanded or have received the like *humiliation* from Spain, or Britain, or any other POWERFUL nation?

No. 4 . . . My last paper assigned several reasons why the safety of the people would be best secured by union against the danger it may be exposed to by JUST causes of war given to other nations; and

those reasons show that such causes would . . . be more easily accommodated, by a national government than either by the State governments or the proposed little confederacies.

But *the safety of the people of America against dangers from FOREIGN force depends not only on their forbearing to give JUST causes of war to other nations, but also on their placing and continuing themselves in such a situation as not to INVITE hostility or insult;* for it need not be observed that there are PRETENDED as well as just causes of war.

It is too true, however disgraceful it may be to human nature, that *nations in general will make war whenever they have a prospect of getting anything by it*; nay, absolute monarchs will often make war when their nations are to get nothing by it, but for the purposes and objects merely personal, such as thirst for military glory, revenge for personal affronts, ambition, or private compacts to aggrandize or support their particular families or partisans. These and a variety of other motives, which affect only the mind of the sovereign, often lead him to engage in wars not sanctified by justice or the voice and interests of his people. But, independent of these inducements to war, which are more prevalent in absolute monarchies, but which well deserve our attention, there are others which affect nations as often as kings; and some of them will on examination be found to grow out of our relative situation and circumstances.

With France and with Britain we are rivals in the fisheries, and can supply their markets cheaper than they can themselves, notwithstanding any efforts to prevent it by bounties on their own or duties on foreign fish. *With them and with most other European nations we are rivals in navigation and the carrying trade;* and we shall deceive ourselves if we suppose that any of them will rejoice to see it flourish; for, as our carrying trade cannot increase without in some degree diminishing theirs, it is more their interest, and will be more their policy, to restrain than to promote it. *In the trade to China and India, we interfere with more than one nation,* inasmuch as it enables us to partake in advantages which they had in a manner monopolized, and as we thereby supply ourselves with commodities which we used to purchase from them. *The extension of our own commerce in our own vessels cannot give pleasure to any nations who possess territories on or near this continent,* because the cheapness and excellence of our productions, added to the circumstance of vicinity, and the enterprise and address of our merchants and navigators, will give us a greater share in the advantages which those territories afford, than consists with the wishes or policy of their respective sovereigns.

Spain thinks it convenient to shut the Mississippi against us on the one side, and Britain excludes us from the Saint Lawrence on the other; nor will either of them permit the other waters which are between them and us to become the means of mutual intercourse and traffic. From these and such like considerations . . . , it is easy to see that jealousies and uneasinesses may gradually slide into the minds and cabinets of other nations, and that we are not to expect that they should regard our advancement in union, in power and consequence by land and by sea, with an eye of indifference and composure.

The people of America are aware that inducements to war may arise out of these circumstances . . . wisely, therefore, do . . . consider union and a good national government as necessary to put and keep them in SUCH A SITUATION as, instead of INVITING war, will tend to repress and discourage it. That situation consists in *the best possible state of defense,* and necessarily *depends on the government, the arms, and the resources of the country.*

As the safety of the whole is the interest of the whole, and cannot be provided for without government, either one or more or many, let us inquire whether one good government is not, relative to the object in question, more competent than any other given number whatever.

One government can collect and avail itself of the talents and experience of the ablest men, in whatever part of the Union they may be found. It can move on uniform principles of policy. It can harmonize, assimilate, and protect the several parts and members, and extend the benefit of its foresight and precautions to each. *In the formation of treaties, it will regard the interest of the whole, and the particular interests of the parts as connected with that of the whole. It can apply the resources and power of the whole to the defense of any particular part,* and that more easily and expeditiously than State governments or separate confederacies can possibly do, for want of concert and unity of system. *It can place the militia under one plan of discipline,* and, by *putting their officers in a proper line of subordination* to the Chief Magistrate, will, as it were, *consolidate them into one corps, and thereby render them more efficient* than if divided into thirteen or into three or four distinct independent companies.

What would the militia of Britain be if the English militia obeyed the government of England, if the Scotch militia obeyed the government of Scotland, and if the Welsh militia obeyed the government of Wales? Suppose an invasion; would those three governments (if they agreed at all) be able, with all their respective forces, to operate against the enemy so effectually as the single government of Great Britain would?

We have heard much of the fleets of Britain, and the time may come, if we are wise, when the fleets of America may engage attention. But if one national government, had not so regulated the navigation of Britain as to make it a nursery for seamen—if one national government had not called forth all the national means and materials for forming fleets, their prowess and their thunder would never have been celebrated. Let England have its navigation and fleet—let Scotland have its navigation and fleet—let Wales have its navigation and fleet—let Ireland have its navigation and fleet—let those four of the constituent parts of the British empire be under four independent governments, and it is easy to perceive how soon they would each dwindle into comparative insignificance.

Apply these facts to our own case. *Leave America divided into thirteen or, if you please, into three or four independent governments—what armies could they raise and pay—what fleets could they ever hope to have?* If one was attacked, would the others fly to its succor, and spend their blood and money in its defense? Would there be no danger of their being flattered into neutrality by its specious promises, or seduced by a too great fondness for peace to decline hazarding their tranquillity and present safety for the sake of neighbors, of whom perhaps they have been jealous, and whose importance they are content to see diminished? Although such conduct would not be wise, it would, nevertheless, be natural. The history of the states of Greece, and of other countries, abounds with such instances, and it is not improbable that what has so often happened would, under similar circumstances, happen again.

But admit that they might be willing to help the invaded State or confederacy.

How, and when, and in what proportion shall aids of men and money be afforded? Who shall command the allied armies, and from which of them shall he receive his orders? Who shall settle the terms of peace, and in case of disputes what umpire shall decide between them and compel acquiescence? Various difficulties and inconveniences would be inseparable from such a situation; whereas *one government, watching over the general and common interests, and combining and directing the powers and resources of the whole, would* be free from all these embarrassments, and *conduce far more to the safety of the people.*

But whatever may be our situation, whether firmly united under one national government, or split into a number of confederacies, certain it is, that *foreign nations* will know and view it exactly as it is; and they will act toward us accordingly. *If they see that our national government is efficient and well administered, our trade prudently regulated, our militia properly organized and disciplined, our resources and finances discreetly managed, our credit re-established, our people free, contented, and united, they will be much more disposed to cultivate our friendship than provoke our resentment. If, on the other hand, they find us either destitute of an effectual government* (each State doing right or wrong, as to its rulers may seem convenient), *or split into three or four independent and probably discordant republics or confederacies,* one inclining to Britain, another to France, and a third to Spain, and perhaps played off against each other by the three, *what a poor, pitiful figure will America make in their eyes! How liable would she become not only to their contempt but to their outrage,* and how soon would dear-bought experience proclaim that when a people or family so divide, it never fails to be against themselves.

No. 5 Queen Anne, in her letter of the 1st July, 1706, to the Scotch Parliament, makes some observations on the importance of the UNION then forming between England and Scotland, which merit our attention . . . : "An entire and perfect union will be the solid foundation of lasting peace: It will secure your religion, liberty, and property; remove the animosities amongst yourselves, and the jealousies and differences betwixt our two kingdoms. It must increase your strength, riches, and trade; and by this union the whole island, being joined in affection and free from all apprehensions of different interest, will be ENABLED TO RESIST ALL ITS ENEMIES . . . ; that the union [is] . . . the only EFFECTUAL way to secure our present and future happiness, and disappoint the designs of our . . . enemies. . . ."

It was remarked in the preceding paper that *weakness and divisions at home would invite dangers from abroad; and that nothing would tend more to secure us from them than union, strength, and good government within ourselves.* . . .

The history of Great Britain . . . gives us many useful lessons. . . . Although it seems obvious to common sense that the people of such an island should be but one nation, yet we find that they were for ages divided into three, and that those three were almost constantly embroiled in quarrels and wars with one another. Notwithstanding their true interest with respect to the continental nations was really the same, yet by the arts and policy and practices of those nations, their mutual jealousies were perpetually kept inflamed, and for a long series of years they were far more inconvenient and troublesome than they were useful and assisting to each other.

Should the people of America divide themselves into three or four nations, would not the same thing happen? Would not similar jealousies arise, and be in like manner cherished? Instead of their being "joined in affection" and free from all apprehension of different "interests," envy and jealousy would soon extinguish confidence and affection, and the partial interests of each confederacy, instead of the general interests of all America, would be the only objects of their policy and pursuits. Hence, like most other BORDERING nations, they would always be either involved in disputes and war, or live in the constant apprehension of them. The most sanguine advocates for three or four confederacies cannot reasonably suppose that they would long remain exactly on an equal footing in point of strength, even if it was possible to form them so at first; but, admitting that to be practicable, yet what human contrivance can secure the continuance of such equality? Independent of those local circumstances which tend to beget and increase power in one part and to impede its progress in another, we must advert to the effects of that superior policy and good management which would probably distinguish the government of one above the rest, and by which their relative equality in strength and consideration would be destroyed. For it cannot be presumed that the same degree of sound policy, prudence, and foresight would uniformly be observed by each of these confederacies for a long succession of years.

Whenever, and from whatever causes, it might happen, and happen it would, that any one of these nations or confederacies should rise on the scale of political importance much above the degree of her neighbors, that moment would those neighbors behold her with envy and with fear. Both those passions would lead them to countenance, if not to promote, whatever might promise to diminish her importance; and would also restrain them from measures calculated to advance or even to secure her prosperity. Much time would not be necessary to enable her to discern these unfriendly dispositions. She would soon begin, not only to lose confidence in her neighbors, but also to feel a disposition equally unfavorable to them.

Distrust naturally creates distrust, and by nothing is good-will and kind conduct more speedily changed than by invidious jealousies and uncandid imputations, whether expressed or implied. The North is generally the region of strength, and many local circumstances render it probable that the most Northern of the proposed confederacies would, at a period not very distant, be unquestionably more formidable than any of the others. No sooner would this become evident than the NORTHERN HIVE would excite the same ideas and sensations in the more southern parts of America which it formerly did in the southern parts of Europe. Nor does it appear to be a rash conjecture that its young swarms might often be tempted to gather honey in the more blooming fields and milder air of their luxurious and more delicate neighbors. They who well consider the history of similar divisions and confederacies will find abundant reason to apprehend that those in contemplation would in no other sense be neighbors than as they would be borderers; that they would neither love nor trust one another, but on the contrary would be a prey to discord, jealousy, and mutual injuries; in short, that they would place us exactly in the situations in which some nations doubtless wish to see us, viz., FORMIDABLE ONLY TO EACH OTHER. *From these considerations it appears that those gentlemen are greatly mistaken who suppose that alliances offensive and defensive might be formed between these confederacies, and would*

produce that combination and union of wills of arms and of resources, which would be necessary to put and keep them in a formidable state of defense against foreign enemies.

When did the independent states, into which Britain and Spain were formerly divided, combine in such alliance, or unite their forces against a foreign enemy? The proposed confederacies will be DISTINCT NATIONS. Each of them would have its commerce with foreigners to regulate by distinct treaties; and as their productions and commodities are different and proper for different markets, so would those treaties be essentially different. *Different commercial concerns must create different interests, and of course different degrees of political attachment to and connection with different foreign nations.* Hence it might and probably would happen that the foreign nation with whom the SOUTHERN confederacy might be at war would be the one with whom the NORTHERN confederacy would be the most desirous of preserving peace and friendship. An alliance so contrary to their immediate interest would not therefore be easy to form, nor, if formed, would it be observed and fulfilled with perfect good faith. Nay, *it is far more probable that in America, as in Europe, neighboring nations, acting under the impulse of opposite interests and unfriendly passions, would frequently be found taking different sides. Considering our distance from Europe, it would be more natural for these confederacies to apprehend danger from one another than from distant nations, and therefore that each of them should be more desirous to guard against the others by the aid of foreign alliances, than to guard against foreign dangers by alliances between themselves.* And here let us not forget how much more easy it is to receive foreign fleets into our ports, and foreign armies into our country, than it is to persuade or compel them to depart.

How many conquests did the Romans and others make in the characters of allies, and what innovations did they under the same character introduce into the governments of those whom they pretended to protect. *Let candid men judge, then, whether the division of America into any given number of independent sovereignties would tend to secure us against the hostilities and improper interference of foreign nations.*

---

11. *[Treaty-Making Powers and Executive-Legislative Concurrence]:* Federalist Paper No. 64

John Jay
(1788)

John Jay, later U.S. Supreme Court justice, tells us here why the Senate was selected to have a greater voice on foreign policy, particularly its role in the ratification of treaties. National interests in relation to foreign powers as well as the interests of "the several States" composing the Union are left to the president and the Senate, "who best understand" these matters as opposed to "a popular assembly [i.e., the House of Representatives] composed of members constantly coming and going in quick succession," thus lacking the knowledge or experience base enjoyed by the Senate. Moreover, the interests of the states are best represented in the Senate where they enjoy equal representation.

. . . The second section gives power to the President, "BY AND WITH THE ADVICE AND CONSENT OF THE SENATE, TO MAKE TREATIES, PROVIDED TWO THIRDS OF THE SENATORS PRESENT CONCUR."

The power of making treaties is an important one, especially as it *relates to war, peace, and commerce;* and it should not be delegated but in such a mode, and with such precautions, as will afford the highest security that it will be exercised by men the best qualified for the purpose, and in the manner most conducive to the public good. . . . That *the President and senators* so chosen will always be of the number of those who best understand our national interests, whether considered in relation to the several States or to foreign nations, who are best able to promote those interests, and whose reputation for integrity inspires and merits confidence. *With such*

men the power of making treaties may be safely lodged.

Although the absolute necessity of system, in the conduct of any business, is universally known and acknowledged, yet the high importance of it in national affairs has not yet become sufficiently impressed on the public mind. *They who wish to commit the power under consideration to a popular assembly,* composed of members constantly coming and going in quick succession, *seem not to recollect that such a body must necessarily be inadequate to the attainment of those great objects,* which require to be steadily contemplated in all their relations and circumstances, and which can only be approached and achieved by measures which not only talents, but also exact information, and often much time, are necessary to concert and to execute. It was wise, therefore, in the convention to provide, not only that the power of making treaties should be committed to able and honest men, but also that they should continue in place a sufficient time to become perfectly acquainted with our national concerns, and to form and introduce a system for the management of them. The duration prescribed is such as will give them an opportunity of greatly extending their political information, and of rendering their accumulating experience more and more beneficial to their country. Nor has the convention discovered less prudence in providing for the frequent elections of senators in such a way as to obviate the inconvenience of periodically transferring those great affairs entirely to new men; for by leaving a considerable residue of the old ones in place, uniformity and order, as well as a constant succession of official information will be preserved.

There are a few who will not admit *that the affairs of trade and navigation should be regulated by a system cautiously formed and steadily pursued; and that both our treaties and our laws should correspond with and be made to promote it.* It is of much consequence *that this correspondence and conformity be carefully maintained;* and they who assent to the truth of this position will see and confess that it is well provided for *by making concurrence of the Senate necessary both to treaties and to laws.*

It seldom happens in the negotiation of treaties, of whatever nature, but that perfect SECRECY and immediate DESPATCH are sometimes requisite. These are cases where the most useful intelligence may be obtained, if the persons possessing it can be relieved from apprehensions of discovery. Those apprehensions will operate on those persons whether they are actuated by mercenary or friendly motives; and there doubtless are many of both descriptions, who would rely on the secrecy of the President, but who would not confide in

that of the Senate, and still less in that of a large popular Assembly. *The convention have done well, therefore, in so disposing of the power of making treaties, that although the President must, in forming them, act by the advice and consent of the Senate, yet he will be able to manage the business of intelligence in such a manner as prudence may suggest. . . .*

So often and so essentially have we heretofore suffered from the want of secrecy and despatch, that the Constitution would have been inexcusably defective, if no attention had been paid to those objects. Those *matters which in negotiations usually require the most secrecy and the most despatch,* are those preparatory and auxiliary measures which are not otherwise important in a national view, than as they tend to facilitate the attainment of the objects of the negotiation. *For these, the President will find no difficulty to provide; and should any circumstance occur which requires the advice and consent of the Senate, he may at any time convene them.* Thus we see that the Constitution provides that our negotiations for treaties shall have every advantage which can be derived from talents, information, integrity, and deliberate investigations, on the one hand, and from secrecy and despatch on the other. . . .

Some are displeased . . . as the *treaties, when made, are to have the force of laws,* they should be made only by men invested with legislative authority. These gentlemen seem not to consider that the judgments of our courts, and the commissions constitutionally given by our governor, are as valid and as binding on all persons whom they concern, as the laws passed by our legislature. All constitutional acts of power, whether in the executive or in the judicial department, have as much legal validity and obligation as if they proceeded from the legislature; and therefore, whatever name be given to the power of making treaties, or however obligatory they may be when made, certain it is, that the people may, with much propriety, commit the power to a distinct body from the legislature, the executive, or the judicial. It surely does not follow, that because they have given the power of making laws to the legislature, that therefore they should likewise give them the power to do every other act of sovereignty by which the citizens are to be bound and affected.

Others, though content that treaties should be made in the mode proposed, are averse to *their being the SUPREME laws of the land.* They insist, and profess to believe, that treaties like acts of assembly, should be repealable at pleasure. This idea seems to be new and peculiar to this country, but new errors, as well as new truths, often appear. These gentlemen would do well to reflect that a treaty is only another name for a bargain, and that it would be impossible to find a nation who would make any bargain with us, which should be binding on them ABSOLUTELY, but on us only so long and so far as we may think proper to be bound by it. They who make laws may, without doubt, amend or repeal them; and it will not be disputed that they who make treaties may alter or cancel them; but still let us not forget that treaties are made, not by only one of the contracting parties, but by both; and consequently, that as the consent of both was essential to their formation at first, so must it ever afterwards be to alter or cancel them. *The proposed Constitution, therefore, has not in the least extended the obligation of treaties. They are just as binding, and just as far beyond the lawful reach of legislative acts now, as they will be at any future period, or under any form of government.*

However useful jealousy may be in republics, yet when like bile in the natural, it abounds too much in the body politic, the eyes of both become very liable to be deceived by the delusive appearances which that malady casts on surrounding objects. From this cause, probably, proceed the fears and apprehensions of some, that the President and Senate may make treaties without an equal eye to the interests of all the States. Others suspect that two thirds will oppress the remaining third, and ask whether those gentlemen are made sufficiently responsible for their conduct; whether, if they act corruptly, they can be punished; and if they make disadvantageous treaties, how are we to get rid of those treaties?

As all the States are equally represented in the Senate, and by men the most able and the most willing to promote the interests of their constituents, they will all have an equal degree of influence in that body, especially while they continue to be careful in appointing proper persons, and to insist on their punctual attendance. In proportion as the United States assume a national form and a national character, so will the good of the whole be more and more an object of attention, and the government must be a weak one indeed, if it should forget that the good of the whole can only be promoted by advancing the good of each of the parts or members which compose the whole. It will not be in the power of the President and Senate to make any treaties by which they and their families and estates will not be equally bound and affected with the rest of the community; and, having no private interests distinct from that of the nation, they will be under no temptations to neglect the latter.

As to corruption, the case is not supposable. He must either have been very unfortunate in his intercourse with the world, or possess a heart very susceptible of such impressions, who can think it probable that the President and two thirds of the Senate will ever be capable of such unworthy conduct. The idea is too gross and too invidious to be entertained. But in such a case, if it should ever happen, the treaty so obtained from us would, like all other fraudulent contracts, be null and void by the law of nations.

With respect to their responsibility, it is difficult to conceive how it could be increased. Every consideration that can influence the human mind, such as honor, oaths, reputations, conscience, the love of country, and family affections and attachments, afford security for their fidelity. In short, as the Constitution has taken the utmost care that they shall be men of talents and integrity, we have reason to be persuaded that the treaties they make will be as advantageous as, all circumstances considered, could be made; and so far as the fear of punishment and disgrace can operate, that motive to good behavior is amply afforded by the article on the subject of impeachments.

---

12. [The Judiciary, Foreign Policy, and National Security]: Federalist Papers Nos. 78–81 and 83

Alexander Hamilton
(1788)

Hamilton's commentary on the judicial branch includes reference to foreign policy and national security matters that would come before federal judges and juries, decisions that could lead to "reprisal and war." He is sensitive to possible difficulties of court decisions adverse to foreign countries or their principals, particularly if state courts were deciding cases within their jurisdiction involving foreigners. In such instances, he sees the federal courts as being better positioned to take on such matters.

No. 78 . . . The Judiciary Department. . . . As nothing can contribute so much to its firmness and independence as permanency in office, this quality may therefore be justly regarded as an indispensable ingredient in its constitution, and, in a great measure, as the citadel of the public justice and the public security. . . .

No. 79 Next to permanency in office, nothing can contribute more to the independence of the judges than a fixed provision for their support. . . .

No. 80 TO JUDGE with accuracy of the proper extent of the federal judicature, it will be necessary to consider, in the first place, what are its proper objects.

It seems scarcely to admit of controversy, that the judiciary authority of the Union ought to extend to these several descriptions of cases: 1st, to all those which arise out of the laws of the United States, passed in pursuance of their just and constitutional powers of legislation; 2d, to all those which concern the execution of the provisions expressly contained in the articles of Union; 3d, to all those in which the United States are a party; 4th, to all those which involve the PEACE of the CONFEDERACY, whether they relate to *the intercourse between the United States and foreign nations,* or to that between the States themselves; 5th, *to all those which originate on the high seas, and are of admiralty or maritime jurisdiction;* and, lastly, to all those in which the State tribunals cannot be supposed to be impartial and unbiased.

The first point depends upon this obvious consideration, that there ought always to be a constitutional method of giving efficacy to constitutional provisions. What, for instance, would avail restrictions on the authority of the State legislatures, without some constitutional mode of enforcing the observance of them? The States, by the plan of the convention, are prohibited from doing a variety of things, some of which are incompatible with the interests of the Union, and others with the principles of good government. The imposition of *duties on imported articles,* and the emission of paper money, are specimens of each kind. No man of sense will believe, that such prohibitions would be scrupulously regarded, without some effectual power in the government to restrain or correct the infractions of them. This power must either be a direct negative on the State laws, or an authority in the federal courts to overrule such as might be in manifest contravention of the articles of Union. There is no third course that I can imagine. The latter appears to have been thought by the convention preferable to the former, and, I presume, will be most agreeable to the States. . . .

The peace of the WHOLE ought not to be left at the disposal of a PART. *The Union will undoubtedly be answerable to foreign powers for the conduct of its members. And the responsibility for an injury ought ever to be accompanied with the faculty of preventing it.* As the denial or perversion of justice by the sentences of courts, as well as in any other manner, is with reason classed among the just causes of war, it will follow that *the federal judiciary ought to have cognizance of all causes in which the citizens of other countries are concerned.* This is not less essential to the preservation of the public faith, than to the security of the public tranquillity. A distinction may perhaps be imagined between *cases arising upon treaties and the laws of nations and those which may stand merely on the footing of the municipal law.* The former kind may be supposed proper for the federal jurisdiction, the latter for that of the States. But it is at least problematical, whether an unjust sentence against a foreigner, where the subject of controversy was wholly relative to the lex loci, would not, if unredressed, be an aggression upon his sovereign, as well as one which violated *the stipulations of a treaty or the general law of nations.* And a still greater objection to the distinction would result from the immense difficulty, if not impossibility, of a practical discrimination between the cases of one complexion and those of the other. *So great a proportion of the cases in which foreigners are parties, involve national questions, that it is by far most safe and most expedient to refer all those in which they are concerned to the national tribunals. . . .*

The most bigoted idolizers of State authority have not thus far shown a disposition to deny the national judiciary the cognizances of *maritime causes.* These *so generally depend on the laws of nations,* and so commonly affect *the rights of foreigners,* that they fall within the considerations which are relative to the public peace. The most important part of them are, by the present Confederation, submitted to federal jurisdiction. . . .

The federal judiciary . . . is to comprehend "all cases in law and equity arising under the Constitution, the laws of the United States, and *treaties made, or which shall be made, under their authority; to all cases affecting ambassadors, other public ministers, and consuls; to all cases of admiralty and maritime jurisdiction; to controversies to which the United States shall be a party;* to controversies between two or more States; between a State and citizens of another State; between citizens of different States; between citizens of the same State claiming lands and grants of different States; and *between a State or the citizens thereof and foreign states, citizens, and subjects."* . . .

The judiciary authority of the Union is to extend . . . to treaties made, or which shall be made, under the authority of the United States, and to all cases affecting ambassadors, other public ministers, and consuls. These . . . have an evident connection with the *preservation of the national peace.* . . .

To cases of *admiralty and maritime jurisdiction.* These form, altogether, the . . . classes of causes proper for the cognizance of the national courts. . . .

To *controversies to which the United States shall be a party.* . . .

To *cases between a State and the citizens thereof, and foreign States, citizens, or subjects* . . . have been already explained to belong to . . . the proper subjects of the national judicature. . . .

No. 81 . . . It is inherent in the nature of sovereignty not to be amenable to the suit of an individual *without its consent.* This is the general sense, and the general practice of mankind. . . .

No. 83 . . . I feel a deep and deliberate conviction that there are many cases in which the trial by jury is an ineligible one. I think it so particularly in cases which concern the public peace with foreign nations— that is, in most cases where the question turns wholly on the laws of nations. . . . *Juries cannot be supposed competent to investigations that require a thorough knowledge of the laws and usages of nations;* and they will sometimes be under the influence of impressions which will not suffer them to pay sufficient regard to those considerations of public policy which ought to guide their inquiries. *There would of course be always danger that the rights of other nations might be infringed by their decisions, so as to afford occasions of reprisal and war. Though the proper province of juries be to determine matters of fact, yet in most cases legal consequences are complicated with fact in such a manner as to render a separation impracticable.*

It will add great weight to this remark, in relation to prize causes, to mention that the method of determining them has been thought worthy of particular regulation in various treaties between different powers of Europe, and that, pursuant to such treaties, they are determinable in Great Britain, in the last resort, before the king himself, in his privy council, where the fact, as well as the law, undergoes a reexamination. This alone demonstrates the impolicy of inserting a fundamental provision in the Constitution which would make the State systems a standard for the national government in the article under consideration, and the danger of encumbering the government with any constitutional provisions the propriety of which is not indisputable. . . .

PART TWO

Constitutional Interpretations on the Conduct of American Foreign Policy

The U.S. Supreme Court, which derives its authority from Article III of the Constitution and from statutes passed by Congress, is not as frequent a player on foreign policy and national security issues as are the "political" branches—the executive and the legislative. That said, the Court has weighed in from time to time, addressing constitutional issues relating to separation of powers, treaties, war powers, and civil liberties in wartime.

Chapter 5 takes up three cases relating to the federal role in foreign policy. We turn in Chapter 6 to four cases on separation of powers in relation to treaties.

Chapter 7 addresses executive and legislative war powers, the former grounded in designation of the president in Article II of the Constitution as being commander in chief of the armed forces—in effect authorizing him *to make war*—and the latter grounded in Article I, Section 8, designating Congress as retaining the right *to declare war.* Finally, wartime demands for domestic security put pressure on civil liberties, the subject of chapter 8.

Chapter 5

The Federal Role in Foreign Policy

1. *Gibbons v. Ogden*

(1824)

John Marshall's landmark opinion in this case rejects "narrow" or "strict construction" in relation to federal government authority, underscoring the importance of the "necessary and proper" (often referred to as the "elastic") clause in Article I, Section 8, of the Constitution, which he interprets as conferring on Congress broad authority to enact legislation consistent with its enumerated powers. Marshall applies this elastic clause to the power of Congress to regulate interstate commerce—among states within the union as well as with foreign states. To Marshall, commerce refers to "every species of commercial intercourse between the United States and foreign nations" and certainly includes "navigation" across waterways. Indeed the word "commerce" is interpreted broadly as referring not merely to "traffic" but to "something more"—"the commercial intercourse between nations, and parts of nations, in all its branches." When federal law conflicts with state law (in this case a New York law dealing with interstate commerce), it is the federal, not state, law that has primacy. In Gibbons v. Ogden we find that Thomas Gibbons, operating with a federal navigation license, has tried to compete with a ferry between New York City and New Jersey run by Aaron Ogden, operating under a thirty-year exclusive steam-powered navigation license for all operations in New York waters, which had been issued by New York state to two prominent New Yorkers, Robert Livingston and Robert Fulton. The New York Supreme Court had ruled in favor of Ogden, granting him an injunction against Gibbons who then appealed to the U.S. Supreme Court. The Court ruled for Gibbons, using the case to establish federal supremacy in interstate commerce—a power that also extends to international commerce.

Opinion by Mr. Chief Justice Marshall.

As preliminary to the very able discussions of the constitution . . . reference has been made to the political situation of these states, anterior to its formation. It has been said that they were sovereign, were completely independent, and were connected with each other only by a league. This is true. But when these allied sovereigns converted their league into a government . . .

empowered to enact laws . . . , the whole character in which the states appear, underwent a change, the extent of which must be determined by a fair consideration of the instrument by which that change was effected.

This instrument [the Constitution] contains an enumeration of powers expressly granted by the people to their government. It has been said that these powers ought to be construed strictly. But why ought they to be so construed? Is there one sentence in the constitution which gives countenance to this rule? In the last of the enumerated powers, that which grants, expressly, the means of carrying all others into execution, Congress is authorized "to make all laws which shall be necessary and proper" for the purpose. . . .

What do gentlemen mean by a strict construction? If they contend . . . for that narrow construction, which would cripple the government and render it unequal to the objects for which it is declared to be instituted, and to which the powers given, as fairly understood, render it competent; then we cannot perceive the propriety of this strict construction, nor adopt it as the rule by which the constitution is to be expounded. . . . We know of no rule for construing the extent of such powers, other than is given by the language of the instrument which confers them, taken in connection with the purposes for which they were conferred. The words are: "*Congress shall have power to regulate commerce with foreign nations, and among the several states, and with the Indian tribes.*"

The subject to be regulated is commerce; and our constitution being, as was aptly said at the bar, one of enumeration, and not of definition, to ascertain the extent of the power it becomes necessary to settle the meaning of the word. The counsel for the appellee would limit it to traffic, to buying and selling, or the interchange of commodities, and do not admit that it comprehends navigation. This would restrict a general term, applicable to many objects, to one of its significations. *Commerce, undoubtedly, is traffic, but it is something more; it is intercourse. It describes the commercial intercourse between nations, and parts of nations, in all its branches, and is regulated by prescribing rules for carrying on that intercourse.* The mind can scarcely conceive a system for regulating commerce between nations, which shall exclude all laws concerning navigation, which shall be silent on the admission of the vessels of the one nation into the ports of the other, and be confined to prescribing rules for the conduct of individuals, in the actual employment of buying and selling or of barter.

If commerce does not include navigation, the government of the Union has no direct power over that subject, and can make no law prescribing what shall constitute American vessels, or requiring that they shall be navigated by American seamen. Yet this power has been exercised from the commencement of the government, has been exercised with the consent of all, and has been understood by all to be a commercial regulation. All America understands, and has uniformly understood, the word "commerce" to comprehend navigation. It was so understood, and must have been so understood, when the constitution was framed. The power over commerce, including navigation, was one of the primary objects for which the people of America adopted their government, and must have been contemplated in forming it. . . . *The word used in the constitution comprehends, and has been always understood to comprehend, navigation within its meaning; and a power to regulate navigation is as expressly granted as if that term had been added to the word "commerce."*

To what commerce does this power extend? The constitution informs us, to commerce "with foreign nations, and among the several states, and with the Indian tribes." It has, we believe, been universally admitted that *these words comprehend every species of commercial intercourse between the United States and foreign nations.* No sort of trade can be carried on between this country and any other, to which this power does not extend. It has been truly said, that commerce, as the word is used in the constitution, is a unit, every part of which is indicated by the term. . . .

The subject to which the power is next applied, is to commerce "among the several states" . . . comprehensive as the word "among" is, it may very properly be restricted to that commerce which concerns more states than one. The phrase is not one which would probably have been selected to indicate the completely interior traffic of a state. . . . The genius and character of the whole government seem to be, that its action is to be applied to all the external concerns of the nation, and to those internal concerns which affect the states generally; but not to those which are completely within a particular state, which do not affect other states, and with which it is not necessary to interfere, for the purpose of executing some of the general powers of the government. The completely internal commerce of a state, then, may be considered as reserved for the state itself. But, *in regulating commerce with foreign nations, the power of Congress does not stop at the jurisdictional lines of the several states. It would be a very useless power if it could not pass those lines. The commerce of the United States with foreign nations, is that of the whole United States.* Every district has a right to participate in it. The deep streams which penetrate our country in every direction, pass through the interior of almost every state

in the Union, and furnish the means of exercising this right. If Congress has the power to regulate it, that power must be exercised whenever the subject exists. *If it exists within the states, if a foreign voyage may commence or terminate at a port within a state, then the power of Congress may be exercised within a state.* . . .

In the regulation of trade with the Indian tribes, the action of the law, especially when the constitution was made, was chiefly within a state. The power of Congress, then, whatever it may be, must be exercised within the territorial jurisdiction of the several states. . . .

What is this power? *It is the power to regulate; that is, to prescribe the rule by which commerce is to be governed. This power, like all others vested in Congress, is complete in itself, may be exercised to its utmost extent, and acknowledges no limitations, other than are prescribed in the constitution.* . . . If, as has always been understood, the sovereignty of Congress, though limited to specified objects, is plenary as to those objects, *the power over commerce with foreign nations,* and among the several States, *is vested in Congress as absolutely as it would be in a single government,* having in its constitution the same restrictions on the exercise of the power as are found in the constitution of the United States. . . .

The power of Congress, then, comprehends navigation within the limits of every State in the Union; so far as that navigation may be in any manner, connected with "commerce with foreign nations, or among the several states, or with the Indian tribes." It may, of consequence, pass the jurisdictional line of New York, and act upon the very waters to which the prohibition now under consideration applies. . . . In exercising the power of regulating their own purely internal affairs, whether of trading or police, the states may sometimes enact laws, the validity of which depends on their interfering with, and being contrary to, an act of Congress passed in pursuance of the constitution, the court will enter upon the inquiry. . . . [If] the laws of New York, as expounded by the highest tribunal of that State, have, in their application to this case, come into collision with an act of Congress, . . . the acts of New York must yield to the law of Congress. . . .

The framers of our constitution foresaw this state of things, and provided for it, by declaring the supremacy not only of itself, but of the laws made in pursuance of it. The nullity of any act, inconsistent with the constitution, is produced by the declaration that the constitution is the supreme law. The appropriate application of that part of the clause which confers the same *supremacy on laws and treaties,* is to such acts of the state legislatures as do not transcend their powers, but, though enacted in the execution of acknowledged state powers, interfere with, or are contrary to the laws of Congress, made in pursuance of the constitution, or some *treaty made under the authority of the United States. In every such case, the act of Congress, or the treaty, is supreme; and the law of the state, though enacted in the exercise of powers not controverted, must yield to it. . . .*

Congress has passed "an act enrolling or licensing ships or vessels to be employed in the coasting trade and fisheries, and for regulating the same." . . . The state of New York cannot prevent an enrolled and licensed vessel . . . from enjoying . . . all the privileges conferred by the act of Congress. . . .

Powerful and ingenious minds, taking, as postulates, that the powers expressly granted to the government of the Union are to be contracted, by construction, into the narrowest possible compass, and that the original powers of the States are retained, if any possible construction will retain them, may, by a course of well digested, but refined and metaphysical reasoning, founded on these premises, explain away the constitution of our country, and leave it a magnificent structure indeed, to look at, but totally unfit for use. They may so entangle and perplex the understanding, as to obscure principles which were before thought quite plain, and induce doubts where, if the mind were to pursue its own course, none would be perceived. In such a case it is peculiarly necessary to recur to safe and fundamental principles, to sustain those principles, and when sustained, to make them the tests of the arguments to be examined.

---

2. *Cherokee Nation v. Georgia*

(1831)

In this case the Supreme Court defines Native American or "Indian" tribes as constituting "dependent nations" within the domestic, sovereign jurisdiction of the United States. The Cherokee nation is neither a "state of the union" nor a "foreign nation" or "foreign state." The Supreme Court does not have original jurisdiction for cases brought by Indian nations because such original jurisdiction is expressly limited in Article III of the U.S. Constitution to "controversies . . . between a state or the citizens thereof, and foreign states, citizens, or subjects." Such matters are thus the domain of domestic, not foreign, policy.

Chief Justice Marshall delivered the opinion of the Court. This bill is brought by the Cherokee nation, praying an injunction to restrain the state of Georgia from the execution of certain laws of that state, which, as is alleged, go directly to annihilate the Cherokees as a political society, and to seize, for the use of Georgia, the lands of the nation which have been assured to them by the United States in solemn treaties repeatedly made and still in force. If courts were permitted to indulge their sympathies, a case better calculated to excite them can scarcely be imagined. . . .

Before we can look into the merits of the case, a preliminary inquiry presents itself. Has this court jurisdiction of the cause? *The third article of the constitution* describes the extent of the judicial power. The second section closes an enumeration of the cases to which it is extended, with "controversies . . . between a state or the citizens thereof, and foreign states, citizens, or subjects." A subsequent clause of the same section *gives the supreme court original jurisdiction in all cases in which a state shall be a party. . . . Is the Cherokee nation a foreign state in the sense in which that term is used in the constitution? . . .*

Counsel have shown conclusively that they are not a state of the union, and have insisted that individually they are aliens, not owing allegiance to the United States. An aggregate of aliens composing a state must, they say, be a foreign state. Each individual being foreign, the whole must be foreign. . . .

Though the Indians are acknowledged to have an unquestionable, and, heretofore, unquestioned right to the lands they occupy, until that right shall be extinguished by a voluntary cession to our government; yet it may well be doubted whether those tribes which reside within the acknowledged boundaries of the United States can,

with strict accuracy, be denominated foreign nations. *They may,* more correctly, perhaps, *be denominated domestic dependent nations.* They occupy a territory to which we assert a title independent of their will, which must take effect in point of possession when their right of possession ceases. Meanwhile they are in a state of pupilage. Their relation to the United States resembles that of a ward to his guardian.

They look to our government for protection; rely upon its kindness and its power; appeal to it for relief to their wants; and address the president as their great father. *They and their country are considered by foreign nations, as well as by ourselves, as being* so *completely under the sovereignty and dominion of the United States,* that any attempt to acquire their lands, or to form a political connexion with them, would be considered by all as an invasion of our territory, and an act of hostility.

These considerations go far to support the opinion, that *the framers of our constitution had not the Indian tribes in view, when they opened the courts of the union to controversies between a state or the citizens thereof, and foreign states. . . .* We should feel much difficulty in considering them as designated by the term foreign state, were there no other part of *the constitution . . . [that] empowers congress to* "regulate commerce with foreign nations, and among the several states, and with the Indian tribes."

In this clause they are as clearly contradistinguished by a name appropriate to themselves, from foreign nations, as from the several states composing the union. They are designated by a distinct appellation; and as this appellation can be applied to neither of the others, neither can the appellation distinguishing either of the others be in fair construction applied to them. *The objects, to which the power of regulating commerce might be directed, are divided into three distinct classes—foreign nations, the several states, and Indian tribes.* When forming this article, the convention considered them as entirely distinct. . . . *The constitution in this article does not comprehend Indian tribes in the general term "foreign nations;"* not we presume because a tribe may not be a nation, but because it is not foreign to the United States. . . .

The court has bestowed its best attention on this question, and, after mature deliberation, *the majority is of opinion that an Indian tribe or nation within the United States is not a foreign state in the sense of the constitution. . . .* If it be true that the Cherokee nation have rights, this is not the tribunal in which those rights are to be asserted.

---

3. *United States v. Curtiss-Wright Export Corporation et al.*
(1936)

This important, landmark decision underscores the primacy of the president over the legislature in foreign affairs. The U.S. Constitution (viz., Article II) is the primary source of this presidential and executive branch authority in foreign affairs and the historical legislative record reflects this deference to executive authority. The British Crown's primacy in foreign affairs was clearly the case in the colonial period, and this authority was transferred on independence to the United States as a unit, not to the states as if they were separate entities.

Appeal from the District Court of the United States for the Southern District of New York. . . . Mr. Justice SUTHERLAND delivered the opinion of the Court.

On January 27, 1936, an indictment was returned . . . which charges that appellees, beginning with the 29th day of May, 1934, conspired to sell in the United States certain arms of war, namely, fifteen machine guns, to Bolivia, a country then engaged in armed conflict in the Chaco, in violation of the Joint Resolution of Congress approved May 28, 1934, and the provisions of a proclamation issued on the same day by the President of the United States. . . .

Whether, if the Joint Resolution had related solely to internal affairs, it would be open to the challenge that it constituted an unlawful delegation of legislative power to the Executive, we find it unnec-essary to determine. *The whole aim of the resolution is to affect a situation entirely external to the United States, and falling within the category of foreign affairs.* The determination which we are called to make, therefore, is whether the Joint Resolution, as applied to that situation, is vulnerable to attack under the rule that forbids a delegation of the lawmaking power. In other words, assuming (but not deciding) that the challenged delegation, if it were confined to internal affairs, would be invalid, may it nevertheless be sustained on the ground that its exclusive aim is to afford a remedy for a hurtful condition within foreign territory?

It will contribute to the elucidation of the question if we first consider the differences between the powers of the federal government in respect of foreign or external affairs and those in respect of domestic or internal affairs. That there are differences between them, and that these differences are fundamental, may not be doubted.

The two classes of powers are different, both in respect of their origin and their nature. The broad statement *that the federal government can exercise no powers except . . . those specifically enumerated in the Constitution, and such implied powers as are necessary and proper to carry into effect the enumerated powers, is categorically true only in respect of our internal affairs. In that field, the primary purpose of the Constitution was to carve from the general mass of legislative powers then possessed by the states such portions as it was thought desirable to vest in the federal government,* leaving those not included in the enumeration still in the states. . . . *That this doctrine applies only to powers which the states had is self-evident. And since the states severally never possessed international powers, such powers* could not have been carved from the mass of state powers but obviously *were transmitted to the United States from some other source. During the Colonial period, those powers were possessed exclusively by and were entirely under the control of the Crown.* By the Declaration of Independence, 'the Representatives of the United States of America' declared the United (not the several) Colonies to be free and independent states, and as such to have 'full Power to levy War, conclude Peace, contract Alliances, establish Commerce and to do all other Acts and Things which Independent States may of right do.'

As a result of the separation from Great Britain by the colonies, acting as a unit, the powers of external sovereignty passed from the Crown not to the colonies severally, but to the colonies in their collective and corporate capacity as the United States of America. Even before the Declaration, the colonies were a unit in foreign affairs, acting through a common agency—namely, the Continental Congress, composed of delegates from the thirteen colonies. That agency exercised the powers of war and peace, raised an army, created a navy, and finally adopted the Declaration of Independence. Rulers come and go; governments end and forms of government change; but sovereignty survives. A political society cannot endure . . . without a supreme will somewhere. Sovereignty is never held in suspense. *When,* therefore, *the external sovereignty of Great Britain in respect of the colonies ceased, it immediately passed to the Union.* . . . That fact was given practical application almost at once. The treaty of peace, made on September 3, 1783, was concluded between his Brittanic [sic] Majesty and the "United States of America." . . .

The Union existed before the Constitution, which was ordained and established among other things to form 'a more perfect Union.' Prior to that event, it is clear that the Union, declared by the Articles of Confederation to be 'perpetual,' was the sole possessor of external sovereignty, and in the Union it remained without change save in so far as the Constitution in express terms qualified its exercise. The Framers' Convention was called and exerted its powers upon the irrefutable postulate that though the states were several their people in respect of foreign affairs were one. . . .

The powers to declare and wage war, to conclude peace, to make treaties, to maintain diplomatic relations with other sovereignties, if they had never been mentioned in the Constitution, would have vested in the federal government as necessary concomitants of nationality. Neither the Constitution nor the laws passed in pursuance of it have any force in foreign territory unless in respect of our own citizens . . . ; and operations of the nation in such territory must be governed by treaties, international understandings and compacts, and the principles of international law. As a member of the family of nations, the right and power of the United States in that field are equal to the right and power of the other members of the international family. Otherwise, the United States is not completely sovereign. The power to acquire territory by discovery and occupation . . . , the power to expel undesirable aliens . . . , the power to make such international agreements as do not constitute treaties in the constitutional sense . . . , none of which is expressly affirmed by the Constitution, nevertheless exist as inherently inseparable from the conception of nationality. This the court recognized, and . . . found the warrant for its conclusions not in the provisions of the Constitution, but in the law of nations.

In Burnet v. Brooks . . . we said, "As a nation with all the attributes of sovereignty, the United States is vested with all the powers of government necessary to maintain an effective control of international relations. . . ." *Not only, as we have shown, is the federal power over external affairs in origin and essential character different from that over internal affairs*, but participation in the exercise of the power is significantly limited. In this vast external realm, with its important, complicated, delicate and manifold problems, *the President alone has the power to speak or listen as a representative of the nation.* He makes treaties with the advice and consent of the Senate; but he alone negotiates. Into the field of negotiation the Senate cannot intrude; and Congress itself is powerless to invade it. *As Marshall said in his great argument of March 7, 1800, in the House of Representatives, 'The President is the sole organ of the nation in its external relations, and its sole representative with foreign nations. . . .' The*

Senate Committee on Foreign Relations at a very early day in our history (February 15, 1816), reported to the Senate, among other things, as follows:

"The President is the constitutional representative of the United States with regard to foreign nations. He manages our concerns with foreign nations and must necessarily be most competent to determine when, how, and upon what subjects negotiation may be urged with the greatest prospect of success. For his conduct he is responsible to the Constitution. The committee considers this responsibility the surest pledge for the faithful discharge of his duty. They think the interference of the Senate in the direction of foreign negotiations calculated to diminish that responsibility and thereby to impair the best security for the national safety. The nature of transactions with foreign nations, moreover, requires caution and unity of design, and their success frequently depends on secrecy and dispatch. . . ."

It is important to bear in mind that we are here dealing not alone with an authority vested in the President by an . . . exertion of legislative power, but with such an authority plus the very delicate, plenary and exclusive power of the President as the sole organ of the federal government in the field of international relations—a power which does not require as a basis for its exercise an act of Congress, but which, of course, like every other governmental power, must be exercised in subordination to the applicable provisions of the Constitution. It is quite apparent that if, in the maintenance of our international relations, embarrassment—perhaps serious embarrassment—is to be avoided and success for our aims achieved, *congressional legislation* which is to be made effective through negotiation and inquiry within the international field *must often accord to the President a degree of discretion and freedom from statutory restriction which would not be admissible were domestic affairs alone involved. Moreover, he, not Congress, has the better opportunity of knowing the conditions which prevail in foreign countries, and especially is this true in time of war.* He has his confidential sources of information. He has his agents in the form of diplomatic, consular and other officials. Secrecy in respect of information gathered by them may be highly necessary, and the premature disclosure of it productive of harmful results. Indeed, so clearly is this true that the first President refused to accede to a request to lay before the House of Representatives the instructions, correspondence and documents relating to the negotiation of the Jay Treaty—a refusal the wisdom of which was recognized by the House itself and has never since been doubted. In his reply to the request, *President Washington said:*

'The nature of foreign negotiations requires caution, and their success must often depend on secrecy; and even when brought to a conclusion a full disclosure of all the measures, demands, or eventual concessions which may have been proposed or contemplated would be extremely . . . impolitic; for this might have a pernicious influence on future negotiations, or produce immediate inconveniences, perhaps danger and mischief, in relation to other powers. The necessity of such caution and secrecy was one cogent reason for vesting the power of making treaties in the President, with the advice and consent of the Senate, the principle on which that body was formed confining it to a small number of members. To admit, then, a right in the House of Representatives to demand and to have as a matter of course all the papers respecting a negotiation with a foreign power would be to establish a dangerous precedent.' . . .

The marked difference between foreign affairs and domestic affairs in this respect is recognized by both houses of Congress in the very *form of their requisitions for information from the executive departments.* In the case of every department except the Department of State, the resolution directs the official to furnish the information. In the case of the State Department, dealing with foreign affairs, the President is requested to furnish the information 'if not incompatible with the public interest.' A statement that to furnish the information is not compatible with the public interest rarely, if ever, is questioned.

When the President is to be authorized by legislation to act in respect of a matter intended to affect a situation in foreign territory, the legislator properly bears in mind the important consideration that the form of the President's action—or, indeed, whether he shall act at all—may well depend, among other things, upon the nature of the confidential information which he has or may thereafter receive, or upon the effect which his action may have upon our foreign relations. This consideration, in connection with what we have already said on the subject discloses the unwisdom of requiring Congress in this field . . . of governmental power to lay down narrowly definite standards by which the President is to be governed. As this court said in Mackenzie v. Hare . . . , "As a government, the United States is invested with all the attributes of sovereignty. As it has the character of nationality it has the powers of nationality, especially those which concern its relations and intercourse with other countries. We should hesitate long before limiting or embarrassing such powers."

In the light of the foregoing observations, it is evident that this court should not be in haste to apply a general rule which will have the effect of condemning legislation like that under review as constituting an unlawful delegation of legislative power. The principles which justify such legislation find overwhelming support in the unbroken legislative practice which has prevailed almost from the inception of the national government to the present day. . . .

The result of holding that the joint resolution here under attack is void and unenforceable as constituting an unlawful delegation of legislative power would be to stamp this multitude of comparable acts and resolutions as likewise invalid. And while this court may not, and should not, hesitate to declare acts of Congress, however many times repeated, to be unconstitutional if beyond all rational doubt it finds them to be so, an impressive array of legislation . . . enacted by nearly every Congress from the beginning of our national existence to the present day, must be given unusual weight in the process of reaching a correct determination of the problem. A legislative practice such as we have here . . . but marked by the movement of a steady stream for a century and a half of time, goes a long way in the direction of proving the presence of unassailable ground for the constitutionality of the practice, to be found in the origin and history of the power involved, or in its nature, or in both combined. . . .

The uniform, long-continued and undisputed legislative practice just disclosed rests upon an admissible view of the Constitution which, even if the practice found far less support in principle than we think it does, we should not feel at liberty at this late day to disturb.

We deem it unnecessary to consider, seriatim, the several clauses which are said to evidence the unconstitutionality of the Joint Resolution as involving an unlawful delegation of legislative power. It is enough to summarize by saying that, both upon principle and in accordance with precedent, *we conclude there is sufficient warrant for the broad discretion vested in the President* to determine whether the enforcement of the statute will have a beneficial effect upon the re-establishment of peace in the affected countries; whether he shall make proclamation to bring the resolution into operation; whether and when the resolution shall cease to operate and to make proclamation accordingly; and to prescribe limitations and exceptions to which the enforcement of the resolution shall be subject. . . .

The judgment of the court below must be reversed and the cause remanded for further proceedings in accordance with the foregoing opinion. . . .

Chapter 6

Separation of Powers and Treaties

4. *Foster & Elam v. Neilson*

(1826)

In this case Chief Justice John Marshall acknowledges constraints on the Supreme Court's intervention in foreign policy matters pursued by the political branches—the executive and legislative. As Marshall puts it: "In a controversy between two nations concerning national boundary, it is scarcely possible that the courts of either should refuse to abide by the measures adopted by its own government." Indeed, he observes that "the judiciary is not that department of the government to which the assertion of its [the country's] interests against foreign powers is confided." Moreover, he reasons that in such matters of state "it is the Province of the Court to conform its decisions to the will of the Legislature if that will has been clearly expressed." Under the U.S. Constitution, a treaty is a contract "to be regarded in courts of justice as equivalent to an act of the Legislature whenever it operates of itself, without the aid of any legislative provision." Accordingly, Marshall reasons that "when either of the parties [in accordance with the "terms" of such agreement] engages to perform a particular act, the treaty addresses itself to the political, not the Judicial, Department, and the Legislature must execute the contract before it can become a rule for the Court."

Mr. Chief Justice MARSHALL delivered the opinion of the Court.

This suit was brought . . . in the Court of the United States for the Eastern District of Louisiana to recover a tract of land . . . in the possession of the defendant. The plaintiffs claimed under a grant . . . of land, made by the Spanish governor . . . and ratified by the King of Spain on the 29th of May, 1804. . . . The defendant excepted to the petition of the plaintiffs, alleging that it does not show a title on which . . . they can recover; that the territory within which the land claimed is situated had been ceded before the grant to France, and by France to the United States; and that the grant is void, being made by persons who had no authority to make it. The court sustained the exception and dismissed the petition. The cause is brought before this Court by a writ of error. . . .

This question has been repeatedly discussed with great talent and research by the Government of the United States and that of Spain. The United States have perseveringly and earnestly insisted that, by the Treaty of St Ildefonso, made on the 1st of October in the year 1800, Spain ceded the disputed territory as part of Louisiana to France, and that France, by the treaty of Paris, signed on the 30th of April, 1803, and ratified on the 21st of October in the same year, ceded it to the United States. Spain has, with equal perseverance and earnestness, maintained that her cession to France comprehended that territory only which was at that time denominated Louisiana, consisting of the island of New Orleans and the country she received from France west of the Mississippi. *The case presents this very intricate, and, at one time, very interesting, question: to whom did the country between the Iberville and the Perdido rightfully belong when the title now asserted by the plaintiffs was acquired? . . .*

The Treaty of the 30th of April, 1803, by which the United States acquired Louisiana . . . proceeds to state that the . . . French Republic doth hereby cede to the United States . . . forever and in full sovereignty, the said territory, with all its rights and appurtenances as fully and in the same manner as they have been acquired by the French Republic. . . . On the 21st of October, 1803, Congress passed an act to enable the President to take possession of the territory ceded by France to the United States, in pursuance of which Commissioners were appointed. . . . The Government of the United States . . . soon manifested the opinion that the whole country originally held by France, and belonging to Spain when the Treaty of St Ildefonso was concluded, was by that Treaty retroceded to France. . . .

Had France and Spain agreed upon the boundaries of the retroceded territory before Louisiana was acquired by the United States, that agreement would undoubtedly have ascertained its limits. But the declarations of France made after parting with the Province cannot be admitted as conclusive. *In questions of this character, political considerations have too much influence over the conduct of nations to permit their declarations to decide the course of an independent Government in a matter vitally interesting to itself. . . .*

Every word in that article of the Treaty of St Ildefonso which ceded Louisiana to France was scanned by the ministers on both sides with all the critical acumen which talents and zeal could bring into their service. . . . We shall say only that the language of the article may admit of either construction, and it is scarcely possible to consider the arguments on either side without believing that they proceed from a conviction of their truth. . . . Had the parties concurred in their intention, a plain mode of expressing that intention would have presented itself to them. But Spain has always manifested infinite repugnance to the surrender of territory, and was probably unwilling to give back more than she had received. The introduction of ambiguous phrases into the Treaty, which power might afterwards construe according to circumstances, was a measure which the strong and the politic might not be disinclined to employ. However this may be, it is, *we think, incontestable that the American construction of the article, if not entirely free from question, is supported by arguments of great strength which cannot be easily confuted.*

In a controversy between two nations concerning national boundary, it is scarcely possible that the courts of either should refuse to abide by the measures adopted by its own government. There being no common tribunal to decide between them, each determines for itself on its own rights, and if they cannot adjust their differences peaceably, the right remains with the strongest. *The judiciary is not that department of the government to which the assertion of its interests against foreign powers is confided,* and its duty commonly is to decide upon individual rights according to those principles which the political departments of the nation have established. If the course of the nation has been a plain one, its courts would hesitate to pronounce it erroneous. We think then, however individual judges might construe the Treaty of St Ildefonso, *it is the Province of the Court to conform its decisions to the will of the Legislature if that will has been clearly expressed.* . . .

After these acts of sovereign power over the territory in dispute asserting the American construction of the treaty by which the government claims it, to maintain the opposite construction in its own courts would certainly be an anomaly in the history and practice of nations. *If those departments which are entrusted with the foreign intercourse of the nation, which assert and maintain its interests against foreign powers, have unequivocally asserted its rights of dominion over a country of which it is in possession and which it claims under a treaty, if the Legislature has acted on the construction thus asserted, it is not in its own courts that this construction is to be denied. A question like this respecting the boundaries of nations is, as has been truly said, more a political than a legal question, and, in its discussion, the courts of every country must respect the pronounced will of the Legislature.* . . . If the Spanish grantee had obtained possession so as to be the defendant, would a Court of the United States maintain his title under a Spanish grant, made subsequent to the acquisition of Louisiana, singly on the principle that the Spanish construction of the Treaty of St Ildefonso was right, and the American construction wrong? Such a decision would, we think, have subverted those *principles* which *govern the relations between the legislative and judicial departments and mark the limits of each.* . . .

A treaty is, in its nature, a contract between two nations, not a legislative act. It does not generally effect, of itself, the object to be accomplished, especially so far as its operation is infra-territorial, but is carried into execution by the sovereign power of the respective parties to the instrument.

In the United States, a different principle is established. *Our Constitution declares a treaty to be the law of the land. It is consequently to be regarded in courts of justice as equivalent to an act of the Legislature whenever it operates of itself, without the aid of any legislative provision. But when the terms of the stipulation import a contract, when either of the parties engages to perform a particular act, the treaty addresses itself to the political, not the Judicial, Department, and the Legislature must execute the contract before it can become a rule for the Court.* . . .

The article under consideration . . . seems to be the language of contract; and if it is, the ratification and confirmation which are promised must be the act of the Legislature. Until such act shall be passed, the Court is not at liberty to disregard the existing laws on the subject. Congress appears to have understood this article as it is understood by the Court. Boards of Commissioners have been appointed for East and West Florida to receive claims for lands. . . . On the 23d of May, 1828, an act was passed . . . which enacts that all claims to land within the territory of Florida embraced by the treaty between Spain and the United States of . . . 1819, which shall not be decided and finally settled under the foregoing provisions of this act . . . shall be received and adjudicated by the judge of the superior court of the district within which the land lies. . . . The act of 1804, erecting Louisiana into two territories . . . annuls all grants for lands in the ceded territories the title whereof was at the date of the Treaty of St Ildefonso in the Crown of Spain. The grant in controversy is not brought within any of the exceptions from the enacting clause. The Legislature has passed many subsequent acts previous to the treaty of 1819 the object of which was to adjust the titles to lands in the country acquired by the treaty of 1803 [and in] 1819 Congress passed an act confirming all complete grants to land from the Spanish Government, contained in the reports made by the Commissioners appointed by the President. . . . Subsequent acts have passed in 1820, 1822 and 1826, but they only confirm claims approved by the Commissioners, among which the plaintiff does not allege his to have been placed.

Congress has reserved to itself the supervision of the titles reported by its Commissioners, and has confirmed those which the Commissioners have approved, but has passed no law withdrawing grants. . . . We are of opinion then, that the court committed no error in dismissing the petition of the plaintiff, and that the judgment ought to be affirmed with costs. This cause came on to be heard on the transcript of the record from the District Court of the United States for the Eastern District of Louisiana. . . . This Court is of opinion that the said district court committed no error in dismissing the petition of the plaintiffs; therefore it is considered, ordered and adjudged by this Court, that the judgment of the said district court in this cause be, and the same is hereby, affirmed with costs.

---

5. *Head Money Cases*

(1884)

Edye v. Robertson; Edye et al. v. Robertson;
and *Cunard Steam-Ship Co., Ltd. v. Robertson*

In what was apparently a unanimous decision, the Supreme Court decided that the statutory authority of Congress allows it to pass acts relating to a treaty's "enforcement, modification, or repeal." The so-called Head Money cases challenged the imposition by statute of fees that were contrary to various treaty provisions. Although both treaties and statutes are constitutionally regarded as the law of the land, the Court concluded that when the two conflict it is the statute that prevails when its passage is later in time.

Opinion by Mr. Justice Miller.

These cases all involve the same questions of law, and have been argued before this court together. . . . The suit is brought to recover from Robertson the sum of money received by him, as collector of the port of New York, from plaintiffs, on account of their landing in that port passengers from foreign ports, not citizens of the United States, at the rate of 50 cents for each of such passengers, under the act of congress of August 3, 1882, entitled 'An act to regulate immigration.' . . .

If it were necessary to prove that the imposition of this contribution on owners of ships is made for the general welfare of the United States, it would not be difficult to show that it is so, and particularly that it is among the means which congress may deem necessary and proper for that purpose, and beyond this we are not permitted to inquire. But the true answer to all these objections is that the power exercised in this instance is not the taxing power. The burden imposed on the shipowner by this statute is the mere incident of the regulation of commerce—of that branch of foreign commerce which is involved in immigration. The title of the act, 'An act to regulate immigration,' is well chosen. It describes, as well as any short sentence can describe it, the real purpose and effect of the statute. Its provisions, from beginning to end, relate to the subject of immigration, and they are aptly designed to mitigate the evils inherent in the business of bringing foreigners to this country, as those evils affect both the immigrant and the people among whom he is suddenly brought and left to his own resources. . . .

We are clearly of opinion that, in the exercise of its power to regulate immigration, and in the very act of exercising that power, it was competent for congress to impose this contribution on the shipowner engaged in that business. Another objection to the validity of this act of congress is that it violates provisions contained in numerous treaties of our government with friendly nations. And several of the articles of these treaties are annexed to the careful brief of counsel. We are not satisfied that this act of congress violates any of these treaties, on any just construction of them. Though laws similar to this have long been enforced by the state of New York in the great metropolis of foreign trade, where four-fifths of these passengers have been landed, no complaint has been made by any foreign nation to ours of the violation of treaty obligations by the enforcement of those laws. But we do not place the defense of the act of congress against this objection upon that suggestion. *We are of opinion that, so far as the provisions in that act may be found to be in conflict with any treaty with a foreign nation, they must prevail in all the judicial courts of this country. . . .*

The precise question involved here, namely, a supposed conflict between an act of congress imposing a customs duty, and a treaty with Russia on that subject, in force when the act was passed, came before the circuit court for the district of Massachusetts in 1855. It received the consideration of that eminent jurist, Mr. Justice Curtis, of this court, who in a very learned opinion exhausted the sources of argument on the subject, holding that if there were such conflict the act of congress must prevail in a judicial forum. . . . And Mr. Justice Field, in a very recent case in the Ninth circuit . . . has delivered an opinion sustaining the same doctrine in reference to a statute regulating the immigration of Chinamen into this country. . . .

It is very difficult to understand how any different doctrine can be sustained. *A treaty is primarily a compact between independent nations. It depends for the enforcement of its provisions on the interest and the honor of the governments which are parties to it. If these fail, its infraction becomes the subject of international negotiations and reclamations, so far as the injured party chooses to seek redress, which may in the end be enforced by actual war. It is obvious that with all this the judicial courts have nothing to do and can give no redress.* But a treaty may also contain provisions which confer certain rights upon the citizens or subjects of one of the nations residing in the territorial limits of the other, which partake of the nature of municipal law, and which are capable of enforcement as between private parties in the courts of the country. An illustration of this character is found in treaties, which regulate the mutual rights of citizens and subjects of the contracting nations in regard to rights of property by descent or inheritance, when the individuals concerned are aliens. The constitution of the United States places such provisions as these in the same category as other laws of congress by its declaration that 'this constitution and the laws made in pursuance thereof, and all treaties made or which shall be made under authority of the United States, shall be the supreme law of the land.' *A treaty, then, is a law of the land as an act of congress is,* whenever its provisions prescribe a rule by which the rights of the private citizen or subject may be determined. And when such rights are of a nature to be enforced in a court of justice, that court resorts to the treaty for a rule of decision for the case before it as it would to a statute. But even in this aspect of the case there is nothing in this law which makes it irrepealable or unchangeable. *The constitution gives it no superiority over an act of congress* in this respect, which may be repealed or modified by an act of a later date. Nor is there anything in its essential character, or in the branches of the government by which the treaty is made, which gives it this superior sanctity. A treaty is made by the president and the senate. Statutes are made by the president, the senate, and the house of representatives.

The addition of the latter body to the other two in making a law certainly does not render it less entitled to respect in the matter of its repeal or modification than a treaty made by the other two. If there be any difference in this regard, it would seem to be in favor of an act in which all three of the bodies participate. And such is, in fact, the case in a declaration of war, which must be made by congress, and which, when made, usually suspends or destroys existing treaties between the nations thus at war. In short, we are of opinion that, *so far as a treaty made by the United States with any foreign nation can become the subject of judicial cognizance in the courts of this country, it is subject to such acts as congress may pass for its enforcement, modification, or repeal.*

Other objections are made to this statute. Some of these relate, not to the power of congress to pass the act, but to the measure, of which congress, and not the courts, are the sole judges. . . . It is enough to say that, congress having the power to pass a law regulating immigration as a part of the commerce of this country with foreign nations, we see nothing in the statute by which it has here exercised that power forbidden by any other part of the constitution. The judgment of the circuit court in all the cases is affirmed.

---

6. *Chae Chan Ping v. United States*

(the "Chinese Exclusion" Case, 1889)

The Court underscores the sovereign authority of the government to exercise complete jurisdiction over U.S. territory. When a treaty "requiring legislation to carry its stipulations into effect" conflicts with statutes that are "within the power of congress, it can be deemed in that particular only the equivalent of a legislative act, to be repealed or modified at the pleasure of congress."

Justice Field wrote the opinion of the Court. This case comes before us on appeal from an order of the circuit court of the United States for the Northern district of California. . . . The appeal involves a consideration of the validity of the act of congress of October 1, 1888, prohibiting Chinese laborers from entering the United States who had departed before its passage, having a certificate issued under the act of 1882 as amended by the act of 1884, granting them permission to return. The validity of the act is assailed as being in effect an expulsion from the country of Chinese laborers, in violation of existing treaties between the United States and the government of China, and of rights vested in them under the laws of congress. . . .

The objection made is that the act of 1888 impairs a right vested under the treaty of 1880, as a law of the United States, and the statutes of 1882 and of 1884 passed in execution of it. It must be conceded that the act of 1888 is in contravention of express stipulations of the treaty of 1868, and of the supplemental treaty of 1880, but it is not on that account invalid, or to be restricted in its enforcement. The treaties were of no greater legal obligation than the act of congress. *By the constitution, laws made in pursuance thereof, and treaties made under the authority of the United States, are both declared to be the supreme law of the land, and no paramount authority is given to one over the other. A treaty,* it is true, is in its nature a contract between nations, and is often merely promissory in its character, *requiring legislation to carry its stipulations into effect.* Such legislation will be open to future repeal or amendment. If the treaty operates by its own force, and relates to a subject within the power of congress, it *can be deemed in that particular only the equivalent of a legislative act, to be repealed or modified at the pleasure of congress.* . . .

Those laborers are not citizens of the United States; they are aliens. That the government of the United States, through the action of the legislative department, can exclude aliens from its territory is a proposition which we do not think open to controversy. *Jurisdiction over its own territory* to that extent *is an incident of every independent nation.* It is a part of its independence. If it could not exclude aliens it would be to that extent subject to the control of another power. . . .

To preserve its independence, and give security against foreign aggression and encroachment, is the highest duty of every nation, and to attain these ends nearly all other considerations are to be subordinated. It matters not in what form such aggression and encroachment come, whether from the foreign nation acting in its national character, or from vast hordes of its people. . . . If, therefore, the government of the United States, through its legislative department, considers the presence of foreigners . . . to be dangerous to its peace and security, their exclusion is not to be stayed because at the time there are no actual hostilities with the nation of which the foreigners are subjects. The existence of war would render the necessity of the proceeding only more obvious and pressing. The same necessity, in a less pressing degree, may arise when war does not exist, and the same authority which adjudges the necessity in one case must also determine it in the other. In both cases its determination is conclusive upon the judiciary. If the government of the country of which the foreigners excluded are subjects is dissatisfied with this action, it can make complaint to the executive head of our government, or resort to any other measure which, in its judgment, its interests or dignity may demand; and there lies its only remedy.

The power of exclusion of foreigners being an incident of sovereignty belonging to the government of the United States as a part of those sovereign powers delegated by the constitution, *the right to its exercise at any time when, in the judgment of the government, the interests of the country require it, cannot be granted away or restrained on behalf of any one.*

---

7. *Missouri v. Holland*

(1920)

The 7–2 majority opinion by Justice Oliver Wendell Holmes underscores the constitutional primacy of treaties over separate rights claimed by states. The treaty at issue called for legislation to protect migratory birds flying between the United States and Canada. Invoking the Tenth Amendment to the U.S. Constitution, the state of Missouri argued that powers not specifically granted to the federal government (as under Article I, Section 8) are reserved to the states. In a carefully worded opinion, the Supreme Court upheld the statute passed by Congress implementing U.S. treaty obligations. Although the Court did "not mean to imply that there are no qualifications to the treaty-making power," it did see a "national interest of very nearly the first magnitude" that could "be protected only by national action in concert with that of another power." Moreover, the birds were "only transitorily within the state" and legislative action by Congress was constitutionally "a necessary and proper means to execute the powers of the government" specified in Article I, Section 8, of the U.S. Constitution.

Holmes, J., for the Court:

This is a bill in equity brought by the State of Missouri to prevent a game warden of the United States from attempting to enforce the Migratory Bird Treaty Act of July 3, 1918 . . . and the regulations made by the Secretary of Agriculture in pursuance of the same. The ground of the bill is that the statute is an unconstitutional interference with the rights reserved to the States by the Tenth Amendment, and that the acts of the defendant done and threatened under that authority invade the sovereign right of the State and contravene its will manifested in statutes. The State also alleges a pecuniary interest, as owner of the wild birds within its borders and otherwise, admitted by the Government to be sufficient, but it is enough that the bill is a reasonable and proper means to assert the alleged quasi sovereign rights of a State. . . . A motion to dismiss was sustained by the District Court on the ground that the act of Congress is constitutional. . . . The State appeals.

On December 8, 1916, a treaty between the United States and Great Britain was proclaimed by the President. It recited that many species of birds in their annual migration traversed certain parts of the United States and of Canada, that they were of great value as a source of food and in destroying insects injurious to vegetation, but were in danger of extermination through lack of adequate protection. It therefore provided for specified closed seasons and protection in other forms, and agreed that the two powers would take or propose to their law-making bodies the necessary measures for carrying the treaty out. . . . The above mentioned Act of

July 3, 1918, entitled an act to give effect to the convention, prohibited the killing, capturing or selling of any of the migratory birds included in the terms of the treaty except as permitted by regulations compatible with those terms, to be made by the Secretary of Agriculture. Regulations were proclaimed on July 3l, and October 25, 1918. . . . *The question* raised *is* the general one *whether the treaty and statute are void as an interference with the rights reserved to the States.*

To answer this question it is not enough to refer to the Tenth Amendment, reserving the powers not delegated to, the United States, because by Article II, section 2, the power to make treaties is delegated expressly, and *by Article VI treaties* made under the authority of the United States, *along with the Constitution and laws* of the United States *made in pursuance thereof, are declared the supreme law of the land. If the treaty is valid there can be no dispute about the validity of the statute under Article I, section 8, as a necessary and proper means to execute the powers of the Government. The language of the Constitution as to the supremacy of treaties being general, the question before us is narrowed to an inquiry into the ground upon which the present supposed exception is placed.*

It is said that a treaty cannot be valid if it infringes the Constitution, that there are limits, therefore, to the treaty-making power, and that one such limit is that what an act of Congress could not do unaided, in derogation of the powers reserved to the States, a treaty cannot do. An earlier act of Congress that attempted by itself and not in pursuance of a treaty to regulate the killing of migratory birds within the States had been held bad in the District Court. . . . Those decisions were supported by arguments that migratory birds were owned by the States in their

sovereign capacity for the benefit of their people, and that . . . this control was one that Congress had no power to displace. The same argument is supposed to apply now with equal force. . . .

Acts of Congress are the supreme law of the land only when made in pursuance of the Constitution, while treaties are declared to be so when made under the authority of the United States. It is open to question whether the authority of the United States means more than the formal acts prescribed to make the convention. *We do not mean to imply that there are no qualifications to the treaty-making power;* but they must be ascertained in a different way. It is obvious that there may be matters of the sharpest exigency for the national well being that an act of Congress could not deal with but that a treaty followed by such an act could, and it is not lightly to be assumed that, in matters requiring national action, "a power which must belong to and somewhere reside in every civilized government" is not to be found. . . .

What was said in that case with regard to the powers of the States applies with equal force to the powers of the nation in cases where the States individually are incompetent to act. We are not yet discussing the particular case before us but only are considering the validity of the test proposed. With regard to that we may add that when we are dealing with words that also are a constituent act, like the Constitution of the United States, we must realize that they have called into life a being the development of which could not have been foreseen completely by the most gifted of its begetters. It was enough for them to realize or to hope that they had created an organism; it has taken a century and has cost their successors much sweat and blood to prove that they created a nation. The case before us must be considered in the light of our whole experience and not merely in that of what was said a hundred years ago. *The treaty in question does not contravene any prohibitory words to be found in the Constitution.* The only question is whether it is forbidden by some invisible radiation from the general terms of the Tenth Amendment. We must consider what this country has become in deciding what that Amendment has reserved.

The State as we have intimated founds its claim of exclusive authority upon an assertion of title to migratory birds, an assertion that is embodied in statute. No doubt it is true that as between a state and its inhabitants the State may regulate the killing and sale of such birds, but it does not follow that its authority is exclusive of paramount powers. To put the claim of the State upon title is to lean upon a slender reed. Wild birds are not in the possession of anyone; and possession is the beginning of ownership. The whole foundation of the State's rights is the presence within their jurisdiction of birds that yesterday had not arrived, tomorrow may be in another State and in a week a thousand miles away. If we are to be accurate we cannot put the case of the State upon higher ground than that the treaty deals with creatures that for the moment are within the State borders, that it must be carried out by officers of the United States within the same territory, and that but for the treaty the State would be free to regulate this subject itself.

As most of the laws of the United States are carried out within the States and as many of them deal with matters which in the silence of such laws the State might regulate, such general grounds are not enough to support Missouri's claim. Valid treaties of course "are as binding within the territorial limits of the States as they are elsewhere throughout the dominion of the United States." . . . *No doubt the great body of private relations usually fall within the control of the State, but a treaty may override its power. . . .* It was assumed by Chief Justice Marshall with regard to the escheat of land to the State in Chirac v. Chirac . . . so as to a limited jurisdiction of foreign consuls within a State. . . . Further illustration seems unnecessary, and it only remains to consider the application of established rules to the present case.

Here a national interest of very nearly the first magnitude is involved. It can be protected only by national action in concert with that of another power. The subject-matter is only transitorily within the State and has no permanent habitat therein. But for the treaty and the statute there soon might be no birds for any powers to deal with. We see nothing in the Constitution that compels the Government to sit by while a food supply is cut off and the protectors of our forests and our crops are destroyed. It is not sufficient to rely upon the States. The reliance is vain, and were it otherwise, the question is whether the United States is forbidden to act. We are of opinion that the treaty and statute must be upheld.

Chapter 7

Executive-Legislative War Powers

8. Prize Cases

(1863)

The Supreme Court upheld President Lincoln's authority as commander in chief to impose a naval blockade in time of war, in this case civil war between the Union and the Confederacy. The blockade was imposed in 1861 shortly after the beginning of hostilities. Compensation was sought for damages from raids conducted by U.S. ships on merchant ships supplying Confederate states. According to the Court: "To legitimate the capture of a neutral vessel or property on the high seas, a war must exist de facto" and "the neutral must have a knowledge or notice of the intention of one of the parties belligerent to use this mode of coercion against a port, city, or territory, in possession of the other." The opinion identifies the conditions under which a state of war can be said to exist, neutral states being precluded under international law from aiding either side. The Court concludes definitively that "the produce of the soil of the hostile territory, as well as other property engaged in the commerce of the hostile power, as the source of its wealth and strength, are always regarded as legitimate prize" and that "all persons residing within this territory whose property may be used to increase the revenues of the hostile power are, in this contest, liable to be treated as enemies."

Opinion by Mr. Justice Grier.

That a blockade de facto actually existed, and was formally declared and notified by the President . . . is an admitted fact in these cases.

That the President, as the Executive Chief of the Government and Commander-in-Chief of the Army and Navy, was the proper person to make such notification, has not been, and cannot be disputed.

The right of prize and capture has its origin in the "jus belli," and is governed and adjudged under the law of nations. *To legitimate the capture of a neutral vessel or property on the high seas, a war must exist de facto, and the neutral must have a knowledge or notice of the intention of one of the parties belligerent to use this mode of coercion against a port, city, or territory, in possession of the other.*

Let us enquire whether, at the time this blockade was instituted, a state of war existed which would justify a resort to these means of subduing the hostile force.

War has been well defined to be, "That state in which a nation prosecutes its right by force." The parties belligerent in a public war are independent nations. But it is not necessary to constitute war, that both parties should be acknowledged as independent nations or sovereign States. A war may exist where one of the belligerents claims sovereign rights as against the other.

Insurrection against a government may or may not culminate in an organized rebellion, but a civil war always begins by insurrection against the lawful authority of the Government. A civil war is never solemnly declared; it becomes such by its accidents—the number, power, and organization of the persons who originate and carry it on. When the party in rebellion occupy and hold in a hostile manner a certain portion of territory; have declared their independence; have cast off their allegiance; have organized armies; have commenced hostilities against their former sovereign, the world acknowledges them as belligerents, and the contest a war. They claim to be in arms to establish their liberty and independence, in order to become a sovereign State, while the sovereign party treats them as insurgents and rebels who owe allegiance and who should be punished with death for their treason. *The laws of war, as established among nations, have their foundation in reason, and all tend to mitigate the cruelties and misery produced by the scourge of war. Hence the parties to a civil war usually concede to each other belligerent rights. They exchange prisoners, and adopt the other courtesies and rules common to public or national wars.*

"A civil war," says Vattel, "breaks the bands of society and government, or at least suspends their force and effect; it produces in the nation two independent parties who consider each other as enemies, and acknowledge no common judge. Those two parties, therefore, must necessarily be considered as constituting, at least for a time, two separate bodies, two distinct societies. Having no common superior to judge between them, they stand in precisely the same predicament as two nations who engage in a contest and have recourse to arms.

"This being the case, it is very evident that the common laws of war—those maxims of humanity, moderation, and honor—ought to be observed by both parties in every civil war. Should the sovereign conceive he has a right to hang up his prisoners as rebels, the opposite party will make reprisals, &c., &c.; the war will become cruel, horrible, and every day more destructive to the nation."

As a civil war is never publicly proclaimed, eo nomine against insurgents, its actual existence is a fact in our domestic history which the Court is bound to notice and to know.

The true test of its existence, as found in the writing of the sages of the common law, may be thus summarily stated: "When the regular course of justice is interrupted by revolt, rebellion, or insurrection, so that the Courts of Justice cannot be kept open, civil war exists and hostilities may be prosecuted on the same footing as if those opposing the Government were foreign enemies invading the land."

By the Constitution, Congress alone has the power to declare a national or foreign war. It cannot declare war against a State, or any number of States, by virtue of any clause in the Constitution. The Constitution confers on the President the whole Executive power. He is bound to take care that the laws be faithfully executed. He is Commander-in-Chief of the Army and Navy of the United States, and of the militia of the several States when called into the actual service of the United States. He has no power to initiate or declare a war either against a foreign nation or a domestic State. But by the Acts of Congress of February 28th, 1795, and 3d of March, 1807, he is authorized to call out the militia and use the military and naval forces of the United States in case of invasion by foreign nations, and to suppress insurrection against the government of a State or of the United States.

If a war be made by invasion of a foreign nation, the President is not only authorized but bound to resist force by force. He does not initiate the war, but is bound to accept the challenge without waiting for any special legislative authority. And whether the hostile party be a foreign invader, or States organized in rebellion, it is none the less a war, although the declaration of it be "unilateral." . . .

This greatest of civil wars was not gradually developed by popular commotion, tumultuous assemblies, or local unorganized insurrections. However long may have been its previous conception, it nevertheless sprung forth suddenly from the parent brain, a Minerva in the full panoply of war. The President was bound to meet it in the shape it presented itself, without waiting for Congress to baptize it with a name; and no name given to it by him or them could change the fact.

It is not the less a civil war, with belligerent parties in hostile array, because it may be called an "insurrection" by one side, and the insurgents . . . considered as rebels or traitors. It is not necessary that the independence of the revolted province or State be acknowledged in order to constitute it a party belligerent in a war according to the law of nations. Foreign nations acknowledge it as war by a declaration of neutrality. The condition of

neutrality cannot exist unless there be two belligerent parties. . . .

As soon as the news of the attack on Fort Sumter, and the organization of a government by the seceding States, assuming to act as belligerents, could become known in Europe, to wit, on the 13th day of May, 1861, the Queen of England issued her proclamation of neutrality, "recognizing hostilities as existing between the Government of the United States of America and certain States styling themselves the Confederate States of America." This was immediately followed by similar declarations or silent acquiescence by other nations.

After such an official recognition by the sovereign, a citizen of a foreign State is estopped to deny the existence of a war, with all its consequences as regards neutrals. They cannot ask a court to affect a technical ignorance of the existence of a war, which all the world acknowledges to be the greatest civil war known in the history of the human race, and thus cripple the arm of the Government and paralyze its power by subtle definitions and ingenious sophisms.

The law of nations is also called the law of nature; it is founded on the common consent as well as the common sense of the world. It contains no such anomalous doctrine as that which this Court are now for the first time desired to pronounce, to wit: That insurgents who have arisen in rebellion against their sovereign, expelled her Courts, established a revolutionary government, organized armies, and commenced hostilities, are not enemies because they are traitors; and a war levied on the Government by traitors, in order to dismember and destroy it, is not a war because it is an "insurrection."

Whether the President in fulfilling his duties, as Commander-in-Chief, in suppressing an insurrection, has met with such armed hostile resistance, and a civil war of such alarming proportions as will compel him to accord to them the character of belligerents, is a question to be decided by him, and this Court must be governed by the decisions and acts of the political department of the Government to which this power was entrusted. "He must determine what degree of force the crisis demands." *The proclamation of blockade is itself official and conclusive evidence to the Court that a state of war existed which demanded and authorized a recourse to such a measure.* . . .

If it were necessary to the technical existence of a war, that it should have a legislative sanction, we find it in almost every act passed at the extraordinary session of the Legislature of 1861, which was wholly employed in enacting laws to enable the Government to prosecute the war with vigor and efficiency. And finally, in 1861, we find Congress "in anticipation of such astute objections, passing an act approving, legalizing, and making valid all the acts, proclamations, and orders of the President, &c., as if they had been issued and done under the previous express authority and direction of the Congress of the United States." . . .

On this first question therefore we are of the opinion that *the President had a right, jure belli, to institute a blockade of ports in possession of the States in rebellion,* which neutrals are bound to regard.

We come now to the consideration of the second question. What is included in the term "enemies' property"?

Is the property of all persons residing within the territory of the States now in rebellion, captured on the high seas, to be treated as "enemies' property" whether the owner be in arms against the Government or not?

The right of one belligerent not only to coerce the other by direct force, but also to cripple his resources by the seizure or destruction of his property, is a necessary result of a state of war. Money and wealth, the products of agriculture and commerce, are said to be the sinews of war, and as necessary in its conduct as numbers and physical force. Hence it is, that *the laws of war recognize the right of a belligerent to cut these sinews of the power of the enemy, by capturing his property on the high seas.*

The appellants contend that the term "enemy" is properly applicable to those only who are subjects or citizens of a foreign State at war with our own. They quote from the pages of the common law, which say "that persons who wage war against the King may be of two kinds, subjects or citizens. The former are not proper enemies, but rebels and traitors; the latter are those that come properly under the name of enemies."

They insist, moreover, that the President himself, in his proclamation, admits that great numbers of the persons residing within the territories in possession of the insurgent government, are loyal in their feelings, and forced by compulsion and the violence of the rebellious and revolutionary party and its "de facto government" to submit to their laws and assist in their scheme of revolution; that the acts of the usurping government cannot legally sever the bond of their allegiance; they have, therefore, a co-relative right to claim the protection of the government for their persons and property, and to be treated as loyal citizens, till legally convicted of having renounced their allegiance and made war against the Government by treasonably resisting its laws.

They contend, also, that insurrection is the act of individuals and not of a government or sovereignty; that the individuals engaged are subjects of law. That confiscation of their property can be effected only under a municipal law. That by the law of the land such confiscation cannot take place without the conviction of the owner of some offence, and finally that the secession ordinances are nullities and ineffectual to release any citizen from his allegiance to the national Government, and consequently that the Constitution and Laws of the United States are still operative over persons in all the States for punishment as well as protection.

This argument rests on the assumption of two propositions, each of which is without foundation on the established law of nations. It assumes that where a civil war exists, the party belligerent claiming to be sovereign, cannot, for some unknown reason, exercise the rights of belligerents, although the revolutionary party may. Being sovereign, he can exercise only sovereign rights over the other party. The insurgent may be killed on the battle-field or by the executioner; his property on land may be confiscated under the municipal law; but the commerce on the ocean, which supplies the rebels with means to support the war, cannot be made the subject of capture under the laws of war, because it is "unconstitutional!!!" Now, it is a proposition never doubted, that the belligerent party who claims to be sovereign, may exercise both belligerent and sovereign rights. Treating the other party as a belligerent and using only the milder modes of coercion which the law of nations has introduced to mitigate the rigors of war, cannot be a subject of complaint by the party to whom it is accorded as a grace or granted as a necessity. We have shown that *a civil war such as that now waged between the Northern and Southern States is properly conducted according to the humane regulations of public law as regards capture on the ocean.*

Under the very peculiar Constitution of this Government, although the citizens owe supreme allegiance to the Federal Government, they owe also a qualified allegiance to the State in which they are domiciled. Their persons and property are subject to its laws.

Hence, in organizing this rebellion, they have acted as States claiming to be sovereign over all persons and property within their respective limits, and asserting a right to absolve their citizens from their allegiance to the Federal Government. Several of these States have combined to form a new confederacy, claiming to be acknowledged by the world as a sovereign State. Their right to do so is now being decided by wager of battle. The ports and territory of each of these States are held in hostility to the General Government. It is no loose, unorganized insurrection, having no defined boundary or possession. It has a boundary marked by lines of bayonets, and which can be crossed only by force—south of this line is enemies' territory, because it is claimed and held in possession by an organized, hostile and belligerent power.

All persons residing within this territory whose property may be used to increase the revenues of the hostile power are, in this contest, liable to be treated as enemies, though not foreigners. They have cast off their allegiance and made war on their Government, and are none the less enemies because they are traitors. . . .

The produce of the soil of the hostile territory, as well as other property engaged in the commerce of the hostile power, as the source of its wealth and strength, are always regarded as legitimate prize, without regard to the domicile of the owner, and much more so if he reside and trade within their territory. . . .

9. *Youngstown Co. v. Sawyer*

(1952)

This important landmark case affirms limits on the president's domestic authority in general and wartime authority in particular. The Korean War was under way, and facing a nationwide strike in the steel industry, President Harry Truman justified federal seizure of the steel mills—nationalizing them—as essential to sustaining production deemed necessary for national security. The Supreme Court found no constitutional or statutory bases for this taking, thus rejecting this expansive interpretation of presidential war powers.

Mr. Justice Black delivered the opinion of the Court.

We are asked to decide whether the President was acting within his constitutional power when he issued an order directing the Secretary of Commerce to take possession of and operate most of the Nation's steel mills. The mill owners argue that the President's order amounts to lawmaking, a legislative function which the Constitution has expressly confided to the Congress and not to the President. *The Government's position is that the order was made on findings of the President that his action was necessary to avert a national catastrophe which would inevitably result from a stoppage of steel production, and that in meeting this grave emergency the President was acting within the aggregate of his constitutional powers as the Nation's Chief Executive and the Commander in Chief of the Armed Forces of the United States. . . .*

Two crucial issues have developed: First. Should final determination of the constitutional validity of the President's order be made in this case which has proceeded no further than the preliminary injunction stage? Second. If so, *is the seizure order within the constitutional power of the President? . . .*

The President's power, if any, to issue the order must stem either from an act of Congress or from the Constitution itself. There is no statute that expressly authorizes the President to take possession of property as he did here. Nor is there any act of Congress to which our attention has been directed from which such a power can fairly be implied. Indeed, we do not understand the Government to rely on statutory authorization for this seizure. There are two statutes which do authorize the President . . . to take both personal and real property under certain conditions. However, the Government admits that these conditions were not met and that the President's order was not rooted in either of the statutes. . . .*

It is clear that if the President had authority to issue the order he did, it must be found in some provision of the Constitution. And it is not claimed that express constitutional language grants this power to the President. *The contention is that presidential power should be implied from the aggregate of his powers under the Constitution. Particular reliance is placed on provisions in Article II which say that "The executive Power shall be vested in a President . . . "; that "he shall take Care that the Laws be faithfully executed"; and that he "shall be Commander in Chief of the Army and Navy of the United States."*

The order cannot properly be sustained as an exercise of the President's military power as Commander in Chief of the Armed Forces. The Government attempts to do so by citing a number of cases upholding broad powers in military commanders engaged in day-to-day fighting in a theater of war. Such cases need not concern us here. Even though "theater of war" be an expanding concept, *we cannot with faithfulness to our*

*constitutional system hold that the Comman-
der in Chief of the Armed Forces has the ultimate power as such to take possession of private property in order to keep labor disputes
from stopping production. This is a job for the
Nation's lawmakers, not for its military
authorities.*

*Nor can the seizure order be sustained be-
cause of the several constitutional provisions
that grant executive power to the President. In
the framework of our Constitution, the President's power to see that the laws are faithfully
executed refutes the idea that he is to be a law-
maker.* The Constitution limits his functions in the lawmaking process to the
recommending of laws he thinks wise and
the vetoing of laws he thinks bad. And the
Constitution is neither silent nor equivo-
cal about who shall make laws which the
President is to execute. The . . . first section of the first article says that "All
legislative Powers herein granted shall
be vested in a Congress of the United
States. . . ." After granting many powers
to the Congress, Article I goes on to provide that Congress may "make all Laws
which shall be necessary and proper for
carrying into Execution the foregoing
Powers, and all other Powers vested by
this Constitution in the Government of
the United States, or in any Department
or Officer thereof."

The President's order does not direct
that a congressional policy be executed in
a manner prescribed by Congress—it directs that a presidential policy be executed
in a manner prescribed by the President.
The preamble of the order itself, like that
of many statutes, sets out reasons why the
President believes certain policies should
be adopted, proclaims these policies as
rules of conduct to be followed, and again,
like a statute, authorizes a government
official to promulgate additional rules and
regulations consistent with the policy
proclaimed and needed to carry that policy into execution. The power of Congress
to adopt such public policies as those
proclaimed by the order is beyond question. It can authorize the taking of private
property for public use. It can make laws
regulating the relationships between em-
ployers and employees, prescribing rules
designed to settle labor disputes, and
fixing wages and working conditions in
certain fields of our economy. The Constitution does not subject this lawmaking
power of Congress to presidential or military supervision or control.

It is said that other Presidents without
congressional authority have taken possession of private business enterprises in
order to settle labor disputes. But even if
this be true, Congress has not thereby
lost its exclusive constitutional authority
to make laws necessary and proper to
carry out the powers vested by the Constitution . . . "in the Government of the
United States, or any Department or
Officer thereof."

*The Founders of this Nation entrusted
the lawmaking power to the Congress alone in
both good and bad times. It would do no
good to recall the historical events, the fears of
power and the hopes for freedom that lay behind their choice. Such a review would but
confirm our holding that this seizure order
cannot stand.*

The judgment of the District Court is
Affirmed.

10. *The War Powers Act*

(1973)

Under Article I, Section 8, of the U.S. Constitution, Congress has the authority or power to "declare war" and to appropriate funds to support and sustain use of the armed forces for such purposes. Presidential power in such matters stems from designation of the president in Article II, Section 2, of the Constitution as commander in chief of the armed forces, which some people claim is constitutional authority to use force or "make war" quite apart from any congressional declaration to this effect. Counter to such an expansive view of executive authority, however, the War Powers Act was passed in 1973 during a period of congressional ascendancy. Both the unpopularity of the seemingly endless Vietnam War and the ongoing Watergate scandal (involving the break-in of the Democratic Party headquarters instigated in 1972 by agents of the Nixon presidential campaign) undermined the legitimacy of the Nixon administration and the presidency itself. Seeing the War Powers Act as encroachment by Congress on executive authority, the president exercised his veto; however, the veto was subsequently overridden by more than a two-thirds vote in both houses of Congress. The War Powers Act became effective November 7, 1973, some ten months before to President Nixon's resignation from office in August 1974.

Joint Resolution

Concerning the war powers of Congress and the President.

Resolved by the Senate and the House of Representatives of the United States of America in Congress assembled,

1. This joint resolution may be cited as the "War Powers Resolution."

2. (a) It is the purpose of this joint resolution to fulfill the intent of the framers of the Constitution of the United States and insure that the collective judgement of both the Congress and the President will apply to the introduction of United States Armed Forces into hostilities, or into situations where imminent involvement in hostilities is clearly indicated by the circumstances, and to the continued use of such forces in hostilities or in such situations. (b) Under article I, section 8, of the Constitution, it is specifically provided that the Congress shall have the power to make all laws necessary and proper for carrying into execution, not only its own powers but also all powers vested by the Constitution in the Government of the United States, or in any department or officer thereof. (c) The constitutional powers of the President as Commander-in-Chief to introduce United States Armed Forces into hostilities, or into situations where imminent involvement in hostilities is clearly indicated by the circumstances, are exercised only pursuant to (1) a declaration of war, (2) specific statutory authorization, or (3) a national emergency created by attack upon the United States, its territories or possessions, or its armed forces.

3. *The President in every possible instance shall consult with Congress before introducing United States Armed Forces into hostilities or into situations where imminent involvement in hostilities is clearly indicated by the circumstances, and after every such introduction shall consult regularly with the Congress until United States Armed Forces are no longer engaged in hostilities or have been removed.*

4. (a) *In the absence of a declaration of war, in any case in which United States Armed Forces are introduced—(1) into hostilities or*

into situations where imminent involvement in hostilities is clearly indicated by the circumstances; (2) into the territory, airspace or waters of a foreign nation, while equipped for combat, except for deployments which relate solely to supply, replacement, repair, or training of such forces; or *(3) in numbers which substantially enlarge United States Armed Forces equipped for combat already located in a foreign nation; the president shall submit within 48 hours* to the Speaker of the House of Representatives and to the President pro tempore of the Senate *a report,* in writing, setting forth—(A) the circumstances necessitating the introduction of United States Armed Forces; (B) the constitutional and legislative authority under which such introduction took place; and (C) the estimated scope and duration of the hostilities or involvement. (b) The President shall provide such other information as the Congress may request in the fulfillment of its constitutional responsibilities with respect to committing the Nation to war and to the use of United States Armed Forces abroad. (c) *Whenever United States Armed Forces are introduced into hostilities* or into any situation described in subsection (a) of this section, *the President shall,* so long as such armed forces continue to be engaged in such hostilities or situation, *report to the Congress periodically on the status of such hostilities or situation as well as on the scope and duration of such hostilities or situation,* but in no event shall he report to the Congress less often than once every six months.

5. (a) Each report submitted pursuant to section 4(a)(1) shall be transmitted to the Speaker of the House of Representatives and to the President pro tempore of the Senate on the same calendar day.... (b) *Within sixty calendar days* after a report is submitted or is required to be submitted pursuant to section 4(a)(1), whichever is earlier, *the President shall terminate any use of United States Armed Forces with respect to which such report was submitted* (or required to be submitted), *unless the Congress (1) has declared war or has enacted a specific authorization for such use of United States Armed Forces, (2) has extended by law such sixty-day period,* or (3) is physically unable to meet as a result of an armed attack upon the United States. *Such sixty-day period shall be extended for not more than an additional thirty days if the President determines and certifies to the Congress in writing that unavoidable military necessity respecting the safety of United States Armed Forces requires the continued use of such armed forces in the course of bringing about a prompt removal of such forces.* (c) *Notwithstanding subsection (b), at any time that United States Armed Forces are engaged in hostilities outside the territory of the United States, its possessions and territories without a declaration of war or specific statutory authorization, such forces shall be removed by the President if the Congress so directs by concurrent resolution.* ...

---

11. *Immigration and Naturalization Service (INS) v. Chadha*

(1983)

The War Powers Act (1973) acknowledges in effect that the executive branch may exercise its power to "make war" under Article II of the U.S. Constitution, but requires congressional concurrence within a specified period in keeping with Congress's Article I power to "declare war."

Without such congressional action, there is a "legislative veto" on the executive continuing the use of force. Although the Chadha case deals with a different issue, the Supreme Court concludes that the legislative veto is unconstitutional because it violates the legislative process specified in the Constitution. Whereas the immigration law in Chadha allowed for legislative veto by either house, the War Powers Act requires concurrence by both houses, allowing either (or both) houses to exercise a legislative veto. The possibility of presidential veto is also bypassed in the War Powers Act as it is in the immigration law at issue in Chadha. Although the Court limited its decision to the Chadha case, the decision did raise serious question about the constitutionality of other legislation: "Our inquiry is sharpened rather than blunted by the fact that Congressional veto provisions are appearing with increasing frequency in statutes which delegate authority to executive and independent agencies." Chadha thus raises question about the constitutionality of the War Powers Act, which as noted also relies on a legislative-veto mechanism.

Chief Justice Burger delivered the opinion of the Court.

We granted certiorari . . . [on] the constitutionality of the provision in . . . the Immigration and Nationality Act . . . authorizing one House of Congress, by resolution, to invalidate the decision of the Executive Branch, pursuant to authority delegated by Congress to the Attorney General of the United States, to allow a particular deportable alien to remain in the United States.

We turn now to the question whether action of one House of Congress under § 244(c)(2) violates strictures of the Constitution. . . . The fact that a given law or procedure is efficient, convenient, and useful in facilitating functions of government, standing alone, will not save it if it is contrary to the Constitution. Convenience and efficiency are not the primary objectives—or the hallmarks—of democratic government and our inquiry is sharpened rather than blunted by the fact that Congressional veto provisions are appearing with increasing frequency in statutes which delegate authority to executive and independent agencies. . . .

Explicit and unambiguous provisions of the Constitution prescribe and define the respective functions of the Congress and of the Executive in the legislative process. . . . The bicameral requirement of Art. I, Sections 1, 7 was of scarcely less concern to the Framers than was the Presidential veto and indeed the two concepts are interdependent. . . . The division of the Congress into two distinctive bodies assures that the legislative power would be exercised only after opportunity for full study and debate in separate settings. The President's unilateral veto power, in turn, was limited by the power of two thirds of both Houses of Congress to overrule a veto thereby precluding final arbitrary action of one person. . . .

Amendment and repeal of statutes, no less than enactment, must conform with Art. I. . . . The nature of the decision implemented by the one-House veto in this case further manifests its legislative character. . . . *Congress made a deliberate choice to delegate to the Executive Branch, and specifically to the Attorney General, the authority to allow deportable aliens to remain in this country in certain specified circumstances.* It is not disputed that this choice to delegate authority is precisely the kind of decision that can be implemented only in accordance with the procedures set out in Art. I. Disagreement with the Attorney General's decision on Chadha's deportation—that is, *Congress' decision to deport Chadha—no less than Congress' original choice to delegate to the Attorney*

General the authority to make that decision, involves determinations of policy that Congress can implement in only one way; bicameral passage followed by presentment to the President. Congress must abide by its delegation of authority [to the Executive] *until that delegation is legislatively altered or revoked. . . .*

The choices we discern as having been made in the Constitutional Convention impose burdens on governmental processes that often seem clumsy, inefficient, even unworkable, but those hard choices were consciously made by men who had lived under a form of government that permitted arbitrary governmental acts to go unchecked. There is no support in the Constitution or decisions of this Court for the proposition that the cumbersomeness and delays often encountered in complying with explicit Constitutional standards may be avoided, either by the Congress or by the President. . . . With all the obvious flaws of delay, untidiness, and potential for abuse, we have not yet found a better way to preserve freedom than by making the exercise of power subject to the carefully crafted restraints spelled out in the Constitution.

We hold that the Congressional veto provision in § 244(c)(2) [of the statute at issue] *is . . . unconstitutional.* Accordingly, the judgment of the Court of Appeals is Affirmed.

Chapter 8

Civil Liberties in Wartime

The issue of wartime liberties has been the subject of Court decisions, legislative acts, and executive orders from the post–Civil War period, two world wars, the Korean and Vietnam wars, and now the campaign against terrorism. As is clear from a review of cases and other documents included in this chapter, the relation between the state and the citizen in times of national danger remains a contentious topic with many legal questions yet to be resolved. As this volume goes to press, the Supreme Court is considering several cases that will expand the documentary record beyond the foundational documents included here on civil liberties and rights of citizens and non-citizens in times of national danger.

12. *Ex parte Milligan*

(1866)

This landmark Supreme Court case severely limits martial law and the jurisdiction of military courts over civilian citizens. Martial law in any part of the country must be militarily necessary, but this "necessity must be actual and present, the invasion real, such as effectually closes the courts and deposes the civil administration." Moreover, martial law "is also confined to the locality of actual war." When civil courts are available civilians should not be tried in military courts. The right of government in such circumstances to suspend habeas corpus, which requires the government to give lawful grounds for imprisoning a citizen, does not in itself suspend the right to trial by jury or other civil liberties.

Mr. Justice DAVIS delivered the opinion of the court.... On the 10th day of May, 1865, Lambdin P. Milligan presented a petition to the Circuit Court of the United States for the District of Indiana to be discharged from an alleged unlawful impris-onment.... *The controlling question in the case is this: upon the facts stated in Milligan's petition and the exhibits filed, had the military commission mentioned in it jurisdiction legally to try and sentence him?* Milligan, not a resident of one of the rebellious states or a prisoner of war, but a citizen of Indiana for twenty years past and never in the military or naval service, is, while at his home, arrested by the military power of the United States, imprisoned, and, on certain criminal charges preferred against him, tried, convicted, and sentenced to be hanged by a military commission, organized under the direction of the military commander of the military district of Indiana. Had this tribunal the legal power and authority to try and punish this man?

No graver question was ever considered by this court, nor one which more nearly concerns the rights of the whole people, for it is the birthright of every American citizen when charged with crime to be tried and punished according to law. . . . By the protection of the law, human rights are secured; withdraw that protection and they are at the mercy of wicked rulers or the clamor of an excited people. If there was law to justify this military trial, it is not our province to interfere; if there was not, it is our duty to declare the nullity of the whole proceedings. . . . The . . . Constitution . . . says "that the trial of all crimes, except in case of impeachment, shall be by jury," and in the fourth, fifth, and sixth articles of the amendments . . . these securities for personal liberty thus embodied were such as wisdom and experience had demonstrated to be necessary for the protection of those accused of crime. . . .

Have any of the rights guaranteed by the Constitution been violated in the case of Milligan?, and, if so, what are they? Every trial involves the exercise of judicial power, and from what source did the military commission that tried him derive their authority? Certainly no part of judicial power of the country was conferred on them, because the Constitution expressly vests it "in one supreme court and such inferior courts as the Congress may from time to time ordain and establish,"

and it is not pretended that the commission was a court ordained and established by Congress. . . .

Another guarantee of freedom was broken when *Milligan was denied a trial by jury. . . . The discipline necessary to the efficiency of the army and navy required other and swifter modes of trial than are furnished by the common law courts, and, in pursuance of the power conferred by the Constitution* [i.e., by Article I, Section 8], Congress has declared the kinds of trial, and the manner in which they shall be conducted, for offences committed while the party is in the military or naval service. Everyone connected with these branches of the public service is amenable to the jurisdiction which Congress has created for their government, and, while thus serving, surrenders his right to be tried by the civil courts. *All other persons, citizens of states where the courts are open, if charged with crime, are guaranteed the inestimable privilege of trial by jury.* This privilege is a vital principle, underlying the whole administration of criminal justice; it is not held by sufferance, and cannot be frittered away on any plea of state or political necessity. . . .

It is claimed that martial law covers with its broad mantle the proceedings of this military commission. The proposition is this: that, *in a time of war, the commander of an armed force* (if, in his opinion, the exigencies of the country demand it, and of which he is to judge) *has the power, within the lines of his military district, to suspend all civil rights and their remedies and subject citizens, as well as soldiers to the rule of his will,* and, in the exercise of his lawful authority, cannot be restrained except by his superior officer or the President of the United States. . . . *Martial law established on such a basis destroys every guarantee of the Constitution, and effectually renders the "military independent of and superior to the civil power"*—the attempt to do which by the King of Great Britain was deemed by our fathers such an offence that they assigned it to the world as one of the causes which impelled them to declare their independence. Civil liberty and this kind of martial law cannot endure together; the antagonism is irreconcilable, and, in the conflict, one or the other must perish. . . .

Our fathers . . . secured the inheritance they had fought to maintain by incorporating in a written constitution the safeguards which time had proved were essential to its preservation. Not one of these safeguards can the President or Congress or the Judiciary disturb, except the one concerning the writ of habeas corpus. . . . In the emergency of the times, an immediate public investigation according to law may not be possible. . . . Unquestionably, there is then an exigency which demands that the government, if it should see fit in the exercise of a proper discretion to make arrests, should not be required to produce the persons arrested in answer to a writ of habeas corpus. The Constitution goes no further. It does not say, after a writ of habeas corpus is denied a citizen, that he shall be tried otherwise than by the course of the common law. . . . *The illustrious men who framed that instrument were guarding the foundations of civil liberty against the abuses of unlimited power.* . . .

It will be borne in mind that this is not a question of the power to proclaim martial law when war exists in a community and the courts and civil authorities are overthrown. Nor is it a question what rule a military commander, at the head of his army, can impose on states in rebellion to cripple their resources and quell the insurrection. . . . *Martial law cannot arise from a threatened invasion. The necessity must be actual and present, the invasion real, such as effectually closes the courts and deposes the civil administration.* It is difficult to see how the safety for the country required martial

law in Indiana. . . . It was as easy to protect witnesses before a civil as a military tribunal, and as there could be no wish to convict except on sufficient legal evidence, surely an ordained and establish court was better able to judge of this than a military tribunal composed of gentlemen not trained to the profession of the law.

It follows from what has been said on this subject that there are occasions when martial rule can be properly applied. If, in foreign invasion or civil war, the courts are actually closed, and it is impossible to administer criminal justice according to law, then, on the theatre of active military operations, where war really prevails, there is a necessity to furnish a substitute for the civil authority, thus overthrown, to preserve the safety of the army and society, and as no power is left but the military, it is allowed to govern by martial rule until the laws can have their free course. As necessity creates the rule, so it limits its duration, for, if this government is continued after the courts are reinstated, it is a gross usurpation of power. *Martial rule can never exist where the courts are open and in the proper and unobstructed exercise of their jurisdiction. It is also confined to the locality of actual war.* . . . In the case of a foreign invasion, martial rule may become a necessity in one state when, in another, it would be "mere lawless violence."

We are not without precedents in English and American history illustrating our views of this question. . . . So sensitive were our Revolutionary fathers on this subject, although Boston was almost in a state of siege, when General Gage issued his proclamation of martial law, they spoke of it as an "attempt to supersede the course of the common law, and, instead thereof, to publish and order the use of martial law." The Virginia Assembly also denounced a similar measure . . . as an assumed power which the king himself cannot exercise, because it annuls the law of the land and introduces the most execrable of all systems, martial law. In some parts of the country, during the war of 1812, our officers made arbitrary arrests and, by military tribunals, tried citizens who were not in the military service. These arrests and trials, when brought to the notice of the courts, were uniformly condemned as illegal. . . .

It is proper to say, although *Milligan's trial and conviction by a military commission was illegal,* yet, if guilty of the crimes imputed to him, and his guilt had been ascertained by an established court and impartial jury, he deserved severe punishment. . . . The suspension of the privilege of the writ of habeas corpus does not suspend the writ itself. The writ issues as a matter of course, and, on the return made

to it, the court decides whether the party applying is denied the right of proceeding any further with it. If the military trial of Milligan was contrary to law, then he was entitled, on the facts stated in his petition, to be discharged from custody. . . .

But it is insisted that Milligan was a prisoner of war, and therefore excluded from the privileges of the statute. It is not easy to see how he can be treated as a prisoner of war when he lived in Indiana for the past twenty years, was arrested there, and had not been, during the late troubles, a resident of any of the states in rebellion. . . . If he cannot enjoy the immunities attaching to the character of a prisoner of war, how can he be subject to their pains and penalties?

---

13. *Posse Comitatus Act*
(June 18, 1878)

The term posse comitatus *normally refers to those persons a county peace officer is authorized to assemble for law enforcement purposes. Because of abuses in the post–Civil War period that came from using military units or personnel for such purposes, this* Posse Comitatus *Act (a provision within the army appropriations bill for fiscal year 1879) became law. In time it became an established doctrine in the United States defining civil-military relations—separating the regular military from domestic law enforcement functions normally performed by the police or, in exceptional circumstances, by the National Guard. Although* posse comitatus *restrictions remain part of U.S. law (see 10 U.S.C. 375 and 18 U.S.C. 1385), there has been some erosion of the doctrine in recent years as the military capabilities of regular units have been used to support federal efforts against illegal drug imports, immigration, and other border activities. Heightened terrorist threats, including possible resort by terrorists to weapons of mass destruction, require regular military participation in Homeland Security planning and implementation—prevention, mitigation of damage, and consequence management, notwithstanding a traditional preference in most states to rely first on National Guard units before turning to regular military forces.*

CHAP. 263—An act making appropriations for the support of the Army for the fiscal year ending June thirtieth, eighteen hundred and seventy-nine, and for other purposes.

SEC. 15. From and after the passage of this act *it shall not be lawful to employ any part of the Army of the United States, as a posse comitatus, or otherwise, for the purpose of executing the laws, except in such cases and* *under such circumstances as such employment of said force may be expressly authorized by the Constitution or by act of Congress; and no money appropriated by this act shall be used to pay any of the expenses incurred in the employment of any troops in violation of this section [sic]. And any person* willfully violating the provisions of this section shall be deemed guilty of a misdemeanor and on conviction thereof shall be punished by fine not exceeding ten thousand dollars or imprisonment not exceeding two years or by both such fine and imprisonment.

---

14. *Schenck v. United States*

(1919)

Oliver Wendell Holmes delivered the opinion of the Supreme Court, arguing that there are limits to free speech in wartime as in other circumstances when the words we use "create a clear and present danger." Holmes concludes: "When a nation is at war, many things that might be said in time of peace are such a hindrance to its effort that their utterance will not be endured so long as men fight, and that no Court could regard them as protected by any constitutional right." Accordingly, the Supreme Court upheld the lower Court ruling against Schenck for printing and circulating a document against conscription intended, contrary to law, to influence draft-eligible citizens from joining the armed services.

Mr. Justice Holmes delivered the opinion of the court. This is an indictment in three counts. The first charges a conspiracy to violate the Espionage Act of June 15, 1917, by causing and attempting to cause insubordination, &c., in the military and naval forces of the United States, and to obstruct the recruiting and enlistment service of the United States, when the United States was at war with the German Empire, to-wit, that the defendants willfully conspired to have printed and circulated to men who had been called and accepted for military service under the Act of May 18, 1917, a document set forth and alleged to be calculated to cause such insubordination and obstruction. The count alleges overt acts in pursuance of the conspiracy, ending in the distribution of the document set forth. The second count alleges a conspiracy to commit an offence against the United States, to-wit, to use the mails for the transmission of matter declared to be nonmailable by . . . the Act of June 15, 1917, to-wit, the above mentioned document, with an averment of the same overt acts. The third count charges an unlawful use of the mails for the transmission of the same matter and otherwise as above. The defendants were found guilty on all the counts. They set up the First Amendment to the Constitution forbidding Congress to make any law abridging the freedom of speech, or of the press, and bringing the case here on that ground have argued some other points also of which we must dispose. . . .

According to the testimony, Schenck said he was general secretary of the Socialist party, and had charge of the Socialist headquarters from which the documents were sent. . . . Without going into confirmatory details that were proved, no reasonable man could doubt that the defendant Schenck was largely instrumental in sending the circulars about. . . . The document in question, upon its first printed side, recited the first section of the Thirteenth Amendment, said that the idea embodied in it was violated by the Conscription Act, and that a conscript is little better than a convict. In impassioned language, it intimated that conscription was despotism in its worst form, and a monstrous wrong against humanity in the interest of Wall Street's chosen few. It said "Do not submit to intimidation," but in form, at least, confined itself to peaceful measures such as a petition for the repeal of the act. The other and later printed side of the sheet was headed "Assert Your Rights." It stated reasons for alleging that anyone violated the Constitution when he refused to recognize "your right to assert your opposition to the draft," and went on: "If you do not assert and support your rights, you are helping to deny or disparage rights which it is the solemn duty of all citizens and residents of the United States to retain."

It described the arguments on the other side as coming from cunning politicians and a mercenary capitalist press, and even silent consent to the conscription law as helping to support an infamous conspiracy. It denied the power to send our citizens away to foreign shores to shoot up the people of other lands, and added that words could not express the condemnation such cold-blooded ruthlessness deserves, &c., &c., winding up, "You must do your share to maintain, support and uphold the rights of the people of this country." Of course, *the document would not have been sent unless it had been intended to have some effect, and we do not see what effect it could be expected to have upon persons subject to the draft except to influence them to obstruct the carrying of it out.* The defendants do not deny that the jury might find against them on this point.

But it is said, suppose that that was the tendency of this circular, it is protected by the First Amendment to the Constitution. . . . We admit that, in many places and in ordinary times, the defendants, in saying all that was said in the circular, would have been within their constitutional rights. But *the character of every act depends upon the circumstances in which it is done. . . . The most stringent protection of free speech would not protect a man in falsely shouting fire in a theatre and causing a panic.* It does not even protect a man from an injunction against uttering words that may have all the effect of force. . . . *The question in every case is whether the words used are used in such circumstances and are of such a nature as to create a clear and present danger that they will bring about the substantive evils that Congress has a right to prevent.* It is a question of proximity and degree. *When a nation is at war, many things that might be said in time of peace are such a hindrance to its effort that their utterance will not be endured so long as men fight, and that no Court could regard them as protected by any constitutional right.* It seems to be admitted that, if an actual obstruction of the recruiting service were proved, liability for words that produced that effect might be enforced. The statute of 1917 . . . punishes conspiracies to obstruct, as well as actual obstruction. If the act (speaking, or circulating a paper), its tendency, and the intent with which it is done are the same, we perceive no ground for saying that success alone warrants making the act a crime. . . . Judgments affirmed.

15. *Gitlow v. People*

(1925)

The Supreme Court held here that there are limits to free speech when such expression is "inimical to the public welfare, tending to corrupt public morals, incite to crime, or disturb the public peace." In this regard, "a State may penalize utterances which openly advocate the overthrow of the representative and constitutional form of government of the United States and the several States, by violence or other unlawful means." Revolutionary movements, whether domestically spawned or linked to external sources, may not advocate or use such unlawful means against the United States or any state. At the same time, there is no prohibition against "utterance or publication of abstract 'doctrine' or academic discussion having no quality of incitement to any concrete action."

Mr. Justice Sanford delivered the opinion of the Court. Benjamin Gitlow was indicted in the Supreme Court of New York, with three others, for the statutory crime of criminal anarchy. . . . He was separately tried, convicted, and sentenced to imprisonment. The judgment was affirmed by the Appellate Division and by the Court of Appeals. . . . The contention here is that the statute, by its terms and as applied in this case, is repugnant to the due process clause of the Fourteenth Amendment [which extends to states due process rights guaranteed in the Fifth Amendment under federal law—Ed.]. Its material provisions are: . . . Criminal anarchy is the doctrine that organized government should be overthrown by force or violence, or by assassination of the executive head or of any of the executive officials of government, or by any unlawful means. The advocacy of such doctrine either by word of mouth or writing is a felony. . . . Any person who . . . by word of mouth or writing advocates, advises or teaches the duty, necessity or propriety of overthrowing or overturning organized government by force or violence, or by assassination of the executive head or of any of the executive officials of government, or by any unlawful means; or, . . . prints, publishes, edits, issues or knowingly circulates, sells, distributes or publicly displays any book, paper, document, or written or printed matter in any form, containing or advocating, advising or teaching the doctrine that organized government should be overthrown by force, violence or any unlawful means is guilty of a felony and punishable by imprisonment or fine, or both. . . .

The precise question presented, and the only question which we can consider under this writ of error . . . is whether the statute, as construed and applied in this case by the state courts, deprived the defendant of his liberty of expression in violation of the due process clause of the Fourteenth Amendment. The statute does not penalize the utterance or publication of abstract "doctrine" or academic discussion having no quality of incitement to any concrete action. It is not aimed against mere historical or philosophical essays. It does not restrain the advocacy of changes in the form of government by constitutional and lawful means. What it prohibits is language advocating, advising or teaching the overthrow of organized government by unlawful means. . . .

For present purposes, we may and do assume that freedom of speech and of the press which are protected by the First Amendment from abridgment by Congress are among the fundamental personal rights and "liberties" protected by the due process clause of the Fourteenth Amendment from impairment by the States.... It is a fundamental principle, long established, that the freedom of speech and of the press which is secured by the Constitution does not confer an absolute right to speak or publish, without responsibility, whatever one may choose, or an unrestricted and unbridled license that gives immunity for every possible use of language and prevents the punishment of those who abuse this freedom.... Reasonably limited, it was said by [Justice] Story . . . , this freedom is an inestimable privilege in a free government; without such limitation, it might become the scourge of the republic.

That a State in the exercise of its police power may punish those who abuse this freedom by utterances inimical to the public welfare, tending to corrupt public morals, incite to crime, or disturb the public peace, is not open to question. . . . A State may punish utterances endangering the foundations of organized government and threatening its overthrow by unlawful means. These imperil its own existence as a constitutional State. . . . *A State may penalize utterances which openly advocate the overthrow of the representative and constitutional form of government of the United States and the several States, by violence or other unlawful means. . . .*

By enacting the present statute, the State has determined, through its legislative body, that utterances advocating the overthrow of organized government by force, violence and unlawful means are so inimical to the general welfare and involve such danger of substantive evil that they may be penalized in the exercise of its police power. That determination must be given great weight. Every presumption is to be indulged in favor of the validity of the statute. . . . *We cannot hold that the present statute is an arbitrary or unreasonable exercise of the police power of the State unwarrantably infringing the freedom of speech or press, and we must and do sustain its constitutionality.* This being so, it may be applied to every utterance—not too trivial to be beneath the notice of the law—which is of such a character and used with such intent and purpose as to bring it within the prohibition of the statute. . . . When the legislative body has determined generally, in the constitutional exercise of its discretion, that utterances of a certain kind involve such danger of substantive evil that they may be punished, the question whether any specific utterance coming within the prohibited class is likely, in and of itself, to bring about the substantive evil is not open to consideration. It is sufficient that the statute itself be constitutional and that the use of the language comes within its prohibition. . . .

Finding, for the reasons stated, that the statute is not, in itself, unconstitutional, and that it has not been applied in the present case in derogation of any constitutional right, the judgment of the Court of Appeals is Affirmed.

---

16. *Ex parte Quirin*

(1942)

This case underscores presidential authority in time of war to establish military tribunals for trying enemy prisoners for offenses against the law of war. The Supreme Court held in effect "that an alien spy, in time of war," may be tried by military tribunal without a jury. Following the attacks by foreign terrorists on the World Trade Center in New York City and the Pentagon in Washington, D.C., on September 11, 2001, President George W. Bush issued an executive order indicating that, given a state of war (albeit no formal declaration of war by Congress), his administration's intent is to try responsible individuals by military tribunal. The administration's claim to constitutional authority for doing so rests in part on interpretation and application of the reasoning in Ex parte Quirin, *which the Supreme Court decided in the midst of World War II.*

Mr. Chief Justice Stone delivered the opinion of the Court. . . . *The question for decision is whether the detention of petitioners by respondent for trial by Military Commission, appointed by Order of the President of July 2, 1942, on charges preferred against them purporting to set out their violations of the law of war and of the Articles of War, is in conformity to the laws and Constitution of the United States.* . . . After the declaration of war between the United States and the German Reich, petitioners received training at a sabotage school near Berlin, Germany, where they were instructed in the use of explosives and in methods of secret writing. Thereafter petitioners . . . proceeded from Germany to a seaport in Occupied France, where petitioners . . . boarded a German submarine which proceeded across the Atlantic to . . . Long Island, New York. The four were there landed from the submarine . . . carrying with them a supply of explosives, fuses and incendiary and timing devices. . . . The remaining four petitioners at the same French port boarded another German submarine, which carried them across the Atlantic to . . . Florida. . . . They came ashore . . . carrying with them a supply of explosives, fuses, and incendiary and timing devices. . . . All were taken into custody in New York or Chicago by agents of the Federal Bureau of Investigation.

The President, as President and Commander in Chief of the Army and Navy, by Order of July 2, 1942, appointed a Military Commission and directed it to try petitioners for offenses against the law of war

and the Articles of War, and prescribed regulations for the procedure on the trial and for review of the record of the trial and of any judgment or sentence of the Commission. On the same day, by Proclamation, the President declared that "all persons who are subjects, citizens or residents of any nation at war with the United States or who give obedience to or act under the direction of any such nation, and who during the time of war enter or attempt to enter the United States . . . and are charged with committing or attempting or preparing to commit sabotage, espionage, hostile or warlike acts, or violations of the law of war, shall be subject to the law of war and to the jurisdiction of military tribunals." The Proclamation also stated . . . that all such persons were denied access to the courts.

Petitioners' main contention is that the President is without any statutory or constitutional authority to order the petitioners to be tried by military tribunal for offenses with which they are charged; that in consequence they are entitled to be tried in the civil courts with the safeguards, including trial by jury, which the Fifth and Sixth Amendments guarantee to all persons charged in such courts with criminal offenses. . . .

We are not here concerned with any question of the guilt or innocence of petitioners. Constitutional safeguards for the protection of all who are charged with offenses are not to be disregarded in order to inflict merited punishment on some who are guilty. But the detention and trial of petitioners—ordered by the President in the declared exercise of his powers as Commander in Chief of the Army in time of war and of grave public danger—are not to be set aside by the courts without the clear conviction that they are in conflict with the Constitution or laws of Congress constitutionally enacted.

The Constitution thus *invests the President* as Commander in Chief with the power to wage war which Congress has declared, and *to carry into effect* all laws passed by Congress for the conduct of war and for the government and regulation of the Armed Forces, and *all laws defining and punishing offences against the law of nations, including those which pertain to the conduct of war.*

From the very beginning of its history this Court has recognized and applied the law of war as including that part of the law of nations which prescribes, for the conduct of war, the status, rights and duties of enemy nations as well as of enemy individuals. *By the Articles of War, and especially Article 15, Congress has explicitly provided, so far as it may constitutionally do so, that military tribunals shall have jurisdiction to try offenders or offenses against the law of war. . . .* It is unnecessary for present purposes to determine to what extent the President as Commander in Chief has constitutional power to create military commissions without the support of Congressional legislation. For here Congress has authorized trial of offenses against the law of war before such commissions. We are concerned only with the question whether it is within the constitutional power of the national government to place petitioners upon trial before a military commission for the offenses with which they are charged. We must therefore first inquire whether any of the acts charged is an offense against the law of war recognizable before a military tribunal, and if so

whether the Constitution prohibits the trial. . . .

The spy who secretly and without uniform passes the military lines of a belligerent in time of war, seeking to gather military information and communicate it to the enemy, or an enemy combatant who without uniform comes secretly through the lines for the purpose of waging war by destruction of life or property, are familiar examples of belligerents who are generally deemed not to be entitled to the status of prisoners of war, but to be offenders against the law of war subject to trial and punishment by military tribunals.

Our Government, by . . . defining lawful belligerents entitled to be treated as prisoners of war, has recognized that there is a class of unlawful belligerents not entitled to that privilege, including those who though combatants do not wear "fixed and distinctive emblems." And by Article 15 of the Articles of War Congress has made provision for their trial and punishment by military commission, according to "the law of war." By a long course of practical administrative construction by its military authorities, our Government has likewise recognized that those who during time of war pass surreptitiously from enemy territory into our own, discarding their uniforms upon entry, for the commission of hostile acts involving destruction of life or property, have the status of unlawful combatants punishable as such by military commission. This precept of the law of war has been so recognized in practice both here and abroad, and has so generally been accepted as valid by authorities on international law that we think it must be regarded as a rule or principle of the law of war recognized by this Government by its enactment of the Fifteenth Article of War.

The law of war cannot rightly treat those agents of enemy armies who enter our territory, armed with explosives intended for the destruction of war industries and supplies, as any the less belligerent enemies than are agents similarly entering for the purpose of destroying fortified places or our Armed Forces. By passing our boundaries for such purposes without uniform or other emblem signifying their belligerent status, or by discarding that means of identification after entry, such enemies become unlawful belligerents subject to trial and punishment.

Citizenship in the United States of an enemy belligerent does not relieve him from the consequences of a belligerency which is unlawful because in violation of the law of war. Citizens who associate themselves with the military arm of the enemy government, and with its aid, guidance and direction enter this country bent on hostile acts are enemy belligerents within the meaning of the Hague Convention and the law of war. . . .

But petitioners insist that even if the offenses with which they are charged are offenses against the law of war, their trial is subject to the requirement of the Fifth Amendment that no person shall be held to answer for a capital or otherwise infamous crime unless on a presentment or indictment of a grand jury, and that such trials . . . must be by jury in a civil court. . . . As this Court has often recognized, it was not the purpose or effect of Section 2 of Article III, read in the light of the common law, to enlarge the then existing right to a jury trial. The object was to preserve unimpaired trial by jury . . . but not to bring within the sweep of the guaranty those cases in which it was then well understood that a jury trial could not be demanded as of right. . . . We must conclude that § 2 of Article III and the Fifth

and Sixth Amendments cannot be taken to have extended the right to demand a jury to trials by military commission, or to have required that offenses against the law of war not triable by jury at common law be tried only in the civil courts. . . .

Section 2 of the Act of Congress of April 10, 1806, derived from the Resolution of the Continental Congress of August 21, 1776, imposed the death penalty on alien spies "according to the law and usage of nations, by sentence of a general court martial." This enactment must be regarded as a contemporary construction of both Article III, § 2, and the Amendments as not foreclosing trial by military tribunals, without a jury, of offenses against the law of war committed by enemies not in or associated with our Armed Forces. It is a construction of the Constitution which has been followed since the founding of our government, and is now continued in the 82nd Article of War. Such a construction is entitled to greatest respect. *It has not hitherto been challenged, and* so far as we are advised *it has never been suggested* in the very extensive literature of the subject *that an alien spy, in time of war, could not be tried by military tribunal without a jury.* . . . Under the original statute authorizing trial of alien spies by military tribunals, the offenders were outside the constitutional guaranty of trial by jury, not because they were aliens but only because they had violated the law of war by committing offenses constitutionally triable by military tribunal. We cannot say that Congress in preparing the Fifth and Sixth Amendments intended to extend trial by jury to the cases of alien or citizen offenders against the law of war otherwise triable by military commission, while withholding it from members of our own armed forces charged with infractions of the Articles of War punishable by death. . . . *We conclude that the Fifth*

*and Sixth Amendments did not restrict what-
ever authority was conferred by the Constitution to try offenses against the law of war by military commission, and that petitioners, charged
with such an offense not required to be tried by
jury at common law, were lawfully placed on
trial by the Commission without a jury.*

Petitioners . . . stress the pronounce-
ment of this Court in the Milligan case that
the law of war "can never be applied to
citizens in states which have upheld the
authority of the government, and where
the courts are open and their process unobstructed.". . . We construe the Court's
statement as to the inapplicability of the
law of war to Milligan's case as having
particular reference to the facts before it.
From them the Court concluded that
Milligan . . . was a non-belligerent, not
subject to the law of war. . . . The Court's
opinion is inapplicable to the case presented by the present record. . . .

17. *Korematsu v. United States*

(1944)

*Military necessity was used by the U.S. government to deny liberties to American citizens of
Japanese descent, excluding them from some areas of the country and sending many to internment camps. Although three justices issued strong dissents because of the violation of civil
liberties and allegations of racism involved, the majority held that the constitutional war power
justified government action. Some four decades after World War II the decision was challenged
in a district court on the grounds that there were errors in the evidence provided at the time to the
Supreme Court. The consensus today is that serious errors made at the time did great harm to
citizens who had committed no crimes.*

Mr. Justice Black delivered the opinion of
the Court.

The petitioner, an American citizen of
Japanese descent, was convicted in a
federal district court for remaining in San
Leandro, California, a "Military Area,"
contrary to Civilian Exclusion Order
No. 34 of the Commanding General of the
Western Command, U.S. Army, which directed that after May 9, 1942, all persons of
Japanese ancestry should be excluded
from that area. No question was raised as
to petitioner's loyalty to the United States.
The Circuit Court of Appeals affirmed, and
the importance of the constitutional question involved caused us to grant certiorari.

It should be noted, to begin with, that
all legal restrictions which curtail the civil
rights of a single racial group are immediately suspect. That is not to say that all
such restrictions are unconstitutional. It is
to say that courts must subject them to the
most rigid scrutiny. Pressing public necessity may sometimes justify the existence of
such restrictions; racial antagonism never
can. . . . Exclusion Order No. 34, which the
petitioner knowingly and admittedly violated, was one of a number of military orders and proclamations. . . . That order,
issued after we were at war with Japan,
declared that "the successful prosecution
of the war requires every possible protection against espionage and against
sabotage to national-defense material,
national-defense premises, and national-
defense utilities. . . ."

In the Hirabayashi case . . . we upheld the curfew order as an exercise of the power of the government to take steps necessary to prevent espionage and sabotage in an area threatened by Japanese attack. In the light of the principles we announced in the Hirabayashi case, we are unable to conclude that it was beyond the war power of Congress and the Executive to exclude those of Japanese ancestry from the West Coast war area at the time they did. . . . Exclusion from a threatened area, no less than curfew, has a definite and close relationship to the prevention of espionage and sabotage. The military authorities, charged with the primary responsibility of defending our shores, concluded that curfew provided inadequate protection and ordered exclusion. They did so, as pointed out in our Hirabayashi opinion, in accordance with Congressional authority to the military to say who should, and who should not, remain in the threatened areas. . . .

We uphold the exclusion order as of the time it was made and when the petitioner violated it. In doing so, we are not unmindful of the hardships imposed by it upon a large group of American citizens. But hardships are part of war, and war is an aggregation of hardships. All citizens alike, both in and out of uniform, feel the impact of war in greater or lesser measure. Citizenship has its responsibilities as well as its privileges, and in time of war the burden is always heavier. Compulsory exclusion of large groups of citizens from their homes, except under circumstances of direst emergency and peril, is inconsistent with our basic governmental institutions. But *when under conditions of modern warfare our shores are threatened by hostile forces, the power to protect must be commensurate with the threatened danger.* . . .

Since the petitioner has not been convicted of failing to report or to remain in an assembly or relocation center, we cannot in this case determine the validity of those separate provisions of the order. It is sufficient here for us to pass upon the order which petitioner violated. . . .

Some of the members of the Court are of the view that evacuation and detention in an Assembly Center were inseparable. After May 3, 1942, the date of Exclusion Order No. 34, Korematsu was under compulsion to leave the area not as he would choose but via an Assembly Center. The Assembly Center was conceived as a part of the machinery for group evacuation. The power to exclude includes the power to do it by force if necessary. And any forcible measure must necessarily entail some degree of detention or restraint whatever method of removal is selected. But whichever view is taken, it results in holding that the order under which petitioner was convicted was valid.

It is said that we are dealing here with the case of imprisonment of a citizen in a concentration camp solely because of his ancestry, without evidence or inquiry concerning his loyalty and good disposition towards the United States. *Our task would be simple, our duty clear, were this a case involving the imprisonment of a loyal citizen in a concentration camp because of racial prejudice.* Regardless of the true nature of the assembly and relocation centers—and we deem it unjustifiable to call them concentration camps with all the ugly connotations that term implies—we are dealing specifically with nothing but an exclusion order. *To cast this case into outlines of racial prejudice, without reference to the real military dangers which were presented, merely confuses the issue.*

Korematsu was not excluded from the Military Area because of hostility to him or his race. *He was excluded because we are at war with the Japanese Empire, because the properly constituted military authorities feared an invasion of our West Coast and felt constrained to take proper security measures,* because they decided that the military urgency of the situation demanded that all citizens of Japanese ancestry be segregated from the West Coast temporarily, and finally, because Congress, reposing its confidence in this time of war in our military leaders—as inevitably it must—determined that they should have the power to do just this. There was evidence of disloyalty on the part of some, the military authorities considered that the need for action was great, and time was short. We cannot—by availing ourselves of the calm perspective of hindsight—now say that at that time these actions were unjustified.

Affirmed.

Mr. Justice Frankfurter, concurring.

. . . The provisions of the Constitution which confer on the Congress and the President powers to enable this country to wage war are as much part of the Constitution as provisions looking to a nation at peace. . . . To talk about *a military order that expresses an allowable judgment of war needs by those entrusted with the duty of conducting war* as "an unconstitutional order" is to suffuse a part of the Constitution with an atmosphere of unconstitutionality. . . . To recognize that military orders are "reasonably expedient military precautions" in time of war and yet to deny them constitutional legitimacy makes of the Constitution an instrument for dialectic subtleties not reasonably to be attributed to the hard-headed Framers, of whom a majority had had actual participation in war. . . . Such action by the military *is as constitutional as would be any authorized action by the Interstate Commerce Commission within the limits of the constitu-*

tional power to regulate commerce. . . . To find that the Constitution does not forbid the military measures now complained of does not carry with it approval of that which Congress and the Executive did. That is their business, not ours.

Mr. Justice Roberts, dissenting.

I dissent, because I think the indisputable facts exhibit a clear violation of Constitutional rights. This is not a case of keeping people off the streets at night as was Hirabayashi v. United States, nor a case of temporary exclusion of a citizen from an area for his own safety or that of the community, nor a case of offering him an opportunity to go temporarily out of an area where his presence might cause danger to himself or to his fellows. On the contrary, *it is the case of convicting a citizen as a punishment for not submitting to imprisonment in a concentration camp, based on his ancestry, and solely because of his ancestry, without evidence or inquiry concerning his loyalty and good disposition towards the United States.* If this be a correct statement of the facts disclosed by this record, and facts of which we take judicial notice, *I need hardly labor the conclusion that Constitutional rights have been violated. . . .* I would reverse the judgment of conviction.

Mr. Justice Murphy, dissenting.

This exclusion of "all persons of Japanese ancestry, both alien and non-alien," from the Pacific Coast area on a plea of military necessity in the absence of martial law ought not to be approved. Such exclusion *goes over "the very brink of constitutional power" and falls into the ugly abyss of racism. . . . Individuals must not be left impoverished of their constitutional rights on a plea of military necessity that has neither substance nor support.* Thus, like other claims conflicting with the asserted constitutional rights of the individual, the military claim must subject itself to the judicial process of having its reasonableness determined and its conflicts with other interests reconciled. . . . I *dissent . . . from this legalization of racism. . . .*

Mr. Justice Jackson, dissenting.

Korematsu was born on our soil, of parents born in Japan. The Constitution makes him a citizen of the United States by nativity and a citizen of California by residence. No claim is made that he is not loyal to this country. There is no suggestion that apart from the matter involved here he is not law-abiding and well disposed. Korematsu, however, has been convicted of an act not commonly a crime. . . . Now, *if any fundamental assumption underlies our system, it is that guilt is personal and not inheritable.* Even if all of one's antecedents had been convicted of treason, *the Constitution* forbids its penalties to be visited upon him, for it *provides that "no attainder of treason shall work corruption of blood, or forfeiture except during the life of the person attained."* But *here is an attempt to make an otherwise innocent act a crime merely because this prisoner is the son of parents as to whom he had no choice, and belongs to a race from which there is no way to resign.*

---

18. *Johnson v. Eisentrager*

(1950)

Citizen rights to constitutional protections are affirmed in this important decision. Resident aliens in peacetime are afforded many of these rights; however, not in wartime: "It is war that exposes the relative vulnerability of the alien's status. The security and protection enjoyed while the nation of his allegiance remains in amity with the United States are greatly impaired when his nation takes up arms against us." Indeed, "the resident enemy alien is constitutionally subject to summary arrest, internment and deportation whenever a 'declared war' exists." Resident enemy aliens in wartime have "no right to the writ of habeas corpus." In this regard, "the Constitution does not confer a right of personal security or an immunity from military trial and punishment upon an alien enemy engaged in the hostile service of a government at war with the United States." The judiciary does not have jurisdiction in such matters outside of territories over which the U.S. is sovereign, the Court noting "that it was the alien's presence within its territorial jurisdiction that gave the Judiciary power to act." Although the issue of citizens who are designated "enemy combatants" is not addressed here, the Court does introduce the distinction between "preventive rather than punitive detention."

Mr. Justice Jackson delivered the opinion of the Court. The ultimate question in this case is one of jurisdiction of civil courts of the United States vis-a-vis military authorities in dealing with enemy aliens overseas. The issues come here in this way:

Twenty-one German nationals petitioned the District Court of the District of Columbia for writs of habeas corpus. . . . These prisoners have been convicted of violating laws of war, by engaging in, permitting or ordering continued military activity against the United States after surrender of Germany and before surrender of Japan. Their hostile operations consisted principally of collecting and furnishing intelligence concerning American forces and their movements to the Japanese armed forces. They, with six others who were acquitted, were taken into custody by the United States Army after the Japanese surrender and were tried and convicted by a Military Commission constituted by our Commanding General at Nanking. . . .

The petition prays an order that the prisoners be produced before the District Court, that it may inquire into their confinement and order them discharged from such offenses and confinement. It is claimed that their trial, conviction and imprisonment violate Articles I and III of the Constitution, and the Fifth Amendment thereto, and other provisions of the Constitution and laws of the United States and provisions of the Geneva Convention governing treatment of prisoners of war.

A rule to show cause issued, to which the United States made return. Thereupon the petition was dismissed. . . . *The Court of Appeals* reversed and, reinstating the petition, remanded for further proceedings. . . . It *concluded that any person, including an enemy alien, deprived of his liberty anywhere under any purported authority of the United States is entitled to the writ if he can show that extension to his case of any constitutional rights or limitations would show his imprisonment illegal;* that, although no statutory jurisdiction of such cases is given, courts must be held to possess it as part of the judicial power of the United States; that where deprivation of liberty by an official act occurs outside the territorial jurisdiction of any District Court, the petition will lie in the District Court which has territorial jurisdiction over officials who have directive power over the immediate jailer.

The obvious importance of these holdings to both judicial administration and military operations impelled us to grant certiorari. . . . The case is before us only on

issues of law. *The writ of habeas corpus* must be granted "unless it appears from the application" that the applicants are not entitled to it. . . .

We are cited to no instance where a court, in this or any other country where the writ is known, *has issued it on behalf of an alien enemy who, at no relevant time and in no stage of his captivity, has been within its territorial jurisdiction. Nothing in the text of the Constitution extends such a right, nor does anything in our statutes. . . .*

I. . . . *With the citizen we* are now little concerned, except to *set his case apart as untouched by this decision and to take measure of the difference between his status and that of all categories of aliens.* Citizenship as a head of jurisdiction and a ground of protection was old when Paul invoked it in his appeal to Caesar. *The years have not destroyed nor diminished the importance of citizenship nor have they sapped the vitality of a citizen's claims upon his government for protection.* If a person's claim to United States citizenship is denied by any official, Congress has directed our courts to entertain his action to declare him to be a citizen "regardless of whether he is within the United States or abroad.". . . This Court long ago extended habeas corpus to one seeking admission to the country to assure fair hearing of his claims to citizenship . . . and has secured citizenship against forfeiture by involuntary formal acts. . . . Because the Government's obligation of protection is correlative with the duty of loyal support inherent in the citizen's allegiance, *Congress has directed the President to exert the full diplomatic and political power of the United States on behalf of any citizen, but of no other, in jeopardy abroad. When any citizen is deprived of his liberty by any foreign government, it is made the duty of the President to demand the reasons and, if the detention appears wrongful, to use means not amounting to acts of war to effectuate his release.* It is neither sentimentality nor chauvinism to repeat that "Citizenship is a high privilege."

... The alien, to whom the United States has been traditionally hospitable, has been accorded a generous and ascending scale of rights as he increases his identity with our society. *Mere lawful presence in the country creates an implied assurance of safe conduct and gives him certain rights; they become more extensive and secure when he makes preliminary declaration of intention to become a citizen, and they expand to those of full citizenship upon naturalization.* During his probationary residence ... this Court has steadily enlarged *his right against Executive deportation except upon full and fair hearing. ... And, at least since 1886, we have extended to the person and property of resident aliens important constitutional guaranties—such as the due process of law of the Fourteenth Amendment. ...*

But, *in extending constitutional protections beyond the citizenry, the Court has been at pains to point out that it was the alien's presence within its territorial jurisdiction that gave the Judiciary power to act. ... Since* most cases involving aliens afford this ground of jurisdiction, and *the civil and property rights of immigrants or transients of foreign nationality so nearly approach equivalence to those of citizens, courts in peace time have little occasion to inquire whether litigants before them are alien or citizen.*

It is war that exposes the relative vulnerability of the alien's status. The security and protection enjoyed while the nation of his allegiance remains in amity with the United States are greatly impaired when his nation takes up arms against us. While his lot is far more humane ... and endurable than the experience of our citizens in some enemy lands, it is still not a happy one. But *disabilities this*

country lays upon the alien who becomes also an enemy are imposed temporarily as an incident of war and not as an incident of alienage. ...

The alien enemy is bound by an allegiance which commits him to lose no opportunity to forward the cause of our enemy; hence the United States, assuming him to be faithful to his allegiance, ... regards him as part of the enemy resources. It therefore takes measures to disable him from commission of hostile acts imputed as his intention because they are a duty to his sovereign. ... Although it obviously denies enemy aliens the constitutional immunities of citizens, it seems not then to have been supposed that a nation's obligations to its foes could ever be put on a parity with those to its defenders.

The resident enemy alien is constitutionally subject to summary arrest, internment and deportation whenever a "declared war" exists. Courts will entertain his plea for freedom from Executive custody *only to ascertain the existence of a state of war and whether he is an alien enemy* and so subject to the Alien Enemy Act. *Once these jurisdictional elements have been determined, courts will not inquire into any other issue as to his internment. ...*

The standing of the enemy alien to maintain any action in the courts of the United States has been often challenged and sometimes denied. ... A unanimous Court recently clarified both the privilege of access to our courts and the limitations upon it. We *said: "The ancient rule against suits by resident alien enemies has survived only so far as necessary to prevent use of the courts to accomplish a purpose which might hamper our own war efforts or give aid to the enemy. This may be taken as the sound principle of the common law today."*

... But the nonresident enemy alien, especially one who has remained in the service of the enemy, does not have even this qualified access to our courts, for he neither has comparable claims upon our institutions nor

could his use of them fail to be helpful to the enemy. . . .

II. . . . We are here confronted with a decision whose basic premise is that these prisoners are entitled, as a constitutional right, to sue in some court of the United States for a writ of habeas corpus. To support that assumption we must hold that a prisoner of our military authorities is constitutionally entitled to the writ, even though he (a) is an enemy alien; (b) has never been or resided in the United States; (c) was captured outside of our territory and there held in military custody as a prisoner of war; (d) was tried and convicted by a Military Commission sitting outside the United States; (e) for offenses against laws of war committed outside the United States; (f) and is at all times imprisoned outside the United States.

We have pointed out that *the privilege of litigation has been extended to aliens, whether friendly or enemy, only because permitting their presence in the country implied . . . protection. No such basis can be invoked here, for* these prisoners at no relevant time were within any territory over which the United States is sovereign, and the scenes of their offense, their capture, *their trial and their punishment were all beyond the territorial jurisdiction of any court of the United States. . . .*

A basic consideration in habeas corpus practice is that the prisoner will be produced before the court. This is the crux of the statutory scheme established by the Congress; indeed, it is inherent in the very term "habeas corpus." . . . The writ, since it is held to be a matter of right, would be equally available to enemies during active hostilities as in the present twilight between war and peace. Such trials would hamper the war effort and bring aid and comfort to the enemy. They would diminish the prestige of our commanders, not

only with enemies but with wavering neutrals. It would be difficult to devise more effective fettering of a field commander than to allow the very enemies he is ordered to reduce to submission to call him to account in his own civil courts and divert his efforts and attention from the military offensive abroad to the legal defensive at home. Nor is it unlikely that the result of such enemy litigiousness would be a conflict between judicial and military opinion highly comforting to enemies of the United States. . . .

Despite this, the doors of our courts have not been summarily closed upon these prisoners. Three courts have considered their application and have provided their counsel opportunity to advance every argument in their . . . support. . . . After hearing all contentions . . . *we arrive at the . . . conclusion . . . that no right to the writ of habeas corpus appears.*

III. The Court of Appeals . . . gave our Constitution an extraterritorial application to embrace our enemies in arms. . . . Resident alien enemies . . . are entitled only to judicial hearing to determine what the petition of these prisoners admits: that they are really alien enemies. When that appears, those resident here may be deprived of liberty by Executive action without hearing. . . . While this is preventive rather than punitive detention, no reason is apparent why an alien enemy charged with having committed a crime should have greater immunities from Executive action than one who it is only feared might at some future time commit a hostile act. . . . *We hold that the Constitution does not confer a right of personal security or an immunity from military trial and punishment upon an alien enemy engaged in the hostile service of a government at war with the United States.*

IV. . . . *The jurisdiction of military authorities, during or following hostilities, to punish* *those guilty of offenses against the laws of war is long-established. . . .* This Court has characterized as "well-established" the "power of the military to exercise jurisdiction over members of the armed forces, those directly connected with such forces, or enemy belligerents, prisoners of war, or others charged with violating the laws of war." . . . And we have held in the Quirin and Yamashita cases . . . *that the Military Commission is a lawful tribunal to adjudge enemy offenses against the laws of war.*

It is not for us to say whether these prisoners were or were not guilty of a war crime, or whether if we were to retry the case we would agree to the findings of fact or the application of the laws of war made by the Military Commission. The petition shows that these prisoners were formally accused of violating the laws of war and fully informed of particulars of these charges. As we observed in the Yamashita case, "If the military tribunals have lawful authority to hear, decide and condemn, their action is not subject to judicial review merely because they have made a wrong decision on disputed . . . facts. Correction of their errors of decision is not for the courts but for the military authorities which are alone authorized to review their decisions." . . .

"We consider here only the lawful power of the commission to try the petitioner for the offense charged."

*. . . Certainly it is not the function of the Judiciary to entertain private litigation—even by a citizen—which challenges the legality, the wisdom, or the propriety of the Commander-in-Chief in sending our armed forces abroad or to any particular region. . . . The issue . . . in-*volves a challenge to conduct of diplomatic and foreign affairs, for which the President is exclusively responsible. . . .

These prisoners do not assert, and could not, that anything in the Geneva Convention makes them immune from prosecution or punishment for war crimes. Article 75 thereof expressly provides that a prisoner of war may be detained until the end of such proceedings and, if necessary, until the expiration of the punishment. . . .

We are unable to find that the petition alleges any fact showing lack of jurisdiction in the military authorities to accuse, try and condemn these prisoners or that they acted in excess of their lawful powers.

V. The . . . judgment of the Court of Appeals is reversed and the judgment of the District Court dismissing the petition is affirmed. Reversed.

---

19. *Toth v. Quarles*

(1955)

Civilians accused of federal crimes customarily are tried in courts constituted under Article III of the U.S. Constitution, which establishes the judiciary as the third branch of the federal government; however, because they are part of the armed forces, military members may fall under jurisdiction of military tribunals—courts martial—constituted under Article I, Section 8, of the Constitution. The Supreme Court notes that military members do not in fact enjoy the same rights as their civilian counterparts precisely because courts martial are not just courts of justice affording all the rights citizens have under the Constitution, but also are federal courts integral to the military discipline system. Although the Court observes efforts to extend greater due process and assure other rights for those in military service, the absence of separation of powers (the military court system is part of the command, i.e., the executive branch, not the judiciary) leads it to conclude that military courts martial are not likely to provide the degree of civil liberties protection enjoyed by civilians. Thus, those not in military service (to include those discharged therefrom) ought not be subject to trial by military courts.

Mr. Justice Black delivered the opinion of the Court.

After serving with the United States Air Force in Korea, Robert W. Toth was honorably discharged. He returned to his home in Pittsburgh and went to work in a steel plant. Five months later he was arrested by military authorities on charges of murder and conspiracy to commit murder while an airman in Korea. At the time of arrest he had no relationship of any kind with the military. He was taken to Korea to stand trial before a court-martial under authority of a 1950 Act of Congress. The Court of Appeals sustained the Act, rejecting the contention that civilian ex-servicemen like Toth could not constitutionally be subjected to trial by court-martial. We granted certiorari to pass upon this important constitutional question.

The 1950 Act cannot be sustained on the constitutional power of Congress "To raise and support Armies," "To declare War," or to punish "Offences against the Law of Nations." And this assertion of military authority over civilians cannot rest on the President's power as commander-in-chief, or on any theory of martial law. See Ex parte Milligan.... The Government's contention is that the Act is a valid exercise of the power granted Congress in Article I of the Constitution "To make Rules for the Government and Regulation of the land and naval Forces," as supplemented by the Necessary and Proper Clause.

This Court has held that the Article I clause just quoted authorizes Congress to subject persons actually in the armed service to trial by court-martial for military and naval offenses. Later it was held that court-martial jurisdiction could be exerted over a dishonorably discharged soldier then a military prisoner serving a sentence imposed by a prior court-martial. It has never been intimated by this Court, however, that Article I military jurisdiction could be extended to civilian ex-soldiers who had severed all relationship with the military and its institutions. To allow this extension of military authority would require an extremely broad construction of the language used in the constitutional provision relied on. For given its natural meaning, *the power granted Congress "To make Rules" to regulate "the land and naval Forces" would seem to restrict court-martial jurisdiction to persons who are actually members or part of the armed forces. There is a compelling reason for construing the clause this way: any expansion of court-martial jurisdiction like that in the 1950 Act necessarily encroaches on the jurisdiction of federal courts set up under Article III of the Constitution where persons on trial are surrounded with more constitutional safeguards than in military tribunals.*

Article III provides for the establishment of a court system as one of the separate but coordinate branches of the National Government. It is the primary, indeed the sole business of these courts to try cases and controversies between individuals and between individuals and the Government. This includes trial of criminal cases. These courts are presided over by judges appointed for life, subject only to removal by impeachment. Their compensation cannot be diminished during their continuance in office. The provisions of Article III were designed to give judges maximum freedom from possible coercion or influence by the executive or legislative branches of the Government. But the Constitution and the Amendments in the Bill of Rights show that the Founders were not satisfied with leaving determination of guilt or innocence to judges, even though wholly independent. They further provided that no person should be held to answer in those courts for capital or other infamous crimes unless on the presentment or indictment of a grand jury drawn from the body of the people. Other safeguards designed to protect defendants against oppressive governmental practices were included. One of these was considered so important to liberty of the individual that it appears in two parts of the Constitution. Article III, 2, commands that the "Trial of all Crimes, except in Cases of Impeachment, shall be by Jury; and such Trial shall be held in the State where the said Crimes shall have been committed; but when not committed within any State, the Trial shall be at such Place or Places as the Congress may by Law have directed." And the Sixth Amendment provides that "In all criminal prosecutions, the accused shall enjoy the right to a speedy and public trial, by an impartial jury of the state and district wherein the crime shall have been committed. . . ." This right of trial by jury ranks very high in our catalogue of constitutional safeguards.

We find nothing in the history or constitutional treatment of military tribunals which entitles them to rank along with Article III courts as adjudicators of the guilt or innocence of people charged with offenses for which they can be deprived of their life, liberty or property. Unlike courts, it is the primary business of armies and navies to fight or be ready to fight wars should the occasion arise. But trial of soldiers to maintain discipline is merely incidental to an army's primary fighting function. To the extent that those responsible for performance of this primary function are diverted from it by the necessity of trying cases, the basic fighting purpose of armies is not served. And conceding to military personnel that high degree of honesty and sense of justice which nearly all of them undoubtedly have, it still remains true that *military tribunals have not been and probably never can be constituted in such way that they can have the same kind of qualifications that the Constitution has deemed essential to fair trials of civilians in federal courts.* For instance, the Constitution does not provide life tenure for those performing judicial functions in military trials. They are appointed by military commanders and may be removed at will. Nor does the Constitution protect their salaries as it does judicial salaries. Strides have been made toward making courts-martial less subject to the will of the executive department which appoints, supervises and ultimately controls them. But from the very nature of things, *courts have more independence in passing on the life and liberty of people than do military tribunals.*

Moreover, there is a great difference between trial by jury and trial by selected members of the military forces. *It is true that military personnel because of their training and experience may be especially competent to try soldiers for infractions of military rules.* Such training is no doubt particularly important where an offense charged against a soldier is purely military, such as disobedience of an order, leaving post, etc. But whether right or wrong, the premise underlying the constitutional method for determining guilt or innocence in federal courts is that laymen are better than specialists to perform this task. This idea is inherent in the institution of trial by jury.

Juries fairly chosen from different walks of life bring into the jury box a variety of different experiences, feelings, intuitions and habits. Such juries may reach completely different conclusions than would be reached by specialists in any single field, including specialists in the military field. On many occasions, fully known to the Founders of this country, jurors—plain people—have manfully stood up in defense of liberty against the importunities of judges and despite prevailing hysteria and prejudices. The acquittal of William Penn is an illustrious example. Unfortunately, instances could also be cited where jurors have themselves betrayed the cause of justice by verdicts based on prejudice or pressures. In such circumstances independent trial judges and independent appellate judges have a most important place under our constitutional plan since they have power to set aside convictions.

The 1950 Act here considered deprives of jury trial and sweeps under military jurisdiction over 3,000,000 persons who have become veterans since the Act became effective. That number is bound to grow from year to year; there are now more than 3,000,000 men and women in uniform. These figures point up what would be the enormous scope of a holding that Congress could subject every ex-serviceman and woman in the land to trial by court-martial for any alleged offense committed while he or she had been a member of the armed forces. Every veteran discharged since passage of the 1950 Act is subject to military trial for any offense punishable by as much as five years' imprisonment unless the offense is now punishable in a civilian court. And one need only glance at the Military Code to see what a vast number and variety of offenses are thus brought under military jurisdiction. Included within these are

crimes such as murder, conspiracy, absence without leave, contempt toward officials, disrespect toward superior officers, willful or neglectful loss, damage, or destruction of government property, making false official statements, dueling, breach of the peace, forgery, fraud, assault, and many others. It is true that with reference to some of these offenses, very minor ones, veterans cannot now be tried because of a presidential order fixing the punishment for such offenses at less than five years. But that amelioration of the Military Code may be temporary, since punishment can be raised or lowered at the will of the President. It is also true that under the present law courts-martial have jurisdiction only if no civilian court does. But that might also be changed by Congress. Thus there is no justification for treating the Act as a mere minor increase of congressional power to expand military jurisdiction. It is a great change, both actually and potentially.

Fear has been expressed that if this law is not sustained discharged soldiers may escape punishment altogether for crimes they commit while in the service. But that fear is not warranted and was not shared by the Judge Advocate General of the Army who made a strong statement against passage of the law. He asked Congress to "confer jurisdiction upon Federal courts to try any person for an offense denounced by the [military] code if he is no longer subject thereto. This would be consistent with the fifth amendment of the Constitution." The Judge Advocate General went on to tell Congress that "If you expressly confer jurisdiction on the Federal courts to try such cases, you preserve the constitutional separation of military and civil courts, you save the military from a lot of unmerited grief, and you provide for a clean, constitutional method for disposing of such cases." It is conceded that it was wholly within the constitutional power of Congress to follow this suggestion and provide for federal district court trials of discharged soldiers accused of offenses committed while in the armed services. This concession is justified. . . . *There can be no valid argument, therefore, that civilian ex-servicemen must be tried by court-martial or not tried at all.* If that is so it is only because Congress has not seen fit to subject them to trial in federal district courts.

None of the other reasons suggested by the Government are sufficient to justify a broad construction of the constitutional grant of power to Congress to regulate the armed forces. That provision itself does not empower Congress to deprive people of trials under Bill of Rights safeguards, and we are not willing to hold that power to circumvent those safeguards should be inferred through the Necessary and Proper Clause. It is impossible to think that the discipline of the Army is going to be disrupted, its morale impaired, or its orderly processes disturbed, by giving ex-servicemen the benefit of a civilian court trial when they are actually civilians. And we are not impressed by the fact that some other countries which do not have our Bill of Rights indulge in the practice of subjecting civilians who were once soldiers to trials by courts-martial instead of trials by civilian courts.

There are dangers lurking in military trials which were sought to be avoided by the Bill of Rights and Article III of our Constitution. Free countries of the world have tried to restrict military tribunals to the narrowest jurisdiction deemed absolutely essential to maintaining discipline among troops in active service. Even as late as the Seventeenth Century standing armies and courts-martial were not established institutions in England. Court-martial jurisdiction sprang from the belief that within the military ranks there is need for a prompt, ready-at-hand means of compelling obedience and order. But Army discipline will not be improved by court-martialing rather than trying by jury some civilian ex-soldier who has been wholly separated from the service for months, years or perhaps decades. Consequently *considerations of discipline provide no excuse for new expansion of court-martial jurisdiction at the expense of the normal and constitutionally preferable system of trial by jury.*

Determining the scope of the constitutional power of Congress to authorize trial by court-martial presents another instance calling for limitation to "the least possible power adequate to the end proposed." *We hold that Congress cannot subject civilians like Toth to trial by court-martial. They, like other civilians, are entitled to have the benefit of safeguards afforded those tried in the regular courts authorized by Article III of the Constitution.*

Reversed.

---

20. *New York Times Co. v. United States*

(1971)

The majority in this landmark Supreme Court case holds that the government did not have legal authority on national security grounds to abridge press freedom and block publication of government documents related to the war in Vietnam—the so-called Pentagon Papers. The strongest view in support of First Amendment press freedoms is that expressed by Justice Hugo Black. Quite apart from First Amendment considerations, none of the justices in the majority find a statutory basis for the Courts in this case to accede to the Executive and prevent publication of the Pentagon Papers. Two justices in the majority (Stewart and White) saw possible ground for censorship as when publication would cause "direct, immediate, and irreparable damage to our Nation or its people"; however, even this concession to the government sets a very high standard they did not see met in this case: "The United States has not satisfied the very heavy burden that it must meet to warrant an injunction against publication in these cases. . . ." Dissenting justices objected to the speed with which the judiciary had moved without in their view proper consideration of facts in relation to law. In his very strong dissent Justice Blackmun also worried about damage to U.S. security interests the decision might cause: "the death of soldiers, the destruction of alliances, the greatly increased difficulty of negotiation with our enemies, the inability of our diplomats to negotiate, . . . prolongation of the war and . . . further delay in the freeing of United States prisoners."

Mr. Justice Black, with whom Mr. Justice Douglas joins, concurring. I adhere to the view that the Government's case against the Washington Post should have been dismissed, and that the injunction against the New York Times should have been vacated without oral argument when the cases were first presented to this Court. I believe that *every moment's continuance of the injunctions against these newspapers amounts to a flagrant, indefensible, and continuing violation of the First Amendment.* Furthermore, after oral argument, I agree completely that we must affirm the judgment of the Court of Appeals for the District of Columbia Circuit and reverse the judgment of the Court of Appeals for the Second Circuit for the reasons stated by my Brothers Douglas and Brennan. In my view, it is unfortunate that some of my Brethren are apparently willing to hold that the publication of news may sometimes be enjoined. Such a holding would make a shambles of the First Amendment.

Our Government was launched in 1789 with the adoption of the Constitution. The Bill of Rights, including the First Amendment, followed in 1791. Now, for the first time in the 182 years since the founding of the Republic, the federal courts are asked to hold that the First Amendment does not mean what it says, but rather means that the Government can halt the publication of current news of vital importance to the people of this country.

In seeking injunctions against these newspapers, and in its presentation to the Court, the Executive Branch seems to have forgotten the essential purpose and history of the First Amendment. When the Constitution was adopted, many people strongly opposed it because the document contained no Bill of Rights to safeguard certain basic freedoms. They especially feared that the new powers granted to a central government might be interpreted to permit the government to curtail freedom of religion, press, assembly, and speech. . . .

In the First Amendment, the Founding Fathers gave the free press the protection it must have to fulfill its essential role in our democracy. The press was to serve the governed, not the governors. The Government's power to censor the press was abolished so that the press would remain forever free to censure the Government. The press was protected so that it could bare the secrets of government and inform the people. *Only a free and unrestrained press can effectively expose deception in government.* And paramount among the responsibilities of a free press is the duty to prevent any part of the government from deceiving the people and sending them off to distant lands to die of foreign fevers and foreign shot and shell. In my view, far from deserving condemnation for their courageous reporting, the New York Times, the Washington Post, and other newspapers should be commended for serving the purpose that the Founding Fathers saw so clearly. *In revealing the workings of government that led to the Vietnam war, the newspapers nobly did precisely that which the Founders hoped and trusted they would do. . . .*

. . . The Government argues in its brief that, in spite of the First Amendment, [t]he authority of the Executive Department *to protect the nation against publication of information whose disclosure would endanger the national security stems from two interrelated sources: the constitutional power of the President over the conduct of foreign affairs and his authority as Commander-in-Chief.* . . . We are asked to hold that, despite the First Amendment's emphatic command, the Executive Branch, the Congress, and the Judiciary can make laws enjoining publication of current news and abridging freedom of the press in the name of "national security." *The Government* does not even attempt to rely on any act of Congress. Instead, it *makes the bold and dangerously far-reaching contention that the courts should take it upon themselves to "make" a law abridging freedom of the press in the name of equity, presidential power and national security, even when the representatives of the people in Congress have adhered to the command of the First Amendment and refused to make such a law. . . . To find that the President has "inherent power" to halt the publication of news by resort to the courts would wipe out the*

First Amendment and destroy the fundamental liberty and security of the very people the Government hopes to make "secure." No one can read the history of the adoption of the First Amendment without being convinced beyond any doubt that it was injunctions like those sought here that Madison and his collaborators intended to outlaw in this Nation for all time.

The word "security" is a broad, vague generality whose contours should not be invoked to abrogate the fundamental law embodied in the First Amendment. The guarding of military and diplomatic secrets at the expense of informed representative government provides no real security for our Republic. The Framers of the First Amendment, fully aware of both the need to defend a new nation and the abuses of the English and Colonial governments, sought to give this new society strength and security by providing that freedom of speech, press, religion, and assembly should not be abridged. This thought was eloquently expressed in 1937 by Mr. Chief Justice Hughes—great man and great Chief Justice that he was—when the Court held a man could not be punished for attending a meeting run by Communists.

The greater the importance of safeguarding the community from incitements to the overthrow of our institutions by force and violence, the more imperative is the need to preserve inviolate the constitutional rights of free speech, free press and free assembly in order to maintain the opportunity for free political discussion, to the end that government may be responsive to the will of the people and that changes, if desired, may be obtained by peaceful means. Therein lies the security of the Republic, the very foundation of constitutional government. . . .

Mr. Justice Douglas, with whom Mr. Justice Black joins, concurring. While I join the opinion of the Court, I believe it necessary to express my views more fully. It should be noted at the outset that the First Amendment provides that "Congress shall make no law . . . abridging the freedom of speech, or of the press." That leaves, in my view, *no room for governmental restraint on the press.* There is, moreover, no statute barring the publication by the press of the material which the Times and the Post seek to use. . . . It is apparent that Congress was capable of, and did, distinguish between publishing and communication in the various sections of the Espionage Act. . . . Moreover, the Act of September 23, 1950, in amending 18 U.S.C. § 793 states in § 1(b) that: *Nothing in this Act shall be construed to authorize, require, or establish military or civilian censorship or in any way to limit or infringe upon freedom of the press or of speech as guaranteed by the Constitution of the United States and no regulation shall be promulgated hereunder having that effect. . . . Thus, Congress has been faithful to the command of the First Amendment in this area. . . .*

Mr. Justice Brennan, concurring. I write separately in these cases only to emphasize what should be apparent: that our judgments in the present cases may not be taken to indicate the propriety, in the future, of issuing temporary stays and restraining orders to block the publication of material sought to be suppressed by the Government. *So far as I can determine, never before has the United States sought to enjoin a newspaper from publishing information in its possession. . . . The First Amendment stands as an absolute bar to the imposition of judicial restraints in circumstances of the kind presented by these cases.* The error that has pervaded these cases from the outset was the granting of any injunctive relief whatsoever, interim or otherwise. . . .

There is no question but that the material sought to be suppressed is within the protection of the First Amendment; the only question is whether, notwithstanding that fact, its publication may be enjoined for a time because of the presence of an overwhelming national interest. Similarly, copyright cases have no pertinence here: the Government is not asserting an interest in the particular form of words chosen in the documents, but is seeking to suppress the ideas expressed therein. And the copyright laws, of course, protect only the form of expression, and not the ideas expressed.

Mr. Justice Stewart, with whom Mr. Justice White joins, concurring. *In the governmental structure created by our Constitution, the Executive is endowed with enormous power in the two related areas of national defense and international relations.* This power, largely unchecked by the Legislative and Judicial branches, has been pressed to the very hilt since the advent of the nuclear missile age. For better or for worse, the simple fact is that a President of the United States possesses vastly greater constitutional independence in these two vital areas of power than does, say, a prime minister of a country with a parliamentary form of government.

In the absence of the governmental checks and balances present in other areas of our national life, the only effective restraint upon executive policy and power in the areas of national defense and international affairs may lie in an enlightened citizenry—in an informed and critical public opinion which alone can here protect the values of democratic government. For this reason, it is perhaps here that a press that is alert, aware, and free most vitally serves the basic purpose of the First Amendment. For, without an informed and free press, there cannot be an enlightened people.

Yet it is elementary that the successful conduct of international diplomacy and the maintenance of an effective national defense require both confidentiality and secrecy. Other nations can hardly deal with this Nation in an atmosphere of mutual trust unless they can be assured that their confidences will be kept. And, within our own executive departments, the development of considered and intelligent international policies would be impossible if those charged with their formulation could not communicate with each other freely, frankly, and in confidence. *In the area of basic national defense, the frequent need for absolute secrecy is, of course, self-evident.*

I think there can be but one answer to this dilemma, if dilemma it be. The responsibility must be where the power is. If the Constitution gives the Executive a large degree of unshared power in the conduct of foreign affairs and the maintenance of our national defense, then, under the Constitution, *the Executive must have the largely unshared duty to determine and preserve the degree of internal security necessary to exercise that power successfully.* It is an awesome responsibility, requiring judgment and wisdom of a high order. I should suppose that moral, political, and practical considerations would dictate that a very first principle of that wisdom would be an insistence upon avoiding secrecy for its own sake. For when everything is classified, then nothing is classified, and the system becomes one to be disregarded by the cynical or the careless, and to be manipulated by those intent on self-protection or self-promotion. I should suppose, in short, that the hallmark of a truly effective internal security system would be the maximum possible disclosure, recognizing that secrecy can best be preserved only when credibility is truly maintained. But, be that as it may, *it is clear to me that it is the constitutional duty of the Executive*—as a matter of sovereign prerogative, and not as a matter of law as the courts know law—through

the promulgation and enforcement of executive regulations, *to protect the confidentiality necessary to carry out its responsibilities in the fields of international relations and national defense.*

This is not to say that Congress and the courts have no role to play. Undoubtedly, Congress has the power to enact specific and appropriate criminal laws to protect government property and preserve government secrets. Congress has passed such laws, and several of them are of very colorable relevance to the apparent circumstances of these cases. And if a criminal prosecution is instituted, it will be the responsibility of the courts to decide the applicability of the criminal law under which the charge is brought. Moreover, if Congress should pass a specific law authorizing civil proceedings in this field, the courts would likewise have the duty to decide the constitutionality of such a law, as well as its applicability to the facts proved.

But in the cases before us, we are asked neither to construe specific regulations nor to apply specific laws. We are asked, instead, to perform a function that the Constitution gave to the Executive, not the Judiciary. We are asked, quite simply, to prevent the publication by two newspapers of material that the Executive Branch insists should not, in the national interest, be published. I am convinced that the Executive is correct with respect to some of the documents involved. But *I cannot say that disclosure of any of them will surely result in direct, immediate, and irreparable damage to our Nation or its people. That being so, there can under the First Amendment be but one judicial resolution of the issues before us.* I join the judgments of the Court.

Mr. Justice White, with whom Mr. Justice Stewart joins, concurring. I concur in today's judgments, but only because of the concededly extraordinary protection against prior restraints enjoyed by the press under our constitutional system. *I do not say that in no circumstances would the First Amendment permit an injunction against publishing information about government plans or operations.* Nor, after examining the materials the Government characterizes as the most sensitive and destructive, can I deny that revelation of these documents will do substantial damage to public interests. Indeed, I am confident that their disclosure will have that result. *But I nevertheless agree that the United States has not satisfied the very heavy burden that it must meet to warrant an injunction against publication in these cases,* at least in the absence of express and appropriately limited congressional authorization for prior restraints in circumstances such as these. . . .

It is thus clear that *Congress has addressed itself to the problems of protecting the security of the country and the national defense from unauthorized disclosure of potentially damaging information. . . . It has not, however, authorized the injunctive remedy against threatened publication.* It has apparently been satisfied to rely on criminal sanctions and their deterrent effect on the responsible, as well as the irresponsible, press. I am not, of course, saying that either of these newspapers has yet committed a crime, or that either would commit a crime if it published all the material now in its possession. That matter must await resolution in the context of a criminal proceeding if one is instituted by the United States. In that event, the issue of guilt or innocence would be determined by procedures and standards quite different from those that have purported to govern these injunctive proceedings.

Mr. Justice Marshall, concurring. . . . I believe the ultimate issue in these cases is . . . whether this Court or the Congress has the power to make law. . . . The problem here is whether, in these particular cases, the Executive Branch has authority to invoke the equity jurisdiction of the courts to protect what it believes to be the national interest. . . . *In some situations,* it may be that, under whatever inherent powers the Government may have, as well as the implicit authority derived from the President's mandate to conduct foreign affairs and to act as Commander in Chief, *there is a basis for the invocation of the equity jurisdiction of this Court as an aid to prevent the publication of material damaging to "national security," however that term may be defined.*

It would, however, *be utterly inconsistent with the concept of separation of powers for this Court to use its power of contempt to prevent behavior that Congress has specifically declined to prohibit.* There would be a similar damage to the basic concept of these co-equal branches of Government if, when the Executive Branch has adequate authority granted by Congress to protect "national security," it can choose, instead, to invoke the contempt power of a court to enjoin the threatened conduct. . . .

In these cases, we are not faced with a situation where Congress has failed to provide the Executive with broad power to protect the Nation from disclosure of damaging state secrets. Congress has, on several occasions, given extensive consideration to the problem of protecting the military and strategic secrets of the United States. This consideration has resulted in the enactment of statutes making it a crime to receive, disclose, communicate, withhold, and publish certain documents, photographs, instruments, appliances, and information. The bulk of these statutes is found in chapter 37 of U.S.C. Title 18, entitled Espionage and Censorship. . . . *It is clear that Congress has specifically rejected passing legislation that would have clearly given the President the power he seeks here* and made the current activity of the newspapers unlawful. . . .

Either the Government has the power under statutory grant to use traditional criminal law to protect the country or, if there is no basis for arguing that Congress has made the activity a crime, it is plain that Congress has specifically refused to grant the authority the Government seeks from this Court. In either case, this Court does not have authority to grant the requested relief. *It is not for this Court to fling itself into every breach perceived by some Government official, nor is it for this Court to take on itself the burden of enacting law, especially a law that Congress has refused to pass.* . . .

Mr. Chief Justice Burger, dissenting. . . . The imperative of a free and unfettered press comes into collision with another imperative, the effective functioning of a complex modern government, and, specifically, the effective exercise of certain constitutional powers of the Executive. Only those who view the First Amendment as an absolute in all circumstances—a view I respect, but reject—can find such cases as these to be simple or easy. . . . These cases are not simple for another and more immediate reason. We do not know the facts of the cases. . . .

I suggest we are in this posture because these cases have been conducted in unseemly haste. . . . The precipitate action of this Court aborting trials not yet completed is not the kind of judicial conduct that ought to attend the disposition of a great issue. . . . An issue of this importance should be tried and heard in a judicial atmosphere conducive to thoughtful, reflective deliberation, especially when haste, in terms of hours, is unwarranted in light of the long period the Times, by its own choice, deferred publication. . . . We all crave speedier judicial processes, but, when judges are pressured, as in these cases, the result is a parody of the judicial function.

Mr. Justice Harlan, with whom The Chief Justice and Mr. Justice Blackmun join, dissenting. . . . I consider that the Court has been almost irresponsibly feverish in dealing with these cases. . . . In order to decide the merits of these cases properly, some or all of the following questions should have been faced: 1. Whether the Attorney General is authorized to bring these suits in the name of the United States. . . . 2. Whether the First Amendment permits the federal courts to enjoin publication of stories which would present a serious threat to national security. . . . 3. Whether the threat to publish highly secret documents is of itself a sufficient implication of national security to justify an injunction on the theory that, regardless of the contents of the documents, harm enough results simply from the demonstration of such a breach of secrecy. 4. Whether the unauthorized disclosure of any of these particular documents would seriously impair the national security. 5. What weight should be given to the opinion of high officers in the Executive Branch of the Government with respect to questions 3 and 4. 6. Whether the newspapers are entitled to retain and use the documents notwithstanding the seemingly uncontested facts that the documents, or the originals of which they are duplicates, were purloined from the Government's possession, and that the newspapers received them with knowledge that they had been feloniously acquired. . . . 7. Whether the threatened harm to the national security or the Government's possessory interest in the documents justifies the issuance of an injunction against publication in light of— a. The strong First Amendment policy against prior restraints on publication;

b. The doctrine against enjoining conduct in violation of criminal statutes; and c. The extent to which the materials at issue have apparently already been otherwise disseminated.

These are difficult questions of fact, of law, and of judgment; the potential consequences of erroneous decision are enormous. The time which has been available to us . . . has been wholly inadequate for giving these cases the kind of consideration they deserve. . . . Forced as I am to reach the merits of these cases, I dissent from the opinion and judgments of the Court. . . .

I think there is another and more fundamental reason why this judgment cannot stand. . . . *It is plain to me that the scope of the judicial function in passing upon the activities of the Executive Branch of the Government in the field of foreign affairs is very narrowly restricted.* This view is, I think, dictated by the concept of separation of powers upon which our constitutional system rests. . . . I agree that, in performance of its duty to protect the values of the First Amendment against political pressures, *the judiciary must review the initial Executive determination to the point of satisfying itself that the subject matter of the dispute does lie within the proper compass of the President's foreign relations power.* . . . Moreover, the judiciary may properly insist that the determination that disclosure of the subject matter would irreparably impair the national security be made by the head of the Executive Department concerned—here, the Secretary of State or the Secretary of Defense—after actual personal consideration by that officer. This safeguard is required in the analogous area of executive claims of privilege for secrets of state. . . .

But, in my judgment, the judiciary may not properly go beyond these two inquiries and redetermine for itself the probable impact of disclosure on the national

security. . . . Even if there is some room for the judiciary to override the executive determination, it is plain that the scope of review must be exceedingly narrow. . . . Accordingly, . . . pending further hearings in each case conducted under the appropriate ground rules, *I would continue the restraints on publication. I cannot believe that the doctrine prohibiting prior restraints reaches to the point of preventing courts from maintaining the* status quo *long enough to act responsibly in matters of such national importance as those involved here.*

Mr. Justice Blackmun, dissenting. I join Mr. Justice Harlan in his dissent. I also am in substantial accord with much that Mr. Justice White says, by way of admonition, in the latter part of his opinion. . . . The country would be none the worse off were the cases tried quickly, to be sure, but in the customary and properly deliberative manner. . . .

The First Amendment, after all, is only one part of an entire Constitution. Article II of the great document vests in the Executive Branch primary power over the conduct of foreign affairs, and places in that branch the responsibility for the Nation's safety. Each provision of the Constitution is important, and I cannot subscribe to a doctrine of unlimited absolutism for the First Amendment at the cost of downgrading other provisions. First Amendment absolutism has never commanded a majority of this Court. . . . *What is needed here is a weighing, upon properly developed standards, of the broad right of the press to print and of the very narrow right of the Government to prevent.* Such standards are not yet developed. The parties here are in disagreement as to what those standards should be. . . . Mr. Justice Holmes gave us a suggestion when he said in *Schenck:* "It is a question of proximity and degree. When a nation is at war, many things that might be said in time of peace are such a hindrance to its effort that their utterance will not be endured so long as men fight and that no Court could regard them as protected by any constitutional right."

. . . It may well be that, if these cases were allowed to develop as they should be developed, and to be tried as lawyers should try them and as courts should hear them, free of pressure and panic and sensationalism, other light would be shed on the situation, and contrary considerations, for me, might prevail. . . . The Court, however, decides the cases today the other way. I

therefore add one final comment. I strongly urge, and sincerely hope, that these two newspapers will be fully aware of their ultimate responsibilities to the United States of America. . . . If, with the Court's action today, these newspapers proceed to publish the critical documents and there results therefrom *the death of soldiers, the destruction of alliances, the greatly increased difficulty of negotiation with our enemies, the inability of our diplomats to negotiate,* to which list I might add the factors of *prolongation of the war* and of *further delay in the freeing of United States prisoners,* then the Nation's people will know where the responsibility for these sad consequences rests.

---

21. *Zadvydas v. Davis et al.*

(2001)

This case was decided in June 2001, before the terrorist attacks on the World Trade Center in New York City and the Pentagon in Washington, D.C., on September 11 of that year. Constitutional rights are specified in Zadvydas vs. Davis et al. *that apply to all "persons" within the United States, whether citizens or aliens. Consistent with this decision, the executive branch has not deemed terrorist-suspect detainees held at Guantánamo in Cuba (or elsewhere outside the United States) as entitled to the same constitutionally based protections that might otherwise have been afforded to the detainees were they held on U.S. soil. Even if a U.S. base in Cuba were construed to be subject to this decision, exceptions relating to terrorist suspects or others posing "danger to the community" likely would be invoked by the executive branch as a matter of law. Indeed, the Supreme Court does acknowledge a dangerousness rationale for indefinite detention as in the special circumstances created by terrorist threats; however, such special-circumstance provisions directed against terrorists and criminals are not to be applied indiscriminately to all aliens.*

Justice Breyer delivered the opinion of the Court.

When an alien has been found to be unlawfully present in the United States and a final order of removal has been entered, the Government ordinarily secures the alien's removal during a subsequent 90-day statutory "removal period," during which time the alien normally is held in custody.

A special statute authorizes further detention if the Government fails to remove the alien during those 90 days. It says:

"An alien ordered removed [1] *who is inadmissible* . . . [2] [or] *removable* [as a result of violations of status requirements or entry conditions, violations of criminal law, or reasons of security or foreign policy] or [3] *who has been determined by the*

Attorney General to be a risk to the community or unlikely to comply with the order of removal, may be detained beyond the removal period and, if released, shall be subject to [certain] terms of supervision. . . ."

In these cases, we must decide whether this post-removal-period statute authorizes the Attorney General to detain a removable alien indefinitely *beyond the removal period or only for a period* reasonably necessary *to secure the alien's removal. We deal here with aliens who were admitted to the United States but subsequently ordered removed.* Aliens who have not yet gained initial admission to this country would present a very different question. . . . *Based on our conclusion that indefinite detention of aliens* in the former category *would raise serious constitutional concerns, we construe the statute to contain an implicit "reasonable time" limitation, the application of which is subject to federal court review. . . .*

We consider two separate instances of detention. . . . We consolidated the two cases for argument; and we now decide them together. We note at the outset that the primary federal habeas corpus statute, . . . confers jurisdiction upon the federal courts to hear these cases. . . .

The post-removal-period detention statute applies to certain categories of aliens who have been ordered removed, namely inadmissible aliens, criminal aliens, aliens who have violated their nonimmigrant status conditions, and aliens removable for certain national security or foreign relations reasons, as well as *any alien "who has been determined by the Attorney General to be a risk to the community or unlikely to comply with the order of removal."* . . . It says that an alien who falls into one of these categories "may be detained beyond the removal period and, if released, shall be subject to [certain] terms of supervision." . . .

The Government argues that the statute means what it literally says. It sets no "limit on the length of time beyond the removal period that an alien who falls within one of the Section 1231(a)(6) categories may be detained." . . . Hence, "whether to continue to detain such an alien and, if so, in what circumstances and for how long" is up to the Attorney General, not up to the courts. . . .

"[I]t is a cardinal principle" of statutory interpretation, however, that when an Act of Congress raises "a serious doubt" as to its constitutionality, "this Court will first ascertain whether a construction of the statute is fairly possible by which the question may be avoided." . . . We have read significant limitations into other immigration statutes in order to avoid their constitutional invalidation . . . (construing a grant of authority to the Attorney General to ask aliens whatever questions he "deem[s] fit and proper" as limited to questions "reasonably calculated to keep the Attorney General advised regarding the continued availability for departure of aliens whose deportation is overdue"). For similar reasons, we read an implicit limitation into the statute before us. *In our view, the statute, read in light of the Constitution's demands,* limits an alien's post-removal-period detention to a period reasonably necessary to bring about that alien's removal from the United States. It *does not permit indefinite detention.*

A statute permitting indefinite detention of an alien would raise a serious constitutional problem. The Fifth Amendment's Due Process Clause forbids the Government to "depriv[e]" any "person of . . . liberty . . . without due process of law." Freedom from imprisonment—from government custody, detention, or other forms of physical restraint—lies at the heart of the liberty that Clause protects. . . .

The second justification—protecting the community—does not necessarily diminish in force over time. But *we have upheld preventive detention based on dangerousness only when limited to specially dangerous individuals and subject to strong procedural protections. . . . In cases in which preventive detention is of potentially* indefinite *duration, we have also demanded that the dangerousness rationale be accompanied by some other special circumstance,* such as mental illness, *that helps to create the danger.*

The civil confinement here at issue is not limited, but potentially permanent. . . . *The provision authorizing detention does not apply narrowly to "a small segment of particularly dangerous individuals,". . . say suspected terrorists,* but broadly to aliens ordered removed for many and various reasons, including tourist visa violations. . . . And, once the flight risk justification evaporates, the only special circumstance present is the alien's removable status itself, which bears no relation to a detainee's dangerousness. . . .

Moreover, the sole procedural protections available to the alien are found in administrative proceedings, where the alien bears the burden of proving he is not dangerous, without (in the Government's view) significant later judicial review. . . . This Court has suggested, however, that the Constitution may well preclude granting "an administrative body the unreviewable authority to make determinations implicating fundamental rights." . . . *The serious constitutional problem arising out of a statute that, in these circumstances, permits an indefinite, perhaps permanent, deprivation of human liberty without any such protection is obvious. . . .*

The distinction between an alien who has effected an entry into the United States and one who has never entered runs throughout immigration law. . . . *It is well established that certain constitutional protections available to persons inside the United States are unavailable to aliens outside of our geographic borders. . . .* (Fifth Amendment's protections do not extend to aliens outside the territorial boundaries). . . . But once an alien enters the country, the legal circumstance changes, for the Due Process Clause applies to all "persons" within the United States, including aliens, whether their presence here is lawful, unlawful, temporary, or permanent. . . . ("[A]liens who have once passed through our gates, even illegally, may be expelled only after proceedings conforming to traditional standards of fairness encompassed in due process of law"). Indeed, *this Court has held that the Due Process Clause protects an alien subject to a final order of deportation, . . . though the nature of that protection may vary depending upon status and circumstance. . . .*

In *Wong Wing* . . . the Court held unconstitutional a statute that imposed a year of hard labor upon aliens subject to a final deportation order. That case concerned substantive protections for aliens who had been ordered removed, not procedural protections for aliens whose removability was being determined. . . . The Court held that punitive measures could not be imposed upon aliens ordered removed because *"all persons within the territory of the United States are entitled to the protection"* of the Constitution. . . .

The Government also looks for support to cases holding that Congress has "plenary power" to create immigration law, and that the judicial branch must defer to executive and legislative branch decisionmaking in that area. . . . But that power is subject to important constitutional limitations. . . . We focus upon those limitations. In doing so, we nowhere deny the right of Congress to remove aliens, to subject them to supervision with conditions when released from detention, or to incarcerate them where appropriate for violations of those conditions. . . . The question before us is not one of "confer[ring] on those admitted the right to remain against the national will" or "sufferance of aliens" who should be removed. . . . Rather, *the issue we address is whether aliens that the Government finds itself unable to remove are to be condemned to an indefinite term of imprisonment within the United States.*

Nor do the cases before us require us to consider the political branches' authority to control entry into the United States. Hence we leave no "unprotected spot in the Nation's armor." . . . *Neither do we consider terrorism or other special circumstances where special arguments might be made for forms of preventive detention and for heightened deference to the judgments of the political branches with respect to matters of national security. The sole foreign policy consideration the Government mentions here is the concern lest courts interfere with "sensitive" repatriation negotiations. . . .* But neither the Government nor the dissents explain how a habeas court's efforts to determine the likelihood of repatriation, if handled with appropriate sensitivity, could make a significant difference in this respect. . . .

Finally, the Government argues that, whatever liberty interest the aliens possess, it is "greatly diminished" by their lack of a legal right to "liv[e] at large in this country." . . . The choice, however, is not between imprisonment and the alien "living at large." . . . It is between imprisonment and supervision under release conditions that may not be violated. . . . And, for the reasons we have set forth, *we believe that an alien's liberty interest is, at the least, strong enough to raise a serious question as to whether, irrespective of the proce-* dures *used, . . . the Constitution permits detention that is indefinite and potentially permanent.*

Despite this constitutional problem, *if* "Congress has made its intent" in the statute "clear, 'we must give effect to that intent.'" . . . *We cannot find here,* however, *any clear indication of congressional intent to grant the Attorney General the power to hold indefinitely in confinement an alien ordered removed. And that is so whether protecting the community from dangerous aliens is a primary or (as we believe) secondary statutory purpose. . . .* But *the statute before us applies not only to terrorists and criminals, but also to ordinary visa violators. . . .*

We have found nothing in the history of these statutes that clearly demonstrates a congressional intent to authorize indefinite, perhaps permanent, detention. Consequently, interpreting the statute to avoid a serious constitutional threat, we conclude that, *once removal is no longer reasonably foreseeable, continued detention is no longer authorized by statute. . . .*

The Government seems to argue that, even under our interpretation of the statute, a federal habeas court would have to accept the Government's view about whether the implicit statutory limitation is satisfied in a particular case, conducting little or no independent review of the matter. In our view, that is not so. *Whether a set of particular circumstances amounts to detention within, or beyond, a period reasonably necessary to secure removal is determinative of whether the detention is, or is not, pursuant to statutory authority. The basic federal habeas corpus statute grants the federal courts authority to answer that question . . . (granting courts authority to determine whether detention is "in violation of the . . . laws . . . of the United States"). In doing so the courts carry out what this Court has described as the "historic purpose of the writ," namely "to relieve detention by executive authorities without judicial trial."* . . .

In answering that basic question, the habeas court must ask whether the detention in question exceeds a period reasonably necessary to secure removal. It should measure reasonableness primarily in terms of the statute's basic purpose, namely assuring the alien's presence at the moment of removal. . . . And if removal is reasonably foreseeable, the habeas court should consider the risk of the alien's committing further crimes as a factor potentially justifying confinement within that reasonable removal period. . . .

Ordinary principles of judicial review in this area recognize primary Executive Branch responsibility. They counsel judges to give expert agencies decisionmaking leeway in matters that invoke their expertise. . . . They *recognize Executive Branch primacy in foreign policy matters. . . . And they consequently require courts to listen with care when the Government's foreign policy judgments, including, for example, the status of repatriation negotiations, are at issue, and to grant the Government appropriate leeway* when its judgments rest upon foreign policy expertise.

We realize that recognizing this necessary Executive leeway will often call for difficult judgments. In order to limit the occasions when courts will need to make them, we think it practically necessary to recognize some presumptively reasonable period of detention. We have adopted similar presumptions in other contexts to guide lower court determinations. . . . We do have reason to believe . . . that Congress previously doubted the constitutionality of detention for more than six months. . . . Consequently, for the sake of uniform administration in the federal courts, we recognize that period. . . . This 6-month presumption, of course, does not mean that every alien not removed must be released after six months. To the contrary, *an alien may be held in confinement until it has been determined that there is no significant likelihood of removal in the reasonably foreseeable future. . . .*

We vacate the decisions below and remand both cases for further proceedings consistent with this opinion.

---

22. *The USA Patriot Act*

(October 24, 2001)

In the aftermath of terrorist attacks on September 11, 2001, Congress passed a statute "Uniting and Strengthening America by Providing Appropriate Tools Required to Intercept and Obstruct Terrorism (USA PATRIOT ACT) Act of 2001," a law strengthening substantially domestic law enforcement capabilities and placing greater restriction on immigration. As always, efforts taken to provide security by enhancing law and order are prone to intrude on privacy and other civil liberties; however, given deep concern for the threat posed by terrorism to national (or homeland) security, the majority in both houses of Congress were willing to make this trade-off. Because of concern for civil liberties over the longer run, the statute does have "sunset" provisions, most of the new governmental authority provisions expiring automatically over time unless specifically renewed by Congress. Because the statute is so lengthy and complex, we include for the reader's reference a partial table of contents that indicates how broad in scope the Patriot Act is. We reprint only a few of the statute's provisions.

AN ACT

To deter and punish terrorist acts in the United States and around the world, to enhance law enforcement investigatory tools, and for other purposes.

Be it enacted by the Senate and House of Representatives of the United States of America in Congress assembled,

Sec. 1. SHORT TITLE AND TABLE OF CONTENTS.

a. SHORT TITLE-This Act may be cited as the 'Uniting and Strengthening America by Providing Appropriate Tools Required to Intercept and Obstruct Terrorism (USA PATRIOT ACT) Act of 2001.'

b. TABLE OF CONTENTS-The table of contents for this Act is as follows: . . .

TITLE I—ENHANCING DOMESTIC SECURITY AGAINST TERRORISM.

Sec. 101. COUNTERTERRORISM FUND.

Sec. 102. SENSE OF CONGRESS CONDEMNING DISCRIMINATION AGAINST ARAB AND MUSLIM AMERICANS.

a. FINDINGS—Congress makes the following findings:

1. Arab Americans, Muslim Americans, and Americans from South Asia play a vital role in our Nation and are entitled to nothing less than the full rights of every American.
2. The acts of violence that have been taken against Arab and Muslim Americans since the September 11, 2001, attacks against the United States should be and are condemned by all Americans who value freedom.
3. The concept of individual responsibility for wrongdoing is sacrosanct in American society, and applies equally to all religious, racial, and ethnic groups.
4. When American citizens commit acts of violence against those who are, or are perceived to be, of Arab or Muslim descent, they should be punished to the full extent of the law.
5. Muslim Americans have become so fearful of harassment that many Muslim women are changing the way they dress to avoid becoming targets.
6. Many Arab Americans and Muslim Americans have acted heroically during the attacks on the United States. . . .

b. SENSE OF CONGRESS—It is the sense of Congress that—

1. the civil rights and civil liberties of all Americans, including Arab Americans, Muslim Americans, and Americans from South Asia, must be protected, and that every effort must be taken to preserve their safety;
2. any acts of violence or discrimination against any Americans be condemned; and
3. the Nation is called upon to recognize the patriotism of fellow citizens from all ethnic, racial, and religious backgrounds.

Sec. 103. INCREASED FUNDING FOR THE TECHNICAL SUPPORT CENTER AT THE FEDERAL BUREAU OF INVESTIGATION.

Sec. 104. REQUESTS FOR MILITARY ASSISTANCE TO ENFORCE PROHIBITION IN CERTAIN EMERGENCIES.

Sec. 105. EXPANSION OF NATIONAL ELECTRONIC CRIME TASK FORCE INITIATIVE.

Sec. 106. PRESIDENTIAL AUTHORITY.

TITLE II—ENHANCED SURVEILLANCE PROCEDURES

Sec. 201. Authority to intercept wire, oral, and electronic communications relating to terrorism.

SEC. 2. CONSTRUCTION; SEVERABILITY.

Any provision of this Act held to be invalid or unenforceable by its terms, or as applied to any person or circumstance, shall be construed so as to give it the maximum effect permitted by law, unless such holding shall be one of utter invalidity or unenforceability, in which event such provision shall be deemed severable from this Act and shall not affect the remainder thereof or the application of such provision to other persons not similarly situated or to other, dissimilar circumstances.

---

23. Detention, Treatment, and Trial of Certain Non-Citizens in the War Against Terrorism

(November 13, 2001)

Given what is defined as a national emergency, we have here an executive order from the president that enhances law enforcement authority in relation to non-citizens, allowing for their detention inside or outside the United States and trial by military tribunal under authority of the secretary of defense. A person who is subject to this order "shall mean any individual who is not a United States citizen" and "there is reason to believe that such individual, at the relevant times, (i) is or was a member of the organization known as al Qaida; (ii) has engaged in, aided or abetted, or conspired to commit, acts of international terrorism, or acts in preparation therefor, that have caused, threaten to cause, or have as their aim to cause, injury to or adverse effects on the United States, its citizens, national security, foreign policy, or economy; or (iii) has knowingly harbored one or more [such] individuals."

President Issues Military Order
By the authority vested in me as President and as Commander in Chief of the Armed Forces of the United States by the Constitution and the laws of the United States of America, including the Authorization for Use of Military Force Joint Resolution . . . , United States Code, it is hereby ordered as follows:

Sec. 1. Findings.
a. International terrorists, including members of al Qaida, have carried out attacks on United States diplomatic and military personnel and facilities abroad and on citizens and property within the United States on a scale that has created a state of armed conflict that requires the use of the United States Armed Forces.

b. In light of grave acts of terrorism and threats of terrorism, including the terrorist attacks on September 11, 2001, on the headquarters of the United States Department of Defense in the national capital region, on the World Trade Center in New York, and on civilian aircraft such as in Pennsylvania, I proclaimed a national emergency on September 14, 2001. . . .

c. Individuals acting alone and in concert involved in international terrorism possess both the capability and the intention to undertake further terrorist attacks against the United States that, if not detected and prevented, will cause mass deaths, mass injuries, and massive destruction of property, and may place at risk the continuity of the operations of the United States Government.

d. The ability of the United States to protect the United States and its citizens, and to help its allies and other cooperating nations protect their nations and their citizens, from such further terrorist attacks depends in significant part upon using the United States Armed Forces to identify terrorists and those who support them, to disrupt their activities, and to eliminate their ability to conduct or support such attacks.

e. To protect the United States and its citizens, and for the effective conduct of military operations and prevention of terrorist attacks, it is necessary for individuals subject to this order pursuant to section 2 hereof to be detained, and, when tried, to be tried for violations of the laws of war and other applicable laws by military tribunals.

f. Given the danger to the safety of the United States and the nature of international terrorism, and to the extent provided by and under this order . . . that it is not practicable to apply in military commissions under this order the principles of law and the rules of evidence generally recognized in the trial of criminal cases in the United States district courts.

g. Having fully considered the magnitude of the potential deaths, injuries, and property destruction that would result from potential acts of terrorism against the United States, and the probability that such acts will occur, I have determined that an extraordinary emergency exists for national defense purposes, that this emergency constitutes an urgent and compelling government interest, and that issuance of this order is necessary to meet the emergency.

Sec. 2. Definition and Policy.
a. The term "individual subject to this order" shall mean any individual who is not a United States citizen with respect to whom I determine from time to time in writing that:

1. there is reason to believe that such individual, at the relevant times,

   i. is or was a member of the organization known as al Qaida;

   ii. has engaged in, aided or abetted, or conspired to commit, acts of international terrorism, or acts in preparation therefor, that have caused, threaten to cause, or have as their aim to cause, injury to or adverse effects on the United States, its citizens, national security, foreign policy, or economy; or

   iii. has knowingly harbored one or more individuals described in subparagraphs (i) or (ii) of subsection 2(a)(1) of this order; and

2. it is in the interest of the United States that such individual be subject to this order.

b. It is the policy of the United States that the Secretary of Defense shall take all necessary measures to ensure that any individual subject to this order is detained in accordance with section 3, and, if the individual is to be tried, that such individual is tried only in accordance with section 4.

c. It is further the policy of the United States that any individual subject to this order who is not already under the control of the Secretary of Defense but who is under the control of any other officer or agent of the United States or any State shall, upon delivery of a copy of such written determination to such officer or agent, forthwith be placed under the control of the Secretary of Defense.

Sec. 3. Detention Authority of the Secretary of Defense. Any individual subject to this order shall be—

a. detained at an appropriate location designated by the Secretary of Defense outside or within the United States;

b. treated humanely, without any adverse distinction based on race, color, religion, gender, birth, wealth, or any similar criteria;

c. afforded adequate food, drinking water, shelter, clothing, and medical treatment;

d. allowed the free exercise of religion consistent with the requirements of such detention; and

e. detained in accordance with such other conditions as the Secretary of Defense may prescribe.

Sec. 4. Authority of the Secretary of Defense Regarding Trials of Individuals Subject to this Order.

a. Any individual subject to this order shall, when tried, be tried by military commission for any and all offenses triable by military commission that such individual is alleged to have committed, and may be punished in accordance with the penalties provided under applicable law, including life imprisonment or death.

b. As a military function and in light of the findings in section 1, including subsection (f) thereof, the Secretary of Defense shall issue such orders and regulations, including orders for the appointment of one or more military commissions, as may be necessary to carry out subsection (a) of this section.

c. Orders and regulations issued under subsection (b) of this section shall include, but not be limited to, rules for the conduct of the proceedings of military commissions, including pretrial, trial, and post-trial procedures, modes of proof, issuance of process, and qualifications of attorneys, which shall at a minimum provide for—

1. military commissions to sit at any time and any place, consistent with such guidance regarding time and place as the Secretary of Defense may provide;

2. a full and fair trial, with the military commission sitting as the triers of both fact and law;

3. admission of such evidence as would, in the opinion of the presiding officer of the military commission (or instead, if any other member of the commission so requests at the time the presiding officer renders that opinion, the opinion of the commission rendered at that time by a majority of the commission), have probative value to a reasonable person;

4. in a manner consistent with the protection of information . . . classified or classifiable. . . , (A) the handling of, admission into evidence of, and access to materials and information, and (B) the conduct, closure of, and access to proceedings;

5. conduct of the prosecution by one or more attorneys designated by the Secretary of Defense and conduct of the defense by attorneys for the individual subject to this order;

6. conviction only upon the concurrence of two-thirds of the members of the commission present at the time of the vote, a majority being present;

7. sentencing only upon the concurrence of two-thirds of the members of the commission present at the time of the vote, a majority being present; and

8. submission of the record of the trial, including any conviction or

sentence, for review and final decision by me or by the Secretary of Defense if so designated by me for that purpose.

Sec. 5. Obligation of Other Agencies to Assist the Secretary of Defense.
Departments, agencies, entities, and officers of the United States shall, to the maximum extent permitted by law, provide to the Secretary of Defense such assistance as he may request to implement this order.

Sec. 6. Additional Authorities of the Secretary of Defense.
a. As a military function and in light of the findings in section 1, the Secretary of Defense shall issue such orders and regulations as may be necessary to carry out any of the provisions of this order.
b. The Secretary of Defense may perform any of his functions or duties, and may exercise any of the powers provided to him under this order. . . .

Sec. 7. Relationship to Other Law and Forums.
a. Nothing in this order shall be construed to—(1) authorize the disclosure of state secrets to any person not otherwise authorized to have access to them; (2) limit the authority of the President as Commander in Chief of the Armed Forces or the power of the President to grant reprieves and pardons; or (3) limit the lawful authority of the Secretary of Defense, any military commander, or any other officer or agent of the United States or of any State to detain or try any person who is not an individual subject to this order.

b. With respect to any individual subject to this order—
   1. military tribunals shall have exclusive jurisdiction with respect to offenses by the individual; and
   2. the individual shall not be privileged to seek any remedy or maintain any proceeding, directly or indirectly, or to have any such remedy or proceeding sought on the individual's behalf, in (i) any court of the United States, or any State thereof, (ii) any court of any foreign nation, or (iii) any international tribunal.
c. This order is not intended to and does not create any right, benefit, or privilege, substantive or procedural, enforceable at law or equity by any party, against the United States, its departments, agencies, or other entities, its officers or employees, or any other person.
d. For purposes of this order, the term "State" includes any State, district, territory, or possession of the United States.
e. I reserve the authority to direct the Secretary of Defense, at any time hereafter, to transfer to a governmental authority control of any individual subject to this order. Nothing in this order shall be construed to limit the authority of any such governmental authority to prosecute any individual for whom control is transferred.

Sec. 8. Publication.
This order shall be published in the Federal Register.

GEORGE W. BUSH
THE WHITE HOUSE,
November 13, 2001.

PART THREE

Statements on Foreign and National Security Policy

Chapter 9

Pre–World War II:
Foreign Policy and
National Security Statements

1. Espionage and Betrayal:
John André and Benedict Arnold

(1780)

As commander of the Continental Army during the Revolutionary War, General George Washington drew a sharp distinction between spies who in loyal service engage in espionage and individuals who betray their country's cause. A British subject and officer in the Royal Army, Major John André, conspired with an American senior officer under Washington's command, General Benedict Arnold. Had Britain accomplished its mission to take West Point at a narrow curve of the Hudson River north of New York City, the British would have divided the colonies strategically along the Hudson River. André was captured by Washington's forces, but Arnold escaped, eventually making his way to England. That André was tried by a very high-level, se-nior court martial board composed entirely of general officers was itself a mark of André's stature, for his rank of major would not normally have called for so distinguished an assemblage: Major Generals Nathaniel Greene, John Laurance (the judge advocate general), William Alexander (Lord Stirling), Arthur St. Clair, the Marquis de Lafayette, Robert Howe, and Baron von Steuben as well as Brigadier Generals Samuel H. Parsons, James Clinton, Henry Knox, John Glover, Edward Hand, John Stark, Jedidiah Huntington, and John Paterson. (Source: Tappantown Historical Society, Tappan, N.Y.) Obviously much more was going on here than might immedi-ately meet the eye. The almost brotherly, compassionate tone, praising rather than condemning André as convicted spy, clearly differentiated him from Arnold, who unceremoniously was viewed as traitor to the American cause. Below are inscriptions from monuments in the town of John André's trial and hanging and in Westminster Abbey in London.

Inscriptions on a Monument on Andre Hill Road in Tappan, New York

HERE DIED October 2, 1780
MAJOR JOHN ANDRE OF THE BRITISH ARMY
AND ENTERING THE AMERICAN LINES
IN A SECRET MISSION TO BENEDICT ARNOLD
FOR THE SURRENDER OF WEST POINT
WAS TAKEN PRISONER, TRIED AND CONDEMNED AS A SPY
HIS DEATH
THOUGH ACCORDING TO THE STERN CODE OF WAR
MOVED EVEN HIS ENEMIES TO PITY
AND BOTH ARMIES MOURNED THE FATE
OF ONE SO YOUNG AND SO BRAVE.
IN 1821 HIS REMAINS WERE REMOVED TO WESTMINSTER ABBEY.
A HUNDRED YEARS AFTER HIS EXECUTION
THIS STONE WAS PLACED ABOVE THE SPOT WHERE HE LAY
BY A CITIZEN OF THE STATES AGAINST WHICH HE FOUGHT
NOT TO PERPETUATE THE RECORD OF STRIFE
BUT IN TOKEN OF THOSE BETTER FEELINGS
WHICH HAVE SINCE UNITED TWO NATIONS. . . .

"HE WAS MORE UNFORTUNATE THAN CRIMINAL;
AN ACCOMPLISHED MAN AND A GALLANT OFFICER."

—George Washington

Inscriptions in Westminster Abbey, London

SACRED to the MEMORY
of
MAJOR JOHN ANDRE
who raised by his merit at an early period of Life to the rank of Adjutant General
of the British Forces in America
and employed in an important but hazardous Enterprise
fell a Sacrifice to his Zeal for his King and Country
on the 2nd of October AD 1780
Aged 29.
Universally Beloved and esteemed by the Army in which he served
and lamented by his
FOES
His gracious Sovereign KING GEORGE the Third
has caused this Monument
to be erected.

The Remains of Major JOHN ANDRE
Were, on the 10th of August 1821, removed from Tappan,
By JAMES BUCHANAN ESQ[R]
His Majesty's Consul at New York.

Under instructions from His Royal Highness
The DUKE of YORK,
And, with the permission of the Dean and Chapter,
Finally deposited in a Grave
Contiguous to the Monument
On the 28th of November 1821.

2. *George Washington's Farewell Address*
(1796)

President George Washington delivered this important farewell address in written form at the end of his second administration. To Washington, the Union of the then thirteen states was essential to both its domestic and international security. He underscores the importance for the United States of its international commerce, but warns against becoming embroiled in the entangling alliances of European balance-of-power politics. This warning established the basis for American neutrality in relation to European countries until World War I (and a return to this policy in the period between World Wars I and II). The United States did intervene diplomatically or militarily in Latin American affairs in the nineteenth and early twentieth centuries, but avoided taking such actions in Europe. Throughout its history, however, the United States has never been isolationist in relation to commerce abroad, which it deemed a continuing and substantial American interest. From the beginning, the United States did impose tariffs on imports (a major source of federal revenue in the eighteenth and nineteenth centuries until introduction of the income tax in the twentieth century). In the twentieth-century period between two world wars the country pursued protectionist trade policies, the Smoot-Hawley tariff legislation the high-water mark of trade protectionism in the 1930s. Because of its strong economic interest in promoting exports, however, the United States never extended its isolationist policies to international commerce. That said, protectionism resulted in retaliatory measures from other countries that substantially reduced the overall volume of American trade. Following World War II, Washington's advice on neutrality finally was set aside; however, promotion of liberal trading arrangements in U.S. postwar foreign policy was seen as serving the same commercial interest about which President Washington had written.

Friends and Citizens:

The period for a new election of a citizen to administer the executive government of the United States being not far distant, and the time actually arrived when your thoughts must be employed in designating the person who is to be clothed with that important trust, it appears to me proper, especially as it may conduce to a more distinct expression of the public voice, that I should now apprise you of the resolution I have formed, to decline being considered among the number of those out of whom a choice is to be made. . . .

The strength of my inclination to do this, previous to the last election, had even led to the preparation of an address to declare it to you; but mature reflection on the then perplexed and critical posture of our affairs with foreign nations, and the unanimous advice of persons entitled to my confidence, impelled me to abandon the idea.

I rejoice that the state of your concerns, external as well as internal, no longer renders the pursuit of inclination incompatible with the sentiment of duty or propriety, and am persuaded, whatever partiality may be retained for my services, that, in the present circumstances of our country, you will not disapprove my determination to retire. . . .

The unity of government which constitutes you one people is also now dear to you. It is justly so, for it is a main pillar in the edifice of your real independence, the support of your tranquility at home, your peace abroad; of your safety; of your prosperity; of that very liberty which you so highly prize. But as it is easy to foresee that, from different causes and from different quarters, much pains will be taken, many artifices employed to weaken in your minds the conviction of this truth; as this is the point in your political fortress against which the batteries of internal and external enemies will be most constantly and actively (though often covertly and insidiously) directed, it is of infinite moment that you should properly estimate the immense value of your national union to your collective and individual happiness; that you should cherish a cordial, habitual, and immovable attachment to it; accustoming yourselves to think and speak of it as of the palladium of your political safety and prosperity; watching for its preservation with jealous anxiety; discountenancing whatever may suggest even a suspicion that it can in any event be abandoned; and *indignantly frowning upon the first dawning of every attempt to alienate any portion of our country from the rest, or to enfeeble the sacred ties which now link together the various parts.*

For this you have every inducement of sympathy and interest. Citizens, by birth or choice, of a common country, that country has a right to concentrate your affections. The name of American, which belongs to you in your national capacity, must always exalt the just pride of patriotism more than any appellation derived from local discriminations. With slight shades of difference, you have the same religion, manners, habits, and political principles. You have in a common cause fought and triumphed together; the independence and liberty you possess are the work of joint counsels, and joint efforts of common dangers, sufferings, and successes.

But these considerations, however powerfully they address themselves to your sensibility, are greatly outweighed by those which apply more immediately to your interest. Here every portion of our country finds the most commanding motives for carefully guarding and preserving the union of the whole.

The North, in an unrestrained intercourse with the South, protected by the equal laws of a common government, finds in the productions of the latter great additional resources of maritime and commercial enterprise and precious materials of manufacturing industry. The South, in the same intercourse, benefiting by the agency of the North, sees its agriculture grow and its commerce expand. Turning partly into its own channels the seamen of the North, it finds its particular navigation invigorated; and, while it contributes, in different ways, to nourish and increase the general mass of the national navigation, it looks forward to *the protection of a maritime strength,* to which itself is unequally adapted. The East, in a like intercourse with the West, already finds, and in the progressive improvement of interior communications by land and water, will more and more find a valuable vent for *the commodities which it brings from abroad,* or manufactures at home. The West derives from the East supplies requisite to its growth and comfort, and, what is perhaps of still greater consequence, it must of necessity owe the secure enjoyment of indispensable outlets for its own productions to the weight, influence, and *the future maritime strength of the Atlantic side of the Union,* directed by an indissoluble community of interest as one nation. Any other tenure by which the West can hold this essential advantage, whether derived from its own separate strength, or from *an apostate and unnatural connection with any foreign power, must be intrinsically precarious.*

While, then, every part of our country thus feels an immediate and particular interest *in union, all the parts combined cannot fail to find in the united mass of means and efforts greater strength, greater resource, proportionably greater security from external danger, a less frequent interruption of their peace by foreign nations; and, what is of inestimable value, they must derive from union an exemption from those broils and wars between themselves, which so frequently afflict neighboring countries not tied together by the same governments, which their own rival ships alone would be sufficient to produce, but which opposite foreign alliances, attachments, and intrigues would stimulate and embitter. Hence, likewise, they will avoid the necessity of those overgrown military establishments which, under any form of government, are inauspicious to liberty, and which are to be regarded as particularly hostile to republican liberty. In this sense it is that your union ought to be considered as a main prop of your liberty, and that the love of the one ought to endear to you the preservation of the other.*

These considerations speak a persuasive language to every reflecting and virtuous mind, and exhibit the continuance of the Union as a primary object of patri-otic desire. Is there a doubt whether a common government can embrace so large a sphere? Let experience solve it. To listen to mere speculation in such a case were criminal. We are authorized to hope that a proper organization of the whole with the auxiliary agency of governments for the respective subdivisions, will afford a happy issue to the experiment. It is well worth a fair and full experiment. With such powerful and obvious motives to union, affecting all parts of our country, while experience shall not have demonstrated its impracticability, there will always be reason to distrust the patriotism of those who in any quarter may endeavor to weaken its bands.

In contemplating the causes which may disturb our Union, it occurs as matter of serious concern that any ground should have been furnished for characterizing parties by geographical discriminations, Northern and Southern, Atlantic and Western; whence designing men may endeavor to excite a belief that there is a real difference of local interests and views. One of the expedients of party to acquire influence within particular districts is to misrepresent the opinions and aims of other districts. You cannot shield yourselves too much against the jealousies and heartburnings which spring from these misrepresentations; they tend to render alien to each other those who ought to be bound together by fraternal affection. *The inhabitants of our Western country* have lately had a useful lesson on this head; they *have seen, in the negotiation by the Executive, and in the unanimous ratification by the Senate, of the treaty with Spain, and in the universal satisfaction at that event, throughout the United States, a decisive proof how unfounded were the suspicions propagated among them of a policy in the General Government and in the Atlantic States unfriendly to their interests in regard to the Mississippi; they have been witnesses to the formation of two treaties, that with Great Britain, and that with Spain, which secure to them everything they could desire, in respect to our foreign relations, towards confirming their prosperity.* Will it not be their wisdom to rely for the preservation of these advantages on the Union by which they were procured? Will they not henceforth be deaf to those advisers, if such there are, who would sever them from their brethren and connect them with aliens?

To the efficacy and permanency of your Union, a government for the whole is indispensable. No alliance, however strict, between the parts can be an adequate substitute; they must inevitably experience the infractions and interruptions which all alliances in all times have experienced. Sensible of this momentous truth, you have improved upon your first essay, by the adoption of a constitution of government better calculated than your former for an intimate union, and for the efficacious management of your common concerns. This government, the offspring of our own choice, uninfluenced and unawed, adopted upon full investigation and mature deliberation, completely free in its principles, in the distribution of its powers, uniting security with energy, and containing within itself a provision for its own amendment, has a just claim to your confidence and your support. Respect for its authority, compliance with its laws, acquiescence in its measures, are duties enjoined by the fundamental maxims of true liberty. The basis of our political systems is the right of the people to make and to alter their constitutions of government. But the Constitution which at any time exists, till changed by an explicit and authentic act of the whole people, is sacredly obligatory upon all. The very idea of the power and the right of the people to establish government presupposes the duty of every individual to obey the established government.

All obstructions to the execution of the laws, all combinations and associations, under whatever plausible character, with the real design to direct, control, counteract, or awe the regular deliberation and action of the constituted authorities, are destructive of this fundamental principle, and of fatal tendency. They serve to organize faction, to give it an artificial and extraordinary force; to put, in the place of the delegated will of the nation the will of a party, often a small but artful and enterprising minority of the community; and, according to the alternate triumphs of different parties, to make the public administration the mirror of the ill-concerted and incongruous projects of faction, rather than the organ of consistent and wholesome plans digested by common counsels and modified by mutual interests.

However combinations or associations of the above description may now and then answer popular ends, they are likely, in the course of time and things, to become potent engines, by which cunning, ambitious, and unprincipled men will be enabled to subvert the power of the people and to usurp for themselves the reins of government, destroying afterwards the very engines which have lifted them to unjust dominion.

Towards the preservation of your government, and the permanency of your present happy state, it is requisite, not only that you steadily discountenance irregular oppositions to its acknowledged authority, but also that you resist with care the spirit of innovation upon its principles, however specious the pretexts. One method of assault may be to effect, in the forms of the Constitution, alterations which will impair the energy of the system, and thus to undermine what cannot be directly overthrown. In all the changes to which you may be invited, remember that time and habit are at least as necessary to fix the true character of governments as of other human institutions; that experience is the surest standard by which to test the real tendency of the existing constitution of a country; that facility in changes, upon the credit of mere hypothesis and opinion, exposes to perpetual change, from the endless variety of hypothesis and opinion; and remember, especially, that for the efficient management of your common interests, in a country so extensive as ours, a government of as much vigor as is consistent with the perfect security of liberty is indispensable. Liberty itself will find in such a government, with powers properly distributed and adjusted, its surest guardian. It is, indeed, little else than a name, where the government is too feeble to withstand the enterprises of faction, to confine each member of the society within the limits prescribed by the laws, and to maintain all in the secure and tranquil enjoyment of the rights of person and property.

I have already intimated to you the danger of parties in the State, with particular reference to the founding of them on geographical discriminations. Let me now take a more comprehensive view, and warn you in the most solemn manner against the baneful effects of the spirit of party generally.

This spirit, unfortunately, is inseparable from our nature, having its root in the strongest passions of the human mind. It exists under different shapes in all governments, more or less stifled, controlled, or repressed; but, in those of the popular form, it is seen in its greatest rankness, and is truly their worst enemy.

The alternate domination of one faction over another, sharpened by the spirit of revenge, natural to party dissension, which in different ages and countries has perpetrated the most horrid enormities, is itself a frightful despotism. But this leads at length to a more formal and permanent despotism. The disorders and miseries which result gradually incline the minds of men to seek security and repose in the absolute power of an individual; and sooner or later the chief of some prevailing faction, more able or more fortunate than his competitors, turns this disposition to the purposes of his own elevation, on the ruins of public liberty.

Without looking forward to an extremity of this kind (which nevertheless ought not to be entirely out of sight), the common and continual mischiefs of the spirit of party are sufficient to make it the interest and duty of a wise people to discourage and restrain it.

It serves always to distract the public councils and enfeeble the public administration. It agitates the community with ill-founded jealousies and false alarms, kindles the animosity of one part against another, foments occasionally riot and insurrection. It opens the door to foreign influence and corruption, which finds a facilitated access to the government itself through the channels of party passions. Thus the policy and the will of one country are subjected to the policy and will of another.

There is an opinion that parties in free countries are useful checks upon the administration of the government and serve to keep alive the spirit of liberty. This within certain limits is probably true; and in governments of a monarchical cast, patriotism may look with indulgence, if not with favor, upon the spirit of party. But in those of the popular character, in governments purely elective, it is a spirit not to be encouraged. From their natural tendency, it is certain there will always be enough of that spirit for every salutary purpose. And there being constant danger of excess, the effort ought to be by force of public opinion, to mitigate and assuage it. A fire not to be quenched, it demands a uniform vigilance to prevent its bursting into a flame, lest, instead of warming, it should consume.

It is important, likewise, that the habits of thinking in a free country should inspire caution in those entrusted with its administration, to confine themselves within their respective constitutional spheres, avoiding in the exercise of the powers of one department to encroach upon another. The spirit of encroachment tends to consolidate the powers of all the departments in one, and thus to create, whatever the form of government, a real despotism. A just estimate of that love of power, and proneness to abuse it, which predominates in the human heart, is sufficient to satisfy us of the truth of this position. The necessity of reciprocal checks in the exercise of political power, by dividing and distributing it into different depositaries, and constituting each the guardian of the public weal against invasions by the others, has been evinced by experiments ancient and modern; some of them in our country and under our own eyes. To preserve them must be as necessary as to institute them. If, in the opinion of the people, the distribution or modification of the constitutional powers be in any particular wrong, let it be corrected by an amendment in the way which the Constitution designates. But let there be no change by usurpation; for though this, in one instance, may be the instrument of good, it is the customary weapon by which free governments are destroyed. The precedent must always greatly overbalance in permanent evil any partial or transient benefit, which the use can at any time yield.

Of all the dispositions and habits which lead to political prosperity, religion and morality are indispensable supports. In vain would that man claim the tribute of patriotism, who should labor to subvert these great pillars of human happiness, these firmest props of the duties of men and citizens. The mere politician, equally with the pious man, ought to respect and to cherish them. A volume could not trace all their connections with private and public felicity. Let it simply be asked: Where is the security for property, for reputation, for life, if the sense of religious obligation desert the oaths which are the instruments of investigation in courts of justice? And let us with caution indulge the supposition that morality can be maintained without religion. Whatever may be conceded to the influence of refined education on minds of peculiar structure, reason and experience both forbid us to expect that national morality can prevail in exclusion of religious principle.

It is substantially true that virtue or morality is a necessary spring of popular government. The rule, indeed, extends with more or less force to every species of free government. Who that is a sincere friend to it can look with indifference upon attempts to shake the foundation of the fabric?

Promote then, as an object of primary importance, institutions for the general diffusion of knowledge. In proportion as the structure of a government gives force to public opinion, it is essential that public opinion should be enlightened.

As a very important source of strength and security, *cherish public credit*. One method of preserving it is to use it as sparingly as possible, *avoiding occasions of expense by cultivating peace, but remembering also that timely disbursements to prepare for danger frequently prevent much greater disbursements to repel it, avoiding likewise the accumulation of debt, not only by shunning occasions of expense, but by vigorous exertion in time of peace to discharge the debts which unavoidable wars may have occasioned, not ungenerously throwing upon posterity the burden which we ourselves ought to bear.* The execution of these maxims belongs to your representatives, but it is necessary that public opinion should co-operate. To facilitate to them the performance of their duty, it is essential that you should practically bear in mind that towards the payment of debts there must be revenue; that to have revenue there must be taxes; that no taxes can be devised which are not more or less inconvenient and unpleasant; that the intrinsic embarrassment, inseparable from the selection of the proper objects (which is always a choice of difficulties), ought to be a decisive motive for a candid construction of the conduct of the government in making it, and for a spirit of acquiescence in the measures for obtaining revenue, which the public exigencies may at any time dictate.

Observe good faith and justice towards all nations; cultivate peace and harmony with all. Religion and morality enjoin this conduct; and can it be, that good policy does not equally enjoin it? It will be worthy of a free, enlightened, and at no distant period, a great nation, to give to mankind the magnanimous and too novel example of a people always guided by an exalted justice and benevolence. Who can doubt that, in the course of time and things, the fruits of such a plan would richly repay any temporary advantages which might be lost by a steady adherence to it ? Can it be that Providence has not connected the permanent felicity of a nation with its virtue? The experiment, at least, is recommended by every sentiment which ennobles human nature. Alas! is it rendered impossible by its vices?

In the execution of such a plan, *nothing is more essential than that permanent, inveterate antipathies against particular nations, and*

passionate attachments for others, should be excluded; and that, *in place of them, just and amicable feelings towards all should be cultivated. The nation which indulges towards another a habitual hatred or a habitual fondness is in some degree a slave. It is a slave to its animosity or to its affection, either of which is sufficient to lead it astray from its duty and its interest. Antipathy in one nation against another disposes each more readily to offer insult and injury, to lay hold of slight causes of umbrage, and to be haughty and intractable, when accidental or trifling occasions of dispute occur. Hence, frequent collisions, obstinate, envenomed, and bloody contests. The nation, prompted by ill-will and resentment, sometimes impels to war the government, contrary to the best calculations of policy. The government sometimes participates in the national propensity, and adopts through passion what reason would reject; at other times it makes the animosity of the nation subservient to projects of hostility instigated by pride, ambition, and other sinister and pernicious motives. The peace often, sometimes perhaps the liberty, of nations, has been the victim.*

So likewise, a passionate attachment of one nation for another produces a variety of evils. Sympathy for the favorite nation, facilitating the illusion of an imaginary common interest in cases where no real common interest exists, and infusing into one the enmities of the other, betrays the former into a participation in the quarrels and wars of the latter without adequate inducement or justification. It leads also to concessions to the favorite nation of privileges denied to others which is apt doubly to injure the nation making the concessions; by unnecessarily parting with what ought to have been retained, and by exciting jealousy, ill-will, and a disposition to retaliate, in the parties from whom equal privileges are withheld. And it gives to ambitious, corrupted, or deluded citizens (who devote themselves to the favorite nation), facility to betray or sacrifice the interests of their own country, without odium, sometimes even with popularity; gilding, with the appearances of a virtuous sense of obligation, a commendable deference for public opinion, or a laudable zeal for public good, the base or foolish compliances of ambition, corruption, or infatuation.

As avenues to foreign influence in innumerable ways, such attachments are particularly alarming to the truly enlightened and independent patriot. How many opportunities do they afford to tamper with domestic factions, to practice the arts of seduction, to mislead public opinion, to influence or awe the public councils? Such an attachment of a small or weak towards a great and powerful nation dooms the former to be the satellite of the latter.

Against the insidious wiles of foreign influence (I conjure you to believe me, fellow-citizens) the jealousy of a free people ought to be constantly awake, since history and experience prove that foreign influence is one of the most baneful foes of republican government. But that jealousy to be useful must be impartial; else it becomes the instrument of the very influence to be avoided, instead of a defense against it. Excessive partiality for one foreign nation and excessive dislike of another cause those whom they actuate to see danger only on one side, and serve to veil and even second the arts of influence on the other. Real patriots who may resist the intrigues of the favorite are liable to become suspected and odious, while its tools and dupes usurp the applause and confidence of the people, to surrender their interests.

The great rule of conduct for us in regard to foreign nations is in extending our commercial relations, to have with them as little political connection as possible. So far as we have already formed engagements, let them be fulfilled with perfect good faith. Here let us stop. Europe has a set of primary interests which to us have none; or a very remote relation. Hence she must be engaged in frequent controversies, the causes of which are essentially foreign to

our concerns. Hence, therefore, it must be unwise in us to implicate ourselves by artificial ties in the ordinary vicissitudes of her politics, or the ordinary combinations and collisions of her friendships or enmities.

Our detached and distant situation invites and enables us to pursue a different course. If we remain one people under an efficient government, the period is not far off when we may defy material injury from external annoyance; when we may take such an attitude as will cause the neutrality we may at any time resolve upon to be scrupulously respected; when belligerent nations, under the impossibility of making acquisitions upon us, will not lightly hazard the giving us provocation; when we may choose peace or war, as our interest, guided by justice, shall counsel.

Why forego the advantages of so peculiar a situation? Why quit our own to stand upon foreign ground? Why, by interweaving our destiny with that of any part of Europe, entangle our peace and prosperity in the toils of European ambition, rivalship, interest, humor or caprice?

It is our true policy to steer clear of permanent alliances with any portion of the foreign world; so far, I mean, as we are now at liberty to do it; for let me not be understood as capable of patronizing infidelity to existing engagements. I hold the maxim no less applicable to public than to private affairs, that honesty is always the best policy. I repeat it, therefore, let those engagements be observed in their genuine sense. But, in my opinion, it is unnecessary and would be unwise to extend them.

Taking care always to keep ourselves by suitable establishments on a respectable defensive posture, we may safely trust to temporary alliances for extraordinary emergencies.

Harmony, liberal intercourse with all nations, are recommended by policy, humanity, and interest. But even our commercial policy should hold an equal and impartial hand; neither seeking nor granting exclusive favors or preferences; consulting the natural course of things; diffusing and diversifying by gentle means the streams of commerce, but forcing nothing; establishing (with powers so disposed, in order to give trade a stable course, to define the rights of our merchants, and to enable the government to support them) conventional rules of intercourse, the best that present circumstances and mutual opinion will permit, but temporary, and liable to be from time to time abandoned or varied, as experience and circumstances shall dictate; constantly keeping in view that it is folly in one nation to look for disinterested favors from another; that it must pay with a portion of its independence for whatever it may accept under that character; that, by such acceptance, it may place itself in the condition of having given equivalents for nominal favors, and yet of being reproached with ingratitude for not giving more. There can be no greater error than to expect or calculate upon real favors from nation to nation. It is an illusion, which experience must cure, which a just pride ought to discard.

In offering to you, my countrymen, these counsels of an old and affectionate friend, I dare not hope they will make the strong and lasting impression I could wish; that they will control the usual current of the passions, or *prevent our nation from running the course which has hitherto marked the destiny of nations.* But, if I may even flatter myself that they may be productive of some partial benefit, some occasional good; that they may now and then recur to moderate the fury of party spirit, *to warn against the mischiefs of foreign intrigue, to guard against the impostures of pretended patriotism;* this hope will be a full recompense for the solicitude for your welfare, by which they have been dictated.

How far in the discharge of my official duties I have been guided by the principles which have been delineated, the public records and other evidences of my conduct must witness to you and to the world. To myself, the assurance of my own conscience is, that I have at least believed myself to be guided by them.

In relation to the still subsisting war in Europe, my proclamation of the twenty-second of April, 1793, is the index of my plan. Sanctioned by your approving voice, and by that of your representatives in both houses of Congress, the spirit of that measure has continually governed me, uninfluenced by any attempts to deter or divert me from it.

After deliberate examination, with the aid of the best lights I could obtain, I was well satisfied that *our country,* under all the circumstances of the case, *had a right to take, and was bound in duty and interest to take, a neutral position.* Having taken it, I determined, as far as should depend upon me, to maintain it, with moderation, perseverance, and firmness.

The considerations which respect the right to hold this conduct, it is not necessary on this occasion to detail. I will only observe that, according to my understanding of the matter, *that right, so far from being denied by any of the belligerent powers, has been virtually admitted by all.*

The duty of holding a neutral conduct may be inferred, without anything more, from the obligation which justice and humanity impose on every nation, in cases in which it is free to act, to maintain inviolate the relations of peace and amity towards other nations.

The inducements of interest for observing that conduct will best be referred to your own reflections and experience. *With me a predominant motive has been to endeavor to gain time to our country to settle and mature its yet recent institutions, and to progress without interruption to that degree of strength and consistency which is necessary to give it, humanly speaking, the command of its own fortunes.*

Though, in reviewing the incidents of my administration, I am unconscious of intentional error, I am nevertheless too sensible of my defects not to think it probable that I may have committed many errors. Whatever they may be, I fervently beseech the Almighty to avert or mitigate the evils to which they may tend. I shall also carry with me the hope that my country will never cease to view them with indulgence; and that, after forty five years of my life dedicated to its service with an upright zeal, the faults of incompetent abilities will be consigned to oblivion, as myself must soon be to the mansions of rest.

Relying on its kindness in this as in other things, and actuated by that fervent love towards it, which is so natural to a man who views in it the native soil of himself and his progenitors for several generations, I anticipate with pleasing expectation that retreat in which I promise myself to realize, without alloy, the sweet enjoyment of partaking, in the midst of my fellow-citizens, the benign influence of good laws under a free government, the ever-favorite object of my heart, and the happy reward, as I trust, of our mutual cares, labors, and dangers.

Geo. Washington.

---

3. *The Monroe Doctrine*

(1823)

In the aftermath of successful independence movements in Latin America directed against Spain and Portugal in the 1820s, President James Monroe articulated in his seventh annual message to Congress, on December 2, 1823, what became known as the Monroe Doctrine. Because of U.S. support for the newly established states and the republican forms of government these states adopted, the aim of the doctrine was to close off the Western Hemisphere to new or further colonization, thus leaving British, French, Dutch, and other colonial possessions intact. Ousting Spain from Cuba and Puerto Rico would have to wait until the Spanish-American War in 1898. The United States did not have the necessary naval and other military capabilities to enforce this policy and had to rely instead on the British Royal Navy for this purpose should the need arise. Indeed, given European balance-of-power rivalry it was also in Britain's interest at the time to curb Spanish, Portuguese, or other colonial presence in the Western Hemisphere even if this effectively allowed the United States to establish for itself a sphere of influence in the hemisphere. Although President Monroe's original intent was to block European powers from intervening in hemispheric affairs, in 1904 President Theodore Roosevelt advanced a corollary that allowed U.S. intervention to put an end to chronic unrest or wrongdoing lest such circumstances invite extra-hemispheric intervention (see the Roosevelt Corollary later in this chapter).

At the proposal of the Russian Imperial Government . . . a full power and instructions have been transmitted to the minister of the United States at St. Petersburg to arrange by amicable negotiation the respective rights and interests of the two nations on the northwest coast of this continent. A similar proposal has been made by His Imperial Majesty to the Government of Great Britain, which has likewise been acceded to. The Government of the United States has been desirous by this friendly proceeding of manifesting the great value which they have invariably attached to the friendship of the Emperor and their solicitude to cultivate the best understanding with his Government. In the discussions to which this interest has given rise and in the arrangements by which they may terminate the occasion has been judged proper for asserting, *as a principle in which the rights and interests of the United States are involved, that the American continents, by the free and independent condition which they have assumed and maintain, are henceforth not to be considered as subjects for future colonization by any European powers. . . .*

It was stated at the commencement of the last session that a great effort was then making in Spain and Portugal to improve the condition of the people of those countries, and that it appeared to be conducted with extraordinary moderation. It need scarcely be remarked that the results have been so far very different from what was then anticipated. Of events in that quarter of the globe, with which we have so much intercourse and from which we derive our origin, we have always been anxious and interested spectators. *The citizens of the United States cherish sentiments the most friendly in favor of the liberty and happiness of their fellow-men on that side of the Atlantic. In the wars of the European powers in matters relating to themselves we have never taken any part, nor does it comport with our policy to do so. It is only when our rights are invaded or seriously menaced that we resent injuries or make preparation for our defense. With the movements in this hemisphere we are of necessity more immediately connected,* and by causes which must be obvious to all enlightened and impartial observers. The political system of the allied powers is essentially different in this respect from that of America.

This difference proceeds from that which exists in their respective Governments; and to the defense of our own, which has been achieved by the loss of so much blood and treasure, and matured by the wisdom of their most enlightened citizens, and under which we have enjoyed unexampled felicity, this whole nation is devoted. *We owe it, therefore, to candor and to the amicable relations existing between the United States and those powers to declare that we should consider any attempt on their part to extend their system to any portion of this hemisphere as dangerous to our peace and safety. With the existing colonies or dependencies of any European power we have not interfered and shall not interfere. But with the Governments who have declared their independence and maintain it, and whose independence we have, on great consideration and on just principles, acknowledged, we could not view any interposition for the purpose of oppressing them, or controlling in any other manner their destiny, by any European power in any other light than as the manifestation of an unfriendly disposition toward the United States.* In the war between those new Governments and Spain we declared our neutrality at the time of their recognition, and to this we have adhered, and shall continue to adhere, provided no change shall occur which, in the judgement of the competent authorities of this Government, shall make a corresponding change on the part of the United States indispensable to their security.

The late events in Spain and Portugal shew that Europe is still unsettled. Of this important fact no stronger proof can be adduced than that the allied powers should have thought it proper, on any principle satisfactory to themselves, to have interposed by force in the internal concerns of Spain. To what extent such interposition may be carried, on the same principle, is a question in which all independent powers whose governments differ from theirs are interested, even those most remote, and surely none of them more so than the United States. Our policy in regard to Europe, which was adopted at an early stage of the wars which have so long agitated that quarter of the globe, nevertheless remains the same, which is, not to interfere in the internal concerns of any of its powers; to consider the government de facto as the legitimate government for us; to cultivate friendly relations with it, and to preserve those relations by a frank, firm, and manly policy, meeting in all instances the just claims of every power, submitting to injuries from none. But in regard to those continents circumstances are eminently and conspicuously different.

It is impossible that the allied powers should extend their political system to any portion of either continent without endangering our peace and happiness; nor can anyone believe that our southern brethren, if left to themselves, would adopt it of their own accord. It is equally impossible, therefore, that we should behold such interposition in any form with indifference. If we look to the comparative strength and resources of Spain and those new Governments, and their distance from each other, it must be obvious that she can never subdue them. It is still the true policy of the United States to leave the parties to themselves, in hope that other powers will pursue the same course.

---

4. *Abraham Lincoln's Gettysburg Address*

(1863)

Delivered on the battlefield at Gettysburg in Pennsylvania on November 19, 1863 after a great Union victory, President Abraham Lincoln not only commemorates the soldiers who fought and died there, but also sees the country and its liberties secured by the union of states he is trying to restore, a constellation then divided in a great civil war.

Four score and seven years ago, our fathers brought forth upon this continent a new nation: conceived in liberty, and dedicated to the proposition that all men are created equal. *Now we are engaged in a great civil war, testing whether that nation, or any nation so conceived and so dedicated, can long endure.* We are met on a great battlefield of that war. We have come to dedicate a portion of that field as a final resting place for *those who here gave their lives that that nation might live.* It is altogether fitting and proper that we should do this.

But, in a larger sense, we cannot dedicate—we cannot consecrate—we cannot hallow—this ground. The brave men, living and dead, who struggled here have consecrated it, far above our poor power to add or detract. The world will little note, nor long remember, what we say here, but it can never forget what they did here.

It is for us the living, rather, to be dedicated here to the unfinished work which they who fought here have thus far so nobly advanced. It is rather for us to be here dedicated to the great task remaining before us—*that from these honored dead we take increased devotion to that cause for which they gave the last full measure of devotion*—that we here highly resolve that these dead shall not have died in vain—

that this nation, under God, shall have a new birth of freedom—and that govern-

ment of the people, by the people, for the people, *shall not perish from the earth.*

5. *The Open Door Policy*
(1899 and 1900)

After the Spanish-American War (1898) and the extension of American interest to East Asia and the Pacific, we find here Secretary of State John Hay on two occasions trying to assure U.S. commercial access to various already established European spheres of influence in China. To advance liberal free-trade understandings and its own commercial interest, the United States sought to equalize treatment of all countries engaged in commerce within China. The Open Door Policy is a commitment to "safeguard for the world the principle of equal and impartial trade."

[September 6, 1899]

Earnestly desirous to remove any cause of irritation and to insure at the same time to the commerce of all nations in China the undoubted benefits which should accrue from a formal recognition by the various powers claiming "spheres of interest" that they shall enjoy perfect equality of treatment for their commerce and navigation within such "spheres," the Government of the United States would . . . give formal assurances and lend its cooperation in securing like assurances from the other interested powers that each within its respective sphere of whatever influence—

First. Will in no way interfere with any treaty or port or any vested interest within any so-called "sphere of influence" or leased territory it may have in China.

Second. That the Chinese treaty tariff . . . shall apply to all merchandise landed or shipped to all such ports as are within said "sphere of interest" . . . no matter what nationality it may belong, and that duties so leviable shall be collected by the Chinese government.

Third. That it will levy no higher harbor dues on vessels of another nationality frequenting any port in such "sphere"

than shall be levied on vessels of its own nationality, and no higher railroad charges over lines . . . within its "sphere" on merchandise belonging to citizens or subjects of other nationalities transported through such "sphere" than shall be levied on similar merchandise belonging to its own nationals transported over equal distances.

[July 3, 1900]

We adhere to the policy . . . of peace with the Chinese nation, of furtherance of lawful commerce, and of protection of lives and property of our citizens. . . , affording all possible protection everywhere in China to American life and property; . . . guarding and protecting all legitimate American interests; and . . . aiding to prevent a spread of disorders. . . . *The policy of the Government of the United States is to* seek a solution which may bring about permanent safety and peace to China, preserve Chinese territorial and administrative entity, protect all rights guaranteed to friendly powers by treaty and international law, and *safeguard for the world the principle of equal and impartial trade with all parts of the Chinese Empire.*

6. *Theodore Roosevelt's Corollary to the Monroe Doctrine*
(1904 and 1905)

In 1902 the United Kingdom, Germany, Italy, and other countries imposed a naval blockade on Venezuela when the country defaulted on its debts. The United States saw this use of force to collect payment as a violation of the Monroe Doctrine. Drawn from Theodore Roosevelt's annual message to Congress on December 6, 1904, the document below opposes external intervention in hemispheric affairs while providing a rationale for U.S. intervention in Latin America. President Roosevelt also tells us the importance he places on military and naval strength to serve U.S. interests. His commentary here follows the realist aphorism attributed to Roosevelt about "speaking softly, but carrying a big stick." At the same time, he holds open the possibility of developing peaceful, legally based mechanisms for maintaining peace. In his annual message a year later, he reiterates this policy supporting U.S. military interventions in Latin America, which occurred from time to time until the 1930s mainly in Central America and the Caribbean, particularly when American business interests were challenged. The Good Neighbor Policy of Franklin Delano Roosevelt (1933) in effect replaced this policy, opting instead for nonintervention as the basis of U.S. foreign policy in the hemisphere, a principle that would become institutionalized after World War II in the Charter of the Organization of American States (OAS).

[December 6, 1904]

In treating of our foreign policy and of the attitude that this great Nation should assume in the world at large, it is absolutely necessary to consider the Army and the Navy, and the Congress, through which the thought of the Nation finds its expression, should keep ever vividly in mind the fundamental fact that it is impossible to treat our foreign policy, whether this policy takes shape in the effort to secure justice for others or justice for ourselves, save as conditioned upon the attitude we are willing to take toward our Army, and especially toward our Navy. *It is not merely unwise, it is contemptible, for a nation,* as for an individual, to use high-sounding language *to proclaim its purposes, or to take positions which are ridiculous if unsupported by potential force, and then to refuse to provide this force.* If there is no intention of providing and keeping the force necessary to back up a strong attitude, then it is far better not to assume such an attitude.

The steady aim of this Nation, as of all enlightened nations, should be to strive to bring ever nearer the day when there shall prevail throughout the world the peace of justice. There are kinds of peace which are highly undesirable, which are in the long run as destructive as any war. Tyrants and oppressors have many times made a wilderness and called it peace. Many times peoples who were slothful or timid or shortsighted, who had been enervated by ease or by luxury, or misled by false teachings, have shrunk in unmanly fashion from doing duty that was stern and that needed self-sacrifice, and have sought to hide from their own minds their shortcomings, their ignoble motives, by calling them love of peace. The peace of tyrannous terror, the peace of craven weakness, the peace of injustice, all these should be shunned as we shun unrighteous war. *The goal to set before us as a nation, the goal which should be set before all mankind, is the attainment of the peace of justice, of the peace which comes when each nation is not merely safe-guarded in its own rights, but scrupulously recognizes and performs its duty toward others.* Generally peace tells for righteousness; but if there is conflict between the two, then our fealty is due first to the cause of righteousness. Unrighteous wars are common, and unrighteous peace is rare; but both should be shunned. The right of freedom and the responsibility for the exercise of that right can not be divorced. One of our great poets has well and finely said that freedom is not a gift that tarries long in the hands of cowards. Neither does it tarry long in the hands of those too slothful, too dishonest, or too unintelligent to exercise it. *The eternal vigilance which is the price of liberty must be exercised, sometimes to guard against outside foes;* although of course far more often to guard against our own selfish or thoughtless shortcomings.

If these self-evident truths are kept before us, and only if they are so kept before us, we shall have a clear idea of what our foreign policy in its larger aspects should be. It is our duty to remember that a nation has no more right to do injustice to another nation, strong or weak, than an individual has to do injustice to another individual; that the same moral law applies in one case as in the other. But we must also remember that *it is* as much *the duty of the Nation to guard its own rights and its own interests* as it is the duty of the individual so to do. Within the Nation the individual has now delegated this right to the State, that is, to the representative of all the individuals, and it is a maxim of the law that for every wrong there is a remedy. But in international law we have not advanced by any means as far as we have advanced in municipal law. There is as yet no judicial way of enforcing a right in international law. When one nation wrongs another or wrongs many others, there is no tribunal before which the wrongdoer can be brought. Either it is necessary supinely to acquiesce in the wrong, and thus put a premium upon brutality and aggression,

or else it is necessary for the aggrieved nation valiantly to stand up for its rights. *Until some method is devised by which there shall be a degree of international control over offending nations, it would be a wicked thing for the most civilized powers, for those with most sense of international obligations and with keenest and most generous appreciation of the difference between right and wrong, to disarm. If the great civilized nations of the present day should completely disarm, the result would mean an immediate recrudescence of barbarism in one form or another.* Under any circumstances a sufficient armament would have to be kept up to serve the purposes of international police; and until international cohesion and the sense of international duties and rights are far more advanced than at present, a nation desirous both of securing respect for itself and of doing good to others must have a force adequate for the work which it feels is allotted to it as its part of the general world duty. Therefore it follows that *a self-respecting, just, and far-seeing nation should on the one hand endeavor by every means to aid in the development of the various movements which tend to provide substitutes for war,* which tend to render nations in their actions toward one another, and indeed toward their own peoples, more responsive to the general sentiment of humane and civilized mankind; and on the other hand that it should keep prepared, while scrupulously avoiding wrongdoing itself, to repel any wrong, and in exceptional cases to take action which in a more advanced stage of international relations would come under the head of the exercise of the international police. *A great free people owes it to itself and to all mankind not to sink into helplessness before the powers of evil.*

We are in every way endeavoring to help on, with cordial good will, every movement which will tend to bring us into more friendly relations with the rest of mankind. *In pursuance of this policy I shall shortly lay before the Senate treaties of arbitration* with all powers which are willing to enter into these treaties with us. It is not possible at this period of the world's development to agree to arbitrate all matters, but there are many matters of possible difference between us and other nations which can be thus arbitrated. Furthermore, at the request of the Interparliamentary Union, an eminent body composed of practical statesmen from all countries, I have asked the Powers to join with this Government in a second Hague conference, at which it is hoped that the work already so happily begun at The Hague may be carried some steps further toward completion. This carries out the desire expressed by the first Hague conference itself.

It is not true that the United States feels any land hunger or entertains any projects as regards the other nations of the Western Hemisphere save such as are for their welfare. All that this country desires is to see the neighboring countries stable, orderly, and prosperous. Any country whose people conduct themselves well can count upon our hearty friendship. *If a nation shows that it knows how to act with reasonable efficiency and decency in social and political matters, if it keeps order and pays its obligations, it need fear no interference from the United States. Chronic wrongdoing, or an impotence which results in a general loosening of the ties of civilized society, may in America, as elsewhere, ultimately require intervention by some civilized nation, and in the Western Hemisphere the adherence of the United States to the Monroe Doctrine may force the United States, however reluctantly, in flagrant cases of such wrongdoing or impotence, to the exercise of an international police power.* If every country washed by the Caribbean Sea would show the progress in stable and just

civilization which with the aid of the Platt Amendment. [With this amendment Congress in 1903 imposed restrictions on Cuba.—Ed.] Cuba has shown since our troops left the island, and which so many of the republics in both Americas are constantly and brilliantly showing, all question of interference by this Nation with their affairs would be at an end. Our interests and those of our southern neighbors are in reality identical. They have great natural riches, and if within their borders the reign of law and justice obtains, prosperity is sure to come to them. While they thus obey the primary laws of civilized society they may rest assured that they will be treated by us in a spirit of cordial and helpful sympathy. We would interfere with them only in the last resort, and then only if it became evident that their inability or unwillingness to do justice at home and abroad had violated the rights of the United States or had invited foreign aggression to the detriment of the entire body of American nations. It is a mere truism to say that every nation, whether in America or anywhere else, which desires to maintain its freedom, its independence, must ultimately realize that the right of such independence can not be separated from the responsibility of making good use of it.

In asserting the Monroe Doctrine, in taking such steps as we have taken in regard to Cuba, Venezuela, and Panama, and in endeavoring to circumscribe the theater of war in the Far East, and to secure the open door in China, we have acted in our own interest as well as in the interest of humanity at large. There are, however, cases in which, while our own interests are not greatly involved, strong appeal is made to our sympathies. Ordinarily it is very much wiser and more useful for us to concern ourselves with striving for our own moral and material betterment here at home than to concern ourselves with trying to better the condition of things in other nations. We have plenty of sins of our own to war against, and under ordinary circumstances we can do more for the general uplifting of humanity by striving with heart and soul to put a stop to civic corruption, to brutal lawlessness and violent race prejudices here at home than by passing resolutions and wrongdoing elsewhere. Nevertheless *there are occasional crimes committed on so vast a scale and of such peculiar horror as to make us doubt whether it is not our manifest duty to endeavor at least to show our disapproval of the deed and our sympathy with those who have suffered by it. The cases must be extreme in which such a course is justifiable.* There must be no effort made to remove the mote from our brother's eye if we refuse to remove the beam from our own. But *in extreme cases action may be justifiable and proper. What form the action shall take must depend upon the circumstances of the case; that is, upon the degree of the atrocity and upon our power to remedy it.* The cases in which we could interfere by force of arms as we interfered to put a stop to intolerable conditions in Cuba are necessarily very few. Yet it is not to be expected that a people like ours, which in spite of certain very obvious shortcomings, nevertheless as a whole shows by its consistent practice its belief in the principles of civil and religious liberty and of orderly freedom, a people among whom even the worst crime, like the crime of lynching, is never more than sporadic, so that individuals and not classes are molested in their fundamental rights—it is inevitable that such a nation should desire eagerly to give expression to its horror on an occasion like that of the massacre of the Jews in Kishenef, or when it witnesses such

systematic and long-extended cruelty and oppression as the cruelty and oppression of which the Armenians have been the victims, and which have won for them the indignant pity of the civilized world.

[December 5, 1905]

It must be understood that under no circumstances will the United States use the Monroe Doctrine as a cloak for territorial aggression. We desire peace with all the world, but perhaps most of all with the other peoples of the American Continent. There are, of course, limits to the wrongs which any self-respecting nation can endure. It is always possible that wrong actions toward this Nation, or toward citizens of this Nation, in some State unable to keep order among its own people, unable to secure justice from outsiders, and unwilling to do justice to those outsiders who treat it well, may result in our having to take action to protect our rights; but such action would not be taken with a view to territorial aggression, and it will be taken at all only with extreme reluctance and when it has become evident that every other resource has been exhausted.

Moreover, we must make it evident that *we do not intend to permit the Monroe Doctrine to be used by any nation on this Continent as a shield to protect it from the consequences of its own misdeeds against foreign nations.* If a republic to the south of us commits a tort against a foreign nation, such as an outrage against a citizen of that nation, then the Monroe Doctrine does not force us to interfere to prevent punishment of the tort, save to see that the punishment does not assume the form of territorial occupation in any shape. The case is more difficult when it refers to a contractual obligation. Our own Government has always refused to enforce such contractual obligations on behalf of its citizens by an appeal to arms. It is much to be wished that all foreign governments would take the same view. But they do not: and in consequence we are liable at anything to be brought face to face with disagreeable alternatives. *On the one hand, this country would certainly decline to go to war to prevent a foreign government from collecting a just debt; on the other hand, it is very inadvisable to permit any foreign power to take possession, even temporarily, of the custom houses of an American Republic in order to enforce the payment of its obligations; for such temporary occupation might turn into a permanent occupation. The only escape from these alternatives may at any time be that we must ourselves undertake to bring about some arrangement by which so much as possible of a just obligation*

shall be paid. It is far better that this country should put through such an arrangement, rather than allow any foreign country to undertake it. To do so insures the defaulting republic from having to pay debt of an improper character under duress, while it also insures honest creditors of the republic from being passed by in the interest of dishonest or grasping creditor. Moreover, for the United States to take such a position offers the only possible way of insuring us against a clash with some foreign power. The position is, therefore the interest of peace as well as in the interest of justice. It is of benefit to our people; it is of benefit to foreign peoples; and most of all it is really of benefit to the people of the country concerned.

---

7. *Woodrow Wilson's Declaration of Neutrality*
(1914)

In keeping with George Washington's late-eighteenth-century view that the United States should avoid entangling itself in European balance-of-power (alliance) politics, upon the outbreak of World War I in Europe President Woodrow Wilson delivered to Congress on August 19, 1914 this declaration of neutrality.

The effect of the war upon the United States will depend upon what American citizens say and do. Every man who really loves America will act and speak in *the true spirit of neutrality, which is the spirit of impartiality and fairness and friendliness to all concerned.* The spirit of the nation in this critical matter will be determined largely by what individuals and society and those gathered in public meetings do and say, upon what newspapers and magazines contain, upon what ministers utter in their pulpits, and men proclaim as their opinions upon the street.

The people of the United States are drawn from many nations, and chiefly

from the nations now at war. It is natural and inevitable that there should be the utmost variety of sympathy and desire among them with regard to the issues and circumstances of the conflict. Some will wish one nation, others another, to succeed in the momentous struggle. It will be easy to excite passion and difficult to allay it. Those responsible for exciting it will assume a heavy responsibility, responsibility for no less a thing than that the people of the United States, whose love of their country and whose loyalty to its government should unite them as Americans all, bound in honor and affection to think first of her and her interests, may be divided in camps of hostile opinion, hot against each other, involved in the war itself in impulse and opinion if not in action.

Such divisions amongst us would be fatal to our peace of mind and might seriously stand in the way of the proper performance of our duty as the one great nation at peace, the one people holding itself ready to play a part of impartial mediation and speak the counsels of peace and accommodation, not as a partisan, but as a friend.

I venture, therefore, my fellow countrymen, to speak a solemn word of warning to you against that deepest, most subtle, most essential breach of neutrality which may spring out of partisanship, out of passionately taking sides. The United States must be neutral in fact, as well as in name, during these days that are to try men's souls. We must be impartial in thought, as well as action, must put a curb upon our sentiments, as well as upon every transaction that might be construed as a preference of one party to the struggle before another.

---

8. *Woodrow Wilson's War Message*

(1917)

In May 1915 almost 1,200 lives (including 128 Americans) were lost in the sinking of the Lusitania, *a British liner, by a German submarine torpedo attack. The Wilson administration protested vigorously on international legal and humanitarian grounds, but Germany persisted in its conduct of submarine warfare directed against commercial and passenger shipping. Emboldened by this casus belli—what Wilson considered a just cause for going to war, he asks the Congress for a declaration of war against Germany. We find in this speech the concept of a world ordered on democratic ideas—that the world may be made safe for democracies. There is reference to self-government, a concept that will take the form of national self-determination in postwar settlements. That authoritarian, autocratic governments tend to be more warlike and that, by contrast, democratic regimes tend to produce peaceful relations is an important idea that not only influenced Wilson, but also leaders during World War II and the cold war. Today, advocates of promoting democracy as a matter of American foreign policy often argue in the Wilsonian spirit that democracies tend not to go to war with other democracies and thus a world composed predominantly of democratic regimes would tend to be a more peaceful one. This ideational foundation differs from Theodore Roosevelt's realist view in which military strength or power is the key component of international security upon which democratic institutions and processes rest.*

Gentlemen of the Congress:

I have called the Congress into extraordinary session because there are serious, very serious, choices of policy to be made, and made immediately, which it was neither right nor constitutionally permissible that I should assume the responsibility of making.

On the 3d of February last I officially laid before you the extraordinary announcement of the Imperial German Government that on and after the 1st day of February it was its purpose to put aside all restraints of law or of humanity and use its submarines to sink every vessel that sought to approach either the ports of

Great Britain and Ireland or the western coasts of Europe or any of the ports controlled by the enemies of Germany within the Mediterranean. . . . *Vessels of every kind, whatever their flag, their character, their cargo, their destination, their errand, have been ruthlessly sent to the bottom* without warning and without thought of help or mercy for those on board, *the vessels of friendly neutrals along with those of belligerents.* Even hospital ships and ships carrying relief to the sorely bereaved and stricken people of Belgium, though the latter were provided with safe-conduct through the proscribed areas by the German Government itself and were distinguished by unmistakable marks of identity, have been sunk with the same reckless lack of compassion or of principle.

I was for a little while unable to believe that such things would in fact be done by any government that had hitherto subscribed to the humane practices of civilized nations. International law had its origin in the attempt to set up some law which would be respected and observed upon the seas, where no nation had right of dominion and where lay the free highways of the world. By painful stage after stage has that law been built up, with meagre enough results, indeed, after all was accomplished that could be accomplished, but always with a clear view, at least, of what the heart and conscience of mankind demanded. This minimum of right the German Government has swept aside. . . . *The present German submarine warfare against commerce is a warfare against mankind.*

It is a war against all nations. American ships have been sunk, American lives taken, in ways which it has stirred us very deeply to learn of, but the ships and people of other neutral and friendly nations have been sunk and overwhelmed in the waters in the same way. There has been

no discrimination. *The challenge is to all mankind.* Each nation must decide for itself how it will meet it. The choice we make for ourselves must be made with a moderation of counsel and a temperateness of judgment befitting our character and our motives as a nation. We must put excited feeling away. *Our motive will not be revenge or the victorious assertion of the physical might of the nation, but only the vindication of right, of human right, of which we are only a single champion.*

When I addressed the Congress on the 26th of February last, I thought that it would suffice to assert our neutral rights with arms, our right to use the seas against unlawful interference, our right to keep our people safe against unlawful violence. But armed neutrality, it now appears, is impracticable. Because submarines are in effect outlaws when used as the German submarines have been used against merchant shipping, it is impossible to defend ships against their attacks as the law of nations has assumed. . . . The German Government denies the right of neutrals to use arms at all within the areas of the sea which it has proscribed. . . . Armed neutrality is ineffectual enough at best; in such circumstances and in the face of such pretensions it is worse than ineffectual; it is likely only to produce what it was meant to prevent; it is practically certain to draw us into the war without either the rights or the effectiveness of belligerents. *There is one choice we can not make, we are incapable of making: we will not choose the path of submission and suffer the most sacred rights of our nation and our people to be ignored or violated.* The wrongs against which we now array ourselves are no common wrongs; they cut to the very roots of human life.

With a profound sense of the solemn and even tragical character of the step I am taking and of the grave responsibilities which it involves, but in unhesitating obedience to what I deem my constitutional duty, *I advise that the Congress declare the recent course of the Imperial German Government to be in fact nothing less than war against the Government and people of the United States; that it formally accept the status of belligerent which has thus been thrust upon it, and that it take immediate steps not only to put the country in a more thorough state of defense but also to exert all its power and employ all its resources to bring the Government of the German Empire to terms and end the war. . . .*

What this will involve is clear. It will involve the utmost practicable cooperation in counsel and action with the governments now at war with Germany, and, as incident to that, the extension to those governments of the most liberal financial credits, in order that our resources may so far as possible be added to theirs. It will involve the organization and mobilization of all the material resources of the country to supply the materials of war and serve the incidental needs of the nation in the most abundant and yet the most economical and efficient way possible. It will involve the immediate full equipment of the Navy . . . [and] the immediate addition to the armed forces . . . of . . . at least 500,000 men, who should, in my opinion, be chosen upon the principle of universal liability to service [i.e., by conscription—the draft]. . . . It will involve also, of course, the granting of adequate credits to the Government, sustained, I hope, so far as they can equitably be sustained by the present generation, by well conceived taxation. . . .

While we do these things, these deeply momentous things, let us be very clear, and make very clear to all the world what our motives and our objects are. . . . *Our object . . . is to vindicate the principles of peace and justice in the life of the world as against selfish and autocratic power and to set up amongst the really free and self-governed peoples of the world such a concert of purpose and of action as will henceforth ensure the observance of those principles. Neutrality is no longer feasible or desirable where the peace of the world is involved and the freedom of its peoples, and the menace to that peace and freedom lies in the existence of autocratic governments backed by organized force which is controlled wholly by their will, not by the will of their people. We have seen the last of neutrality in such circumstances.* We are at the beginning of an age in which it will be insisted that the same standards of conduct and of responsibility for wrong done shall be observed among nations and their governments that are observed among the individual citizens of civilized states.

We have no quarrel with the German people. We have no feeling towards them but one of sympathy and friendship. It was not upon their impulse that their Government acted in entering this war. It was not with their previous knowledge or approval. It was a war determined upon . . . in the interest of dynasties or of little groups of ambitious men who were accustomed to use their fellow men as pawns and tools. *Self-governed nations do not fill their neighbour states with spies or set the course of intrigue to bring about some critical posture of affairs which will give them an opportunity to strike and make conquest.* Such designs can be successfully worked out only under cover and where no one has the right to ask questions. Cunningly contrived *plans of deception or aggression,* carried, it may be, from generation to generation, can be worked out and kept from the light only within the privacy of courts or behind the carefully guarded confidences of a narrow and privileged class. They *are happily impossible where public opinion commands and insists upon full information concerning all the nation's affairs.*

A steadfast concert for peace can never be maintained except by a partnership of democratic nations. No autocratic government could be trusted to keep faith within it or observe its covenants. It must be a league of honour, a partnership of opinion. Intrigue would eat its vitals away; the plottings of inner circles who could plan what they would and render account to no one would be a corruption seated at its very heart. Only free peoples can hold their purpose and their honour steady to a common end and prefer the interests of mankind to any narrow interest of their own. . . .

Does not every American feel that assurance has been added to our hope for the future peace of the world by the wonderful and heartening things that have been happening within the last few weeks in Russia? Russia was known by those who knew it best to have been always in fact democratic at heart, in all the vital habits of her thought, in all the intimate relationships of her people that spoke their natural instinct, their habitual attitude towards life. *The autocracy that crowned the summit of her political structure, long as it had stood and terrible as was the reality of its power, was not in fact Russian in origin, character, or purpose; and now it has been shaken off and the great, generous Russian people have been added in all their naive majesty and might to the forces that are fighting for freedom in the world, for justice, and for peace. Here is a fit partner for a league of honour.*

One of the things that has served to convince us that *the Prussian autocracy was not and could never be our friend* is that from the very outset of the present war it has filled our unsuspecting communities and even our offices of government with spies and set criminal intrigues everywhere afoot against our national unity of coun-

sel, our peace within and without our industries and our commerce. Indeed it is now evident that its spies were here even before the war began. . . . Disturbing the peace and dislocating the industries of the country have been carried on at the instigation, with the support, and even under the personal direction of official agents of the Imperial Government. . . . Their source lay, not in any hostile feeling or purpose of the German people towards us (who were, no doubt, as ignorant of them as we ourselves were), but only in the selfish designs of a Government that did what it pleased and told its people nothing. But they have played their part in serving to convince us at last that that Government entertains no real friendship for us and means to act against our peace and security at its convenience. . . .

We are accepting this challenge of hostile purpose because we know that in such a government, following such methods, we can never have a friend; and that *in the presence of its organized power, always lying in wait to accomplish we know not what purpose, there can be no assured security for the democratic governments of the world.* We are now about to accept gage of battle with this natural foe to liberty and shall, if necessary, spend the whole force of the nation to check and nullify its pretensions and its power. *We are glad,* now that we see the facts with no veil of false pretence about them, *to fight thus for the ultimate peace of the world and for the liberation of its peoples,* the German peoples included: for *the rights of nations great and small and the privilege of men everywhere to choose their way of life and of obedience. The world must be made safe for democracy. Its peace must be planted upon the tested foundations of political liberty. We have no selfish ends to serve. We desire no conquest, no dominion. We seek no indemnities for ourselves, no material compensation for the sacrifices we shall freely make. We are but one of the champions of the rights of mankind. We shall be satisfied when those rights have been made as secure as the faith and the freedom of nations can make them.

Just because we fight without rancour and without selfish object, seeking nothing for ourselves but what we shall wish to share with all free peoples, we shall, *I feel confident, conduct our operations as belligerents without passion and ourselves observe with proud punctilio the principles of right and of fair play we profess to be fighting for....* We enter this war only where we are clearly forced into it because there are no other means of defending our rights.

It will be all the easier for us to conduct ourselves as belligerents in a high spirit of right and fairness because we act without animus, not in enmity towards a people or with the desire to bring any injury or disadvantage upon them, but only in armed opposition to an irresponsible government which has thrown aside all considerations of humanity and of right and is running amuck. *We are,* let me say again, *the sincere friends of the German people, and shall desire nothing so much as the early reestablishment of intimate relations of mutual advantage between us*—however hard it may be for them, for the time being, to believe that this is spoken from our hearts. We have borne with their present government through all these bitter months because of that friendship— exercising a patience and forbearance which would otherwise have been impossible. We shall, happily, still have an opportunity to prove that friendship in our daily attitude and actions towards the millions of men and women of German birth

and native sympathy, who live amongst us and share our life, and we shall be proud to prove it towards all who are in fact loyal to their neighbours and to the Government in the hour of test. They are, most of them, as true and loyal Americans as if they had never known any other fealty or allegiance. They will be prompt to stand with us in rebuking and restraining the few who may be of a different mind and purpose. If there should be disloyalty, it will be dealt with with a firm hand of stern repression; but, if it lifts its head at all, it will lift it only here and there and without countenance except from a lawless and malignant few.

It is a distressing and oppressive duty, gentlemen of the Congress, which I have performed in thus addressing you. There are, it may be, many months of fiery trial and sacrifice ahead of us. *It is a fearful thing to lead this great peaceful people into war, into the most terrible and disastrous of all wars, civilization itself seeming to be in the balance. But the right is more precious than peace, and we shall fight for the things which we have always carried nearest our hearts—for democracy, for the right of those who submit to authority to have a voice in their own governments for the rights and liberties of small nations, for a universal dominion of right by such a concert of free peoples as shall bring peace and safety to all nations and make the world itself at last free.* To such a task we can dedicate our lives and our fortunes, everything that we are and everything that we have, with the pride of those who know that the day has come when America is privileged to spend her blood and her might for the principles that gave her birth and happiness and the peace which she has treasured. God helping her, she can do no other.

9. *Woodrow Wilson's Fourteen Points*

(1918)

The Wilsonian preference for national self-determination as the basis for forming states is central to his concept of a peace based on democratic principles. He advances fourteen points on January 8, 1918, as bases for the peace settlement to follow in 1918. It is a liberal vision in which there no longer are secret treaties, navigation and trade are free, armaments are reduced, and popular interests are represented. His optimism about Russia no longer under the dynastic dominance of the Romanovs would later change as Wilson came to understand better the Bolshevik regime that seized power in 1917.

It will be our wish and purpose that the processes of peace, when they are begun, shall be absolutely open and that they shall involve and permit henceforth no secret understandings of any kind. The day of conquest and aggrandizement is gone by; so is also the day of secret covenants entered into in the interest of particular governments and likely at some unlooked-for moment to upset the peace of the world. It is this happy fact, now clear to the view of every public man whose thoughts do not still linger in an age that is dead and gone, which makes it possible for every nation whose purposes are consistent with justice and the peace of the world to avow nor or at any other time the objects it has in view.

We entered this war because violations of right had occurred which touched us to the quick and made the life of our own people impossible unless they were corrected and the world secure once for all against their recurrence. What we demand in this war, therefore, is nothing peculiar to ourselves. It is that the world be made fit and safe to live in; and particularly that it be made safe for every peace-loving nation which, like our own, wishes to live its own life, determine its own institutions, be assured of justice and fair dealing by the other peoples of the world as against force and selfish aggression. All the peoples of the world are in effect partners in this interest, and for our own part we see very clearly that unless justice be done to others it will not be done to us. The programme of the world's peace, therefore, is our programme; and that programme, the only possible programme, as we see it, is this:

I. *Open covenants of peace, openly arrived at,* after which there shall be no private international understandings of any kind but diplomacy shall proceed always frankly and in the public view.

II. *Absolute freedom of navigation upon the seas,* outside territorial waters, alike in peace and in war, except as the seas may be closed in whole or in part by international action for the enforcement of international covenants.

III. *The removal, so far as possible, of all economic barriers and the establishment of an equality of trade conditions* among all the nations consenting to the peace and associating themselves for its maintenance.

IV. *Adequate guarantees given and taken that national armaments will be reduced* to the lowest point consistent with domestic safety.

V. *A free, open-minded, and absolutely impartial adjustment of all colonial claims, based upon a strict observance of the principle that in determining all such questions of sovereignty the interests of the populations concerned* must have equal weight with the equitable claims of the government whose title is to be determined.

VI. *The evacuation of all Russian territory and such a settlement of all questions affecting Russia as will secure the best and freest cooperation* of the other nations of the world in obtaining for her an unhampered and unembarrassed opportunity for the independent determination of her own political development and national policy and assure her of a sincere welcome into the society of free nations under institutions of her own choosing; and, more than a welcome, assistance also of every kind that she may need and may herself desire. The treatment accorded Russia by her sister nations in the months to come will be the acid test of their good will, of their comprehension of her needs as distinguished from their own interests, and of their intelligent and unselfish sympathy.

VII. *Belgium, the whole world will agree, must be evacuated and restored, without any attempt to limit the sovereignty which she enjoys* in common with all other free nations. No other single act will serve as this will serve to restore confidence among the nations in the laws which they have themselves set and determined for the government of their relations with one another. Without this healing act the whole structure and validity of international law is forever impaired.

VIII. *All French territory should be freed and the invaded portions restored,* and the wrong done to France by Prussia in 1871 in the matter of Alsace-Lorraine, which has unsettled the peace of the world for nearly fifty years, should be righted, in order that peace may once more be made secure in the interest of all.

IX. *A readjustment of the frontiers of Italy should be effected along clearly recognizable lines of nationality.*

X. *The peoples of Austria-Hungary,* whose place among the nations we wish to see safeguarded and assured, *should be accorded the freest opportunity to autonomous development.*

XI. *Rumania, Serbia, and Montenegro should be evacuated; occupied territories restored;* Serbia accorded free and secure access to the sea; and the relations of the several Balkan states to one another determined by friendly counsel along historically established lines of allegiance and nationality; and international guarantees of the political and economic independence and territorial integrity of the several Balkan states should be entered into.

XII. *The turkish [sic] portion of the present Ottoman Empire should be assured a secure sovereignty, but the other nationalities which are now under Turkish rule should be assured an undoubted security of life and an absolutely unmolested opportunity of autonomous development,* and the Dardanelles should be permanently opened as a free passage to the ships and commerce of all nations under international guarantees.

XIII. *An independent Polish state should be erected* which should include the territories inhabited by indisputably Polish populations, which should be assured a free and secure access to the sea, and whose political and economic independence and territorial integrity should be guaranteed by international covenant.

XIV. *A general association of nations must be formed under specific covenants for the purpose of affording mutual guarantees of political independence and territorial integrity to great and small states alike.*

In regard to these essential rectifications of wrong and assertions of right *we feel ourselves to be intimate partners of all the governments and peoples associated together against the Imperialists. We cannot be separated in interest or divided in purpose. We stand together until the end.*

For such arrangements and covenants we are willing to fight and to continue to fight until they are achieved; but only because we wish the right to prevail and desire *a just and stable peace such as can be secured only by removing the chief provocations to war,* which this programme does remove. *We have no jealousy of German greatness,* and there is nothing in this programme that impairs it. We grudge her no achievement or distinction of learning or of pacific enter-prise such as have made her record very bright and very enviable. We do not wish to injure her or to block in any way her legitimate influence or power. We do not wish to fight her either with arms or with hostile arrangements of trade if she is willing to associate herself with us and the other peace-loving nations of the world in covenants of justice and law and fair dealing. *We wish her only to accept a place of equality among the peoples of the world,—the new world in which we now live,—instead of a place of mastery.*

---

10. The Kellogg-Briand Pact
(1928)

In reaction to the carnage of World War I, the United States entered into this treaty outlawing war on August 7, 1928. Viewed by many as utopian, the intent was to eliminate war and the use of force as a matter of law. Instead of power and balance-of-power alliances (which were seen as causally related to the outbreak of war in 1914), world order would be based on respect for an international law prohibiting war and the use of force as means for settling disputes or conflicts.

I. The High Contracting Parties solemnly declare in the names of their respective peoples that they condemn recourse to war for the solution of international controversies, and renounce it, as an instrument of national policy in their relations with one another.

II. The High Contracting Parties agree that the settlement or solution of all disputes or conflicts of whatever nature or of whatever origin they may be, which may arise among them, shall never be sought except by pacific means. . . . This Treaty shall . . . remain open as long as may be necessary for adherence by all the other Powers of the world. . . .

---

11. The Good Neighbor Policy
(1933)

In his inaugural address on March 4, 1933, President Franklin Delano Roosevelt first mentioned what would become his "good neighbor" policy: "In the field of world policy, I would dedicate this Nation to the policy of the good neighbor." He expanded on this theme in relation to Latin

America in an address on April 12, 1933, to the governing board of the Pan American Union (predecessor to the post–World War II Organization of American States, the OAS). Although preserving the Monroe Doctrine against further colonization or acquisition of territory in the Western Hemisphere, the policy effectively reversed the interventionist corollary that President Theodore Roosevelt had advanced earlier in the century. Indeed, Central America and the Caribbean witnessed numerous interventions, usually for commercial or business interests, by U.S. military forces over the three decades following proclamation of the Roosevelt corollary in 1904.

Franklin Roosevelt's aim was to set that interventionist policy aside, replacing it with mutual understanding and cooperation among "good neighbors," and to call for liberalization of commerce as a foundation stone for a lasting and prosperous hemispheric peace. Nonintervention in the domestic affairs of other states in the hemisphere would become institutionalized as a guiding principle after World War II in the OAS Charter.

In practice, however, the United States continued to intervene from time to time in Latin American affairs—overturning the Jacobo Arbenz (said to be communist) regime in Guatemala in 1954; attempting to overthrow Fidel Castro's regime in Cuba, particularly during the 1960s; sending military forces into the Dominican Republic in 1965, again said to be directed against communist forces at work there; covert actions in the early 1970s contributing to the overthrow of Salvador Allende's socialist regime in Chile; and in the 1980s and 1990s military invasion to depose the left in Grenada, covert action in Nicaragua against left-leaning Sandinistas, military intervention against the Manuel Noriega regime in Panama, and for humanitarian purposes in Haiti. Although some of these interventions were clearly unilateral in orientation, particularly covert actions, efforts were made in other cases to multilateralize the interventions under OAS auspices or other coalition efforts in response to hemispheric threats.

I rejoice in this opportunity to participate in the celebration of "Pan American Day" and to extend on behalf of the people of the United States a fraternal greeting to our sister American Republics. . . . This celebration commemorates a movement based upon the policy of fraternal cooperation. In my Inaugural Address I stated that I would "dedicate this Nation to *the policy of the good neighbor—the neighbor who resolutely respects himself and, because he does so, respects the rights of others—the neighbor who respects his obligations and respects the sanctity of his agreements in and with a world of neighbors."* Never before has the significance of the words "good neighbor" been so manifest in international relations. *Never have the need and benefit of neighborly cooperation in every form of human activity been so evident as they are today.*

Friendship among Nations, as among individuals, calls for *constructive efforts to muster the forces of humanity in order that an* *atmosphere of close understanding and cooperation may be cultivated. It involves mutual obligations and responsibilities, for it is only by sympathetic respect for the rights of others and a scrupulous fulfillment of the corresponding obligations by each member of the community that a true fraternity can be maintained.*

The essential qualities of a true Pan Americanism must be the same as those which constitute *a good neighbor, namely, mutual understanding,* and, through such understanding, a sympathetic appreciation of the other's point of view. It is only in this manner that we can hope *to build up a system of which confidence, friendship and good will are the cornerstones.*

In this spirit the people of every Republic on our continent are coming to a deep understanding of the fact that *the Monroe Doctrine,* of which so much has been written and spoken for more than a century *was and is directed at the maintenance of independence by the peoples of the continent. It was aimed and is aimed against the acquisition in any manner of the control of additional territory in this hemisphere by any non-American power.*

Hand in hand with this Pan American doctrine of continental self-defense, the peoples of the American Republics understand more clearly, with the passing years, that the independence of each Republic must recognize the independence of every other Republic. Each one of us must grow by an advancement of civilization and social well-being and not by the acquisition of territory at the expense of any neighbor.

In this spirit of mutual understanding and of cooperation on this continent you and I cannot fail to be disturbed by any armed strife between neighbors.... Your Americanism and mine must be a structure built of confidence cemented by a sympathy which recognizes only equality and fraternity. It finds its source and being in the hearts of men and dwells in the temple of the intellect.

We all of us have peculiar problems, and, to speak frankly, the interest of our own citizens must, in each instance, come first. But it is equally true that it is of vital importance to every Nation of this Continent that the American Governments, individually, take, without further delay, *such action as may be possible to abolish all unnecessary and artificial barriers and restrictions which now hamper the healthy flow of trade between the peoples of the American Republics.*

I am glad to deliver this message to you, Gentlemen of the Governing Board of the Pan American Union, for I look upon the Union as the outward expression of the spiritual unity of the Americas. It is to this unity which must be courageous and vital in its element that humanity must look for one of the great stabilizing influences in world affairs....

---

12. *The Munich Pact*

(1938)

Still in its isolationist period, the United States was not a party to the Munich Pact; however, the agreement would become symbolically important in American foreign policy as an example of appeasement. Britain and France made concessions on September 29, 1938 to accommodate territorial demands by Germany, albeit at the expense of Czechoslovakia. After all, borders for a newly constructed state, Czechoslovakia, had been drawn up hastily after World War I; a few "adjustments" might be necessary to keep from having to go to war yet again. Whatever the expectations of making "peace in our time," as British prime minister Neville Chamberlain put it, the arrangement did buy time for Britain and France to prepare for what some foresaw as the inevitability of war with the German Reich and its allies. The "lesson" many drew from Munich, however, was the futility of appeasing dictators bent on aggression—that appeasement would only whet the appetite of such dictators for further aggression. Avoiding another round of mass carnage just twenty years after the first world war was the great hope, which tragically was dashed when Germany invaded Poland in 1939. The "lesson" of Munich subsequently became part of American post–World War II foreign policy. For example, many policy makers at the time saw the Vietnam War as necessary to stop aggression by communist forces. Indeed, advocates of using force have often represented Munich as metaphor for what happens when a stand against aggression is not taken.

Germany, the United Kingdom, France and Italy, taking into consideration the agreement, which has been already reached in principle for the cession to Germany of the Sudeten German territory [The Germans called the part of Bohemia in western Czechoslovakia in which many ethnic Germans lived the Sudetenland.—Ed.], have agreed on the following terms and conditions governing the said cession and the measures consequent thereon, and by this agreement they each hold themselves responsible for the steps necessary to secure its fulfilment:

1. The evacuation will begin on 1st October.
2. The United Kingdom, France and Italy agree that the evacuation of the territory shall be completed by the 10th October, without any existing installations having been destroyed, and that the Czechoslovak Government will be held responsible for carrying out the evacuation without damage to the said installations.
3. The conditions governing the evacuation will be laid down in detail by an international commission composed of representatives of Germany, the United Kingdom, France, Italy and Czechoslovakia.
4. The occupation by stages of the predominantly German territory by German troops will begin on 1st October. . . . The remaining territory of preponderantly German character will be ascertained by the aforesaid international commission forthwith and be occupied by German troops by the 10th of October.
5. The international commission . . . will determine the territories in which a plebiscite is to be held. These territories will be occupied by international bodies until the plebiscite has been completed. . . .
6. The final determination of the frontiers will be carried out by the international commission. The commission will also be entitled to recommend to the four Powers, Germany, the United Kingdom, France and Italy, in certain exceptional cases, minor modifications in the strictly ethnographical determination of the zones which are to be transferred without plebiscite.
7. There will be a right of option into and out of the transferred territories, the option to be exercised within six months from the date of this agreement. A German-Czechoslovak commission shall determine the details of the option, consider ways of facilitating the transfer of population and settle questions of principle arising out of the said transfer.
8. The Czechoslovak Government will within a period of four weeks from the date of this agreement release from their military and police forces any Sudeten Germans who may wish to be released, and the Czechoslovak Government will within the same period release Sudeten German prisoners who are serving terms of imprisonment for political offences.

Munich, September 29, 1938.
ADOLF HITLER [Germany],
NEVILLE CHAMBERLAIN [United Kingdom],
EDOUARD DALADIER [France],
BENITO MUSSOLINI [Italy].

13. *The Atlantic Charter*

(1941)

Britain was already at war in August 1941, when Franklin Roosevelt joined Winston Churchill in laying out general objectives for constructing a post–World War II world order. Theirs was a liberal internationalist vision of national self-determination, free trade, freedom of navigation, economic and social collaboration, and human security through abandonment of the use of force and disarmament.

The President of the United States of America and the Prime Minister, Mr. Churchill, representing His Majesty's Government in the United Kingdom, being met together, deem it right to make known certain common principles in the national policies of their respective countries on which they base their hopes for a better future for the world.

First, their countries *seek no aggrandizement*, territorial or other;

Second, they *desire to see no territorial changes that do not accord with the freely expressed wishes of the peoples concerned*;

Third, they *respect the right of all peoples to choose the form of government under which they will live*; and they wish to see sovereign rights and self government restored to those who have been forcibly deprived of them;

Fourth, they *will endeavor*, with due respect for their existing obligations, *to further the enjoyment by all States, great or small, victor or vanquished, of access, on equal terms, to the trade and to the raw materials of the world which are needed for their economic prosperity*;

Fifth, they *desire to bring about the fullest collaboration between all nations in the economic field* with the object of securing, for all, improved labor standards, economic advancement and social security;

Sixth, after the final destruction of the Nazi tyranny, they *hope to see established a peace which will afford to all nations the means of dwelling in safety within their own boundaries, and which will afford assurance that all the men in all lands may live out their lives in freedom from fear and want*;

Seventh, *such a peace should enable all men to traverse the high seas and oceans without hindrance*;

Eighth, they believe *that all of the nations of the world*, for realistic as well as spiritual reasons *must come to the abandonment of the use of force*. Since no future peace can be maintained if land, sea or air armaments continue to be employed by nations which threaten, or may threaten, aggression outside of their frontiers, they believe, pending the establishment of a wider and permanent system of general security, that the disarmament of such nations is essential. They will likewise aid and encourage all other practicable measure which will *lighten for peace-loving peoples the crushing burden of armaments*.

Franklin D. Roosevelt
Winston S. Churchill

Chapter 10

World War II and Its Settlement: Foreign and National Security Policy Statements

14. Lend-Lease: The United States Lends, the United Kingdom Leases

(1940)

President Franklin Roosevelt held a press conference on December 17, 1940 to explain his idea of a lend-lease proposal by which the United States could transfer military equipment and war-related matériel to the United Kingdom. Given American neutrality, lend-lease offered a way around the prohibition against taking sides by providing direct support to one party engaged in warfare (in this case, Britain, which was at war with Germany). Roosevelt also represented lend-lease as being in the U.S. interest to support the United Kingdom. Moreover, it was not so much as a profit-oriented venture or merely an effort to defend a democratic country as it was also a way of stimulating domestic defense production in the event that capacity were needed should the United States go to war. The "fire hose" metaphor to justify the new policy is classic Roosevelt. Congress would authorize lend-lease in the new year. It was in fact a first step away from the strictures imposed by neutrality.

In the present world situation ... there is absolutely no doubt in the mind of a very overwhelming number of Americans that the best immediate defense of the United States is the success of Great Britain in defending itself; and that, therefore, quite aside from our historic and current inter-est in the survival of democracy, in the world as a whole, *it is equally important from a selfish point of view of American defense, that we should do everything to help the British Empire to defend itself.* . . .

I go back to the idea that *the one thing necessary for American national defense is additional productive facilities;* and the more we increase those facilities—factories, shipbuilding ways, munition plants, . . . and so on—the stronger American national defense is.

Orders from Great Britain are therefore a tremendous asset to American national defense; because they automatically create additional facilities. I am talking selfishly, from the American point of view—nothing else. Therefore, from the selfish point of view, that production must be encouraged by us. . . .

It is possible—I will put it that way—*for the United States to take over British orders,* and, because they are essentially the same kind of munitions that we use ourselves, turn them into American orders. We have enough money to do it. *And thereupon, as to such portion of them as the military events of the future determine to be right and proper for us to allow to go to the other side, either lease or sell the materials, subject to mortgage, to the people on the other side. That would be on the general theory that it may still prove true that the best defense of Great Britain is the best defense of the United States,* and therefore that these materials would be more useful to the defense of the United States if they were used in Great Britain, than if they were kept in storage here.

Now, what I am trying to do is to eliminate the dollar sign. That is something brand new in the thoughts of practically everybody in this room, I think—get rid of the silly, foolish old dollar sign.

Well, let me give you an illustration: Suppose my neighbor's home catches fire, and I have a length of garden hose four or five hundred feet away. If he can take my garden hose and connect it up with his hydrant, I may help him to put out his fire. Now, what do I do? I don't say to him before that operation, "Neighbor, my garden hose cost me $15; you have to pay me $15 for it." What is the transaction that goes on? I don't want $15—I want my garden hose back after the fire is over. All right. If it goes through the fire all right, intact, without any damage to it, he gives it back to me and thanks me very much for the use of it. But suppose it gets smashed up—holes in it—during the fire; we don't have to have too much formality about it, but I say to him, "I was glad to lend you that hose; I see I can't use it any more, it's all smashed up." He says, "How many feet of it were there?" I tell him, "There were 150 feet of it." He says, "All right, I will replace it." Now, if I get a nice garden hose back, I am in pretty good shape.

In other words, if you lend certain munitions and get the munitions back at the end of the war, if they are intact, haven't been hurt—you are all right; if they have been damaged or have deteriorated or have been lost completely, it seems to me you come out pretty well if you have them replaced by the fellow to whom you have lent them.

I can't go into details; and there is no use asking legal questions about how you would do it, because that is the thing that is now under study; but *the thought is that we would take over not all, but a very large number of, future British orders; and when they came off the line, whether they were planes or guns or something else, we would enter into some kind of arrangement for their use by the British* on the ground that it was the best thing for American defense, *with the understanding that* when the show was over, *we would get repaid sometime in kind,* thereby leaving out the dollar mark in the form of a dollar debt and substituting for it a gentleman's obligation to repay in kind. I think you all get it.

15. *Declaration of War Speeches Against Japan and Germany*

(1941)

The day after the surprise attack on Pearl Harbor in the American Territory of Hawaii, President Franklin Roosevelt responded the next day with a call to Congress for a war against Japan. Because of American isolationism in the interwar period, President Roosevelt had been constrained in preparations for war. It took a direct attack on American territory to secure a declaration of war from Congress. Even then, Roosevelt did not expand his war request to include Japan's European allies, Germany and Italy, in the absence of direct provocation. For their part, Germany and Italy took it upon themselves to declare war on the United States. Because these acts produced a state of war, the president followed up with what amounted to a supplemental request for recognizing formally this state of war against Germany and Italy.

[December 8, 1941]

To the Congress of the United States:

Yesterday, Dec. 7, 1941—a date which will live in infamy—the United States of America was suddenly and deliberately attacked by naval and air forces of the Empire of Japan. The United States was at peace with that nation and, at the solicitation of Japan, was still in conversation with the government and its emperor looking toward the maintenance of peace in the Pacific.

Indeed, one hour after Japanese air squadrons had commenced bombing in Oahu, the Japanese ambassador to the United States and his colleagues delivered to the Secretary of State a formal reply to a recent American message. While this reply stated that it seemed useless to continue the existing diplomatic negotiations, it contained no threat or hint of war or armed attack.

It will be recorded that the distance of Hawaii from Japan makes it obvious that the attack was deliberately planned many days or even weeks ago. During the intervening time, the Japanese government has deliberately sought to deceive the United States by false statements and expressions of hope for continued peace.

The attack yesterday on the Hawaiian islands has caused severe damage to American naval and military forces. Very many American lives have been lost. In addition, American ships have been reported torpedoed on the high seas between San Francisco and Honolulu. Yesterday, the Japanese government also launched an attack against Malaya. Last night, Japanese forces attacked Hong Kong. Last night, Japanese forces attacked Guam. Last night, Japanese forces attacked the Philippine Islands. Last night, the Japanese attacked Wake Island. This morning, the Japanese attacked Midway Island.

Japan has, therefore, undertaken a surprise offensive extending throughout the Pacific area. The facts of yesterday speak for themselves. The people of the United States have already formed their opinions and well understand the implications to the very life and safety of our nation.

As commander in chief of the Army and Navy, I have directed that all measures be taken for our defense. Always will we remember the character of the onslaught against us. *No matter how long it may take us to overcome this premeditated invasion, the American people in their righteous might will win through to absolute victory.*

I believe I interpret the will of the Congress and of the people when I assert that we will not only defend ourselves to the uttermost, but will make very certain that this form of treachery shall never endanger us again. Hostilities exist. There is no blinking at the fact that our people, our territory and our interests are in grave danger.

With confidence in our armed forces—with the unbounding determination of our people—we will gain the inevitable triumph—so help us God. *I ask that the Congress declare that since the unprovoked and dastardly attack by Japan on Sunday, December 7, a state of war has existed between the United States and the Japanese empire.*

[December 11, 1941]
To the Congress of the United States:
On the morning of Dec. 11 the Government of Germany, pursuing its course of world conquest, declared war against the United States. The long-known and the long-expected has thus taken place. The forces endeavoring to enslave the entire world now are moving toward this hemisphere.

Never before has there been a greater challenge to life, liberty and civilization. Delay invites great danger. Rapid and united effort by all of the peoples of the world who are determined to remain free will insure a world victory of the forces of justice and of righteousness over the forces of savagery and of barbarism.

Italy also has declared war against the United States. I therefore request the Congress to recognize a state of war between the United States and Germany, and between the United States and Italy.

Franklin D. Roosevelt

---

16. *Dumbarton Oaks*

(1944)

An outline for the United Nations Charter was drafted at Dumbarton Oaks, a nineteenth-century mansion in Georgetown, Washington, D.C. Completed on October 7, 1944, the charter provided the objectives, principles, and details of a United Nations organization in construction. We reprint here only a portion of this document; most of its provisions can be found in the charter finalized in San Francisco the following year and included in part 5 of this volume.

There should be established an international organization under the title of The United Nations, the Charter of which should contain provisions necessary to give effect to the proposals which follow. The purposes of the Organization should be:

1. *To maintain international peace and security; and to that end to take effective collective measures for the prevention and removal of threats to the peace and the suppression of acts of aggression or other breaches of the peace, and to bring about by peaceful means adjustment or settlement of international disputes which may lead to a breach of the peace; 2. To develop friendly relations among nations and to* take other appropriate measures to strengthen universal peace; 3. *To achieve international cooperation in the solution of international economic, social and other humanitarian problems; and 4. To afford a center for harmonizing the actions of nations* in the achievement of these common ends. . . .

In pursuit of the[se] purposes . . . the Organization and its members should act in accordance with the following principles: 1. The Organization is based on the *principle of the sovereign equality* of all peace-loving states. 2. All members of the Organization undertake, in order to ensure to all of them the rights and benefits resulting from membership in the Organization, to fulfill the obligations assumed by them in accordance with the Charter. 3. *All members of the Organization shall settle their disputes by peaceful means in such a manner that international peace and security are not endangered.* . . . 4. *All members of the Organization shall refrain* in their international relations *from the threat or use of force in any manner inconsistent with the purposes of the Organization.* 5. All members of the Organization shall give every assistance to the Organization in any action undertaken by it in accordance with the provisions of the Charter. 6. All members of the Organization shall refrain from giving assistance to any state against which preventive or enforcement action is being undertaken by the Organization.

The Organization should ensure that states not members of the Organization act in accordance with these principles so far as may be necessary for the *maintenance of international peace and security.* . . . Membership of the Organization should be open to all peace-loving states. . . . *The Organization should have as its principal organs: a. A General Assembly; b. A Security Council; c. An international court of justice; and d. A Secretariat [and]* the Organization should have *such subsidiary agencies as may be found necessary.* . . .

[Because in final form they are found in the United Nations Charter, we omit details here concerning these principal organs, arrangements for maintaining international peace and security, international economic and social cooperation, the charter amendment process, and transitional arrangements for establishing the United Nations organization.]

---

17. *The Yalta Conference*
(1945)

The Yalta Conference held in the Soviet Crimea in February 1945 was the last great summit for Roosevelt (who would die shortly thereafter), Churchill (who would be replaced as prime minister in a forthcoming British election), and Stalin (who would remain in power until his death in 1953). The Yalta agreement set in place terms for the post–World War II order. Many in the United States criticized the agreement for conceding to Soviet demands concerning Poland and other issues; however, the Soviet Red Army's liberation of most of Eastern Europe from German control put Stalin in a strong position to insist on terms favorable to Soviet interests.

The Crimea Conference of the heads of the Governments of the United States of America, the United Kingdom, and the Union of Soviet Socialist Republics, which took place from Feb. 4 to 11, came to the following conclusions:

I. World Organization

It was decided . . . that a United Nations conference on the proposed world organization should be summoned for Wednesday, 25 April, 1945, and should be held in the United States of America. . . .

II. Declaration of Liberated Europe

. . . The Premier of the Union of Soviet Socialist Republics, the Prime Minister of the United Kingdom and the President of the United States . . . jointly declare their mutual agreement to concert during the temporary period of instability in liberated Europe the policies of their three Governments in assisting the peoples liberated. . . .

The *establishment of order in Europe and the rebuilding of national economic life* must be achieved by processes which will enable the liberated peoples to destroy the last vestiges of nazism and fascism and to create democratic institutions of their own choice. This is a principle of the Atlantic Charter—*the right of all people to choose the form of government under which they will live*—the restoration of sovereign rights and self-government to those peoples who have been forcibly deprived to them by the aggressor nations.

To foster the conditions in which the liberated people may exercise these rights, the three governments will jointly assist the people in any European liberated state or former Axis state in Europe where, in their judgment conditions require, (a) to establish conditions of internal peace; (b) to carry out emergency relief measures for the relief of distressed peoples; (c) to form interim governmental authorities broadly representative of all democratic elements in the population and pledged to the earliest possible establishment through free elections of Governments responsive to the will of the people; and (d) to facilitate where necessary the holding of such elections. . . . By this declaration *we reaffirm our faith in the principles of the* Atlantic Charter, *our pledge in the Declaration by the United Nations and our determination to build in cooperation with other peace-loving nations world order, under law, dedicated to peace, security, freedom and general well-being of all mankind.* . . .

III. Dismemberment of Germany

The United Kingdom, the United States of America and the Union of Soviet Socialist Republics shall possess supreme authority with respect to Germany. In the exercise of such authority they will take such steps, including the complete dismemberment of Germany as they deem requisite for future peace and security. . . .

IV. Zone of Occupation for the French Control Council for Germany

It was agreed that a zone in Germany, to be occupied by the French forces, should be allocated [to] France. This zone would be formed out of the British and American zones and its extent would be settled by the British and Americans in consultation with the French Provisional Government. It was also agreed that the French Provisional Government should be invited to become a member of the Allied Control Council for Germany.

V. Reparation

Germany must pay in kind for the losses caused by her to the Allied nations in the course of the war. Reparations are to be received in the first instance by those countries which have borne the main burden of the war, have suffered the heaviest losses and have organized victory over the enemy. . . .

VI. Major War Criminals

The conference agreed that the question of the major war criminals should be the subject of inquiry by the three Foreign Secretaries for report in due course after the close of the conference.

VII. Poland

A new situation has been created in Poland as a result of her complete liberation by the Red Army. This calls for the establishment of a Polish Provisional Government which can be more broadly based than was possible before the recent liberation of the western part of Poland. The Provisional Government which is now functioning in Poland should therefore be reorganized on a broader democratic basis with the inclusion of democratic leaders from Poland itself and from Poles abroad.... This Polish Provisional Government of National Unity shall be pledged to the holding of free and unfettered elections as soon as possible on the basis of universal suffrage and secret ballot.... The eastern frontier of Poland should follow the Curzon Line.... The new Polish Provisional Government of National Unity should be sought in due course of the extent of these accessions and that the final delimitation of the western frontier of Poland should thereafter await the peace conference.

VIII. Yugoslavia

It was agreed ... that as soon as the new Government has been formed it should declare: (I) That the Anti-Fascist Assembly of the National Liberation (AVNOJ) will be extended to include members of the last Yugoslav Skupstina who have not compromised themselves by collaboration with the enemy, thus forming a body to be known as a temporary Parliament and (II) That legislative acts passed by ... AVNOJ will be subject to subsequent ratification by a Constituent Assembly....

IX. Italo-Yugoslav Frontier [and] Italo-Austrian Frontier

Notes on these subjects were put in by the British delegation and the American and Soviet delegations agreed to consider them and give their views later.

X. Yugoslav-Bulgarian Relations

There was an exchange of views between the Foreign Secretaries on the question of the desirability of a Yugoslav-Bulgarian pact of alliance. The question at issue was whether a state still under an armistice regime could be allowed to enter into a treaty with another state....

XI. Southeastern Europe

The British delegation put in notes for the consideration of their colleagues on the following subjects: (a) The Control Commission in Bulgaria. (b) Greek claims upon Bulgaria, more particularly with reference to reparations. (c) Oil equipment in Rumania.

XII. Iran

Mr. Eden, Mr. Stettinius and Mr. Molotov exchanged views on the situation in Iran. It was agreed that this matter should be pursued through the diplomatic channel....

XIII. Meetings of the Three Foreign Secretaries

The conference agreed that permanent machinery should be set up for consultation between the three Foreign Secretaries; they should meet as often as necessary, probably about every three or four months. These meetings will be held in rotation in the three capitals....

XIV. The Montreux Convention and the Straits

It was agreed that at the next meeting of the three Foreign Secretaries ... they should consider proposals which it was understood the Soviet Government would put forward in relation to the Montreux Convention [This is a reference to the 1936 agreement, that put the straits between the Black and Mediterranean seas under Turkish military control, reserving to Turkey the right to close the straits to warships when at war or threatened by aggression while, at the same time, permitting passage of merchant ships from countries not at war with Turkey— Ed.], and report to their Governments. The Turkish Government should be informed at the appropriate moment. . . .

The forgoing protocol was approved and signed by the three Foreign Secretaries at the Crimean Conference Feb. 11, 1945.

E. R. Stettinius Jr., M. Molotov, Anthony Eden

Agreement Regarding Japan

The leaders of the three great powers—the Soviet Union, the United States of America and Great Britain—have agreed that *in two or three months after Germany has surrendered and the war in Europe is terminated, the Soviet Union shall enter into war against Japan on the side of the Allies* on condition that: 1. The status quo in Outer Mongolia (the Mongolian People's Republic) shall be preserved. 2. *The former rights of Russia* violated by the treacherous attack of Japan in 1904 shall be restored, *viz.:* (a) *The southern part of Sakhalin as well as the islands adjacent to it shall be returned to the Soviet Union;* (b) The commercial port of Dairen shall be internationalized, the pre-eminent interests of the Soviet Union in this port being safeguarded, and the lease of Port Arthur as a naval base of the U.S.S.R. restored; (c) The Chinese-Eastern Railroad and the South Manchurian Railroad, which provide an outlet to Dairen, shall be jointly operated by the establishment of a joint Soviet-Chinese company, it being understood that the pre-eminent interests of the Soviet Union shall be safeguarded and that China shall retain sovereignty in Manchuria; 3. *The Kurile Islands shall be handed over to the Soviet Union.* It is understood that the agreement concerning Outer Mongolia and the ports and railroads referred to above will require concurrence of Generalissimo Chiang Kai-shek. The President will take measures in order to maintain this concurrence on advice from Marshal Stalin. The heads of the three great powers have agreed that these claims of the Soviet Union shall be unquestionably fulfilled after Japan has been defeated. For its part, the Soviet Union expresses it readiness to conclude with the National Government of China a pact of friendship and alliance between the U.S.S.R. and China in order to render assistance to China with its armed forces for the purpose of liberating China from the Japanese yoke.

Joseph Stalin, Franklin D. Roosevelt, Winston S. Churchill
February 11, 1945.

---

18. *The United Nations Charter*

(1945)

Dumbarton Oaks provided an outline for the United Nations organization then under construction. The United Nations charter was signed on June 26, 1945 in San Francisco, California. The charter is reprinted in its entirety in part 5, chapter 18.

19. The Potsdam Conference
(1945)

After Yalta, a new U.S.-U.K.-Soviet summit meeting was convened just outside Berlin in Potsdam, Germany, between July 17 and August 2, 1945. Harry Truman had assumed office after President Roosevelt's death; Clement Attlee replaced Churchill as prime minister after the Labour Party won an election; only Stalin remained of the three principal wartime allied leaders. Building on the Yalta accords as a starting point, the Potsdam Conference established borders and terms of occupation of Germany and other countries in central and Eastern Europe. Taken together, Yalta and Potsdam were the subject of great debate for many years in the United States, critics arguing that both Roosevelt and Truman had yielded too much to Stalin in central and eastern Europe. As a practical matter, however, the presence of the Soviet Red Army in occupation of these countries gave the United States and Britain much less say in defining the outcome of Yalta and Potsdam than they otherwise might have had. The lines drawn in these agreements in time became the cold war dividing lines between East and West.

Protocol of the Proceedings, August 1, 1945

The Berlin Conference of the Three Heads of Government of the U.S.S.R., U.S.A., and U.K., which took place from July 17 to August 2, 1945, came to the following conclusions:

I. Establishment of a Council of Foreign Ministers.

The Governments of the United Kingdom, the United States and the U.S.S.R. consider it necessary to begin without delay the essential preparatory work upon the peace settlements in Europe. To this end they are agreed that there should be established a Council of the Foreign Ministers of the Five Great Powers to prepare treaties of peace with the European enemy States, for submission to the United Nations. The Council would also be empowered to propose settlements of outstanding territorial questions in Europe and to consider such other matters as member Governments might agree to refer to it. . . . It was felt that further work of a detailed character for the coordination of Allied policy for the control of Germany and Austria would in future fall within the competence of the Control Council at Berlin and the Allied Commission at Vienna. . . .

II. The Principles to Govern the Treatment of Germany. . . .

A. Political Principles.

1. In accordance with the Agreement on Control Machinery in Germany, supreme authority in Germany is exercised, on instructions from their respective Governments, by the Commanders-in-Chief of the armed forces of the United States of America, the United Kingdom, the Union of Soviet Socialist Republics, and the French Republic, each in his own zone of occupation, and also jointly, in matters affecting Germany as a whole, in their capacity as members of the Control Council.

2. So far as is practicable, there shall be uniformity of treatment of the German population throughout Germany.

3. The purposes of the occupation of Germany by which the Control Council shall be guided are: (i) The complete disarmament and demilitarization of Germany and the elimination or control of all German industry that could be used for

military production. . . . (ii) To convince the German people that they have suffered a total military defeat and that they cannot escape responsibility for what they have brought upon themselves, since their own ruthless warfare and the fanatical Nazi resistance have destroyed German economy and made chaos and suffering inevitable. (iii) To destroy the National Socialist Party and its affiliated and supervised organizations, to dissolve all Nazi institutions, to ensure that they are not revived in any form, and to prevent all Nazi and militarist activity or propaganda. (iv) To prepare for the eventual reconstruction of German political life on a democratic basis and for eventual peaceful cooperation in international life by Germany.

4. All Nazi laws which provided the basis of the Hitler regime or established discriminations on grounds of race, creed, or political opinion shall be abolished. No such discriminations, whether legal, administrative or otherwise, shall be tolerated.

5. War criminals and those who have participated in planning or carrying out Nazi enterprises involving or resulting in atrocities or war crimes shall be arrested and brought to judgment. Nazi leaders, influential Nazi supporters and high officials of Nazi organizations and institutions and any other persons dangerous to the occupation or its objectives shall be arrested and interned.

6. All members of the Nazi Party who have been more than nominal participants in its activities and all other persons hostile to Allied purposes shall be removed from public and semi-public office, and from positions of responsibility in important private undertakings. Such persons shall be replaced by persons who, by their political and moral qualities, are deemed capable of assisting in developing genuine democratic institutions in Germany.

7. German education shall be so controlled as completely to eliminate Nazi and militarist doctrines and to make possible the successful development of democratic ideas.

8. The judicial system will be reorganized in accordance with the principles of democracy, of justice under law, and of equal rights for all citizens without distinction of race, nationality or religion.

9. The administration in Germany should be directed towards the decentralization of the political structure and the development of local responsibility. . . . To this end:—(i) local self-government shall be restored throughout Germany on democratic principles. . . ; (ii) all democratic political parties with rights of assembly and of public discussion shall be allowed and encouraged throughout Germany; (iii) representative and elective principles shall be introduced into regional, provincial and state (Land) administration as rapidly as may be justified by the successful application of these principles in local self-government; (iv) for the time being, no central German Government shall be established. Notwithstanding this, however, certain essential central German administrative departments, headed by State Secretaries, shall be established, particularly in the fields of finance, transport, communications, foreign trade and industry. Such departments will act under the direction of the Control Council.

10. Subject to the necessity for maintaining military security, freedom of speech, press and religion shall be permitted, and religious institutions shall be respected. Subject likewise to the maintenance of military security, the formation of free trade unions shall be permitted.

B. Economic Principles.

11. In order to eliminate Germany's war potential, the production of arms, ammunition and implements of war as well as all types of aircraft and sea-going ships shall be prohibited and prevented. Production of metals, chemicals, machinery and other items that are directly necessary to a war economy shall be rigidly controlled.... Productive capacity not needed for permitted production shall be removed in accordance with the reparations plan....

12. At the earliest practicable date, the German economy shall be decentralized for the purpose of eliminating the present excessive concentration of economic power as exemplified in particular by cartels, syndicates, trusts and other monopolistic arrangements.

13. In organizing the German Economy, primary emphasis shall be given to the development of agriculture and peaceful domestic industries.

14. During the period of occupation Germany shall be treated as a single economic unit. To this end common policies shall be established in regard to: (a) mining and industrial production and its allocation; (b) agriculture, forestry and fishing; (c) wages, prices and rationing; (d) import and export programs for Germany as a whole; (e) currency and banking, central taxation and customs; (f) reparation and removal of industrial war potential; (g) transportation and communications. In applying these policies account shall be taken, where appropriate, of varying local conditions.

15. Allied controls shall be imposed upon the German economy but only to the extent necessary....

16. In the imposition and maintenance of economic controls established by the Control Council, German administrative machinery shall be created and the German authorities shall be required to the fullest extent practicable to proclaim and assume administration of such controls. Thus it should be brought home to the German people that the responsibility for the administration of such controls and any break-down in these controls will rest with themselves. Any German controls which may run counter to the objectives of occupation will be prohibited.

17. Measures shall be promptly taken: (a) to effect essential repair of transport; (b) to enlarge coal production; (c) to maximize agricultural output; and (d) to erect emergency repair of housing and essential utilities.

18. Appropriate steps shall be taken by the Control Council to exercise control and the power of disposition over German-owned external assets not already under the control of United Nations which have taken part in the war against Germany.

19. Payment of Reparations should leave enough resources to enable the German people to subsist without external assistance. In working out the economic balance of Germany the necessary means must be provided to pay for imports approved by the Control Council in Germany. The proceeds of exports from current production and stocks shall be available in the first place for payment for such imports....

III. Reparations from Germany.

1. Reparation claims of the U.S.S.R. shall be met by removals from the zone of Germany occupied by the U.S.S.R., and from appropriate German external assets.

2. The U.S.S.R. undertakes to settle the reparation claims of Poland from its own share of reparations.

3. The reparation claims of the United States, the United Kingdom and other countries entitled to reparations shall be

met from the Western Zones and from appropriate German external assets.

4. In addition to the reparations to be taken by the U.S.S.R. from its own zone of occupation, the U.S.S.R. shall receive additionally from the Western Zones: (a) 15 per cent of such usable and complete industrial capital equipment. . . . (b) 10 per cent of such industrial capital equipment as is unnecessary for the German peace economy and should be removed from the Western Zones. . . .

8. The Soviet Government renounces all claims in respect of reparations to shares of German enterprises which are located in the Western Zones of Germany as well as to German foreign assets in all countries except those specified in paragraph 9 below.

9. The Governments of the U.K. and U.S.A. renounce all claims in respect of reparations to shares of German enterprises which are located in the Eastern Zone of occupation in Germany, as well as to German foreign assets in Bulgaria, Finland, Hungary, Rumania and Eastern Austria.

10. The Soviet Government makes no claims to gold captured by the Allied troops in Germany.

IV. Disposal of the German Navy and Merchant Marine

A. The following principles for the distribution of the German Navy were agreed:

1. The total strength of the German surface navy, excluding ships sunk and those taken over from Allied Nations, but including ships under construction or repair, shall be divided equally among the U.S.S.R., U.K., and U.S.A.

2. Ships under construction or repair mean those ships whose construction or repair may be completed within three to six months, according to the type of ship. Whether such ships under construction or repair shall be completed or repaired shall be determined by the technical commission appointed by the Three Powers. . . .

3. The larger part of the German submarine fleet shall be sunk. . . .

4. All stocks of armament, ammunition and supplies of the German Navy appertaining to the vessels transferred . . . shall be handed over to the respective powers receiving such ships.

5. The Three Governments agree to constitute a tripartite naval commission. . . .

6. The Three Governments agreed that transfers, including those of ships under construction and repair, shall be completed as soon as possible. . . .

B. The following principles for the distribution of the German Merchant Marine were agreed:—The German Merchant Marine, surrendered to the Three Powers and wherever located, shall be divided equally among the U.S.S.R., the U.K., and the U.S.A. . . .

V. City of Koenigsberg and the Adjacent Area.

The Conference examined a proposal by the Soviet Government to the effect that pending the final determination of territorial questions at the peace settlement, the section of the western frontier of the Union of Soviet Socialist Republics which is adjacent to the Baltic Sea should pass from a point on the eastern shore of the Bay of Danzig to the east, north of Braunsberg-Goldap, to the meeting point of the frontiers of Lithuania, the Polish Republic and East Prussia. The Conference has agreed in principle to the proposal of the Soviet Government concerning the ultimate transfer to the Soviet Union of the City of Koenigsberg and the area adjacent to it. . . .

VI. War Criminals. The Three Governments have taken note of the discussions which have been proceeding in recent weeks . . . with a view to reaching agreement on the methods of trial of those major war criminals whose crimes under the Moscow Declaration of October, 1943 have no particular geographical localization. The Three Governments reaffirm their intention to bring these criminals to swift and sure justice. They hope that the negotiations in London will result in speedy agreement being reached for this purpose, and they regard it as a matter of great importance that the trial of these major criminals should begin at the earliest possible date. . . .

VII. Austria. The Conference examined a proposal by the Soviet Government on the extension of the authority of the Austrian Provisional Government to all of Austria. The three governments agreed that they were prepared to examine this question after the entry of the British and American forces into the city of Vienna. It was agreed that reparations should not be exacted from Austria.

VIII. Poland.

A. Declaration. We have taken note with pleasure of . . . the formation . . . of a Polish Provisional Government of National Unity recognized by the Three Powers. . . . The Three Powers are anxious to assist . . . in facilitating the return to Poland as soon as practicable of all Poles abroad who wish to go. . . . The Three Powers note that the Polish Provisional Government . . . has agreed to the holding of free and unfettered elections as soon as possible on the basis of universal suffrage

and secret ballot in which all democratic and anti-Nazi parties shall have the right to take part and to put forward candidates, and that representatives of the Allied press shall enjoy full freedom to report to the world upon developments in Poland before and during the elections.

B. Western Frontier of Poland. . . . The three Heads of Government agree that, pending the final determination of Poland's western frontier, the former German territories cast of a line running from the Baltic Sea . . . along the Oder River to the confluence of the western Neisse River and along the Western Neisse to the Czechoslovak frontier [i.e., what became known as the Oder-Neisse line between East Germany and Poland—Ed.], including that portion of East Prussia not placed under the administration of the Union of Soviet Socialist Republics in accordance with the understanding reached at this conference and including the area of the former free city of Danzig, shall be under the administration of the Polish State and for such purposes should not be considered as part of the Soviet zone of occupation in Germany.

IX. Conclusion on Peace Treaties and Admission to the United Nations Organization. The three Governments consider it desirable that the present anomalous position of Italy, Bulgaria, Finland, Hungary and Rumania should be terminated by the conclusion of Peace Treaties. . . . As regards the admission of other States into the United Nations Organization, Article 4 of the *Charter of the United Nations* declares that: 1: Membership in the United Nations is open to all other peace-loving States who accept the obligations contained in the present Charter and, in the judgment of the organization, are able and willing to carry out these obligations; 2. The admission of any such State to membership in the United Nations will be effected by a decision of the General Assembly upon the recommendation of the Security Council. The three Governments ... will support applications for membership from those States which have remained neutral during the war and which fulfill the qualifications set out above. The three Governments feel bound however to make it clear that they for their part would not favour any application for membership put forward by the present Spanish Government, which, having been founded with the support of the Axis Powers, does not, in view of its origins, its nature, its record and its close association with the aggressor States, possess the qualifications necessary to justify such membership.

X. Territorial Trusteeship. The Conference examined a proposal by the Soviet Government on the question of trusteeship territories as defined in the decision of the Crimea Conference [i.e., Yalta] and in the Charter of the United Nations Organization. After an exchange of views on this question it was decided that the disposition of any former Italian colonial territories was one to be decided in connection with the preparation of a peace treaty for Italy and that the question of Italian colonial territory would be considered by the September Council of Ministers of Foreign Affairs.

XI. Revised Allied Control Commission Procedure in Rumania, Bulgaria and Hungary. The three Governments took note that the Soviet Representatives on the Allied Control Commissions in Rumania, Bulgaria, and Hungary, have communicated to their United Kingdom and United States colleagues proposals for improving the work of the Control Commissions, now that hostilities in Europe have ceased.

The three Governments agreed that the revision of the procedures of the Allied Control Commissions in these countries would now be undertaken, taking into account the interests and responsibilities of the three Governments. . . .

XII. Orderly Transfer of German Populations. The Three Governments, having considered the question in all its aspects, recognize that the transfer to Germany of German populations, or elements thereof, remaining in Poland, Czechoslovakia and Hungary, will have to be undertaken. They agree that any transfers that take place should be effected in an orderly and humane manner. Since the influx of a large number of Germans into Germany would increase the burden already resting on the occupying authorities, they consider that the Control Council in Germany should in the first instance examine the problem, with special regard to the question of the equitable distribution of these Germans among the several zones of occupation. . . .

XIII. Oil Equipment in Rumania. The Conference agreed to set up two bilateral commissions of experts . . . as a basis for the settlement of questions arising from the removal of oil equipment in Rumania. . . .

XIV. Iran. It was agreed that Allied troops should be withdrawn immediately from Tehran, and that further stages of the withdrawal of troops from Iran should be considered at the meeting of the Council of Foreign Ministers to be held in London in September, 1945.

XV. The International Zone of Tangier. A proposal by the Soviet Government was examined and the following decisions were reached: Having examined the question of the Zone of Tangier, the three Governments have agreed that this Zone, which includes the City of Tangier and the area adjacent to it, in view of its special strategic importance, shall remain international. The question of Tangier will be discussed in the near future at a meeting in Paris of representatives of the Governments of the Union of Soviet Socialist Republics, the United States of America, the United Kingdom and France.

XVI. The Black Sea Straits. The Three Governments recognized that the Convention concluded at Montreux should be revised as failing to meet present-day conditions. It was agreed that as the next step the matter should be the subject of direct conversations between each of the three Governments and the Turkish Government.

XVII. International Inland Waterways. The Conference considered a proposal of the U.S. Delegation on this subject and agreed to refer it for consideration to the forthcoming meeting of the Council of Foreign Ministers in London.

XVIII. European Inland Transport Conference. The British and U.S. Delegations to the Conference informed the Soviet Delegation of the desire of the British and U.S. Governments to reconvene the European Inland Transport Conference. . . . The Soviet Government agreed that it would participate in this conference.

XIX. Directives to Military Commanders on Allied Control Council for Germany. The Three Governments agreed that each would send a directive to its representative on the Control Council for Germany informing him of all decisions of the Conference affecting matters within the scope of his duties.

XX. Use of Allied Property for Satellite Reparations or War Trophies. The

proposal (Annex II) presented by the United States Delegation was accepted in principle by the Conference, but the drafting of an agreement on the matter was left to be worked out through diplomatic channels.

XXI. Military Talks. During the Conference there were meetings between the Chiefs of Staff of the Three Governments on military matters of common interest.

ANNEX I . . . In view of the changed situation in connection with the termination of the war against Germany, the Soviet Government finds it necessary to establish the following order of work for the Allied Control Commission in Hungary. . . . The British and American representatives in the ACC will take part in general conferences of heads of divisions and delegates of the ACC, convoked by the President of the ACC, which meetings will be regular in nature. The British and American representatives will also participate personally or through their representatives in appropriate instances in mixed commissions created by the President of the ACC for questions connected with the execution by the ACC of its functions. Free movement by the American and British representatives in the country will be permitted provided that the ACC is previously informed of the time and route of the journeys. . . .

ANNEX II . . . The burden of reparation and "war trophies" should not fall on Allied nationals. *Capital Equipment*—We object to the removal of such Allied property as reparations, "war trophies", or under any other guise. . . . The United States looks to the other occupying powers for the return of any equipment already removed and the cessation of removals. . . . These principles apply to all property wholly or substantially owned by Allied nationals.... *Current Production*—While the U.S. does not oppose reparation out of current production of Allied investments, the satellite must provide immediate and adequate compensation to the Allied nationals including sufficient foreign exchange or products so that they can recover reasonable foreign currency expenditures and transfer a reasonable return on their investment....

Proclamation Defining Terms for Japanese Surrender, July 26, 1945

We—The President of the United States, the President of the National Government of the Republic of China, and the Prime Minister of Great Britain, representing the hundreds of millions of our countrymen, have conferred and agree that Japan shall be given an opportunity to end this war. The prodigious land, sea and air forces of the United States, the British Empire and of China, many times reinforced by their armies and air fleets from the west, are poised to strike the final blows upon Japan. This military power is sustained and inspired by the determination of all the Allied Nations to prosecute the war against Japan until she ceases to resist.... The full application of our military power, backed by our resolve ... mean the inevitable and complete destruction of the Japanese armed forces and just as inevitably the utter devastation of the Japanese homeland.... There must be eliminated for all time the authority and influence of those who have deceived and misled the people of Japan into embarking on world conquest, for we insist that a new order of peace security and justice will be impossible until irresponsible militarism is driven from the world. Until such a new order is established and until

there is convincing proof that Japan's war-making power is destroyed, points in Japanese territory to be designated by the Allies shall be occupied to secure the achievement of the basic objectives we are here setting forth. The terms of the Cairo Declaration shall be carried out and Japanese sovereignty shall be limited to the islands of Honshu, Hokkaido, Kyushu, Shikoku and such minor islands as we determine.... We do not intend that the Japanese shall be enslaved as a race or destroyed as a nation, but stern justice shall be meted out to all war criminals, including those who have visited cruelties upon our prisoners. The Japanese Government shall remove all obstacles to the revival and strengthening of democratic tendencies among the Japanese people. Freedom of speech, of religion, and of thought, as well as respect for the fundamental human rights shall be established. Japan shall be permitted to maintain such industries as will sustain her economy and permit the exaction of just reparations in kind, but not those which would enable her to re-arm for war. To this end, access to, as distinguished from control of, raw materials shall be permitted. Eventual Japanese participation in world trade relations shall be permitted. The occupying forces of the Allies shall be withdrawn from Japan as soon as these objectives have been accomplished and there has been established in accordance with the freely expressed will of the Japanese people a peacefully inclined and responsible government. We call upon the government of Japan to proclaim now the unconditional surrender of all Japanese armed forces, and to provide proper and adequate assurances of their good faith in such action. The alternative for Japan is prompt and utter destruction.

Chapter 11

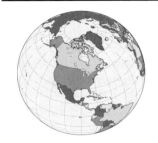

The Onset of the Cold War: Foreign and National Security Policy Statements

20. *Toward Containment: George Kennan's Long Telegram*
(1946)

On February 22, 1946, George Kennan, foreign service officer in the U.S. embassy in Moscow, replied apologetically to a State Department inquiry, saying, "answer . . . involves questions so intricate, so delicate, so strange to our form of thought, and so important to analysis of our international environment that I cannot compress answers into single brief message without yielding to what I feel would be dangerous degree of oversimplification." In fact, this long telegram would provide a basis for what would become the containment *doctrine, articulated publicly the following year in the anonymous "X" article written by Kennan in* Foreign Affairs, *the journal of the Council on Foreign Relations in New York. We reprint here his policy prescriptions for dealing with the Soviet Union. In this telegram he argues: The Soviet Union does not tend to "take unnecessary risks" and "is highly sensitive to logic of force, . . . it can easily withdraw—and usually does—when strong resistance is encountered at any point. Thus, if the adversary has sufficient force and makes clear his readiness to use it, he rarely has to do so. If situations are properly handled there need be no prestige-engaging showdowns." This clearly represents the idea of* containment *as originally conceived by George Kennan.*

In summary, *we have here a political force committed fanatically to the belief that with US there can be no permanent* modus vivendi, *that it is desirable and necessary that the internal harmony of our society be disrupted, our traditional way of life be destroyed, the international authority of our* state be broken, if Soviet power is to be secure. This political force has complete power of disposition over energies of one of world's greatest peoples and resources of world's richest national territory, and is borne along by deep and powerful currents of Russian nationalism. In addition, *it has an elaborate and far-flung apparatus for exertion of its influence in other countries, an apparatus of amazing flexibility and versatility, managed by people whose experience and skill in underground methods are presumably without parallel in history.* Finally, it is seemingly inaccessible to considerations of reality in its basic reactions. For it, the vast fund of objective fact about human society is not, as with us, the measure against which outlook is constantly being tested and re-formed, but a grab bag from which individual items are selected arbitrarily and tendenciously to bolster an outlook already preconceived. This is admittedly not a pleasant picture. Problem of how to cope with this force undoubtedly [is] greatest task our diplomacy has ever faced and probably greatest it will ever have to face. It should be point of departure from which our political general staff work at present juncture should proceed. It should be approached with same thoroughness and care as solution of major strategic problem in war and, if necessary, with no smaller outlay in planning effort. I cannot attempt to suggest all answers here. But I would like to record *my conviction that problem is within our power to solve—and that without recourse to any general military conflict.* And in support of this conviction there are certain observations for a more encouraging nature I should like to make.

(1) *Soviet power,* unlike that of Hitlerite Germany, is neither schematic nor adventuristic. It does not work by fixed plans. It *does not take unnecessary risks.* Impervious to logic of reason, and *it is highly sensitive to logic of force.* For this reason it can easily withdraw—and usually does—when strong resistance is encountered at any point. *Thus, if the adversary has sufficient force and makes clear his readiness to use it, he rarely has to do so.* If situations are properly handled there need be no prestige-engaging showdowns.

(2) Gauged against Western world as a whole, *Soviets are still by far the weaker force.* Thus, their success will really depend on degree of cohesion, firmness and vigor which Western world can muster. And this is factor which it is within our power to influence.

(3) Success of Soviet system, as form of internal power, is not yet finally proven. It has yet to be demonstrated that it can survive supreme test of successive transfer of power from one individual or group to another. Lenin's death was first such transfer, and its effects wracked Soviet state for 15 years. After Stalin's death or retirement will be second. But even this will not be final test. Soviet internal system will now be subjected, by virtue of recent territorial expansions, to series of additional strains which once proved severe tax on Tsardom. We here are convinced that never since termination of civil war have mass of Russian people been emotionally farther removed from doctrines of Communist Party than they are today. *In Russia, party has now become a* great and—for the moment—highly *successful apparatus of dictatorial administration, but it has ceased to be a source of emotional inspiration.* Thus, internal soundness and permanence of movement need not yet be regarded as assured.

(4) All *Soviet propaganda* beyond Soviet security sphere is basically negative and destructive. It *should* therefore *be relatively easy to combat* it by any intelligent and really constructive program.

For these reasons I think we may approach calmly and with good heart problem of how to deal with Russia. As to how this approach should be made, I only wish to advance, by way of conclusion, following comments:

(1) Our first step must be to apprehend, and recognize for what it is, the nature of the movement with which we are dealing. We must study it with same courage, detachment, objectivity, and same determination not to be emotionally provoked or unseated by it, with which doctor studies unruly and unreasonable individual.

(2) *We must see that our public is educated to realities of Russian situation.* I cannot overemphasize importance of this. Press cannot do this alone. It must be done mainly by Government, which is necessarily more experienced and better informed on practical problems involved. In this we need not be deterred by [the negative appearance] of picture. I am convinced that there would be far less hysterical anti-Sovietism in our country today if realities of this situation were better understood by our people. There is nothing as dangerous or as terrifying as the unknown. It may also be argued that to reveal more information on our difficulties with Russia would reflect unfavorably on Russian-American relations. I feel that if there is any real risk here involved, it is one which we should have courage to face, and sooner the better. But I cannot see what we would be risking. Our stake in this country, even coming on heels of tremendous demonstrations of our friendship for Russian people, is remarkably small. We have here no investments to guard, no actual trade to lose, virtually no citizens to protect, few cultural contacts to preserve. Our only stake [lies] in what we hope rather than what we have; and *I am con-*

vinced we have better chance of realizing those hopes *if our public is enlightened and if our dealings with Russians are placed entirely on realistic and matter-of-fact basis.*

(3) *Much depends on health and vigor of our own society.* World communism is like malignant parasite which feeds only on diseased tissue. This is point at which domestic and foreign policies meet. *Every courageous and incisive measure to solve internal problems of our own society, to improve self-confidence, discipline, morale and community spirit of our own people, is a diplomatic victory over Moscow worth a thousand diplomatic notes and joint communiqués.* If we cannot abandon fatalism and indifference in face of deficiencies of our own society, Moscow will profit—Moscow cannot help profiting by them in its foreign policies.

(4) *We must formulate and put forward for other nations a much more positive and constructive picture of sort of world we would like to see* than we have put forward in past. It is not enough to urge people to develop political processes similar to our own. Many foreign peoples, in Europe at least, are tired and frightened by experiences of past, and are less interested in abstract freedom than in security. They are seeking guidance rather than responsibilities. We should be better able than Russians to give them this. And, unless we do, Russians certainly will.

(5) Finally *we must have courage and self-confidence to cling to our own methods and conceptions of human society. After all, the greatest danger that can befall us in coping with this problem of Soviet communism is that we shall allow ourselves to become like those with whom we are coping.*

21. Winston Churchill's "Sinews of Peace": The Iron Curtain Speech

(1946)

Accompanied by President Harry Truman to his home state, former British prime minister Winston Churchill (still leader of the Loyal Opposition in the British parliament) delivered this landmark address on March 5, 1946 at Westminster College in Fulton, Missouri. His hope is for the success of multilateral diplomacy within the context of the new United Nations organization as a means for avoiding war and tyranny in a post–World War II period. Rather than engage yet again in balance-of-power politics, he underscores the importance of military strength as a foundation for successful multilateral diplomacy, the Anglo-American link a core building block for success in achieving peace and advancing the human condition. On the other hand, he also takes full account of the extension of the Soviet sphere into central Europe, which posed a challenge to regimes in Western European countries. Indeed, the "iron curtain" that he already saw as dividing East from West became the cold war geopolitical definition of a newly constructed postwar Europe.

. . . *The United States stands at this time at the pinnacle of world power.* It is a solemn moment for the American Democracy. For with primacy in power is also joined an awe-inspiring accountability to the future. If you look around you, *you must feel* not only *the sense of duty* done but also you must feel anxiety lest you fall below the level of achievement. *Opportunity is here now,* clear and shining for both our countries. . . .

When American military men approach some serious situation they are wont to write at the head of their directive the words "over-all strategic concept." There is wisdom in this, as it leads to clarity of thought. What then is the over-all strategic concept which we should inscribe today? It is nothing less than the safety and welfare, the freedom and progress, of all the homes and families of all the men and women in all the lands. . . . To give security to these countless homes, they must be shielded from the two giant marauders, war and tyranny. . . . Our supreme task and duty is to guard the homes of the common people from the horrors and miseries of another war. We are all agreed on that.

Our American military colleagues, after having proclaimed their "over-all strategic concept" and computed available resources, always proceed to the next step—namely, the method. Here again there is widespread agreement. *A world organization has already been erected for the prime purpose of preventing war, UNO [i.e., United Nations Organization], the successor of the League of Nations, with the decisive addition of the United States and all that means, is already at work.* We must make sure that its work is fruitful, that it is a reality and not a sham, that it is a force for action, and not merely a frothing of words, that it is a true temple of peace in which the shields of many nations can some day be hung up, and not merely a cockpit in a Tower of Babel. *Before we cast away the solid assurances of national armaments for self-preservation we must be certain that our temple is built, not upon shifting sands or quagmires, but upon the rock.* Anyone can see with his eyes open that our path will be difficult and also long, but if we persevere together as we did in the two world wars—though not, alas, in the interval between them—I cannot doubt that we shall achieve our common purpose in the end.

I have, however, a definite and practical proposal to make for action. Courts and magistrates may be set up but they cannot function without sheriffs and constables. *The United Nations Organization must immediately begin to be equipped with an international armed force.* . . . This might be started on a modest scale and would grow as confidence grew. I wished to see this done after the first world war, and I devoutly trust it may be done forthwith.

It would nevertheless be wrong and imprudent to entrust the secret knowledge or experience of the atomic bomb, which the United States, Great Britain, and Canada now share, to the world organization, while it is still in its infancy. It would be criminal madness to cast it adrift in this still agitated and un-united world. . . . Ultimately, when the essential brotherhood of man is truly embodied and expressed in a world organization with all the necessary practical safeguards to make it effective, these powers would naturally be confided to that world organization.

Now I come to the second danger of these two marauders which threatens the cottage, the home, and the ordinary people—namely, tyranny. . . . *The power of the State is exercised without restraint, either by dictators or by compact oligarchies operating through a privileged party and a political police. It is not our duty at this time when difficulties are so numerous to interfere forcibly in the internal affairs of countries which we have not conquered in war.* But we must never cease to proclaim in fearless tones the great principles of freedom and the rights of man which are the joint inheritance of the English-speaking world and which through Magna Carta, the Bill of Rights, the Habeas Corpus, trial by jury, and the English common law find their

most famous expression in the American Declaration of Independence.

All this means that the people of any country have the right, and should have the power by constitutional action, by free unfettered elections, with secret ballot, to choose or change the character or form of government under which they dwell; that freedom of speech and thought should reign; that courts of justice, independent of the executive, unbiased by any party, should administer laws which have received the broad assent of large majorities or are consecrated by time and custom. Here are the title deeds of freedom which should lie in every cottage home. Here is the message of the British and American peoples to mankind. Let us preach what we practice—let us practice what we preach.

I have now stated the two great dangers which menace the homes of the people: War and Tyranny. I have not yet spoken of poverty and privation which are in many cases the prevailing anxiety. But *if the dangers of war and tyranny are removed, there is no doubt that science and co-operation can bring* in the next few years to the world, certainly in the next few decades newly taught in the sharpening school of war, *an expansion of material well-being beyond anything that has yet occurred in human experience.* . . . Now, while still pursuing the method of realizing our overall strategic concept, *I come to the crux of what I have traveled here to say. Neither the sure prevention of war, nor the continuous rise of world organization will be gained without what I have called the fraternal association of the English-speaking peoples. This means a special relationship between the British Commonwealth and Empire and the United States.* . . .

I spoke earlier of *the Temple of Peace. Workmen from all countries must build that temple.* If two of the workmen know each other particularly well and are old friends, . . . why cannot they work together at the common task as friends and partners? Why cannot they share their tools and thus increase each other's working powers? Indeed they must do so or else the temple may not be built, or, being built, it may collapse, and we shall all be proved again unteachable and have to go and try to learn again for a third time in a school of war, incomparably more rigorous than that from which we have just been released. The dark ages may return, the Stone Age may return on the gleaming wings of science, and what might now shower immeasurable material blessings upon mankind, may even bring about its total destruction. Beware, I say; time may be short. *Do not let us take the course of allowing events to drift along until it is too late.* If there is to be *a fraternal association* of the kind I have described, *with all the extra strength and security which both our countries can derive from it,* let us make sure that that great fact is known to the world, and that it *plays its part in steadying and stabilizing the foundations of peace.* There is the path of wisdom. *Prevention is better than cure.*

A shadow has fallen upon the scenes so lately lighted by the Allied victory. Nobody knows what Soviet Russia and its Communist international organization intends to do in the immediate future, or what are the limits, if any, to their expansive and proselytizing tendencies. I have a strong admiration and regard for the valiant Russian people and for my wartime comrade, Marshal Stalin. There is deep sympathy and goodwill in Britain—and I doubt not here also—towards the peoples of all the Russias and a resolve to persevere through many differences and rebuffs in establishing lasting friendships. *We understand the Russian need to be secure on her western frontiers by the removal of all possibility of German aggres-*

sion. *We welcome Russia to her rightful place among the leading nations of the world.* We welcome her flag upon the seas. Above all, we welcome constant, frequent and growing contacts between the Russian people and our own people on both sides of the Atlantic. *It is my duty, however,* for I am sure you would wish me to state the facts as I see them to you, *to place before you certain facts about the present position in Europe.*

From Stettin in the Baltic to Trieste in the Adriatic, an iron curtain has descended across the Continent. Behind that line lie all the capitals of the ancient states of Central and Eastern Europe. Warsaw, Berlin, Prague, Vienna, Budapest, Belgrade, Bucharest and Sofia, all these famous cities and the populations around them lie in what I must call the Soviet sphere, and all are subject in one form or another, not only to Soviet influence but to a very high and, in many cases, increasing measure of control from Moscow. . . . *Whatever conclusions may be drawn from these facts—and facts they are—this is certainly not the Liberated Europe we fought to build up. Nor is it one which contains the essentials of permanent peace.*

The safety of the world requires a new unity in Europe, from which no nation should be permanently outcast. It is from the quarrels of the strong parent races in Europe that the world wars we have witnessed, or which occurred in former times, have sprung. Twice in our own lifetime we have seen the United States, against their wishes and their traditions, against arguments, the force of which it is impossible not to comprehend, drawn by irresistible forces, into these wars in time to secure the victory of the good cause, but only after frightful slaughter and devastation had occurred. *Twice the United States has had to send several millions of its young men across the Atlantic to find the war; but now war can find any nation,* wherever it may dwell between dusk and dawn. *Surely we should work with conscious purpose for a grand pacification of Europe, within the structure of the United Nations and in accordance with its Charter.* That I feel is an open cause of policy of very great importance.

In front of the iron curtain which lies across Europe [i.e., what would come to be called "the West"—Ed.] *are other causes for anxiety.* In a great number of countries, far from the Russian frontiers and throughout the world, Communist fifth columns are established and work in complete unity and absolute obedience to the directions they receive from the Communist center. Except in the British Commonwealth and in the United States where Communism is in its infancy, the Communist parties or fifth columns constitute a growing challenge. . . .

The outlook is also anxious in the Far East. . . . The Agreement which was made at Yalta, to which I was a party, was extremely favorable to Soviet Russia, but it was made at a time when no one could say that the German war might not extend all through the summer and autumn of 1945 and when the Japanese war was expected to last for a further 18 months from the end of the German war. . . .

I have felt bound to portray the shadow which, alike in the west and in the east, falls upon the world. I was a high minister at the time of the Versailles Treaty and a close friend of Mr. Lloyd-George, who was the head of the British delegation at Versailles. . . . In those days there were high hopes and unbounded confidence that the wars were over, and that the League of Nations would become all-powerful. I do not see or feel that same confidence or even the same hopes in the haggard world at the present time.

On the other hand I repulse the idea that a new war is inevitable; still more that it is imminent. It is because I am sure that our fortunes are still in our own hands and that we hold the power to save the future, that I feel the duty to speak out now that I have the occasion and the opportunity to do so. *I do not believe that Soviet Russia desires war. What they desire is the fruits of war and the indefinite expansion of their power and doctrines. But what we have to consider here today while time remains, is the permanent prevention of war and the establishment of conditions of freedom and democracy as rapidly as possible in all countries.* . . .

From what I have seen of our Russian friends and Allies during the war, I am convinced that there is nothing they admire so much as strength, and there is nothing for which they have less respect than for weakness, especially military weakness. For that reason the old doctrine of a balance of power is unsound. We cannot afford, if we can help it, to work on narrow margins, offering temptations to a trial of strength. *If the Western Democracies stand together in strict adherence to the principles of the United Nations Charter, their influence for furthering those principles will be immense* and no one is likely to molest them. If however they become divided or falter in their duty and if these all-important years are allowed to slip away then indeed catastrophe may overwhelm us all. . . .

Last time I saw it all coming and cried aloud to my own fellow-countrymen and to the world, but no one paid any attention. Up till the year 1933 or even 1935, Germany might have been saved from the awful fate which has overtaken her and we might all have been spared the miseries Hitler let loose upon mankind. *There never was a war in all history easier to prevent by timely action than the one which has just desolated such great areas of the globe.* It could have been prevented in my belief without the firing of a single shot, and Germany might be powerful, prosperous and honored to-day; but no one would listen and one by one we were all sucked into the awful whirlpool. We surely must not let that happen again. This can only be achieved by reaching now, in 1946, *a good understanding on all points with Russia under the general authority of the United Nations Organization and by the maintenance of that good understanding through many peaceful years,* by the world instrument, supported by the whole strength of the English-speaking world and all its connections. There is the solution which I respectfully offer to you in this Address to which I have given the title "The Sinews of Peace." . . .

If the population of the English-speaking Commonwealths be added to that of the United States with all that such

co-operation implies in the air, on the sea, all over the globe and in science and in industry, and in moral force, there will be no quivering, precarious balance of power to offer its temptation to ambition or adventure. On the contrary, there will be an overwhelming assurance of security. If we adhere faithfully to the Charter of the United Nations and walk forward in sedate and sober strength seeking no one's land or treasure, seeking to lay no arbitrary control upon the thoughts of men; if all British moral and material forces and convictions are joined with your own in fraternal association, the high-roads of the future will be clear, not only for us but for all, not only for our time, but for a century to come.

---

22. *The Truman Doctrine*

(1947)

President Harry Truman justifies this call on March 12, 1947 for aid to Greece and Turkey as an early postwar anticommunist effort. Strengthening noncommunist regimes through foreign aid and other assistance is core to the Truman Doctrine. Like Kennan's Long Telegram and the containment doctrine, the Truman Doctrine treats the Soviet Union and communist movements it supports as rivals. Truman also puts aid to Greece and Turkey in a West-versus-East context. The cold war clearly is under way.

Mr. President, Mr. Speaker, Members of the Congress of the United States:

The gravity of the situation which confronts the world today necessitates my appearance before a joint session of the Congress. The foreign policy and the national security of this country are involved.

One aspect of the present situation, which I wish to present to you at this time for your consideration and decision, concerns Greece and Turkey. *The United States has received from the Greek Govern-*

ment an urgent appeal for financial and economic assistance. Preliminary reports from the American Economic Mission now in Greece and reports from the American Ambassador in Greece corroborate the statement of the Greek Government that *assistance is imperative if Greece is to survive as a free nation.* I do not believe that the American people and the Congress wish to turn a deaf ear to the appeal of the Greek Government. . . .

The very existence of the Greek state is today threatened by the terrorist activities of several thousand armed men, led by Communists, who defy the government's authority at a number of points, particularly along the northern boundaries. A Commission appointed by the United Nations Security Council is at present investigating disturbed conditions in northern Greece and alleged border violations along the frontier between Greece on the one hand and Albania, Bulgaria, and Yugoslavia on the other.

Meanwhile, the Greek Government is unable to cope with the situation. The Greek army is small and poorly equipped. It needs supplies and equipment if it is to restore the authority of the government throughout Greek territory. *Greece must have assistance if it is to become a self-supporting and self-respecting democracy. The United States must supply that assistance.* We have already extended to Greece certain types of relief and economic aid but these are inadequate.

There is no other country to which democratic Greece can turn. No other nation is willing and able to provide the necessary support for a democratic Greek government. The British Government, which has been helping Greece, can give no further financial or economic aid after March 31. Great Britain finds itself under the necessity of reducing or liquidating its commitments in several parts of the world, including Greece.

We have considered how the United Nations might assist in this crisis. But the situation is an urgent one requiring immediate action and the United Nations and its related organizations are not in a position to extend help of the kind that is required. . . .

Greece's neighbor, *Turkey, also deserves our attention. The future of Turkey as an independent and economically sound state is* *clearly no less important to the freedom-loving peoples of the world than the future of Greece. . . .* The British government has informed us that, owing to its own difficulties can no longer extend financial or economic aid to Turkey. As in the case of Greece, if Turkey is to have the assistance it needs, the United States must supply it. We are the only country able to provide that help. . . .

One of the primary objectives of the foreign policy of the United States is the creation of conditions in which we and other nations will be able to work out a way of life free from coercion. . . . I believe that it must be the policy of the United States to support free peoples who are resisting attempted subjugation by armed minorities or by outside pressures. I believe that we must assist free peoples to work out their own destinies in their own way. I believe that our help should be primarily through economic and financial aid which is essential to economic stability and orderly political processes. . . .

Should we fail to aid Greece and Turkey in this fateful hour, the effect will be far reaching to the West as well as to the East. We must take immediate and resolute action. I therefore ask the Congress to provide authority for assistance to Greece and Turkey in the amount of $400,000,000 for the period ending June 30, 1948. . . .

This is a serious course upon which we embark. I would not recommend it except that the alternative is much more serious. *The United States contributed $341,000,000,000 toward winning World War II.* This is an investment in world freedom and world peace. *The assistance that I am recommending for Greece and Turkey amounts to little more than one tenth of one per cent of this investment.* It is only common sense that we should safeguard this investment and make sure that it was not in vain. The seeds of totalitarian regimes are nurtured by misery and want. They spread and grow in the evil soil of poverty and strife. They reach their full growth when the hope of a people for a better life has died. We must keep that hope alive.

The free peoples of the world look to us for support in maintaining their freedoms. If we falter in our leadership, we may endanger the peace of the world—and we shall surely endanger the welfare of our own nation. Great responsibilities have been placed upon us by the swift movement of events. I am confident that the Congress will face these responsibilities squarely.

---

23. *The Marshall Plan*
(1947)

As a speaker at Harvard University commencement exercises on June 5, 1947, Secretary of State George C. Marshall unveiled a plan for economic recovery through American capital transfers. In his call for European relief, Marshall says the focus is "not against any country or doctrine but against hunger, poverty, desperation, and chaos." In addition to humanitarian, charitable reasons for such foreign aid, rebuilding postwar European economies was seen by many to be consistent with the Truman Doctrine and as a bulwark against communism, especially against communist expansion into western European countries. Marshall saw such aid in multilateral terms—"a joint one, agreed to by a number, if not all European nations." The plan also put dollars in European hands, some of which would be spent on imports from the United States, thus contributing as well to the employment of American workers at home. Indeed, Marshall comments on adverse consequences for the U.S. economy of failure to take action to remedy the economic situation in Europe. It was also smart politics at the time for the Truman administration to highlight General (now Secretary of State) Marshall as author of this plan for transferring American capital abroad, which underscored its importance for national security.

I need not tell you gentlemen that the world situation is very serious. That must be apparent to all intelligent people. I think one difficulty is that the problem is one of such enormous complexity that the very mass of facts presented to the public by press and radio make it exceedingly difficult for the man in the street to reach a clear appraisement of the situation. Furthermore, the people of this country are distant from the troubled areas of the earth and it is hard for them to comprehend the plight and consequent reaction of the long-suffering peoples, and the effect of those reactions on their governments in connection with our efforts to promote peace in the world.

In considering the requirements for the rehabilitation of Europe the physical loss of life, the visible destruction of cities, factories, mines, and railroads was correctly estimated, but it has become obvious during recent months that this visible destruction was probably less serious than the dislocation of the entire fabric of European economy. . . . *The rehabilitation of the economic structure of Europe quite evidently will require a much longer time and greater effort than had been foreseen. . . .*

The truth of the matter is that Europe's requirements for the next three or four years of foreign food and other essential products—principally from America—are so much greater than her present ability to pay that she must have substantial additional help, or face economic, social, and political deterioration of a very grave character. *The remedy lies in breaking the vicious circle and restoring the confidence of the European people in the economic future of their own countries and of Europe as a whole.* The manufacturer and the farmer throughout wide areas must be able and willing to exchange their products for currencies the continuing value of which is not open to question.

Aside from the demoralizing effect on the world at large and the possibilities of disturbances arising as a result of the desperation of the people concerned, the consequences to the economy of the United States should be apparent to all. It is logical that the United States should do whatever it is able to do to assist in the return of normal economic health in the world, without which there can be no political stability and no assured peace. *Our policy is directed not against any country or doctrine but against hunger, poverty, desperation, and chaos.* Its purpose should be the revival of working economy in the world so as to permit the emergence of political and social conditions in which free institutions can exist. *Such assistance, I am convinced, must not be on a piecemeal basis as various crises develop. Any assistance that this Government may render in the future should provide a cure rather than a mere palliative. Any government that is willing to assist in the task of recovery will find full cooperation,* I am sure, on the part of the United States

Government. Any government which maneuvers to block the recovery of other countries cannot expect help from us. Furthermore, governments, political parties, or groups which seek to perpetuate human misery in order to profit therefrom politically or otherwise will encounter the opposition of the United States.

It is already evident that, before the United States Government can proceed much further in its efforts to alleviate the situation and help start the European world on its way to recovery, there must be some agreement among the countries of Europe as to the requirements of the situation and the part those countries themselves will take in order to give proper effect to whatever action might be undertaken by this Government. It would be neither fitting nor efficacious for this Government to undertake to draw up unilaterally a program designed to place Europe on its feet economically. This is the business of the Europeans. The initiative, I think, must come from Europe. *The role of this country should consist of friendly aid in the drafting of a European program so far as it may be practical for us to do so. The program should be a joint one, agreed to by a number, if not all European nations.*

An essential part of any successful action on the part of the United States is an understanding on the part of the people of America of the character of the problem and the remedies to be applied. Political passion and prejudice should have no part. With foresight, and a willingness on the part of our people to face up to the vast responsibilities which history has clearly placed upon our country, the difficulties I have outlined can and will be overcome.

24. Containment as Cold War Doctrine: George Kennan's "Sources of Soviet Conduct"

(1947)

In the Long Telegram George Kennan understands the importance for the U.S. government of bringing the American public on board with an understanding of the threat and the U.S. response thereto. This anonymous article attributed in the July 1947 issue of Foreign Affairs *to "X" was an obvious indication to most readers that this was a statement by a U.S. government official. Building on the foundation in the then still-classified Long Telegram, Kennan lays out a strategy for dealing with the Soviet Union through* containment *of what are understood to be its expansionist tendencies: "Soviet pressure against the free institutions of the western world is something that can be contained by the adroit and vigilant application of counter-force at a series of constantly shifting geographical and political points, corresponding to the shifts and maneuvers of Soviet policy." He predicts that, accompanied by active measures, containment over time can transform the Soviet Union itself: "The United States has it in its power to increase enormously the strains under which Soviet policy must operate, to force upon the Kremlin a far greater degree of moderation and circumspection than it has had to observe in recent years, and in this way to promote tendencies which must eventually find their outlet in either the breakup or the gradual mellowing of Soviet power"—a vision finally attained at the end of the cold war in 1989, a process completed in 1991 with a failed military coup attempt followed by the breakup of the Communist Party and the subsequent collapse of the Soviet Union.*

The political personality of Soviet power as we know it today is the product of ideology and circumstances: ideology inherited by the present Soviet leaders from the movement in which they had their political origin, and circumstances of the power which they now have exercised for nearly three decades in Russia. There can be few tasks of psychological analysis more difficult than to try to trace the interaction of these two forces and the relative role of each in the determination of official Soviet conduct. Yet the attempt must be made if that conduct is to be understood and effectively countered. . . .

Tremendous emphasis has been placed on the original Communist thesis of a basic antagonism between the capitalist and Socialist worlds. It is clear, from many indications, that this emphasis is not founded in reality. The real facts concerning it have been confused by the existence abroad of genuine resentment provoked by Soviet philosophy and tactics and occasionally by the existence of great centers of military power, notably the Nazi regime in Germany and the Japanese Government of the late 1930s, which indeed have [had] aggressive designs against the Soviet Union. But there is ample evidence that the stress laid in Moscow on the menace confronting Soviet society from the world outside its borders is founded not in the realities of foreign antagonism but in the necessity of explaining away the maintenance of dictatorial authority at home.

Now the maintenance of this pattern of Soviet power, namely, the pursuit of unlimited authority domestically, accompanied by the cultivation of the semi-myth of implacable foreign hostility, has gone far to shape the actual machinery of Soviet power as we know it. . . . Today the major part of the structure of Soviet power is committed to the perfection of the dictatorship and to the maintenance of the concept of Russia as in a state of siege, with the enemy lowering beyond the walls. And the millions of human beings who form that part of the structure of power must defend at all costs this concept of Russia's position, for without it they are themselves superfluous. . . .

But least of all can the rulers dispense with the fiction by which the maintenance of dictatorial power has been defended. For this fiction has been canonized in Soviet philosophy by the excesses already committed in its name; and it is now anchored in the Soviet structure of thought by bonds far greater than those of mere ideology. . . .

It must inevitably be assumed in Moscow that the aims of the capitalist world are antagonistic to the Soviet regime, and therefore to the interests of the peoples it controls. If the Soviet government occasionally sets it signature to documents which would indicate the contrary, this is to [be] regarded as a tactical maneuver permissible in dealing with the enemy (who is without honor) and should be taken in the spirit of *caveat emptor*. Basically, the antagonism remains. It is postulated. And from it flow many of the phenomena which we find disturbing in the Kremlin's conduct of foreign policy: the secretiveness, the lack of frankness, the duplicity, the wary suspiciousness, and the basic unfriendliness of purpose. These phenomena are there to stay, for the foreseeable future. There can be variations of degree and of emphasis. When there is something the Russians want from us, one or the other of these features of their policy may be thrust temporarily into the background; and when that happens there will always be Americans who will leap forward with gleeful announcements that "the Russians have changed," and some who will even try to take credit for having brought about such "changes." But we should not be misled by tactical maneuvers. These characteristics of Soviet policy, like the postulate from which they flow, are basic to the internal nature of Soviet power, and will be with us, whether in the foreground or the background, until the internal nature of Soviet power is changed.

This means we are going to continue for long time to find the Russians difficult to deal with. . . . This brings us to the second of the concepts important to contemporary Soviet outlook. That is the infallibility of the Kremlin. The Soviet concept of power, which permits no focal points of organization outside the Party itself, requires that the Party leadership remain in theory the sole repository of truth. For if truth were to be found elsewhere, there would be justification for its expression in organized activity. But it is precisely that which the Kremlin cannot and will not permit. . . . On the principle of infallibility there rests the iron discipline of the Communist Party. . . .

But we have seen that the Kremlin is under no ideological compulsion to accomplish its purposes in a hurry. Like the Church, it is dealing in ideological concepts which are of long-term validity, and it can afford to be patient. It has no right to risk the existing achievements of the revolution for the sake of vain baubles of the future. The very teachings of Lenin himself require great caution and flexibility in the pursuit of Communist purposes. . . . Thus *the Kremlin has no compunction about retreating in the face of superior forces*. And being under the compulsion of no timetable, it does not get panicky under the necessity for such retreat. *Its political action is a fluid stream which moves constantly, wherever it is permitted to move, toward a given goal.* Its main concern is to make sure that it has filled every nook and cranny available to it in the basin of world power. But *if it finds unassailable barriers in its path, it accepts these philosophically and accommodates itself to them.* The main thing is that there should always be pressure, unceasing constant pressure, toward the desired goal. There is no trace of any feeling in Soviet psychology that that goal must be reached at any given time.

These considerations make Soviet diplomacy at once easier and more difficult to deal with than the diplomacy of individual aggressive leaders like Napoleon and Hitler. On the one hand it is more sensitive to contrary force, more ready to yield on individual sectors of the diplomatic front when that force is felt to be too strong, and thus more rational in the logic and rhetoric of power. On the other hand it cannot be easily defeated or discouraged by a single victory on the part of its opponents. And *the patient persistence by which it is animated means that it can be effectively countered not by sporadic acts* which represent the momentary whims of democratic opinion *but only be intelligent long-range policies on the part of Russia's adversaries—policies no less steady in their purpose, and no less variegated and resourceful in their application, than those of the Soviet Union itself.*

In these circumstances it is clear that *the main element of any United States policy toward the Soviet Union must be that of long-term, patient but firm and vigilant containment of Russian expansive tendencies.* It is important to note, however, that such a policy has nothing to do with outward histrionics: with threats or blustering or superfluous gestures of outward "toughness." While the Kremlin is basically flexible in its reaction to political realities, it is by no means unamenable to considerations of prestige. Like almost any other

government, it can be placed by tactless and threatening gestures in a position where it cannot afford to yield even though this might be dictated by its sense of realism. The Russian leaders are keen judges of human psychology, and as such they are highly conscious that loss of temper and of self-control is never a source of strength in political affairs. They are quick to exploit such evidences of weakness. For these reasons it is a *sine qua non* of successful dealing with Russia that the foreign government in question should remain at all times cool and collected and that its demands on Russian policy should be put forward in such a manner as to leave the way open for a compliance not too detrimental to Russian prestige.

In the light of the above, it will be clearly seen that the *Soviet pressure against the free institutions of the western world is something that can be contained by the adroit and vigilant application of counter-force at a series of constantly shifting geographical and political points, corresponding to the shifts and maneuvers of Soviet policy,* but which cannot be charmed or talked out of existence. The Russians look forward to a duel of infinite duration, and they see that already they have scored great successes. It must be borne in mind that there was a time when the Communist Party represented far more of a minority in the sphere of Russian national life than Soviet power today represents in the world community.

But if the ideology convinces the rulers of Russia that truth is on their side and they can therefore afford to wait, those of us on whom that ideology has no claim are free to examine objectively the validity of that premise. The Soviet thesis not only implies complete lack of control by the west over its own economic destiny, it likewise assumes Russian unity, discipline and patience over an infinite period.

Let us bring this apocalyptic vision down to earth, and *suppose that the western world finds the strength and resourcefulness to contain Soviet power* over a period of ten to fifteen years. What does that spell for Russia itself? . . .

It is always possible that another transfer of pre-eminent power may take place quietly and inconspicuously, with no repercussions anywhere. But again, it is possible that the questions involved may unleash, to use some of Lenin's words, one of those "incredibly swift transitions" from "delicate deceit" to "wild violence" which characterize Russian history, and may shake Soviet power to its foundations. . . .

If disunity were ever to seize and paralyze the Party, the chaos and weakness of Russian society would be revealed in forms beyond description. . . . If . . . anything were ever to occur to disrupt the unity and efficacy of the Party as a political instrument, *Soviet Russia might be changed overnight from one of the strongest to one of the weakest and most pitiable of national societies.*

Thus the future of Soviet power may not be by any means as secure as Russian capacity for self-delusion would make it appear to the men of the Kremlin. That they can quietly and easily turn it over to others remains to be proved. Meanwhile, the hardships of their rule and the vicissitudes of international life have taken a heavy toll of the strength and hopes of the great people on whom their power rests. . . . But the possibility remains (and in the opinion of this writer it is a strong one) that *Soviet power, like the capitalist world of its conception, bears within it the seeds of its own decay, and that the sprouting of these seeds is well advanced.*

It is clear that *the United States* cannot expect *in the foreseeable future* to enjoy political intimacy with the Soviet regime. It *must continue to regard the Soviet Union as a rival, not a partner, in the political arena. It must continue* to expect that Soviet policies will reflect no abstract love of peace and stability, no real faith in the possibility of a permanent happy coexistence of the Socialist and capitalist worlds, but rather *a cautious, persistent pressure toward the disruption and, weakening of all rival influence and rival power.*

Balanced against this are the facts that Russia, as opposed to the western world in general, is still by far the weaker party, that Soviet policy is highly flexible, and that *Soviet society may well contain deficiencies which will eventually weaken its own total potential. This would of itself warrant the United States entering with reasonable confidence upon a policy of firm containment, designed to confront the Russians with unalterable counter-force at every point where they show signs of encroaching upon the interests of a peaceful and stable world.*

But in actuality the possibilities for American policy are by no means limited to holding the line and hoping for the best. *It is entirely possible for the United States to influence by its actions the internal developments, both within Russia and throughout the international Communist movement*, by which Russian policy is largely determined. This is not only a question of the modest measure of informational activity which this government can conduct in the Soviet Union and elsewhere, although that, too, is important. *It is* rather *a question of the degree to which the United States can create among the peoples of the world generally the impression of a country which knows what it wants, which is coping successfully with the problem of its internal life and with the responsibilities of a World Power, and which has a spiritual vitality capable of holding its own among the major ideological currents of the time.* To the extent that such an impression can be created and maintained, the aims of

Russian Communism must appear sterile and quixotic, the hopes and enthusiasm of Moscow's supporters must wane, and added strain must be imposed on the Kremlin's foreign policies. For the palsied decrepitude of the capitalist world is the keystone of Communist philosophy. Even the failure of the United States to experience the early economic depression which the ravens of the Red Square have been predicting with such complacent confidence since hostilities ceased would have deep and important repercussions throughout the Communist world.

By the same token, exhibitions of indecision, disunity and internal disintegration within this country have an exhilarating effect on the whole Communist movement. At each evidence of these tendencies, a thrill of hope and excitement goes through the Communist world; a new jauntiness can be noted in the Moscow tread; new groups of foreign supporters climb on to what they can only view as the band wagon of international politics; and Russian pressure increases all along the line in international affairs.

It would be an exaggeration to say that American behavior unassisted and alone could exercise a power of life and death over the Communist movement and bring about the early fall of Soviet power in Russia. But *the United States has it in its power to increase enormously the strains under which Soviet policy must operate, to force upon the Kremlin a far greater degree of moderation and circumspection than it has had to observe in recent years, and in this way to promote tendencies which must eventually find their outlet in either the breakup or the gradual mellowing of Soviet power.* For no mystical, Messianic movement—and particularly not that of the Kremlin—can face frustration indefinitely without eventually adjusting itself in one way or another to the logic of that state of affairs.

Thus the decision will really fall in large measure in this country itself. *The issue of Soviet-American relations is in essence a test of the overall worth of the United States as a nation among nations. To avoid destruction the United States need only measure up to its own best traditions* and prove itself worthy of preservation as a great nation.

Surely, there was never a fairer test of national quality than this. In the light of these circumstances, the thoughtful observer of Russian-American relations will find no cause for complaint in the Kremlin's challenge to American society. He will rather experience a certain gratitude to a Providence which, by providing the American people with this implacable challenge, has made their entire security as a nation dependent on their pulling themselves together and accepting the responsibilities of moral and political leadership that history plainly intended them to bear.

25. *The Berlin Blockade and Airlift*

(1948)

This policy statement printed in the Department of State Bulletin *of July 6, 1948 provides the rationale for the Berlin airlift. After the Soviet Union imposed a blockade of rail and road access to the city on June 24, President Truman chose to airlift supplies rather than confront the Red*

Army on the ground in East Germany. The successful aerial supply of Berlin forced the Soviet Union finally to change policy and lift the blockade on May 12, 1949. Berlin can be viewed as the first battle of the cold war—a test of wills, but one that successfully avoided armed conflict.

The United States Government wishes to call to the attention of the Soviet Government the extremely serious international situation which has been brought about by the actions of the Soviet Government in imposing restrictive measures on transport which amount now to a blockade against the sectors in Berlin occupied by the United States, United Kingdom and France. The United States Government regards these measures of blockade as a clear violation of existing agreements concerning the administration of Berlin by the four occupying powers. . . .

The United States Government is therefore obliged to insist that in accordance with existing agreements the arrangements for the movement of freight and passenger traffic between the western zones and Berlin be fully restored. There can be no question of delay in the restoration of these essential services, since the needs of the civilian population in the Berlin area are imperative. . . .

26. *The North Atlantic Treaty*

(1949)

Excerpts from the North Atlantic Treaty are reprinted in part 5, chapter 18.

27. *NSC-68: United States Objectives and Programs for National Security*

(April 14, 1950)

National Security Council Document No. 68 was a top-secret report prepared in response to President Truman's January 31, 1950 directive. NSC-68 offered an alternative to seemingly exclusive U.S. reliance on nuclear weapons by calling for a major buildup by the United States and its allies of their conventional, nonnuclear forces. Although for different reasons than those given in NSC-68, the outbreak of war in Korea in fact focused Washington's attention on building up conventional arms capabilities to sustain American forces engaged in the war effort. After ceasefire in Korea was achieved in 1953, the new Eisenhower administration chose not to follow the NSC-68 prescription for a very costly conventional arms buildup to match extensive conventional capabilities in Europe of the Soviet Union and its allies. The administration opted instead for what was presented as a less costly, greater reliance on nuclear weapons. Throughout the cold war reference was often made by both policy makers and scholars to NSC-68 as a document that not only operationalized containment, economic growth, and liberal values as part of national security strategy, but also provided a benchmark for comparing the relative priority or mix of nuclear and conventional forces in U.S. and allied arsenals. Among the authors was Paul Nitze, who played a substantial role as both strategist and negotiator in subsequent decades.

The assault on free institutions is world-wide now, and in the context of the present polarization of power a defeat of free institutions anywhere is a defeat everywhere. . . . Thus unwillingly our free society finds itself mortally challenged by the Soviet system. No other value system is so wholly irreconcilable with ours, so implacable in its purpose to destroy ours, so capable of turning to its own uses the most dangerous and divisive trends in our own society, no other so skillfully and powerfully evokes the elements of irrationality in human nature everywhere, and no other has the support of a great and growing center of military power. . . .

Thus we must make ourselves strong, both in the way in which we affirm our values in the conduct of our national life, and in the development of our military and economic strength. . . . In a shrinking world, which now faces the threat of atomic warfare, it is not an adequate objective merely to seek to check the Kremlin design, for the absence of order among nations is becoming less and less tolerable. *This fact imposes on us, in our own interests, the responsibility of world leadership.* It demands that we make the attempt, and accept the risks inherent in it, to bring about order and justice by means consistent with the principles of freedom and democracy. . . .

For us the role of military power is to serve the national purpose by deterring an attack upon us while we seek by other means to create an environment in which our free society can flourish, and by fighting, if necessary, to defend the integrity and vitality of our free society and to defeat any aggressor. . . . But if war comes, what is the role of force? . . . In the words

of the Federalist (No. 28) "The means to be employed must be proportioned to the extent of the mischief." The mischief may be a global war or it may be a Soviet campaign for limited objectives. In either case *we should take no avoidable initiative which would cause it to become a war of annihilation, and if we have the forces to defeat a Soviet drive for limited objectives it may well be to our interest not to let it become a global war.* Our aim in applying force must be to compel the acceptance of terms consistent with our objectives, and our capabilities for the application of force should, therefore, within the limits of what we can sustain over the long pull, be congruent to the range of tasks which we may encounter. . . .

[Specifying the Soviet Threat]
The Soviet Union is developing the military capacity to support its design for world domination. The Soviet Union actually possesses armed forces far in excess of those necessary to defend its national territory. These armed forces are probably not yet considered by the Soviet Union to be sufficient to initiate a war which would involve the United States. This excessive strength, coupled now with an atomic capability, provides the Soviet Union with great coercive power for use in time of peace in furtherance of its objectives and serves as a deterrent to the victims of its aggression from taking any action in opposition to its tactics which would risk war. . . .

Unless the military strength of the Western European nations is increased on a much larger scale than under current programs and at an accelerated rate, it is more than likely that those nations will not be able to oppose even by 1960 the Soviet armed forces in war with any degree of effectiveness. Considering the Soviet Union military capability, the *long-range allied military objective in Western Europe must envisage an increased military strength in that area sufficient possibly to deter the Soviet Union from a major war or, in any event, to delay materially the overrunning of Western Europe.* . . .

At the time the Soviet Union has a substantial atomic stockpile and if it is assumed that it will strike a strong surprise blow and if it is assumed further that its atomic attacks will be met with no more effective defense opposition than the United States and its allies have programmed, results of those attacks could include: (a) Laying waste to the British Isles and thus depriving the Western Powers of their use as a base; (b) Destruction of the vital centers and of the communications of Western Europe, thus precluding effective defense by the Western Powers; and (c) Delivering devastating attacks on certain vital centers of the United States and Canada. . . .

[U.S. Response to the Soviet Threat]
Our overall policy at the present time may be described as one designed to foster a world environment in which the American system can survive and flourish. It therefore *rejects the concept of isolation and affirms the necessity of our positive participation in the world community.* . . . This broad intention embraces two subsidiary policies. One is a policy which we would probably pursue even if there were no Soviet threat. It is a *policy of attempting to develop a healthy international community.* The other is the *policy of "containing" the Soviet system.* These two policies are closely interrelated and interact on one another. . . . In a world of polarized power, the policies designed to develop a healthy international community are more than ever necessary to our own strength. . . .

It was and continues to be cardinal in this policy that we possess superior overall power in ourselves or in dependable combination with other likeminded nations. One of the most important ingredients of power is military strength. In the concept of "containment," the maintenance of a strong military posture is deemed to be essential. . . . Without *superior aggregate military strength,* in being and readily mobilizable, a policy of "containment"—which is in effect a policy of calculated and gradual coercion—is no more than a policy of bluff.

At the same time, it is essential to the successful conduct of a policy of "containment" that we always leave open the possibility of negotiation with the USSR. . . . In "containment" it is desirable to exert pressure in a fashion which will avoid so far as possible directly challenging Soviet prestige, to keep open the possibility for the USSR to retreat before pressure with a minimum loss of face and to secure political advantage from the failure of the Kremlin to yield or take advantage of the openings we leave it. . . .

In the face of obviously mounting Soviet military strength ours has declined relatively. Partly as a byproduct of this, but also for other reasons, we now find ourselves at a diplomatic impasse with the Soviet Union, with the Kremlin growing bolder. . . . The capabilities of our allies are, in an important sense, a function of our own. An affirmative decision to summon up the potential within ourselves would evoke the potential strength within others and add it to our own. . . .

The capability of the American economy to support a build-up of economic and military strength at home and to assist a build-up abroad is limited not, as in the case of the Soviet Union, so much by the ability to produce as by the decision on the proper allocation of resources to this and other purposes. Even Western Europe could afford to assign a substantially larger proportion of its resources to defense, if the necessary foundation in public understanding and will could be laid, and if the assistance needed to meet its dollar deficit were provided.... United States foreign economic policy has been designed to assist in ... The strengthening of the free world and therefore to the frustration of the Kremlin design....

The United States now possesses the greatest military potential of any single nation in the world. *The military weaknesses of the United States vis-à-vis the Soviet Union, however, include its numerical inferiority in forces in being and in total manpower.* Coupled with the inferiority of forces in being, the United States also lacks tenable positions from which to employ its forces in event of war and munitions power in being and readily available....

If the potential military capabilities of the United States and its allies were rapidly and effectively developed, *sufficient forces could be produced probably to deter war, or if the Soviet Union chooses war, to withstand the initial Soviet attacks, to stabilize supporting attacks, and to retaliate in turn with even greater impact on the Soviet capabilities.* From the military point of view alone, however, this would require not only the generation of the necessary military forces but also the development and stockpiling of improved weapons of all types.... If such a course of increasing our military power is adopted now, the United States would have the capability of eliminating the disparity between its military strength and the exigencies of the situation we face; eventually of gaining the initiative in the "cold" war and of materially delaying if not stopping the Soviet offensives in war itself.

[Risk Assessment]

It is quite clear from Soviet theory and practice that the Kremlin seeks to bring the free world under its dominion by the methods of the cold war.... The Soviet Union is seeking to create overwhelming military force, in order to back up infiltration with intimidation. In the only terms in which it understands strength, it is seeking to demonstrate to the free world that force and the will to use it are on the side of the Kremlin....

The possession of atomic weapons at each of the opposite poles of power, and the inability (for different reasons) of either side to place any trust in the other, puts a premium on a surprise attack against us. It equally puts a premium on a more violent and ruthless prosecution of its design by cold war, especially if the Kremlin is sufficiently objective to realize the improbability of our prosecuting a preventive war. It also puts a premium on piecemeal aggression against others, counting on our unwillingness to engage in atomic war unless we are directly attacked. We run all these risks.... It is clear that our present weakness would prevent us from offering effective resistance at any of several vital pressure points. The only deterrent we can present to the Kremlin is the evidence we give that we may make any of the critical points which we cannot hold the occasion for a global war of annihilation.

The risk of having no better choice than to capitulate or precipitate a global war at any of a number of pressure points is bad enough in itself, but it is multiplied by the weakness it imparts to our position in the cold war. Instead of appearing strong and resolute we are continually at the verge of appearing and being alternately irresolute and desperate; yet it is the cold war which we must win, because both the Kremlin design, and our fundamental purpose give it the first priority.

The frustration of the Kremlin design, however, cannot be accomplished by us alone.... Strength at the center, in the

United States, is only the first of two essential elements. The second is that our allies and potential allies do not as a result of a sense of frustration or of Soviet intimidation drift into a course of neutrality eventually leading to Soviet domination. If this were to happen in Germany the effect upon Western Europe and eventually upon us might be catastrophic.

But there are risks in making ourselves strong.... At any point in the process of demonstrating our will to make good our fundamental purpose, the Kremlin may decide to precipitate a general war, or in testing us, may go too far. These are risks we will invite by making ourselves strong, but they are lesser risks than those we seek to avoid. Our fundamental purpose is more likely to be defeated from lack of the will to maintain it, than from any mistakes we may make or assault we may undergo because of asserting that will. No people in history have preserved their freedom who thought that by not being strong enough to protect themselves they might prove inoffensive to their enemies.

[Nuclear Weapons and Deterrence]
The United States now has an atomic capability, including both numbers and deliverability, estimated to be adequate, if effectively utilized, to deliver a serious blow against the war-making capacity of the USSR. It is doubted whether such a blow, even if it resulted in the complete destruction of the contemplated target systems, would cause the USSR to sue for terms or prevent Soviet forces from occupying Western Europe against such ground resistance as could presently be mobilized....

As the atomic capability of the USSR increases, it will have an increased ability to hit at our atomic bases and installations and thus seriously hamper the ability of the United States to carry out an attack such as that outlined above....

From the foregoing analysis it appears that *it would be to the long-term advantage of the United States if atomic weapons were to be effectively eliminated from national peacetime armaments....* In the absence of such elimination ... , it would appear that we have no alternative but to increase our atomic capability as rapidly as other considerations make appropriate. In either case, *it appears to be imperative to increase as rapidly as possible our general air, ground, and sea strength and that of our allies to a point where we are militarily not so heavily dependent on atomic weapons....*

[Against Any No First Use of Nuclear Weapons Pledge]
It has been suggested that we announce that we will not use atomic weapons except in retaliation against the prior use of such weapons by an aggressor.... In our present situation of relative unpreparedness in conventional weapons, such a declaration would be interpreted by the USSR as an admission of great weakness and by our allies as a clear indication that we intended to abandon them. Furthermore, it is doubtful whether such a declaration would be taken sufficiently seriously by the Kremlin.... Unless we are prepared to abandon our objectives, we cannot make such a declaration in good faith until we are confident that we will be in a position to attain our objectives without war, or, in the event of war, without recourse to the use of atomic weapons for strategic or tactical purposes....

[Difficulties with Nuclear Arms Control Efforts]
No system of international control could prevent the production and use of atomic weapons in the event of a prolonged war.... In order to assure an appreciable

time lag between notice of violation and the time when atomic weapons might be available in quantity, it would be necessary to destroy all plants capable of making large amounts of fissionable material. Such action would, however, require a moratorium on those possible peacetime uses which call for large quantities of fissionable materials.

Effective control over the production and stockpiling of raw materials might further extend the time period which effective international control would assure. Now that the Russians have learned the technique of producing atomic weapons, the time between violation of an international control agreement and production of atomic weapons will be shorter. . . .

Conclusions

The United States now faces the contingency that within the next four or five years the Soviet Union will possess the military capability of delivering a surprise atomic attack of such weight that *the United States must have substantially increased general air, ground, and sea strength, atomic capabilities, and air and civilian defenses to deter war and to provide reasonable assurance, in the event of war, that it could survive the initial blow and go on to the eventual attainment of its objectives.* In return, this contingency requires the intensification of our efforts in the fields of intelligence and research and development. . . .

The gravest threat to the security of the United States within the foreseeable future *stems from the hostile designs and formidable power of the USSR,* and from the nature of the Soviet system. . . . The risk of war with the USSR is sufficient to warrant, in common prudence, timely and adequate preparation by the United States. . . . Now and for the foreseeable future *there is a continuing danger that war will arise* either through Soviet miscalculation of the determination of the United States to use all the means at its command to safeguard its security, through Soviet misinterpretation of our intentions, or through U.S. miscalculation of Soviet reactions to measures which we might take. . . . Soviet domination of the potential power of Eurasia, whether achieved by armed aggression or by political and subversive means, would be strategically and politically unacceptable to the United States. . . .

Our current security programs and strategic plans are based upon these objectives, aims, and measures: (a) To reduce the power and influence of the USSR to limits which no longer constitute a threat to the peace, national independence, and stability of the world family of nations. (b) To bring about a basic change in the conduct of international relations by the government in power in Russia, to conform with the purposes and principles set forth in the UN Charter. In pursuing these objectives, due care must be taken to avoid permanently impairing our economy and the fundamental values and institutions inherent in our way of life. We should endeavor to achieve our general objectives by methods short of war. . . .

Attainment of these aims requires that the United States: (a) Develop a level of military readiness which can be maintained as long as necessary as a deterrent to Soviet aggression . . . and as an adequate basis for immediate military commitments and for rapid mobilization should war prove unavoidable. (b) Assure the internal security of the United States against dangers of sabotage, subversion, and espionage. (c) Maximize our economic potential, including the strengthening of our peacetime economy and the establishment of essential reserves readily available in the event of war. (d) Strengthen the orientation toward the United States of the non-Soviet nations; and help such of those nations as are able and willing to make an important contribution to U.S. security, to increase their economic and political stability and their military capability. (e) Place the maximum strain on the Soviet structure of power and particularly on the relationships between Moscow and the satellite countries. (f) Keep the U.S. public fully informed and cognizant of the threats to our national security so that it will be prepared to support the measures which we must accordingly adopt. . . .

A continuation of present trends would result in a serious decline in the strength of the free world relative to the Soviet Union and its satellites. This unfavorable trend arises from the inadequacy of current programs and plans rather than from any error in our objectives and aims. These trends lead in the direction of isolation, not by deliberate decision but by lack of the necessary basis for a vigorous initiative in the conflict with the Soviet Union.

Our position as the center of power in the free world places a heavy responsibility upon the United States for leadership. We must organize and enlist the energies and resources of the free world in a positive program for peace which will frustrate the Kremlin design for world domination by creating a situation in the free world to which the Kremlin will be compelled to adjust. Without such a cooperative effort, led by the United States, we will have to make gradual withdrawals under pressure until we discover one day that we have sacrificed positions of vital interest.

It is imperative that this trend be reversed by a much more rapid and concerted build-up of the actual strength of both the United States and the other nations of the free world. The analysis shows that *this will be costly and will involve significant domestic financial and economic adjustments.* . . .

This program should include a plan for negotiation with the Soviet Union, developed and agreed with our allies and which is consonant with our objectives. The United States and its allies, particularly the United Kingdom and France, should always be ready to negotiate with the Soviet Union on terms consistent with our objectives. The present world situation, however, is one which militates against successful negotiations with the Kremlin. . . .

In summary, *we must, by means of a rapid and sustained build-up of the political, economic, and military strength of the free world, and by means of an affirmative program intended to wrest the initiative from the Soviet Union, confront it with convincing evidence of the determination and ability of the free world to frustrate the Kremlin design of a world dominated by its will.* Such evidence is the only means short of war which eventually may force the Kremlin to abandon its present course of action and to negotiate acceptable agreements on issues of major importance.

The whole success of the proposed program hangs ultimately on recognition by this Government, the American people, and all free peoples, that *the cold war is in fact a real war in which the survival of the free world is at stake.* Essential prerequisites to success are consultations with Congressional leaders designed to make the program the object of non-partisan legislative support, and a presentation to the public of a full explanation of the facts and implications of the present international situation. The prosecution of the program will require of us all the ingenuity, sacrifice, and unity demanded by the vital importance of the issue and the tenacity to persevere until our national objectives have been attained. . . .

28. *The Korean Conflict*

(1950)

In this State Department press release of June 27, 1950, President Truman explains U.S. involvement in the Korean conflict. Rather than seek a declaration of war, he turns to the United Nations Security Council (UNSC) under Article 42 of the UN Charter, which authorizes collective security action in line with the UNSC responsibility to maintain international peace and security. This precedent for using force without a congressional declaration of war in what the administration referred to as a "police action" would be emulated by President Truman's successors, whether acting under UN auspices or not. Indeed, often resorting instead to resolutions authorizing the Executive branch to use force instead, Congress issued the last formal declarations of war against Japan, Germany, and Italy in 1941. The press of action in Korea also effectively shelved NSC-68 plans for restructuring U.S. forces.

In Korea the Government forces . . . were attacked by invading forces from North Korea. The Security Council of the United Nations called upon troops to cease hostilities to withdraw to the 38th parallel. This they have not done, but on the contrary have pressed the attack. The Security Council called upon all members of the United Nations to render every assistance to the United Nations in the execution of this resolution. In these circumstances I have ordered United States air and sea forces to give the Korean Government troops cover and support.

The attack upon Korea makes it plain beyond all doubt that Communism has passed beyond the use of subversion to conquer independent nations and will now use armed force and war. It has defied orders of the Security Council of the United Nations to preserve international peace and security. . . .

I know that all members of the United Nations will consider carefully the consequences of this latest aggression in Korea in defiance of the Charter of the United Nations. A return to the rule of force in international relations would have far reaching effects. The United States will continue to uphold the rule of law.

---

29. *General Douglas MacArthur's Farewell Address to Congress*

(1951)

Because of a dispute on conduct of the war in Korea, President Truman removed General Douglas MacArthur from command of U.S. forces there. The incident was in many respects a test of presidential authority over military commanders, particularly one like General MacArthur, who had earned so distinguished a record as a commander in World Wars I and II. MacArthur returned home and delivered a farewell address to a sympathetic Congress on April 19, 1951, providing his geopolitical view of Asia as a whole and the conflict in Korea in relation to China in particular.

Mr. President, Mr. Speaker, and Distinguished Members of the Congress:

I stand on this rostrum with a sense of deep humility and great pride—humility in the weight of those great American architects of our history who have stood here before me; pride in the reflection that this home of legislative debate represents human liberty in the purest form yet devised. . . . I address you with neither rancor nor bitterness in the fading twilight of life, with but one purpose in mind: to serve my country. The issues are global and so interlocked that to consider the problems of one sector, oblivious to those of another, is but to court disaster for the whole. *While Asia is commonly referred to as the Gateway to Europe, it is no less true that Europe is the Gateway to Asia, and the broad influence of the one cannot fail to have its impact upon the other. There are those who claim our strength is inadequate to protect on both fronts, that we cannot divide our effort. I can think of no greater expression of defeatism. If a potential enemy can divide his strength on two fronts, it is for us to counter his effort. The Communist threat is a global one. Its successful advance in one sector threatens the destruction of every other sector. You can not appease or otherwise surrender to communism in Asia without simultaneously undermining our efforts to halt its advance in Europe. . . .*

Of more direct and immediately bearing upon our national security are the changes wrought in the strategic potential of the Pacific Ocean in the course of the past war. . . . The Pacific was a potential area of advance for any predatory force intent upon striking at the bordering land areas. All this was changed by our Pacific victory. Our strategic frontier then shifted to embrace the entire Pacific Ocean, which became a vast moat to protect us as long as we held it. Indeed, it acts as a protective shield for all of the Americas and all free lands of the Pacific Ocean area. We control it to the shores of Asia by a chain of islands extending in an arc from the Aleutians to the Mariannas held by us and our free allies. From this island chain we can dominate with sea and air power every Asiatic port from Vladivostok to Singapore—with sea and air power every port, as I said, from Vladivostok to Singapore—and prevent any hostile movement into the Pacific. . . . The Pacific no longer represents menacing avenues of approach for a prospective invader. It assumes, instead, the friendly aspect of a peaceful lake. Our line of defense is a natural one and can be maintained with a minimum of military effort and expense. . . .

I now turn to the Korean conflict. While I was not consulted prior to the President's decision to intervene in support of the Republic of Korea, that decision from a military standpoint proved a sound one, as we hurled back the invader and decimated his forces. Our victory was complete, and our objectives within reach, when Red China intervened with numerically superior ground forces. This created a new war and an entirely new situation, a situation not contemplated when our forces were committed against the North Korean invaders; a situation which called for new decisions in the diplomatic sphere to permit the realistic adjustment of military strategy. Such decisions have not been forthcoming. *While no man in his right mind would advocate sending our ground forces into continental China,* and such was never given a thought, the new situation did urgently demand a drastic revision of strategic planning if our political aim was to defeat this new enemy as we had defeated the old.

Apart from the military need, as I saw It, to neutralize the sanctuary protection given the enemy north of the Yalu, I felt that military necessity in the conduct of the war made necessary: first the intensification of our economic blockade against

China; two the imposition of a naval blockade against the China coast; three removal of restrictions on air reconnaissance of China's coastal areas and of Manchuria; four removal of restrictions on the forces of the Republic of China on Formosa, with logistical support to contribute to their effective operations against the common enemy. . . .

I called for reinforcements but was informed that reinforcements were not available. . . . We could hold in Korea by constant maneuver and in an approximate area where our supply line advantages were in balance with the supply line disadvantages of the enemy, but we could hope at best for only an indecisive campaign with its terrible and constant attrition upon our forces if the enemy utilized its full military potential. I have constantly called for the new political decisions essential to a solution.

Efforts have been made to distort my position. It has been said, in effect, that I was a warmonger. *Nothing* could be further from the truth. I know war as few other men now living know it, and nothing to me is more revolting. . . . But *once war is forced upon us, there is no other alternative than to apply every available means to bring it to a swift end. War's very object is victory, not prolonged indecision. In war there is no substitute for victory.*

There are some who, for varying reasons, would appease Red China. They are blind to history's clear lesson, for history teaches with unmistakable emphasis that appeasement but begets new and bloodier war. It points to no single instance where this end has justified that means, where appeasement has led to more than a sham peace. Like blackmail, it lays the basis for new and successively greater demands until, as in blackmail, violence becomes the only other alternative. . . .

Why, my soldiers asked of me, surrender military advantages to an enemy in the field? I could not answer. Some may say: to avoid spread of the conflict into an all-out war with China; others, to avoid Soviet intervention. Neither explanation seems valid, for China is already engaging with the maximum power it can commit, and the Soviet will not necessarily mesh its actions with our moves. *Like a cobra, any new enemy will more likely strike whenever it feels that the relativity in military or other potential is in its favor on a worldwide basis.*

The tragedy of Korea is further heightened by the fact that its military action is confined to its territorial limits. . . . Of the nations of the world, Korea alone, up to now, is the sole one which has risked its all against communism. The magnificence of the courage and fortitude of the Korean people defies description. They have chosen to risk death rather than slavery. Their last words to me were: "Don't scuttle the Pacific!"

I have just left your fighting sons in Korea. They have met all tests there, and I can report to you without reservation that they are splendid in every way. . . . I am closing my 52 years of military service. When I joined the Army, even before the turn of the century, it was the fulfillment of all of my boyish hopes and dreams. The world has turned over many times since I took the oath on the plain at West Point, and the hopes and dreams have long since vanished, but I still remember the refrain of one of the most popular barrack ballads of that day which proclaimed most proudly that "old soldiers never die; they just fade away." And like the old soldier of that ballad, I now close my military career and just fade away, an old soldier who tried to do his duty as God gave him the light to see that duty. Good Bye.

Chapter 12

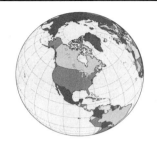

The Cold War:
Foreign and National
Security Policy Statements

As in the earlier periods covered in chapters 9–11, there is a vast number of documents related to foreign policy and national security covering the cold war period. We make no pretense here to presenting an all-inclusive diplomatic history. Instead, we exercise great selectivity with an eye to including those documents that have had lasting relevance or impact on the conduct of American foreign and national security policy.

30. *Secretary of State Dulles and Deterrence Through Threat of Massive Retaliation*

(1954)

As early as May 19, 1952, during General Dwight Eisenhower's presidential campaign against Governor Adlai Stevenson, John Foster Dulles expressed his misgivings about containment in Life, *then a wide-circulation weekly magazine. He wrote instead that "There is one solution and only one: that is for the free world to develop the will and organize the means to* retaliate *in-stantly against open aggression by Red Armies, so that, if it occurred anywhere, we could and would strike back where it hurts, by means of our choosing. . . . Today atomic energy, coupled with strategic air and sea power, provides the community of free nations with vast new possibil-ities of organizing a community power to stop open aggression before it starts and reduce, to the vanishing point, the risk of general* war." *Shelving the fiscally expensive proposals in NSC-68 for conventional capabilities to balance those of the Soviet Union and its allies, the Eisenhower administration favored a less costly alternative—reliance primarily on nuclear forces to deter aggression. Secretary of State Dulles articulated the essence of the strategy in the* Department of State Bulletin *on January 12, 1954. The massive-retaliation doctrine proved difficult to apply practically to policy issues. Indeed, in the 1952* Life *article Dulles observed that "Brute liberation from the yoke of Moscow will not occur for a very long time, and courage in neighboring lands will not be sustained, unless the United States makes it publicly known that it wants and expects liberation to occur." Notwithstanding the moral support he offered for "liberation," no U.S. military action, nuclear or nonnuclear, was taken in response to Soviet military intervention in Hungary in 1956. Although the idea of a graduated nuclear response to aggression found advocates within the Eisenhower administration, it would take the Kennedy administration to replace such heavy reliance on nuclear retaliation with an alternative doctrine of "flexible response," posturing U.S. conventional and nuclear forces to meet threats with a level of force deemed appropriate to a particular contingency. (See the Kennedy Doctrine later in this chapter.) General Maxwell D. Taylor, later Kennedy's chairman of the Joint Chiefs of Staff, first articulated this flexible-response doctrine in his book* The Uncertain Trumpet *(1958). Senator Kennedy referred to flexible response in his 1960 presidential campaign against then vice president Richard Nixon.*

[January 25, 1954, in *State Department Bulletin*]

We live in a world where emergencies are always possible, and our survival may depend upon our capacity to meet emergencies. . . . We need allies and collective security. Our purpose is to make these relations more effective, less costly. This can be done by *placing more reliance on deterrent power and less dependence on local defensive power*. . . . What the Eisenhower administration seeks is . . . for ourselves and the other free nations, a maximum deterrent at a bearable cost.

Local defense will always be important. But there is no local defense which alone will contain the mighty landpower of the Communist world. *Local defenses must be reinforced by the further deterrent of massive retaliatory power.* A potential aggressor must know that he cannot always prescribe battle conditions that suit him. Otherwise, for example, a potential aggressor, who is glutted with manpower, might be tempted to attack in confidence that resistance would be confined to manpower. He might be tempted to attack in places where his superiority was decisive.

The way to deter aggression is for the free community to be willing and able to respond vigorously at places and with means of its own choosing. So long as our basic policy concepts were unclear, our military leaders could not be selective in building our military power. . . .

Before military planning could be changed, the President and his advisers . . . had to make some basic policy decisions. This has been done. The basic decision was *to depend primarily upon a great capacity to retaliate, instantly, by means and at places of our choosing*. . . . That permits . . . a selection of military means instead of a multiplication of means. As a result, it is now possible to get, and share, more basic security at less cost. . . .

If we can deter such aggression as would mean general war, and that is our confident resolve, *then we can let time and fundamentals work for us*. . . .

31. *The Domino Theory of Communist Aggression*
(1954)

In a press conference on April 7, 1954, President Dwight D. Eisenhower responded to a question on security in Southeast Asia. Concerned about the effects of French losses in Vietnam, the president said that communist success in Vietnam would be followed by gains in other countries, which would fall metaphorically like a row of dominoes. Eisenhower's fears prompted the United States to negotiate a Southeast Asia Treaty Organization (SEATO), which would take its place alongside other multilateral and bilateral alliances ringing the Soviet Union and China.

Question: Mr. President, would you mind commenting on the strategic importance of Indochina for the free world? I think there has been, across the country, some lack of understanding on just what it means to us.

The President: You have, of course, both the specific and the general when you talk about such things. First of all, you have the specific value of a locality in its production of materials that the world needs. Then you have the possibility that many human beings pass under a dictatorship that is inimical to the free world. Finally, *you have broader considerations that might follow what you would call the "falling domino" principle. You have a row of dominoes set up, you knock over the first one, and what will happen to the last one is the certainty that it will go over very quickly. So you could have a beginning of a disintegration that would have the most profound influences.*

Now, with respect to the first one, two of the items from this particular area that the world uses are tin and tungsten. They are very important. There are others, of course, the rubber plantations and so on. Then *with respect to more people passing under this domination, Asia, after all, has already lost some 450 million of its peoples to the Communist dictatorship, and we simply can't afford greater losses. But when we come to the possible sequence of events, the loss of Indochina, of Burma, of Thailand, of the Peninsula and Indonesia following, now you begin to talk about areas that not only multiply the disadvantages that you would suffer* through the loss of materials, sources of materials, but now you are talking about millions and millions of people.

Finally, the geographical position achieved thereby does many things. It turns the so-called island defensive chain of Japan, Formosa, of the Philippines and to the southward; it moves in to threaten Australia and New Zealand. It takes away, in its economic aspects, that region that Japan must have as a trading area or Japan, in turn, will have only one place in the world to go—that is, toward the Communist areas in order to live. So, the possible consequences of the loss are just incalculable to the free world.

---

32. *The Eisenhower Doctrine*
(1957)

On January 5, 1957, President Eisenhower addressed Congress on the Middle East. Following Egypt's nationalization of the Suez Canal (1956) and in the aftermath of British and French support for Israel in its subsequent short war with Egypt, the Eisenhower Doctrine underscored U.S. willingness to support Middle East countries to buttress their independence and provide both economic and "military assistance and cooperation . . . to include the employment of the armed forces of the United States." Given this commitment, the U.S. intervened militarily in Lebanon the following year in response to a request by the Lebanese president for U.S. support in dealing with domestic turmoil. Beyond the issues at hand, the intervention was intended as a signal that the U.S. was not only capable, but also willing to intervene (thus confirming its stake) in the Middle East against "international communism."

There is . . . a special situation in the Middle East which I feel I should, even now, lay before you. Before doing so it is well to remind ourselves that our basic national objective in international affairs remains peace—a world peace based on justice. Such a peace must include all areas, all peoples of the world if it is to be enduring. There is no nation, great or small, with which we would refuse to negotiate, in mutual good faith, with patience and in the determination to secure a better understanding between us. Out of such understandings must, and eventually will, grow confidence and trust, indispensable ingredients to a program of peace and to plans for lifting from us all the burdens of expensive armaments. To promote these objectives, our government works tirelessly, day by day, month by month, year by year. But until a degree of success crowns our efforts that will assure to all nations peaceful existence, we must, in the interests of peace itself, remain vigilant, alert and strong.

The Middle East has abruptly reached a new and critical stage in its long and important history. . . . The area has been often troubled. Persistent cross-currents of distrust and fear with raids back and forth across national boundaries have brought about a high degree of instability in much of the Mid East. Just recently there have been hostilities involving Western European nations that once exercised much influence in the area. Also the relatively large attack by Israel in October

has intensified the basic differences between that nation and its Arab neighbors. *All this instability has been heightened and, at times, manipulated by International Communism.* Russia's rulers have long sought to dominate the Middle East. That was true of the Czars and it is true of the Bolsheviks. . . . The reason for Russia's interest in the Middle East is solely that of power politics. Considering her announced purpose of Communizing the world, it is easy to understand her hope of dominating the Middle East. . . .

Under these circumstances I deem it necessary to seek the cooperation of the Congress. . . . Thus, the United States through the joint action of the President and the Congress, or, in the case of treaties, the Senate, has manifested in many endangered areas its purpose to support free and independent governments—and peace—against external menace, notably the menace of International Communism. Thereby we have helped to maintain peace and security during a period of great danger. It is now essential that the United States should manifest through joint action of the President and the Congress our determination to assist those nations of the Mid East area, which desire that assistance.

The action which I propose would have the following features: It would, *first* of all, *authorize the United States to cooperate with and assist any nation or group of nations in the general area of the Middle East in the development of economic strength* dedicated to the maintenance of national independence. It would, in the *second* place, authorize the Executive to undertake in the same region *programs of military assistance and cooperation* with any nation or group of nations which desires such aid. It would, in the *third* place, authorize such assistance and cooperation to include *the employment of the armed forces of the United States to secure and protect the territorial integrity and political independence of such nations,* requesting such aid, against overt armed aggression from any nation controlled by International Communism. These measures would have to be consonant with the treaty obligations of the United States, including the Charter of the United Nations. . . . The present proposal would, in the *fourth* place, authorize the President to employ, for economic and defensive military purposes, sums available under the Mutual Security Act of 1954. . . .

Experience shows that *indirect aggression rarely if ever succeeds where there is reasonable security against direct aggression;* where the government disposes of loyal security forces, and where economic conditions are such as not to make Communism seem an attractive alternative. *The program I suggest deals with* all three aspects of this matter and thus with *the problem of indirect aggression.*

---

33. *Eisenhower and the Military-Industrial Complex*
(1961)

President Eisenhower gave a radio and television farewell address to the country on January 17, 1961, in which he discussed the growth of a new military-industrial complex. He expressed concern about its increasing influence as well as the centralization of research and development related to government contracts, a wish for disarmament and lasting peace his parting sentiment.

A vital element in keeping the peace is our military establishment. Our arms must be mighty, ready for instant action, so that no potential aggressor may be tempted to risk his own destruction. Our military organization today bears little relation to that known by any of my predecessors in peacetime, or indeed by the fighting men of World War II or Korea.

Until the latest of our world conflicts, the United States had no armaments industry. American makers of plowshares could, with time and as required, make swords as well. But now we can no longer risk emergency improvisation of national defense; we have been compelled to create a permanent armaments industry of vast proportions. Added to this, three and a half million men and women are directly engaged in the defense establishment. We annually spend on military security more than the net income of all United States corporations. American makers of plowshares could, with time and as required, make swords as well. But now we can no longer risk emergency improvisation of national defense; we have been compelled to create a permanent armaments industry of vast proportions.

This conjunction of an immense military establishment and a large arms industry is new in the American experience. The total influence—economic, political, even spiritual—is felt in every city, every State-house, every office of the Federal government. We recognize the imperative need for this development. Yet we must not fail to comprehend its grave implications. Our toil, resources and livelihood are all involved; so is the very structure of our society.

In the councils of government, we must guard against the acquisition of unwarranted influence, whether sought or unsought, by the military-industrial complex. The potential for the disastrous rise of misplaced power exists and will persist. We must never let the weight of this combination endanger our liberties or democratic processes. We should take nothing for granted. Only an alert and knowledgeable citizenry can compel the proper meshing of the huge industrial and military machinery of defense with our peaceful methods and goals, so that security and liberty may prosper together.

Akin to, and largely responsible for the sweeping changes in our industrial-military posture, has been the technological revolution during recent decades. In this revolution, research has become central, it also becomes more formalized, complex, and costly. A steadily increasing share is conducted for, by, or at the direction of, the Federal government.

Today, the solitary inventor, tinkering in his shop, has been overshadowed by task forces of scientists in laboratories and testing fields. In the same fashion, the free university, historically the fountainhead of free ideas and scientific discovery, has experienced a revolution in the conduct of research. Partly because of the huge costs involved, a government contract becomes virtually a substitute for intellectual curiosity. For every old blackboard there are now hundreds of new electronic computers. The prospect of domination of the nation's scholars by Federal employment, project allocations, and the power of money is ever present—and is gravely to be regarded.

Yet, in holding scientific research and discovery in respect, as we should, we must also be alert to the equal and opposite danger that public policy could itself become the captive of a scientific-technological elite. The prospect of domination of the nation's scholars by Federal employment, project allocations, and the power of money is ever present—and is gravely to be regarded. It is the task of statesmanship to mold, to balance, and to integrate these and other forces, new and old, within the principles of our democratic system—ever aiming toward the supreme goals of our free society. . . . Disarmament, with mutual honor and confidence, is a continuing imperative. Together we must learn how to compose differences, not with arms, but with intellect and decent purpose. Because this need is so sharp and apparent I confess that I lay down my official responsibilities in this field with a definite sense of disappointment. As one who has witnessed the horror and the lingering sadness of war—as one who knows that another war could utterly destroy this civilization which has been so slowly and painfully built over thousands of years—I wish I could say tonight that a lasting peace is in sight. Happily, I can say that war has been avoided. Steady progress toward our ultimate goal has been made. But, so much remains to be done. . . .

34. *John Kennedy's Inaugural Address and the Kennedy Doctrine*

(1961)

We include the inaugural address delivered by President John F. Kennedy on January 20, 1961, at the height of the cold war precisely because it is almost entirely devoted to his vision of foreign policy and national security. These were the outlines of what came to be called the Kennedy Doctrine—*a willingness to "pay any price, bear any burden, meet any hardship, support any friend, oppose any foe" in a worldwide struggle against communism. Calls for military strength and unity in the struggle against communism are balanced with hopes for disarmament and global cooperation. Even in his presidential campaign, Kennedy referred to relying on "flexible response" rather than limiting presidential options to retaliation with nuclear weapons. Indeed, the United States would require forces capable not only of counterimg regular, conventional, or nuclear forces in Europe, but also of engaging in counterinsurgency warfare directed against enemy irregulars conducting guerrilla activities—such contingencies as would occur in Southeast Asia or Latin America. Military preparedness for a wide spectrum of nuclear and nonnuclear options required a large military buildup of both nuclear and nonnuclear forces that began in the Kennedy years and continued during the Johnson administration. Flexible response later would also become NATO doctrine (1967).*

Let every nation know, whether it wishes us well or ill, that we shall pay any price, bear any burden, meet any hardship, support any friend, oppose any foe, in order to assure the survival and the success of liberty. This much we pledge—and more. To those old allies whose cultural and spiritual origins we share, we pledge the loyalty of faithful friends. United, there is little we cannot do in a host of cooperative ventures. Divided, there is little we can do—for we dare not meet a powerful challenge at odds and split asunder.

To those new States whom we welcome to the ranks of the free, we pledge our word that one form of colonial control shall not have passed away merely to be replaced by a far more iron tyranny. We shall not always expect to find them supporting our view. But we shall always hope to find them strongly supporting their own freedom—and to remember that, in the past, those who foolishly sought power by riding the back of the tiger ended up inside.

To those peoples in the huts and villages across the globe struggling to break the bonds of mass misery, we pledge our best efforts to help them help themselves, for whatever period is required—not because the Communists may be doing it, not because we seek their votes, but because it is right. If a free society cannot help the many who are poor, it cannot save the few who are rich.

To our sister republics south of our border, we offer a special pledge—to convert our good words into good deeds—in a new alliance for progress—to assist free men and free governments in casting off the chains of poverty. But this peaceful revolution of hope cannot become the prey of hostile powers. Let all our neighbors know that we shall join with them to oppose aggression or subversion anywhere in the Americas. And let every other power know that this Hemisphere intends to remain the master of its own house.

To that world assembly of sovereign states, the United Nations, our last best hope in an age where the instruments of war have far outpaced the instruments of peace, we renew our pledge of support—to prevent it from becoming merely a forum for invective—to strengthen its shield of the new and the weak—and to enlarge the area in which its writ may run.

Finally, to those nations who would make themselves our adversary, we offer not a pledge but a request: that both sides begin anew the quest for peace, before the dark powers of destruction unleashed by science engulf all humanity in planned or accidental self-destruction. *We dare not tempt them with weakness. For only when our arms are sufficient beyond doubt can we be certain beyond doubt that they will never be employed.*

But neither can two great and powerful groups of nations take comfort from our present course—both sides overburdened by the cost of modern weapons, both rightly alarmed by the steady spread of the deadly atom, yet both racing to alter that uncertain balance of terror that stays the hand of mankind's final war.

So let us begin anew—remembering on both sides that civility is not a sign of weakness, and sincerity is always subject to proof. *Let us never negotiate out of fear. But let us never fear to negotiate.* Let both sides explore what problems unite us instead of belaboring those problems which divide us. Let both sides, for the first time, formulate serious and precise proposals for the inspection and control of arms—and bring the absolute power to destroy other nations under the absolute control of all nations.

Let both sides seek to invoke the wonders of science instead of its terrors. Together let us explore the stars, conquer the deserts, eradicate disease, tap the ocean depths, and encourage the arts and commerce. Let both sides unite to heed in all corners of the earth the command of Isaiah—to "undo the heavy burdens . . . and to let the oppressed go free."

And if a beachhead of cooperation may push back the jungle of suspicion, let both sides join in creating a new endeavor, not a new balance of power, but a new world of law, where the strong are just and the weak secure and the peace preserved. All this will not be finished in the first 100 days. Nor will it be finished in the first 1,000 days, nor in the life of this Administration, nor even perhaps in our lifetime on this planet. But let us begin.

In your hands, my fellow citizens, more than in mine, will rest the final success or failure of our course. Since this country was founded, each generation of Americans has been summoned to give testimony to its national loyalty. The graves of young Americans who answered the call to service surround the globe. Now the trumpet summons us again—not as a call to bear arms, though arms we need; not as a call to battle, though embattled we are—but a call to bear the burden of a long twilight struggle, year in and year out, "rejoicing in hope, patient in tribulation"—a struggle against the common enemies of man: tyranny, poverty, disease, and war itself.

Can we forge against these enemies a grand and global alliance, North and South, East and West, that can assure a more fruitful life for all mankind? Will you join in that historic effort? In the long history of the world, only a few generations have been granted the role of defending freedom in its hour of maximum danger. I do not shrink from this responsibility—I welcome it. I do not believe that any of us would exchange places with any other people or any other generation. The energy, the faith, the devotion which we bring to this endeavor will light our country and all who serve it—and the glow from that fire can truly light the world.

And so, my fellow Americans: ask not what your country can do for you—ask what you can do for your country. My fellow citizens of the world: ask not what America will do for you, but what together we can do for the freedom of man. Finally, whether you are citizens of America or citizens of the world, ask of us the same high standards of strength and sacrifice which we ask of you. With a good conscience our only sure reward, with history the final judge of our deeds, let us go forth to lead the land we love, asking His blessing and His help, but knowing that here on earth God's work must truly be our own.

---

35. John Kennedy's Alliance for Progress with Latin America

(1961)

On March 13, 1961, almost two months after taking office, President John F. Kennedy addressed Latin American diplomats and members of Congress at a White House reception, using the occasion to outline his proposal—an "Alliance for Progress" in the Western Hemisphere. The project would focus on the economic and social aspects of development with the aim of establishing more firmly a democratic, market-oriented bulwark against what he saw as the threat of communism posed by Fidel Castro and other Marxist revolutionaries in various Latin American countries with backing by Cuban, Soviet, or other external supporters. Social and economic aspects of the Alliance for Progress are also linked explicitly to multilateral defense arrangements within the Organization of American States.

Our continents are bound together by a common history—the endless exploration of new frontiers. Our nations are the product of a common struggle—the revolt from colonial rule. And our people share a common heritage—the quest for the dignity and the freedom of man. . . . As a citizen of the United States let me be the first to admit that we North Americans have not always grasped the significance of this common mission, just as it is also true that many in your own countries have not fully understood the urgency of the need to lift people from poverty and ignorance and despair. But we must turn from these mistakes—from the failures and the misunderstandings of the past—to a future full of peril but bright with hope.

Throughout Latin America . . . millions of men and women suffer the daily degradations of hunger and poverty. They lack decent shelter or protection from disease. Their children are deprived of the education or the jobs which are the gateway to a better life. . . . If we are to meet a problem so staggering in its dimensions, our approach must itself be equally bold, an approach consistent with the majestic concept of Operation Pan America. Therefore *I have called on all the people of the hemisphere to join in a new Alliance for Progress— Alianza para Progreso—a vast cooperative effort, unparalleled in magnitude and nobility of purpose, to satisfy the basic needs of the American people* for homes, work and land, health and schools. . . .

I propose that the American Republics begin on a vast new 10-year plan for the Americas, a plan to transform the 1960's into an historic decade of democratic progress . . . And if we are successful, if our effort is bold enough and determined enough, then the close of this decade will mark the beginning of a new era in the

American experience. The living standards of every American family will be on the rise, basic education will be available to all, hunger will be a forgotten experience, the need for massive outside help will have passed, most nations will have entered a period of self-sustaining growth.... Let me stress that only the most determined efforts of the American nations themselves can bring success to this effort. They, and they alone, can mobilize their resources, enlist the energies of their people, and modify their social patterns so that all, and not just a privileged few, share in the fruits of growth....

I have this evening signed a request to the Congress for $500 million as a first step in fulfilling the Act of Bogotá.... *The money will be used to combat illiteracy, improve the productivity and use of their land, wipe out disease, attack archaic tax and land-tenure structures, provide educational opportunities, and offer a broad range of projects designed to make the benefits of increasing abundance available to all....*

We must support all economic integration which is a genuine step toward larger markets and greater competitive opportunity. The fragmentation of Latin American economies is a serious barrier to industrial growth.... We must rapidly expand the training of those needed to man the economies of rapidly developing countries. This means expanded technical training programs, for which the Peace Corps, for example, will be available where needed. It also means assistance to Latin American universities, graduate schools, and research institutes....

We [also] reaffirm our pledge to come to the defense of any American nation whose independence is endangered. As confidence in the collective security system of the OAS [Organization of American States] spreads, it will be possible to devote to constructive use a major share of those resources now spent on the instruments of war....

With steps such as these we propose to complete the revolution of the Americas, to build a hemisphere where all men can hope for a suitable standard of living and all can live out their lives in dignity and in freedom.... To achieve this goal political freedom must accompany material progress. Our Alliance for Progress is an alliance of free governments—and it must work to eliminate tyranny from a hemisphere in which it has no rightful place. Therefore let us express our special friendship to the people of Cuba and the Dominican Republic—and the hope they will soon rejoin the society of free men, uniting with us in our common effort.

This political freedom must be accompanied by social change. For unless necessary social reforms, including land and tax reform, are freely made, unless we broaden the opportunity of all of our people, unless the great mass of Americans share in increasing prosperity, then our alliance, our revolution, our dream, and our freedom will fail. But we call for social change by free men—change in the spirit of Washington and Jefferson, of Bolivar and San Martín and Martí—not change which seeks to impose on men tyrannies which we cast out a century and a half ago. Our motto is what it has always been—progress yes, tyranny no—*Progreso si, tirania no!*

But our greatest challenge comes from within—the task of creating an American civilization where spiritual and cultural values are strengthened by an ever-broadening base of material advance, where, within the rich diversity of its own traditions, each nation is free to follow its own path toward progress.... Let us once again transform the American Continent into a vast crucible of revolutionary ideas and efforts, a tribute to the power of the creative energies of free men and women, an example to all the world that liberty and progress walk hand in hand. Let us once again awaken our American revolution until it guides the struggles of people everywhere—not with an imperi-alism of force or fear but the rule of courage and freedom and hope for the future of man.

---

36. Civil-Military Relations: The Role of the Military in Civil Society
(1962)

In his speech on May 12, 1962 to the corps of cadets at the U.S. Military Academy at West Point, New York, General Douglas MacArthur dealt with "duty, honor, country" as his theme, but used the occasion to define a focus on the profession of arms rather than broader engagement in matters not directly related to combat and other military concerns. By contrast, at graduation ceremonies on June 6, 1962, President John F. Kennedy offered a broader vision. Never fully resolved, the debate continues in civil society on the proper role the professional military should play—a narrowly focused versus broad view of its service to the making and implementation of U.S. foreign and national security policy.

[General MacArthur, May 12, 1962]

Duty, honor, country: Those three hallowed words reverently dictate what you ought to be, what you can be, what you will be. They are your rallying point to build courage when courage seems to fail, to regain faith when there seems to be little cause for faith, to create hope when hope becomes forlorn. . . .

You now face a new world, a world of change. The thrust into outer space of the satellite, spheres, and missiles marks a beginning of another epoch in the long story of mankind. In the five or more billions of years the scientists tell us it has taken to form the earth, in the three or more billion years of development of the human race, there has never been a more abrupt or staggering evolution.

We deal now, not with things of this world alone, but with the illimitable distances and as yet unfathomed mysteries of the universe. We are reaching out for a new and boundless frontier. We speak in strange terms of harnessing the cosmic energy, of making winds and tides work for us, of creating unheard of synthetic materials to supplement or even replace our old standard basics; to purify sea water for our drink; of mining ocean floors for new fields of wealth and food; of disease preventatives to expand life into the hundred of years; of controlling the weather for a more equitable distribution of heat and cold, of rain and shine; of spaceships to the moon; of the primary target in war, no longer limited to the armed forces of an enemy, but instead to include his civil populations; of ultimate conflict between a united human race and the sinister forces of some other planetary galaxy; of such dreams and fantasies as to make life the most exciting of all times.

And through all this welter of change and development your mission remains fixed, determined, inviolable. It is to win our wars. Everything else in your professional career is but corollary to this vital dedication. All other public purposes, all other public projects, all other public needs, great or small, will find others for their accomplishment; but you are the ones who are trained to fight.

Yours is the profession of arms, the will to win, the sure knowledge that in war there is no substitute for victory, that if you lose, the Nation will be destroyed, that the very obsession of your public service must be duty, honor, country. Others will debate the controversial issues, national and international, which divide men's minds. But *serene, calm, aloof, you stand as the Nation's war guardian, as its lifeguard from the raging tides of international conflict, as its gladiator in the arena of battle.* For a century and a half you have defended, guarded, and protected its hallowed traditions of liberty and freedom, of right and justice.

Let civilian voices argue the merits or demerits of our processes of government: Whether our strength is being sapped by deficit financing indulged in too long, by Federal paternalism grown too mighty, by power groups grown too arrogant, by politics grown too corrupt, by crime grown too rampant, by morals grown too low, by taxes grown too high, by extremists grown too violent; whether our personal liberties are as thorough and complete as they should be.

These great national problems are not for your professional participation or military solution. Your guidepost stands out like a ten-fold beacon in the night: Duty, honor, country. You are the leaven which binds together the entire fabric of our national system of defense. From your ranks come the great captains who hold the Nation's destiny in their hands the moment the war tocsin sounds.

The long, gray line [a reference to West Point alumni, more broadly the Army—Ed.] has never failed us. Were you to do so, a million ghosts in olive drab, in brown khaki, in blue and gray, would rise from their white crosses, thundering those magic words: Duty, honor, country. This does not mean that you are warmongers. On the contrary, the soldier above all other people prays for peace, for he must suffer

and bear the deepest wounds and scars of war. But always in our ears ring the ominous words of Plato, that wisest of all philosophers: "Only the dead have seen the end of war."

The shadows are lengthening for me. The twilight is here. My days of old have vanished—tone and tint. They have gone glimmering through the dreams of things that were. Their memory is one of wondrous beauty, watered by tears and coaxed and caressed by the smiles of yesterday. I listen vainly, but with thirsty ear, for the witching melody of faint bugles blowing reveille, of far drums beating the long roll. In my dreams I hear again the crash of guns, the rattle of musketry, the strange, mournful mutter of the battlefield. But in the evening of my memory always I come back to West Point. Always there echoes and re-echoes: Duty, honor, country.

Today marks my final roll call with you. But I want you to know that when I cross the river, my last conscious thoughts will be of the corps, and the corps, and the corps. I bid you farewell.

[President Kennedy, June 6, 1962]

I have spoken thus far only on the military challenges which your education must prepare you for. *The nonmilitary problems which you will face will also be most demanding—diplomatic, political, and economic.*

In the years ahead, some of you will serve as advisers to foreign aid missions or even foreign governments; some will negotiate terms of a cease-fire, with broad political as well as military ramifications; some of you will go to the far corners of the earth and to the far reaches of space; some of you will sit in the highest Councils of the Pentagon; others will hold delicate command posts which are international in character; still others will advise on plans to abolish arms instead of using them to abolish others.

Whatever your position, the scope of your decisions will not be confined to the traditional tenets of military competence and training. You will need to know and understand not only the foreign policy of the United States, but [also] the foreign policy of all countries scattered around the world who 20 years ago were distant names to us. You will need to give orders in different tongues and read maps by different systems.

You will be involved in economic judgments. . . . In many countries your posture and performance will provide the local population with the only evidence of what our country is really like. In other countries, your military mission, its advice and action, will play a key role in determining whether those people will remain free.

You will need to understand the importance of military power and also the limits of military power. . . . *Our forces . . . must fulfill a broader role—as a complement to our diplomacy, as an arm of our diplomacy, as a deterrent to our adversaries and as a symbol to our allies of our determination to support them.*

---

37. *Kennedy and the Cuban Missile Crisis*
(1962)

In what some at the time referred to as the first nuclear standoff or diplomatic "battle" of the cold war, Soviet deployment of nuclear weapons in Cuba, just ninety miles from Florida and in firing range of the American East Coast and Midwest, produced an American response that in addition to diplomatic efforts imposed a naval blockade (referred to as a "quarantine") around Cuba and threatened invasion with accompanying air strikes to take the missiles out. The United States and the Soviet Union understood that the conflict could easily escalate to nuclear warfare. As a result of diplomatic efforts backed by this use of force, the Soviet Union finally relented and removed the missiles. President Kennedy's October 27, 1962 note to Chairman Nikita Khrushchev specifies the terms of the agreement. It would be learned later that the United States also agreed separately to remove its nuclear warhead ballistic missiles then deployed in Turkey in target range of the Soviet Union. Significantly, the terms of this agreement in relation to Cuba and Turkey would remain in place throughout the cold war as neither the United States nor the Soviet Union wished to come again to the brink of nuclear war.

As I read your letter, the key elements of your proposals—which seem generally acceptable as I understand them—are as follows: 1) You would agree to remove these weapons systems from Cuba under appropriate United Nations observation and supervision; and undertake, with suitable safeguards, to halt the further introduction of such weapons systems into Cuba. 2) We, on our part, would agree—upon the establishment of adequate arrangements through the United Nations to ensure the carrying out and continuation of these commitments— (a) to remove promptly the quarantine measures now in effect and (b) to give assurances against an invasion of Cuba. . . . There is no reason why we should not be able to complete these arrangements and announce them to the world within a couple of days. The effect of such a settlement on easing world tensions would enable us to work toward a more general arrangement regarding "other armaments" [apparently a reference to U.S. missiles in Turkey—Ed.], as proposed in your second letter which you made public. . . .

---

38. *The Tonkin Gulf Resolution*

(1964)

In a message to Congress on August 5, 1964, President Lyndon Johnson alleged that "the North Vietnamese regime had conducted further deliberate attacks against U.S. naval vessels operating in international waters." Congress provides the president a broad grant of authority on August 7, which President Johnson (and his successors) used as a basis for prosecuting war in Southeast Asia. As in Korea, no declaration of war as such is passed. Congress continued to appropriate funds for the Vietnam War even in the absence of any declaration of war; however, late in the war Congress would reassert its war power by passing a War Powers Act (see part 2, chapter 7).

Resolved by the Senate and House of Representatives of the United States of America in Congress assembled, That *the Congress approves and supports the determination of the President, as Commander in Chief, to take all necessary measures to repel any armed attack against the forces of the United States and to prevent further aggression.*

Section 2. The United States regards as vital to its national interest and to world peace the maintenance of international peace and security in southeast Asia. Consonant with the Constitution of the United States and the Charter of the United Nations and in accordance with its obligations under the Southeast Asia Collective Defense Treaty, *the United States is,* therefore, *prepared, as the President determines, to take all necessary steps, including the use of armed force, to assist any member or protocol state of the Southeast Asia Collective Defense Treaty requesting assistance in defense of its freedom.*

Section 3. This resolution shall expire when the President shall determine that the peace and security of the area is reasonably assured by international conditions created by action of the United Nations or otherwise, except that it may be terminated earlier by concurrent resolution of the Congress.

---

39. *The Johnson Doctrine*

(1965)

Responding to revolutionary turbulence in the Dominican Republic, President Johnson directed American armed forces to intervene both for humanitarian purposes (saving lives) and to prevent what was said to be an imminent threat of communist takeover. In this May 2, 1965, statement, the Johnson Doctrine *effectively made intervention to forestall a communist takeover an exception to the inter-American pledge not to intervene in the domestic affairs of another hemispheric state.*

The American nations cannot, must not, and will not *permit the establishment of another Communist government in the Western hemisphere.* This was the unanimous view of all the American nations when, in January 1962, they declared, and I quote: "The principles of communism are incompatible with the principles of the Inter-American system." . . .

We believe that change . . . should come through peaceful process. But revolution in any country is a matter for that country to deal with. It becomes a matter calling for hemispheric action only—repeat, only—when the object is the establishment of a Communist dictatorship. . . . We are there to save the lives of our citizens and to save the lives of all people. Our goal, in keeping with the great principles of the inter-American system, is to help prevent another Communist state in this hemisphere. And we would like to do this without bloodshed or without large-scale fighting.

---

40. *The United States, the Security Council, and Middle East Peace*
(1967 and 1973)

The Six Days' War in June 1967 resulted in Israeli victory over Egypt and territorial gains taken in Israel's security interest from neighboring Arab states. Another round of war in October 1973 finally ended in cease-fire when the United States intervened diplomatically. In 1979 with the good offices of President Jimmy Carter at Camp David, the presidential retreat in Maryland, Israel agreed to surrender occupied Egyptian territory in exchange for diplomatic recognition by Egypt of Israeli sovereignty as a state, both sides also making mutual security guarantees. The framework for peace established by UN Security Council Resolution 242 (November 22, 1967) and reaffirmed by UN Security Council Resolution 338 (October 22, 1973) contains central elements that remain unresolved in the stop-and-go peace process under way from time to time since Camp David.

[UNSC 242, November 22, 1967]
  The Security Council . . .

1. *Affirms* that the fulfilment of Charter principles requires the establishment of a just and lasting peace in the Middle East which should include the application of both of the following principles:
   i. Withdrawal of Israel armed forces from territories occupied in the recent conflict;
   ii. Termination of all claims or states of belligerency and respect for and *acknowledgement of the sovereignty,*
territorial integrity and political independence of every State in the area and their right to live in peace within secure and recognized boundaries free from threats or acts of force;

2. *Affirms further* the necessity (a) For *guaranteeing freedom of navigation* through international waterways in the area; (b) For *achieving a just settlement of the refugee problem;* (c) For *guaranteeing the territorial inviolability and political independence of every State in the area,* through measures including the establishment of demilitarized zones.

[UNSC 338, October 22, 1973]
The Security Council

1. *Calls upon* all parties to the present fighting to cease all firing and terminate all military activity immediately, no later than 12 hours after the moment of the adoption of this decision, in the positions they now occupy;
2. *Calls upon* the parties concerned to start immediately after the cease-fire the implementation of Security Council Resolution 242 (1967) in all of its parts;
3. *Decides* that, immediately and concurrently with the cease-fire, *negotiations shall start between the parties concerned under appropriate auspices aimed at establishing a just and durable peace in the Middle East.*

---

41. *The Nixon Doctrine*
(1969)

In this November 3, 1969 address to the nation on the war in Vietnam, President Richard M. Nixon advances the idea that U.S. commitments to allies in Asia will be kept, but these countries will increasingly have to rely on their own ground forces to bear the burden of national defense. In Vietnam this would eventually take the form of "Vietnamization" with reduction in numbers of U.S. forces over time. The decade had begun with the Kennedy Doctrine—to "pay any price, bear any burden, meet any hardship, support any friend, oppose any foe," ending with looking "to the nation directly threatened to assume the primary responsibility of providing the manpower for its defense."

Good Evening, my fellow Americans:

Tonight I want to talk to you on a subject of deep concern to all Americans and to many people in all parts of the world—the war in Vietnam. . . . Before any American troops were committed to Vietnam, a leader of another Asian country expressed this opinion to me when I was traveling in Asia as a private citizen. He said: "When you are trying to assist another nation defend its freedom, U.S. policy should be to help them fight the war but not to fight the war for them."

Well, in accordance with this wise counsel, I laid down in Guam three principles as guidelines for future American policy toward Asia: First, *the United States will keep all of its treaty commitments*; Second, *we shall provide a shield if a nuclear power threatens the freedom of a nation allied with us or of a nation whose survival we consider vital to our security*; Third, *in cases involving other types of aggression, we shall furnish military and economic assistance when requested in accordance with our treaty commitments. But we shall look to the nation directly threatened to assume the primary responsibility of providing the manpower for its defense. . . .*

My fellow Americans, I am sure you can recognize from what I have said that we really only have two choices open to us if we want to end this war. I can order an immediate, precipitate withdrawal of all Americans from Vietnam without regard to the effects of that action. Or we can persist in our search for a just peace through a negotiated settlement if possible, or through continued implementation of our plan for Vietnamization if necessary—a plan in which we will withdraw all of our forces from Vietnam on a schedule in accordance with our program, as the

South Vietnamese become strong enough to defend their own freedom. I have chosen the second course. It is not the easy way. It is the right way. It is a plan which will end the war and serve the cause of peace—not just in Vietnam but in the Pacific and in the world. . . . As President I hold the responsibility for choosing the best path to that goal and then leading the Nation along it.

42. *The Shanghai Communiqué*

(1972)

After difficult negotiations that would define the future course of U.S.-China relations, the parties reached agreement on what became known as the Shanghai Communiqué of February 28, 1972. Representing so major a break with the past, the normalization process would proceed through the decade. President Carter's administration agreed finally to exchange ambassadors, thus raising the level of diplomatic representation between the two countries.

President Richard Nixon of the United States of America visited the People's Republic of China at the invitation of Premier Chou En-lai of the People's Republic of China. . . . President Nixon met with Chairman Mao Tsetung of the Communist Party of China on February 21. The two leaders had a serious and frank exchange of views on Sino-U.S. relations and world affairs. During the visit, extensive, earnest and frank discussions were held between President Nixon and Premier Chou En-lai on the normalization of relations between the United States of America and the People's Republic of China, as well as on other matters of interest to both sides. In addition, Secretary of State William Rogers and Foreign Minister Chi Peng-fei held talks in the same spirit. . . .

There are essential differences between China and the United States in their social systems and foreign policies. However, the two sides agreed that countries, regardless of their social systems, should conduct their relations on the principles of respect for the sovereignty and territorial integrity of all states, non-aggression against other states, non-interference in the internal affairs of other states, equality and mutual benefit, and peaceful coexistence. International disputes should be settled on this basis, without resorting to the use or threat of force. The United States and the People's Republic of China are prepared to apply these principles to their mutual relations.

With these principles of international relations in mind the two sides stated that: *progress toward the normalization of relations between China and the United States is in the interests of all countries;* both wish to reduce the danger of international military conflict; neither should seek hegemony in the Asia-Pacific region and each is opposed to efforts by any other country or group of countries to establish such hegemony; neither is prepared to negotiate on behalf of any third party or to enter into agreements or understandings with the other directed at other states. Both sides are of the view that it would be against the interests of the peoples of the world for any major country to collude with another against other countries, or for major countries to divide up the world into spheres of interest.

The two sides reviewed the long-standing serious disputes between China and the United States. *The Chinese side reaffirmed its position:* the Taiwan question is the crucial question obstructing the normalization of relations between China and the United States; *the Government of the People's Republic of China is the sole legal government of China; Taiwan is a province of China which has long been returned to the motherland; the liberation of Taiwan is China's internal affair in which no other country has the right to interfere;* and *all U.S. forces and military installations must be withdrawn from Taiwan.* The Chinese Government firmly opposes any activities which aim at the creation of "one China, one Taiwan", "one China, two governments", "two Chinas", an "independent Taiwan" or advocate that "the status of Taiwan remains to be determined".

The U.S. side declared: The United States acknowledges that all Chinese on either side of the Taiwan Strait maintain there is but one China and that Taiwan is a part of China. The United States Government does not challenge that position. It reaffirms its interest in a peaceful settlement of the Taiwan question by the Chinese themselves. With this prospect in mind, it affirms the ultimate objective of the withdrawal of all U.S. forces and military installations from Taiwan. In the meantime, it will progressively reduce its forces and military installations on Taiwan as the tension in *the area diminishes.* The two sides agreed that it is desirable to broaden the understanding between the two peoples. To this end, they discussed specific areas in such fields as science, technology, culture, sports and journalism, in which people-to-people contacts and exchanges would be mutually beneficial. Each side undertakes to facilitate the further development of such contacts and exchanges. Both sides view bilateral trade as another area from which mutual benefit can be derived, and agreed that economic relations based on equality and mutual benefit are in the interest of the peoples of the two countries. They agree to facilitate the progressive development of trade between their two countries.

The two sides agreed that they will stay in contact through various channels, including the sending of a senior U.S. representative to Peking from time to time for concrete consultations to further the normalization of relations between the two countries and continue to exchange views on issues of common interest.

The two sides expressed the hope that the gains achieved during this visit would open up new prospects for the relations between the two countries. They believe that the normalization of relations between the two countries is not only in the interest of the Chinese and American peoples but also contributes to the relaxation of tension in Asia and the world.

---

43. The Ford Doctrine on the Pacific

(1975)

Following the end of the Vietnam War, President Gerald Ford's December 7, 1975 speech (thirty-four years to the day after Japan attacked Pearl Harbor and other targets in the Pacific) set forth a new policy for Asian and Pacific countries. Elements of the Nixon Doctrine are retained, notably reliance on local countries as the primary source of their defense; however, Ford also defines the United States as a Pacific power and advocates continued engagement in the region (to include normalization of relations with China, a process begun by President Nixon).

America, a nation of the Pacific Basin, has a very vital stake in Asia and a responsibility to take a leading part in lessening tensions, preventing hostilities, and preserving peace. World stability and our own security depend upon our Asian commitments. . . .

The center of political power in the United States has shifted westward. Our Pacific interests and concerns have increased. We have exchanged the freedom of action of an isolationist state for the responsibilities of a great global power. . . .

The *first* premise of a new Pacific doctrine is that *American strength is basic to any stable balance of power in the Pacific.* We must reach beyond our concern for security; but without security, there can be neither peace nor progress. The preservation of the sovereignty and the independence of our Asian friends and allies remains a paramount objective of American policy. We recognize that force alone is insufficient to assure security. Popular legitimacy and social justice are vital prerequisites of resistance against subversion or aggression. Nevertheless, we owe it to ourselves and those whose independence depends upon our continued support to preserve a flexible and balanced position of strength throughout the Pacific. The *second* basic premise . . . is that *partnership with Japan is a pillar of our strategy.* . . . The *third* premise . . . is the *normalization of relations with the People's Republic of China,* the strengthening of our new ties with this great nation. . . . A *fourth* principle . . . is our continuing stake in stability and security in Southeast Asia.

---

44. *Jimmy Carter's Inaugural Address*

(1977)

Delivered on January 20, 1977, President Jimmy Carter's inaugural address is one of the clearest statements of not only his commitment to human rights (and eventually nuclear disarmament), but also his view of the importance of the spiritual or ideational aspect of policy, both foreign and domestic. He was criticized by many at the time for his strong stance on human rights (including those critics who felt he took a too narrow, individualistic view of the subject); however, subsequent presidents would come to make human rights part of their agendas as well.

This inauguration ceremony marks a new beginning, a new dedication within our Government, and a new spirit among us all. A President may sense and proclaim that new spirit, but only a people can provide it. Two centuries ago our Nation's birth was a milestone in the long quest for freedom, but the bold and brilliant dream which excited the founders of this Nation still awaits its consummation. I have no new dream to set forth today, but rather urge a fresh faith in the old dream. . . .

Ours was the first society openly to define itself in terms of both spirituality and of human liberty. It is that unique self-definition which has given us an exceptional appeal, but it also imposes on us a special obligation, to take on those moral duties which, when assumed, seem invariably to be in our own best interests. . . .

We have already found a high degree of personal liberty, and we are now struggling to enhance equality of opportunity. *Our commitment to human rights must be absolute, our laws fair, our natural beauty preserved; the powerful must not persecute the weak, and human dignity must be enhanced. . . .* Our Nation can be strong abroad only if it is strong at home. And we know that the best way to enhance freedom in other lands is to demonstrate here that our democratic system is worthy of emulation.

To be true to ourselves, we must be true to others. We will not behave in foreign places so as to violate our rules and standards here at home, for we know that the trust which our Nation earns is essential to our strength. The world itself is now dominated by a new spirit. Peoples more numerous and more politically aware are craving and now demanding their place in the sun—not just for the benefit of their own physical condition, but *for basic human rights.*

The passion for freedom is on the rise. Tapping this new spirit, there can be no nobler nor more ambitious task for America to undertake on this day of a new beginning than to help shape a just and peaceful world that is truly humane. We are a strong nation, and we will maintain strength so sufficient that it need not be proven in combat—a quiet strength based not merely on the size of an arsenal, but on the nobility of ideas. . . .

We will be ever vigilant and never vulnerable, and we will fight our wars against poverty, ignorance, and injustice— for those are the enemies against which our forces can be honorably marshaled.

We are a purely idealistic Nation, but let no one confuse our idealism with weakness. Because we are free we can never be indifferent to the fate of freedom elsewhere. *Our moral sense dictates a clearcut preference for these societies which share with us an abiding respect for individual human rights.* We do not seek to intimidate, but it is clear that a world which others can dominate with impunity would be inhospitable to decency and a threat to the well-being of all people.

The world is still engaged in a massive armaments race designed to ensure continuing equivalent strength among potential adversaries. We pledge perseverance and wisdom in our efforts to limit the world's armaments to those necessary for each nation's own domestic safety. And we will move this year a step toward ultimate goal—the elimination of all nuclear weapons from this Earth. We urge all other people to join us, for success can mean life instead of death.

Within us, the people of the United States, there is evident a serious and purposeful rekindling of confidence. And I join in the hope that when my time as your President has ended, people might say this about our Nation: that we had remembered the words of Micah and renewed our search for humility, mercy, and justice; that we had torn down the barriers that separated those of different race and region and religion, and where there had been mistrust, built unity, with a respect for diversity; that we had found productive work for those able to perform it; that we had strengthened the American family, which is the basis of our society; that we had ensured respect for the law, and equal treatment under the law, for the weak and the powerful, for the rich and the poor; and that we had enabled our people to be proud of their own Government once again.

I would hope that the nations of the world might say that we had built a lasting peace, built not on weapons of war but on international policies which reflect our own most precious values. These are not just my goals, and they will not be my accomplishments, but the affirmation of our Nation's continuing moral strength and our belief in an undiminished, ever-expanding American dream.

45. The Camp David Accords

(1978)

From September 5 to September 17, 1978, President Jimmy Carter used his good offices as president of the United States to facilitate negotiations between Egyptian president Anwar el-Sadat and Israeli prime minister Menachem Begin at Camp David, the presidential retreat in Maryland. The resulting accords exchanged lands taken by Israel in the Six Days' War (1967) for Egypt's recognition of the Israeli state and its government as part of the process of normalizing relations between the two countries. Getting the parties to agree was a major accomplishment by President Carter for which he finally was awarded the Nobel Peace Prize in 2002.

In order to achieve peace between them, Israel and Egypt agree to negotiate in good faith with a goal of concluding within three months of the signing of this framework a peace treaty between them. It is agreed that: the site of the negotiations will be under a United Nations flag at a location or locations to be mutually agreed; all of the principles of U.N. Resolution 242 [see above in this chapter] will apply in this resolution of the dispute between Israel and Egypt; unless otherwise mutually agreed, terms of the peace treaty will be implemented between two and three years after the peace treaty is signed; the following matters are agreed between the parties: 1. the full exercise of Egyptian sovereignty up to the internationally recognized border between Egypt and mandated Palestine; 2. the withdrawal of Israeli armed forces from the Sinai; 3. the use of airfields left by the Israelis near al-Arish, Rafah, Ras en-Naqb, and Sharm el-Sheikh for civilian purposes only, including possible commercial use only by all nations; 4. the right of free passage by ships of Israel through the Gulf of Suez and the Suez Canal on the basis of the Constantinople Convention of 1888 applying to all nations; the Strait of Tiran and Gulf of Aqaba are international waterways to be open to all nations for unimpeded and nonsuspendable freedom of navigation and overflight; 5. the construction of a highway between the Sinai and Jordan near Eilat with guaranteed free and peaceful passage by Egypt and Jordan; and 6. the stationing of military forces listed below [Details of these locations are omitted here.—Ed.]. . . .

After a peace treaty is signed, and after the interim withdrawal is complete, *normal relations will be established between Egypt and Israel, including full recognition, including diplomatic, economic and cultural relations; termination of economic boycotts and barriers to the free movement of goods and people; and mutual protection of citizens by the due process of law.*

46. The Carter Doctrine

(1980)

In his January 21, 1980 State of the Union Address, President Jimmy Carter presented to Congress what came to be known as the Carter Doctrine, which tried to dissuade the Soviet Union or any other outside power from trying to dominate the Persian Gulf. In very clear language, Carter asserts: "An attempt by any outside force to gain control of the Persian Gulf region will be regarded as an assault on the vital interests of the United States of America, and such an assault will be repelled by any means necessary, including military force."

. . . At this time in Iran, 50 Americans are still held captive, innocent victims of terrorism and anarchy. Also at this moment, massive Soviet troops are attempting to subjugate the fiercely independent and deeply religious people of Afghanistan. These two acts—one of international terrorism and one of military aggression—present a serious challenge to the United States of America and indeed to all the nations of the world. Together, we will meet these threats to peace.

I'm determined that the United States will remain the strongest of all nations, but our power will never be used to initiate a threat to the security of any nation or to the rights of any human being. We seek to be and to remain secure—a nation at peace in a stable world. But to be secure we must face the world as it is.

Three basic developments have helped to shape our challenges: the steady growth and increased projection of Soviet military power beyond its own borders; the overwhelming dependence of the Western democracies on oil supplies from the Middle East; and the press of social and religious and economic and political change in the many nations of the developing world, exemplified by the revolution in Iran. . . .

We continue to pursue these specific goals: first, to protect the present and long-range interests of the United States; secondly, to preserve the lives of the American hostages and to secure, as quickly as possible, their safe release . . . ; to enlist the help of other nations in condemning this act of violence, which is shocking and violates the moral and the legal standards of a civilized world; and also to convince and to persuade the Iranian leaders that the real danger to their nation lies in the north, in the Soviet Union and from the Soviet troops now in Afghanistan, and that the unwarranted Iranian quarrel with the United States hampers their response to this far greater danger to them. . . .

Let our position be absolutely clear: An attempt by any outside force to gain control of the Persian Gulf region will be regarded as an assault on the vital interests of the United States of America, and such an assault will be repelled by any means necessary, including military force. During the past three years, you have joined with me to improve our own security and the prospects for peace, not only in the vital oil-producing area of the Persian Gulf region but around the world. We've increased annually our real commitment for defense. . . .

We are also improving our capability to deploy U.S. military forces rapidly to distant areas. . . . We've increased and strengthened our naval presence in the Indian Ocean, and we are now making arrangements for key naval and air facilities to be used by our forces in the region of northeast Africa and the Persian Gulf.

47. *Executive Order 12333: U.S. Intelligence Activities*

(December 4, 1981)

U.S. law and constitutional rights and liberties of citizens are to be observed in the collection of intelligence. As U.S. government covert actions in the 1950s and 1960s became known in the 1970s in media disclosures and congressional hearings (notably the Church and Pike committees), efforts were taken to limit or proscribe such activities. Thus, President Reagan's Executive Order 12333 prohibits assassination and other unlawful conduct by U.S. intelligence and other agencies and their employees. It replaced an earlier order of a similar nature by President Carter. In the political climate at the time, had presidential executive orders not been issued, Congress likely would have imposed by statute its own prohibitions on assassination and limits on other covert actions as tactics in the conduct of American foreign and national security policy. The order does give the president some latitude as in authorizing "such other intelligence activities as the President may direct from time to time," which allows for presidential interpretation of the guidelines in cases not specifically covered by the executive order. Some also have seen the order as being limited territorially to where U.S. law applies; however, others have interpreted it more broadly as legitimating the extraterritorial application of this executive order prohibiting assassinations and other unlawful activities by intelligence and other government agencies and employees. Quite apart from moral considerations, nothing as a matter of law precludes a given president from issuing additional orders to cover particular contingencies as in the Bush administration's campaign against terrorism. On the other hand, a new executive order completely rescinding the assassination ban likely would generate greater congressional opposition, motivating some to seek a statutory prohibition and thus legally constraining presidential discretion.

Timely and accurate information about the activities, capabilities, plans, and intentions of foreign powers, organizations, and persons, and their agents, is essential to the national security of the United States. *All reasonable and lawful means must be used* to ensure that the United States will receive the best intelligence available. For that purpose, by virtue of the authority vested in me by the Constitution and statutes of the United States of America, including the National Security Act of 1947, as amended . . . , and as President of the United States of America, in order to provide for the effective conduct of United States intelligence activities and the protection of constitutional rights, it is hereby ordered as follows:

. . . *All means, consistent with applicable United States law and this Order, and with full consideration of the rights of United States*

persons, shall be used to develop intelligence information for the President and the National Security Council. . . . *The agencies within the Intelligence Community shall, in accordance with applicable United States law and with the other provisions of this Order, conduct intelligence activities necessary for the conduct of foreign relations and the protection of the national security of the United States* . . . [and] such other intelligence activities as the President may direct from time to time. . . .

The heads of departments and agencies with organizations in the Intelligence Community or the heads of such organizations, as appropriate, *shall . . . report to the Attorney General possible violations of federal criminal laws by employees and of specified federal criminal laws by any other person. . . .* [and] report to the [Congressional] Intelligence Oversight Board, and keep the Director of Central Intelligence appropriately informed, concerning any intelligence activities of their organizations that they have reason to believe may be unlawful or contrary to Executive order or Presidential directive. . . .

Agencies within the Intelligence Community shall use the least intrusive collection techniques feasible within the United States or directed against United States persons abroad. Agencies are not authorized to use such techniques as electronic surveillance, unconsented physical search, mail surveillance, physical surveillance, or monitoring devices unless they are in accordance with procedures established by the head of the agency concerned and approved by the Attorney General. Such procedures shall protect constitutional and other legal rights and limit use of such information to lawful governmental purposes. . . .

Nothing in this Order shall be construed to authorize any activity in violation of the Constitution or statutes of the United States. . . . No agency within the Intelligence Community shall sponsor, contract for or conduct research on human subjects except in accordance with guidelines issued by the Department of Health and Human Services. The subject's informed consent shall be documented as required by those guidelines. . . . *No person employed by or acting on behalf of the United States Government shall engage in, or conspire to engage in, assassination. . . .* No agency of the Intelligence Community shall participate in or request any person to undertake activities forbidden by this Order. . . .

For the purposes of this Order . . . *counterintelligence means information gathered and activities conducted to protect against espionage, other intelligence activities, sabotage, or assassinations conducted for or on behalf of foreign powers, organizations or persons, or international terrorist activities. . . .* United States person means a United States citizen, an alien known by the intelligence agency concerned to be a permanent resident alien, an unincorporated association substantially composed of United States citizens or permanent resident aliens, or a corporation incorporated in the United States, except for a corporation directed and controlled by a foreign government or governments. . . .

Ronald Reagan.

---

48. *Freedom versus Totalitarian Evil*

(1982)

President Ronald Reagan in a speech early in his administration delivered to the British House of Commons on June 8, 1982, made clear his view that such totalitarian regimes as existed in the U.S.S.R. were inherently evil. He would later be identified as referring to the Soviet Union with the phrase "evil empire." In a March 8, 1983 speech before the National Association of Evangelicals in Orlando, Florida, President Reagan urged them not "to ignore the facts of history and the aggressive impulses of an evil empire," seeing U.S.-Soviet relations as a "struggle between right and wrong and good and evil." As it turned out, the Soviet Union would collapse within a decade of further competition with the West. Indeed, Reagan identified the economic problems facing the Soviet Union, which were exacerbated by the military arms competition that persisted during the 1980s.

We're approaching the end of a bloody century plagued by a terrible political invention—totalitarianism. Optimism comes less easily today, not because democracy is less vigorous, but because democracy's enemies have refined their instruments of repression. Yet optimism is in order because day by day democracy is proving itself to be a not at all fragile flower. From Stettin on the Baltic to Varna on the Black Sea, the regimes planted by totalitarianism have had more than thirty years to establish their legitimacy. But none—not one regime—has yet been able to risk free elections. Regimes planted by bayonets do not take root. . . .

If history teaches anything, it teaches self-delusion in the face of unpleasant facts is folly. We see around us today the marks of our terrible dilemma—predictions of doomsday, antinuclear demonstrations, an arms race in which the West must, for its own protection, be an unwilling participant. At the same time we see totalitarian forces in the world who seek subversion and conflict around the globe to further their barbarous assault on the human spirit. What, then, is our course? Must civilization perish in a hail of fiery atoms? *Must freedom wither in a quiet, deadening accommodation with totalitarian evil?* . . .

In an ironic sense Karl Marx was right. *We are witnessing today a great revolutionary crisis, a crisis where the demands of the economic order are conflicting directly with those of the political order. But the crisis is happening not in the free, non-Marxist West but in the home of Marxism-Leninism, the Soviet Union.* It is the Soviet Union that runs against the tide of history by denying human freedom and human dignity to its citizens. *It also is in deep economic difficulty. The rate of growth in the national product has been steadily declining since the fifties and is less than half of what it was then.* . . . What we see here is a political structure that no longer corresponds to its economic base, a society where productive forced are hampered by political ones. . . .

The objective I propose is quite simple to state: to foster the infrastructure of democracy, the system of a free press, unions, political parties, universities, which allows a people to choose their own way to develop their own culture, to reconcile their own differences through peaceful means. This is not cultural imperialism; it is providing the means for genuine self-determination and protection for diversity. Democracy already flourishes in countries with very different cultures and historical experiences. It would be cultural condescension, or worse, to say that any people prefer dictatorship to democracy. . . .

Our military strength is a prerequisite to peace, but let it be clear we maintain this strength in the hope it will never be used, for the ultimate determinant in the struggle that's now going on in the world will not be bombs and rockets but a test of wills and ideas, a trial of spiritual resolve, the values we hold, the beliefs we cherish, the ideals to which we are dedicated.

The British people know that, *given strong leadership, time, and a little bit of hope, the forces of good ultimately rally and triumph over evil.* Here among you is the cradle of self-government, the Mother of Parliaments. Here is the enduring greatness of the British contribution to mankind, the great civilized ideas: individual liberty, representative government, and the rule of law under God.

I've often wondered about the shyness of some of us in the West about standing for these ideals that have done so much to ease the plight of man and the hardships of our imperfect world. . . .

Well, the task I've set forth will long outlive our own generation. But together, we too have come through the worst. Let us now begin a major effort to secure the best—a crusade for freedom that will engage the faith and fortitude of the next generation. For the sake of peace and justice, let us move toward a world in which all people are at last free to determine their own destiny.

---

49. *The Reagan Doctrine*

(1985)

In his 1985 State of the Union address to Congress, President Ronald Reagan indicated the United States would support democratic forces (e.g., the "Contras" who were fighting the Sandinistas in Nicaragua) "whose struggle is tied to our own security." Given this commitment (but contrary to the will of Congress), members of the National Security Council staff authorized Israeli sale of U.S.-manufactured military equipment to Iran, net revenues flowing therefrom to support the Contras. This was the genesis of what was referred to at the time as the Iran-Contra scandal.

We must stand by all our democratic allies. And we must not break faith with those who are risking their lives—on every continent, from Afghanistan to Nicaragua—to defy Soviet-supported aggression and secure rights which have been ours from birth. The Sandinista dictatorship of Nicaragua, with full Cuban-Soviet bloc support, not only persecutes its people, the church, and denies a free press, but [also] arms and provides bases for Communist terrorists attacking neighboring states. *Support for freedom fighters is self-defense and totally consistent with the OAS and U.N. Charters. It is essential that the Congress continue all facets of our assistance to Central America. I want to work with you to support the democratic forces whose struggle is tied to our own security.*

Chapter 13

After the Cold War:
Foreign and National
Security Policy Statements

50. *The Gulf War Resolution*

(1991)

On January 12, 1991, responding to Iraq's invasion of Kuwait, Congress passed a resolution granting President George H. W. Bush authority to use force against Iraq. The grant of authority to President Bush explicitly conformed to the 1973 War Powers Act (see part 2, chapter 7).

JOINT RESOLUTION

 To authorize the use of United States Armed Forces Pursuant to United Nations Security Council resolution 678. . . .

 Resolved by the Senate and House of Representatives of the United States of America in Congress assembled,

a. *. . . The President is authorized*, subject to subsection (b), *to use United States Armed Forces pursuant to United Nations Security Council Resolution 678* (1990) in order to achieve implementation of Security Council Resolutions 660, 661, 662, 664, 665, 666, 667, 669, 670, 674, and 677. . . .

b. . . . Before exercising the authority granted in subsection (a), the President shall make available to the Speaker of the House of Representatives and the President *pro tempore* of the Senate his determination that—(1) the United States has used all appropriate diplomatic and other peaceful means to obtain compliance by Iraq with the United Nations Security Council resolutions cited in subsection (a); and (2) that those efforts have not been successful in obtaining such compliance.

c. *. . . Consistent with* section 8(a)(1) of *the War Powers Resolution, the Congress declares that this section is intended to constitute specific statutory authorization* within the meaning of section 5(b) of the War Powers Resolution. . . . Nothing in this resolution supersedes any requirement of the War Powers Resolution. . . .

At least once every 60 days, the President shall submit to the Congress a summary on the status of efforts to obtain compliance by Iraq with the resolutions adopted by the United Nations Security Council in response to Iraq's aggression.

51. *The Dayton Peace Accords*

(1995)

The Clinton administration finally engaged in a major diplomatic effort to bring Bosnia and Herzegovina, Croatia, and Serbia from war to a peaceful settlement. The agreement among the parties reached in Dayton, Ohio, was signed in Paris on November 21, 1995. After this and other experiences, the administration gradually developed what came to be called the Clinton Doctrine—*a willingness to intervene militarily for humanitarian purposes, subject to some limitations (as in avoiding "quagmires" that could cause U.S. military forces to bog down and providing an exit strategy for withdrawal of American forces).*

I. The Republic of Bosnia and Herzegovina, the Republic of Croatia and the Federal Republic of Yugoslavia [i.e., Serbia] (the "Parties"), have agreed as follows:

The Parties shall conduct their relations in accordance with the principles set forth in the United Nations Charter, as well as the Helsinki Final Act and other documents of the Organization for Security and Cooperation in Europe. In particular, the Parties shall fully respect the sovereign equality of one another, shall settle disputes by peaceful means, and shall refrain from any action, by threat or use of force or otherwise, against the territorial integrity or political independence of Bosnia and Herzegovina or any other State;

The Parties welcome and endorse the arrangements that have been made concerning: the military aspects of the peace settlement and aspects of regional stabilization; . . . the boundary demarcation between the two Entities, the Federation of Bosnia and Herzegovina and Republika Srpska; . . . the elections program for Bosnia and Herzegovina; . . . the Constitution of Bosnia and Herzegovina; . . .

[and] the establishment of an arbitration tribunal, a Commission on Human Rights, a Commission on Refugees and Displaced Persons, a Commission to Preserve National Monuments, and Bosnia and Herzegovina Public Corporations;

Recognizing that the observance of human rights and the protection of refugees and displaced persons are of vital importance in achieving a lasting peace, the Parties agree to and shall comply fully with the provisions concerning human rights . . . ; The Parties welcome and endorse the arrangements that have been made concerning the implementation of this peace settlement, including in particular those pertaining to the civilian (non-military) implementation . . . ; The Parties shall cooperate fully with all entities involved in implementation of this peace settlement . . . ; *The Federal Republic of Yugoslavia and the Republic of Bosnia and Herzegovina recognize each other as sovereign independent States within their international borders.* Further aspects of their mutual recognition will be subject to subsequent discussions.

52. *The Bush Doctrine & the "War" on Terrorism*

(2001 and 2002)

In two messages delivered to joint sessions of the Congress, President George W. Bush sets forth his response to the provocation of the September 11, 2001 attacks on the World Trade Center in New York and the Pentagon in Washington, D.C.—a "war", not just a "campaign" against terrorism. In his September 20th message just nine days after the attacks, he announces creation of a cabinet-level Homeland Security office and outlines a multi-prong, global approach including military, diplomatic, intelligence, law enforcement, and financial means to foil terrorist activities. In the State of the Union Message on January 29, 2002 he announces substantially increased funding for both military and homeland-security efforts, focused on four key areas: bioterrorism, emergency response, airport and border security, and improved intelligence. His address at the U.S. Military Academy at West Point, New York, on June 1, 2002 gives notice of what will become the Bush doctrine—a "preemptive" strategy of going after terrorists and the regimes that support them before they attack, not waiting to be attacked. This becomes formalized in September 2002 with publication of his administration's U.S. National Security strategy, which not only makes the case for preemption, but also for the importance of maintaining American military superiority and a willingness to engage in unilateral action, if necessary.

[Congress, Post-9/11 Speech, September 20, 2001]:

. . . On September the 11th, enemies of freedom committed an act of war against our country . . . Americans are asking: How will we fight and win this *war? We will direct every resource at our command—every means of diplomacy, every tool of intelligence, every instrument of law enforcement, every financial influence, and every necessary weapon of war—to the disruption and to the defeat of the global terror network.* . . . Dozens of federal departments and agencies, as well as state and local governments, have responsibilities affecting homeland security. These efforts must be coordinated at the highest level. So tonight I announce the creation of a Cabinet-level position reporting directly to me—the Office of Homeland Security. . . . And tonight, a few miles from the damaged Pentagon, I have a message for our military: Be re ady. I've called the Armed Forces to alert, and there is a reason. The hour is coming when America will act, and you will make us proud. . . .

[Congress, State of the Union Address, January 29, 2002]:

As we gather tonight, *our Nation is at war.* . . . Our Nation will continue to be steadfast, and patient, and persistent in the pursuit of two great objectives. *First, we will shut down terrorist camps, disrupt terrorist plans, and bring terrorists to justice. Second, we must prevent the terrorists and regimes who seek chemical, biological, or nuclear weapons from threatening the United States and the world.* . . .

Our second goal is *to prevent regimes that sponsor terror from threatening America or our friends and allies with weapons of mass destruction.* . . . North Korea is a regime arming with missiles and weapons of mass destruction, while starving its citizens. Iran aggressively pursues these weapons and exports terror, while an unelected few repress the Iranian people's hope for freedom. Iraq continues to flaunt its hostility toward America and to support terror. The Iraqi regime has plotted to develop anthrax, and nerve gas, and nuclear weapons for over a decade. This is a regime that has already used poison gas to murder thousands of its own citizens—leaving the bodies of mothers huddled over their dead children. This is a regime that agreed to international inspections—then kicked out the inspectors. This is a regime that has something to hide from the civilized world.

States like these, and their terrorist allies, constitute an axis of evil, arming to threaten the peace of the world. By seeking weapons of mass destruction, these regimes pose a grave and growing danger. . . . We will be deliberate, yet time is not on our side. *I will not wait on events, while dangers gather.* I will not stand by, as peril draws closer and closer. The United States of America will not permit the world's most dangerous regimes to threaten us with the world's most destructive weapons.

Our war on terror is well begun, but it is only begun. This campaign may not be finished on our watch—yet it must be and it will be waged on our watch. . . . *My budget includes the largest increase in defense spending in two decades*—because while the price of freedom and security is high, it is never too high. Whatever it costs to defend our country, we will pay it.

The next priority of my budget is to do everything possible to protect our citizens and strengthen our Nation against the ongoing threat of another attack. . . . My budget nearly doubles funding for *a sustained strategy of homeland security, focused on four key areas: bioterrorism, emergency response, airport and border security, and improved intelligence. . . .*

[West Point, June 1, 2002]
. . . *New threats also require new thinking.* Deterrence, the promise of massive retaliation against nations, means nothing against shadowy terrorist networks with no nation or citizens to defend. Containment is not possible when unbalanced dictators with weapons of mass destruction can deliver those weapons on missiles or secretly provide them to terrorist allies. . . .

Homeland defense and missile defense are part of a stronger security. They're essential priorities for America. Yet *the war on terror will not be won on the defensive. We must take the battle to the enemy, disrupt his plans and confront the worst threats before they emerge. In the world we have entered the only path to safety is the path of action. And this nation will act.*

Our security will require the best intelligence. . . . Our security will require modernizing domestic agencies, such as the F.B.I., so they are prepared to act and act quickly against danger. Our security will require transforming the military you will lead. A military that must be ready to strike at a moment's notice in any dark corner of the world. *And our security will require all Americans to be forward looking and resolute, to be ready for preemptive action when necessary to defend our liberty and to defend our lives. . . .* We will send diplomats where they are needed. And *we will send you, our soldiers, where you're needed. . . .*

[U.S. National Security Strategy, September 2002]
. . . *The United States possesses unprecedented—and unequaled—strength and influence in the world. . . . The United States will:* champion aspirations for human dignity; *strengthen alliances to defeat global terrorism and work to prevent attacks against us and our friends; work with others to defuse regional conflicts; prevent our enemies from threatening us, our allies, and our friends, with weapons of mass destruction;* ignite a new era of global economic growth through

free markets and free trade; expand the circle of development by opening societies and building the infrastructure of democracy; *develop agendas for cooperative action with other main centers of global power;* and *transform America's national security institutions to meet the challenges and opportunities of the twenty-first century. . . .*

. . . The United States of America is fighting a war against terrorists of global reach. The enemy is not a single political regime or person or religion or ideology. The enemy is terrorism—premeditated, politically motivated violence perpetrated against innocents. In many regions, *legitimate grievances prevent the emergence of a lasting peace. Such grievances deserve to be, and must be, addressed within a political process. But no cause justifies terror.* The United States will make no concessions to terrorist demands and strike no deals with them. *We make no distinction between terrorists and those who knowingly harbor or provide aid to them. . . .* Our priority will be first to disrupt and destroy terrorist organizations of global reach. . . .

Our immediate focus will be those terrorist organizations of global reach and any terrorist or state sponsor of terrorism which attempts to gain or use weapons of mass destruction (WMD) or their precursors; defending the United States, the American people, and our interests at home and abroad by *identifying and destroying the threat before it reaches our borders.* While the United States will constantly strive to enlist the support of the international community, *we will not hesitate to act alone,* if necessary, *to exercise our right of self defense by acting preemptively against such terrorists, to prevent them from doing harm against our people and our country;* and denying further sponsorship, support, and sanctuary to terrorists by convincing or compelling states to accept their sovereign

responsibilities. We will also wage a war of ideas to win the battle against international terrorism . . .

While we recognize that our best defense is a good offense, *we are also strengthening America's homeland security* to protect against and deter attack. . . . Centered on a new Department of Homeland Security and including a new unified military command and a fundamental reordering of the FBI, our comprehensive plan to secure the homeland encompasses every level of government and the cooperation of the public and the private sector. . . .

. . . But new deadly challenges have emerged from rogue states and terrorists. . . . We must be prepared to stop rogue states and their terrorist clients before they are able to threaten or use weapons of mass destruction against the United States and our allies and friends. Our response must take full advantage of strengthened alliances, the establishment of new partnerships with former adversaries, innovation in the use of military forces, modern technologies, including the development of an effective missile defense system, and increased emphasis on intelligence collection and analysis.

Our comprehensive strategy to combat WMD includes: [A] *Proactive counterproliferation efforts.* We must deter and defend against the threat before it is unleashed. We must ensure that key capabilities— detection, active and passive defenses, and counterforce capabilities—are integrated into our defense transformation and our homeland security systems. . . ; [B] *Strengthened nonproliferation efforts to prevent rogue states and terrorists from acquiring the materials, technologies, and expertise necessary for weapons of mass destruction. . . ;* [C] *Effective consequence management to respond to the effects of WMD use, whether by terrorists or hostile states.* Minimizing the effects of WMD use against our people will help deter those who possess such weapons and dissuade those who seek to acquire them by persuading enemies that they cannot attain their desired ends. The United States must also be prepared to respond to the effects of WMD use against our forces abroad, and to help friends and allies if they are attacked.

. . . The United States can no longer solely rely on a reactive posture as we have in the past. The inability to deter a potential attacker, the immediacy of today's threats, and the magnitude of potential harm that could be caused by our adversaries' choice of weapons, do not permit that option. *We cannot let our enemies strike first. . . .* Traditional concepts of deterrence will not work against a terrorist enemy whose avowed tactics are wanton destruction and the targeting of innocents; whose so-called soldiers seek martyrdom in death and whose most potent protection is statelessness. The overlap between states that sponsor terror and those that pursue WMD compels us to action.

For centuries, international law recognized that *nations need not suffer an attack before they can lawfully take action to defend themselves against forces that present an imminent danger of attack.* Legal scholars and international jurists often conditioned *the legitimacy of preemption on the existence of an imminent threat*—most often a visible mobilization of armies, navies, and air forces preparing to attack. *We must adapt the concept of imminent threat to the capabilities and objectives of today's adversaries. . . . The United States has long maintained the option of preemptive actions to counter a sufficient threat to our national security.* The greater the threat, the greater is the risk of inaction—and the more compelling *the case for taking anticipatory action to defend*

ourselves, even if uncertainty remains as to the time and place of the enemy's attack. *To forestall or prevent such hostile acts by our adversaries, the United States will, if necessary, act preemptively. . . .*

. . . America will implement its strategies by organizing coalitions—as broad as practicable—of states able and willing to promote a balance of power that favors freedom. . . . *We are attentive to the possible renewal of old patterns of great power competition. Several potential great powers are now in the midst of internal transition—most importantly Russia, India, and China.* In all three cases, recent developments have encouraged our hope that a truly global consensus about basic principles is slowly taking shape. . . .

The major institutions of American national security were designed in a different era to meet different requirements. All of them must be transformed. *It is time to reaffirm the essential role of American military strength. . . . The unparalleled strength of the United States armed forces,* and their forward presence, have maintained the peace in some of the world's most strategically vital regions. . . . Through *our willingness to use force in our own defense and in defense of others,* the United States demonstrates its resolve *to maintain a balance of power that favors freedom. . . .* Innovation within the armed forces will rest on experimentation with new approaches to warfare, strengthening joint operations, exploiting U.S. intelligence advantages, and taking full advantage of science and technology. . . . While maintaining near-term readiness and the ability to fight the war on terrorism, *the goal must be to provide the President with a wider range of military options to discourage aggression or any form of coercion* against the United States, our allies, and our friends.

We know from history that deterrence can fail; and we know from experience that some enemies cannot be deterred. *The United States must and will maintain the capability to defeat any attempt by an enemy—whether a state or non-state actor—to impose its will on the United States, our allies, or our friends.* We will maintain the forces sufficient to support our obligations, and to defend freedom. *Our forces will be strong enough to dissuade potential adversaries from pursuing a military build-up in hopes of surpassing, or equaling, the power of the United States....*

We will make hard choices in the coming year and beyond to ensure the right level and allocation of government spending on national security. The United States Government must strengthen its defenses to win this war. *At home, our most important priority is to protect the homeland for the American people.*

Today, the distinction between domestic and foreign affairs is diminishing. In a globalized world, events beyond America's borders have a greater impact inside them.... *In exercising our leadership, we will respect the values, judgment, and interests of our friends and partners. Still, we will be prepared to act apart when our interests and unique responsibilities require....* Ultimately, the foundation of American strength is at home. It is in the skills of our people, the dynamism of our economy, and the resilience of our institutions. A diverse, modern society has inherent, ambitious, entrepreneurial energy. Our strength comes from what we do with that energy. That is where our national security begins.

---

53. *Resolution Authorizing War against Iraq*

(2003)

Because of concern over Iraqi weapons of mass destruction and alleged involvement with terrorist groups, President George W. Bush sought congressional backing to employ U.S. forces against Iraq. On October 11, 2002, Congress, abiding by the 1973 War Powers Act, passed a resolution authorizing use of force against Iraq (see part 2, chapter 7).

To authorize the use of United States Armed Forces against Iraq.

Now, therefore, be it resolved by the Senate and House of Representatives of the United States of America in Congress assembled, The Congress of the United States supports the efforts by the President to: Strictly enforce through the United Nations Security Council all relevant Security Council resolutions regarding Iraq and encourages him in those efforts and obtain prompt and decisive action by the Security Council to ensure that Iraq abandons its strategy of delay, evasion and non-compliance and promptly and strictly complies with all relevant Security Council resolutions regarding Iraq.

a. *... The President is authorized to use the Armed Forces of the United States as he determines to be necessary and appropriate in order to: (1) Defend the national security of the United States against the continuing threat posed by Iraq; and (2) Enforce all relevant United Nations Security Council resolutions regarding Iraq.*

b. . . . In connection with the exercise of the authority granted in subsection (a) to use force the President shall, prior to such exercise or as soon thereafter as may be feasible, but no later than 48 hours after exercising such authority, make available to the Speaker of the House of Representatives and the President *pro tempore* of the Senate his determination that: (1) Reliance by the United States on further diplomatic or other peaceful means alone either (A) will not adequately protect the national security of the United States against the continuing threat posed by Iraq or (B) is not likely to lead to enforcement of all relevant United Nations Security Council resolutions regarding Iraq; and (2) Acting pursuant to this joint resolution is consistent with the United States and other countries continuing to take the necessary actions against international terrorist and terrorist organizations, including those nations, organizations, or persons who planned, authorized, committed or aided the terrorist attacks that occurred on September 11, 2001.

c. War Powers Resolution Requirements: (1) Specific Statutory Authorization: Consistent with section 8(a)(1) of the War Powers Resolution, the Congress declares that this section is intended to constitute specific statutory authorization within the meaning of section 5(b) of the War Powers Resolution. (2) Applicability of other requirements: Nothing in this joint resolution supersedes any requirement of the War Powers Resolution.

Reports to Congress

The President shall, at least once every 60 days, submit to the Congress a report on matters relevant to this joint resolution. . . .

PART FOUR

Arms Control

Arms control efforts are not new. The late-nineteenth- and early-twentieth-century Hague Conventions related to the conduct and use of force. The Washington Naval Treaty (1922) and the Protocol Against Using Chemical and Bacteriological Weapons (1925) are also early examples; however, arms control and disarmament efforts achieved their greatest success in the years since the late 1950s.

Objectives sought in pursuing arms control and disarmament (actual force reductions) are diverse. Some seek to reduce the likelihood of war or, should war occur, reduce or mitigate the damage wrought. Another motivation is to achieve economies by saving scarce resources consumed in arms races, allocating them instead to other purposes. Still others see arms control as an integral part of national strategy—a means to secure strategic advantage, buy time in competitive arms races, or serve other national purposes.

The rules that states agree on set limits of one kind or another, and associated institutions they construct constitute what we call an arms control *regime.* To make sense of the large number of arms control treaties and agreements constituting arms control regimes, we organize them under three broad categories—efforts to constrain armaments quantitatively or qualitatively (chapter 14), arms control rules that identify geographically or spatially certain areas in which states should be constrained from deploying or using military forces (chapter 15), and agreed functional measures aimed at limiting armed conflicts or the likelihood of resorting to the use of force (chapter 16). It is convenient to place these treaties and other agreements into one or another of these three categories; however, we are careful to note that these are not air-tight, mutually exclusive categories. Any given treaty or other agreement may indeed contain provisions that fit into more than one category. Nevertheless, the main thrust of a particular treaty or agreement gives us a basis for its categorization and placement in one of the three chapters in this part.

Because of space limitations, the length of many of these agreements obviously precludes our reprinting them here in their entirety; however, as an overview of the arms control component of American foreign policy and national security, every effort has been made to be inclusive of significant arms control agreements, underscoring their major provisions.

There are those who see arms control merely as an artifact of the cold war; however, the challenges and dangers posed by conventional armaments and weapons of mass destruction on Earth and prospects for weaponization of space strongly suggest a substantial future for arms control.

Chapter 14

Controlling Armaments

We collect here several sets of treaties and other agreements that constitute arms control regimes—the rules and associated institutions that aim to constrain or reduce armaments. When the main thrust of a particular treaty or agreement is to set quantitative or qualitative restraints on weapons or weapons systems (as in specifying numbers, types, or locations of military equipment, units, or personnel), we identify the effort as one of controlling armaments. The documents in this chapter are organized categorically by types of *regimes:* chemical and biological weapons, nuclear test bans, nuclear nonproliferation, strategic defense and strategic offense, and conventional weapons and weapons systems.

1. *The Washington Naval Treaty*
(1922)

We include this treaty as an early and classic effort to establish a naval armaments regime by placing limits on numbers and types of armaments (ultimately unsuccessful), the focus being on aircraft carriers and capital ships—the latter a term referring, for example, to such armed vessels as battleships or cruisers (ships typically carrying more than ten thousand tons displacement). In an effort to prevent a naval arms race, on November 12, 1921, the United States, the United Kingdom, France, Italy, and Japan convened a Conference on the Limitation of Armament, which concluded its work on February 6, 1922. The degree of attention to detail in the Washington Naval Treaty, although abbreviated here, would not be matched until the SALT and START agreements and treaties of the 1970s, 1980s, and 1990s.

The United States of America, the British Empire, France, Italy and Japan . . . have agreed as follows:

I. *The Contracting Powers agree to limit their respective naval armament* as provided in the present Treaty.

II. *The Contracting Powers may retain respectively the capital ships which are specified. . . .* On the coming into force of the present Treaty . . . *all other capital ships, built or building, of the United States, the British Empire and Japan shall be disposed of. . . .*

III. . . . *The Contracting Powers shall abandon their respective capital ship building programs, and no new capital ships shall be constructed or acquired by any of the Contracting Powers except replacement tonnage which may be constructed or acquired.* . . . Ships which are replaced . . . shall be disposed of. . . .

IV. The total capital ship replacement tonnage of each of the Contracting Powers shall not exceed in standard displacement, for the United States 525,000 tons (533,400 metric tons); for the British Empire 525,000 tons (533,400 metric tons); for France 175,000 tons (177,800 metric tons); for Italy 175,000 tons (177,800 metric tons); for Japan 315,000 tons (320,040 metric tons).

V. No capital ship exceeding 35,000 tons (35,560 metric tons) standard displacement shall be acquired by, or constructed by, for, or within the jurisdiction of, any of the Contracting Powers.

VI. No capital ship of any of the Contracting Powers shall carry a gun with a calibre in excess of 16 inches (406 millimetres).

VII. The total tonnage for aircraft carriers of each of the Contracting Powers shall not exceed in standard displacement, for the United States 135,000 tons (137,160 metric tons); for the British Empire 135,000 tons (137,160 metric tons); for France 60,000 tons (60,960 metric tons); for Italy 60,000 tons (60,960 metric tons); for Japan 81,000 tons (82,296 metric tons).

VIII. The replacement of aircraft carriers shall be effected only as prescribed. . . .

IX. No aircraft carrier exceeding 27,000 tons (27,432 metric tons) standard displacement shall be acquired by, or constructed by, for or within the jurisdiction of, any of the Contracting Powers. However, any of the Contracting Powers may, provided that its total tonnage allowance of aircraft carriers is not thereby exceeded, build not more than two aircraft carriers, each of a tonnage of not more than 33,000 tons (33,528 metric tons) standard displacement, and in order to effect economy any of the Contracting Powers may use for this purpose any two of their ships, whether constructed or in course of construction, which would otherwise be scrapped. . . . The armament of any aircraft carriers exceeding 27,000 tons (27,432 metric tons) standard displacement shall be in accordance with the requirements of Article X, except that the total number of guns to be carried in case any of such guns be of a calibre exceeding 6 inches (152 millimetres), except anti-aircraft guns and guns not exceeding 5 inches (127 millimetres), shall not exceed eight.

X. No aircraft carrier of any of the Contracting Powers shall carry a gun with a calibre in excess of 8 inches (203 millimetres). Without prejudice to the provisions of Article IX, if the armament carried includes guns exceeding 6 inches (152 millimetres) in calibre the total number of guns carried, except anti-aircraft guns and guns not exceeding 5 inches (127 millimetres), shall not exceed ten. If alternatively the armament contains no guns exceeding 6 inches (152 millimetres) in calibre, the number of guns is not limited. In either case the number of anti-aircraft guns and of guns not exceeding 5 inches (127 millimetres) is not limited.

XI. No vessel of war exceeding 10,000 tons (10,160 metric tons) standard displacement, other than a capital ship or aircraft carrier, shall be acquired by, or constructed by, for, or within the jurisdiction of, any of the Contracting Powers. Vessels not specifically built as fighting ships nor taken in time of peace under government control for fighting purposes, which are employed on fleet duties or as troop transports or in some other way for the purpose of assisting in the prosecution of hostilities otherwise than as fighting ships, shall not be within the limitations of this Article.

XII. No vessel of war of any of the Contracting Powers, hereafter laid down, other than a capital ship, shall carry a gun with a calibre in excess of 8 inches (203 millimetres).

XIII. Except as provided in Article IX, no ship designated in the present Treaty to be scrapped may be reconverted into a vessel of war.

XIV. No preparations shall be made in merchant ships in time of peace for the installation of warlike armaments for the purpose of converting such ships into vessels of war, other than the necessary stiffening of decks for the mounting of guns not exceeding 6 inch (152 millimetres) calibre.

XV. No vessel of war constructed within the jurisdiction of any of the Contracting Powers for a non-Contracting Power shall exceed the limitations as to displacement and armament prescribed by the present Treaty for vessels of a similar type which may be constructed by or for any of the Contracting Powers; provided, however, that the displacement for aircraft carriers constructed for a non-Contracting Power shall in no case exceed 27,000 tons (27,432 metric tons) standard displacement.

XVI. If the construction of any vessel of war for a non-Contracting Power is undertaken within the jurisdiction of any of the Contracting Powers, such Power shall promptly inform the other Contracting Powers of the date of the signing of the contract and the date on which the keel of the ship is laid; and shall also communicate to them the particulars relating to the ship. . . .

XVII. In the event of a Contracting Power being engaged in war, such Power shall not use as a vessel of war any vessel of war which may be under construction within its jurisdiction for any other Power, or which may have been constructed within its jurisdiction for another Power and not delivered.

XVIII. Each of the Contracting Powers undertakes not to dispose by gift, sale or any mode of transfer of any vessel of war in such a manner that such vessel may become a vessel of war in the Navy of any foreign Power.

XIX. The United States, the British Empire and Japan agree that the status quo at the time of the signing of the present Treaty, with regard to fortifications and naval bases, shall be maintained in their respective territories and possessions. . . . The maintenance of the status quo under the foregoing provisions implies that no new fortifications or naval bases shall be established in the territories and possessions specified; that no measures shall be taken to increase the existing naval facilities for the repair and maintenance of naval forces, and that no increase shall be made in the coast defences of the territories and possessions above specified. This restriction, however, does not preclude such repair and replacement of worn-out weapons and equipment as is customary in naval and military establishments in time of peace. . . .

XXI. *If during the term of the present Treaty the requirements of the national security of any Contracting Power in respect of naval defence are, in the opinion of that Power, materially affected by any change of circumstances, the Contracting Powers will, at the request of such Power, meet in conference with a view to the reconsideration of the provisions of the Treaty* and its amendment by mutual agreement. In view of possible technical and scientific developments, the United States, after consultation with the other Contracting Powers, shall arrange for a conference of all the Contracting Powers which shall convene as soon as possible after the expiration of eight years from the coming into force of the present Treaty to consider what changes, if any, in the Treaty may be necessary to meet such developments.

XXII. *Whenever any Contracting Power shall become engaged in a war which in its opinion affects the naval defence of its national security, such Power may after notice to the other Contracting Powers suspend for the period of hostilities its obligations under the present Treaty other than those under Articles XIII and XVII,* provided that such Power shall notify the other Contracting Powers that the emergency is of such a character as to require such suspension. The remaining Contracting Powers shall in such case consult together with a view to agreement as to what temporary modifications if any

should be made in the Treaty as between themselves. Should such consultation not produce agreement, duly made in accordance with the constitutional methods of the respective Powers, *any one of said Contracting Powers may, by giving notice to the other Contracting Powers, suspend for the period of hostilities its obligations under the present Treaty,* other than those under Articles XIII and XVII. On the cessation of hostilities the Contracting Powers will meet in conference to consider what modifications, if any, should be made in the provisions of the present Treaty.

XXIII. The present Treaty shall remain in force until December 31st, 1936, and in case none of the Contracting Powers shall have given notice two years before that date of its intention to terminate the treaty, it shall continue in force until the expiration of two years from the date on which notice of termination shall be given by one of the Contracting Powers, whereupon the Treaty shall terminate as regards all the Contracting Powers.

2.–4. *Chemical and Biological Weapons Regimes*
(1925, 1972, and 1993)

Given the searing experience with the use in World War I of such weapons as chlorine, phosgene, mustard gas, and similar weapons, the regime began with agreement in 1925 on prohibiting use of chemical and biological weapons. Agreement to destroy biological and chemical weapons would have to wait until 1972 and 1993, respectively.

2. *The Protocol against Using Chemical and Bacteriological Weapons*
(1925)

The formal name of this treaty is the Protocol for the Prohibition of the Use in War of Asphyxiating, Poisonous or Other Gases, and of Bacteriological Methods of Warfare—an early effort to control chemical and biological weapons use in warfare, underscored by the adverse experience with gases used on battlefields in World War I. Of particular importance here is the protocol's foundational role in relation to arms control efforts undertaken decades later to control chemical and biological weapons.

Whereas the use in war of asphyxiating, poisonous or other gases, and of all analogous liquids, materials or devices, has been justly condemned . . . and whereas the prohibition of such use has been declared in Treaties . . . , *the High Contracting Parties,* so far as they are not already Parties to Treaties prohibiting such use, accept this prohibition, agree to *extend this prohibition to the use of bacteriological methods of warfare* and agree to be bound as between themselves according to the terms of this declaration.

The High Contracting Parties will exert every effort to induce other States to accede to the present Protocol. . . .

---

3. *The Biological Weapons Convention*
(1972)

By banning development, production, and stockpiling of biological weapons, this 1972 biological weapons treaty (formally the Convention on the Prohibition of the Development, Production and Stockpiling of Bacteriological [Biological] and Toxin Weapons and on Their Destruction) goes well beyond merely prohibiting their use as had long been established in the 1925 protocol against use of chemical and biological weapons.

I. *Each State Party to this Convention undertakes never in any circumstance to develop, produce, stockpile or otherwise acquire or retain: (1) Microbial or other biological agents, or toxins* whatever their origin or method of production, of types and in quantities that have no justification for prophylactic, protective or other peaceful purposes; (2) *Weapons, equipment or means of delivery designed to use such agents or toxins for hostile purposes or in armed conflict.*

II. *Each State Party to this Convention undertakes to destroy, or to divert to peaceful purposes,* as soon as possible but not later than nine months after the entry into force of the Convention, *all agents, toxins, weapons, equipment and means of delivery* specified in article I of the Convention, which are in its possession or under its jurisdiction or control. In implementing the provisions of this article all necessary safety precautions shall be observed to protect populations and the environment.

III. *Each State Party to this Convention undertakes not to transfer to any recipient whatsoever,* directly or indirectly, and not in any way to assist, encourage, or induce any State, group of States or international organizations to manufacture or otherwise acquire *any of the agents, toxins, weapons, equipment or means of delivery specified* in article I of the Convention.

IV. *Each State Party to this Convention shall,* in accordance with its constitutional processes, *take any necessary measures to prohibit and prevent the development, production, stockpiling, acquisition or retention of the agents, toxins, weapons, equipment and means of delivery* specified in article I of the Convention, *within the territory of such State, under its jurisdiction or under its control anywhere.*

V. The States Parties to this Convention undertake to consult one another and to cooperate in solving any problems which may arise in relation to the objective of, or in the application of the provisions of, the Convention. Consultation and cooperation pursuant to this article may also be undertaken through appropriate international procedures within the framework of the United Nations and in accordance with its Charter.

VI. Any State Party to this Convention which finds that any other State Party is acting in breach of obligations deriving from the provisions of the Convention may lodge a complaint with the Security Council of the United Nations. Such a complaint should include all possible evidence confirming its validity, as well as a request for its consideration by the Security Council. . . .

X. *The States Parties to this Convention undertake to facilitate, and have the right to participate in, the fullest possible exchange of equipment, materials and scientific and technological information for the use of bacteriological (biological) agents and toxins for peaceful purposes.* . . .

XIII. This Convention shall be of unlimited duration. (2) Each State Party to this Convention shall in exercising its natural sovereignty have the right to withdraw from the Convention if it decides that extraordinary events, related to the subject matter of the Convention, have jeopardized the supreme interests of its country. . . .

XIV. This Convention shall be open to all States for signature. . . .

---

4. The Chemical Weapons Convention

(1993)

The Chemical Weapons Convention eliminates as a matter of law an entire category of weaponry, except for those chemicals (such as tear gas) declared for riot-control purposes, which may not be used as a method of warfare. Intrusive measures are provided for on-site inspection and verification of compliance with the terms of the treaty. The treaty creates the Organization for the Prohibition of Chemical Weapons, located at The Hague in the Netherlands. Supportive of controls on transfer of chemicals that could have weapons applications is the multistate "Australia Group," which meets annually on regulating exports of chemical and biological materials.

The States Parties to this Convention have agreed as follows:

I. *General Obligations. Each State Party to this Convention undertakes never* under any circumstances: (a) *To develop, produce, otherwise acquire, stockpile or retain chemical weapons, or transfer, directly or indirectly, chemical weapons to anyone;* (b) *To use chemical weapons;* (c) *To engage in any military*

preparations to use chemical weapons; (d) *To assist,* encourage or induce, in any way, *anyone to engage in any activity prohibited to a State Party under this Convention. Each State Party undertakes to destroy chemical weapons it owns or possesses,* or that are located in any place under its jurisdiction or control, all chemical weapons it abandoned on the territory of another State Party, . . . any chemical weapons production facilities it owns or possesses, or that are located in any place under its jurisdiction or control, . . . [and] not to use riot control agents as a method of warfare.

II. *Definitions and Criteria.* . . .

III. *Declarations.* [The article specifies an obligation by each state party to make declarations on chemical weapons, production, and related facilities to include] *whether it owns or possesses any chemical weapons,* or whether there are any chemical weapons located in any place under its jurisdiction or control [and] . . . the precise location, aggregate quantity and detailed inventory of chemical weapons it owns or possesses; . . . *whether it has or has had any chemical weapons production facility under its ownership or possession . . .* [and] the precise location, nature and general scope of activities of any facility or establishment under its ownership or possession, or located in any place under its jurisdiction or control . . . primarily for development of chemical weapons. Such declaration shall include, inter alia, laboratories and test and evaluation sites . . . ; [and] . . . the chemical name, structural formula and Chemical Abstracts Service (CAS) registry number, if assigned, of *each chemical it holds for riot control purposes.*

IV. *Chemical Weapons.* . . . All locations at which chemical weapons . . . are stored or destroyed shall be subject to systematic verification through on-site inspection and monitoring with on-site instruments. . . . Each State Party shall . . . Provide access to chemical weapons . . . for the purpose of systematic verification of the declaration through on-site inspection. Thereafter, each State Party shall not remove any of these chemical weapons, except to a chemical weapons destruction facility. It shall provide access to such chemical weapons, for the purpose of systematic on-site

verification. Each State Party shall provide access to any chemical weapons destruction facilities and their storage areas, that it owns or possesses, or that are located in any place under its jurisdiction or control, for the purpose of systematic verification through on-site inspection and monitoring with on-site instruments. Each State Party shall destroy all chemical weapons specified. . . . [And] certify . . . that all chemical weapons specified . . . have been destroyed. . . . Each State Party, during transportation, sampling, storage and destruction of chemical weapons, shall assign the highest priority to ensuring the safety of people and to protecting the environment. Each State Party shall transport, sample, store and destroy chemical weapons in accordance with its national standards for safety and emissions. . . . Each State Party shall meet the costs of destruction of chemical weapons it is obliged to destroy. It shall also meet the costs of verification of storage and destruction of these chemical weapons unless the Executive Council decides otherwise. . . .

V. *Chemical Weapons Production Facilities.* The provisions of this Article and the detailed procedures for its implementation shall apply to any and all chemical weapons production facilities owned or possessed by a State Party, or that are located in any place under its jurisdiction or control. . . . All *chemical weapons production facilities* specified . . . *shall be subject to systematic verification through on-site inspection and monitoring with on-site instruments.* . . . Each State Party shall cease immediately all activity at chemical weapons production facilities specified . . . except activity required for closure. *No State Party shall construct any new chemical weapons production facilities or modify any existing facilities for the purpose of chemical weapons production* or for any other activity prohibited under this Convention. *Each State Party shall . . . provide access to chemical weapons production facilities* specified . . . *for the purpose of systematic verification* of the declaration through on-site inspection. *Each State Party shall:* (a) *Close . . . all chemical weapons production facilities* specified . . . and give notice thereof; and (b) *Provide access to chemical weapons production facilities* specified . . . *subsequent to closure, for the purpose of systematic verification* through on-site inspection and monitoring with on-site instruments in order to ensure that the facility remains closed and is subsequently destroyed. *Each State Party shall destroy all chemical weapons production facilities* specified . . . and related facilities and equipment . . . in accordance with an agreed rate and sequence of destruction (hereinafter referred to as "order of destruction"). . . . A State Party is not precluded from destroying such facilities at a faster rate. . . . A State Party may request, in exceptional cases of compelling need, permission to use a chemical weapons production facility specified . . . for purposes not prohibited under this Convention. . . . Each State Party shall meet the costs of destruction of chemical weapons production facilities it is obliged to destroy. It shall also meet the costs of verification under this Article unless the Executive Council decides otherwise. . . .

VI. *Activities not Prohibited Under this Convention. Each State Party has the right,* subject to the provisions of this Convention, *to develop, produce, otherwise acquire, retain, transfer and use toxic chemicals and their precursors for purposes not prohibited under this Convention.* Each State Party shall adopt the necessary measures to ensure that toxic chemicals and their precursors are only developed, produced, otherwise acquired, retained, transferred, or used within its territory or in any other place under its jurisdiction or control for purposes not prohibited under this Convention. . . .

VII. *National Emplementation Measures.* Each State Party shall, in accordance with its constitutional processes, adopt the necessary measures to implement its obligations under this Convention. . . . Each State Party undertakes to cooperate with the Organization in the exercise of all its functions and in particular to provide assistance to the Technical Secretariat.

VIII. *The Organization. The States Parties* to this Convention hereby *establish the Organization for the Prohibition of Chemical Weapons* to achieve the object and purpose of this Convention, to ensure the implementation of its provisions, including those for international verification of compliance with it, and to provide a forum for consultation and cooperation among States Parties. All States Parties to this Convention shall be members of the Organization. A State Party shall not be deprived of its membership in the Organization. *The seat of the Headquarters of the Organization shall be The Hague, Kingdom of the Netherlands.* There are hereby established as the organs of the Organization: the Conference of the States Parties, the Executive Council, and the Technical Secretariat. The Organization shall conduct its verification activities provided for under this Convention in the least intrusive manner possible consistent with the timely and efficient accomplishment of their objectives. It shall request only the information and data necessary to fulfil its responsibilities under this Convention. . . .

IX. *Consultations, Cooperation and Fact-Finding.* States Parties shall consult and cooperate, directly among themselves, or through the Organization or other appropriate international procedures, including procedures within the framework of the United Nations and in accordance with its Charter, on any matter which may be raised relating to the object and purpose, or the implementation of the provisions, of this Convention. Without prejudice to the right of any State Party to request a challenge inspection, States Parties should, whenever possible, first make every effort to clarify and resolve, through exchange of information and consultations among themselves, any matter which may cause doubt about compliance. . . .

X. *Assistance and Protection Against Chemical Weapons.* . . . Nothing in this Convention shall be interpreted as impeding the right of any State Party to conduct research into, develop, produce, acquire, transfer or use means of protection against chemical weapons, for purposes not prohibited under this Convention. Each State Party undertakes to facilitate, and shall have the right to participate in, the fullest possible exchange of equipment, material and scientific and technological information concerning means of protection against chemical weapons. For the purposes of increasing the transparency of national programmes related to protective purposes, each State Party shall provide annually . . . information on its programme. . . .

XI. *Economic and Technological Development.* The provisions of this Convention shall be implemented in a manner which avoids hampering the economic or technological development of States Parties, and international cooperation in the field of chemical activities for purposes not prohibited under this Convention including the international exchange of scientific and technical information and chemicals and equipment for the production,

processing or use of chemicals for purposes not prohibited under this Convention. Subject to the provisions of this Convention and without prejudice to the principles and applicable rules of international law, the *States Parties shall:* (a) *Have the right, individually or collectively, to conduct research with, to develop, produce, acquire, retain, transfer, and use chemicals;* (b) Undertake to facilitate, and have the right to participate in, the fullest possible exchange of chemicals, equipment and scientific and technical information relating to the development and application of chemistry for purposes not prohibited under this Convention; (c) Not maintain among themselves any restrictions, including those in any international agreements, incompatible with the obligations undertaken under this Convention, which would restrict or impede trade and the development and promotion of scientific and technological knowledge in the field of chemistry for industrial, agricultural, research, medical, pharmaceutical or other peaceful purposes; (d) Not use this Convention as grounds for applying any measures other than those provided for, or permitted, under this Convention nor use any other international agreement for pursuing an objective inconsistent with this Convention; (e) Undertake to review their existing national regulations in the field of trade in chemicals in order to render them consistent with the object and purpose of this Convention.

XII. *Measures to Redress a Situation and to Ensure Compliance Including Sanctions.* The Conference shall take the necessary measures . . . to ensure compliance with this Convention and to redress and remedy any situation which contravenes the provisions of this Convention.

5.–8. *The Nuclear Test-Ban Regime*
(1963, 1974, 1976, and 1996)

One response to the Cuban missile crisis of October 1962 (during which the United States and the Soviet Union came to the brink of nuclear war) was the beginning of an effort to limit further tests of nuclear weapons. The process began by excluding tests in the atmosphere, in outer space, and under water (1963), limiting underground tests to 150 kilotons or less (1974), and culminating in a comprehensive or complete test ban (1996) that has yet to be ratified. Limiting (and ultimately excluding) nuclear weapons tests was intended as a means of reducing arms-race tensions and curbing adverse environmental effects in the atmosphere and the oceans. As a practical matter, arms controllers also saw these restrictions as inhibiting to some extent further development of nuclear weapons technologies.

5. *The Treaty Banning Nuclear Weapon Tests in the Atmosphere, Outer Space and Under Water*
(1963)

The nuclear test-ban regime began with this treaty negotiated in the months following the missile crisis in Cuba that had brought the United States and Soviet Union to the brink of nuclear war.

The Governments of the United States of America, the United Kingdom of Great Britain and Northern Ireland, and the Union of Soviet Socialist Republics, hereinafter referred to as the "Original Parties" . . . have agreed as follows:

I. 1. *Each of the Parties to this Treaty undertakes to prohibit, to prevent, and not to carry out any nuclear weapon test explosion, or any other nuclear explosion, at any place under its jurisdiction or control: (a) in the atmosphere; beyond its limits, including outer space; or under water, including territorial waters or high seas; or (b) in any other environment if such explosion causes radioactive debris to be present outside the territorial limits of the State under whose jurisdiction or control such explosion is conducted. It is understood in this connection that the provisions of this subparagraph* are without prejudice to the conclusion of a Treaty resulting in the permanent banning of all nuclear test explosions, including all such explosions underground, the conclusion of which . . . they seek to achieve.

2. Each of the Parties to this Treaty undertakes furthermore to refrain from causing, encouraging, or in any way participating in, the carrying out of any nuclear weapon test explosion, or any other nuclear explosion, anywhere which would take place in any of the environments described, or have the effect referred to, in paragraph 1 of this Article. . . .

III. This Treaty shall be open to all States for signature. . . .

IV. This Treaty shall be of unlimited duration.

6. *The Limitation of Underground Nuclear Weapon Tests*
(1974)

This threshold test-ban treaty, though concluded in 1974, did not formally go into force until 1990 when post–cold war U.S.-Soviet negotiations finally provided the verification and compliance measures necessary for U.S. Senate ratification.

The United States of America and the Union of Soviet Socialist Republics, hereinafter referred to as the Parties, . . . have agreed as follows:

I. 1. *Each Party undertakes to prohibit, to prevent, and not to carry out any underground nuclear weapon test having a yield exceeding 150 kilotons at any place under its jurisdiction or control,* beginning March 31, 1976.

2. Each Party shall limit the number of its underground nuclear weapon tests to a minimum.

3. The Parties shall continue their negotiations with a view toward achieving a solution to the problem of the cessation of all underground nuclear weapon tests.

II. 1. For the purpose of providing assurance of compliance with the provisions of this Treaty, each Party shall use national technical means of verification at its disposal in a manner consistent with the generally recognized principles of international law.

2. Each Party undertakes not to interfere with the national technical means of verification of the other Party operating in accordance with paragraph 1 of this Article.

3. To promote the objectives and implementation of the provisions of this Treaty the Parties shall, as necessary, consult with each other, make inquiries and furnish information in response to such inquiries.

III. *The provisions of this Treaty do not extend to underground nuclear explosions carried out by the Parties for peaceful purposes.* Underground nuclear explosions for peaceful purposes shall be governed by an agreement which is to be negotiated and concluded by the Parties at the earliest possible time. . . .

7. *Peaceful Nuclear Explosions (PNE)*
(1976)

This peaceful nuclear explosions (PNE) treaty (formally called the Treaty on Underground Nuclear Explosions for Peaceful Purposes), though concluded in 1976, did not formally go into force until 1990 when post–cold war U.S.-Soviet negotiations finally provided the verification and compliance measures necessary for U.S. Senate ratification. Details on implementation of the agreement are contained in a protocol not reprinted here.

The United States of America and the Union of Soviet Socialist Republics, hereinafter referred to as the Parties . . . have agreed as follows:

I. The Parties enter into this Treaty to satisfy the obligations in Article III of the Treaty on the Limitation of Underground Nuclear Weapon Tests, and assume additional obligations in accordance with the provisions of this Treaty. *This Treaty shall govern all underground nuclear explosions for peaceful purposes conducted by the Parties. . . .*

III. 1. Each Party, subject to the obligations assumed under this Treaty and other international agreements, reserves the right to: (a) carry out explosions at any place under its jurisdiction or control . . . ; and (b) carry out, participate or assist in carrying out explosions in the territory of another State at the request of such other State.

2. *Each Party undertakes to prohibit,* to prevent and not to carry out at any place under its jurisdiction or control, and further undertakes not to carry out, participate or assist in carrying out anywhere: (a) *any individual explosion having a yield exceeding 150 kilotons;* (b) any group explosion: (1) having an aggregate yield exceeding 150 kilotons except in ways that will permit identification of each individual explosion and determination of the yield of each individual explosion in the group in accordance with the provisions of Article IV of and the Protocol to this Treaty; (2) having an aggregate yield exceeding one and one-half megatons; (c) any explosion which does not carry out a peaceful application; (d) any explosion except in compliance with the provisions of the Treaty Banning Nuclear Weapon Tests in the Atmosphere,

in Outer Space and Under Water, the Treaty on the Non-Proliferation of Nuclear Weapons, and other international agreements entered into by that Party.

3. The question of carrying out any individual explosion having a yield exceeding the yield specified in paragraph 2(a) of this article will be considered by the Parties at an appropriate time to be agreed.

IV. 1. *For the purpose of providing assurance of compliance* with the provisions of this Treaty, *each Party shall:* (a) *use national technical means of verification* at its disposal in a manner consistent with generally recognized principles of international law; and (b) *provide to the other Party information and access to sites of explosions* and furnish assistance in accordance with the provisions set forth in the Protocol to this Treaty. 2. *Each Party undertakes not to interfere with the national technical means of verification of the other Party. . . .*

V. To promote the objectives and implementation of the provisions of this Treaty, the Parties shall establish promptly a Joint Consultative Commission. . . .

VI. The Parties will develop cooperation on the basis of mutual benefit, equality, and reciprocity in various areas related to carrying out underground nuclear explosions for peaceful purposes. . . .

---

8. *The Comprehensive Nuclear Test-Ban Treaty*
(1996)

Although the United States was a principal negotiator of this treaty, political opposition to date has precluded its ratification. Accordingly, there is no legal prohibition at present to nuclear testing within the limits of the threshold test-ban treaty [see Document No. 6 above].

I. *Basic Obligations*

1. *Each State Party undertakes not to carry out any nuclear weapon test explosion or*

any other nuclear explosion, and to prohibit and prevent any such nuclear explosion at any place under its jurisdiction or control.

2. Each State Party undertakes, further-more, to refrain from causing, encouraging, or in any way participating in the carrying out of any nuclear weapon test explosion or any other nuclear explosion.

II. *The Organization*

A. *General Provisions.* The States Parties hereby establish the Comprehensive Nuclear Test-Ban Treaty Organization (hereinafter referred to as "the Organization") to achieve the object and purpose of this Treaty, to ensure the implementation of its provisions, including those for international verification of compliance with it, and to provide a forum for consultation and cooperation among States Parties. . . . The seat of the Organization shall be Vienna, Republic of Austria. . . . The Organization shall conduct its verification activities provided for under this Treaty in the least intrusive manner possible consistent with the timely and efficient accomplishment of their objectives. . . .

B. *The Conference of the States Parties.* . . . Each State Party shall have one representative in the Conference, who may be accompanied by alternates and advisers. . . . The Conference shall meet in regular sessions. . . . The Conference shall be the principal organ of the Organization. It shall consider any questions, matters or issues within the scope of this Treaty. . . . It may make recommendations and take decisions on any questions, matters or issues within the scope of this Treaty. . . .

C. *The Executive Council . . .* shall be the executive organ of the Organization. It shall be responsible to the Conference. It shall carry out the powers and functions entrusted to it in accordance with this Treaty. . . .

D. *The Technical Secretariat . . .* shall assist States Parties in the implementation of this Treaty. The Technical Secretariat shall assist the Conference and the Executive Council in the performance of their functions. The Technical Secretariat shall carry out the verification and other functions entrusted to it by this Treaty. . . . The Director-General shall assume responsibility for the activities of an inspection team. . . .

III. *National Implementation Measures*

Each State Party shall, in accordance with its constitutional processes, take any necessary measures to implement its obligations under this Treaty. . . .

IV. *Verification. . . .* In order to verify compliance with this Treaty, a verification regime shall be established consisting of the following elements: (a) An International Monitoring System; (b) Consultation and clarification; (c) On-site inspections; and (d) Confidence-building measures. . . .

9.–10. A Nuclear Nonproliferation Regime

(1968 and 1980)

The nuclear nonproliferation regime aims to stem the flow "horizontally" of nuclear weapons and related technologies to states not possessing them as well as to reduce "vertically" the massive stockpiles presently in the inventories of nuclear weapons states. The International Atomic Energy Agency (IAEA) in Vienna plays an instrumental role in helping to maintain the nuclear nonproliferation treaty (NPT) regime by monitoring compliance and taking enforcement measures authorized by treaty—the IAEA statute and NPT Treaty—or by UN Security Council resolutions.

The multistate Nuclear Suppliers Group (or "London Club") and the NPT Exporters Committee (or "Zangger Committee") also have been engaged since the mid-1970s in initiatives to maintain the NPT regime by monitoring items related to production of nuclear weapons. Finally, efforts since the 1990s have been made to negotiate a Fissile Material Cutoff Treaty to end the production of fissile material for nuclear weapons; however, to date this remains to be accomplished.

9. The NPT Regime: Treaty on the Nonproliferation of Nuclear Weapons

(1968)

The Nuclear Nonproliferation Treaty (NPT) enjoyed substantial bipartisan support, which assured relatively smoother sailing through the ratification process than was the case for many later arms control treaties. Indeed, it was signed in Washington, London, and Moscow on July 1, 1968, late in the Johnson administration. After ratification was "advised" by the U.S. Senate on March 13, 1969, President Nixon subsequently ratified the treaty on November 24, 1969, and finally proclaimed it on March 5, 1970, when it formally entered into force. Focusing on both weapons and weapons-related technology, the treaty prohibits nuclear states from transferring (and nonnuclear states are prohibited from receiving) nuclear weapons or nuclear weapons manufacturing capabilities. The treaty in effect limits the nuclear club to those then possessing such weapons capabilities, promising nonnuclear weapons states in exchange for not acquiring such capabilities that nuclear weapons states will "pursue negotiations in good faith" toward "cessation of the nuclear arms race" and "nuclear disarmament" as well as "general and complete disarmament under strict and effective international control." Both nuclear and nonnuclear states may engage in "research, production and use of nuclear energy for peaceful purposes"; however, provision is also made in the NPT "regime" for "safeguards"—a verification and compliance enforcement mechanism institutionally linked to the International Atomic Energy Agency (IAEA) in Vienna to assure that such "peaceful" efforts do not result in nonnuclear weapons states acquiring such capabilities.

I. *Each nuclear-weapon State Party to the Treaty undertakes not to transfer to any recipient whatsoever nuclear weapons or other nuclear explosive devices or control over such weapons or explosive devices* directly, or indirectly; and not in any way to assist, encourage, or induce any non-nuclear weapon State to manufacture or otherwise acquire nuclear weapons or other nuclear explosive devices, or control over such weapons or explosive devices.

II. *Each non-nuclear-weapon State Party to the Treaty undertakes not to receive the transfer from any transferor whatsoever of nuclear weapons or other nuclear explosive devices or of control over such weapons or explosive devices* directly, or indirectly; not to manufacture or otherwise acquire nuclear weapons or other nuclear explosive devices; and not to seek or receive any assistance in the manufacture of nuclear weapons or other nuclear explosive devices.

III. 1. *Each non-nuclear-weapon State Party to the Treaty undertakes to accept safeguards,* as set forth in an agreement to be negotiated and concluded with the International Atomic Energy Agency in accordance with the Statute of the International Atomic Energy Agency and the Agency's safeguards system, *for the exclusive purpose of verification of the fulfillment of its obligations assumed under this Treaty with a view to preventing diversion of nuclear energy from peaceful uses to nuclear weapons or other nuclear explosive devices.* Procedures for the safeguards required by this article shall be followed with respect to source or special fissionable material whether it is being produced, processed or used in any principal nuclear facility or is outside any such facility. The safeguards required by this article shall be applied to all source or special fissionable material in all peaceful nuclear activities within the territory of such State, under its jurisdiction, or carried out under its control anywhere. 2. Each State Party to the Treaty undertakes not to provide: (a) source or special fissionable material, or (b) equipment or material especially designed or prepared for the processing, use or production of special fissionable material, to any non-nuclear-weapon State for peaceful purposes, unless the source or special fissionable material shall be subject to the safeguards required by this article. 3. The safeguards required by this article shall be implemented in a manner designed to comply with article IV of this Treaty, and to avoid hampering the economic or technological development of the Parties or international cooperation in the field of peaceful nuclear activities, including the international exchange of nuclear material and equipment for the processing, use or production of nuclear material for peaceful purposes in accordance with the

provisions of this article and the principle of safeguarding set forth in the Preamble of the Treaty. 4. Non-nuclear-weapon States Party to the Treaty shall conclude agreements with the International Atomic Energy Agency to meet the requirements of this article either individually or together with other States in accordance with the Statute of the International Atomic Energy Agency. . . .

IV. 1. *Nothing in this Treaty shall be interpreted as affecting the inalienable right of all the Parties to the Treaty to develop research, production and use of nuclear energy for peaceful purposes without discrimination and in conformity with articles I and II of this Treaty.* 2. All the Parties to the Treaty undertake to facilitate, and have the right to participate in, the fullest possible exchange of equipment, materials and scientific and technological information for the peaceful uses of nuclear energy. Parties to the Treaty in a position to do so shall also cooperate in contributing alone or together with other States or international organizations to the further development of the applications of nuclear energy for peaceful purposes, especially in the territories of non-nuclear-weapon States Party to the Treaty, with due consideration for the needs of the developing areas of the world.

V. Each party to the Treaty undertakes to take appropriate measures to ensure that, in accordance with this Treaty, under appropriate international observation and through appropriate international procedures, potential benefits from any peaceful applications of nuclear explosions will be made available to non-nuclear-weapon States Party to the Treaty on a nondiscriminatory basis and that the charge to such Parties for the explosive devices used will be as low as possible and exclude any charge for research and development. . . .

VI. *Each of the Parties to the Treaty undertakes to pursue negotiations in good faith on effective measures relating to cessation of the nuclear arms race at an early date and to nuclear disarmament, and on a Treaty on general and complete disarmament under strict and effective international control.*

VII. Nothing in this Treaty affects the right of any group of States to conclude regional treaties in order to assure the total absence of nuclear weapons in their respective territories.

VIII. Any Party to the Treaty may propose amendments to this Treaty. . . .

IX. This Treaty shall be open to all States for signature. . . .

X. 1. *Each Party shall in exercising its national sovereignty have the right to withdraw from the Treaty if it decides that extraordinary events,* related to the subject matter of this Treaty, *have jeopardized the supreme interests of its country. It shall give notice of such withdrawal* to all other Parties to the Treaty and to the United Nations Security Council *three months in advance.* Such notice shall include a statement of the extraordinary events it regards as having jeopardized its supreme interests. 2. Twenty-five years after the entry into force of the Treaty, a conference shall be convened to decide whether the Treaty shall continue in force indefinitely, or shall be extended for an additional fixed period or periods. [Consistent with this provision, the treaty has been extended indefinitely.—Ed.] This decision shall be taken by a majority of the Parties to the Treaty. . . .

10. *Protection of Nuclear Material*
(1980)

In effect an adjunct to terms of the Nonproliferation Treaty (1968), the Convention on the Physical Protection of Nuclear Material, signed in 1980 (and formally going into force in 1987), addresses protecting nuclear material in transit as well as recovering and returning nuclear material stolen by either state or nonstate actors should such material be weaponized by them.

The States Parties to This Convention . . . have Agreed as follows:

I. For the purposes of this Convention: (a) "nuclear material" means plutonium except that with isotopic concentration exceeding 80% in plutonium . . . ; (b) "uranium enriched in the isotopes 235 or 233" . . . ; (c) "international nuclear transport" means the carriage of a consignment of nuclear material by any means of transportation intended to go beyond the territory of the State where the shipment originates beginning with the departure from a facility of the shipper in that State and ending with the arrival at a facility of the receiver within the State of ultimate destination.

II. 1. *The Convention shall apply to nuclear material used for peaceful purposes while in international nuclear transport. 2. . . . This Convention shall also apply to nuclear material used for peaceful purposes while in domestic use, storage and transport. 3. . . . This Con-* vention shall be interpreted as affecting the sovereign rights of a State regarding the domestic use, storage and transport of such nuclear material.

III. *Each State Party shall take appropriate steps . . . that, during international nuclear transport, nuclear material within its territory, or on board a ship or aircraft under its jurisdiction insofar as such ship or aircraft is engaged in the transport to or from that State, is protected. . . .*

IV. 1. *Each State Party shall not export or authorize the export of nuclear material unless* the State Party has received assurances that *such material will be protected during the international nuclear transport. . . .* 2. *Each State Party shall not import or authorize the*

import of nuclear material from a State not party to this Convention unless the State Party has received assurances that such material will during the international nuclear transport be protected. . . .

V. *States Parties shall identify and make known to each other* directly or through the International Atomic Energy Agency . . . *any unauthorized removal, use or alteration of nuclear material or in the event of credible threat thereof. In the case of theft, robbery or any other unlawful taking of nuclear material or of credible threat thereof, States Parties shall . . . provide co-operation and assistance to the maximum feasible extent* in the recovery and protection of such material to any State that so requests. . . .

---

11. A Strategic Defense Regime: The Antiballistic Missile (ABM) Treaty and Its Abrogation

(1972)

Signed in Moscow by Soviet general secretary Leonid I. Brezhnev and U.S. president Richard M. Nixon on May 26, 1972, the Antiballistic Missile (ABM) Treaty limited strategic defenses consistent with an offense-dominant deterrence posture. Referred to at the time as mutually assured destruction, if neither the Soviet Union nor the United States could effectively defend against a massive nuclear attack, neither party rationally would choose to attack the other. Provisions of the ABM Treaty were an obstacle to testing and deploying such defensive systems as the Reagan-Bush Strategic Defense Initiative (SDI) or the more modest Clinton-Bush National Missile Defense (NMD) programs. In the Reagan-Bush years, a "broad" or permissive interpretation of space-based testing prohibitions competed with a "narrow" interpretation later adopted by the Clinton administration that prohibited such tests. Arms control advocates underscored the value of the ABM Treaty precisely because of its qualitative curbs that constrain tests and deployments of new arms programs; however, "breaking out" of the ABM Treaty—withdrawal under Article XV—was advocated by those seeing its restrictions as inhibiting testing and developing space-based components of missile defense systems.

In 2002 President George W. Bush consulted with his Russian counterpart, President Vladimir Putin, notifying him of the U.S. decision to withraw from the treaty and underscoring his view that relations between the two countries had so improved in the post–cold war period as to make the treaty's restrictions out of date. To President Bush, the need to develop missile defenses against states newly acquiring nuclear and missile-delivery capabilities necessitated withdrawing from the ABM Treaty.

I. 1. Each Party undertakes to limit anti-ballistic missile (ABM) systems and to adopt other measures in accordance with the provisions of this Treaty. 2. Each Party undertakes *not to deploy ABM systems for a defense of the territory of its country* and not to provide a base for such a defense, *and not to deploy ABM systems for defense of an individual region except as provided for in Article III* of this Treaty.

II. 1. For the purpose of this Treaty *an ABM system is a system to counter strategic ballistic missiles or their elements in flight trajectory,* currently consisting of: (a) ABM interceptor missiles, which are interceptor missiles constructed and deployed for an ABM role, or of a type tested in an ABM mode; (b) ABM launchers, which are launchers constructed and deployed for launching ABM interceptor missiles; and (c) ABM radars, which are radars constructed and deployed for an ABM role, or of a type tested in an ABM mode. 2. The ABM system components listed in paragraph 1 of this Article include those which are: (a) operational; (b) under construction; (c) undergoing testing; (d) undergoing overhaul, repair or conversion; or (e) mothballed.

III. Each Party undertakes not to deploy ABM systems or their components except that: (a) within one ABM system deployment area having a radius of one hundred and fifty kilometers and centered on the Partys [sic] national capital, a Party may deploy: (1) no more than one hundred ABM launchers and no more than one hundred ABM interceptor missiles at launch sites, and (2) ABM radars within no more than six ABM radar complexes, the area of each complex being circular and having a diameter of no more than three kilometers; and (b) within one ABM system deployment area having a radius

of one hundred and fifty kilometers and containing ICBM silo launchers, a Party may deploy: (1) no more than one hundred ABM launchers and no more than one hundred ABM interceptor missiles at launch sites, (2) two large phased-array ABM radars comparable in potential to corresponding ABM radars operational or under construction on the date of signature of the Treaty in an ABM system deployment area containing ICBM silo launchers, and (3) no more than eighteen ABM radars each having a potential less than the potential of the smaller of the above-mentioned two large phased-array ABM radars.

IV. The limitations provided for in Article III shall not apply to ABM systems or their components used for development or testing, and located within current or additionally agreed test ranges. Each Party may have no more than a total of fifteen ABM launchers at test ranges.

V. 1. Each Party undertakes *not to develop, test, or deploy ABM systems or components which are sea-based, air-based, space-based, or mobile land-based.* 2. Each Party undertakes not to develop, test or deploy ABM launchers for launching more than one ABM interceptor missile at a time from each launcher, not to modify deployed launchers to provide them with such a capacity, not to develop, test, or deploy automatic or semi-automatic or other similar systems for rapid reload of ABM launchers.

VI. To enhance assurance of the effectiveness of the limitations on ABM systems and their components provided by the Treaty, each Party undertakes: (a) *not to give missiles, launchers, or radars, other than ABM interceptor missiles, ABM launchers, or ABM radars, capabilities to counter strategic ballistic missiles or their elements in flight trajectory, and not to test them in an ABM* *mode;* and (b) *not to deploy in the future radars for early warning of strategic ballistic missile attack except at locations along the periphery of its national territory and oriented outward.*

VII. Subject to the provisions of this Treaty, modernization and replacement of ABM systems or their components may be carried out.

VIII. ABM systems or their components in excess of the numbers or outside the areas specified in this Treaty, as well as ABM systems or their components prohibited by this Treaty, shall be destroyed or dismantled under agreed procedures within the shortest possible agreed period of time.

IX. To assure the viability and effectiveness of this Treaty, each Party undertakes *not to transfer to other States, and not to deploy outside its national territory, ABM systems or their components limited by this Treaty.*

X. Each Party undertakes not to assume any international obligations which would conflict with this Treaty.

XI. The Parties undertake to continue active negotiations for limitations on strategic offensive arms.

XII. 1. For the purpose of providing assurance or compliance with the provisions of this Treaty, each Party shall use national technical means of verification at its disposal in a manner consistent with generally recognized principles of international law. 2. Each Party undertakes not to interfere with the national technical means of verification of the other Party operating in accordance with paragraph 1 of this Article. 3. Each Party undertakes not to use deliberate concealment measures which impede verification by national

technical means of compliance with the provisions of this Treaty. This obligation shall not require changes in current construction, assembly, conversion, or overhaul practices.

XIII. 1. To promote the objectives and implementation of the provisions of this Treaty, the Parties shall establish promptly a Standing Consultative Commission, within the framework of which they will: (a) consider questions concerning compliance with the obligations assumed and related situations which may be considered ambiguous; (b) provide on a voluntary basis such information as either Party considers necessary to assure confidence in compliance with the obligations assumed; (c) consider questions involving unintended interference with national technical means of verification; (d) consider possible changes in the strategic situation which have a bearing on the provisions of this Treaty; (e) agree upon procedures and dates for destruction or dismantling of ABM systems or their components in cases provided for by the provisions of this Treaty; (f) consider, as appropriate, possible proposals for further increasing the viability of this Treaty; including proposals for amendments in accordance with the provisions of this Treaty; (g) consider, as appropriate, proposals for further measures aimed at limiting strategic arms. 2. The Parties through consultation shall establish, and may amend as appropriate, Regulations for the Standing Consultative Commission governing procedures, composition and other relevant matters.

XIV. 1. Each Party may propose amendments to this Treaty. Agreed amendments shall enter into force in accordance with the procedures governing the entry into force of this Treaty. 2. Five years after entry into force of this Treaty, and at five-year intervals thereafter, the Parties shall together conduct a review of this Treaty.

XV. 1. *This Treaty shall be of unlimited duration.* 2. *Each Party shall, in exercising its national sovereignty, have the right to withdraw from this Treaty if it decides that extraordinary events related to the subject matter of this Treaty have jeopardized its supreme interests. It shall give notice of its decision to the other Party six months prior to withdrawal from the Treaty.* Such notice shall include a statement of the extraordinary events the notifying Party regards as having jeopardized its supreme interests. . . .

AGREED STATEMENTS: [A] The Parties understand that, in addition to the ABM radars which may be deployed in accordance with subparagraph (a) of Article III of the Treaty, those non-phased-array ABM radars operational on the date of signature of the Treaty within the ABM system deployment area for defense of the national capital may be retained. [B] The Parties understand that the potential (the product of mean emitted power in watts and antenna area in square meters) of the smaller of the two large phased-array ABM radars referred to in subparagraph (b) of Article III of the Treaty is considered for purposes of the Treaty to be three million. [C] The Parties understand that the center of the ABM system deployment area centered on the national capital and the center of the ABM system deployment area containing ICBM silo launchers for each Party shall be separated by no less than thirteen hundred kilometers. [D] In order to insure fulfillment of the obligation not to deploy ABM systems and their components except as provided in Article III of the Treaty, the Parties agree that *in the event ABM systems based on other physical principles and including components capable of substituting for ABM interceptor missiles,* *ABM launchers, or ABM radars are created in the future, specific limitations on such systems and their components would be subject to discussion in accordance with Article XIII and agreement in accordance with Article XIV of the Treaty.* [E] The Parties understand that Article V of the Treaty includes obligations not to develop, test or deploy ABM interceptor missiles for the delivery by each ABM interceptor missile of more than one independently guided warhead. [F] The Parties agree not to deploy phased-array radars having a potential (the product of mean emitted power in watts and antenna area in square meters) exceeding three million, except as provided for in Articles III, IV, and VI of the Treaty, or except for the purposes of tracking objects in outer space or for use as national technical means of verification. [G] The Parties understand that Article IX of the Treaty includes the obligation of the United States and the USSR *not to provide to other States technical descriptions or blueprints specially worked out for the construction of ABM systems and their components limited by the Treaty.*

COMMON UNDERSTANDINGS: Common understanding of the Parties on the following matters was reached during the negotiations: A. *Location of ICBM Defenses* The U.S. Delegation made the following statement on May 26, 1972: Article III of the ABM Treaty provides for each side one ABM system deployment area centered on its national capital and one ABM system deployment area containing ICBM silo launchers. The two sides have registered agreement on the following statement: "The Parties understand that the center of the ABM system deployment area centered on the national capital and the center of the ABM system deployment area containing ICBM silo launchers for each Party shall be separated by no less than thirteen hundred kilometers." In this connection, the U.S. side notes that its ABM system deployment area for defense of ICBM silo launchers, located west of the Mississippi River, will be centered in the Grand Forks ICBM silo launcher deployment area. (See Agreed Statement [C].) B. *ABM Test Ranges* The U.S. Delegation made the following statement on April 26, 1972: Article IV of the ABM Treaty provides that "the limitations provided for in Article III shall not apply to ABM systems or their components used for development or testing, and located within current or additionally agreed test ranges." We believe it would be useful to assure that there is no misunderstanding as to current ABM test ranges. It is our understanding that ABM test ranges encompass the area within which ABM components are located for test purposes. The current U.S. ABM test ranges are at White Sands, New Mexico, and at Kwajalein Atoll, and the current Soviet ABM test range is near Sary Shagan in Kazakhstan. We consider that non-phased array radars of types used for range safety or instrumentation purposes may be located outside of ABM test ranges. We interpret the reference in Article IV to "additionally agreed test ranges" to mean that ABM components will not be located at any other test ranges without prior agreement between our Governments that there will be such additional ABM test ranges. On May 5, 1972, the Soviet Delegation stated that there was a common understanding on what ABM test ranges were, that the use of the types of non-ABM radars for range safety or instrumentation was not limited under the Treaty, that the reference in Article IV to "additionally agreed" test ranges was sufficiently clear, and that national means permitted identifying current test ranges. C. *Mobile ABM Systems* On January 29, 1972, the U.S. Delegation made the

following statement: Article V(1) of the Joint Draft Text of the ABM Treaty includes *an undertaking not to develop, test, or deploy mobile land-based ABM systems and their components.* On May 5, 1971, the U.S. side indicated that, in its view, a prohibition on development of mobile ABM systems and components *would rule out the deployment of ABM launchers and radars which were not permanent fixed types.* At that time, we asked for the Soviet view of this interpretation. Does the Soviet side agree with the U.S. sides interpretation put forward on May 5, 1971? On April 13, 1972, the Soviet Delegation said there is a general common understanding on this matter. D. *Standing Consultative Commission* Ambassador Smith made the following statement on May 22, 1972: The United States proposes that the sides agree that, with regard to initial implementation of the ABM Treaty's Article XIII on the Standing Consultative Commission (SCC) and of the consultation Articles to the Interim Agreement on offensive arms and the Accidents Agreement [This refers to Article 7 of the September 30, 1971 US-USSR Agreement to Reduce the Risk of Outbreak of Nuclear War.] agreement establishing the SCC will be worked out early in the follow-on SALT negotiations; until that is completed, the following arrangements will prevail: when SALT is in session, any consultation desired by either side under these Articles can be carried out by the two SALT Delegations; when SALT is not in session, ad hoc arrangements for any desired consultations under these Articles may be made through diplomatic channels. Minister Semenov replied that, on an *ad referendum* basis, he could agree that the U.S. statement corresponded to the Soviet understanding. E. *Standstill* On May 6, 1972, Minister Semenov made the following statement: In an effort to accommodate the wishes of the U.S. side, the Soviet

Delegation is prepared to proceed on the basis that the two sides will in fact observe the obligations of both the Interim Agreement and the ABM Treaty beginning from the date of signature of these two documents. In reply, the U.S. Delegation made the following statement on May 20, 1972: The United States agrees in principle with the Soviet statement made on May 6 concerning observance of obligations beginning from date of signature but we would like to make clear our understanding that this means that, pending ratification and acceptance, neither side would take any action prohibited by the agreements after they had entered into force. This understanding would continue to apply in the absence of notification by either signatory of its intention not to proceed with ratification or approval. The Soviet Delegation indicated agreement with the U.S. statement.

UNILATERAL STATEMENTS: The following noteworthy unilateral statements were made during the negotiations by the United States Delegation: A. *Withdrawal from the ABM Treaty* On May 9, 1972, Ambassador Smith made the following statement: The U.S. Delegation has stressed the importance the U.S. Government attaches to achieving agreement on more complete limitations on strategic offensive arms, following agreement on an ABM Treaty and on an Interim Agreement on certain measures with respect to the limitation of strategic offensive arms. The U.S. Delegation believes that an objective of the follow-on negotiations should be to constrain and reduce on a long-term basis threats to the survivability of our respective strategic retaliatory forces. The USSR Delegation has also indicated that the objectives of SALT would remain unfulfilled without the achievement of an agreement providing for more complete limitations on strategic offensive arms. Both sides recognize that the initial agreements would be steps toward the achievement of complete limitations on strategic arms. If an agreement providing for more complete strategic offensive arms limitations were not achieved within five years, U.S. supreme interests could be jeopardized. Should that occur, it would constitute a basis for withdrawal from the ABM Treaty. The United States does not wish to see such a situation occur, nor do we believe that the USSR does. It is because we wish to prevent such a situation that we emphasize the importance the U.S. Government attaches to achievement of more complete limitations on strategic offensive arms. The U.S. Executive will inform the Congress, in connection with Congressional consideration of the ABM Treaty and the Interim Agreement, of this statement of the U.S. position. B. *Tested in an ABM Mode* On April 7, 1972, the U.S. Delegation made the following statement: Article II of the Joint Text Draft uses the term *"tested in an ABM mode,"* in defining ABM components, and Article VI includes certain obligations concerning such testing. *We believe that the sides should have a common understanding of this phrase.* First, we would note that the testing provisions of the ABM Treaty are intended to apply to testing which occurs after the date of signature of the Treaty, and not to any testing which may have occurred in the past. Next, we would amplify the remarks we have made on this subject during the previous Helsinki phase by setting forth the objectives which govern the U.S. view on the subject, namely, *while prohibiting testing of non-ABM components for ABM purposes: not to prevent testing of ABM components, and not to prevent testing of non-ABM components for non-ABM purposes.* To clarify our interpretation of "tested in an ABM mode," we note that *we would consider a launcher, missile or radar to be "tested in an*

ABM mode" if, for example, any of the following events occur: (1) a launcher is used to
launch an ABM interceptor missile, (2) an interceptor missile is flight tested against a target vehicle which has a flight trajectory with
characteristics of a strategic ballistic missile
flight trajectory, or is flight tested in conjunction with the test of an ABM interceptor missile or an ABM radar at the same test range,
or is flight tested to an altitude inconsistent
with interception of targets against which air
defenses are deployed, (3) a radar makes measurements on a cooperative target vehicle of
the kind referred to in item (2) above during
the reentry portion of its trajectory or makes
measurements in conjunction with the test of
an ABM interceptor missile or an ABM radar
at the same test range. Radars used for purposes such as range safety or instrumentation
would be exempt from application of these criteria. C. No-Transfer Article of ABM Treaty
On April 18, 1972, the U.S. Delegation

made the following statement: In regard
to this Article [IX], I have a brief and I believe self-explanatory statement to make.
The U.S. side wishes to make clear that
the provisions of this Article do not set
a precedent for whatever provision may
be considered for a Treaty on Limiting
Strategic Offensive Arms. The question of
transfer of strategic offensive arms is a
far more complex issue, which may require a different solution. D. *No Increase in
Defense of Early Warning Radars* On
July 28, 1970, the U.S. Delegation made
the following statement: Since Hen House
[Soviet ballistic missile early warning]
radars can detect and track ballistic missile warheads at great distances, they
have a significant ABM potential. Accordingly, the United States would regard any
increase in the defenses of such radars by
surface-to-air missiles as inconsistent
with an agreement.

[A 1974 protocol further limited ABM deployments in Article III to one system either defending the national capital or an ICBM field.—Ed.]

12.–19. *Strategic Offensive Armaments Regime: SALT, START, and Other Agreements*

(1972, 1979, 1987, 1991, 1993, 1996, 1997, and 2002)

Initially putting caps on (and later reducing quantities of) strategic offensive weapons systems has been a major undertaking since 1968, reaching initial agreement in the Strategic Arms Limitation Talks (SALT) in 1972. The Strategic Arms Reductions Talks (START) began in the 1980s and went from merely putting caps on arsenals to actual reductions.

12. *SALT I*

(1972)

Coupled with the ABM Treaty that limited ballistic missile defenses, this Interim Agreement Between the United States of America and the Union of Soviet Socialist Republics on Certain Measures with Respect to the Limitation of Strategic Offensive Arms was the outcome of the first-phase Strategic Arms Limitations Talks (SALT). National technical means of verification (e.g., intelligence gathered from satellites, ground- and sea-based stations, and aerial platforms) would be used to assure compliance. Institutionally, issues between the United States and the Soviet Union could be discussed in the Standing Consultative Commission (SCC) in Geneva. As an executive agreement, the SALT I accord was seen as an interim measure until a treaty could be agreed. At the time, American understanding of deterrence through the threat of mutually assured destruction (MAD) was used to justify minimizing strategic defenses while putting caps on strategic offensive weapons systems. In such circumstances both sides would remain vulnerable to attack by the other, but each would have sufficient offensive forces with which to retaliate—a "second-strike" capability. Knowing this, both countries would be deterred—neither would be expected to use nuclear weapons against the other because doing so would invite retaliatory attack. In addition to the Interim Agreement and Protocol, a supplement not included here contained details in agreed statements, common understandings, and separate national positions or interpretations.

The United States of America and the Union of Soviet Socialist Republics, hereinafter referred to as the Parties . . . have agreed as follows:

I. The Parties undertake *not to start construction of additional fixed land-based intercontinental ballistic missile (ICBM) launchers.* . . .

II. The Parties undertake *not to convert land-based launchers for light ICBMs, or for ICBMs of older types* deployed prior to 1964, *into land-based launchers for heavy ICBMs* of types deployed after that time.

III. The Parties undertake *to limit submarine-launched ballistic missile (SLBM) launchers and modern ballistic missile submarines* to the numbers operational and under construction on the date of signature of this Interim Agreement, and in addition to launchers and submarines constructed under procedures established by the Parties as replacements for an equal number of ICBM launchers of older types deployed prior to 1964 or for launchers on older submarines.

IV. Subject to the provisions of this Interim Agreement, *modernization and replacement of strategic offensive ballistic mis-*siles *and launchers* covered by this Interim Agreement *may be undertaken.*

V. 1. For the purpose of providing assurance of compliance with the provisions of this Interim Agreement, *each Party shall use national technical means of verification* at its disposal in a manner consistent with generally recognized principles of international law.

2. Each Party undertakes *not to interfere with the national technical means of verification of the other Party* operating in accordance with paragraph 1 of this Article.

3. Each Party undertakes *not to use deliberate concealment measures which impede verification by national technical means of compliance* with the provisions of this Interim Agreement. This obligation shall not require changes in current construction, assembly, conversion, or overhaul practices.

VI. To promote the objectives and implementation of the provisions of this Interim Agreement, the Parties shall use the Standing Consultative Commission established under Article XIII of the Treaty on the Limitation of Anti-Ballistic Missile Systems in accordance with the provisions of that Article.

VII. The Parties undertake to continue active negotiations for limitations on strategic offensive arms. The obligations provided for in this Interim Agreement shall not prejudice the scope or terms of the limitations on strategic offensive arms which may be worked out in the course of further negotiations.

VIII. This Interim Agreement shall enter into force upon exchange of written notices of acceptance by each Party. . . . Each Party shall, in exercising its national sovereignty, have the right to withdraw from this Interim Agreement if it decides that extraordinary events related to the subject matter of this Interim Agreement have jeopardized its supreme interests. It shall give notice of its decision to the other Party six months prior to withdrawal from this Interim Agreement. Such notice shall include a statement of the extraordinary events the notifying Party regards as having jeopardized its supreme interests.

Protocol to the Interim Agreement
. . . The Parties understand that . . . the United States may have no more than 710 ballistic missile launchers on submarines (SLBMs) and no more than 44 modern ballistic missile submarines. The Soviet Union may have no more than 950 ballistic missile launchers on submarines and no more than 62 modern ballistic missile submarines. Additional ballistic missile launchers on submarines up to the above-mentioned levels, in the United States—over 656 ballistic missile launchers on nuclear-powered submarines, and in the USSR—over 740 ballistic missile launchers on nuclear-powered submarines, operational and under construction, may become operational as replacements for equal numbers of ballistic missile launchers of older types deployed prior to 1964 or of ballistic missile launchers on older submarines. The deployment of modern SLBMs on any submarine, regardless of type, will be counted against the total level of SLBMs permitted for the United States and the USSR. This Protocol shall be considered an integral part of the Interim Agreement.

---

13. SALT II

(1979)

The United States and the Soviet Union finally reached agreement on terms of a treaty on strategic arms limitations, going beyond the interim agreement (SALT I) that had been agreed in 1972. A worsening of U.S.-Soviet relations, particularly U.S. opposition to Soviet intervention in Afghanistan in 1979, made it politically impossible for the Carter administration to secure the necessary two-thirds vote for ratification in the U.S. Senate. Although the Reagan administration that took office in January 1981 had little interest in securing ratification, it nevertheless held the Soviet Union accountable for compliance with its terms in the SCC. Both the Soviet Union and the United States in effect treated the SALT II accords as a binding Executive Agreement in much the same way as they had the SALT I Interim Agreement on offensive arms. Principal terms are reprinted here; however, the full text also includes a complex set of agreed statements and common understandings of these terms. The treaty exhibits great attention to detail in setting limits or caps on strategic offensive forces.

The United States of America and the Union of Soviet Socialist Republics, hereinafter referred to as the Parties, . . . have agreed as follows:

I. *Each Party undertakes*, in accordance with the provisions of this Treaty, *to limit strategic offensive arms quantitatively and qualitatively, to exercise restraint in the development of new types of strategic offensive arms*, and to adopt other measures provided for in this Treaty.

II. For the purposes of this Treaty: 1. *Intercontinental ballistic missile* (ICBM) *launchers* are land-based launchers of ballistic missiles capable of a range in excess of the shortest distance between the northeastern border of the continental part of the territory of the United States of America and the northwestern border of the continental part of the territory of the Union of Soviet Socialist Republics, that is, a range in excess of 5,500 kilometers. . . . 2. *Submarine-launched ballistic missile* (SLBM) *launchers* are launchers of ballistic missiles installed on any nuclear-powered submarine or launchers of modern ballistic missiles installed on any submarine, regardless of its type. 3. *Heavy bombers* are considered to be: (a) currently, for the United States of America, bombers of the B-52 and B-1 types, and for the Union of Soviet Socialist Republics, bombers of the Tupolev-95 and Myasishchev types; (b) in the future, types of bombers which can carry out the mission of a heavy bomber in a manner similar or superior to that of bombers listed in subparagraph (a) above; (c) types of bombers equipped for cruise missiles capable of a range in excess of 600 kilometers; and (d) types of bombers equipped for ASBMs. . . . 4. *Air-to-surface ballistic missiles* (ASBMs) are any such missiles capable of a range in excess of 600 kilometers and installed in an aircraft or on its external

mountings. 5. *Launchers of ICBMs and SLBMs equipped with multiple independently targetable reentry vehicles (MIRVs)* are launchers of the types developed and tested for launching ICBMs or SLBMs equipped with MIRVs. . . . 6. *ASBMs equipped with MIRVs are ASBMs of the* types which have been flight-tested with MIRVs. . . . 7. *Heavy ICBMs are ICBMs which have a launch-weight greater or a throw-weight greater than that of the heaviest*, in terms of either launch-weight or throw-weight, respectively, *of the light ICBMs deployed by either Party* as of the date of signature of this Treaty. . . . 8. Cruise missiles are unmanned, self-propelled, guided, weapon-delivery vehicles which sustain flight through the use of aerodynamic lift over most of their flight path and which are flight-tested from or deployed on aircraft, that is, air-launched cruise missiles, or such vehicles which are referred to as cruise missiles in subparagraph 1(b) of Article IX. . . .

III. 1. Upon entry into force of this Treaty, *each Party undertakes to limit ICBM launchers, SLBM launchers, heavy bombers, and ASBMs to an aggregate number not to exceed 2,400. 2. Each Party undertakes to limit . . . strategic offensive arms . . . to an aggregate number not to exceed 2,250*, and to initiate reductions of those arms which as of that date would be in excess of this aggregate number. . . .

IV. 1. Each Party undertakes not to start construction of additional fixed ICBM launchers. 2. Each Party undertakes not to relocate fixed ICBM launchers. 3. Each Party undertakes not to convert launchers of light ICBMs, or of ICBMs of older types deployed prior to 1964, into launchers of heavy ICBMs of types deployed after that time. 4. Each Party undertakes in the process of modernization and replacement of ICBM silo launchers not to increase the original internal volume of an ICBM silo launcher by more than thirty-two percent. Within this limit each Party has the right to determine whether such an increase will be made through an increase in the original diameter or in the original depth of an ICBM silo launcher, or in both of these dimensions. . . . 5. Each Party undertakes: (a) not to supply ICBM launcher deployment areas with intercontinental ballistic missiles in excess of a number consistent with normal deployment, maintenance, training, and replacement requirements; (b) not to provide storage facilities for or to store ICBMs in excess of normal deployment requirements at launch sites of ICBM launchers; (c) not to develop, test, or deploy systems for rapid reload of ICBM launchers. . . . 6. Subject to the provisions of this Treaty, each Party undertakes not to have under construction at any time strategic offensive arms . . . in excess of numbers consistent with a normal construction schedule. . . . 7. Each Party undertakes not to develop, test, or deploy ICBMs which have a launch-weight greater or a throw-weight greater than that of the heaviest, in terms of either launch-weight or throw-weight, respectively, of the heavy ICBMs deployed by either Party as of the date of signature of this Treaty. . . . 8. Each Party undertakes not to convert land-based launchers of ballistic missiles which are not ICBMs into launchers for launching ICBMs, and not to test them for this purpose. . . . 9. Each Party undertakes not to flight-test or deploy new types of ICBMs . . . except that each Party may flight-test and deploy one new type of light ICBM. . . . 10. Each Party undertakes not to flight-test or deploy ICBMs . . . with a number of reentry vehicles greater than the maximum number of reentry vehicles with which an ICBM of that type has been flight-tested. . . . 11. Each Party undertakes not to flight-test or deploy ICBMs of the one

new type permitted pursuant to paragraph 9 of this Article with a number of reentry vehicles greater than . . . ten. . . . 12. Each Party undertakes not to flight-test or deploy SLBMs with a number of reentry vehicles greater than . . . fourteen. . . . 13. Each Party undertakes not to flight-test or deploy ASBMs with a number of reentry vehicles greater than . . . ten. . . . 14. Each Party undertakes not to deploy at any one time on heavy bombers equipped for cruise missiles capable of a range in excess of 600 kilometers a number of such cruise missiles which exceeds the product of 28 and the number of such heavy bombers. . . .

V. 1. Within the aggregate numbers provided for in paragraphs 1 and 2 of Article III, each Party undertakes to limit launchers of ICBMs and SLBMs equipped with MIRVs, ASBMs equipped with MIRVs, and heavy bombers equipped for cruise missiles capable of a range in excess of 600 kilometers to an aggregate number not to exceed 1,320,455. 2. Within the aggregate number provided for in paragraph 1 of this Article, each Party undertakes to limit launchers of ICBMs and SLBMs equipped with MIRVs, and ASBMs equipped with MIRVs to an aggregate number not to exceed 1,200. 3. Within the aggregate number provided for in paragraph 2 of this Article, each Party undertakes to limit launchers of ICBMs equipped with MIRVs to an aggregate number not to exceed 820. 4. For each bomber of a type equipped for ASBMs equipped with MIRVs, the aggregate numbers provided for in paragraphs 1 and 2 of this Article shall include the maximum number of ASBMs for which a bomber of that type is equipped for one operational mission. . . . 5. Within the aggregate numbers provided for in paragraphs 1, 2, and 3 of this Article and subject to the provisions of this Treaty, each Party has the right to determine the composition of these aggregates.

VI. The limitations provided for in this Treaty shall apply to those arms which are: (a) operational; (b) in the final stage of construction; (c) in reserve, in storage, or mothballed; (d) undergoing overhaul, repair, modernization, or conversion. . . . In accordance with the provisions of Article XVII, the Parties will agree in the Standing Consultative Commission upon procedures to implement the provisions of this Article.

VII. 1. The limitations provided for in Article III shall not apply to ICBM and SLBM test and training launchers or to space vehicle launchers for exploration and use of outer space. ICBM and SLBM test and training launchers are ICBM and SLBM launchers used only for testing or training. . . . 2. The Parties agree that: (a) there shall be no significant increase in the number of ICBM or SLBM test and training launchers or in the number of such launchers of heavy ICBMs; (b) construction or conversion of ICBM launchers at test ranges shall be undertaken only for purposes of testing and training; (c) there shall be no conversion of ICBM test and training launchers or of space vehicle launchers into ICBM launchers subject to the limitations provided for in Article III. . . .

VIII. 1. Each Party undertakes not to flight-test cruise missiles capable of a range in excess of 600 kilometers or ASBMs from aircraft other than bombers or to convert such aircraft into aircraft equipped for such missiles. . . . 2. Each Party undertakes not to convert aircraft other than bombers into aircraft which can carry out the mission of a heavy bomber as referred to in subparagraph 3(b) of Article II.

IX. 1. Each Party undertakes not to develop, test, or deploy: (a) ballistic missiles capable of a range in excess of 600 kilometers for installation on waterborne vehicles other than submarines, or launchers of such missiles; . . . (b) fixed ballistic or cruise missile launchers for emplacement on the ocean floor, on the seabed, or on the beds of internal waters and inland waters, or in the subsoil thereof, or mobile launchers of such missiles, which move only in contact with the ocean floor, the seabed, or the beds of internal waters and inland waters, or missiles for such launchers; . . . (c) systems for placing into Earth orbit nuclear weapons or any other kind of weapons of mass destruction, including fractional orbital missiles; . . . (d) mobile launchers of heavy ICBMs; (e) SLBMs which have a launch-weight greater or a throw-weight greater than that of the heaviest, in terms of either launch-weight or throw-weight, respectively, of the light ICBMs deployed by either Party as of the date of signature of this Treaty, or launchers of such SLBMs; or (f) ASBMs which have a launch-weight greater or a throw-weight greater than that of the heaviest, in terms of either launch-weight or throw-weight, respectively, of the light ICBMs deployed by either Party as of the date of signature of this Treaty. . . . 2. Each Party undertakes not to flight-test from aircraft cruise missiles capable of a range in excess of 600 kilometers which are equipped with multiple independently targetable warheads and not to deploy such cruise missiles on aircraft. . . .

X. Subject to the provisions of this Treaty, modernization and replacement of strategic offensive arms may be carried out.

XI. Strategic offensive arms which would be in excess of the aggregate numbers provided for in this Treaty as well as strategic offensive arms prohibited by this Treaty shall be dismantled or destroyed under procedures to be agreed upon in the Standing Consultative Commission. . . .

XII. In order to ensure the viability and effectiveness of this Treaty, each Party undertakes not to circumvent the provisions of this Treaty, through any other state or states, or in any other manner.

XIII. Each Party undertakes not to assume any international obligations which would conflict with this Treaty.

XIV. The Parties undertake to begin, promptly after the entry into force of this Treaty, active negotiations with the objective of achieving, as soon as possible, agreement on further measures for the limitation and reduction of strategic arms. It is also the objective of the Parties to conclude well in advance of 1985 an agreement limiting strategic offensive arms to replace this Treaty upon its expiration.

XV. 1. For the purpose of providing assurance of compliance with the provisions of this Treaty, each Party shall use national technical means of verification at its disposal in a manner consistent with generally recognized principles of international law. 2. Each party undertakes not to interfere with the national technical means of verification of the other Party. . . . 3. Each Party undertakes not to use deliberate concealment measures which impede verification by national technical means of compliance with the provisions of this Treaty. This obligation shall not require changes in current construction, assembly, conversion, or overhaul practices. . . .

XVI. 1. Each Party undertakes, before conducting each planned ICBM launch, to notify the other Party well in advance on a case-by-case basis that such a launch will occur, except for single ICBM launches from test ranges or from ICBM launcher deployment areas, which are not planned to extend beyond its national territory. . . . 2. The Parties shall agree in the Standing Consultative Commission upon procedures to implement the provisions of this Article.

XVII. 1. To promote the objectives and implementation of the provisions of this Treaty, the Parties shall use the Standing Consultative Commission established . . . December 21, 1972. 2. *Within the framework of the Standing Consultative Commission,* with respect to this Treaty, *the Parties will:* (a) *consider questions concerning compliance* with the obligations assumed and related situations which may be considered ambiguous; (b) *provide on a voluntary basis such information as either Party considers necessary to assure confidence in compliance* with the obligations assumed; (c) *consider questions involving unintended interference with national technical means of verification,* and questions involving unintended impeding of verification by national technical means of compliance with the provisions of this Treaty; (d) *consider possible changes in the strategic situation* which have a bearing on the provisions of this Treaty; (e) *agree upon procedures for replacement, conversion, and dismantling or destruction, of strategic offensive arms* in cases provided for in the provisions of this Treaty *and upon procedures for removal of such arms* from the aggregate numbers when they otherwise cease to be subject to the limitations provided for in this Treaty, and at regular sessions of the Standing Consultative Commission, notify each other in accordance with the aforementioned procedures, at least twice annually, of actions completed and those in process; (f) *consider,* as appropriate, possible *proposals for further increasing the viability of this Treaty* . . . ; (g) consider, as appropriate, proposals for further measures limiting strategic offensive arms.

3. In the Standing Consultative Commission the Parties shall maintain by category the agreed data base on the numbers of strategic offensive arms.

---

14. *The INF (Intermediate-Range Nuclear Forces) Treaty*
(1987)

Negotiated toward the end of the cold war, this disarmament treaty eliminated an entire class of armaments—not just Soviet and U.S. intermediate-range (1,000–5,500 kilometers), but also shorter-range (500–1,000 kilometers) ballistic and cruise missiles. Principal impact was on missiles both sides had deployed or planned to deploy in Europe, on-site inspections being an important precedent.

The United States of America and the Union of Soviet Socialist Republics, hereinafter referred to as the Parties, . . . have agreed as follows:

I. In accordance with the provisions of this Treaty . . . *each Party shall eliminate its intermediate-range and shorter-range missiles,* not have such systems thereafter, and carry out the other obligations set forth in this Treaty.

II. For the purposes of this Treaty: 1. The term "ballistic missile" means a missile that has a ballistic trajectory over most of its flight path. The term "ground-launched ballistic missile (GLBM)" means a ground-launched ballistic missile that is a weapon-delivery vehicle. 2. The term "cruise missile" means an unmanned, self-propelled vehicle that sustains flight through the use of aerodynamic lift over most of its flight path. The term "ground-launched cruise missile (GLCM)" means a ground-launched cruise missile that is a weapon-delivery vehicle. 3. The term "GLBM launcher" means a fixed launcher or a mobile land-based transporter-erector-launcher mechanism for launching a GLBM. 4. The term "GLCM launcher" means a fixed launcher or a mobile land-based transporter-erector-launcher mechanism for launching a GLCM. 5. The term *"intermediate-range missile" means a GLBM or a GLCM having a range capability in excess of 1000 kilometers but not in excess of 5500 kilometers.* 6. The term *"shorter-range missile" means a GLBM or a GLCM having a range capability equal to or in excess of 500 kilometers but not in excess of 1000 kilometers.* . . .

VII. For the purposes of this Treaty: If a ballistic missile or a cruise missile has been flight-tested or deployed for weapon delivery, all missiles of that type shall be considered to be weapon-delivery vehicles. . . .

XI. For the purpose of ensuring verification of compliance with the provisions of this Treaty, each Party shall have the right to conduct on-site inspections. . . .

XII. 1. For the purpose of ensuring verification of compliance with the provisions of this Treaty, *each Party shall use national technical means of verification* at its disposal in a manner consistent with generally recognized principles of international law. 2. *Neither Party shall:* (a) *interfere with national technical means of verification of the other Party* . . . or (b) *use concealment measures which impede verification of compliance.*

15. *START I*

(1991)

Soon after coming to office in January 1981, President Ronald Reagan shifted the orientation of U.S. arms control efforts—not just setting limitations (caps or ceilings on strategic offensive armaments as in SALT), but also seeking actual arms reductions or disarmament, hence the change in label from SALT (Strategic Arms Limitation Talks) to START (Strategic Arms Reductions Talks). Indeed, the treaty that finally emerged at the end of the cold war referred formally to both "the Reduction and Limitation of Strategic Offensive Arms." Extremely detailed, only highlights of the treaty are included here. Agreeing to cut strategic nuclear warheads roughly in half to 6,000 for each side was a major achievement as were incorporation of extensive data sharing and on-site inspections to aid verification and compliance.

The United States of America and the Union of Soviet Socialist Republics, hereinafter referred to as the Parties, have agreed as follows:

I. Each Party shall reduce and limit its strategic offensive arms. . . .

II. 1. *Each Party shall reduce and limit its ICBMs and ICBM launchers, SLBMs and SLBM launchers, heavy bombers, ICBM warheads, SLBM warheads, and heavy bomber armaments,* so that . . . the aggregate numbers . . . do not exceed: (a) 1600, for deployed ICBMs and their associated launchers, deployed SLBMs and their associated launchers, and deployed heavy bombers, including 154 for deployed heavy ICBMs and their associated launchers; . . . (b) *6000, for warheads attributed to deployed ICBMs,* deployed SLBMs, and deployed heavy bombers. . . . (i) 4900, for warheads attributed to deployed ICBMs and deployed SLBMs; . . . (ii) 1100, for warheads attributed to deployed ICBMs on mobile launchers of ICBMs; . . . (iii) 1540, for warheads attributed to deployed heavy ICBMs. . . . 2. Each Party shall implement the reductions pursuant to paragraph 1 of this Article in three phases. . . .

V. . . . Modernization and replacement of strategic offensive arms may be carried out. Each Party undertakes not to: (a) produce, flight-test, or deploy heavy ICBMs of a new type, or increase the launch weight . . . of heavy ICBMs of an existing type; (b) produce, flight-test, or deploy heavy SLBMs; (c) produce test, or deploy mobile launchers of heavy ICBMs. . . .

VIII. A data base pertaining to the obligations under this Treaty . . . are listed according to categories of data. . . . In order to ensure the fulfillment of its obligations with respect to this Treaty, each Party shall notify the other Party of changes in data. . . . *Each Party shall use the Nuclear Risk Reduction Centers, which provide for continuous communication between the Parties, to provide and receive notifications. . . .*

IX. For the purpose of ensuring verification of compliance with the provisions of this Treaty, *each Party shall use national technical means of verification* at its disposal in a manner consistent with generally recognized principles of international law. *Each Party undertakes not to interfere with the national technical means of verification of the other Party. . . . Each Party undertakes not to use concealment measures that impede verification, by national technical means of verification, of compliance with the provisions of this Treaty. . . .*

X. During each flight test of an ICBM or SLBM, the Party conducting the flight test shall make on-board technical measurements and shall broadcast all telemetric information obtained from such measurements. . . . *During each flight test of an ICBM or SLBM, the Party conducting the flight test undertakes not to engage in any activity that denies full access to telemetric information,* including: (a) the use of encryption; (b) the use of jamming; (c) broadcasting telemetric information from an ICBM or SLBM using narrow directional beaming; and (d) encapsulation of telemetric information, including the use of ejectable capsules or recoverable reentry vehicles. . . . After each flight test of an ICBM or SLBM, *the Party conducting the flight test shall provide . . . data associated with the analysis of the telemetric information. . . .*

XI. For the purpose of ensuring verification of compliance with the provisions of this Treaty, *each Party shall have the right to conduct inspections and continuous monitoring activities* and shall conduct exhibitions. . . . Each Party shall have the right to conduct . . . data inspections at facilities to confirm the accuracy of data on the numbers and types of items specified for such facilities. . . .

XII. To enhance the effectiveness of national technical means of verification, each Party shall, if the other Party makes a request . . . , carry out the following cooperative measures: (a) a display in the open of the road-mobile launchers of ICBMs located within restricted areas specified by the requesting Party. . . . (b) a display in the open of the rail-mobile launchers of ICBMs located at parking sites specified by the requesting Party. . . . (c) a display in the open of all heavy bombers. . . .

XIII. Each Party shall have the right to conduct exercise dispersal of deployed mobile launchers of ICBMs and their associated missiles from restricted areas or rail garrisons. . . . An exercise dispersal shall be completed no later than 30 days after it begins. Exercise dispersals shall not be conducted . . . more than two times in any period of two calendar years. . . . A major strategic exercise involving heavy bombers . . . shall begin no more than one time in any calendar year, and shall be completed no later than 30 days after it begins. . . .

XIV. Each Party shall have the right to conduct operational dispersals of deployed mobile launchers of ICBMs and their associated missiles, ballistic missile submarines, and heavy bombers. There shall be no limit on the number and duration of operational dispersals. . . .

XV. *To promote the objectives and implementation of the provisions of this Treaty, the Parties hereby establish the Joint Compliance and Inspection Commission.* The Parties agree that, if either Party so requests, they shall meet within the framework of the Joint Compliance and Inspection Commission to: (a) *resolve questions relating to compliance with the obligations assumed;* (b) *agree upon such additional measures as may be necessary to improve the viability and effectiveness of this Treaty;* and (c) *resolve questions related to the application of relevant provisions of this Treaty to a new kind of strategic offensive arm. . . .*

XVI. To ensure the viability and effectiveness of this Treaty, each Party shall not assume any international obligations or undertakings that would conflict with its provisions.

16. *Nunn-Lugar and Cooperative Threat Reduction*
(1991)

Most arms control initiatives have come from the executive branch; however, the Nunn-Lugar proposal to include the Cooperative Threat Reduction Program that grew from it is an example of arms control through legislative action. Indeed, on U.S. Senate initiative, a post–cold war effort to assist the Soviet Union (as of January 1992, the Russian Federation and other post-Soviet republics) in the destruction of nuclear weapons would after 1997 be extended to chemical and biological weapons. The following text is drawn from a U.S. Senate debate on the Conventional Forces in Europe Treaty Implementation Act of 1991 reprinted in the Congressional Record, *November 25, 1991, pages S18039–40.*

Mr. Byrd [West Virginia]. . . . The distinguished Senator from Georgia [Mr. Nunn] has developed an important, far-reaching proposal which should be considered on an urgent basis. I sat in the Chair earlier today and listened to the debate on the proposal and I was very much persuaded to support that proposal. The Soviet nuclear weapons inventory is vast, mindless, and dangerous. In some cases, I understand that the integrity of the command-control system may be in question, and the security of the weapons cannot be guaranteed. We cannot afford to leave opportunities for the black market sale of such weapons to terrorist organizations, unreliable nations, and thereby set into motion nightmare scenarios of blackmail and threats that could ensue from the diversion of these weapons. . . .

The amendment pending by Mr. Nunn, Mr. Lugar [Indiana], and Mr. Boren [Oklahoma] . . . gives the Soviet Union an opportunity to use our help to destroy these weapons and reduce the threat of proliferation and instability. It provides an opportunity to take weapons that may exist in areas where compromise or diversion might occur, and transport them to secure sites. The issue of nuclear proliferation is an extremely worrisome one in the present circum-

stances of instability present in the areas of the Soviet Union and its former and present Republics. This is a question of vital practical importance and I commend the vision of the Senators from Georgia, Oklahoma, and Indiana, for offering the proposal. . . .

I now have the copy of the letter that has just been delivered to me and I ask unanimous consent that letter, with the approval of the Senator from Georgia and the Senator from Indiana, Mr. Lugar, be included in the *Record* at the conclusion of my remarks. There being no objection, the letter was ordered to be printed in the *Record*, as follows:

November 25, 1991
U.S. Senate, Washington, D.C.
Hon. Robert C. Byrd, Chairman.
Hon. Mark O. Hatfield, Ranking Minority
    Member, Committee on Appropriations, U.S. Senate, Washington, D.C.

Dear Robert and Mark: Later this afternoon, we hope the Senate will give overwhelming approval to an amendment concerning U.S. assistance in destroying Soviet nuclear weapons that we and 24 other Senators have offered to HR3807, the "Conventional Forces in Europe Treaty Implementation Act of 1991." We have attached a copy of the amendment.

Sec. 221 of the amendment provides as follows:

"(a) FUNDING(1) *The President may,* to the extent provided in appropriations Acts, *transfer from amounts appropriated to the Department of Defense* . . . such *amounts* as may be provided in appropriations Acts, not to exceed $500,000,000, *for reducing the Soviet nuclear threat.* . . .

We would respectfully request that you consider action to provide the appropriations authority and funding required to implement this critical program. In our view, the deteriorating situation in the former Soviet Union is of such urgency that we could well miss an historic opportunity to reduce the Soviet threat if, prior to adjournment *sine die* later this week, we do not complete the process of providing the President with full legislative authority to conduct this program. We would, therefore, urge you to incorporate relevant appropriations authority and funding in the course of your on-going conference on HJRES157, the Dire Emergency Supplemental Act.

Sincerely,
Sam Nunn,
Richard G. Lugar,
U.S. Senators.

Mr. Byrd: Mr. President, I yield to the Senator from Oklahoma.

Mr. Boren: . . . I agree with the comments made by the Senator from Georgia in response to the comments of our distinguished President *pro tempore* [Mr. Byrd] that the matter is urgent. Without going into any classified matters on the floor, I say to my colleagues that we are investigating significant warnings from the intelligence community about the instability of the Soviet Union and the dangers of the proliferation of weapons.

---

17. *Missile Technology Control Regime (MTCR) Guidelines*
(1996)

This regime aims to curtail proliferation of missile technologies and missiles as delivery systems for weapons of mass destruction. In fact, this has proven to be very difficult. The initiative for an MTCR began in the Reagan administration and now has some thirty-three member states. Guidelines are policy statements by participating countries.

The United States Government has, after careful consideration and subject to its international treaty obligations, decided that, when considering the transfer of equipment and technology related to missiles, it will act in accordance with . . . Guidelines. . . .

1. The purpose of these Guidelines is *to limit the risks of proliferation of weapons of mass destruction* (i.e. nuclear, chemical and biological weapons), *by controlling transfers that could make a contribution to delivery systems* (other than manned aircraft) for such weapons. *The Guidelines are not designed to impede national space programs for international cooperation* in such programs as long as such programs could not contribute to delivery systems for weapons of mass destruction. These Guidelines . . .

form the basis for controlling transfers to any destination beyond the Government's jurisdiction or control of all delivery systems (other than manned aircraft) capable of delivering weapons of mass destruction, and of equipment and technology relevant to missiles whose performance in terms of payload and range exceeds stated parameters. Restraint will be exercised in the consideration of all transfers of items. . . . The Government will implement the Guidelines in accordance with national legislation.

2. . . . Category I items . . . are those items of greatest sensitivity. . . . Particular restraint will be exercised in the consideration of Category I transfers regardless of their purpose, and there will be a strong presumption to deny such transfers. Particular restraint will also be exercised in the consideration of transfers of any . . . missiles . . . if the Government judges, on the basis of all available, persuasive information, evaluated according to factors including those in paragraph 3, that they are intended to be used for the delivery of weapons of mass destruction, and there will be a strong presumption to deny such transfers. . . .

3. In the evaluation of transfer applications . . . the following factors will be taken into account: A. Concerns about the proliferation of weapons of mass destruction; B. The capabilities and objectives of the missile and space programs of the recipient state; C. The significance of the transfer in terms of the potential development of delivery systems (other than manned aircraft) for weapons of mass destruction; D. The assessment of the end-use of the transfers, including the relevant assurances of the recipient states . . . ; E. The applicability of relevant multilateral agreements.

4. The transfer of design and production technology . . . will be subject to as great a degree of scrutiny and control as will the equipment itself, to the extent permitted by national legislation.

5. Where the transfer could contribute to a delivery system for weapons of mass destruction, the Government will authorize transfers of items . . . only on receipt of appropriate assurances from the government of the recipient state that: A. The items will be used only for the purpose stated and that such use will not be modified nor the items modified or replicated without the prior consent of the United States Government; B. Neither the items nor replicas nor derivatives thereof will be retransferred without the consent of the United States Government.

6. In furtherance of the effective operation of the Guidelines, the United States Government will, as necessary and appropriate, exchange relevant information with other governments applying the same Guidelines.

7. The adherence of all States to these Guidelines in the interest of international peace and security would be welcome.

---

18. START II

(1993 and 1997)

Deadlines for compliance specified in this 1993 treaty on Further Reduction and Limitation of Strategic Arms were modified in a 1997 protocol, allowing by mutual agreement more time for compliance with reductions in offensive arms—the new dates reflected in the text below. Strategic nuclear warhead limits are reduced here to 3,500 or fewer, the parties institutionalizing their disarmament collaboration within a Bilateral Implementation Commission they have established.

The United States of America and the Russian Federation, hereinafter referred to as the Parties, . . . have agreed as follows:

I. 1. Each Party shall reduce and limit its intercontinental ballistic missiles (ICBMs) and ICBM launchers, submarine-launched ballistic missiles (SLBMs) and SLBM launchers, heavy bombers, ICBM warheads, SLBM warheads, and heavy bomber armaments, so that . . . *the aggregate number for each Party . . . does not exceed,* for warheads attributed to deployed ICBMs, deployed SLBMs, and deployed heavy bombers, a number between *3800 and 4250* or such lower number as each Party shall decide for itself, but *in no case shall such number exceed 4250.* 2. Within the limitations provided for in paragraph 1 of this Article, the aggregate numbers for each Party shall not exceed: (a) 2160, for warheads attributed to deployed SLBMs; (b) 1200 for warheads attributed to deployed ICBMs of types to which more than one warhead is attributed; and (c) 650, for warheads attributed to deployed heavy ICBMs. 3. Upon fulfillment of the obligations provided for in paragraph 1 of this Article, *each Party shall further reduce and limit its ICBMs and ICBM launchers, SLBMs and SLBM launchers, ICBM warheads, SLBM warheads, and heavy bomber armaments, so that* no later than . . . December 31, 2007, and thereafter, *the aggregate number for each Party . . . does not exceed,* for warheads attributed to deployed ICBMs, deployed SLBMS, and deployed heavy bombers, *a number between 3000 and 3500* or such lower number as each Party shall decide for itself, *but in no case shall such number exceed 3500.* 4. Within the limitations provided for in paragraph 3 of this Article, the aggregate numbers for each Party shall not exceed:

(a) a number between 1700 and 1750, for warheads attributed to deployed SLBMs or such lower number as each Party shall decide for itself, but in no case shall such number exceed 1750; (b) zero, for warheads attributed to deployed ICBMs of types to which more than one warhead is attributed; and (c) zero, for warheads attributed to deployed heavy ICBMs. . . .

II. No later than . . . December 31, 2007, each Party undertakes to have eliminated or to have converted to launchers of ICBMs to which one warhead is attributed all its deployed and non-deployed launchers of ICBMs to which more than one warhead is attributed. . . . No later than . . . December 31, 2007, each Party undertakes to have eliminated all of its deployed and non-deployed heavy ICBMs and their launch canisters. . . . Each Party shall have the right to conduct inspections in connection with the elimination of heavy ICBMs and their launch canisters, as well as inspections in connection with the conversion of silo launchers of heavy ICBMs. . . .

V. Except as provided for in this Treaty, the provisions of the START Treaty, including the verification provisions, shall be used for implementation of this Treaty. *To promote the objectives and implementation of the provisions of this Treaty, the Parties hereby establish the Bilateral Implementation Commission.* The Parties agree that, if either Party so requests, they shall meet within the framework of the Bilateral Implementation Commission to: (a) resolve questions relating to compliance with the obligations assumed; and (b) agree upon such additional measures as may be necessary to improve the viability and effectiveness of this Treaty.

19. *Strategic Offensive Reductions Treaty*
(2002)

This short agreement further reduced strategic nuclear warheads down to the 1,700–2,200 range for each party—an 80–85 percent reduction from the 12,000-plus levels sustained to the end of the cold war.

The United States of America and the Russian Federation, hereinafter referred to as the Parties, . . . have agreed as follows:

I. *Each Party shall reduce and limit strategic nuclear warheads . . . so that* by December 31, 2012 *the aggregate number of such warheads does not exceed 1700–2200 for each Party.* Each Party shall determine for itself the composition and structure of its strategic offensive arms, based on the established aggregate limit for the number of such warheads.

II. The Parties agree that the START Treaty remains in force in accordance with its terms.

III. For purposes of implementing this Treaty, the Parties shall hold meetings at least twice a year of a Bilateral Implementation Commission. . . .

20.–22. *Conventional Arms Control Regimes: UN Register, Land Mines, and Small Arms*
(1991, 1996, 1997, and 2001)

We document here ongoing efforts to construct conventional arms control regimes related to transparency through informational exchange, controlling the small arms and light weapons trade, and prohibiting land mines. Although the Missile Technology Control Regime Guidelines could be included in this section, because they have more to do with delivery platforms for weapons of mass destruction than with conventional armaments, we place this document (No. 17 above) in the strategic offensive armaments regime category.

20. *Transparency in Armaments Transfers*
(1991 and 2001)

Although United Nations General Assembly or other resolutions are not in themselves legally binding under international law, they often represent (as with work by the Committee on Disarmament in Geneva and other international meetings) development of a foundational consensus on which arms control regimes are constructed. On December 9, 1991, the UN General Assembly passed Resolution 46/36 L, which provided for establishing a register on international conventional arms transfers to include battle tanks, armored combat vehicles, large caliber artillery systems, combat aircraft, attack helicopters, warships, and missiles or missile systems. A decade later on July 20, 2001, another effort pursued in a conference of UN members resolved to establish an informational basis useful in efforts to control transfers of small arms and light weapons, more formally a Programme of Action to Prevent, Combat and Eradicate the Illicit Trade in Small Arms and Light Weapons in All Its Aspects. Particularly controversial in the United States are provisions relating to tracking of domestic manufacture, transfer, and ownership of such weapons.

(1991)

The General Assembly . . . recognizes that an increased level of openness and transparency in the field of armaments would enhance confidence, promote stability, help States to exercise restraint, ease tensions and strengthen regional and international peace and security . . . ; requests the Secretary-General to establish and maintain at United Nations Headquarters in New York a universal and non-discriminatory Register of Conventional Arms, to include data on international arms transfers as well as information provided by Member States on military holdings, procurement through national production and relevant policies . . . ; [and] invites Member States . . . also to provide to the Secretary-General, with their annual report on imports and exports of arms, available background information regarding their military holdings, procurement through national production and relevant policies, and requests the Secretary-General to record this material and to make it available for consultation by Member States at their request. . . .

ANNEX: The Register of Conventional Arms ("the Register") shall be established, with effect from 1 January 1992, and maintained at the Headquarters of the United Nations in New York. . . .

(2001)

. . . We, the States participating in this Conference, bearing in mind the different situations, capacities and priorities of States and regions, undertake the following measures to prevent, combat and eradicate the illicit trade in small arms and light weapons in all its aspects:

To put in place, where they do not exist, adequate laws, regulations and administrative procedures to exercise effective control over the production of small arms and light weapons within their areas of jurisdiction and over the export, import, transit or retransfer of such weapons, in order to prevent illegal manufacture of and illicit trafficking in small arms and light weapons, or their diversion to unauthorized recipients. . . .

To identify, where applicable, groups and individuals engaged in the illegal manufacture, trade, stockpiling, transfer, possession, as well as financing for acquisition, of illicit small arms and light weapons, and take action under appropriate national law against such groups and individuals.

To ensure that henceforth licensed manufacturers apply an appropriate and reliable marking on each small arm and light weapon as an integral part of the production process. This marking should be unique and should identify the country of manufacture and also provide information that enables the national authorities of that country to identify the manufacturer and serial number so that the authorities concerned can identify and trace each weapon. . . .

To ensure that comprehensive and accurate records are kept for as long as possible on the manufacture, holding and transfer of small arms and light weapons under their jurisdiction. These records should be organized and maintained in such a way as to ensure that accurate information can be promptly retrieved and collated by competent national authorities. . . .

To assess applications for export authorizations according to strict national regulations and procedures that cover all small arms and light weapons. . . . Likewise, to establish or maintain an effective national system of export and import licensing or authorization, as well as measures on international transit, for the transfer of all small arms and light weapons, with a view to combating the illicit trade in small arms and light weapons.

To put in place and implement adequate laws, regulations and administrative procedures to ensure the effective control over the export and transit of small arms and light weapons, including the use of authenticated end-user certificates and effective legal and enforcement measures. . . .

To develop adequate national legislation or administrative procedures regulating the activities of those who engage in small arms and light weapons brokering. . . .

To establish or designate, as appropriate, a point of contact within subregional and regional organizations to act as liaison on matters relating to the implementation of the Programme of Action. . . .

To cooperate with the United Nations system to ensure the effective implementation of arms embargoes decided by the United Nations Security Council in accordance with the Charter of the United Nations. . . .

To encourage States and the World Customs Organization, as well as other relevant organizations, to enhance cooperation with the International Criminal Police Organization (Interpol) to identify those groups and individuals engaged in the illicit trade in small arms and light weapons in all its aspects in order to allow national authorities to proceed against them in accordance with their national laws.

21. *The Wassenaar Arrangement*
(1996)

Meeting in the Netherlands, the United States and other participant states adopted the Wassenaar Arrangement on Export Controls for Conventional Arms and Dual-Use Goods and Technologies in July 1996. The regime calls on participants to provide notifications of arms transfers and denials, thus enhancing transparency in the conventional arms trade market—an effort to prevent accumulations understood to be destabilizing.

I. *Purposes:* The *Wassenaar Arrangement* has been established in order to contribute to regional and international security and stability, by *promoting transparency and greater responsibility in transfers of conventional arms and dual-use goods and technologies, thus preventing destabilising accumulations.* Participating States will seek, through their national policies, to ensure that transfers of these items do not contribute to the development or enhance-

ment of military capabilities which undermine these goals, and are not diverted to support such capabilities. . . .

II. *Scope:* Participating States will meet on a regular basis *to ensure that transfers of conventional arms and transfers in dual-use goods and technologies are carried out responsibly and in furtherance of international and regional peace and security.* To this end, Participating States will *exchange, on a voluntary* *basis, information that will enhance transparency,* will lead to *discussions* among all Participating States *on arms transfers, as well as on sensitive dual-use goods and technologies,* and will assist in developing common understandings of the risks associated with the transfer of these items.... *Participating States agree to notify transfers and denials.* These notifications will apply to all non-participating states.... A participating State will notify, preferably within 30 days, but no later than within 60 days, all other Participating States of an approval of a license which has been denied by another Participating State for an essentially identical transaction during the last three years.... Upon the commencement of this arrangement, Participating States agree that work on further guidelines and procedures will continue expeditiously and taking into account experience acquired. This will include, in particular, a review of the scope of conventional arms to be covered with a view to extending information and notifications....

III. *Control Lists:* Participating States will control all items set forth in the [agreed] List of Dual-Use Goods and Technologies and in the Munitions List ... with the objective of preventing unauthorised transfers or re-transfers of those items.... The lists will be reviewed regularly to reflect technological developments and experience gained by Participating States, including in the field of dual-use goods and technologies which are critical for indigenous military capabilities....

IV. *Procedures for the General Information Exchange:* Participating States agree to exchange general information on risks associated with transfers of conventional arms and dual-use goods and technologies in order to consider, where necessary, the

scope for co-ordinating national control policies to combat these risks....

V. *Procedures for the Exchange of Information on Dual-Use Goods and Technology:* Participating States will notify licenses denied to non-participants with respect to items on the List of Dual-Use Goods and Technologies, where the reasons for denial are relevant to the purposes of the arrangement....

VI. *Procedures for the Exchange of Information on Arms:* Participating States agree that the information to be exchanged on arms will include any matters which individual Participating States wish to bring to the attention of others, such as emerging trends in weapons programmes and the accumulation of particular weapons systems, where they are of concern, for achieving the objectives of the arrangement....

VII. *Meetings and Administration:* Participating States will meet periodically to take decisions regarding this arrangement, its purposes and its further elaboration, to review the lists of controlled items, to consider ways of co-ordinating efforts to promote the development of effective export control systems, and to discuss other relevant matters of mutual interest, including information to be made public. Plenary meetings will be held at least once a year....

VIII. *Participation:* The new arrangement will be open, on a global and non-discriminatory basis, to prospective adherents....

IX. *Confidentiality:* Information exchanged will remain confidential and be treated as privileged diplomatic communications. This confidentiality will extend to any use made of the information and any discussion among Participating States.

22. The Land Mines Convention
(1997)

Because the U.S. Army continues to rely on mines mainly for defense positions in South Korea, the United States has not agreed to this Convention on the Prohibition of the Use, Stockpiling, Production and Transfer of Anti-Personnel Mines and on their Destruction. Owing to world-wide support on humanitarian and other grounds for this land mines convention and the regime it constructs, we can expect domestic and international advocates to continue to urge the United States to join the antimines effort. Indeed, provision is made to invite the United States and other nonparties to participate as observers in international meetings and review conferences.

The States Parties . . . have agreed as follows:

1. *General obligations: Each State Party undertakes never* under any circumstances: a) *To use anti-personnel mines;* b) *To develop, produce, otherwise acquire, stockpile, retain or transfer to anyone, directly or indirectly, anti-personnel mines;* c) To assist, encourage or induce, in any way, anyone to engage in any activity prohibited to a State Party under this Convention. 2. *Each State Party undertakes to destroy or ensure the destruction of all anti-personnel mines* in accordance with the provisions of this Convention. . . .

2. *Definitions.* . . .

3. *Exceptions:* . . . The retention or transfer of a number of anti-personnel mines for the development of and training in mine detection, mine clearance, or mine destruction techniques is permitted. The amount of such mines shall not exceed the minimum number absolutely necessary for the above-mentioned purposes. The transfer of anti-personnel mines for the purpose of destruction is permitted.

4. *Destruction of stockpiled anti-personnel mines:* Except as provided for in Article 3, *each State Party undertakes to destroy or ensure the destruction of all stockpiled anti-personnel mines it owns or possesses,* or that are under its jurisdiction or control, as soon as possible but not later than four

years after the entry into force of this Convention for that State Party.

5. *Destruction of anti-personnel mines in mined areas: Each State Party undertakes to destroy or ensure the destruction of all anti-personnel mines in mined areas under its jurisdiction or control,* as soon as possible but not later than ten years after the entry into force of this Convention for that State Party. . . .

6. *International cooperation and assistance:* In fulfilling its obligations under this Convention each State Party has the right to seek and receive assistance, where feasible, from other States Parties to the extent possible. . . .

7. *Transparency measures:* Each State Party shall report to the Secretary-General of the United Nations . . . national implementation measures. . . . The information provided in accordance with this Article shall be updated by the States Parties annually. . . . The Secretary-General of the United Nations shall transmit all such reports received to the States Parties.

8. *Facilitation and clarification of compliance:* The States Parties agree to consult and cooperate with each other regarding the implementation of the provisions of this Convention, and to work together in a spirit of cooperation to facilitate compliance by States Parties with their obligations under this Convention. . . .

9. *National implementation measures:* Each State Party shall take all appropriate legal, administrative and other measures, including the imposition of penal sanctions, to prevent and suppress any activity prohibited to a State Party under this Convention undertaken by persons or on territory under its jurisdiction or control.

10. *Settlement of disputes:* The States Parties shall consult and cooperate with each other to settle any dispute that may arise with regard to the application or the interpretation of this Convention. Each State Party may bring any such dispute before the Meeting of the States Parties. . . .

11. *Meetings of the States Parties:* The States Parties shall meet regularly in order to consider any matter with regard to the application or implementation of this Convention. . . . *States not parties to this Convention,* as well as the United Nations, other relevant international organizations or institutions, regional organizations, the International Committee of the Red Cross and relevant non-governmental organizations *may be invited to attend these meetings as observers.* . . .

12. *Review Conferences:* A Review Conference shall be convened by the Secretary-General of the United Nations five years after the entry into force of this Convention. Further Review Conferences shall be convened by the Secretary-General of the United Nations if so requested . . . provided that the interval between Review Conferences shall in no case be less than five years. . . . *States not parties to this Convention,* as well as the United Nations, other relevant international organizations or institutions, regional organizations, the International Committee of the Red Cross and relevant non-governmental organizations *may be invited to attend each Review Conference as observers.*

Chapter 15

Arms Control through Geographic or Spatial Measures

We deal here with arms control efforts within a region, area, or place. Although the rules of each regime necessarily concern armaments or functional measures as in documents presented in chapters 14 and 16, respectively, their overall thrust is to assure security, spatially attending to region, area, or place. From Antarctica to Europe to space (as a place), we address armaments, confidence-and-security building, and other functional measures.

23. *The Antarctic Treaty*

(1959)

This treaty demilitarizes Antarctica and mandates that the area be used for peaceful, scientific purposes. As such it set an important precedent for arms control focused on a particular region or area. It was signed in Washington on December 1, 1959, the U.S. Senate advised ratification on August 10, 1960, and President Eisenhower carried out ratification on August 18, 1960, the treaty entering into force on June 23, 1961.

I. *Antarctica shall be used for peaceful purposes only. There shall be prohibited,* inter alia, *any measures of a military nature, such as the establishment of military bases and fortifications, the carrying out of military maneuvers, as well as the testing of any type of weapons.* The present treaty shall not prevent the use of military personnel or equipment for scientific research or for any other peaceful purposes.

II. Freedom of scientific investigation in Antarctica and cooperation toward that end, as applied during the International Geophysical Year, shall continue, subject to the provisions of the present treaty.

III. 1. In order to promote international cooperation in scientific investigation in Antarctica . . . the Contracting Parties agree that, to the greatest extent feasible and practicable: (a) *information regarding plans for scientific programs in Antarctica shall be exchanged* to permit maximum economy and efficiency of operations; (b) *scientific personnel shall be exchanged in Antarctica between expeditions and stations;* (c) *scientific observations and results from Antarctica shall be exchanged and made freely available.* 2. In implementing this Article, every encouragement shall be given to the establishment of cooperative working relations with those Specialized Agencies of the United Nations and other international organizations having a scientific or technical interest in Antarctica.

IV. Nothing contained in the present treaty shall be interpreted as: (a) a renunciation by any Contracting Party of previously asserted rights of or claims to territorial sovereignty in Antarctica; (b) a renunciation or diminution by any Contracting Party of any basis of claim to territorial sovereignty in Antarctica which it may have whether as a result of its activities or those of its nationals in Antarctica, or otherwise; (c) prejudicing the position of any Contracting Party as regards its recognition or non-recognition of any other States right of or claim or basis of claim to territorial sovereignty in Antarctica. No acts or activities taking place while the present treaty is in force shall constitute a basis for asserting, supporting or denying a claim to territorial sovereignty in Antarctica or create any rights of sovereignty in Antarctica. *No new claim, or enlargement of an existing claim, to territorial sovereignty in Antarctica shall be asserted while the present treaty is in force.*

V. *Any nuclear explosions in Antarctica and the disposal there of radioactive waste material shall be prohibited.* In the event of the conclusion of international agreements concerning the use of nuclear energy, including nuclear explosions and the disposal of radioactive waste material, to which all of the Contracting Parties . . . are parties, the rules established under such agreements shall apply in Antarctica.

VI. The provisions of the present treaty shall apply to the area south of 60 degrees South Latitude, including all ice shelves, but nothing in the present treaty shall prejudice or in any way affect the rights, or the exercise of the rights, of any State under international law with regard to the high seas within that area.

VII. In order to promote the objectives and ensure the observance of the provisions of the present treaty, *each Contracting Party . . . shall have the right to designate observers to carry out any inspection provided for by the present Article.* Observers shall be nationals of the Contracting Parties which designate them. The names of observers shall be communicated to every other Contracting Party. . . . *Each observer . . . shall have complete freedom of access at any time to any or all areas of Antarctica. All areas of Antarctica,* including all stations, installations and equipment within those areas, and all ships and aircraft at points of discharging or embarking cargoes or personnel in Antarctica, *shall be open at all times to inspection by any observers designated in accordance with paragraph 1 of this Article. Aerial observation may be carried out at any time* over any or all areas of Antarctica by any of the Contracting Parties having the right to designate observers. Each Contracting Party shall . . . give . . . notice in advance, of (a) all expeditions to and within Antarctica, on the part of its ships or nationals, and all expeditions to Antarctica organized in or proceeding from its territory; (b) all stations in Antarctica occupied by its nationals; and (c) any military personnel or equipment intended to be introduced by it into Antarctica subject to the conditions prescribed in . . . Article I of the present treaty.

VIII. In order to facilitate the exercise of their functions . . . observers . . . and scientific personnel . . . and members of the staffs accompanying any such persons, shall be subject only to the jurisdiction of the Contracting Party of which they are nationals. . . . The Contracting Parties concerned in any case of dispute with regard to the exercise of jurisdiction in Antarctica shall immediately consult together with a view to reaching a mutually acceptable solution.

IX. Representatives of the Contracting Parties . . . shall meet . . . at suitable intervals and places, for the purpose of exchanging information, consulting together on matters of common interest pertaining to Antarctica, and formulating and considering, and recommending to their Governments, measures in furtherance of the principles and objectives of the treaty, including measures regarding: (a) use of Antarctica for peaceful purposes only; (b) facilitation of scientific research in Antarctica; (c) facilitation of international scientific cooperation in Antarctica; (d) facilitation of the exercise of the rights of inspection provided for in Article VII of the treaty; (e) questions relating to the exercise of jurisdiction in Antarctica; (f) preservation and conservation of living resources in Antarctica. . . . Each Contracting Party . . . shall be entitled to appoint representatives to participate in [these] meetings . . . during such time as that Contracting Party demonstrates its

interest in Antarctica by conducting substantial scientific research activity there, such as the establishment of a scientific station or the despatch of a scientific expedition. Reports from the observers referred to in Article VII of the present treaty shall be transmitted to the representatives of the Contracting Parties. . . .

X. Each of the Contracting Parties undertakes to exert appropriate efforts, consistent with the Charter of the United Nations, to the end that no one engages in any activity in Antarctica contrary to the principles or purposes of the present treaty.

XI. If any dispute arises between two or more of the Contracting Parties concerning the interpretation or application of the present treaty, those Contracting Parties shall consult among themselves with a view to having the dispute resolved by negotiation, inquiry, mediation, conciliation, arbitration, judicial settlement or other peaceful means of their own choice. Any dispute of this character not so resolved shall, with the consent, in each case, of all parties to the dispute, be referred to the International Court of Justice for settlement; but failure to reach agreement on reference to the International Court shall not absolve parties to the dispute from the responsibility of continuing to seek to resolve it by any of the various peaceful means referred to in paragraph 1 of this Article.

XII. The present treaty may be modified or amended at any time by unanimous agreement of the Contracting Parties. . . . If . . . any of the Contracting Parties . . . so requests . . . , a Conference of all the Contracting Parties shall be held as soon as practicable to review the operation of the treaty. Any modification or amendment to the present treaty which is approved at such a Conference by a majority of the Contracting Parties . . . shall be communicated . . . to all the Contracting Parties. . . . If any such modification or amendment has not entered into force . . . within a period of two years after the date of its communication to all the Contracting Parties, any Contracting Party may at any time after the expiration of that period give notice . . . of its withdrawal from the present treaty; and such withdrawal shall take effect two years after . . . The notice. . . .

XIII. The present treaty shall be . . . open for accession by any State which is a Member of the United Nations, or by any other State which may be invited to accede to the treaty with the consent of all the Contracting Parties.

---

24. *Treaty for the Prohibition of Nuclear Weapons in Latin America*

(1967)

Signed in Mexico City on February 14, 1967, the Treaty of Tlatelolco entered into force on April 22, 1968. The United States and other members of the Organization of American States (OAS) were reacting in particular to the Soviet introduction in 1962 of nuclear weapons to Cuba, which were subsequently withdrawn in the aftermath of the crisis that brought the United States and the Soviet Union to the brink of nuclear war. By making Latin America "off-limits" for nuclear weapons, the Treaty of Tlatelolco followed the Antarctic Treaty (1959) and established a precedent for nuclear-free zones as a regional arms-control measure in the South Pacific (1985), Southeast Asia, (1995), and Africa (1996).

I. *The Contracting Parties hereby undertake to use exclusively for peaceful purposes the nuclear material and facilities which are under their jurisdiction, and to prohibit and prevent in their respective territories:* (a) *The testing, use, manufacture, production or acquisition by any means whatsoever of any nuclear weapons, by the Parties themselves, directly or indirectly, on behalf of anyone else or in any other way,* and (b) *The receipt, storage, installation, deployment and any form of possession of any nuclear weapons, directly or indirectly, by the Parties themselves, by anyone on their behalf or in any other way.* The Contracting Parties also undertake *to refrain from* engaging in, encouraging or authorizing, directly or indirectly, or in any way participating in *the testing, use, manufacture,* production, possession or control of any nuclear weapon. . . .

III. For the purposes of this Treaty, the term "territory" shall include the territorial sea, air space and any other space over which the State exercises sovereignty in accordance with its own legislation.

IV. The zone of application of this Treaty is the whole of the territories for which the Treaty is in force. . . .

V. For the purposes of this Treaty, a nuclear weapon is any device which is capable of releasing nuclear energy in an uncontrolled manner and which has a group of characteristics that are appropriate for use for warlike purposes. . . .

VI. At the request of any of the signatory States or if the Agency established by article VII should so decide, a meeting of all the signatories may be convoked to consider in common questions which may affect the very essence of this instrument, including possible amendments to it. . . .

VII. In order to ensure compliance with the obligations of this Treaty, the Contracting Parties hereby establish an international organization to be known as the "Agency for the Prohibition of Nuclear Weapons in Latin America," hereinafter referred to as "the Agency." . . . The headquarters of the Agency shall be in Mexico City.

VIII. There are hereby established as principal organs of the Agency a General Conference, a Council and a Secretariat. Such subsidiary organs as are considered necessary by the General Conference may be established. . . .

XII. For the purpose of verifying compliance with the obligations entered into by the Contracting Parties . . . *a control system shall be established.* . . . The control system shall be used in particular *for the purpose of verifying:* (a) *That devices, services and facilities intended for peaceful uses of nuclear energy are not used in the testing or manufacture of nuclear weapons,* (b) *That none of the activities prohibited in article I of this Treaty are carried out in the territory of the Contracting Parties with nuclear materials or weapons introduced from abroad,* and (c) *That explosions for peaceful purposes are compatible with article XVIII of this Treaty.*

XIII. Each Contracting Party shall negotiate multilateral or bilateral agreements with the International Atomic Energy Agency for the application of its safeguards to its nuclear activities. . . .

XIV. The Contracting Parties shall submit to the Agency and to the International Atomic Energy Agency, for their information, semi-annual reports stating that no activity prohibited under this Treaty has occurred in their respective territories. . . .

XV. With the authorization of the Council, the General Secretary may request any of the Contracting Parties to provide the Agency with complementary or supplementary information regarding any event or circumstance connected with compliance with this Treaty, explaining his reasons. The Contracting Parties undertake to co-operate promptly and fully with the General Secretary. The General Secretary shall inform the Council and the Contracting Parties forthwith of such requests and of the respective replies.

XVI. *The International Atomic Energy Agency and the Council . . . have the power of carrying out special inspections.* . . . The Contracting Parties undertake to grant the inspectors carrying out such special inspections full and free access to all places and all information which may be necessary for the performance of their duties and which are directly and intimately connected with the suspicion of violation of this Treaty. . . . The Council may decide, or any Contracting Party may request, the convening of a special session of the General Conference for the purpose of considering the reports resulting from any special inspection. . . . The General Conference . . . may make recommendations to the Contracting Parties and submit reports to the Secretary-General of the United Nations to be transmitted to the United Nations Security Council and the General Assembly.

XVII. Nothing in the provisions of this Treaty shall prejudice the rights of the Contracting Parties, in conformity with this Treaty, to use nuclear energy for peaceful purposes, in particular for their economic development and social progress.

XVIII. *The Contracting Parties may carry out explosions of nuclear devices for peaceful purposes*—including explosions which involve devices similar to those used in nuclear weapons—or collaborate with third parties for the same purpose, provided that they do so in accordance with the provisions of this article and the other articles of the Treaty, particularly articles I and V. . . . Contracting Parties intending to carry out, or to cooperate in carrying out, such an explosion shall notify the Agency and the International Atomic Energy Agency. . . . The General Secretary and the technical personnel designated by the Council and the International Atomic Energy Agency may observe all the preparations, including the explosion of the device, and shall have unrestricted access to any area in the vicinity of the site of the explosion. . . .

XIX. The Agency may conclude such agreements with the International Atomic Energy Agency as are authorized by the General Conference and as it considers likely to facilitate the efficient operation of the control system established by this Treaty. . . .

XX. The General Conference shall take note of all cases in which, in its opinion, any Contracting Party is not complying fully with its obligations under this Treaty and shall draw the matter to the attention of the Party concerned, making such recommendations as it deems appropriate. If, in its opinion, such non-compliance constitutes a violation of this Treaty which might endanger peace and security, the General Conference shall report thereon

simultaneously to the United Nations Security Council and the General Assembly through the Secretary-General of the United Nations, and to the Council of the Organization of American States. The General Conference shall likewise report to the International Atomic Energy Agency. . . .

XXIV. Unless the Parties concerned agree on another mode of peaceful settlement, any question or dispute concerning the interpretation or application of this Treaty which is not settled shall be referred to the International Court of Justice with the prior consent of the Parties to the controversy. . . .

XXIX. Any Contracting Party may propose amendments to this Treaty . . . for the adoption of which a two-thirds majority of the Contracting Parties present and voting shall be required. . . .

XXX. *This Treaty shall be of a permanent nature and shall remain in force indefinitely, but any Party may denounce it* by notifying the General Secretary of the Agency *if, in the opinion of the denouncing State, there have arisen or may arise circumstances* connected with the content of this Treaty or of the annexed Additional Protocols I and II *which affect its supreme interests or the peace and security of one or more Contracting Parties.* The denunciation shall take effect three months after the delivery to the General Secretary of the Agency of the notification. . . .

Additional Protocol I (Signed May 26, 1977, and ratified in November 1981)

The undersigned Plenipotentiaries, furnished with full powers by their respective Governments, . . . , have agreed . . . to undertake to apply the statute of denuclearization in respect of warlike purposes as defined in . . . the Treaty . . . in territories for which, de jure or de facto, they are internationally responsible and which lie within the limits of the geographical zone established in that Treaty. . . .

Additional Protocol II (Signed April 1, 1968, and ratified in May 1971)

I. The statute of denuclearization of Latin America in respect of warlike purposes . . . shall be fully respected by the Parties to this Protocol in all its express aims and provisions.

II. The Governments . . . undertake . . . not to contribute in any way to the performance of acts involving a violation of the obligations of article I of the Treaty in the territories to which the Treaty applies. . . .

III. The Governments represented by the undersigned Plenipotentiaries also undertake not to use or threaten to use nuclear weapons against the Contracting Parties of the Treaty for the Prohibition of Nuclear Weapons in Latin America. . . .

Proclamation by President Nixon (May 1971)

That as regards the undertaking in Article III of Protocol II not to use or threaten to use nuclear weapons against the Contracting Parties, the United States Government would have to consider that an armed attack by a Contracting Party, in which it was assisted by a nuclear-weapon state, would be incompatible with the Contracting Party's corresponding obligations under Article I of the Treaty. . . .

That the United States Government considers that the technology of making nuclear explosive devices for peaceful purposes is indistinguishable from the technology of making nuclear weapons. . . . Therefore, the United States Government understands the definition contained in Article V of the Treaty as necessarily encompassing all nuclear explosive devices. . . .

That the United States Government understands that . . . Article XVIII of the Treaty permits, and that United States adherence to Protocol II will not prevent, collaboration by the United States with Contracting Parties for the purpose of carrying out explosions of nuclear devices for peaceful purposes in a manner consistent with a policy of not contributing to the proliferation of nuclear weapons capabilities.

25. *The Outer Space Treaty*

(1967)

Taking a spatial approach, this important Treaty on Principles Governing the Activities of States in the Exploration and Use of Outer Space, Including the Moon and Other Celestial Bodies follows precedent set by the Antarctic Treaty. Deployment of weapons of mass destruction in orbit is prohibited in outer space as are certain military activities on the moon or other celestial bodies. The treaty also provides a basis for cooperative activities in outer space.

The States Parties to this Treaty . . . have agreed on the following:

I. The exploration and use of outer space, including the moon and other celestial bodies, shall be carried out for the benefit and in the interests of all countries, irrespective of their degree of economic or scientific development, and shall be the province of all mankind. *Outer space, including the moon and other celestial bodies, shall be free for exploration and use by all States without discrimination of any kind, on a basis of equality and in accordance with international law, and there shall be free access to all areas of celestial bodies. There shall be freedom of scientific investigation in outer space, including the moon and other celestial bodies, and States shall facilitate and encourage international co-operation in such investigation.*

II. *Outer space, including the moon and other celestial bodies, is not subject to national appropriation* by claim of sovereignty, by means of use or occupation, or by any other means.

III. *States Parties to the Treaty shall carry on activities in the exploration and use of outer space,* including the moon and other celestial bodies, in accordance with international law, including the Charter of the United Nations, *in the interest of maintaining international peace and security and promoting international co-operation and understanding.*

IV. States Parties to the Treaty undertake *not to place in orbit around the Earth any objects carrying nuclear weapons or any other kinds of weapons of mass destruction, install such weapons on celestial bodies, or station such weapons in outer space in any other manner. The Moon and other celestial bodies shall be used by all States Parties to the Treaty exclusively for peaceful purposes. The establishment of military bases, installations*

and fortifications, the testing of any type of weapons and the conduct of military maneuvers on celestial bodies shall be forbidden. The use of military personnel for scientific research or for any other peaceful purposes shall not be prohibited. The use of any equipment or facility necessary for peaceful exploration of the Moon and other celestial bodies shall also not be prohibited.

V. States Parties to the Treaty shall regard *astronauts as envoys of mankind in outer space and shall render to them all possible assistance in the event of accident, distress, or emergency landing on the territory of another State Party or on the high seas.* When astronauts make such a landing, they shall be safely and promptly returned to the State of registry of their space vehicle. In carrying on activities in outer space and on celestial bodies, the astronauts of one State Party shall render all possible assistance to the astronauts of other States Parties. States Parties to the Treaty shall immediately inform the other States Parties to the Treaty or the Secretary-General of the United Nations of any phenomena they discover in outer space, including the Moon and other celestial bodies, which could constitute a danger to the life or health of astronauts.

VI. States Parties to the Treaty shall bear international responsibility for national activities in outer space, including the Moon and other celestial bodies, whether such activities are carried on by governmental agencies or by non-governmental entities, and for assuring that national activities are carried out in conformity with the provisions set forth in the present Treaty. The activities of non-governmental entities in outer space, including the Moon and other celestial bodies, shall require authorization and continuing supervision by the appropriate State Party to the

Treaty. When activities are carried on in outer space, including the Moon and other celestial bodies, by an international organization, responsibility for compliance with this Treaty shall be borne both by the international organization and by the States Parties to the Treaty participating in such organization.

VII. Each State Party to the Treaty that launches or procures the launching of an object into outer space, including the Moon and other celestial bodies, and each State Party from whose territory or facility an object is launched, is internationally liable for damage to another State Party to the Treaty or to its natural or juridical persons by such object or its component parts on the Earth, in air space or in outer space, including the Moon and other celestial bodies.

VIII. A State Party to the Treaty on whose registry an object launched into outer space is carried shall retain jurisdiction and control over such object, and over any personnel thereof, while in outer space or on a celestial body. Ownership of objects launched into outer space, including objects landed or constructed on a celestial body, and of their component parts, is not affected by their presence in outer space or on a celestial body or by their return to the Earth. Such objects or component parts found beyond the limits of the State Party to the Treaty on whose registry they are carried shall be returned to that State Party, which shall, upon request, furnish identifying data prior to their return.

IX. In the exploration and use of outer space, including the Moon and other celestial bodies, States Parties to the Treaty shall be guided by the principle of co-operation and mutual assistance and shall conduct all their activities in outer space, including the Moon and other celestial bodies, with due regard to the corresponding interests of all other States Parties to the Treaty. States Parties to the Treaty shall pursue studies of outer space, including the Moon and other celestial bodies, and conduct exploration of them so as to avoid their harmful contamination and also adverse changes in the environment of the Earth resulting from the introduction of extraterrestrial matter and, where necessary, shall adopt appropriate measures for this purpose. If a State Party to the Treaty has reason to believe that an activity or experiment planned by it or its nationals in outer space, including the Moon and other celestial bodies, would cause potentially harmful interference with activities of other States Parties in the peaceful exploration and use of outer space, including the Moon and other celestial bodies, it shall undertake appropriate international consultations before proceeding with any such activity or experiment. A State Party to the Treaty which has reason to believe that an activity or experiment planned by another State Party in outer space, including the Moon and other celestial bodies, would cause potentially harmful interference with activities in the peaceful exploration and use of outer space, including the Moon and other celestial bodies, may request consultation concerning the activity or experiment.

X. In order to promote international co-operation in the exploration and use of outer space, including the Moon and other celestial bodies, in conformity with the purposes of this Treaty, the States Parties to the Treaty shall consider on a basis of equality any requests by other States Parties to the Treaty to be afforded an opportunity to observe the flight of space objects launched by those States. The nature of such an opportunity for observation and the conditions under which it could be afforded shall be determined by agreement between the States concerned.

XI. In order to promote international cooperation in the peaceful exploration and use of outer space, States Parties to the Treaty conducting activities in outer space, including the Moon and other celestial bodies, agree to inform the Secretary-General of the United Nations as well as the public and the international scientific community, to the greatest extent feasible and practicable, of the nature, conduct, locations and results of such activities. On receiving the said information, the Secretary-General of the United Nations should be prepared to disseminate it immediately and effectively.

XII. All stations, installations, equipment and space vehicles on the Moon and other celestial bodies shall be open to representatives of other States Parties to the Treaty on a basis of reciprocity. Such representatives shall give reasonable advance notice of a projected visit, in order that appropriate consultations may be held and that maximum precautions may be taken to assure safety and to avoid interference with normal operations in the facility to be visited.

XIII. The provisions of this Treaty shall apply to the activities of States Parties to the Treaty in the exploration and use of outer space, including the Moon and other celestial bodies, whether such activities are carried on by a single State Party to the Treaty or jointly with other States, including cases where they are carried on within the framework of international intergovernmental organizations. Any practical questions arising in connection with activities carried on by international inter-governmental organizations in the exploration and use of outer space, including the Moon and other celestial bodies, shall be resolved by the States Parties to the Treaty either with the appropriate international organization or with one ormore States members of that international organization, which are Parties to this Treaty.

---

26. *The Seabed Treaty*

(1971)

Like Antarctica and outer space, the seabed is declared off-limits to nuclear or other weapons of mass destruction that could be stored there or launched therefrom.

The States Parties to this Treaty have agreed as follows:

I. *The States Parties* to this Treaty *undertake not to emplant or emplace on the seabed and the* *ocean floor and in the subsoil thereof* beyond the outer limit of a seabed zone, as defined in article II, *any nuclear weapons or any other types of weapons of mass destruction* as well as structures, launching installations or any other facilities specifically designed for storing, testing or using such weapons. . . .

II. For the purpose of this Treaty, the outer limit of the seabed zone referred to in article I shall be coterminous with the twelve-mile outer limit of the . . . Territorial Sea. . . .

III. In order to promote the objectives of and insure compliance with the provisions of this Treaty, each State Party to the Treaty shall have the right to verify through observations the activities of other States Parties to the Treaty on the seabed and the ocean floor and in the subsoil thereof. . . .

---

27. The Conference on Security and Cooperation in Europe: The Helsinki Final Act

(1975)

The Conference on Security and Cooperation in Europe (CSCE) convened in July 1973, concluding its work at Helsinki on August 1, 1975. The CSCE area as the subject of these talks extended by agreement of the parties from the Atlantic in the west (including the United States and Canada) to the Ural Mountains, thus including the Russian and other western parts of the Soviet Union. The CSCE focused on three "baskets," or clusters, of issues: security; economics, science and technology, and the environment; and human contacts, information, cooperation, and exchanges in the fields of culture and education. We include here a statement of general principles and provisions. (The confidence- and security-building document in the Helsinki Final Act is included in the next chapter on functional measures in arms control.) Finally, provision is made for continuing conferences in what came to be known as the CSCE process, the more formal institutionalization at the end of the cold war being the Organization for Security and Cooperation in Europe (OSCE).

I. *Sovereign equality, respect for the rights inherent in sovereignty:* The participating States will respect each other's sovereign equality and individuality as well as all the rights inherent in and encompassed by its sovereignty, including in particular the right of every State to juridical equality, to territorial integrity and to freedom and political independence. . . . They also have the right to belong or not to belong to international organizations, to be or not to be a party to bilateral or multilateral treaties including the right to be or not to be a party to treaties of alliance; they also have the right to neutrality.

II. *Refraining from the threat or use of force. The participating States will refrain in their mutual relations,* as well as in their international relations in general, *from the threat or use of force against the territorial integrity or political independence of any State.* . . .

III. *Inviolability of frontiers. The participating States regard as inviolable . . . the frontiers of all States in Europe* and therefore they will refrain now and in the future from assaulting these frontiers. Accordingly, they will also refrain from any demand for, or act of, seizure and usurpation of part or all of the territory of any participating State.

IV. *Territorial integrity of States.* The participating States will respect the territorial integrity of each of the participating States . . . and in particular from any such action constituting a threat or use of force. . . .

V. *Peaceful settlement of disputes.* The participating States will settle disputes among them by peaceful means in such a manner as not to endanger international peace and security, and justice. . . .

VI. *Non-intervention in internal affairs.* The participating States will refrain from any intervention, direct or indirect, individual or collective, in the internal or external affairs falling within the domestic jurisdiction of another participating State. . . .

VII. *Respect for human rights and fundamental freedoms, including the freedom of thought, conscience, religion or belief.* . . .

VIII. *Equal rights and self-determination of peoples.* . . .

IX. *Cooperation among States.* . . .

X. *Fulfilment in good faith of obligations under international law.* . . .

The participating States . . . declare their intention . . . to seek, by further improving their relations with the non-participating Mediterranean States, to increase mutual confidence, so as to promote security and stability in the Mediterranean area as a whole. . . . In order to advance the objectives set forth above, the participating States also declare their intention of maintaining and amplifying the contacts and dialogue as initiated by the CSCE with the non-participating Mediterranean States to include all the States of the Mediterranean, with the purpose of contributing to peace, reducing armed forces in the region, strengthening security, lessening tensions in the region, and widening the scope of cooperation, ends in which all share a common interest, as well as with the purpose of defining further common objectives.

---

28. *Conventional Armed Forces in Europe (CFE)*

(1990 and 1992)

With the end of the cold war, negotiations in Vienna moved quickly to define operationally the Atlantic-to-the-Urals area as one in which ideally there would be enough military forces for a country to defend itself, but not enough to provoke neighboring states. Numbers, types, and locations of military forces were important quantitative and qualitative factors in the European security construction. The agreement reached in 1990 dealt with military equipment; personnel caps were finally specified by agreement in 1992.

(1990)
The States Parties . . . have agreed as follows:

I. *Each State Party shall carry out the obligations set forth in this Treaty in accordance* with its provisions, including those obligations *relating to the following five categories of conventional armed forces: battle tanks, armoured combat vehicles, artillery, combat aircraft and combat helicopters.* Each State

Party also shall carry out the other measures set forth in this Treaty designed to ensure security and stability both during the period of reduction of conventional armed forces and after the completion of reductions. . . .

IV. Within the area of application . . . each State Party shall limit and, as necessary, reduce its battle tanks, armoured combat vehicles, artillery, combat aircraft and attack helicopters so that, 40 months after entry into force of this Treaty and thereafter, for the group of States Parties to which it belongs . . . the aggregate numbers do not exceed: (A) 20,000 battle tanks, of which no more than 16,500 shall be in active units; (B) 30,000 armoured combat vehicles, of which no more than 27,300 shall be in active units. Of the 30,000 armoured combat vehicles, no more than 18,000 shall be armoured infantry fighting vehicles and heavy armament combat vehicles; of armoured infantry fighting vehicles and heavy armament combat vehicles, no more than 1,500 shall be heavy armament combat vehicles; (C) 20,000 pieces of artillery, of which no more than 17,000 shall be in active units; (D) 6,800 combat aircraft; and (E) 2,000 attack helicopters. . . . [The treaty lists here detail sublimits within each category that apply to each State Party group.—Ed.]

VII. In order that the limitations set forth . . . are not exceeded, no State Party shall exceed, from 40 months after entry into force of this Treaty, the maximum levels which it has previously agreed upon within its group of States Parties. . . .

XIII. For the purpose of ensuring verification of compliance with the provisions of this Treaty, each State Party shall provide notifications and exchange information pertaining to its conventional armaments and equipment. . . .

XIV. For the purpose of ensuring verification of compliance with the provisions of this Treaty, each State Party shall have the right to conduct, and the obligation to accept, within the area of application, inspections. . . .

XV. For the purpose of ensuring verification of compliance with the provisions of this Treaty, a State Party shall have the right to use . . . national or multinational technical means of verification at its disposal in a manner consistent with generally recognised principles of international law. A State Party shall not interfere with national or multinational technical means of verification of another State Party. . . . A State Party shall not use concealment measures that impede verification of compliance with the provisions of this Treaty by national or multinational technical means of verification of another State Party. . . .

XVI. To promote the objectives and implementation of the provisions of this Treaty, the States Parties hereby establish a Joint Consultative Group.

(1992)

. . . The participating States . . . have adopted the following: Each participating State will limit its military personnel based on land within the area of application in the categories of conventional armed forces specified . . . so that . . . the aggregate number of such personnel will not exceed the number representing its national personnel limit as specified in this paragraph: . . . The Republic of Belarus 100,000; The Kingdom of Belgium 70,000; The Republic of Bulgaria 104,000; Canada 10,660; The Czech and Slovak

Federal Republic 140,000; The Kingdom of Denmark 39,000; The French Republic 325,000; The Republic of Georgia 40,000; The Federal Republic of Germany 345,000; The Hellenic Republic 158,621; The Republic of Hungary 100,000; The Republic of Iceland 0; The Italian Republic 315,000; The Republic of Kazakhstan 0; The Grand Duchy of Luxembourg 900; The Republic of Moldova; The Kingdom of the Netherlands 80,000; The Kingdom of Norway 32,000; The Republic of Poland 234,000; The Portuguese Republic 75,000; Romania 230,000; The Russian Federation 1,450,000; The Kingdom of Spain 300,000; The Republic of Turkey 530,000; Ukraine 450,000; The United Kingdom of Great Britain and Northern Ireland 260,000; [and] The United States of America 250,000. . . .

Chapter 16

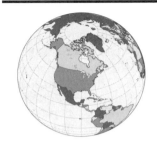

Arms Control through Functional Measures

In this chapter we look to conflict and arms control regimes through functional measures—telecommunications in the form of "hot lines" between adversaries, risk-reduction centers, missile launch notices, and other confidence- and security-building measures.

29. The U.S.-Soviet Hot Line Agreement

(1963)

In the wake of the 1962 Cuban missile crisis, which brought the two superpowers to the brink of nuclear war, this memorandum of understanding established a "direct communications link" between the White House in Washington and the Kremlin in Moscow. This "hot line" agreement was a response to difficulties the parties had had contacting each other in times of crisis. Upgrades in the hot line would occur as telecommunications technologies improved over the passing decades.

The direct communications link between Washington and Moscow established in accordance with the Memorandum, and the operation of such link, shall be governed by the following provisions: The direct communications link shall consist of two terminal points with telegraph-teleprinter equipment between which communications shall be directly exchanged. . . . In case of interruption of the wire circuit, transmission of messages shall be effected via the radio circuit, and for this purpose provision shall be made at the terminal points for the capability of prompt switching of all necessary equipment from one circuit to another. The terminal points of the link shall be so equipped as to provide for the transmission and reception of messages from Moscow to Washington in the Russian language and from Washington to Moscow in the English language.

30. *The Nuclear Incidents Agreement*
(1971)

The two superpowers agreed on confidence- and security-building measures to prevent an accidental detonation of a nuclear weapon from causing them to go to war.

The United States of America and the Union of Soviet Socialist Republics, hereinafter referred to as the Parties . . . have agreed as follows: *Each Party undertakes to maintain and to improve,* as it deems necessary, *its existing organizational and technical arrangements to guard against the accidental or unauthorized use of nuclear weapons under its control.* The Parties undertake to notify each other immediately in the event of an accidental, unauthorized or any other unexplained incident involving a possible detonation of a nuclear weapon which could create a risk of outbreak of nuclear war. *In the event of such an incident, the Party whose nuclear weapon is involved will immediately make every effort to take necessary measures to render harmless or destroy such weapon without its causing damage. The Parties undertake to notify each other immediately in the event of detection by missile warning* systems *of unidentified objects,* or in the event of signs of interference with these systems or with related communications facilities, *if such occurrences could create a risk of outbreak of nuclear war* between the two countries. *Each Party undertakes to notify the other Party in advance of any planned missile launches if such launches will extend beyond its national territory in the direction of the other Party.* Each Party, in other situations involving unexplained nuclear incidents, undertakes to act in such a manner as to reduce the possibility of its actions being misinterpreted by the other Party. . . . For transmission of urgent information, notifications and requests for information in situations requiring prompt clarification, the Parties shall make primary use of the Direct Communications Link between the Governments [i.e., the hot line—Ed.]. . . .

---

31. *Incidents on the High Seas*
(1972)

In this U.S.-Soviet agreement on the prevention of incidents on and over the high seas, functional measures were applied to avoid or manage conflicts on the high seas or in the airspace above that could escalate to the use of armed force.

The Government of the United States of America and the Government of the Union of Soviet Socialist Republics . . . have decided to conclude this Agreement and have agreed as follows: . . .

II. *The Parties shall take measures* to instruct the commanding officers of their respective ships *to observe strictly the letter and spirit of the International Regulations for Preventing Collisions at Sea, hereinafter referred to as the Rules of the Road.* . . .

III. In all cases ships operating in proximity to each other, except when required to maintain course and speed under the Rules of the Road, shall remain well clear to *avoid risk of collision.* Ships meeting or operating in the vicinity of a formation of the other Party shall, while conforming to the Rules of the Road, avoid maneuvering in a manner which would hinder the evolutions of the formation.... *Ships of the Parties shall not simulate attacks* by aiming guns, missile launchers, torpedo tubes, and other weapons in the direction of a passing ship of the other Party, not launch any object in the direction of passing ships of the other Party, and not use searchlights or other powerful illumination devices to illuminate the navigation bridges of passing ships of the other Party. When conducting exercises with submerged submarines, exercising ships shall show the appropriate signals ... to warn ships of the presence of submarines in the area.... Ships of one Party when approaching ships of the other Party conducting operations ... and particularly ships engaged in launching or landing aircraft as well as ships engaged in replenishment underway, shall take appropriate measures *not to hinder maneuvers* of such ships and shall remain well clear.

IV. Commanders of aircraft of the Parties shall use the greatest *caution and prudence in approaching aircraft and ships of the other Party* operating on and over the high seas, in particular, ships engaged in launching or landing aircraft, and in the interest of mutual safety shall *not permit: simulated attacks* by the simulated use of weapons against aircraft and ships, *or performance of various aerobatics over ships,* or dropping various objects near them in such a manner as to be hazardous to ships or to constitute a hazard to navigation.

V. Ships of the Parties operating in sight of one another shall raise proper signals concerning their intent to begin launching or landing aircraft. Aircraft of the Parties flying over the high seas in darkness or under instrument conditions shall, whenever feasible, display navigation lights.

VI. *Both Parties shall:* 1. *Provide* through the established system of radio *broadcasts of information and warning to mariners,* not less than 3 to 5 days in advance as a rule, notification *of actions on the high seas which represent a danger to navigation or to aircraft in flight.* 2. Make increased use of the informative signals ... to *signify the intentions of their respective ships when maneuvering in proximity to one another....*

VII. *The Parties shall exchange appropriate information concerning* instances of *collision, incidents which result in damage, or other incidents at sea between ships and aircraft of the Parties.* The United States Navy shall provide such information through the Soviet Naval Attache in Washington and the Soviet Navy shall provide such information through the United States Naval Attache in Moscow.

---

32. *Prevention of Nuclear War*

(1973)

The two superpowers adopt here confidence- and security-building measures designed to prevent nuclear war between them or with other countries.

The United States of America and the Union of Soviet Socialist Republics, hereinafter referred to as the Parties . . . have agreed as follows: . . . that an objective of their policies is to remove the danger of nuclear war and of the use of nuclear weapons. Accordingly, *the Parties agree that they will act in such a manner as to prevent the development of situations capable of causing a dangerous exacerbation of their relations, as to avoid military confrontations, and as to exclude the outbreak of nuclear war between them* and between either of the Parties and other countries. The Parties agree . . . to proceed from the premise that *each Party will refrain from the threat or use of force against the other Party, against the allies of the other Party and against other countries, in circumstances which may endanger international peace and security.* The Parties agree that they will be guided by these considerations in the formulation of their foreign policies and in their actions in the field of international relations. . . . If at any time relations between the Parties or between either Party and other countries appear to involve the risk of a nuclear conflict, or if relations between countries not parties to this Agreement appear to involve the risk of nuclear war . . . the United States and the Soviet Union . . . shall immediately enter into urgent consultations with each other and make every effort to avert this risk.

33. *Confidence- and Security-Building Measures (CSBMs): The Helsinki Final Act*

(1975)

As discussed in chapter 15, the Conference on Security and Cooperation in Europe (CSCE) concluded its initial work at Helsinki in August 1975. We include here the confidence- and security-building document in the Helsinki Final Act as an example of functional measures, which would be expanded substantially in follow-on negotiations in the 1980s and early 1990s in Stockholm and Vienna.

The participating States . . . have adopted the following:

Prior notification of major military manoeuvres. They will notify their major military manoeuvres to all other participating States through usual diplomatic channels in accordance with the following provisions: Notification will be given of major military manoeuvres exceeding a total of 25,000 troops, independently or combined with any possible air or naval components. . . . Notification will be given of major military manoeuvres which take place on the territory, in Europe, of any participating State as well as, if applicable, in the adjoining sea area and air space. . . .

Prior notification of other military manoeuvres. The participating States recognize that they can contribute further to strengthening confidence and increasing security and stability, and to this end may also notify smaller-scale military manoeuvres to other participating States, with special regard for those near the area of such manoeuvres. To the same end, the participating States also recognize that they may notify other military manoeuvres conducted by them.

Exchange of observers. The participating States will invite other participating States, voluntarily and on a bilateral basis, in a spirit of reciprocity and goodwill towards all participating States, to send observers to attend military manoeuvres. . . .

Prior notification of major military movements. . . . The participating States recognize that they may, at their own discretion and with a view to contributing to confidence-building, notify their major military movements. . . .

Other confidence-building measures. The participating States recognize that there are other means by which their common objectives can be promoted. In particular, they will, with due regard to reciprocity and with a view to better mutual understanding, *promote exchanges by invitation among their military delegations.* . . . The participating States, when conducting their military activities in the area covered by the provisions for the prior notification of major military manoeuvres, will duly take into account and respect this objective. They also recognize that the experience gained by the implementation of the provisions set forth above, together with further efforts, could lead to developing and enlarging measures aimed at strengthening confidence.

Questions relating to disarmament. The participating States recognize the interest of all of them in efforts aimed at lessening military confrontation and promoting disarmament which are designed to complement political détente in Europe and to strengthen their security. They are convinced of the necessity to take effective measures in these fields which by their scope and by their nature constitute steps towards the ultimate achievement of general and complete disarmament under strict and effective international control, and which should result in strengthening peace and security throughout the world. . . .

General considerations. Having considered the views expressed on various subjects related to the strengthening of security in Europe through joint efforts aimed at promoting détente and disarmament, the participating States, when engaged in such efforts, will, in this context, proceed, in particular, from the following essential considerations: *the complementary nature of the political and military aspects of security; the interrelation between the security of each participating State and security in Europe as a whole* and the relationship which exists, in the broader context of world security, between security in Europe and security in the Mediterranean area; respect for the security interests of all States participating in the Conference on Security and Cooperation in Europe inherent in their sovereign equality; the importance that participants in negotiating fora see to it that information about relevant developments, progress and results is provided on an appropriate basis to other States participating in the Conference on Security and Cooperation in Europe and, in return, the justified interest of any of those States in having their views considered.

---

34. *The Conference on Disarmament in Europe (CDE)*

(1986)

Because of a CSCE mandate, the Conference on Confidence- and Security-Building Measures and Disarmament in Europe (CDE) was convened in Stockholm in January 1984. Work was completed with this document on September 19, 1986 that expanded substantially the confidence- and security-building regime in Europe. Quantitative thresholds were set for notifications of military exercises, allowing observers of these maneuvers, providing one- and two-year notification calendars, and allowing verification and compliance inspections—the last of these a major breakthrough at the time.

. . . The participating States have declared the following:

Refraining from the Threat or Use of Force: The participating States . . . reaffirm their commitment to respect and put into practice the principle of refraining from the threat or use of force, as laid down in the Final Act. . . . No occupation or acquisition of territory resulting from the threat or use of force in contravention of international law, will be recognized as legal. . . . They stress their commitment to the principle of peaceful settlement of disputes as contained in the Final Act. . . .

Prior Notification of Certain Military Activities: The participating States will give notification in writing through diplomatic channels in an agreed form of content, to all other participating States 42 days or more in advance of the start of notifiable military activities in the zone of application for confidence- and security-building measures (CSBMs). . . .

Each of the following military activities in the field conducted as a single activity . . . *at or above the levels defined below, will be notified:* (1) The engagement of formations of land forces of the participating States in the same exercise activity conducted under a single operational command independently or in combination with any possible air or naval components. This military activity will be subject to notification whenever it involves at any time during the activity: *at least 13,000 troops,* including support troops, *or at least 300 battle tanks,* if organized into a divisional structure or at least two brigades/regiments, not necessarily subordinate to the same division; the participation of air forces of the partic-

ipating States will be included in the notification if it is foreseen that in the course of *the activity 200 or more sorties by aircraft,* excluding helicopters, will be flown. (2) The engagement of military forces either in an amphibious landing or in a parachute assault by airborne forces . . . ; these military activities will be subject to notification *whenever the amphibious landing involves at least 3,000 troops or whenever the parachute drop involves at least 3,000 troops.* (3) The engagement of formations of land forces of the participating States in a transfer from outside the zone of application for CSBMs to arrival points in the zone, or from inside the zone of application for CSBMs to points of concentration in the zone, to participate in a notifiable exercise activity or to be concentrated. The arrival or concentration of these forces will be subject to notification whenever it involves, at any time during the activity: at least 13,000 troops, including support troops, or at least 300 battle tanks if organized into a divisional structure or at least two brigades/regiments, not necessarily subordinate to the same division. Forces which have been transferred into the zone will be subject to all provisions of agreed CSBMs when they depart their arrival points to participate in a notifiable exercise activity or to be concentrated within the zone of application for CSBMs. . . .

Observation of Certain Military Activities: The participating States will invite observers from all other participating States to the following notifiable military activities: (1) The engagement of formations of land forces of the participating States in the same exercise activity conducted under a single operational command independently or in combination with any possible air or naval components. (2) The engagement of military forces either in an amphibious landing or in a parachute assault by airborne forces in the zone of application for CSBMs.... The above-mentioned activities will be subject to observation whenever the number of troops engaged meets or exceeds 7,000 troops, except in the case of either an amphibious landing or a parachute assault by airborne forces, which will be subject to observation whenever the number of troops engaged meets or exceeds 5,000 troops.... Each participating State may send up to two observers to the military activity to be observed....

Annual Calendars: Each participating State will exchange, with all other participating States, *an annual calendar of its military activities subject to prior notification,* within the zone of application for CSBMs, forecast for the subsequent calendar year. It will be transmitted every year, in writing, through diplomatic channels.... *Each participating State will communicate,* in writing, to all other participating States ... information concerning military activities subject to prior notification involving more than 40,000 troops, which *it plans to carry out in the second subsequent calendar year.*... Participating States will not carry out military activities subject to prior notification involving more than 75,000 troops, unless they have been the object of communication.... Participating States will not carry out military activities subject to prior notification involving more than 40,000 troops unless they have been included in the annual calendar.... If military activities subject to prior notification are carried out in

addition to those contained in the annual calendar, they should be as few as possible.

Compliance and Verification: ...The participating States recognize that *national technical means can play a role in monitoring compliance* with agreed confidence- and security-building measures. In accordance with the provisions contained in this document *each participating State has the right to conduct inspections on the territory of any other participating State within the zone of application for CSBMs.*... No participating State will be obliged to accept on its territory within the zone of application for CSBMS, more than three inspections per calendar year. No participating State will be obliged to accept more than one inspection per calendar year from the same participating State.... In the specified area the representatives of the inspecting State accompanied by the representatives of the receiving State will be permitted access, entry and unobstructed survey, except for areas or sensitive points to which access is normally denied or restricted, military and other defence installations, as well as naval vessels, military vehicles and aircraft.... Inspection will be permitted on the ground, from the air, or both....

The participating States stress that these confidence- and security-building measures are designed to reduce the dangers of armed conflict and of misunderstanding or miscalculation of military activities and emphasize that their implementation will contribute to these objectives. Reaffirming the relevant objectives of the Final Act, the participating States are determined to continue building confidence, to lessen military confrontation and to enhance security for all. They are also determined to achieve progress in disarmament.

35. *The Vienna Conference on CSBMs*

(1990)

Separate from the CFE negotiations (see chapter 15, Document No. 28.) in Vienna were those in the same city from March 1989 to November 1990 on confidence- and security-building measures. The final agreement greatly expanded CSBMs that had been agreed five years earlier in Stockholm, calling for annual exchange of detailed information, risk reduction measures, military-to-military contacts, prior notification and observation of certain military activities, exchange of annual calendars, constraining provisions, compliance and verification mechanisms, communications, and annual assessment meetings. Further CSBM accords followed in 1992, 1994, and 1999.

The participating States have adopted the present document which integrates a set of new confidence- and security-building measures with measures adopted in the Document of the Stockholm Conference which have been further developed in the light of experience gained. . . .

Information Exchange

The participating States will exchange annually information on their military forces concerning the military organization, manpower and major weapon and equipment systems, as specified below, in the zone of application for confidence- and security-building measures (CSBMs). . . . The participating States will exchange annually information on their military budgets for the forthcoming fiscal year. . . .

Risk Reduction

Participating States will, in accordance with the following provisions, consult and co-operate with each other about any unusual and unscheduled activities of their military forces outside their normal peacetime locations which are militarily significant, within the zone of application for CSBMs and about which a participating State expresses its security concern. . . . Participating States will co-operate by reporting and clarifying hazardous incidents of a military nature within the zone of application for CSBMs in order to prevent possible misunderstandings and mitigate the effects on another participating State. . . .

Contacts

Each participating State with air combat units . . . will arrange visits for representatives of all other participating States to one of its normal peacetime air bases on which such units are located. . . . To improve further their mutual relations in the interest of strengthening the process of confidence- and security-building, the participating States will, as appropriate, promote and facilitate: exchanges and visits between senior military / defence representatives; contacts between relevant military institutions; attendance by military representatives of other participating States at courses of instruction; exchanges between military commanders and officers of commands down to brigade / regiment or equivalent level; exchanges and contacts between academics and experts in military studies and related areas; sporting and cultural events between members of their armed forces.

Notifications

The participating States will give notification in writing through diplomatic channels in an agreed form of content, to all other participating States 42 days or more in advance of the start of notifiable military activities in the zone of application for confidence- and security-building measures (CSBMs). . . . Each of the following military activities in the field conducted as a single activity in the zone of application for CSBMs at or above the levels defined below, will be notified: The engagement of formations of land forces of the participating States in the same exercise activity conducted under a single operational command independently or in combination with any possible air or naval components. . . . This military activity will be subject to notification whenever it involves at any time during the activity: at least 13,000 troops, including support troops, or at least 300 battle tanks if organized into a divisional structure or at least two brigades/regiments, not necessarily subordinate to the same division. The participation of air forces of the participating States will be included in the notification if it is foreseen that in the course of the activity 200 or more sorties by aircraft, excluding helicopters, will be flown. The engagement of military forces either in an amphibious landing or in a parachute assault by airborne forces in the zone of application for CSBMs. These military activities will be subject to notification whenever the amphibious landing involves at least 3,000 troops or whenever the parachute drop involves at least 3,000 troops.

The engagement of formations of land forces of the participating States in a transfer from outside the zone of application for CSBMs to arrival points in the zone, or from inside the zone of application for CSBMs to points of concentration in the zone, to participate in a notifiable exercise activity or to be concentrated. The arrival or concentration of these forces will be subject to notification whenever it involves, at any time during the activity: at least

13,000 troops, including support troops, or at least 300 battle tanks if organized into a divisional structure or at least two brigades/regiments, not necessarily subordinate to the same division. . . .

Observations

The participating States will invite observers from all other participating States to . . . notifiable military activities.

Annual Calendars

Each participating State will exchange, with all other participating States, an annual calendar of its military activities subject to prior notification, within the zone of application for CSBMs, forecast for the subsequent calendar year. . . .

Constraining Conditions

Each participating State will communicate, in writing, to all other participating States . . . information concerning military activities subject to prior notification involving more than 40,000 troops, which it plans to carry out or host in the second subsequent calendar year. . . . Participating States will not carry out military activities subject to prior notification involving more than 40,000 troops, unless they have been the object of communication as defined above. Participating States will not carry out military activities subject to prior notification involving more than 40,000 troops unless they have been included in the annual calendar. . . .

Compliance and Verification

According to the Madrid Mandate, the confidence- and security-building measures to be agreed upon "will be provided with adequate forms of verification which correspond to their content". The participating States recognize that national technical means can play a role in monitoring compliance with agreed confidence- and security-building measures. In accordance with the provisions contained in this document each participating State has the right to conduct inspections on the territory of any other participating State within the zone of application for CSBMs. . . . Inspection will be permitted on the ground, from the air, or both. . . .

Evaluation

Information provided under the provisions on Information on Military Forces and on Information on Plans for the Deployment of Major Weapon and Equipment Systems will be subject to evaluation. . . . The communications concerning compliance and verification will be transmitted preferably through the CSBM communications network. The participating States will establish a network of direct communications between their capitals for the transmission of messages relating to agreed measures. . . . The participating States will hold each year a meeting to discuss the present and future implementation of agreed CSBMs. . . . The Conflict Prevention Centre will serve as the forum for such meetings.

36. *Nuclear Risk Reduction Centers*

(1987)

Institutionalizing a mechanism for notifications and related communications takes the form here of nuclear risk reduction centers, this institutionalization itself a confidence- and security-building measure.

The United States of America and the Union of Soviet Socialist Republics, hereinafter referred to as *the Parties . . . have agreed . . . [to] establish, in its capital, a national Nuclear Risk Reduction Center* that shall operate on behalf of and under the control of its respective Government. The Parties shall use the Nuclear Risk Reduction Centers *to transmit notifications. . . .* The Parties shall establish a special facsimile communications link between their national Nuclear Risk Reduction Centers. . . . The Parties shall staff their national Nuclear Risk Reduction Centers as they deem appropriate, so as to ensure their normal functioning. *The Parties shall hold regular meetings* between representatives of the Nuclear Risk Reduction Centers at least once each year to consider matters related to the functioning of such Centers.

37. *Launch Notifications*

(1988)

To reduce the likelihood that test missile launches could be misinterpreted as an attack, the United States and the Soviet Union agreed that the parties would provide notice in advance of all strategic missile launches—a confidence- and security-building measure between them.

The United States of America and the Union of Soviet Socialist Republics, hereinafter referred to as the Parties . . . have agreed as follows: *Each Party shall provide the other Party notification, through the Nuclear Risk Reduction Centers* of the United States of America and the Union of Soviet Socialist Republics, *no less than twenty-four hours in advance, of the planned date, launch area, and area of impact for any launch of a strategic ballistic missile:* an intercontinental ballistic missile (hereinafter "ICBM") or a submarine-launched ballistic missile (hereinafter "SLBM"). A notification of a planned launch of an ICBM or an SLBM shall be valid for four days. . . . For launches of ICBMs or SLBMs from land, the notification shall indicate the area from which the launch is planned to take place. For launches of SLBMs from submarines, the notification shall indicate the general area from which the missile will be launched. . . . For all launches of ICBMs or SLBMs, the notification shall indicate the geographic coordinates of the planned impact area or areas of the reentry vehicles.

---

38. *The Treaty on Open Skies*
(1992)

As a confidence- and security-building measure, the Treaty on Open Skies creates a reconnaissance overflight regime.

The States concluding this Treaty, hereinafter referred to collectively as the States Parties or individually as a State Party . . . have agreed as follows: *This Treaty establishes the regime, to be known as the Open Skies regime, for the conduct of observation flights by States Parties over the territories of other States Parties,* and sets forth the rights and obligations of the States Parties relating thereto. . . . Each State Party shall have the right to conduct observation flights in accordance with the provisions of this Treaty. Each State Party shall be obliged to accept observation flights over its territory in accordance with the provisions of this Treaty. Each State Party shall have the right to conduct a number of observation flights over the territory of any other State Party equal to the number of observation flights which that other State Party has the right to conduct over it.

PART FIVE

American Foreign Policy and National Security: The U.S. Government and International Organizations

We conclude this volume with two chapters that examine the legal foundations of domestic institutions and international organizations most relevant to the formation and implementation of U.S. foreign and national security policy.

Chapter 17

State, Defense, Homeland Security, and the National Security Council

We focus in this chapter on the statutory authority of those cabinet offices most concerned with foreign policy and national security—the Departments of State, Defense, and Homeland Security as well as the National Security Council (NSC) within the Executive Office of the President—that brings these and other departments and agencies together under presidential authority.

Statutes on these and other matters are consolidated and updated in the U.S. Code, which is divided into some fifty titles containing sections variously aggregated as parts or chapters. Particularly relevant in this chapter are Title 10 (Armed Forces), Title 22 (Foreign Relations and Intercourse), and Title 50 (War and National Defense). Conventional reference is to a title as prefix to the U.S. Code (U.S.C.), the suffix being the particular section. For example, Title 22, Section 2656, which deals with the management of foreign affairs, can be abbreviated simply as 22 U.S.C. 2656.

In the documents excerpted below we follow the U.S. Code's format; however, as legal documents they are structured formally in a cumbersome style with numerous alphabetical and numerical divisions in the text. While careful not to alter meaning, to facilitate reading the documents, we have deleted letters and numbers designating some passages and made related changes in punctuation and marks as in underlining internal labels.

1. The Department of State

(1789–present)

The Department of State has primary responsibility in foreign affairs and diplomacy. The secretary of state is the senior member of the cabinet. Indeed, fellow Virginian Thomas Jefferson held the position in President George Washington's original cabinet that also included Secretary of the Treasury Alexander Hamilton (New York), Secretary of War Henry Knox (Massachusetts), and Attorney General Edmund Randolph (Virginia). This excerpt from the U.S. Code, Title 22, summarizes the present-day legal basis for the secretary of state and the State Department, which is organized in regional (e.g., Europe) and functional (e.g., intelligence and research or political-military) bureaus, some of which are specified by statute.

Sec. 2656. *Management of foreign affairs:* The Secretary of State shall perform such duties as shall from time to time be enjoined on or intrusted to him by the President relative to correspondences, commissions, or instructions to or with public ministers or consuls from the United States, or to negotiations with public ministers from foreign states or princes, or to memorials or other applications from foreign public ministers or other foreigners, or to such other matters respecting foreign affairs as the President of the United States shall assign to the Department, and he shall conduct the business of the Department in such manner as the President shall direct.

Sec. 2651. *Establishment of Department.* There shall be at the seat of government an executive department to be known as the "Department of State", and a Secretary of State, who shall be the head thereof.

Sec. 2651a. *Organization of Department of State.*

a. *Secretary of State:* (1) The Department of State shall be administered . . . under the supervision and direction of the Secretary of State (hereinafter referred to as the "Secretary"). (2) The Secretary, the Deputy Secretary of State, and the Deputy Secretary of State for Management and Resources shall be appointed by the President, by and with the advice and consent of the Senate. (3) (A) Notwithstanding any other provision of law and except as provided in this section, the Secretary shall have and exercise any authority vested by law in any office or official of the Department of State. The Secretary shall administer, coordinate, and direct the Foreign Service of the United States and the personnel of the Department of State, except where authority is inherent in or vested in the President. (B) (i) The Secretary shall not have the authority of the Inspector General or the Chief Financial Officer. (ii) The Secretary shall not have any authority given expressly to diplomatic or consular officers. [Ambassadors and other emissaries appointed by the president may in principle be tasked by (and thus work directly for) the president.—Ed.] (4) The Secretary is authorized to promulgate such rules and regulations as may be necessary to carry out the functions of the Secretary of State and the Department of State. Unless otherwise specified in law, the Secretary may delegate authority to perform any of the functions of the Secretary or the Department to officers and employees under the direction and supervision of the Secretary. The Secretary may delegate the authority to redelegate any such functions.

b. *Under Secretaries:* (1) *In general:* There shall be in the Department of State not more than 6 Under Secretaries of State, who shall be appointed by the President, by and with the advice and consent of the Senate. . . . (2) *Under Secretary for Arms Control and International Security:* There shall be in the

Department of State, among the Under Secretaries . . . an Under Secretary for Arms Control and International Security, who shall assist the Secretary and the Deputy Secretary in matters related to international security policy, arms control, and nonproliferation. Subject to the direction of the President, the Under Secretary may attend and participate in meetings of the National Security Council in his role as Senior Advisor to the President and the Secretary of State on Arms Control and Nonproliferation Matters. (3) *Under Secretary for Public Diplomacy:* There shall be in the Department of State . . . an Under Secretary for Public Diplomacy, who shall have primary responsibility to assist the Secretary and the Deputy Secretary in the formation and implementation of United States public diplomacy policies and activities, including international educational and cultural exchange programs, information, and international broadcasting. (4) *Nomination of Under Secretaries:* Whenever the President submits to the Senate a nomination of an individual for appointment . . . the President shall designate the particular Under Secretary position in the Department of State that the individual shall have.

c. *Assistant Secretaries:* (1) *In general:* There shall be in the Department of State not more than 24 Assistant Secretaries of State, each of whom shall be appointed by the President, by and with the advice and consent of the Senate. . . . (2) *Assistant Secretary of State for Democracy, Human Rights, and Labor:* (A) There shall be in the Department of State an Assistant Secretary of State for Democracy, Human Rights, and Labor who shall be responsible to the Secretary of State for matters pertaining to human rights and humanitarian affairs (including matters relating to prisoners of war and members of the United States Armed Forces missing in action) in the conduct of foreign policy and such other related duties as the Secretary may from time to time designate. . . . (3) *Nomination of Assistant Secretaries:* Whenever the President submits to the Senate a nomination of an individual for appointment to a position in the Department of State . . . , the President shall designate the regional or functional bureau or bureaus of the Department of State with respect to which the individual shall have responsibility.

d. *Other senior officials:* In addition to officials of the Department of State who are otherwise authorized to be appointed by the President, by and with the advice and consent of the Senate. . . .

e. *Coordinator for Counterterrorism:* (1) *In general:* There is within the office of the Secretary of State a Coordinator for Counterterrorism (in this paragraph referred to as the "Coordinator") who shall be appointed by the President, by and with the advice and consent of the Senate. (2) *Duties:* . . . The principal duty of the Coordinator shall be the overall supervision (including policy oversight of resources) of international counterterrorism activities. . . . (3) *Rank and status of Ambassador:* The Coordinator shall have the rank and status of Ambassador at Large.

UNITED STATES DEPARTMENT OF STATE

Revised June 13, 2003

SECRETARY OF STATE (S)

U.S. Agency for International Development (USAID)
Administrator

U.S. Permanent Representative to the United Nations (USUN)

Deputy Secretary of State (D)

Executive Secretariat (S/ES)
Executive Secretary

Chief of Staff (S/COS)

Under Secretary for Political Affairs (P)

Under Secretary for Economic, Business and Agricultural Affairs (E)

Economic and Business Affairs (EB)
Assistant Secretary

African Affairs (AF)
Assistant Secretary

East Asian and Pacific Affairs (EAP)
Assistant Secretary

European and Eurasian Affairs (EUR)
Assistant Secretary

South Asian Affairs (SA)
Assistant Secretary

Near Eastern Affairs (NEA)
Assistant Secretary

International Organizations (IO)
Assistant Secretary

Western Hemisphere Affairs (WHA)
Assistant Secretary

Under Secretary for Arms Control and International Security Affairs (T)

Arms Control (AC)
Assistant Secretary

Nonproliferation (NP)
Assistant Secretary

Political-Military Affairs (PM)
Assistant Secretary

Verification and Compliance (VC)
Assistant Secretary

Under Secretary for Public Diplomacy and Public Affairs (R)

Educational and Cultural Affairs (ECA)
Assistant Secretary

Public Affairs (PA)
Assistant Secretary

International Information Programs (IIP)
Director

Under Secretary (M)

Office of Management Policy (M/P)

Consular Affairs (CA)
Assistant Secretary

Administration (A)
Assistant Secretary

Human Resources (HR)
Director General of the Foreign Service and Director of Human Resources

Diplomatic Security (DS)
Assistant Secretary

Overseas Buildings Operations (OBO)
Director

Information Resource Management (IRM)
Chief Information Officer

Office of White House Liaison (M/WHL)
Director

Foreign Service Institute (FSI)
Director

Under Secretary for Global Affairs (G)

Democracy, Human Rights and Labor (DRL)
Assistant Secretary

International Narcotics and Law Enforcement (INL)
Assistant Secretary

Oceans and International Environmental and Scientific Affairs (OES)
Assistant Secretary

Population, Refugees and Migration (PRM)
Assistant Secretary

Office of Science and Technology Adviser (STAS)

Inspector General (OIG)

Policy Planning Staff (S/P)
Director

Office of Civil Rights (S/OCR)
Director

Legal Adviser (L)

Legislative Affairs (H)
Assistant Secretary

Intelligence and Research (INR)
Assistant Secretary

Resource Management (RM)
Assistant Secretary and Chief Financial Officer

Chief of Protocol (S/CPR)
Ambassador

Counterterrorism (S/CT)
Coordinator and Ambassador at Large

War Crimes Issues (S/WCI)
Ambassador at Large

Counselor (C)

2. *The Department of Defense*

(1947–present)

Postwar planners saw separate, virtually independent War (Army) and Navy cabinet departments as inadequate, particularly after recent World War II experience in which coordination of ground, naval, and air forces was so essential to assuring victory in Europe and the Pacific. Accordingly, the National Security Act of 1947 created the U.S. Air Force as a new service department alongside the Departments of the Army and the Navy, the latter also including as before the U.S. Marine Corps. In addition to a secretary of defense and staff, the act also created a Joint Chiefs of Staff (JCS) essentially as a coordinating body for the four armed services. In bringing separate services together in a single executive department that included a JCS and staff, an effort was made to avoid any semblance of a Prussian-style general staff with centralized power and authority. This concern is reflected in Section 155(e) in attention paid to civilian control and explicit denial of executive authority to the JCS joint staff. In relation to the unified and specified combatant commands, the military chiefs of staff are not designated as combat commanders in the chain of command. In this regard, Section 162(b) states: "Unless otherwise directed by the President, the chain of command to a unified or specified combatant command runs from the President to the Secretary of Defense; and from the Secretary of Defense to the commander of the combatant command." Indeed, the Department of Defense (DoD) is a complex bureaucracy with numerous power centers. In the 1940s and 1950s, the locus of power and authority in day-to-day activities for organizing, training, and equipping ground, sea, and air forces remained primarily with the service secretaries and their chiefs of staff who report separately to civilian service secretaries who, in turn, report to the secretary of defense, also a civilian. Although the service departments would retain these functions, statutory reform efforts strengthened the Office of Secretary of Defense (OSD) (1958) and the JCS, the Joint Staff, and Joint Commands (1987), reducing somewhat the relative power and authority within the DoD of the service departments. In addition to the OSD, the JCS, and service departments are such DoD agencies dealing with logistics, intelligence, security assistance, and other defense functions not tied to a particular service. This excerpt is taken from the U.S. Code, Titles 10 and 50.

Title 10, Subtitle A

The Department of Defense and Secretary of Defense

Sec. 111. *Executive department* The Department of Defense is an executive department of the United States. The Department is composed of the following: (1) The Office of the Secretary of Defense. (2) The Joint Chiefs of Staff. (3) The Joint Staff. (4) The Defense Agencies. (5) Department of Defense Field Activities. (6) The Department of the Army. (7) The Department of the Navy. (8) The Department of the Air Force. (9) The unified and specified combatant commands. (10) Such other offices, agencies, activities, and commands as may be established or designated by law or by the President. (11) All offices, agencies, activities, and commands under the control or supervision of any element named in paragraphs (1) through (10). If the President establishes or designates an office, agency, activity, or command in the Department of Defense of a kind other than those described [above] . . . , the President shall notify Congress not later than 60 days thereafter.

Sec. 113. *Secretary of Defense*

a. There is a Secretary of Defense, who is the head of the Department of Defense, appointed from civilian life by the President, by and with the advice and consent of the Senate. A person may not be appointed as Secretary of Defense within 10 years after relief from active duty as a commissioned officer of a regular component of an armed force.

b. The Secretary is the principal assistant to the President in all matters relating to the Department of Defense. Subject to the direction of the President and to this title and section 2 of the National Security Act of 1947 (50 U.S.C. 401), he has authority, direction, and control over the Department of Defense.

c. The Secretary shall report annually in writing to the President and the Congress on the expenditures, work, and accomplishments of the Department of Defense during the period covered by the report, together with a report from each military department on the expenditures, work, and accomplishments of that department; itemized statements showing the savings of public funds, and the eliminations of unnecessary duplications . . . ; [and] such recommendations as he considers appropriate. At the same time that the Secretary submits the annual report . . . , the Secretary shall transmit to the President and Congress a separate report from the Reserve Forces Policy Board on the reserve programs of the Department of Defense and on any other matters that the Reserve Forces Policy Board considers appropriate to include in the report.

d. Unless specifically prohibited by law, the Secretary may, without being relieved of his responsibility, perform any of his functions or duties, or exercise any of his powers through, or with the aid of, such persons in, or organizations of, the Department of Defense as he may designate.

e. The Secretary shall include in his annual report to Congress . . . a description of the major military missions and of the military force structure of the United States for the next fiscal year; an explanation of the relationship of those military missions to that force structure; and the justification for those military missions and that force structure. In preparing . . . [this report], the Secretary shall take into consideration the content of the annual national security strategy report of the President under section 108 of the National Security Act of 1947 (50 U.S.C. 404a) for the fiscal year concerned.

f. When a vacancy occurs in an office within the Department of Defense and the office is to be filled by a person appointed from civilian life by the President, by and with the advice and consent of the Senate, the Secretary of Defense shall inform the President of the qualifications needed by a person serving in that office to carry out effectively the duties and responsibilities of that office.

g. The Secretary of Defense, with the advice and assistance of the Chairman of the Joint Chiefs of Staff, shall provide annually to the heads of Department of Defense components written policy guidance for the preparation and review of the program recommendations and budget proposals of their respective components. Such guidance shall include guidance on national security objectives and policies; the priorities of military missions; and the resource levels projected to be available for the period of time for which such recommendations and proposals are to be effective. The Secretary of Defense, with the approval of the President and after consultation with the Chairman of the Joint Chiefs of Staff, shall provide to the Chairman written policy guidance for the preparation and review of contingency plans. Such guidance shall be provided every two years or more frequently as needed and shall include guidance on the specific force levels and specific supporting resource levels projected to be available for the period of time for which such plans are to be effective.

h. The Secretary of Defense shall keep the Secretaries of the military departments informed with respect to military operations and activities of the Department of Defense that directly affect their respective responsibilities.

i. The Secretary of Defense shall transmit to Congress each year a report that contains a comprehensive net assessment of the defense capabilities and programs of the armed forces of the United States and its allies as compared with those of their potential adversaries. . . . Such report shall be transmitted in both classified and unclassified form.

j. Not later than April 8 of each year, the Secretary of Defense shall submit to the Committee on Armed Services and the Committee on Appropriations of the Senate and the Committee on Armed Services and the Committee on Appropriations of the House of Representatives a report on the cost of stationing United States forces outside of the United States. . . .

k. The Secretary of Defense, with the advice and assistance of the Chairman of the Joint Chiefs of Staff, shall provide annually to the Secretaries of the military departments and to the commanders of the combatant commands written guidelines to direct the effective detection and monitoring of all potential aerial and maritime threats to the national security of the United States. Those guidelines shall include guidance on the specific force levels and specific supporting resources to be made available for the period of time for which the guidelines are to be in effect. . . .

l. The Secretary shall include in the annual report to Congress. [Statistical data are specified here on missions and military and civilian personnel.—Ed.] . . .

m. *Information To Accompany Funding Request for Contingency Operation.* Whenever the President submits to Congress a request for appropriations for costs associated with a contingency operation that involves, or likely will involve, the deployment of more than 500 members of the armed forces, the Secretary of Defense shall submit to Congress a report on the objectives of the operation. The report shall include a discussion of the following: (1) What clear and distinct objectives guide the activities of United States forces in the operation. (2) What the President has identified on the basis of those objectives as the date, or the set of conditions, that defines the endpoint of the operation.

Sec. 131. *Office of the Secretary of Defense*

a. There is in the Department of Defense an Office of the Secretary of Defense. The function of the Office is to assist the Secretary of Defense in carrying out his duties and responsibilities and to carry out such other duties as may be prescribed by law.

b. The Office of the Secretary of Defense is composed of the following: (1) The

Deputy Secretary of Defense. (2) The Under Secretary of Defense for Acquisition, Technology, and Logistics. (3) The Under Secretary of Defense for Policy. (4) The Under Secretary of Defense (Comptroller). (5) The Under Secretary of Defense for Personnel and Readiness. (6) The Director of Defense Research and Engineering. (7) The Assistant Secretaries of Defense. (8) The Director of Operational Test and Evaluation. (9) The General Counsel of the Department of Defense. (10) The Inspector General of the Department of Defense. (11) Such other offices and officials as may be established by law or the Secretary of Defense may establish or designate in the Office.

c. Officers of the armed forces may be assigned or detailed to permanent duty in the Office of the Secretary of Defense. However, the Secretary may not establish a military staff in the Office of the Secretary of Defense.

d. The Secretary of each military department, and the civilian employees and members of the armed forces under the jurisdiction of the Secretary, shall cooperate fully with personnel of the Office of the Secretary of Defense to achieve efficient administration of the Department of Defense and to carry out effectively the authority, direction, and control of the Secretary of Defense.

The Joint Chiefs of Staff, the Joint Staff, and Combatant Commands

Sec. 151. *Joint Chiefs of Staff: composition; functions*

a. *Composition.* There are in the Department of Defense the Joint Chiefs of Staff, headed by the Chairman of the Joint Chiefs of Staff. The Joint Chiefs of Staff consist of the following:

(1) The Chairman. (2) The Vice Chairman. (3) The Chief of Staff of the Army. (4) The Chief of Naval Operations. (5) The Chief of Staff of the Air Force. (6) The Commandant of the Marine Corps.

b. *Function as Military Advisers.* The Chairman of the Joint Chiefs of Staff is the principal military adviser to the President, the National Security Council, and the Secretary of Defense. The other members of the Joint Chiefs of Staff are military advisers to the President, the National Security Council, and the Secretary of Defense as specified in subsections (d) and (e).

c. *Consultation by Chairman.* In carrying out his functions, duties, and responsibilities, the Chairman shall, as he considers appropriate, consult with and seek the advice of the other members of the Joint Chiefs of Staff and the commanders of the unified and specified combatant commands. Subject to subsection (d), in presenting advice with respect to any matter to the President, the National Security Council, or the Secretary of Defense, the Chairman shall, as he considers appropriate, inform the President, the National Security Council, or the Secretary of Defense, as the case may be, of the range of military advice and opinion with respect to that matter.

d. *Advice and Opinions of Members Other Than Chairman.* A member of the Joint Chiefs of Staff (other than the Chairman) may submit to the Chairman advice or an opinion in disagreement with, or advice or an opinion in addition to, the advice presented by the Chairman to the President, the National Security Council, or the Secretary of Defense. If a member submits such advice or opinion, the Chairman shall

DEPARTMENT OF DEFENSE

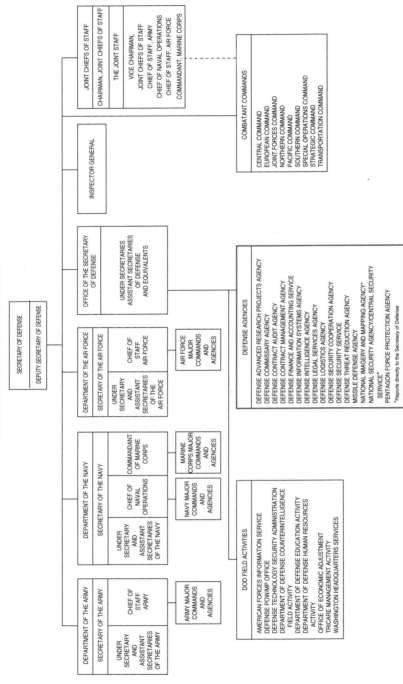

SECRETARY OF DEFENSE

DEPUTY SECRETARY OF DEFENSE

DEPARTMENT OF THE ARMY

SECRETARY OF THE ARMY

- UNDER SECRETARY AND ASSISTANT SECRETARIES OF THE ARMY
- CHIEF OF STAFF ARMY
- ARMY MAJOR COMMANDS AND AGENCIES

DEPARTMENT OF THE NAVY

SECRETARY OF THE NAVY

- UNDER SECRETARY AND ASSISTANT SECRETARIES OF THE NAVY
- CHIEF OF NAVAL OPERATIONS
- COMMANDANT OF MARINE CORPS
- NAVY MAJOR COMMANDS AND AGENCIES
- MARINE CORPS MAJOR COMMANDS AND AGENCIES

DEPARTMENT OF THE AIR FORCE

SECRETARY OF THE AIR FORCE

- UNDER SECRETARY AND ASSISTANT SECRETARIES OF THE AIR FORCE
- CHIEF OF STAFF AIR FORCE
- AIR FORCE MAJOR COMMANDS AND AGENCIES

OFFICE OF THE SECRETARY OF DEFENSE

- UNDER SECRETARIES ASSISTANT SECRETARIES OF DEFENSE AND EQUIVALENTS

INSPECTOR GENERAL

JOINT CHIEFS OF STAFF

CHAIRMAN, JOINT CHIEFS OF STAFF

THE JOINT STAFF

- VICE CHAIRMAN, JOINT CHIEFS OF STAFF
- CHIEF OF STAFF, ARMY
- CHIEF OF NAVAL OPERATIONS
- CHIEF OF STAFF, AIR FORCE
- COMMANDANT, MARINE CORPS

COMBATANT COMMANDS

- CENTRAL COMMAND
- EUROPEAN COMMAND
- JOINT FORCES COMMAND
- NORTHERN COMMAND
- PACIFIC COMMAND
- SOUTHERN COMMAND
- SPECIAL OPERATIONS COMMAND
- STRATEGIC COMMAND
- TRANSPORTATION COMMAND

DEFENSE AGENCIES

- DEFENSE ADVANCED RESEARCH PROJECTS AGENCY
- DEFENSE COMMISSARY AGENCY
- DEFENSE CONTRACT AUDIT AGENCY
- DEFENSE CONTRACT MANAGEMENT AGENCY
- DEFENSE FINANCE AND ACCOUNTING SERVICE
- DEFENSE INFORMATION SYSTEMS AGENCY
- DEFENSE INTELLIGENCE AGENCY
- DEFENSE LEGAL SERVICES AGENCY
- DEFENSE LOGISTICS AGENCY
- DEFENSE SECURITY COOPERATION AGENCY
- DEFENSE SECURITY SERVICE
- DEFENSE THREAT REDUCTION AGENCY
- MISSILE DEFENSE AGENCY
- NATIONAL IMAGERY AND MAPPING AGENCY*
- NATIONAL SECURITY AGENCY/CENTRAL SECURITY SERVICE*
- PENTAGON FORCE PROTECTION AGENCY

*Reports directly to the Secretary of Defense

DOD FIELD ACTIVITIES

- AMERICAN FORCES INFORMATION SERVICE
- DEFENSE POW/MP OFFICE
- DEFENSE TECHNOLOGY SECURITY ADMINISTRATION
- DEPARTMENT OF DEFENSE COUNTERINTELLIGENCE FIELD ACTIVITY
- DEPARTMENT OF DEFENSE EDUCATION ACTIVITY
- DEPARTMENT OF DEFENSE HUMAN RESOURCES ACTIVITY
- OFFICE OF ECONOMIC ADJUSTMENT
- TRICARE MANAGEMENT ACTIVITY
- WASHINGTON HEADQUARTERS SERVICES

present the advice or opinion of such member at the same time he presents his own advice to the President, the National Security Council, or the Secretary of Defense, as the case may be. The Chairman shall establish procedures to ensure that the presentation of his own advice to the President, the National Security Council, or the Secretary of Defense is not unduly delayed by reason of the submission of the individual advice or opinion of another member of the Joint Chiefs of Staff.

e. *Advice on Request.* The members of the Joint Chiefs of Staff, individually or collectively, in their capacity as military advisers, shall provide advice to the President, the National Security Council, or the Secretary of Defense on a particular matter when the President, the National Security Council, or the Secretary requests such advice.

f. *Recommendations to Congress.* After first informing the Secretary of Defense, a member of the Joint Chiefs of Staff may make such recommendations to Congress relating to the Department of Defense as he considers appropriate.

g. *Meetings of JCS.* The Chairman shall convene regular meetings of the Joint Chiefs of Staff. Subject to the authority, direction, and control of the President and the Secretary of Defense, the Chairman shall preside over the Joint Chiefs of Staff; provide agenda for the meetings of the Joint Chiefs of Staff (including, as the Chairman considers appropriate, any subject for the agenda recommended by any other member of the Joint Chiefs of Staff); assist the Joint Chiefs of Staff in carrying on their business as promptly as practicable; and determine when issues under consideration by the Joint Chiefs of Staff shall be decided.

Sec. 155. *Joint Staff*

a. *Appointment of Officers to Joint Staff.* There is a Joint Staff under the Chairman of the Joint Chiefs of Staff. The Joint Staff assists the Chairman and, subject to the authority, direction, and control of the Chairman, the other members of the Joint Chiefs of Staff in carrying out their responsibilities. Officers of the armed forces (other than the Coast Guard) assigned to serve on the Joint Staff shall be selected by the Chairman in approximately equal numbers from the Army; the Navy and the Marine Corps; and the Air Force. Selection of officers of an armed force to serve on the Joint Staff shall be made by the Chairman from a list of officers submitted by the Secretary of the military department having jurisdiction over that armed force. Each officer whose name is submitted shall be among those officers considered to be the most outstanding officers of that armed force. The Chairman may specify the number of officers to be included on any such list.

b. *Director.* The Chairman of the Joint Chiefs of Staff, after consultation with the other members of the Joint Chiefs of Staff and with the approval of the Secretary of Defense, may select an officer to serve as Director of the Joint Staff.

c. *Management of Joint Staff.* The Chairman of the Joint Chiefs of Staff manages the Joint Staff and the Director of the Joint Staff. The Joint Staff shall perform such duties as the Chairman prescribes and shall perform such duties under such procedures as the Chairman prescribes.

d. *Operation of Joint Staff.* The Secretary of Defense shall ensure that the Joint Staff is independently organized and operated so that the Joint Staff supports the

Chairman of the Joint Chiefs of Staff in meeting the congressional purpose . . . to provide: for the unified strategic direction of the combatant forces; for their operation under unified command; and for their integration into an efficient team of land, naval, and air forces.

e. *Prohibition of Function as Armed Forces General Staff.* The Joint Staff shall not operate or be organized as an overall Armed Forces General Staff and shall have no executive authority. The Joint Staff may be organized and may operate along conventional staff lines.

f. *Tour of Duty of Joint Staff Officers.* An officer who is assigned or detailed to permanent duty on the Joint Staff may not serve for a tour of duty of more than four years. However, such a tour of duty may be extended with the approval of the Secretary of Defense. In accordance with procedures established by the Secretary of Defense, the Chairman of the Joint Chiefs of Staff may suspend from duty and recommend the reassignment of any officer assigned to the Joint Staff. Upon receipt of such a recommendation, the Secretary concerned shall promptly reassign the officer. An officer completing a tour of duty with the Joint Staff may not be assigned or detailed to permanent duty on the Joint Staff within two years after relief from that duty except with the approval of the Secretary. [These restrictions] . . . do not apply in time of war or during a national emergency declared by the President or Congress.

g. *Composition of Joint Staff.* The Joint Staff is composed of all members of the armed forces and civilian employees assigned or detailed to permanent duty in the executive part of the Department

of Defense to perform the functions and duties prescribed under subsections (a) and (c). The Joint Staff does not include members of the armed forces or civilian employees assigned or detailed to permanent duty in a military department.

Sec. 161. *Combatant commands: establishment*

a. *Unified and Specified Combatant Commands.* With the advice and assistance of the Chairman of the Joint Chiefs of Staff, the President, through the Secretary of Defense, shall establish unified combatant commands and specified combatant commands to perform military missions and prescribe the force structure of those commands.

b. *Periodic Review.* The Chairman periodically (and not less often than every two years) shall review the missions, responsibilities (including geographic boundaries), and force structure of each combatant command and recommend to the President, through the Secretary of Defense, any changes to such missions, responsibilities, and force structures as may be necessary. Except during time of hostilities or imminent threat of hostilities, the President shall notify Congress not more than 60 days after establishing a new combatant command or significantly revising the missions, responsibilities, or force structure of an existing combatant command.

c. *Definitions.* . . . The term "unified combatant command" means a military command which has broad, continuing missions and which is composed of forces from two or more military departments. The term "specified combatant command" means a military command which has broad, continuing missions and which is normally composed of forces from a single military department. The term "combatant command" means a unified combatant command or a specified combatant command.

Sec. 162. *Combatant commands: assigned forces; chain of command*

a. *Assignment of Forces. . . .* The Secretaries of the military departments shall assign all forces under their jurisdiction to unified and specified combatant commands or to the United States element of the North American Aerospace Defense Command to perform missions assigned to those commands. Such assignments shall be made as directed by the Secretary of Defense, including direction as to the command to which forces are to be assigned. The Secretary of Defense shall ensure that such assignments are consistent with the force structure prescribed by the President for each combatant command. Except as otherwise directed by the Secretary of Defense, forces to be assigned by the Secretaries of the military departments to the combatant commands or to the United States element of the North American Aerospace Defense Command . . . do not include forces assigned to carry out functions of the Secretary of a military department . . . or forces assigned to multinational peacekeeping organizations. A force assigned to a combatant command or to the United States element of the North American Aerospace Defense Command under this section may be transferred from the command to which it is assigned only by authority of the Secretary of Defense and under procedures prescribed by the Secretary and approved by the President. Except as otherwise directed by the Secretary of Defense, all forces oper-

ating within the geographic area assigned to a unified combatant command shall be assigned to, and under the command of, the commander of that command. The preceding sentence applies to forces assigned to a specified combatant command only as prescribed by the Secretary of Defense.

b. *Chain of Command.* Unless otherwise directed by the President, the chain of command to a unified or specified combatant command runs from the President to the Secretary of Defense; and from the Secretary of Defense to the commander of the combatant command.

The Military Service Departments

Title 50

Sec. 409. *Definitions of military departments*

a. The term "Department of the Army" . . . shall be construed to mean the Department of the Army at the seat of the government and all field headquarters, forces, reserve components, installations, activities, and functions under the control or supervision of the Department of the Army.

b. The term "Department of the Navy" . . . shall be construed to mean the Department of the Navy at the seat of the government; the headquarters, United States Marine Corps; the entire operating forces of the United States Navy, including naval aviation, and of the United States Marine Corps, including the reserve components of such forces; all field activities, headquarters, forces, bases, installations, activities, and functions under the control or supervision of the Department of the Navy; and the United States Coast Guard when operating as a part of the Navy pursuant to law.

c. The term "Department of the Air Force" . . . shall be construed to mean the Department of the Air Force at the seat of the government and all field headquarters, forces, reserve components, installations, activities, and functions under the control or supervision of the Department of the Air Force.

Title 10

The Department of the Army

Sec. 3011. *Organization* The Department of the Army is separately organized under the Secretary of the Army. It operates under the authority, direction, and control of the Secretary of Defense.

Sec. 3013. *Secretary of the Army*

a. There is a Secretary of the Army, appointed from civilian life by the President, by and with the advice and consent of the Senate. The Secretary is the head of the Department of the Army. A person may not be appointed as Secretary of the Army within five years after relief from active duty as a commissioned officer of a regular component of an armed force.

b. Subject to the authority, direction, and control of the Secretary of Defense and subject to the provisions of . . . this title, the Secretary of the Army is responsible for, and has the authority necessary to conduct, all affairs of the Department of the Army, including the following functions: recruiting; organizing; supplying; equipping (including research and development); training, servicing, mobilizing; demobilizing; administering (including the morale and welfare of personnel); maintaining; the construction, outfitting, and repair of military equipment; the construction, maintenance, and repair of buildings, structures, and utilities and the acquisi-

tion of real property and interests in real property necessary to carry out the responsibilities specified in this section.

c. Subject to the authority, direction, and control of the Secretary of Defense, the Secretary of the Army is also responsible to the Secretary of Defense for the functioning and efficiency of the Department of the Army; the formulation of policies and programs by the Department of the Army that are fully consistent with national security objectives and policies established by the President or the Secretary of Defense; the effective and timely implementation of policy, program, and budget decisions and instructions of the President or the Secretary of Defense relating to the functions of the Department of the Army; carrying out the functions of the Department of the Army so as to fulfill (to the maximum extent practicable) the current and future operational requirements of the unified and specified combatant commands; effective cooperation and coordination between the Department of the Army and the other military departments and agencies of the Department of Defense to provide for more effective, efficient, and economical administration and to eliminate duplication; the presentation and justification of the positions of the Department of the Army on the plans, programs, and policies of the Department of Defense; and the effective supervision and control of the intelligence activities of the Department of the Army.

d. The Secretary of the Army is also responsible for such other activities as may be prescribed by law or by the President or Secretary of Defense.

e. After first informing the Secretary of Defense, the Secretary of the Army may make such recommendations to Congress relating to the Department of Defense as he considers appropriate.

f. The Secretary of the Army may assign such of his functions, powers, and duties as he considers appropriate to the Under Secretary of the Army and to the Assistant Secretaries of the Army. Officers of the Army shall, as directed by the Secretary, report on any matter to the Secretary, the Under Secretary, or any Assistant Secretary.

g. The Secretary of the Army may assign, detail, and prescribe the duties of members of the Army and civilian personnel of the Department of the Army; change the title of any officer or activity of the Department of the Army not prescribed by law; and prescribe regulations to carry out his functions, powers, and duties under this title.

Sec. 3033. *Chief of Staff*

a. There is a Chief of Staff of the Army, appointed for a period of four years by the President, by and with the advice and consent of the Senate, from the general officers of the Army. He serves at the pleasure of the President. In time of war or during a national emergency declared by Congress, he may be reappointed for a term of not more than four years. The President may appoint an officer as Chief of Staff only if the officer has had significant experience in joint duty assignments; and such experience includes at least one full tour of duty in a joint duty assignment . . . as a general officer. The President may waive . . . [this requirement] in the case of an officer if the President determines such action is necessary in the national interest.

b. The Chief of Staff, while so serving, has the grade of general without vacating his permanent grade.

c. Except as otherwise prescribed by law . . . , the Chief of Staff performs his duties under the authority, direction, and control of the Secretary of the Army and is directly responsible to the Secretary.

d. Subject to the authority, direction, and control of the Secretary of the Army, the Chief of Staff shall preside over the Army Staff; transmit the plans and recommendations of the Army Staff to the Secretary and advise the Secretary with regard to such plans and recommendations; after approval of the plans or recommendations of the Army Staff by the Secretary, act as the agent of the Secretary in carrying them into effect; exercise supervision, consistent with the authority assigned to commanders of unified or specified combatant commands . . . over such of the members and organizations of the Army as the Secretary determines; perform the duties prescribed for him by . . . provisions of law; and perform such other military duties, not otherwise assigned by law, as are assigned to him by the President, the Secretary of Defense, or the Secretary of the Army.

e. The Chief of Staff shall also perform the duties prescribed for him as a member of the Joint Chiefs of Staff. . . . To the extent that such action does not impair the independence of the Chief of Staff in the performance of his duties as a member of the Joint Chiefs of Staff, the Chief of Staff shall inform the Secretary regarding military advice rendered by members of the Joint Chiefs of Staff on matters affecting the Department of the Army. Subject to the authority, direction, and control of the Secretary of Defense, the Chief of Staff shall keep the Secretary of the Army fully informed of significant military operations affecting the duties and responsibilities of the Secretary.

The Department of the Navy

Sec. 5011. *Organization* The Department of the Navy is separately organized under the Secretary of the Navy. It operates under the authority, direction, and control of the Secretary of Defense.

Sec. 5013. *Secretary of the Navy*

a. There is a Secretary of the Navy, appointed from civilian life by the President, by and with the advice and consent of the Senate. The Secretary is the head of the Department of the Navy. A person may not be appointed as Secretary of the Navy within five years after relief from active duty as a commissioned officer of a regular component of an armed force.

b. Subject to the authority, direction, and control of the Secretary of Defense and subject to the provisions of . . . this title, the Secretary of the Navy is responsible for, and has the authority necessary to conduct, all affairs of the Department of the Navy, including the following functions: recruiting; organizing; supplying; equipping (including research and development); training, servicing, mobilizing; demobilizing; administering (including the morale and welfare of personnel); maintaining; the construction, outfitting, and repair of military equipment; the construction, maintenance, and repair of buildings, structures, and utilities and the acquisition of real property and interests in real property necessary to carry out the responsibilities specified in this section.

c. Subject to the authority, direction, and control of the Secretary of Defense, the Secretary of the Navy is also responsible to the Secretary of Defense for the

functioning and efficiency of the Department of the Navy; the formulation of policies and programs by the Department of the Navy that are fully consistent with national security objectives and policies established by the President or the Secretary of Defense; the effective and timely implementation of policy, program, and budget decisions and instructions of the President or the Secretary of Defense relating to the functions of the Department of the Navy; carrying out the functions of the Department of the Navy so as to fulfill (to the maximum extent practicable) the current and future operational requirements of the unified and specified combatant commands; effective cooperation and coordination between the Department of the Navy and the other military departments and agencies of the Department of Defense to provide for more effective, efficient, and economical administration and to eliminate duplication; the presentation and justification of the positions of the Department of the Navy on the plans, programs, and policies of the Department of Defense; and the effective supervision and control of the intelligence activities of the Department of the Navy.

d. The Secretary of the Navy is also responsible for such other activities as may be prescribed by law or by the President or Secretary of Defense.

e. After first informing the Secretary of Defense, the Secretary of the Navy may make such recommendations to Congress relating to the Department of Defense as he considers appropriate.

f. The Secretary of the Navy may assign such of his functions, powers, and duties as he considers appropriate to the Under Secretary of the Navy and to the Assistant Secretaries of the Navy. Officers of the Navy and the Marine

Corps shall, as directed by the Secretary, report on any matter to the Secretary, the Under Secretary, or any Assistant Secretary.

g. The Secretary of the Navy may assign, detail, and prescribe the duties of members of the Navy and Marine Corps and civilian personnel of the Department of the Navy; change the title of any officer or activity of the Department of the Navy not prescribed by law; and prescribe regulations to carry out his functions, powers, and duties under this title.

Sec. 5033. *Chief of Naval Operations*

a. There is a Chief of Naval Operations, appointed by the President, by and with the advice and consent of the Senate. The Chief of Naval Operations shall be appointed for a term of four years, from officers on the active-duty list in the line of the Navy who are eligible to command at sea and who hold the grade of rear admiral or above. He serves at the pleasure of the President. In time of war or during a national emergency declared by Congress, he may be reappointed for a term of not more than four years. The President may appoint an officer as the Chief of Naval Operations only if the officer has had significant experience in joint duty assignments; and such experience includes at least one full tour of duty in a joint duty assignment . . . as a flag officer. The President may waive . . . [this requirement] in the case of an officer if the President determines such action is necessary in the national interest.

b. The Chief of Naval Operations, while so serving, has the grade of admiral without vacating his permanent grade. In the performance of his duties within the Department of the Navy, the Chief of Naval Operations takes precedence above all other officers of the naval service.

c. Except as otherwise prescribed by law . . . the Chief of Naval Operations performs his duties under the authority, direction, and control of the Secretary of the Navy and is directly responsible to the Secretary.

d. Subject to the authority, direction, and control of the Secretary of the Navy, the Chief of Naval Operations shall preside over the Office of the Chief of Naval Operations; transmit the plans and recommendations of the Office of the Chief of Naval Operations to the Secretary and advise the Secretary with regard to such plans and recommendations; after approval of the plans or recommendations of the Office of the Chief of Naval Operations by the Secretary, act as the agent of the Secretary in carrying them into effect; exercise supervision, consistent with the authority assigned to commanders of unified or specified combatant commands . . . over such of the members and organizations of the Navy and the Marine Corps as the Secretary determines; perform the duties prescribed for him by . . . this title and other provisions of law; and perform such other military duties, not otherwise assigned by law, as are assigned to him by the President, the Secretary of Defense, or the Secretary of the Navy.

e. The Chief of Naval Operations shall also perform the duties prescribed for him as a member of the Joint Chiefs of Staff. . . . To the extent that such action does not impair the independence of the Chief of Naval Operations in the performance of his duties as a member of the Joint Chiefs of Staff, the Chief of Naval Operations shall inform the Secretary regarding military advice rendered by members of the Joint Chiefs of

Staff on matters affecting the Department of the Navy. Subject to the authority, direction, and control of the Secretary of Defense, the Chief of Naval Operations shall keep the Secretary of the Navy fully informed of significant military operations affecting the duties and responsibilities of the Secretary.

Sec. 5043. *Commandant of the Marine Corps*

a. There is a Commandant of the Marine Corps, appointed by the President, by and with the advice and consent of the Senate. The Commandant shall be appointed for a term of four years from officers on the active-duty list of the Marine Corps not below the grade of colonel. He serves at the pleasure of the President. In time of war or during a national emergency declared by Congress, he may be reappointed for a term of not more than four years. The President may appoint an officer as Commandant of the Marine Corps only if the officer has had significant experience in joint duty assignments; and such experience includes at least one full tour of duty in a joint duty assignment . . . as a general officer. The President may waive . . . [this requirement] in the case of an officer if the President determines such action is necessary in the national interest.

b. The Commandant of the Marine Corps, while so serving, has the grade of general without vacating his permanent grade.

c. Repealed. . . .

d. Except as otherwise prescribed by law . . . the Commandant performs his duties under the authority, direction, and control of the Secretary of the Navy and is directly responsible to the Secretary.

e. Subject to the authority, direction, and control of the Secretary of the Navy, the Commandant shall preside over the Headquarters, Marine Corps; transmit the plans and recommendations of the Headquarters, Marine Corps, to the Secretary and advise the Secretary with regard to such plans and recommendations; after approval of the plans or recommendations of the Headquarters, Marine Corps, by the Secretary, act as the agent of the Secretary in carrying them into efect; exercise supervision, consistent with the authority assigned to commanders of unified or specified combatant commands under chapter 6 of this title, over such of the members and organizations of the Marine Corps and the Navy as the Secretary determines; perform the duties prescribed for him . . . and other provisions of law; and perform such other military duties, not otherwise assigned by law, as are assigned to him by the President, the Secretary of Defense, or the Secretary of the Navy.

f. The Commandant shall also perform the duties prescribed for him as a member of the Joint Chiefs of Staff. . . . To the extent that such action does not impair the independence of the Commandant in the performance of his duties as a member of the Joint Chiefs of Staff, the Commandant shall inform the Secretary regarding military advice rendered by members of the Joint Chiefs of Staff on matters affecting the Department of the Navy. Subject to the authority, direction, and control of the Secretary of Defense, the Commandant shall keep the Secretary of the Navy fully informed of significant military operations affecting the duties and responsibilities of the Secretary.

The Department of the Air Force

Sec. 8011. *Organization* The Department of the Air Force is separately organized under the Secretary of the Air Force. It operates under the authority, direction, and control of the Secretary of Defense.

Sec. 8013. *Secretary of the Air Force*

a. There is a Secretary of the Air Force, appointed from civilian life by the President, by and with the advice and consent of the Senate. The Secretary is the head of the Department of the Air Force. A person may not be appointed as Secretary of the Air Force within five years after relief from active duty as a commissioned officer of a regular component of an armed force. Subject to the authority, direction, and control of the Secretary of Defense and subject to the provisions of . . . this title, the Secretary of the Air Force is responsible for, and has the authority necessary to conduct, all affairs of the Department of the Air Force, including the following functions: recruiting; organizing; supplying; equipping (including research and development); training, servicing, mobilizing; demobilizing; administering (including the morale and welfare of personnel); maintaining; the construction, outfitting, and repair of military equipment; the construction, maintenance, and repair of buildings, structures, and utilities and the acquisition of real property and interests in real property necessary to carry out the responsibilities specified in this section.

c. Subject to the authority, direction, and control of the Secretary of Defense, the Secretary of the Air Force is also responsible to the Secretary of Defense for the functioning and efficiency of the Department of the Air Force; the formulation of policies and programs by the Department of the Air Force that are fully consistent with national security objectives and policies established by the President or the Secretary of Defense; the effective and timely implementation of policy, program, and budget decisions and instructions of the President or the Secretary of Defense relating to the functions of the Department of the Air Force; carrying out the functions of the Department of the Air Force so as to fulfill (to the maximum extent practicable) the current and future operational requirements of the unified and specified combatant commands; effective cooperation and coordination between the Department of the Air Force and the other military departments and agencies of the Department of Defense to provide for more effective, efficient, and economical administration and to eliminate duplication; the presentation and justification of the positions of the Department of the Air Force on the plans, programs, and policies of the Department of Defense; and the effective supervision and control of the intelligence activities of the Department of the Air Force.

d. The Secretary of the Air Force is also responsible for such other activities as may be prescribed by law or by the President or Secretary of Defense.

e. After first informing the Secretary of Defense, the Secretary of the Air Force may make such recommendations to Congress relating to the Department of Defense as he considers appropriate.

f. The Secretary of the Air Force may assign such of his functions, powers, and duties as he considers appropriate to the Under Secretary of the Air Force and to the Assistant Secretaries of the Air Force. Officers of the Air Force shall, as directed by the Secretary, report on any matter to the Secretary, the Under Secretary, or any Assistant Secretary.

g. The Secretary of the Air Force may assign, detail, and prescribe the duties of members of the Air Force and civilian personnel of the Department of the Air Force; change the title of any officer or activity of the Department of the Air Force not prescribed by law; and prescribe regulations to carry out his functions, powers, and duties under this title.

Sec. 8033. *Chief of Staff*

a. There is a Chief of Staff of the Air Force, appointed for a period of four years by the President, by and with the advice and consent of the Senate, from the general officers of the Air Force. He serves at the pleasure of the President. In time of war or during a national emergency declared by Congress, he may be reappointed for a term of not more than four years. The President may appoint an officer as Chief of Staff only if the officer has had significant experience in joint duty assignments; and such experience includes at least one full tour of duty in a joint duty assignment . . . as a general officer. The President may waive . . . [this requirement] in the case of an officer if the President determines such action is necessary in the national interest.

b. The Chief of Staff, while so serving, has the grade of general without vacating his permanent grade.

c. Except as otherwise prescribed by law . . . the Chief of Staff performs his duties under the authority, direction, and control of the Secretary of the Air Force and is directly responsible to the Secretary.

d. Subject to the authority, direction, and control of the Secretary of the Air Force, the Chief of Staff shall preside over the Air Staff; transmit the plans and recommendations of the Air Staff to the Secretary and advise the Secretary with regard to such plans and recommendations; after approval of the plans or recommendations of the Air Staff by the Secretary, act as the agent of the Secretary in carrying them into effect; exercise supervision, consistent with the authority assigned to commanders of unified or specified combatant commands under chapter 6 of this title, over such of the members and organizations of the Air Force as the Secretary determines; perform the duties prescribed for him by . . . provisions of law; and perform such other military duties, not otherwise assigned by law, as are assigned to him by the President, the Secretary of Defense, or the Secretary of the Air Force.

e. The Chief of Staff shall also perform the duties prescribed for him as a member of the Joint Chiefs of Staff. . . . To the extent that such action does not impair the independence of the Chief of Staff in the performance of his duties as a member of the Joint Chiefs of Staff, the Chief of Staff shall inform the Secretary regarding military advice rendered by members of the Joint Chiefs of Staff on matters affecting the Department of the Air Force. Subject to the authority, direction, and control of the Secretary of Defense, the Chief of Staff shall keep the Secretary of the Air Force fully informed of significant military operations affecting the duties and responsibilities of the Secretary.

3. *The National Security Council*
(1947)

In the years following World War II the need became apparent for an organization within the Executive Office of the President that would coordinate efforts taken by the State and Defense Departments and other cabinet departments and government agencies in the foreign policy and national security arena. The work of the National Security Council (NSC) and its staff would be a mechanism available for presidential use not only in crises, but also in day-to-day policy matters orchestrated from the White House. With the help of the NSC staff the national security advisor also provides direct input to the president. In practice each president tends to put a particular stamp on the way the NSC performs its work and on the role played by the national security advisor. The NSC has been modified by statute since its original formulation in 1947, its present form described in this excerpt from Title 50, U.S. Code.

Sec. 401. *Congressional declaration of purpose.* In enacting this legislation, it is the intent of Congress to provide a comprehensive program for the future security of the United States; to provide for the establishment of integrated policies and procedures for the departments, agencies, and functions of the Government relating to the national security; to provide a Department of Defense, including the three military Departments of the Army, the Navy (including naval aviation and the United States Marine Corps), and the Air Force under the direction, authority, and control of the Secretary of Defense; to provide that each military department shall be separately organized under its own Secretary and shall function under the direction, authority, and control of the Secretary of Defense; to provide for their unified direction under civilian control of the Secretary of Defense but not to merge these departments or services; to provide for the establishment of unified or specified combatant commands, and a clear and direct line of command to such commands; to eliminate unnecessary duplication in the Department of Defense, and particularly in the field of research and engineering by vesting its overall direction and control in the Secretary of Defense; to provide more effective, efficient, and economical administration in the Department of Defense; to provide for the unified strategic direction of the combatant forces, for their operation under unified command, and for their integration into an efficient team of land, naval, and air forces but not to establish a single Chief of Staff over the armed forces nor an overall armed forces general staff. . . .

Sec. 402. *National Security Council*

a. *Establishment; presiding officer; functions; composition:* There is established a council to be known as the National Security Council (hereinafter in this section referred to as the "Council"). The President of the United States shall preside over meetings of the Council: Provided, That in his absence he may designate a member of the Council to preside in his place. The function of the Council shall be to advise the President with respect to the integration of domestic, foreign, and military policies relating to the national security so as to enable the military services and the other departments and agencies of the Government to cooperate more effectively in matters involving the national security. The Council shall be composed of: (1) the President; (2) the Vice President; (3) the Secretary of State; (4) the Secretary of Defense; (5) the Director for Mutual Security; (6) the Chairman of the National Security Resources Board; and (7) the Secretaries and Under Secretaries of other executive departments and of the military departments, the Chairman of the Munitions Board, and the Chairman of the Research and Development Board, when appointed by the President by and with the advice and consent of the Senate, to serve at his pleasure.

b. *Additional functions:* In addition to performing such other functions as the President may direct, for the purpose of more effectively coordinating the policies and functions of the departments and agencies of the Government relating to the national security, it shall, subject to the direction of the President, be the duty of the Council: (1) to assess and appraise the objectives, commitments, and risks of the United States in relation to our actual and potential military power, in the interest of national security, for the purpose of making recommendations to the President in connection therewith; and (2) to consider policies on matters of common interest to the departments and agencies of the Government concerned with the national security, and to make recommendations to the President in connection therewith.

c. *Executive secretary; appointment; staff employees:* The Council shall have a staff to be headed by a civilian executive secretary who shall be appointed by the President. The executive secretary, subject to the direction of the

Council, is authorized . . . to appoint and fix the compensation of such personnel as may be necessary to perform such duties as may be prescribed by the Council in connection with the performance of its functions.

d. *Recommendations and reports:* The Council shall, from time to time, make such recommendations, and such other reports to the President as it deems appropriate or as the President may require.

e. *Participation of Chairman or Vice Chairman of Joint Chiefs of Staff:* The Chairman (or in his absence the Vice Chairman) of the Joint Chiefs of Staff may, in his role as principal military adviser to the National Security Council and subject to the direction of the President, attend and participate in meetings of the National Security Council.

f. *Participation by Director of National Drug Control Policy:* The Director of National Drug Control Policy may, in the role of the Director as principal adviser to the National Security Council on national drug control policy, and subject to the direction of the President, attend and participate in meetings of the National Security Council.

g. *Board for Low Intensity Conflict:* The President shall establish within the National Security Council a board to be known as the "Board for Low Intensity Conflict". The principal function of the board shall be to coordinate the policies of the United States for low intensity conflict.

h. *Committee on Foreign Intelligence:* (1) There is established within the National Security Council a committee to be known as the Committee on Foreign Intelligence (in this subsection referred to as the "Committee"). (2) The Committee shall be composed of the following: (A) The Director of Central Intelligence. (B) The Secretary of State.

(C) The Secretary of Defense. (D) The Assistant to the President for National Security Affairs, who shall serve as the chairperson of the Committee. (E) Such other members as the President may designate. (3) The function of the Committee shall be to assist the Council in its activities by: (A) identifying the intelligence required to address the national security interests of the United States as specified by the President; (B) establishing priorities (including funding priorities) among the programs, projects, and activities that address such interests and requirements; and (C) establishing policies relating to the conduct of intelligence activities of the United States, including appropriate roles and missions for the elements of the intelligence community and appropriate targets of intelligence collection activities. (4) In carrying out its function, the Committee shall: (A) conduct an annual review of the national security interests of the United States; (B) identify on an annual basis, and at such other times as the Council may require, the intelligence required to meet such interests and establish an order of priority for the collection and analysis of such intelligence; and (C) conduct an annual review of the elements of the intelligence community in order to determine the success of such elements in collecting, analyzing, and disseminating the intelligence identified under subparagraph (B). (5) The Committee shall submit each year to the Council and to the Director of Central Intelligence a comprehensive report on its activities during the preceding year. . . .

i. *Committee on Transnational Threats:* (1) There is established within the National Security Council a committee to be known as the Committee on Transnational Threats (in this subsec-

tion referred to as the "Committee"). (2) The Committee shall include the following members: (A) The Director of Central Intelligence. (B) The Secretary of State. (C) The Secretary of Defense. (D) The Attorney General. (E) The Assistant to the President for National Security Affairs, who shall serve as the chairperson of the Committee. (F) Such other members as the President may designate. (3) The function of the Committee shall be to coordinate and direct the activities of the United States Government relating to combatting transnational threats. (4) In carrying out its function, the Committee shall: (A) identify transnational threats; (B) develop strategies to enable the United States Government to respond to transnational threats . . . ; (C) monitor implementation of such strategies; (D) make recommendations as to appropriate responses to specific transnational threats; (E) assist in the resolution of operational and policy differences among Federal departments and agencies in their responses to transnational threats; (F) develop policies and procedures to ensure the effective sharing of information about transnational threats among Federal departments and agencies, including law enforcement agencies and the elements of the intelligence community; and (G) develop guidelines to enhance and improve the coordination of activities of Federal law enforcement agencies and elements of the intelligence community outside the United States with respect to transnational threats. (5) For purposes of this subsection, the term "transnational threat" means the following: (A) Any transnational activity (including international terrorism, narcotics trafficking, the proliferation of weapons of mass destruction and the delivery systems for such weapons, and organized crime) that threatens the national security of the United States. (B) Any individual or group that engages in an activity referred to [above] in subparagraph (A).

j. *Participation of Director of Central Intelligence:* The Director of Central Intelligence (or, in the Director's absence, the Deputy Director of Central Intelligence) may, in the performance of the Director's duties under this Act and subject to the direction of the President, attend and participate in meetings of the National Security Council.

k. *Special Adviser to the President on International Religious Freedom:* It is the sense of the Congress that there should be within the staff of the National Security Council a Special Adviser to the President on International Religious Freedom, whose position should be comparable to that of a director within the Executive Office of the President. The Special Adviser should serve as a resource for executive branch officials, compiling and maintaining information on the facts and circumstances of violations of religious freedom . . . and making policy recommendations. The Special Adviser should serve as liaison with the Ambassador at Large for International Religious Freedom, the United States Commission on International Religious Freedom, Congress and, as advisable, religious nongovernmental organizations.

Sec. 402a.-Coordination of counterintelligence activities

a. *Establishment of Counterintelligence Policy Board:* There is established within the executive branch of Government a National Counterintelligence Policy Board (in this section referred to as the "Board"). The Board shall report to the President through the National Security Council.

b. *Function of Board:* The Board shall serve as the principal mechanism for: (1) developing policies and procedures for the approval of the President to govern the conduct of counterintelligence activities; and (2) resolving conflicts, as directed by the President, which may arise between elements of the Government which carry out such activities. . . .

4. *The Homeland Security Act*

(2002)

Responding not only to the terrorist attacks on the World Trade Center in New York and the Pentagon in Washington, D.C., on September 11, 2001, but also to a continuation of such threats, the Bush administration and Congress agreed to establish a new cabinet department and a Homeland Security Council. The president may call the secretary of homeland security to sit on the National Security Council; however, that body remains for the most part externally focused. The new Homeland Security Council includes both the secretary of homeland security and the secretary of defense as statutory members. The Homeland Security Department includes a number of agencies previously part of other cabinet departments. These functions are reflected in the titles of various undersecretaries and other officers specified in this excerpt from the Homeland Security Act (Public Law 107-296, 107th Congress).

An Act: To establish the Department of Homeland Security, and for other purposes. Be it enacted by the Senate and House of Representatives of the United States of America in Congress assembled. . . .

Title I—Department of Homeland Security

Sec. 101. *Executive Department; Mission.*

a. *Establishment.*—There is established a Department of Homeland Security, as an executive department of the United States. . . .
b. *Mission.*—(1) In general: The primary mission of the Department is to: (A) prevent terrorist attacks within the United States; (B) reduce the vulnerability of the United States to terrorism; (C) minimize the damage, and assist in the recovery, from terrorist attacks that do occur within the United States; (D) carry out all functions of entities transferred to the Department, including by acting as a focal point regarding natural and manmade crises and emergency planning; (E) ensure that the functions of the agencies and subdivisions within the Department that are not related directly to securing the homeland are not diminished or neglected except by a specific explicit Act of Congress; (F) ensure that the overall economic security of the United States is not diminished by efforts, activities, and programs aimed at securing the homeland; and (G) monitor connections between illegal drug trafficking and terrorism, coordinate efforts to sever such connections, and otherwise contribute to efforts to interdict illegal drug trafficking. (2) *Responsibility for investigating and prosecuting terrorism:* Except as specifically provided by law with respect to entities transferred to the Department under this Act, primary responsibility for investigating and prosecuting acts of terrorism shall be vested not in the Department, but rather in Federal, State, and local law enforcement agencies with jurisdiction over the acts in question.

Sec. 102. *Secretary; Functions.*

a. *Secretary:* (1) *In general:* There is a Secretary of Homeland Security, appointed by the President, by and with the advice and consent of the Senate. (2) *Head of department:* The Secretary is the head of the Department and shall have direction, authority, and control over it. (3) *Functions vested in secretary:* All functions of all officers, employees, and organizational units of the Department are vested in the Secretary.
b. *Functions:* (1) except as otherwise provided by this Act, may delegate any of the Secretary's functions to any officer, employee, or organizational unit of the Department; (2) shall have the authority to make contracts, grants, and cooperative agreements, and to enter into agreements with other executive agencies, as may be necessary and proper to carry out the Secretary's responsibilities under this Act or otherwise provided by law; and (3) shall take reasonable steps to ensure that information systems and databases of the Department are compatible with each other and with appropriate databases of other Departments.
c. *Coordination With Non-Federal Entities:* With respect to homeland security, the Secretary shall coordinate through the Office of State and Local Coordination . . . with State and local government personnel, agencies, and authorities, with the private sector, and with other entities. . . .

DEPARTMENT OF HOMELAND SECURITY

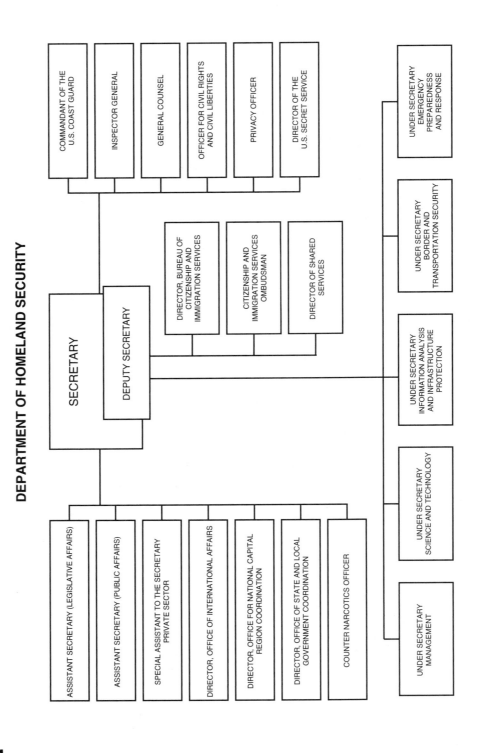

d. *Meetings of National Security Council.*— The Secretary may, subject to the direction of the President, attend and participate in meetings of the National Security Council. . . .

Sec. 103. *Other Officers.*

a. *Deputy Secretary; Under Secretaries:* There are the following officers, appointed by the President, by and with the advice and consent of the Senate: (1) A Deputy Secretary of Homeland Security, who shall be the Secretary's first assistant. . . . (2) An Under Secretary for Information Analysis and Infrastructure Protection. (3) An Under Secretary for Science and Technology. (4) An Under Secretary for Border and Transportation Security. (5) An Under Secretary for Emergency Preparedness and Response. (6) A Director of the Bureau of Citizenship and Immigration Services. (7) An Under Secretary for Management. (8) Not more than 12 Assistant Secretaries. (9) A General Counsel, who shall be the chief legal officer of the Department.

b. *Inspector General:* There is an Inspector General. . . .

c. *Commandant of the Coast Guard:* To assist the Secretary in the performance of the Secretary's functions, there is a Commandant of the Coast Guard, who . . . shall report directly to the Secretary. . . .

d. *Other Officers:* To assist the Secretary in the performance of the Secretary's functions, there are the following officers, appointed by the President: (1) A Director of the Secret Service. (2) A Chief Information Officer. (3) A Chief Human Capital Officer. (4) A Chief Financial Officer. (5) An Officer for Civil Rights and Civil Liberties. . . .

Title IX—National Homeland Security Council

Sec. 901. *National Homeland Security Council.* There is established within the Executive Office of the President a council to be known as the "Homeland Security Council" (in this title referred to as the "Council").

Sec. 902. *Function.* The function of the Council shall be to advise the President on homeland security matters.

Sec. 903. *Membership.* The members of the Council shall be the following: (1) The President. (2) The Vice President. (3) The Secretary of Homeland Security. (4) The Attorney General. (5) The Secretary of Defense. (6) Such other individuals as may be designated by the President.

Sec. 904. *Other Functions and Activities.* For the purpose of more effectively coordinating the policies and functions of the United States Government relating to homeland security, the Council shall: (1) assess the objectives, commitments, and risks of the United States in the interest of homeland security and to make resulting recommendations to the President; (2) oversee and review homeland security policies of the Federal Government and to make resulting recommendations to the President; and (3) perform such other functions as the President may direct.

Sec. 905. *Staff Composition.* The Council shall have a staff, the head of which shall be a civilian Executive Secretary, who shall be appointed by the President. . . .

Sec. 906. *Relation to the National Security Council.* The President may convene joint meetings of the Homeland Security Council and the National Security Council with participation by members of either Council or as the President may otherwise direct.

Chapter 18

International Organizations

The United States belongs to a large number of international organizations, only a few of which are represented here. We have selected those with the greatest role in foreign policy and national security. We begin with the post–World War I Covenant of the League of Nations (1919) and proceed to its post–World War II successor document, the United Nations Charter (1945). Indeed, the UN Charter was constructed to correct for what were understood to be shortcomings in the League. Thus, *collective defense* as in alliances or other coalitions (Article 51) was added to *collective security* understood as international law enforcement. Hemispheric relations formalized in the late nineteenth century in what came to be known as the Pan American Union were expanded substantially as an Inter-American "system" by the Act of Chapultepec, a declaration produced by a multilateral hemispheric meeting held in Mexico (1945), the Rio Treaty (1947), and finally the Organization of American States (OAS, 1948). Concerning Europe, the North Atlantic Treaty Organization (1949) remains most important in terms of U.S. participation in European security arrangements. Another regional organization, also compatible with Article 52 of the UN Charter is the Organization for Security and Cooperation in Europe (OSCE). The OSCE began in 1973 as a "process" of periodic meetings of the Conference on Security and Cooperation in Europe (CSCE), which was given supporting institutions in 1990 and renamed OSCE in 1994. Finally, we include a brief excerpt of the North American Free Trade Agreement (NAFTA, 1993).

5. *The Covenant of the League of Nations*
(negotiated 1919; includes amendments adopted through 1924)

Following through with his Fourteen Points (part 3, chapter 9), President Woodrow Wilson was a principal architect of the League of Nations, his frustration being failure to secure ratification of the League Covenant by the U.S. Senate. Indeed, there was a decided inclination at the time, particularly in conservative circles, to disengage and return to the neutrality and nonentanglement in external affairs that had been prescribed in President Washington's Farewell Address (part 3, chapter 9). Even Wilson's success in carving out an important American exception—specifying in Article 21 the legitimacy of the Monroe Doctrine (part 3, chapter 9)—was insufficient in overcoming political obstacles to Senate ratification.

Indeed, in the 1920s and 1930s the United States became increasingly isolated, trade and commerce accentuating this isolation during the Depression years when high tariffs and devaluation of the dollar in the 1930s drove down substantially the overall volume of international trade. That said, as a collective security organization the League of Nations was to have been the principal mechanism for international law enforcement and, as such, a replacement for reliance on alliances (or balance of power) as the basis for security: "Any war or threat of war . . . is hereby declared a matter of concern to the whole League, and the League shall take any action that may be deemed wise and effectual to safeguard the peace of nations" (Article 11). Rather than use force, states were to refer their disputes to arbitration, to judicial settlement by the Permanent Court of International Justice, or to the League's machinery in the Council or in the Assembly (Articles 12 and 13); however, "should any Member of the League resort to war," the Council would "recommend to the several Governments concerned what effective military, naval or air force the Members of the League shall severally contribute to the armed forces to be used to protect the covenants of the League" violated by the law-breaking state (Article 16).

Located in Geneva, Switzerland, the League's principal organs included an Assembly, a Council, and a Secretariat (Article 2), forerunners respectively of the UN General Assembly, Security Council, and Secretariat. All treaties were to be registered with the League (Article 18) to avoid secret agreements such as those understood to have been causally related to the outbreak of World War I. League members were also to engage in arms reductions seen as core to maintaining peace (Article 8).

Beyond its historical interest, we include the League's Covenant because its basic collective-security and institutional provisions would be retained in the UN Charter albeit in modified form. Thus, international law enforcement as collective security in the League would also find its place in the United Nations organization, mainly the Security Council. If the League's Council had been hamstrung in any resort to using force, this was altered in the UN Charter, which gave the Security Council in Chapter VII (particularly Article 42) the right to authorize use of force. Added to that, the Charter also provided for formation of alliances and coalitions (Articles 51 and 52), but in principle subordinated such collective-defense arrangements to the Security Council.

The High Contracting Parties, In order *to promote international co-operation and to achieve international peace and security by the acceptance of obligations not to resort to war,* by the prescription of open, just and honourable relations between nations, by the *firm establishment of the understandings of international law as the actual rule of conduct among Governments,* and by the maintenance of justice and a scrupulous respect for all treaty obligations in the dealings of organised peoples with one another, Agree to this Covenant of the League of Nations.

Article 1. The original Members of the League of Nations shall be those of the Signatories which are named in the Annex to this Covenant and also such of those other States named in the Annex as shall accede without reservation to this Covenant. Such accession shall be effected by a Declaration deposited with the Secretariat within two months of the coming into force of the Covenant. Notice thereof shall be sent to all other Members of the League. *Any fully self-governing State,* Dominion or Colony not named in the Annex *may become a Member of the League if its admission is agreed to by* *two-thirds of the Assembly, provided that it shall give effective guarantees of its sincere intention to observe its international obligations, and shall accept such regulations as may be prescribed by the League in regard to its military, naval and air forces and armaments.* Any Member of the League may, after two years' notice of its intention so to do, withdraw from the League, provided that all its international obligations and all its obligations under this Covenant shall have been fulfilled at the time of its withdrawal.

Article 2. The action of the League under this Covenant shall be effected through the instrumentality of an Assembly and of a Council, with a permanent Secretariat.

Article 3. The Assembly shall consist of Representatives of the Members of the League. The Assembly shall meet at stated intervals and from time to time as occasion may require at the Seat of the League or at such other place as may be decided upon. *The Assembly may deal at its meetings with any matter* within the sphere of action of the League or *affecting the peace of the world.* At meetings of the Assembly each Member of the League shall have one vote, and may have not more than three Representatives.

Article 4. The Council shall consist of Representatives of the Principal Allied and Associated Powers, together with Representatives of four other Members of the League. These four Members of the League shall be selected by the Assembly from time to time in its discretion. Until the appointment of the Representatives of the four Members of the League first selected by the Assembly, Representatives of Belgium, Brazil, Spain and Greece shall be members of the Council. With the approval of the majority of the Assembly, the Council may name additional Members of the League whose Representatives shall always be members of the Council; the Council, with like approval may increase the number of Members of the League to be selected by the Assembly for representation on the Council. The Council shall meet from time to time as occasion may require, and at least once a year, at the Seat of the League, or at such other place as may be decided upon. *The Council may deal at its meetings with any matter within the sphere of action of the League or affecting the peace of the world.* Any Member of the League not represented on the Council shall be invited to send a Representative to sit as a member at any meeting of the Council during the consideration of matters specially affecting the interests of that Member of the League. At meetings of the Council, each Member of the League represented on the Council shall have one vote, and may have not more than one Representative.

Article 5. *Except where otherwise expressly provided* in this Covenant or by the terms of the present Treaty, *decisions at any meeting of the Assembly or of the Council shall require the agreement of all the Members of the League represented at the meeting.* All matters of procedure at meetings of the Assembly or of the Council, including the appointment of Committees to investigate particular matters, shall be regulated by the Assembly or by the Council and may be decided by a majority of the Members of the League represented at the meeting. The first meeting of the Assembly and the first meeting of the Council shall be summoned by the President of the United States of America.

Article 6. The permanent Secretariat shall be established at the Seat of the League. The Secretariat shall comprise a Secretary

General and such secretaries and staff as may be required. The first Secretary General shall be the person named in the Annex; thereafter the Secretary General shall be appointed by the Council with the approval of the majority of the Assembly. The secretaries and staff of the Secretariat shall be appointed by the Secretary General with the approval of the Council. The Secretary General shall act in that capacity at all meetings of the Assembly and of the Council. The expenses of the League shall be borne by the Members of the League in the proportion decided by the Assembly.

Article 7. The Seat of the League is established at Geneva. The Council may at any time decide that the Seat of the League shall be established elsewhere. All positions under or in connection with the League, including the Secretariat, shall be open equally to men and women. Representatives of the Members of the League and officials of the League when engaged on the business of the League shall enjoy diplomatic privileges and immunities. The buildings and other property occupied by the League or its officials or by Representatives attending its meetings shall be inviolable.

Article 8. The Members of the League recognise that *the maintenance of peace requires the reduction of national armaments to the lowest point consistent with national safety and the enforcement by common action of international obligations. The Council,* taking account of the geographical situation and circumstances of each State, *shall formulate plans for such reduction for the consideration and action of the several Governments.* Such plans shall be subject to reconsideration and revision at least every ten years. After these plans shall have been adopted by the several Governments, the limits of armaments therein fixed shall not be exceeded without the concurrence of the Council. The Members of the League agree that *the manufacture by private enterprise of munitions and implements of war is open to grave objections.* The Council shall advise how the evil effects attendant upon such manufacture can be prevented, due regard being had to the necessities of those Members of the League which are not able to manufacture the munitions and implements of war necessary for their safety. *The Members of the League undertake to interchange full and frank information as to the scale of their armaments, their military, naval and air programmes and the condition of such of their industries as are adaptable to war-like purposes.*

Article 9. *A permanent Commission shall be constituted to advise the Council* on the execution of the provisions of Articles 1 and 8 and *on military, naval and air questions* generally.

Article 10. *The Members of the League undertake to respect and preserve as against external aggression the territorial integrity and existing political independence of all Members of the League. In case of any such aggression or in case of any threat or danger of such aggression the Council shall advise upon the means by which this obligation shall be fulfilled.*

Article 11. *Any war or threat of war, whether immediately affecting any of the Members of the League or not, is hereby declared a matter of concern to the whole League, and the League shall take any action that may be deemed wise and effectual to safeguard the peace of nations.* In case any such emergency should arise the Secretary General shall on the request of any Member of the League forthwith summon a meeting of the Council. It is also declared to be the friendly *right of each Member of the League to bring to the attention* *of the Assembly or of the Council any circumstance whatever affecting international relations which threatens to disturb international peace or the good understanding between nations upon which peace depends.*

Article 12. The Members of the League agree that, *if there should arise between them any dispute likely to lead to a rupture they will submit the matter either to arbitration or judicial settlement or to enquiry by the Council,* and they agree in no case to resort to war until three months after the award by the arbitrators or the judicial decision, or the report by the Council. In any case under this Article the award of the arbitrators or the judicial decision shall be made within a reasonable time, and the report of the Council shall be made within six months after the submission of the dispute.

Article 13. *The Members* of the League agree that *whenever any dispute shall arise* between them which they recognise to be *suitable for submission to arbitration or judicial settlement and which cannot be satisfactorily settled by diplomacy,* they *will submit the whole subject-matter to arbitration or judicial settlement. Disputes as to the interpretation of a treaty, as to any question of international law,* as to the existence of any fact which if established would constitute a breach of any international obligation, or as to the extent and nature of the reparation to be made for any such breach, are declared to be among those which are generally suitable for submission to arbitration or judicial settlement. For the consideration of any such dispute, the court to which the case is referred *shall be the Permanent Court of International Justice,* established in accordance with **Article 14,** or any tribunal agreed on by the parties to the dispute or stipulated in any convention existing between them. The Members of the League agree that they will carry out in full good

faith any award or decision that may be rendered, and that they will not resort to war against a Member of the League which complies therewith. In the event of any failure to carry out such an award or decision, the Council shall propose what steps should be taken to give effect thereto.

Article 14. The Council shall formulate and submit to the Members of the League for adoption plans for the establishment of a Permanent Court of International Justice. The Court shall be competent to hear and determine any dispute of an international character which the parties thereto submit to it. The Court may also give an advisory opinion upon any dispute or question referred to it by the Council or by the Assembly.

Article 15. If there should arise between Members of the League any dispute likely to lead to a rupture, which is not submitted to arbitration or judicial settlement in accordance with **Article 13,** the Members of the League agree that they will submit the matter to the Council. Any party to the dispute may effect such submission by giving notice of the existence of the dispute to the Secretary General, who will make all necessary arrangements for a full investigation and consideration thereof. For this purpose the parties to the dispute will communicate to the Secretary General, as promptly as possible, statements of their case with all the relevant facts and papers, and the Council may forthwith direct the publication thereof. The Council shall endeavour to effect a settlement of the dispute, and if such efforts are successful, a statement shall be made public giving such facts and explanations regarding the dispute and the terms of settlement thereof as the Council may deem appropriate. If the dispute is not thus settled, *the*

Council either unanimously or by a majority vote shall make and publish a report containing a statement of the facts of the dispute and the recommendations which are deemed just and proper in regard thereto.

Any Member of the League represented on the Council may make public a statement of the facts of the dispute and of its conclusions regarding the same. If a report by the Council is unanimously agreed to by the members thereof other than the Representatives of one or more of the parties to the dispute, *the Members of the League agree that they will not go to war with any party to the dispute which complies with the recommendations of the report.* If the Council fails to reach a report which is unanimously agreed to by the members thereof, other than the Representatives of one or more of the parties to the dispute, the Members of the League reserve to themselves the right to take such action as they shall consider necessary for the maintenance of right and justice.

If the dispute between the parties is claimed by one of them, and is found by the Council, to arise out of a matter which by international law is solely within the domestic jurisdiction of that party, the Council shall so report, and shall make no recommendation as to its settlement. The Council may in any case under this Article refer the dispute to the Assembly. The dispute shall be so referred at the request of either party to the dispute, provided that such request be made within fourteen days after the submission of the dispute to the Council.

In any case referred to the Assembly, all the provisions of this Article and of **Article 12** relating to the action and powers of the Council shall apply to the action and powers of the Assembly, provided that a report made by the Assembly, if concurred in by the Representatives of those Members of the League represented on the Council and of a majority of the other Members of the League, exclusive in each case of the Representatives of the parties to the dispute, shall have the same force as a report by the Council concurred in by all the members thereof other than the Representatives of one or more of the parties to the dispute.

Article 16. *Should any Member of the League resort to war* in disregard of its covenants under **Articles 12, 13** or **15,** *it shall* ipso facto *be deemed to have committed an act of war against all other Members of the League,* which hereby undertake immediately to subject it to the severance of all trade or financial relations, the prohibition of all intercourse between their nationals and the nationals of the covenant-breaking State, and the prevention of all financial, commercial or personal intercourse between the nationals of the covenant-breaking State and the nationals of any other State, whether a Member of the League or not. *It shall be the duty of the Council in such case to recommend to the several Governments concerned what effective military, naval or air force the Members of the League shall severally contribute to the armed forces to be used to protect the covenants of the League.* The Members of the League agree, further, that they will mutually support one another in the financial and economic measures which are taken under this Article, in order to minimise the loss and inconvenience resulting from the above measures, and that they will mutually support one another in resisting any special measures aimed at one of their number by the covenant-breaking State, and that they will take the necessary steps to afford passage through their territory to the forces of any of the Members of the League which are co-operating to protect the covenants of the League. Any Member of the League which has violated any covenant of the League may be declared to be no longer a Member of the League by a vote of the Council concurred in by the Representatives of all the other Members of the League represented thereon.

Article 17. In the event of a dispute between a Member of the League and a State which is not a Member of the League, or between States not Members of the League, the State or States not Members of the League shall be invited to accept the obligations of membership in the League for the purposes of such dispute, upon such conditions as the Council may deem just. If such invitation is accepted, the provisions of **Articles 12 to 16** inclusive shall be applied with such modifications as may be deemed necessary by the Council. Upon such invitation being given the Council shall immediately institute an inquiry into the circumstances of the dispute and recommend such action as may seem best and most effectual in the circumstances. *If a State so invited shall refuse to accept the obligations of membership in the League* for the purposes of such dispute, *and shall resort to war against a Member of the League, the provisions of* **Article 16** *shall be applicable as against the State taking such action.* If both parties to the dispute when so invited refuse to accept the obligations of membership in the League for the purposes of such dispute, the Council may take such measures and make such recommendations as will prevent hostilities and will result in the settlement of the dispute.

Article 18. *Every treaty or international engagement entered into hereafter by any Member of the League shall be forthwith registered with the Secretariat and shall as soon as possible be published by it. No such treaty or international engagement shall be binding until so registered.*

Article 19. *The Assembly may from time to time advise the reconsideration* by Members of the League *of treaties which have become inapplicable and the consideration of international conditions whose continuance might endanger the peace of the world.*

Article 20. The Members of the League severally agree that this Covenant is accepted as abrogating all obligations or understandings *inter se* [i.e., among themselves] which are inconsistent with the terms thereof, and solemnly undertake that they will not hereafter enter into any engagements inconsistent with the terms thereof. In case any Member of the League shall, before becoming a Member of the League, have undertaken any obligations inconsistent with the terms of this Covenant, it shall be the duty of such Member to take immediate steps to procure its release from such obligations.

Article 21. *Nothing in this Covenant shall be deemed to affect the validity of international engagements, such as treaties of arbitration or regional understandings like the Monroe doctrine, for securing the maintenance of peace.*

Article 22. *To those colonies and territories which as a consequence of the late war have ceased to be under the sovereignty of the States which formerly governed them* and which are inhabited by peoples not yet able to stand by themselves under the strenuous conditions of the modern world, there should be applied the principle that the well-being and development of such peoples form a sacred trust of civilisation and that securities for the performance of this trust should be embodied in this Covenant. The best method of giving practical effect to this principle is that *the tutelage of such peoples should be entrusted to advanced nations who by reason of their resources, their experience or their geographical position can best* *undertake this responsibility, and who are willing to accept it, and that this tutelage should be exercised by them as Mandatories on behalf of the League.*

The character of the mandate must differ according to the stage of the development of the people, the geographical situation of the territory, its economic conditions and other similar circumstances. Certain communities formerly belonging to the Turkish Empire have reached a stage of development where their existence as independent nations can be provisionally recognized subject to the rendering of administrative advice and assistance by a Mandatory until such time as they are able to stand alone. The wishes of these communities must be a principal consideration in the selection of the Mandatory. Other peoples, especially those of Central Africa, are at such a stage that the Mandatory must be responsible for the administration of the territory under conditions which will guarantee freedom of conscience and religion, subject only to the maintenance of public order and morals, *the prohibition of* abuses such as the slave trade, *the arms traffic* and the liquor traffic, and the prevention of the establishment of fortifications or military and naval bases and of military training of the natives for other than police purposes and the defence of territory, and will also secure equal opportunities for the trade and commerce of other Members of the League. There are territories, such as South-West Africa and certain of the South Pacific Islands, which, owing to the sparseness of their population, or their small size, or their remoteness from the centres of civilisation, or their geographical contiguity to the territory of the Mandatory, and other circumstances, can be best administered under the laws of the Mandatory as integral portions of its territory, subject to the safeguards above mentioned in the interests of the indigenous population.

In every case of mandate, the Mandatory shall render to the Council an annual report in reference to the territory committed to its charge. The degree of authority, control, or administration to be exercised by the Mandatory shall, if not previously agreed upon by the Members of the League, be explicitly defined in each case by the Council. A permanent Commission shall be constituted to receive and examine the annual reports of the Mandatories and to advise the Council on all matters relating to the observance of the mandates.

Article 23. Subject to and in accordance with the provisions of international conventions existing or hereafter to be agreed upon, the Members of the League: (a) will endeavour to secure and maintain fair and humane conditions of labour for men, women, and children, both in their own countries and in all countries to which their commercial and industrial relations extend, and for that purpose will establish and maintain the necessary international organisations; (b) undertake to secure just treatment of the native inhabitants of territories under their control; (c) will entrust the League with the general supervision over the execution of agreements with regard to the traffic in women and children, and the traffic in opium and other dangerous drugs; (d) *will entrust the League with the general supervision of the trade in arms and ammunition with the countries in which the control of this traffic is necessary in the common interest;* (e) will make provision to secure and maintain freedom of communications and of transit and equitable treatment for the commerce of all Members of the League. In this connection, the special necessities of the regions devastated during the war of 1914–1918 shall be borne in mind; (f) will endeavour to take steps in matters of international concern for the prevention and control of disease.

Article 24. There shall be placed under the direction of the League all international bureaux already established by general treaties if the parties to such treaties consent. All such international bureaux and all commissions for the regulation of matters of international interest hereafter constituted shall be placed under the direction of the League. In all matters of international interest which are regulated by general convention but which are not placed under the control of international bureaux or commissions, the Secretariat of the League shall, subject to the consent of the Council and if desired by the parties, collect and distribute all relevant information and shall render any other assistance which may be necessary or desirable. The Council may include as part of the ex-

penses of the Secretariat the expenses of any bureau or commission which is placed under the direction of the League.

Article 25. The Members of the League agree to encourage and promote the establishment and co-operation of duly authorised voluntary national Red Cross organisations having as purposes the improvement of health, the prevention of disease and the mitigation of suffering throughout the world.

Article 26. Amendments to this Covenant will take effect when ratified by the Members of the League whose Representatives compose the Council and by a majority of the Members of the League whose Representatives compose the Assembly. No such amendments shall bind any Member of the League which signifies its dissent therefrom, but in that case it shall cease to be a Member of the League.

---

6. *The United Nations Charter*

(1945)

The United Nations Charter, signed in San Francisco on June 26, 1945, recognizes the sovereignty of its member states, but also establishes an important exception to the state's sovereign claim by allowing UN intervention in matters involving international peace and security (Article 2, Sections 1 and 7, and Chapter VII). The General Assembly (Chapter IV) has broad authority to take up issues of global importance including international peace and security, which is the primary responsibility of the Security Council (Chapter V). The Secretariat (Chapter XV) supports the work of these two organs as well as the Economic and Social Council (Chapter X), Trusteeship Council (Chapter XIII), and the International Court of Justice (Chapter XIV). The charter lays out a global plan for dealing with international peace and security (especially in Chapters V–VIII), international economic and social cooperation (Chapters IX and X), the administration and supervision of "non-self-governing territories" as in the former colonies of defeated powers (Chapters XI–XIII), and judicial settlement of disputes among states (Chapter XIV).

    Responsibility for collective security (i.e., international law enforcement as in collective action against aggression) remained primarily with the Security Council (the counterpart of the

League of Nations' Council); however, use (or threatened use) of the Article 27 veto power during the cold war owing to U.S.-Soviet and other divisions among the great powers on the Security Council with few exceptions effectively kept it from taking many actions, restricting itself primarily to peacekeeping and related measures.

Facing the threat of Soviet veto, the United States and its allies turned in the 1950s and early 1960s to the General Assembly for what were called Uniting for Peace resolutions; however, this effort was abandoned in the 1960s when the United States lost its working majority in the General Assembly because many new member states (mostly former colonies of European powers) disagreed with the American agenda. In these circumstances, during the cold war the United States relied primarily on NATO and other Article 51 collective-defense alliances or coalitions.

Since the end of the cold war there has been greater reliance on collective-security actions under the Security Council, but the veto power held by the permanent members continues to block actions when there is no great-power consensus on what is to be done. Because of its importance, the United Nations Charter is provided here in its entirety.

We the peoples of the United Nations determined to save succeeding generations from the scourge of war, which twice in our lifetime has brought untold sorrow to mankind, and to reaffirm faith in fundamental human rights, in the dignity and worth of the human person, in the equal rights of men and women and of nations large and small, and to establish conditions under which justice and respect for the obligations arising from treaties and other sources of international law can be maintained, and to promote social progress and better standards of life in larger freedom, and for these ends to practice tolerance and live together in peace with one another as good neighbours, and *to unite our strength to maintain international peace and security,* and *to ensure,* by the acceptance of principles and the institution of methods, *that armed force shall not be used, save in the common interest,* and to employ international machinery for the promotion of the economic and social advancement of all peoples, have resolved to combine our efforts to accomplish these aims. Accordingly, our respective Governments, through representatives assembled in the city of San Francisco, who have exhibited their full powers found to be in good and due form, have agreed to the present Charter of the United Nations and do hereby establish an international organization to be known as the United Nations.

Chapter I. *Purposes and Principles*

Article 1. The Purposes of the United Nations are: 1. *To maintain international peace and security, and to that end: to take effective collective measures for the prevention and removal of threats to the peace, and for the suppression of acts of aggression or other breaches of the peace, and to bring about by peaceful means, and in conformity with the principles of justice and international law, adjustment or settlement of international disputes or situations which might lead to a breach of the peace;* 2. *To develop friendly relations among nations based on respect for the principle of equal rights and self-determination of peoples, and to take other appropriate measures to strengthen universal peace;* 3. To achieve international co-operation in solving international problems of an economic, social, cultural, or humanitarian character, and in promoting and encouraging respect for human rights and for fundamental freedoms for all without distinction as to race, sex, language, or religion; and 4. To be a centre for harmonizing the actions of nations in the attainment of these common ends.

Article 2. The Organization and its Members, in pursuit of the Purposes stated in Article 1, shall act in accordance with the following Principles. 1. *The Organization is based on the principle of the sovereign equality of all its Members.* 2. All Members, in order to ensure to all of them the rights and benefits resulting from membership, shall fulfill in good faith the obligations assumed by them in accordance with the present Charter. 3. *All Members shall settle their international disputes by peaceful means in such a manner that international peace and security, and justice, are not endangered.* 4. *All Members shall refrain in their international relations from the threat or use of force against the territorial integrity or political independence of any state,* or in any other manner inconsistent with the Purposes of the United Nations. 5. All Members shall give the United Nations every assistance in any action it takes in accordance with the present Charter, and shall refrain from giving assistance to any state against which the United Nations is taking preventive or enforcement action. 6. *The Organization shall ensure that states which are not Members of the United Nations act in accordance with these Principles so far as may be necessary for the maintenance of international peace and security.* 7. *Nothing contained in the present Charter shall authorize the United Nations to intervene in matters which are essentially within the domestic jurisdiction of any state or shall require the Members to submit such matters to settlement under the present Charter; but this principle shall not prejudice the application of enforcement measures under Chapter VII.*

Chapter II. *Membership*

Article 3. The original Members of the United Nations shall be the states which, having participated in the United Nations Conference on International Organization at San Francisco, or having previously signed the Declaration by United Nations of 1 January 1942, sign the present Charter and ratify it in accordance with Article 110.

Article 4. 1. Membership in the United Nations is open to all other peace-loving states which accept the obligations contained in the present Charter and, in the judgment of the Organization, are able and willing to carry out these obligations. 2. The admission of any such state to membership in the United Nations will be effected by a decision of the General Assembly upon the recommendation of the Security Council.

Article 5. A Member of the United Nations against which preventive or enforcement action has been taken by the Security Council may be suspended from the exercise of the rights and privileges of membership by the General Assembly upon the recommendation of the Security Council. The exercise of these rights and privileges may be restored by the Security Council.

Article 6. A Member of the United Nations which has persistently violated the Principles contained in the present Charter may be expelled from the Organization by the General Assembly upon the recommendation of the Security Council.

Chapter III. *Organs*

Article 7. 1. There are established as the principal organs of the United Nations: a General Assembly, a Security Council, an Economic and Social Council, a Trusteeship Council, an International Court of Justice, and a Secretariat. 2. Such subsidiary organs as may be found necessary may be established in accordance with the present Charter.

Article 8. The United Nations shall place no restrictions on the eligibility of men and women to participate in any capacity and under conditions of equality in its principal and subsidiary organs.

Chapter IV. *The General Assembly*

Composition

Article 9. 1. The General Assembly shall consist of all the Members of the United Nations. 2. Each Member shall have not more than five representatives in the General Assembly.

Functions and Powers

Article 10. *The General Assembly may discuss any questions or any matters within the scope of the present Charter or relating to the powers and functions of any organs provided for in the present Charter, and, except as provided in Article 12, may make recommendations to the Members of the United Nations or to the Security Council or to both on any such questions or matters.*

Article 11. 1. *The General Assembly may consider the general principles of co-operation in the maintenance of international peace and security, including the principles governing disarmament and the regulation of armaments, and may make recommendations with regard to such principles to the Members or to the Security Council or to both.* 2. *The General Assembly may discuss any questions relating to the maintenance of international peace and security brought before it by any Member of the United Nations, or by the Security Council, or by a state which is not a Member of the United Nations* in accordance with Article 35, paragraph 2, and, except as provided in Article 12, may make recommendations with regard to any such questions to the state or states concerned or to the Security Council or to both. Any such question on which action is necessary shall be referred to the Security Council by the General Assembly either before or after discussion. 3. *The General Assembly may call the attention of the Security Council to situations which are likely to endanger international peace and security.* 4. The powers of the General Assembly set forth in this Article shall not limit the general scope of Article 10.

Article 12. 1. *While the Security Council is exercising in respect of any dispute or situation the functions assigned to it in the present Charter, the General Assembly shall not make any recommendation with regard to that dispute or situation unless the Security Council so requests.* 2. *The Secretary-General, with the consent of the Security Council, shall notify the General Assembly at each session of any matters relative to the maintenance of international peace and security which are being dealt with by the Security Council and shall similarly notify the General Assembly, or the Members of the United Nations if the General Assembly is not in session, immediately the Security Council ceases to deal with such matters.*

Article 13. 1. The General Assembly shall initiate studies and make recommendations for the purpose of: a. promoting international co-operation in the political field and encouraging the progressive development of international law and its codification; b. promoting international co-operation in the economic, social, cultural, educational, and health fields, and assisting in the realization of human rights and fundamental freedoms for all without distinction as to race, sex, language, or religion. 2. The further responsibilities, functions and powers of the General Assembly with respect to matters mentioned in paragraph 1 (b) above are set forth in Chapters IX and X.

Article 14. Subject to the provisions of Article 12, the General Assembly may recommend measures for the peaceful adjustment of any situation, regardless of origin, which it deems likely to impair the general welfare or friendly relations among nations, including situations resulting from a violation of the provisions of the present Charter setting forth the Purposes and Principles of the United Nations.

Article 15. 1. The General Assembly shall receive and consider annual and special reports from the Security Council; these reports shall include an account of the measures that the Security Council has decided upon or taken to maintain international peace and security. 2. The General Assembly shall receive and consider reports from the other organs of the United Nations.

Article 16. The General Assembly shall perform such functions with respect to the international trusteeship system as are assigned to it under Chapters XII and XIII, including the approval of the trusteeship agreements for areasnot designated as strategic.

Article 17. 1. The General Assembly shall consider and approve the budget of the Organization. 2. The expenses of the Organization shall be borne by the Members as apportioned by the General Assembly. 3. The General Assembly shall consider and approve any financial and budgetary arrangements with specialized agencies referred to in Article 57 and shall examine the administrative budgets of such specialized agencies with a view to making recommendations to the agencies concerned.

Voting

Article 18. 1. Each member of the General Assembly shall have one vote. 2. *Decisions of the General Assembly on important questions shall be made by a two-thirds major-*

ity of the members present and voting. These questions shall include: recommendations with respect to the maintenance of international peace and security, the election of the non-permanent members of the Security Council, the election of the members of the Economic and Social Council, the election of members of the Trusteeship Council in accordance with paragraph 1 (c) of Article 86, the admission of new Members to the United Nations, the suspension of the rights and privileges of membership, the expulsion of Members, questions relating to the operation of the trusteeship system, and budgetary questions. 3. Decisions on other questions, including the determination of additional categories of questions to be decided by a two-thirds majority, shall be made by a majority of the members present and voting.

Article 19. A Member of the United Nations which is in arrears in the payment of its financial contributions to the Organization shall have no vote in the General Assembly if the amount of its arrears equals or exceeds the amount of the contributions due from it for the preceding two full years. The General Assembly may, nevertheless, permit such a Member to vote if it is satisfied that the failure to pay is due to conditions beyond the control of the Member.

Procedure

Article 20. The General Assembly shall meet in regular annual sessions and in such special sessions as occasion may require. Special sessions shall be convoked by the Secretary-General at the request of the Security Council or of a majority of the Members of the United Nations.

Article 21. The General Assembly shall adopt its own rules of procedure. It shall elect its President for each session.

Article 22. The General Assembly may establish such subsidiary organs as it deems necessary for the performance of its functions.

Chapter V. *The Security Council*

Composition

Article 23. 1. The Security Council shall consist of fifteen Members of the United Nations. The Republic of China, France, the Union of Soviet Socialist Republics, the United Kingdom of Great Britain and Northern Ireland, and the United States of America shall be permanent members of the Security Council. The General Assembly shall elect ten other Members of the United Nations to be non-permanent members of the Security Council, due regard being specially paid, in the first instance to the contribution of Members of the United Nations to the maintenance of international peace and security and to the other purposes of the Organization, and also to equitable geographical distribution. 2. The non-permanent members of the Security Council shall be elected for a term of two years. In the first election of the non-permanent members after the increase of the membership of the Security Council from eleven to fifteen, two of the four additional members shall be chosen for a term of one year. A retiring member shall not be eligible for immediate reelection. 3. Each member of the Security Council shall have one representative.

Functions and Powers

Article 24. 1. In order to ensure prompt and effective action by the United Nations, its Members confer on *the Security Council primary responsibility for the maintenance of international peace and security,* and agree that in carrying out its duties under this responsibility the Security Council

acts on their behalf. 2. In discharging these duties the Security Council shall act in accordance with the Purposes and Principles of the United Nations. The specific powers granted to the Security Council for the discharge of these duties are laid down in Chapters VI, VII, VIII, and XII. 3. The Security Council shall submit annual and, when necessary, special reports to the General Assembly for its consideration.

Article 25. The Members of the United Nations agree to accept and carry out the decisions of the Security Council in accordance with the present Charter.

Article 26. *In order to promote the establishment and maintenance of international peace and security with the least diversion for armaments of the world's human and economic resources, the Security Council shall be responsible for formulating,* with the assistance of the Military Staff Committee referred to in Article 47, *plans to be submitted to the Members of the United Nations for the establishment of a system for the regulation of armaments.*

Voting

Article 27. 1. Each member of the Security Council shall have one vote. 2. Decisions of the Security Council on procedural matters shall be made by an affirmative vote of nine members. 3. *Decisions of the Security Council on all other matters shall be made by an affirmative vote of nine members including the concurring votes of the permanent members;* provided that, in decisions under Chapter VI, and under paragraph 3 of Article 52, a party to a dispute shall abstain from voting.

Procedure

Article 28. 1. The Security Council shall be so organized as to be able to function continuously. Each member of the

Security Council shall for this purpose be represented at all times at the seat of the Organization. 2. The Security Council shall hold periodic meetings at which each of its members may, if it so desires, be represented by a member of the government or by some other specially designated representative. 3. The Security Council may hold meetings at such places other than the seat of the Organization as in its judgment will best facilitate its work.

Article 29. The Security Council may establish such subsidiary organs as it deems necessary for the performance of its functions.

Article 30. The Security Council shall adopt its own rules of procedure, including the method of selecting its President.

Article 31. Any Member of the United Nations which is not a member of the Security Council may participate, without vote, in the discussion of any question brought before the Security Council whenever the latter considers that the interests of that Member are specially affected.

Article 32. *Any Member of the United Nations* which is not a member of the Security Council or any state which is not a Member of the United Nations, *if it is a party to a dispute under consideration by the Security Council, shall be invited to participate, without vote, in the discussion relating to the dispute.* The Security Council shall lay down such conditions as it deems just for the participation of a state which is not a Member of the United Nations.

Chapter VI. *Pacific Settlement of Disputes*

Article 33. 1. *The parties to any dispute, the continuance of which is likely to endanger the maintenance of international peace and secu-*

rity, shall, first of all, seek a solution by negotiation, enquiry, mediation, conciliation, arbitration, judicial settlement, resort to regional agencies or arrangements, or other peaceful means of their own choice. 2. The Security Council shall, when it deems necessary, call upon the parties to settle their dispute by such means.

Article 34. *The Security Council may investigate any dispute, or any situation which might lead to international friction or give rise to a dispute, in order to determine whether the continuance of the dispute or situation is likely to endanger the maintenance of international peace and security.*

Article 35. 1. *Any Member of the United Nations may bring any dispute, or any situation of the nature referred to in Article 34, to the attention of the Security Council or of the General Assembly.* 2. A state which is not a Member of the United Nations may bring to the attention of the Security Council or of the General Assembly any dispute to which it is a party if it accepts in advance, for the purposes of the dispute, the obligations of pacific settlement provided in the present Charter. 3. The proceedings of the General Assembly in respect of matters brought to its attention under this Article will be subject to the provisions of Articles 11 and 12.

Article 36. 1. *The Security Council may, at any stage of a dispute of the nature referred to in Article 33 or of a situation of like nature, recommend appropriate procedures or methods of adjustment.* 2. The Security Council should take into consideration any procedures for the settlement of the dispute which have already been adopted by the parties. 3. In making recommendations under this Article the Security Council should also take into consideration that *legal disputes should as a general rule be* referred by the parties to the International Court of Justice in accordance with the provisions of the Statute of the Court.

Article 37. 1. *Should the parties to a dispute of the nature referred to in Article 33 fail to settle it* by the means indicated in that Article, they *shall refer it to the Security Council.* 2. *If the Security Council deems that the continuance of the dispute is in fact likely to endanger the maintenance of international peace and security, it shall decide whether to take action under Article 36 or to recommend such terms of settlement as it may consider appropriate.*

Article 38. Without prejudice to the provisions of Articles 33 to 37, *the Security Council may, if all the parties to any dispute so request, make recommendations to the parties with a view to a pacific settlement of the dispute.*

Chapter VII. *Action with Respect to Threats to the Peace, Breaches of the Peace, and Acts of Aggression*

Article 39. *The Security Council shall determine the existence of any threat to the peace, breach of the peace, or act of aggression and shall make recommendations, or decide what measures shall be taken in accordance with Articles 41 and 42, to maintain or restore international peace and security.*

Article 40. In order to prevent an aggravation of the situation, *the Security Council may,* before making the recommendations or deciding upon the measures provided for in Article 39, *call upon the parties concerned to comply with such provisional measures as it deems necessary or desirable.* Such provisional measures shall be without prejudice to the rights, claims, or position of the parties concerned. The Security Council shall duly take account of failure to comply with such provisional measures.

Article 41. *The Security Council may decide what measures not involving the use of armed force are to be employed to give effect to its decisions, and it may call upon the Members of the United Nations to apply such measures. These may include complete or partial interruption of economic relations and of rail, sea, air, postal, telegraphic, radio, and other means of communication, and the severance of diplomatic relations.*

Article 42. *Should the Security Council consider that measures provided for in Article 41 would be inadequate or have proved to be inadequate, it may take such action by air, sea, or land forces as may be necessary to maintain or restore international peace and security. Such action may include demonstrations, blockade, and other operations by air, sea, or land forces of Members of the United Nations.*

Article 43. 1. *All Members of the United Nations, in order to contribute to the maintenance of international peace and security, undertake to make available to the Security Council, on its call and in accordance with a special agreement or agreements, armed forces, assistance, and facilities, including rights of passage, necessary for the purpose of maintaining international peace and security.* 2. Such agreement or agreements shall govern the numbers and types of forces, their degree of readiness and general location, and the nature of the facilities and assistance to be provided. 3. The agreement or agreements shall be negotiated as soon as possible on the initiative of the Security Council. They shall be concluded between the Security Council and Members or between the Security Council and groups of Members and shall be subject to ratification by the signatory states in accordance with their respective constitutional processes.

Article 44. When the Security Council has decided to use force it shall, before calling upon a Member not represented on it to provide armed forces in fulfilment of the obligations assumed under Article 43, invite that Member, if the Member so desires, to participate in the decisions of the Security Council concerning the employment of contingents of that Member's armed forces.

Article 45. In order to enable the United Nations to take urgent military measures, Members shall hold immediately available national air-force contingents for combined international enforcement action. The strength and degree of readiness of these contingents and plans for their combined action shall be determined within the limits laid down in the special agreement or agreements referred to in Article 43, by the Security Council with the assistance of the Military Staff Committee.

Article 46. Plans for the application of armed force shall be made by the Security Council with the assistance of the Military Staff Committee.

Article 47. 1. There shall be established a Military Staff Committee to advise and assist the Security Council on all questions relating to the Security Council's military requirements for the maintenance of international peace and security, the employment and command of forces placed at its disposal, the regulation of armaments, and possible disarmament. 2. The Military Staff Committee shall consist of the Chiefs of Staff of the permanent members of the Security Council or their representatives. Any Member of the United Nations not permanently represented on the Committee shall be invited by the Committee to be associated with it when the efficient discharge of the Committee's responsibilities requires the participation of that Member in its work. 3. The Military Staff Commit-

tee shall be responsible under the Security Council for the strategic direction of any armed forces placed at the disposal of the Security Council. Questions relating to the command of such forces shall be worked out subsequently. 4. The Military Staff Committee, with the authorization of the Security Council and after consultation with appropriate regional agencies, may establish regional sub-committees.

Article 48. 1. *The action required to carry out the decisions of the Security Council for the maintenance of international peace and security shall be taken by all the Members of the United Nations or by some of them, as the Security Council may determine.* 2. Such decisions shall be carried out by the Members of the United Nations directly and through their action in the appropriate international agencies of which they remembers.

Article 49. The Members of the United Nations shall join in affording mutual assistance in carrying out the measures decided upon by the Security Council.

Article 50. If preventive or enforcement measures against any state are taken by the Security Council, any other state, whether a Member of the United Nations or not, which finds itself confronted with special economic problems arising from the carrying out of those measures shall have the right to consult the Security Council with regard to a solution of those problems.

Article 51. *Nothing in the present Charter shall impair the inherent right of individual or collective self-defence if an armed attack occurs against a Member of the United Nations, until the Security Council has taken measures necessary to maintain international peace and security. Measures taken by Members in the exercise of this right of self-defence shall be immediately reported to the Security Council and shall not in any way affect the authority* and responsibility of the Security Council under the present Charter to take at any time such action as it deems necessary in order to maintain or restore international peace and security.

Chapter VIII. *Regional Arrangements*

Article 52. 1. *Nothing in the present Charter precludes the existence of regional arrangements or agencies for dealing with such matters relating to the maintenance of international peace and security as are appropriate for regional action* provided that such arrangements or agencies and their activities are consistent with the Purposes and Principles of the United Nations. 2. The Members of the United Nations entering into such arrangements or constituting such agencies shall make every effort to achieve pacific settlement of local disputes through such regional arrangements or by such regional agencies before referring them to the Security Council. 3. *The Security Council shall encourage the development of pacific settlement of local disputes through such regional arrangements or by such regional agencies either on the initiative of the states concerned or by reference from the Security Council.* 4. This Article in no way impairs the application of Articles 34 and 35.

Article 53. 1. *The Security Council shall, where appropriate, utilize such regional arrangements or agencies for enforcement action under its authority.* But no enforcement action shall be taken under regional arrangements or by regional agencies without the authorization of the Security Council, with the exception of measures against any enemy state, as defined in paragraph 2 of this Article, provided for pursuant to Article 107 or in regional arrangements directed against renewal of aggressive policy on the part of any such state, until such time as the Organization

may, on request of the Governments concerned, be charged with the responsibility for preventing further aggression by such a state. 2. The term enemy state as used in paragraph 1 of this Article applies to any state which during the Second World War has been an enemy of any signatory of the present Charter.

Article 54. *The Security Council shall at all times be kept fully informed of activities undertaken or in contemplation under regional arrangements or by regional agencies for the maintenance of international peace and security.*

Chapter IX. *International Economic and Social Co-operation*

Article 55. With a view to the creation of conditions of stability and well-being which are necessary for peaceful and friendly relations among nations based on respect for the principle of equal rights and self-determination of peoples, the United Nations shall promote: a. higher standards of living, full employment, and conditions of economic and social progress and development; b. solutions of international economic, social, health, and related problems; and international cultural and educational cooperation; and c. universal respect for, and observance of, human rights and fundamental freedoms for all without distinction as to race, sex, language, or religion.

Article 56. All Members pledge themselves to take joint and separate action in co-operation with the Organization for the achievement of the purposes set forth in Article 55.

Article 57. 1. The various specialized agencies, established by intergovernmental agreement and having wide international responsibilities, as defined in their basic instruments, in economic, social, cultural, educational, health, and related fields, shall be brought into relationship with the United Nations in accordance with the provisions of Article 63. 2. Such agencies thus brought into relationship with the United Nations are hereinafter referred to as specialized agencies.

Article 58. The Organization shall make recommendations for the co-ordination of the policies and activities of the specialized agencies.

Article 59. The Organization shall, where appropriate, initiate negotiations among the states concerned for the creation of any new specialized agencies required for the accomplishment of the purposes set forth in Article 55.

Article 60. Responsibility for the discharge of the functions of the Organization set forth in this Chapter shall be vested in the General Assembly and, under the authority of the General Assembly, in the Economic and Social Council, which shall have for this purpose the powers set forth in Chapter X.

Chapter X. *The Economic and Social Council*

Composition

Article 61. 1. The Economic and Social Council shall consist of fifty-four Members of the United Nations elected by the General Assembly. 2. Subject to the provisions of paragraph 3, eighteen members of the Economic and Social Council shall be elected each year for a term of three years. A retiring member shall be eligible for immediate re-election. 3. At the first election after the increase in the membership of the Economic and Social Council from twenty-seven to fifty-four members, in addition to the members elected in place of the nine members whose term of office expires at the end of that year, twenty-seven additional members shall be elected. Of these twenty-seven additional members, the term of office of nine members so elected shall expire at the end of one year, and of nine other members at the end of two years, in accordance with arrangements made by the General Assembly. 4. Each member of the Economic and Social Council shall have one representative.

Functions and Powers

Article 62. 1. The Economic and Social Council may make or initiate studies and reports with respect to international economic, social, cultural, educational, health, and related matters and may make recommendations with respect to any such matters to the General Assembly to the Members of the United Nations, and to the specialized agencies concerned. 2. It may make recommendations for the purpose of promoting respect for, and observance of, human rights and fundamental freedoms for all. 3. It may prepare draft conventions for submission to the General Assembly, with respect to matters falling within its competence. 4. It may call, in accordance with the rules prescribed by the United Nations, international conferences on matters falling within its competence.

Article 63. 1. The Economic and Social Council may enter into agreements with any of the agencies referred to in Article 57, defining the terms on which the agency concerned shall be brought into relationship with the United Nations. Such agreements shall be subject to approval by the General Assembly. 2. It may co-ordinate the activities of the specialized agencies through consultation with and recommendations to such agencies and through recommendations to the General

Assembly and to the Members of the United Nations.

Article 64. 1. The Economic and Social Council may take appropriate steps to obtain regular reports from the specialized agencies. It may make arrangements with the Members of the United Nations and with the specialized agencies to obtain reports on the steps taken to give effect to its own recommendations and to recommendations on matters falling within its competence made by the General Assembly. 2. It may communicate its observations on these reports to the General Assembly.

Article 65. The Economic and Social Council may furnish information to the Security Council and shall assist the Security Council upon its request.

Article 66. 1. The Economic and Social Council shall perform such functions as fall within its competence in connexion with the carrying out of the recommendations of the General Assembly. 2. It may, with the approval of the General Assembly, perform services at the request of Members of the United Nations and at the request of specialized agencies. 3. It shall perform such other functions as are specified elsewhere in the present Charter or as may be assigned to it by the General Assembly.

Voting

Article 67. 1. Each member of the Economic and Social Council shall have one vote. 2. Decisions of the Economic and Social Council shall be made by a majority of the members present and voting.

Procedure

Article 68. The Economic and Social Council shall set up commissions in economic and social fields and for the promotion of human rights, and such other commissions as may be required for the performance of its functions.

Article 69. The Economic and Social Council shall invite any Member of the United Nations to participate, without vote, in its deliberations on any matter of particular concern to that Member.

Article 70. The Economic and Social Council may make arrangements for representatives of the specialized agencies to participate, without vote, in its deliberations and in those of the commissions established by it, and for its representatives to participate in the deliberations of the specialized agencies.

Article 71. The Economic and Social Council may make suitable arrangements for consultation with non-governmental organizations which are concerned with matters within its competence. Such arrangements may be made with international organizations and, where appropriate, with national organizations after consultation with the Member of the United Nations concerned.

Article 72. 1. The Economic and Social Council shall adopt its own rules of procedure, including the method of selecting its President. 2. The Economic and Social Council shall meet as required in accordance with its rules, which shall include provision for the convening of meetings on the request of a majority of its members.

Chapter XI. *Declaration Regarding Non-Self-Governing Territories*

Article 73. Members of the United Nations which have or assume responsibilities for the administration of territories whose peoples have not yet attained a full measure of self-government recognize the principle that the interests of the inhabitants of these territories are paramount, and accept as a sacred trust the obligation to promote to the utmost, within the system of international peace and security established by the present Charter, the well-being of the inhabitants of these territories, and, to this end: a. to ensure, with due respect for the culture of the peoples concerned, their political, economic, social, and educational advancement, their just treatment, and their protection against abuses; b. to develop self-government, to take due account of the political aspirations of the peoples, and to assist them in the progressive development of their free political institutions, according to the particular circumstances of each territory and its peoples and their varying stages of advancement; c. to further international peace and security; d. to promote constructive measures of development, to encourage research, and to co-operate with one another and, when and where appropriate, with specialized international bodies with a view to the practical achievement of the social, economic, and scientific purposes set forth in this Article; and e. to transmit regularly to the Secretary-General for information purposes, subject to such limitation as security and constitutional considerations may require, statistical and other information of a technical nature relating to economic, social, and educational conditions in the territories for which they are respectively responsible other than those territories to which Chapters XII and XIII apply.

Article 74. Members of the United Nations also agree that their policy in respect of the territories to which this Chapter applies, no less than in respect of their metropolitan areas, must be based on the general principle of good-neighbourliness, due account being taken of the interests and well-being of the rest of the world, in social, economic, and commercial matters.

Chapter XII. *International Trusteeship System*

Article 75. The United Nations shall establish under its authority an international trusteeship system for the administration and supervision of such territories as may be placed thereunder by subsequent individual agreements. These territories are hereinafter referred to as trust territories.

Article 76. The basic objectives of the trusteeship system, in accordance with the Purposes of the United Nations laid down in Article 1 of the present Charter, shall be: a. to further international peace and security; b. to promote the political, economic, social, and educational advancement of the inhabitants of the trust territories, and their progressive development towards self-government or independence as may be appropriate to the particular circumstances of each territory and its peoples and the freely expressed wishes of the peoples concerned, and as may be provided by the terms of each trusteeship agreement; c. to encourage respect for human rights and for fundamental freedoms for all without distinction as to race, sex, language, or religion, and to encourage recognition of the interdependence of the peoples of the world; and d. to ensure equal treatment in social, economic, and commercial matters for all Members of the United Nations and their nationals, and also equal treatment for the latter in the administration of justice, without prejudice to the attainment of the foregoing objectives and subject to the provisions of Article 80.

Article 77. 1. The trusteeship system shall apply to such territories in the following categories as may be placed thereunder by means of trusteeship agreements: a. territories now held under mandate; b. territories which may be detached from enemy states as a result of the Second World War; and c. territories voluntarily placed under the system by states responsible for their administration. 2. It will be a matter for subsequent agreement as to which territories in the foregoing categories will be brought under the trusteeship system and upon what terms.

Article 78. The trusteeship system shall not apply to territories which have become Members of the United Nations, relationship among which shall be based on respect for the principle of sovereign equality.

Article 79. The terms of trusteeship for each territory to be placed under the trusteeship system, including any alteration or amendment, shall be agreed upon by the states directly concerned, including the mandatory power in the case of territories held under mandate by a Member of the United Nations, and shall be approved as provided for in Articles 83 and 85.

Article 80. 1. Except as may be agreed upon in individual trusteeship agreements, made under Articles 77, 79, and 81, placing each territory under the trusteeship system, and until such agreements have been concluded, nothing in this Chapter shall be construed in or of itself to alter in any manner the rights whatsoever of any states or any peoples or the terms of existing international instruments to which Members of the United Nations may respectively be parties. 2. Paragraph 1 of this Article shall not be interpreted as giving grounds for delay or postponement of the negotiation and conclusion of agreements for placing mandated and other territories under the trusteeship system as provided for in Article 77.

Article 81. The trusteeship agreement shall in each case include the terms under which the trust territory will be administered and designate the authority which will exercise the administration of the trust territory. Such authority, hereinafter called the administering authority, may be one or more states or the Organization itself.

Article 82. There may be designated, in any trusteeship agreement, a strategic area or areas which may include part or all of the trust territory to which the agreement applies, without prejudice to any special agreement or agreements made under Article 43.

Article 83. 1. All functions of the United Nations relating to strategic areas, including the approval of the terms of the trusteeship agreements and of their alteration or amendment shall be exercised by the Security Council. 2. The basic objectives set forth in Article 76 shall be applicable to the people of each strategic area. 3. The Security Council shall, subject to the provisions of the trusteeship agreements and without prejudice to security considerations, avail itself of the assistance of the Trusteeship Council to perform those functions of the United Nations under the trusteeship system relating to political, economic, social, and educational matters in the strategic areas.

Article 84. It shall be the duty of the administering authority to ensure that the trust territory shall play its part in the maintenance of international peace and security. To this end the administering authority may make use of volunteer forces, facilities, and assistance from the trust territory in carrying out the obligations towards the Security Council undertaken in this regard by the administering authority, as well as for local defence and the maintenance of law and order within the trust territory.

Article 85. 1. The functions of the United Nations with regard to trusteeship agreements for all areas not designated as strategic, including the approval of the terms of the trusteeship agreements and of their alteration or amendment, shall be exercised by the General Assembly. 2. The Trusteeship Council, operating under the authority of the General Assembly shall assist the General Assembly in carrying out these functions.

Chapter XIII. *The Trusteeship Council*

Composition

Article 86. 1. The Trusteeship Council shall consist of the following Members of the United Nations: a. those Members administering trust territories; b. such of those Members mentioned by name in Article 23 as are not administering trust territories; and c. as many other Members elected for three-year terms by the General Assembly as may be necessary to ensure that the total number of members of the Trusteeship Council is equally divided between those Members of the United Nations which administer trust territories and those which do not. 2. Each member of the Trusteeship Council shall designate one specially qualified person to represent it therein.

Functions and Powers

Article 87. The General Assembly and, under its authority, the Trusteeship Council, in carrying out their functions, may: a. consider reports submitted by the administering authority; b. accept petitions and examine them in consultation with the administering authority; c. provide for periodic visits to the respective trust territories at times agreed upon with the ad-

ministering authority; and d. take these and other actions in conformity with the terms of the trusteeship agreements.

Article 88. The Trusteeship Council shall formulate a questionnaire on the political, economic, social, and educational advancement of the inhabitants of each trust territory, and the administering authority for each trust territory within the competence of the General Assembly shall make an annual report to the General Assembly upon the basis of such questionnaire.

Voting

Article 89. 1. Each member of the Trusteeship Council shall have one vote. 2. Decisions of the Trusteeship Council shall be made by a majority of the members present and voting.

Procedure

Article 90. 1. The Trusteeship Council shall adopt its own rules of procedure, including the method of selecting its President. 2. The Trusteeship Council shall meet as required in accordance with its rules, which shall include provision for the convening of meetings on the request of a majority of its members.

Article 91. The Trusteeship Council shall, when appropriate, avail itself of the assistance of the Economic and Social Council and of the specialized agencies in regard to matters with which they are respectively concerned.

Chapter XIV. *The International Court of Justice*

Article 92. The International Court of Justice shall be the principal judicial organ of the United Nations. It shall function in accordance with the annexed Statute, which is based upon the Statute of the Permanent Court of International Justice and forms an integral part of the present Charter.

Article 93. 1. All Members of the United Nations are *ipso facto* parties to the Statute of the International Court of Justice. 2. A state which is not a Member of the United Nations may become a party to the Statute of the International Court of Justice on conditions to be determined in each case by the General Assembly upon the recommendation of the Security Council.

Article 94. 1. Each Member of the United Nations undertakes to comply with the decision of the International Court of Justice in any case to which it is a party. 2. If any party to a case fails to perform the obligations incumbent upon it under a judgment rendered by the Court, the other party may have recourse to the Security Council, which may, if it deems necessary, make recommendations or decide upon measures to be taken to give effect to the judgment.

Article 95. Nothing in the present Charter shall prevent Members of the United Nations from entrusting the solution of their differences to other tribunals by virtue of agreements already in existence or which may be concluded in the future.

Article 96. 1. The General Assembly or the Security Council may request the International Court of Justice to give an advisory opinion on any legal question. 2. Other organs of the United Nations and specialized agencies, which may at any time be so authorized by the General Assembly, may also request advisory opinions of the Court on legal questions arising within the scope of their activities.

Chapter XV. *The Secretariat*

Article 97. The Secretariat shall comprise a Secretary-General and such staff as the Organization may require. The Secretary-General shall be appointed by the General Assembly upon the recommendation of the Security Council. He shall be the chief administrative officer of the Organization.

Article 98. The Secretary-General shall act in that capacity in all meetings of the General Assembly, of the Security Council, of the Economic and Social Council, and of the Trusteeship Council, and shall perform such other functions as are entrusted to him by these organs. The Secretary-General shall make an annual report to the General Assembly on the work of the Organization.

Article 99. *The Secretary-General may bring to the attention of the Security Council any matter which in his opinion may threaten the maintenance of international peace and security.*

Article 100. 1. In the performance of their duties the Secretary-General and the staff shall not seek or receive instructions from any government or from any other authority external to the Organization. They shall refrain from any action which might reflect on their position as international officials responsible only to the Organization. 2. Each Member of the United Nations undertakes to respect the exclusively international character of the responsibilities of the Secretary-General and the staff and not to seek to influence them in the discharge of their responsibilities.

Article 101. 1. The staff shall be appointed by the Secretary-General under regulations established by the General Assembly. 2. Appropriate staffs shall be permanently assigned to the Economic and Social Council, the Trusteeship Council, and, as required, to other organs of the United Nations. These staffs shall form a part of the Secretariat. 3. The paramount consideration in the employment of the staff and in the determination of the conditions of service shall be the necessity of securing the highest standards of efficiency, competence, and integrity. Due regard shall be paid to the importance of recruiting the staff on as wide a geographical basis as possible.

Chapter XVI. *Miscellaneous Provisions*

Article 102. 1. Every treaty and every international agreement entered into by any Member of the United Nations after the present Charter comes into force shall as soon as possible be registered with the Secretariat and published by it. 2. No party to any such treaty or international agreement which has not been registered in accordance with the provisions of paragraph 1 of this Article may invoke that treaty or agreement before any organ of the United Nations.

Article 103. In the event of a conflict between the obligations of the Members of the United Nations under the present Charter and their obligations under any other international agreement, their obligations under the present Charter shall prevail.

Article 104. The Organization shall enjoy in the territory of each of its Members such legal capacity as may be necessary for the exercise of its functions and the fulfilment of its purposes.

Article 105. 1. The Organization shall enjoy in the territory of each of its Members such privileges and immunities as are necessary for the fulfilment of its purposes. 2. Representatives of the Members of the United Nations and officials of the Organization shall similarly enjoy such privileges and immunities as are necessary for the independent exercise of their functions in connexion with the Organization. 3. The General Assembly may make

recommendations with a view to determining the details of the application of paragraphs 1 and 2 of this Article or may propose conventions to the Members of the United Nations for this purpose.

Chapter XVII. *Transitional Security Arrangements*

Article 106. Pending the coming into force of such special agreements referred to in Article 43 as in the opinion of the Security Council enable it to begin the exercise of its responsibilities under Article 42, the parties to the Four-Nation Declaration, signed at Moscow, 30 October 1943, and France, shall, in accordance with the provisions of paragraph 5 of that Declaration, consult with one another and as occasion requires with other Members of the United Nations with a view to such joint action on behalf of the Organization as may be necessary for the purpose of maintaining international peace and security.

Article 107. Nothing in the present Charter shall invalidate or preclude action, in relation to any state which during the Second World War has been an enemy of any signatory to the present Charter, taken or authorized as a result of that war by the Governments having responsibility for such action.

Chapter XVIII. *Amendments*

Article 108. Amendments to the present Charter shall come into force for all Members of the United Nations when they have been adopted by a vote of two thirds of the members of the General Assembly and ratified in accordance with their respective constitutional processes by two thirds of the Members of the United Nations, including all the permanent members of the Security Council.

Article 109. 1. A General Conference of the Members of the United Nations for the purpose of reviewing the present Charter may be held at a date and place to be fixed by a two-thirds vote of the members of the General Assembly and by a vote of any nine members of the Security Council. Each Member of the United Nations shall have one vote in the conference. 2. Any alteration of the present Charter recommended by a two-thirds vote of the conference shall take effect when ratified in accordance with their respective constitutional processes by two thirds of the Members of the United Nations including all the permanent members of the Security Council. 3. If such a conference has not been held before the tenth annual session of the General Assembly following the coming into force of the present Charter, the proposal to call such a conference shall be placed on the agenda of that session of the General Assembly, and the conference shall be held if so decided by a majority vote of the members of the General Assembly and by a vote of any seven members of the Security Council.

Chapter XIX. Ratification and Signature

Article 110. 1. The present Charter shall be ratified by the signatory states in accordance with their respective constitutional processes. 2. The ratifications shall be deposited with the Government of the United States of America, which shall notify all the signatory states of each deposit as well as the Secretary-General of the Organization when he has been appointed. 3. The present Charter shall come into force upon the deposit of ratifications by the Republic of China, France, the Union of Soviet Socialist Republics, the United Kingdom of Great Britain and Northern Ireland, and the United States of America, and by a majority of the other signatory states. A protocol of the ratifications deposited shall thereupon be drawn up by the Government of the United States of America which shall communicate copies thereof to all the signatory states. 4. The states signatory to the present Charter which ratify it after it has come into force will become original Members of the United Nations on the date of the deposit of their respective ratifications.

Article 111. The present Charter, of which the Chinese, French, Russian, English, and Spanish texts are equally authentic, shall remain deposited in the archives of the Government of the United States of America. Duly certified copies thereof shall be transmitted by that Government to the Governments of the other signatory states.

IN FAITH WHEREOF the representatives of the Governments of the United Nations have signed the present Charter. DONE at the city of San Francisco the twenty-sixth day of June, one thousand nine hundred and forty-five.

7. *The Rio Treaty*

(1947)

Building on the Act of Chapultepec, a declaration produced by a multilateral hemispheric meeting held in Mexico (1945), the Inter-American Treaty of Reciprocal Assistance (or Rio Treaty) signed on September 2, 1947, provides a framework for security in the Western Hemisphere following Articles 51 and 52 of the UN Charter (1945), which would be institutionalized later in the Organization of American States (OAS). At least since the Monroe Doctrine (1823), the United States has viewed security in the Americas as principally an intra-hemispheric matter.

Article 1. *The High Contracting Parties formally condemn war and undertake in their international relations not to resort to the threat or the use of force in any manner inconsistent with the provisions of the Charter of the United Nations or of this Treaty.*

Article 2. As a consequence of the principle set forth in the preceding Article, *the High Contracting Parties undertake to submit every controversy which may arise between them to methods of peaceful settlement and to endeavor to settle any such controversy among themselves by means of the procedures in force in the Inter-American System before referring it to the General Assembly or the Security Council of the United Nations.*

Article 3. 1. The High Contracting Parties agree *that an armed attack by any State against an American State shall be considered as an attack against all the American States and, consequently, each one of the said Contracting Parties undertakes to assist in meeting the attack in the exercise of the inherent right of individual or collective self-defense recognized by Article 51 of the Charter of the United Nations.* 2. On the request of the State or States directly attacked and until the decision of the Organ of Consultation of the Inter-American System, each one of the Contracting Parties may determine the immediate measures which it may individually take in fulfillment of the obligation contained in the preceding paragraph and in accordance with the principle of continental solidarity. The Organ of Consultation shall meet without delay for the purpose of examining those measures and agreeing upon the measures of a collective character that should be taken. 3. The provisions of this Article shall be applied in case of any armed attack which takes place within the region described in Article 4 or within the territory of an American State. When the attack takes place outside of the said areas, the provisions of Article 6 shall be applied. 4. Measures of self-defense provided for under this Article may be taken until the Security Council of the United Nations has taken the measures necessary to maintain international peace and security.

Article 4. The region to which this Treaty refers is bounded as follows: beginning at the North Pole [geographic description of North and South America follows]. . . .

Article 5. The High Contracting Parties shall immediately send to the Security Council of the United Nations, in conformity with Articles 51 and 54 of the Charter of the United Nations, complete information concerning the activities undertaken or in contemplation in the exercise of the right of self-defense or for the purpose of maintaining inter-American peace and security.

Article 6. *If the inviolability or the integrity of the territory or the sovereignty or political independence of any American State should be affected by an aggression which is not an armed attack or by an extracontinental or intra-continental conflict, or by any other fact or situation that might endanger the peace of America, the Organ of Consultation shall meet immediately in order to agree on the measures which must be taken in case of aggression to assist the victim of the aggression or, in any case, the measures which should be taken for the common defense and for the maintenance of the peace and security of the Continent.*

Article 7. *In the case of a conflict between two or more American States,* without prejudice to the right of self-defense in conformity with Article 51 of the Charter of the United Nations, *the High Contracting Parties,* meeting in consultation *shall call upon the contending States to suspend hostilities and restore matters to the* status quo ante bellum [i.e., conditions as they were before the war], *and shall take in addition all other necessary measures to reestablish or maintain inter-American peace and security and for the solution of the conflict by peaceful means.* The rejection of the pacifying action will be considered in the determination of the aggressor and in the application of the measures which the consultative meeting may agree upon.

Article 8. For the purposes of this Treaty, the *measures* on which the Organ of Consultation *may* agree will *comprise one or more of the following:* recall of chiefs of diplomatic missions; breaking of diplomatic relations; breaking of consular relations; partial or complete interruption of economic relations or of rail, sea, air, postal, telegraphic, telephonic, and radiotelephonic or radiotelegraphic communications; and *use of armed force.*

Article 9. In addition to other acts which the Organ of Consultation may characterize as *aggression,* the following shall be considered as such: a. *Unprovoked armed attack by a State against the territory, the people, or the land, sea or air forces of another State;* b. *Invasion, by the armed forces of a State, of the territory of an American State,* through the trespassing of boundaries demarcated in accordance with a treaty, judicial decision, or, arbitral award, or, in the absence of frontiers thus demarcated, invasion affecting a region which is under the effective jurisdiction of another State.

Article 10. None of the provisions of this Treaty shall be construed as impairing the rights and obligations of the High Contracting Parties under the Charter of the United Nations.

Article 11. The consultations to which this Treaty refers shall be carried out by means of the Meetings of Ministers of Foreign Affairs of the American Republics which have ratified the Treaty, or in the manner or by the organ which in the future may be agreed upon.

Article 12. The Governing Board of the Pan American Union may act provisionally as an organ of consultation until the meeting of the Organ of Consultation referred to in the preceding Article takes place.

Article 13. The consultations shall be initiated at the, request addressed to the Governing Board of the Pan American Union by any of the Signatory States which has ratified the Treaty.

Article 14. In the voting referred to in this Treaty only the representatives of the Signatory States which have ratified the Treaty may take part.

Article 15. The Governing Board of the Pan American Union shall act in all matters concerning this Treaty as an organ of liaison among the Signatory States which have ratified this Treaty and between these States and the United Nations.

Article 16. The decisions of the Governing Board of the Pan American Union referred to in Articles 13 and 15 above shall be taken, by an absolute majority of the Members entitled to vote.

Article 17. The Organ of Consultation shall take its decisions by a vote of two-thirds of the Signatory States which have ratified the Treaty.

Article 18. In the case of a situation or dispute between American States, the parties directly interested shall be excluded from the voting referred to in the two preceding Articles. . . .

---

8. *The Charter of the Organization of American States (OAS)*
(1948 as amended in 1967, 1985, 1992, and 1993)

Inter-American relations were institutionalized in 1890 in what came to be called the Pan American Union (1910). The terms of the Rio Treaty (1947) were incorporated in the OAS Charter (1948). This Act of Bogotá remains a living document. Originally signed on May 2, 1948, it has been amended several times (the Protocol of Buenos Aires [1967], the Protocol of Cartagena de Indias [1985], the Protocol of Washington [1992], and the Protocol of Managua [1993]), mainly to establish and expand upon social and economic commitments (see Chapter VII in particular). The principle of nonintervention in the domestic affairs of another hemispheric state is emphasized in Articles 1, 3, 13, and especially 19, 28, and 29. Disputes are to be settled peacefully. A central concept is that an attack on one is an attack on all, thus inviting a hemispheric response by the OAS.

PART ONE

Chapter I: Nature and Purposes

Article 1. The American States establish by this Charter the international organization that they have developed to achieve an order of peace and justice, to promote their solidarity, to strengthen their collaboration, and *to defend their sovereignty, their territorial integrity, and their independence.* Within the United Nations, the Organization of American States is a regional agency. The Organization of American States has no powers other than those expressly conferred upon it by this Charter, none of whose provisions authorizes it to intervene in matters that are within the internal jurisdiction of the Member States.

Article 2. The Organization of American States, in order to put into practice the principles on which it is founded and to fulfill its regional obligations under the Charter of the United Nations, proclaims the following essential purposes: a) *To strengthen the peace and security of the continent;* b) To promote and consolidate representative democracy, with due respect for the principle of nonintervention; c) To prevent possible causes of difficulties and *to ensure the pacific settlement of disputes* that may arise among the Member States; d) *To provide for common action on the part of those States in the event of aggression;* e) To seek the solution of political, juridical, and economic problems that may arise among them; f) To promote, by cooperative action, their economic, social, and cultural development; g) To eradicate extreme poverty, which constitutes an obstacle to the full democratic development of the peoples of the hemisphere; and h) To achieve an effective limitation of conventional weapons that will make it possible to devote the largest amount of resources to the economic and social development of the Member States.

Chapter II: Principles

Article 3. The American States reaffirm the following principles: a) International law is the standard of conduct of States in their reciprocal relations; b) International order consists essentially of respect for the personality, sovereignty, and independence of States, and the faithful fulfillment of obligations derived from treaties and other sources of international law; c) Good faith shall govern the relations between States; d) The solidarity of the American States and the high aims which are sought through it require the political organization of those States on the basis of the effective exercise of representative democracy; e) *Every State has the right to choose, without external interference, its political, economic, and social system and to organize itself in the way best suited to it, and has the duty to abstain from intervening in the affairs of another State.* Subject to the foregoing, the American States shall cooperate fully among themselves, independently of the nature of their political, economic, and social systems; f) The elimination of extreme poverty is an essential part of the promotion and consolidation of representative democracy and is the common and shared responsibility of the American States; g) *The American States condemn war of aggression:* victory does not give rights; h) *An act of aggression against one American State is an act of aggression against all the other American States;* i) *Controversies of an international character arising between two or more American States shall be settled by peaceful procedures;* j) Social justice and social security are bases of lasting peace; k) Economic cooperation is essential to the common welfare and prosperity of the peoples of the continent; l) The American States proclaim the fundamental rights of the individual without distinction as to race, nationality, creed, or sex; m) The spiritual unity of the continent is based on respect for the cultural values of the American countries and requires their close cooperation for the high purposes of civilization; n) The education of peoples should be directed toward justice, freedom, and peace.

Chapter III: Members

Article 4. All American States that ratify the present Charter are Members of the Organization.

Article 5. Any new political entity that arises from the union of several Member States and that, as such, ratifies the present Charter, shall become a Member of the Organization. The entry of the new political entity into the Organization shall result in the loss of membership of each one of the States which constitute it.

Article 6. Any other independent American State that desires to become a Member of the Organization should so indicate. . . .

Article 7. The General Assembly, upon the recommendation of the Permanent Council of the Organization, shall determine whether it is appropriate that the Secretary General be authorized to permit the applicant State to sign the Charter and to accept the deposit of the corresponding instrument of ratification. Both the recommendation of the Permanent Council and the decision of the General Assembly shall require the affirmative vote of two thirds of the Member States.

Article 8. Membership in the Organization shall be confined to independent States of the Hemisphere that were Members of the United Nations as of

December 10, 1985, and the nonautonomous territories . . . when they become independent.

Article 9. *A Member of the Organization whose democratically constituted government has been overthrown by force may be suspended from the exercise of the right to participate* in the sessions of the General Assembly, the Meeting of Consultation, the Councils of the Organization and the Specialized Conferences as well as in the commissions, working groups and any other bodies established. . . .

Chapter IV: Fundamental Rights and Duties of States

Article 10. States are juridically equal, enjoy equal rights and equal capacity to exercise these rights, and have equal duties. The rights of each State depend not upon its power to ensure the exercise thereof, but upon the mere fact of its existence as a person under international law.

Article 11. Every American State has the duty to respect the rights enjoyed by every other State in accordance with international law.

Article 12. The fundamental rights of States may not be impaired in any manner whatsoever.

Article 13. The political existence of the State is independent of recognition by other States. Even before being recognized, *the State has the right to defend its integrity and independence,* to provide for its preservation and prosperity, and consequently to organize itself as it sees fit, to legislate concerning its interests, to administer its services, and to determine the jurisdiction and competence of its courts. The exercise of these rights is limited only by the exercise of the rights of other States in accordance with international law.

Article 14. Recognition implies that the State granting it accepts the personality of the new State, with all the rights and duties that international law prescribes for the two States.

Article 15. The right of each State to protect itself and to live its own life does not authorize it to commit unjust acts against another State.

Article 16. The jurisdiction of States within the limits of their national territory is exercised equally over all the inhabitants, whether nationals or aliens.

Article 17. Each State has the right to develop its cultural, political, and economic life freely and naturally. In this free development, the State shall respect the rights of the individual and the principles of universal morality.

Article 18. Respect for and the faithful observance of treaties constitute standards for the development of peaceful relations among States. International treaties and agreements should be public.

Article 19. *No State or group of States has the right to intervene, directly or indirectly, for any reason whatever, in the internal or external affairs of any other State. The foregoing principle prohibits not only armed force but also any other form of interference or attempted threat against the personality of the State or against its political, economic, and cultural elements.*

Article 20. No State may use or encourage the use of coercive measures of an economic or political character in order to force the sovereign will of another State and obtain from it advantages of any kind.

Article 21. The territory of a State is inviolable; it may not be the object, even temporarily, of military occupation or of other measures of force taken by another State, directly or indirectly, on any grounds whatever. No territorial acquisitions or special advantages obtained either by force or by other means of coercion shall be recognized.

Article 22. *The American States bind themselves in their international relations not to have recourse to the use of force, except in the case of self-defense in accordance with existing treaties or in fulfillment thereof.*

Article 23. Measures adopted for the maintenance of peace and security in accordance with existing treaties do not constitute a violation of the principles set forth in Articles 19 and 21.

Chapter V: Pacific Settlement of Disputes

Article 24. *International disputes between Member States shall be submitted to the peaceful procedures set forth in this Charter.* This provision shall not be interpreted as an impairment of the rights and obligations of the Member States under Articles 34 and 35 of the Charter of the United Nations.

Article 25. The following are peaceful procedures: direct negotiation, good offices, mediation, investigation and conciliation, judicial settlement, arbitration, and those which the parties to the dispute may especially agree upon at any time.

Article 26. In the event that a dispute arises between two or more American States which, in the opinion of one of them, cannot be settled through the usual diplomatic channels, the parties shall agree on some other peaceful procedure that will enable them to reach a solution.

Article 27. A special treaty will establish adequate means for the settlement of disputes and will determine pertinent procedures for each peaceful means such that no dispute between American States may remain without definitive settlement within a reasonable period of time.

Chapter VI: Collective Security

Article 28. *Every act of aggression by a State against the territorial integrity or the inviolability of the territory or against the sovereignty or political independence of an American State shall be considered an act of aggression against the other American States.*

Article 29. *If the inviolability or the integrity of the territory or the sovereignty or political independence of any American State should be affected by an armed attack or by an act of aggression that is not an armed attack, or by an extracontinental conflict, or by a conflict between two or more American States, or by any other fact or situation that might endanger the peace of America, the American States, in furtherance of the principles of continental solidarity or collective self-defense, shall apply the measures and procedures established in the special treaties on the subject.*

Chapter VII: Integral Development

Article 30. The Member States, inspired by the principles of inter-American solidarity and cooperation, pledge themselves to a united effort to ensure international social justice in their relations and integral development for their peoples, as conditions essential to peace and security. Integral development encompasses the economic, social, educational, cultural, scientific, and technological fields through which the goals that each country sets for accomplishing it should be achieved.

Article 31. Inter-American cooperation for integral development is the common and joint responsibility of the Member States, within the framework of the democratic principles and the institutions of the inter-American system. . . .

Article 32. Inter-American cooperation for integral development should be continuous and preferably channeled through multilateral organizations, without prejudice to bilateral cooperation between Member States. . . .

Article 33. Development is a primary responsibility of each country and should constitute an integral and continuous process for the establishment of a more just economic and social order that will make possible and contribute to the fulfillment of the individual.

Article 34. The Member States agree that equality of opportunity, the elimination of extreme poverty, equitable distribution of wealth and income and the full participation of their peoples in decisions relating to their own development are, among others, basic objectives of integral development. . . .

Article 35. The Member States should refrain from practicing policies and adopting actions or measures that have serious adverse effects on the development of other Member States.

Article 36. Transnational enterprises and foreign private investment shall be subject to the legislation of the host countries and to the jurisdiction of their competent courts and to the international treaties and agreements to which said countries are parties, and should conform to the development policies of the recipient countries.

Article 37. The Member States agree to join together in seeking a solution to urgent or critical problems that may arise whenever the economic development or stability of any Member State is seriously affected by conditions that cannot be remedied through the efforts of that State.

Article 38. The Member States shall extend among themselves the benefits of science and technology by encouraging the exchange and utilization of scientific and technical knowledge in accordance with existing treaties and national laws.

Article 39. The Member States, recognizing the close interdependence between foreign trade and economic and social development, should make individual and united efforts to bring about the following: a) Favorable conditions of access to world markets for the products of the developing countries of the region . . . ; b) Continuity in their economic and social development. . . .

Article 40. The Member States reaffirm the principle that when the more developed countries grant concessions in international trade agreements that lower or eliminate tariffs or other barriers to foreign trade so that they benefit the less-developed countries, they should not expect reciprocal concessions from those countries that are incompatible with their economic development, financial, and trade needs.

Article 41. The Member States, in order to accelerate their economic development, regional integration, and the expansion and improvement of the conditions of their commerce, shall promote improvement and coordination of transportation and communication in the developing countries and among the Member States.

Article 42. The Member States recognize that integration of the developing countries of the Hemisphere is one of the objectives of the inter-American system and, therefore, shall orient their efforts and take the necessary measures to accelerate the integration process, with a view to establishing a Latin American common market in the shortest possible time.

Article 43. In order to strengthen and accelerate integration in all its aspects, the Member States agree to give adequate priority to the preparation and carrying out of multinational projects and to their financing, as well as to encourage economic and financial institutions of the inter-American system to continue giving their broadest support to regional integration institutions and programs.

Article 44. The Member States agree that technical and financial cooperation that seeks to promote regional economic integration should be based on the principle of harmonious, balanced, and efficient development, with particular attention to the relatively less-developed countries, so that it may be a decisive factor that will enable them to promote, with their own efforts, the improved development of their infrastructure programs, new lines of production, and export diversification.

Article 45. The Member States [are] convinced that man can only achieve the full realization of his aspirations within a just social order, along with economic development and true peace. . . .

Article 46. The Member States recognize that, in order to facilitate the process of Latin American regional integration, it is necessary to harmonize the social legislation of the developing countries, especially in the labor and social security fields, so that the rights of the workers shall be equally protected, and they agree to make the greatest efforts possible to achieve this goal.

Article 47. The Member States will give primary importance within their development plans to the encouragement of education, science, technology, and culture, oriented toward the overall improvement of the individual, and as a foundation for democracy, social justice, and progress.

Article 48. The Member States will cooperate with one another to meet their educational needs, to promote scientific research, and to encourage technological progress for their integral development. They will consider themselves individually and jointly bound to preserve and enrich the cultural heritage of the American peoples.

Article 49. The Member States will exert the greatest efforts, in accordance with their constitutional processes, to ensure the effective exercise of the right to education. . . .

Article 50. The Member States will give special attention to the eradication of illiteracy. . . .

Article 51. The Member States will develop science and technology through educational, research, and technological development activities. . . .

Article 52. The Member States, with due respect for the individuality of each of them, agree to promote cultural exchange as an effective means of consolidating inter-American understanding. . . .

PART TWO

Chapter VIII: The Organs

Article 53. The Organization of American States accomplishes its purposes by means of: a) The General Assembly; b) The Meeting of Consultation of Ministers of Foreign Affairs; c) The Councils; d) The Inter-American Juridical Committee; e) The Inter-American Commission on Human Rights; f) The General Secretariat; g) The Specialized Conferences; and h) The Specialized Organizations. There may be established, in addition to those provided for in the Charter and in accordance with the provisions thereof, such subsidiary organs, agencies, and other entities as are considered necessary.... [Most of the remainder of the treaty provides details on the responsibilities, authority, and operational rules related these OAS institutions.]

---

9. *The North Atlantic Treaty*

(1949)

This treaty, signed on April 4, 1949, provides the authority and bases for action of the North Atlantic Treaty Organization (NATO), the United States being a charter member. Although the United Nations Security Council retains the principal authority and responsibility under the UN Charter for collective security, NATO assumes an additional, regional collective defense role also permitted under Article 51 (see also Article 52) of the UN Charter. Collective security and collective defense are related but have different technical meanings: collective security refers to the same international law-enforcement authority against lawbreaking aggressors that existed under the League of Nations after World War I, whereas collective defense is understood as allowing the formation of alliances or coalitions based on countervailing power so long as the parties defer to the prerogatives, when exercised, of the UN Security Council.

The North Atlantic Treaty was signed and ratified early in the cold war with the understanding that the security of NATO countries would be enhanced by U.S. participation as a counter to Soviet power in the East and as an assurance against Germany returning to its aggressive posture that had threatened both East and West in World Wars I and II. The treaty thus focused on security in a European and North Atlantic area identified in Article 6—a geographical scope that also included the United States and Canada.

Because of U.S. unwillingness to defend the colonial empires of its allies, defining the NATO area this way thus excluded from any NATO security guarantee extensive British, French, Dutch, and Portuguese colonial interests at the time in Asia, Africa, and the Western Hemisphere. These empires were subsequently dismantled mainly in the 1960s and 1970s, but the North Atlantic area as geographic restriction still applied, thus rendering engagements elsewhere in the world technically as "out-of-area" and thus beyond the formal geographic scope of NATO's authority. More recently, expansion of NATO membership and a broadening interpretation of geographic scope—applying Article 4 to post–cold war security challenges—have tended to relax this limitation on NATO actions.

Following post–World War I understandings that events in 1914 had triggered automatic alliance responses that themselves contributed to the outbreak of war, Article 5 does not specify the particular action NATO will take in response to attack on any member; the treaty does not mandate an automatic use of force. Finally, should one consider NATO only a military alliance, Article 2 makes clear that NATO as an international organization has responsibilities and authority in service of democratic principles that also extend to nonmilitary, political, and economic matters.

The Parties to this Treaty reaffirm their faith in the purposes and principles of the Charter of the United Nations and their desire *to live in peace with all peoples and all governments.* They are determined *to safeguard the freedom, common heritage and civilisation of their peoples,* founded on the principles of democracy, individual liberty and the rule of law. They seek *to promote stability and well-being* in the North Atlantic area. They are resolved to unite their efforts for *collective defense* and for the *preservation of peace and security.* They therefore agree to this North Atlantic Treaty:

Article 1. The Parties undertake, as set forth in the Charter of the United Nations, to settle any international dispute in which they may be involved by *peaceful means* in such a manner that *international peace and security and justice* are not endangered, and *to refrain* in their international relations *from the threat or use of force in any manner inconsistent with the purposes of the United Nations.*

Article 2. The Parties will contribute toward the further development of peaceful and friendly international relations by *strengthening their free institutions,* by bringing about a better understanding of the principles upon which these institutions are founded, and by *promoting conditions of stability and well-being.* They will seek to *eliminate conflict in their international economic policies* and will *encourage economic collaboration* between any or all of them.

Article 3. In order more effectively to achieve the objectives of this Treaty, *the Parties,* separately and jointly, by means of continuous and effective self-help and mutual aid, *will maintain and develop their individual and collective capacity to resist armed attack.*

Article 4. *The Parties will consult together whenever,* in the opinion of any of them, the *territorial integrity, political independence or security of any of the Parties is threatened.*

Article 5. *The Parties agree that an armed attack against one or more of them in Europe or North America shall be considered an attack against them all* and consequently they agree that, *if such an armed attack occurs, each of them, in exercise of the right of individual or collective self-defence recognised by Article 51 of the Charter of the United Nations, will assist the Party or Parties so attacked by taking forthwith, individually and in concert with the other Parties, such action as it deems necessary, including the use of armed force, to restore and maintain the security of the North Atlantic area.* Any such armed attack and all measures taken as a result thereof shall immediately be reported to the Security Council. Such *measures shall be terminated when the Security Council has taken the measures necessary to restore and maintain international peace and security.*

Article 6. For the purpose of Article 5, an armed attack on one or more of the Parties is deemed to include an armed attack: *on the territory of any of the Parties in Europe or North America,* on the Algerian Departments of France [reference to Algeria no longer applies since Algeria became independent of France in 1962], *on the territory of Turkey or on the Islands under the jurisdiction of any of the Parties in the North Atlantic area north of the Tropic of Cancer; on the forces, vessels, or aircraft of any of the Parties, when in or over these territories* or any other area in Europe in which occupation forces of any of the Parties were stationed on the date when the Treaty entered into force *or the Mediterranean Sea or the North Atlantic area north of the Tropic of Cancer.*

Article 7. *This Treaty does not affect,* and shall not be interpreted as affecting in any way the rights and obligations under the Charter of the Parties which are members of the United Nations, or *the primary responsibility of the Security Council for the maintenance of international peace and security.*

Article 8. Each Party declares that none of the international engagements now in force between it and any other of the Parties or any third State is in conflict with the provisions of this Treaty, and undertakes not to enter into any international engagement in conflict with this Treaty.

Article 9. *The Parties hereby establish a Council,* on which each of them shall be represented, to consider matters concerning the implementation of this Treaty. The Council shall be so organised as to be able to meet promptly at any time. *The Council shall set up such subsidiary bodies as may be necessary; in particular it shall establish immediately a defence committee* which shall recommend measures for the implementation of Articles 3 and 5.

Article 10. *The Parties may, by unanimous agreement, invite any other European State* in a position to further the principles of this Treaty and to contribute to the security of the North Atlantic area *to accede to this Treaty. . . .*

Article 11. This Treaty shall be ratified and its provisions carried out by the Parties in accordance with their respective constitutional processes. . . .

Article 12. After the Treaty has been in force for ten years, or at any time thereafter, the Parties shall, if any of them so requests, consult together for the purpose of reviewing the Treaty. . . .

Article 13. After the Treaty has been in force for twenty years, any Party may cease to be a Party one year after its notice of denunciation has been given. . . .

Article 14. This Treaty, of which the English and French texts are equally authentic, shall be deposited in the archives of the Government of the United States.

---

10. *The OSCE: The Charter of Paris for a New Europe and Budapest Summit*

(1990 and 1994, respectively)

The Conference on Security and Cooperation in Europe (CSCE) began in 1973, concluding its initial work in the Helsinki Final Act in 1975 (part 4, chapter 15). Unlike NATO's selective membership, the CSCE was an inclusive Atlantic-to-the-Urals "process," as it was called, that during the cold war included thirty-five member states and principalities in Europe as well as the United States and Canada. (The post–cold war breakup of Czechoslovakia, the Soviet Union, and Yugoslavia into component states has swelled membership to some fifty-five states and principalities.) Agreements of the CSCE process in arms control can be found above in part 4 (chapters 15 and 16). A decision to add institutional support to the CSCE process was made at a Paris summit meeting on November 21, 1990; a secretariat was constituted in Prague to support the CSCE Council composed of the foreign ministers of member states (in the United States, the secretary of state) as were a Conflict Prevention Center in Vienna and an Office for Free Elections in Warsaw. Four years later at a Budapest summit on December 6, 1994, the CSCE "process" formally became an "organization"—designated the OSCE, or Organization for Security and Cooperation in Europe.

[Paris Document: November 21, 1990]

We, the Heads of State or Government of the States participating in the Conference on Security and Co-operation in Europe, have assembled in Paris at a time of profound change and historic expectations. The era of confrontation and division of Europe has ended. . . . Our common efforts to consolidate respect for human rights, democracy and the rule of law, to strengthen peace and to promote unity in Europe require a new quality of political dialogue and co-operation and thus development of the structures of the CSCE. . . .

In order to provide administrative support . . . we establish a Secretariat in Prague. . . . We decide to create a Conflict Prevention Centre in Vienna to assist the Council in reducing the risk of conflict. We decide to establish an Office for Free Elections in Warsaw to facilitate contacts and the exchange of information on elections within participating States. Recognizing the important role parliamentarians can play in the CSCE process, we call for greater parliamentary involvement in the CSCE, in particular through the creation of a CSCE parliamentary assembly, involving members of parliaments from all participating States. To this end, we urge that contacts be pursued at parliamentary level to discuss the field of activities, working methods and rules of procedure of such a CSCE parliamentary structure, drawing on existing experience and work already undertaken in this field. . . . Procedural and organizational modalities . . . are set out in the Supplementary Document which is adopted together with the Charter of Paris. We entrust to the Council the further steps which may be required to ensure the implementation of decision. . . .

Done at Paris, on 21 November 1990

Institutional Arrangements

A. The Council: The Council, consisting of Ministers for Foreign Affairs of the participating States, provides the central forum for regular political consultations within the CSCE process. The Council will consider issues relevant to the Conference on Security and Co-operation in Europe and take appropriate decisions; prepare the meetings of Heads of State or Government of the participating States and implement tasks defined and decisions taken by these meetings. The Council will hold meetings regularly and at least once a year. The participating States may agree to hold additional meetings of the Council. The Chair throughout each meeting of the Council will be taken by the representative of the host country. An agenda for the meetings of the Council, including proposals for the venue on a basis of rotation and date of the next meeting, will be prepared by the Committee of Senior Officials.

B. The Committee of Senior Officials: A Committee of Senior Officials will prepare the work of the Council, carry out its decisions, review current issues and consider future work of the CSCE including its relations with other international fora. . . .

C. Emergency Mechanism: The Council will discuss the possibility of establishing a mechanism for convening meetings of the Committee of Senior Officials in emergency situations.

D. Follow-up Meetings: Follow-up meetings of the participating States will be held as a rule every two years. Their duration will not exceed three months, unless otherwise agreed.

E. The CSCE Secretariat: The Secretariat will provide administrative support to the meetings of the Council and of the Committee of Senior Officials; maintain an archive of CSCE documentation and circulate documents as requested by the participating States; provide information in the public domain regarding the CSCE to individuals, NGOs, international organizations and non-participating States; provide support as appropriate to the Executive Secretaries of CSCE summit meetings, follow-up meetings and inter-sessional meetings. The Secretariat will carry out other tasks assigned to it by the Council or the Committee of Senior Officials. . . .

F. The Conflict Prevention Centre (CPC): The Conflict Prevention Centre (CPC) will assist the Council in reducing the risk of conflict. The Centre's functions and structure are described below. During its initial stage of operations the Centre's role will consist in giving support to the implementation of CSBMs such as mechanism for consultation and co-operation as regards unusual military activities; annual exchange of military information; communications network; annual implementation assessment meetings; [and] co-operation as regards hazardous incidents of a military nature. The Centre might assume other functions and the above tasks are without prejudice to any additional tasks concerning a procedure for the conciliation of disputes as well as broader tasks relating to dispute settlement, which may be assigned to it in the future by the Council of the Foreign Ministers. . . .

G. The Office for Free Elections: The function of the Office for Free Elections will be to facilitate contacts and the exchange of information on elections within participating States. . . . To this end, the Office will compile information . . . on the dates, procedures and official results of scheduled national elections within participating States, as well as reports of election observations, and provide these on request to governments, parliaments and interested private organizations; serve to facilitate contact among governments, parliaments or private organizations wishing to observe elections and competent authorities of the States in which elections are to take place; [and] organize and serve as the venue for seminars or other meetings related to election procedures and democratic institutions at the request of the participating States. . . .

[Budapest Document, December 6, 1994]

Towards a Genuine Partnership in a New Era

We, the Heads of State or Government of the States participating in the Conference on Security and Co-operation in Europe, have met in Budapest. . . . We believe in the central role of the CSCE in building a secure and stable CSCE community, whole and free. . . . The CSCE is the security structure embracing States from Vancouver to Vladivostok. We are determined to give a new political impetus to the CSCE, thus enabling it to play a cardinal role in meeting the challenges of the twenty-first century. To reflect this determination, the CSCE will henceforth be known as the Organization for Security and Co-operation in Europe (OSCE).

11. *North American Free Trade Agreement (NAFTA)*
(1993)

This is an extraordinarily detailed, lengthy free-trade agreement negotiated by the Bush administration with Canada and Mexico. Congressional approval was secured by the Clinton administration in 1993. We include here only the preamble and objectives.

The Government of Canada, the Government of the United Mexican States and the Government of the United States of America, resolved to: STRENGTHEN the special bonds of friendship and cooperation among their nations; CONTRIBUTE to the harmonious development and expansion of world trade and provide a catalyst to broader international cooperation; CREATE an expanded and secure market for the goods and services produced in their territories; REDUCE distortions to trade; ESTABLISH clear and mutually advantageous rules governing their trade; ENSURE a predictable commercial framework for business planning and investment; BUILD on their respective rights and obligations under the General Agreement on Tariffs and Trade and other multilateral and bilateral instruments of cooperation; ENHANCE the competitiveness of their firms in global markets; FOSTER creativity and innovation, and promote trade in goods and services that are the subject of intellectual property rights; CREATE new employment opportunities and improve working conditions and living standards in their respective territories; UNDERTAKE each of the preceding in a manner consistent with environmental protection and conservation; PRESERVE their flexibility to safeguard the public welfare; PROMOTE sustainable development; STRENGTHEN the development and enforcement of environmental laws and regulations; and PROTECT, enhance and enforce basic workers' rights; HAVE AGREED as follows:

Article 101: *Establishment of the Free Trade Area* The Parties to this Agreement, consistent with ... the General Agreement on Tariffs and Trade, hereby establish a free trade area.

Article 102: *Objectives* ... The objectives of this Agreement, as elaborated more specifically through its principles and rules, including national treatment, most-favored-nation treatment and transparency are to: (a) *eliminate barriers to trade* in, and facilitate the cross border movement of, goods and services between the territories of the Parties; (b) *promote conditions of fair competition* in the free trade area; (c) *increase substantially investment opportunities* in their territories; (d) *provide adequate and effective protection and enforcement of intellectual property rights* in each Party's territory; (e) *create effective procedures for* the implementation and application of this Agreement, and for its joint administration and *the resolution of disputes*; and (f) *establish a framework for further trilateral, regional and multilateral cooperation* to expand and enhance the benefits of this Agreement. ...

Index